Less managing. More teaching. Greater learning.

INSTRUCTORS...

Would you like your **students** to show up for class **more prepared**? *(Let's face it, class is much more fun if everyone is engaged and prepared...)*

Want an **easy way to assign** homework online and track student **progress**? *(Less time grading means more time teaching...)*

Want an **instant view** of student or class performance relative to learning objectives? *(No more wondering if students understand...)*

Need to **collect data and generate reports** required for administration or accreditation? *(Say goodbye to manually tracking student learning outcomes...)*

Want to **record and post your lectures** for students to view online?

With **McGraw-Hill's** *Connect*™ **Plus Accounting,**

INSTRUCTORS GET:

- Simple **assignment management**, allowing you to spend more time teaching.
- **Auto-graded** assignments, quizzes, and tests.
- **Detailed Visual Reporting** where student and section results can be viewed and analyzed.
- Sophisticated **online testing** capability.
- A **filtering and reporting** function that allows you to easily assign and report on materials that are correlated to accreditation standards, learning outcomes, and Bloom's taxonomy.
- An easy-to-use **lecture capture** tool.
- The option to **upload course documents** for student access.

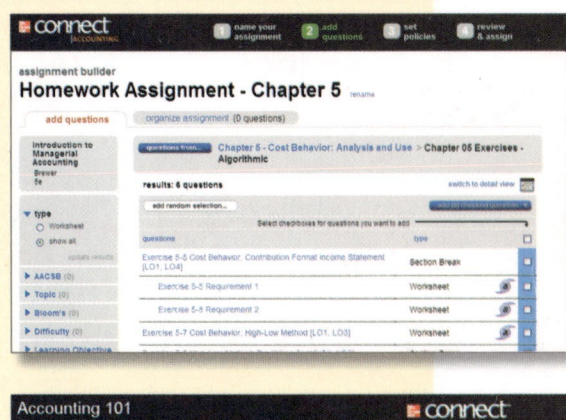

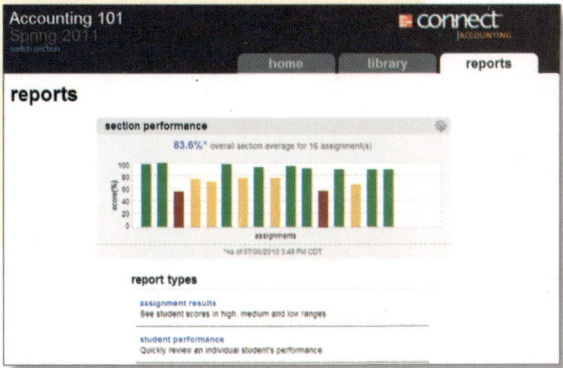

Want an online, searchable version of your textbook?

Wish your textbook could be **available online** while you're doing your assignments?

 ### Connect™ Plus Accounting eBook

If you choose to use *Connect™ Plus Accounting*, you have an affordable and searchable online version of your book integrated with your other online tools.

Connect™ Plus Accounting eBook offers features like:

- Topic search
- Direct links from assignments
- Adjustable text size
- Jump to page number
- Print by section

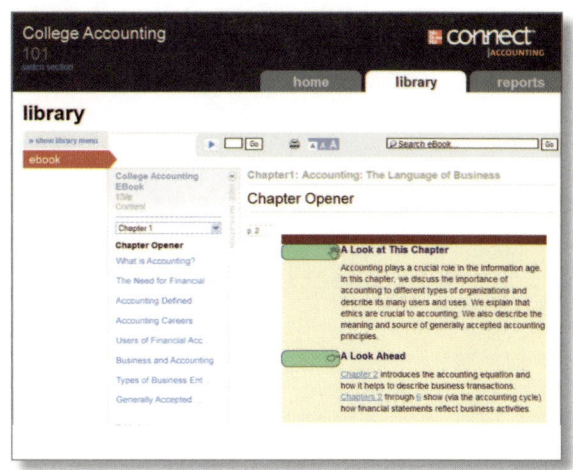

 Want to get more value from your textbook purchase?

Think learning accounting should be a bit more **interesting**?

 ### Check out the STUDENT RESOURCES section under the *Connect™* Library tab.

Here you'll find a wealth of resources designed to help you achieve your goals in the course. You'll find things like **quizzes, PowerPoints, and Internet activities** to help you study. Every student has different needs, so explore the STUDENT RESOURCES to find the materials best suited to you.

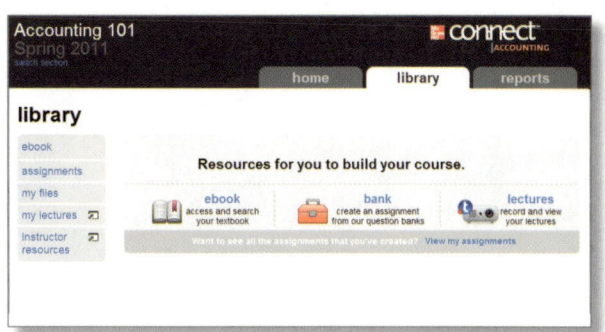

second edition

College Accounting: A Contemporary Approach

second edition

College Accounting: A Contemporary Approach

M. DAVID HADDOCK, JR., Ed.D., CPA
Professor of Accounting Emeritus
Chattanooga State Community College
Director of Training
Lattimore Black Morgan & Cain, PC
Brentwood, Tennessee

JOHN ELLIS PRICE, Ph.D., CPA
President and Professor of Accounting
University of North Texas at Dallas
Dallas, Texas

MICHAEL J. FARINA, MBA, CPA
Professor of Accounting
Cerritos College
Norwalk, California

McGraw-Hill Irwin

McGraw-Hill Irwin

COLLEGE ACCOUNTING: A CONTEMPORARY APPROACH

Published by McGraw-Hill/Irwin, a business unit of The McGraw-Hill Companies, Inc., 1221 Avenue of the Americas, New York, NY, 10020. Copyright © 2012, 2010 by The McGraw-Hill Companies, Inc. All rights reserved. No part of this publication may be reproduced or distributed in any form or by any means, or stored in a database or retrieval system, without the prior written consent of The McGraw-Hill Companies, Inc., including, but not limited to, in any network or other electronic storage or transmission, or broadcast for distance learning.

Some ancillaries, including electronic and print components, may not be available to customers outside the United States.

This book is printed on acid-free paper.

3 4 5 6 7 8 9 0 DOW/DOW 1 0 9 8 7 6 5 4 3

ISBN: 978-0-07-339695-8
MHID: 0-07-339695-8

Vice president and editor-in-chief: *Brent Gordon*
Editorial director: *Stewart Mattson*
Publisher: *Tim Vertovec*
Executive editor: *Steve Schuetz*
Executive director of development: *Ann Torbert*
Development editor: *Rebecca Mann*
Vice president and director of marketing: *Robin J. Zwettler*
Marketing director: *Brad Parkins*
Marketing manager: *Michelle Heaster*
Vice president of editing, design, and production: *Sesha Bolisetty*
Senior project manager: *Diane L. Nowaczyk*
Senior buyer: *Michael R. McCormick*
Lead designer: *Matthew Baldwin*
Senior photo research coordinator: *Keri Johnson*
Photo researcher: *Ira C. Roberts*
Senior media project manager: *Bruce Gin*
Media project manager: *Ron Nelms*
Cover image: *@ Getty Images*
Typeface: *10.5/12 Times Roman*
Compositor: *Laserwords Private Limited*
Printer: *R. R. Donnelley*

Library of Congress Cataloging-in-Publication Data

Haddock, M. David.
    College accounting : a contemporary approach / M. David Haddock, Jr.,
John Ellis Price, Michael J. Farina. — 2nd ed.
        p. cm.
    Includes index.
    ISBN-13: 978-0-07-339695-8 (alk. paper)
    ISBN-10: 0-07-339695-8 (alk. paper)
    1. Accounting. I. Price, John Ellis. II. Farina, Michael J. III. Title.
HF5636.H33 2012
657'.044—dc22
                                                                2011009915

About the Authors

M. DAVID HADDOCK, JR., is currently director of training for Lattimore, Black, Morgan, & Cain, PC, one of the largest financial services firms in the Southeast. He is located in the Brentwood, Tennessee, office. He recently retired from a 35-year career in higher education, having served in faculty and administrative roles at Auburn University at Montgomery, the University of Alabama in Birmingham, the University of West Georgia, and Chattanooga State Community College. He retired as professor of accounting at Chattanooga State Community College in Tennessee. In addition to his teaching, he maintained a sole proprietorship tax practice for 20 years prior to taking his current position.

He received his BS in accounting and MS in adult education from the University of Tennessee, and the DE degree in administration of higher education from Auburn University. He is a licensed CPA in Tennessee.

Professor Haddock was elected treasurer of the Tennessee Society of Certified Public Accountants in 2008 after serving on the board of directors and as the Chattanooga TSCPA chapter president. He is also active in the American Institute for Certified Public Accountants and the Tennessee Society of Accounting Educators. He is a frequent speaker for Continuing Professional Education programs.

JOHN ELLIS PRICE is president and professor of accounting of the University of North Texas at Dallas. Dr. Price has previously held positions of professor and assistant professor, as well as chair and dean, at the University of North Texas, Jackson State University, and the University of Southern Mississippi. Dr. Price has also been active in the Internal Revenue Service as a member of the Commissioner's Advisory Group for two terms and as an Internal Revenue agent.

Professor Price is a certified public accountant who has twice received the UNT College of Business Administration's Outstanding Teaching Award and the university's President's Council Award. Majoring in accounting, he received his BBA and MS degrees from the University of Southern Mississippi and his Ph.D. in accounting from the University of North Texas.

Dr. Price is a member of the Mississippi Society of Certified Public Accountants, the American Accounting Association, and the American Taxation Association (serving as past chair of the Subcommittee on Relations with the IRS and Treasury). Dr. Price has also served as chair of the American Institute of Certified Public Accountants Minority Initiatives Committee and as a member of the Foundation Trustees.

MICHAEL J. FARINA is professor of accounting and finance at Cerritos College in California. Prior to joining Cerritos College, Professor Farina was a manager in the audit department at a large multinational firm of certified public accountants and held management positions with other companies in private industry.

He received an AA in business administration from Cerritos College, a BA in business administration from California State University, Fullerton, and an MBA from the University of California, Irvine. Professor Farina is a member of Beta Gamma Sigma, an honorary fraternity for graduate business students. He is a licensed certified public accountant in California and a member of the American Institute of Certified Public Accountants and the California Society of Certified Public Accountants.

Professor Farina is currently the cochair of the Accounting and Finance Department at Cerritos College. Professor Farina received an Outstanding Faculty award from Cerritos College in 2008.

Haddock/Price/Farina

For students just embarking on a college career, an accounting course can seem daunting, like a rushing river with no clear path to the other side. New concepts and language come fast and furious, and it's easy to feel overwhelmed. Haddock/Price/Farina **bridges the rushing river,** offering first-time accounting students a path to understanding and mastery. Not only is Haddock clear and readable, with many opportunities for students to practice what they've learned, but it also includes **no special journals!** Stripping out this topic allows you to focus on the fundamentals of the introductory accounting course. With one less thing to overwhelm them, your students will be able to achieve solid footing on that bridge to success.

As in their flagship text, Price et al.'s *College Accounting,* the authors have adhered to a common philosophy about textbooks: They should be readable, contain many opportunities for practice, and make accounting relevant for all.

> This text does not use special journals—hurrah!
>
> —Anna Marie Boulware
> St. Charles Community College

Bridges College to Career

- **Encourages Reading** The authors' writing style and clear step-by-step examples make key concepts easy to grasp. *College Accounting*'s concise chapters are broken into manageable sections to avoid overwhelming students who might be seeing the material for the first time. Features like the Business Transaction Analysis Model make it easy for students to see how to analyze business transactions. The Important and Recall margin elements briefly highlight important concepts and remind students of key term definitions as the topics begin to build on each other.

- **Emphasizes Practice** Self reviews at the end of each section give students the opportunity to practice what they've just learned before moving on to the next topic. The author-created end-of-chapter material includes A and B problem sets, exercises, critical thinking problems, and Business Connection problems that utilize real-world companies and scenarios and address important topics like ethics. Mini-practice sets included within the text itself allow students to put theory into practice without paying additional money for a separate practice set. End-of-chapter content is tied to templates in **Excel** and **Quickbooks** allowing students to practice using software they are likely to encounter in the real world.

- **Answers the Question "Why Is Accounting Important?"** The "Why It's Important" explanation that accompanies each learning objective explains to students why the topics they're studying matter. Well-known companies like Google, Southwest, and Urban Outfitters are used in vignettes and examples throughout the text, making a clear bridge for students between the concepts they're learning and how those concepts are applied in the real world.

> The textbook introduces a beginner to the essential concepts and skills needed to succeed in further study of accountancy. For non-business students needing only a basic understanding of the principles, the hands-on instruction teaches the application of a variety of business transactions. The chapters are concise, the effective visuals help motivate the students to actively read, while each chapter's resources encourage practice that leads to retention. It is one of the best introductory accounting texts I have used in my 30+ years of teaching.
>
> —Gisela Dicklin
> Edmonds Community College

How Does Haddock/Price/Farina Bridge the Gap from Learning to Mastery?

College Accounting: A Contemporary Approach is designed to help students learn and master the material.

Chapter Opener

Brief features about **real-world companies**—like **Google, Williams-Sonoma, Urban Outfitters, and Clif Bar**—allow students to see how the chapter's information and insights apply to the world outside the classroom. Thinking Critically questions stimulate thought on the topics to be explored in the chapter.

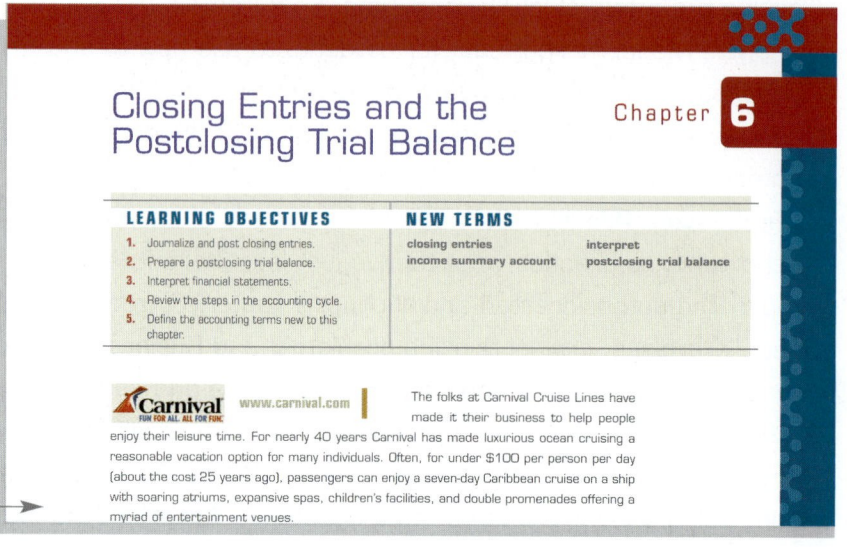

Closing Entries and the Postclosing Trial Balance — Chapter 6

LEARNING OBJECTIVES
1. Journalize and post closing entries.
2. Prepare a postclosing trial balance.
3. Interpret financial statements.
4. Review the steps in the accounting cycle.
5. Define the accounting terms new to this chapter.

NEW TERMS
closing entries
income summary account
interpret
postclosing trial balance

Carnival FUN FOR ALL. ALL FOR FUN. www.carnival.com

The folks at Carnival Cruise Lines have made it their business to help people enjoy their leisure time. For nearly 40 years Carnival has made luxurious ocean cruising a reasonable vacation option for many individuals. Often, for under $100 per person per day (about the cost 25 years ago), passengers can enjoy a seven-day Caribbean cruise on a ship with soaring atriums, expansive spas, children's facilities, and double promenades offering a myriad of entertainment venues.

Learning Objectives

Appearing in the chapter opener and within the margins of the text, learning objectives alert students to what they should expect as they progress through the chapter. Many students question the relevance of what they're learning, which is why we explain **"Why It's Important."**

> An exciting, colorful text with a great approach and layout. Lots of problems and illustrations that will help students learn effectively. A variety of teaching methods that will provide a variety of learning opportunities for students.
>
> —Julia Angel
> North Arkansas College

Section 2

SECTION OBJECTIVES
>> 4. Record cash payments in a cash payments journal.
   WHY IT'S IMPORTANT
   The cash payments journal is an efficient option for recording payments by check.
>> 5. Post from the cash payments journal to subsidiary and general ledgers.
   WHY IT'S IMPORTANT
   The subsidiary and general ledgers must hold accurate, up-to-date information about cash transactions.
>> 6. Demonstrate a knowledge of procedures for a petty cash fund.
   WHY IT'S IMPORTANT
   Businesses use the petty cash fund to pay for small operating expenditures.
>> 7. Demonstrate a knowledge of internal control procedures for cash.
   WHY IT'S IMPORTANT
   Internal controls safeguard business assets.

Cash Payments

A good system of internal control requires that payments be made by check. In a good control system, one employee approves payments, another employee prepares the another employee records the transactions.

The Cash Payments Journal

Unless a business has just a few cash payments each month, the process of record transactions in the general journal is time consuming. The **cash payments journal**

Recall and Important!

Recall is a series of brief reinforcements that serve as reminders of material covered in *previous* chapters that are relevant to the new information being presented. **Important!** draws students' attention to critical materials introduced in the *current* chapter.

important!

For liability T accounts
- right side shows increases,
- left side shows decreases.

Business Transaction Analysis Models

Instructors say mastering the ability to properly analyze transactions is critical to success in this course. Haddock's step-by-step transaction analysis illustrations show how to identify the appropriate general ledger accounts affected, determine debit or credit activity, present the transaction in T-account form, and record the entry in the general journal.

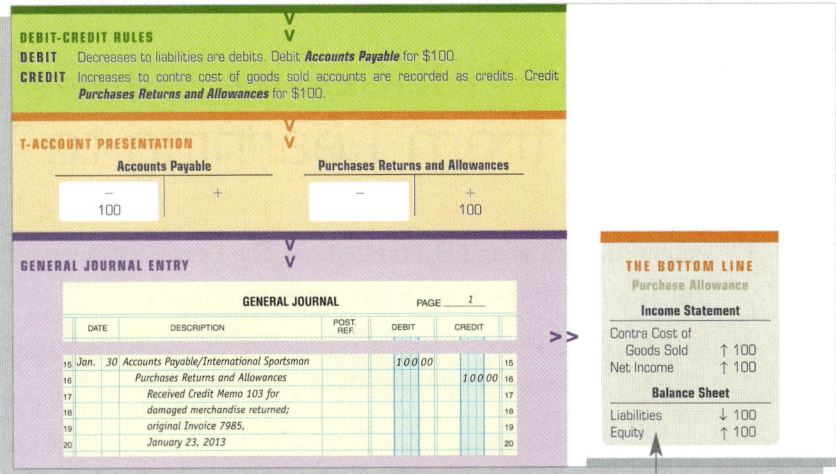

The Bottom Line

Appears in the margins alongside select transactions and concepts in the text. These visuals offer a summary of the effects of these transactions—the end result—on the financial statements of a business.

> The Haddock text flows smoothly from topic to topic and follows the flow of business transactions. The different transactions are illustrated with journal entries and with the calculations needed to compute different numbers. The narrative is succinct and easy to read. The explanations are thorough.
>
> —Marjorie Ashton
> Truckee Meadows Community College

Managerial Implications

Puts your students in the role of managers and asks them to apply the concepts learned in the chapter.

MANAGERIAL IMPLICATIONS <<

- The statement of owner's equity shows the change in owner's equity during the period.
- The balance sheet summarizes the assets, liabilities, and owner's equity of the business on a given date.
- Owners, managers, creditors, banks, and many others use financial statements to make decisions about the business.

THINKING CRITICALLY

What are some possible consequences of not recording financial data correctly?

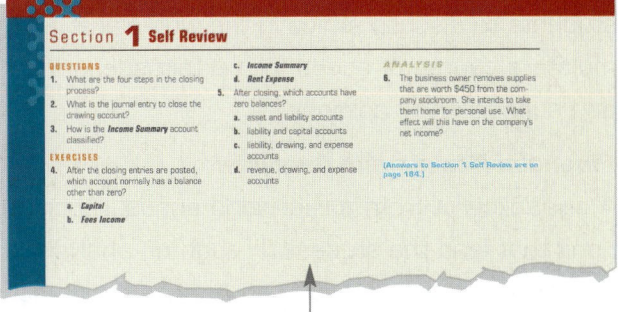

ABOUT ACCOUNTING

Employee Fraud

According to the U.S. Chamber of Commerce, businesses lose billions of dollars each year to employee fraud. The best defense against fraud is to use good internal controls: Have multiple employees in contact with suppliers and screen employees and vendors to reduce fraud opportunities.

About Accounting

These marginal notes contain interesting examples of how accounting is used in the real world, providing relevance to students who might not be going on to a career in accounting.

Self Review

Each section concludes with a Self Review that includes questions, multiple-choice exercises, and an analysis assignment. A Comprehensive Self Review appears at the end of each chapter. Answers are provided at the end of the chapter.

How Can Haddock/Price/Farina Bridge the Gap from Learning to "Doing"?

Problem Sets A and B and Critical Thinking Problems conclude with an **Analyze** question asking the student to evaluate each problem critically.

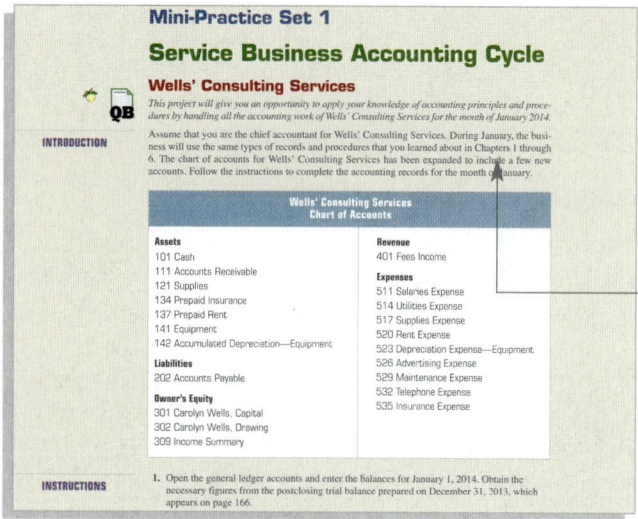

Mini-Practice Sets

In addition to two full-length practice sets that are available to your students for purchase with the textbook, Haddock/Price/Farina offers a number of mini-practice sets right in the book. This means additional practice, but less cost, for your students.

Business Connections

Reinforces chapter materials from practical and real-world perspectives:

Managerial Focus: Applies accounting concepts to business situations.

Ethical Dilemma: Provides the opportunity for students to discuss ethics in the workplace, formulate a course of action for certain scenarios, and support their opinions.

Financial Statement Analysis:

A brief excerpt from a real-world annual report and questions that lead the student through an analysis of the statement, concluding with an Analyze Online activity where students research the company's most recent financial reports on the Internet.

TeamWork: Each chapter contains a collaborative learning activity to prepare students for team-oriented projects and work environments.

Internet Connection: These activities give students the opportunity to conduct online research about major companies, accounting trends, organizations, and government agencies.

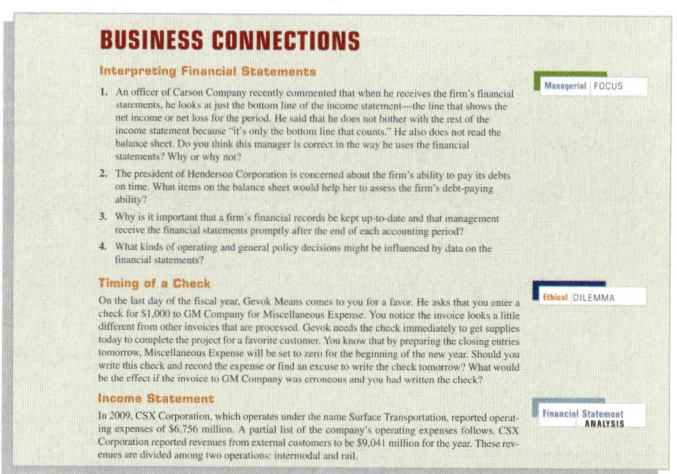

> You have done an excellent job at introducing ethics, something which I haven't found in the other text we are using!! I always introduce ethics to my classes!!
>
> —Joanne Salas
> Olympic College

New to the Second Edition

- **NEW** chapter openers for select chapters feature: **AT&T, indi, Williams-Sonoma, New Castle Hotels, Urban Outfitters, Google,** and **Whole Foods**

- Updates to real-world examples throughout text

- Revised and updated end-of-chapter exercises, problems, and critical thinking problems throughout the text

- Condensed and revised Business Connections section of end-of-chapter material:
  - Financial Statement Analysis questions have been updated to include the latest financial data
  - Streetwise: Questions from the Real World, Extending the Thought, and Business Communication questions have been removed based on user feedback

- Revised Mini-Practice Sets covering the Service Business Accounting Cycle, Merchandising Business Accounting Cycle, Corporation Accounting Cycle, and Financial Analysis and Decision Making

- Modified design of worksheets for added clarity and learning

- Simplified labels in the Business Transaction Analysis Model so students can clearly understand how a transaction affects both sides of the accounting equation

- **NEW** section on online banking in Chapter 9

- Examples in Chapter 10 reflecting the latest earnings base for the Social Security tax and minimum hourly rate of pay

- Deletion of section on Checks Written on Regular Checking Account from Chapter 10 to reflect that most businesses write payroll checks from a separate payroll bank account

- **NEW** McGraw-Hill *Connect Accounting,* an online assignment and assessment solution that connects students with the tools and resources needed to achieve success through faster learning, more efficient studying, and higher retention of knowledge

What Can McGraw-Hill Technology Offer You?

McGraw-Hill *Connect Accounting*

Connect Accounting offers a number of powerful tools and features to make managing assignments easier, so faculty can spend more time teaching. With *Connect Accounting*, students can engage with their coursework anytime and anywhere, making the learning process more accessible and efficient. *Connect Accounting* offers you the features described below.

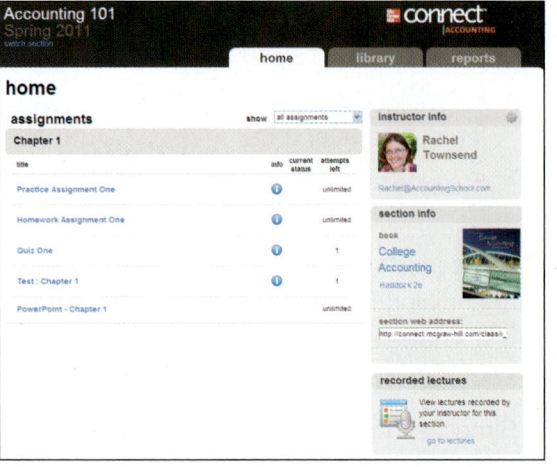

Simple assignment management and auto grading

With *Connect Accounting*, creating assignments is easier than ever, so you can spend more time teaching and less time managing. *Connect Accounting* enables you to:

- Create and deliver assignments easily with select end-of-chapter questions and test bank items.
- Go paperless with the eBook and online submission and grading of student assignments.
- Have assignments scored automatically, giving students immediate feedback on their work and side-by-side comparisons with correct answers.
- Access and review each response; manually change grades or leave comments for students to review.
- Reinforce classroom concepts with practice tests and instant quizzes.
- Guided Examples in *Connect Accounting* provide a narrated, animated, step-by-step walk-through of select exercises similar to those assigned. These short presentations provide reinforcement when students need it most.

Student reporting

Connect Accounting keeps instructors informed about how each student, section, and class is performing, allowing for more productive use of lecture and office hours. The reporting function enables you to:

- View scored work immediately and track individual or group performance with assignment and grade reports.
- Access an instant view of student or class performance relative to learning objectives.
- Collect data and generate reports required by many accreditation organizations, such as AACSB and AICPA.

Instructor library

The *Connect Accounting* Instructor Library is your repository for additional resources to improve student engagement in and out of class. You can select and use any asset that enhances your lecture. The *Connect Accounting* Instructor Library includes access to the eBook version of the text, PowerPoint files,

Solutions Manual, Instructor Resource Manual, and Test Bank. The *Connect Accounting* Instructor Library also allows you to upload your own files. Your students can access these files through the student library.

Student library

The *Connect Accounting* Student Study Center gives access to additional resources such as recorded lectures, online practice materials, an eBook, and more.

McGraw-Hill *Connect Plus Accounting*

McGraw-Hill reinvents the textbook learning experience for the modern student with *Connect Plus Accounting*. A seamless integration of an eBook and *Connect Accounting*, *Connect Plus Accounting* provides all of the *Connect Accounting* features plus the following:

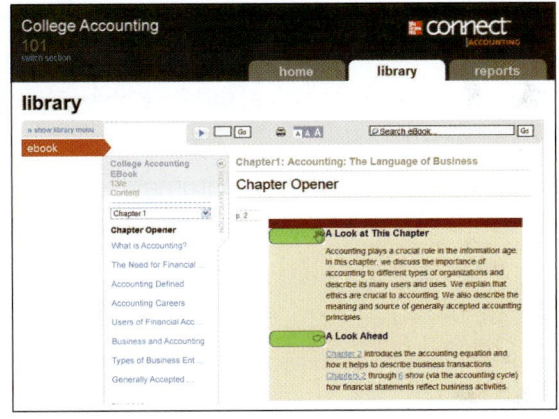

- An integrated eBook, allowing for anytime, anywhere access to the textbook.
- Dynamic links between the problems or questions you assign to your students and the location in the eBook where that problem or question is covered.
- A powerful search function to pinpoint and connect key concepts in a snap.

For more information about Connect, go to **www.mcgrawhillconnect.com,** or contact your local McGraw-Hill sales representative.

Record your lectures for student access with Tegrity Campus

Included in *Connect* is Tegrity Campus, the leading class-capture solution for impacting learning and increasing student satisfaction and retention. With Tegrity's simple one-click recording capability, you can give your students access to your recorded lectures 24 hours a day in just seconds.

With patented Tegrity "search anything" technology, students instantly recall key class moments for replay online or on iPods and mobile devices. At their leisure, they can clear up confusion in their notes or review a discussion on difficult concepts before an exam. Tegrity is another way *Connect* can help your students study and review more effectively and efficiently.

To learn more about Tegrity, watch a two-minute Flash demo at **http://tegrity-campus.mhhe.com.**

How Can Text-Related Web Resources Enrich My Course?

Do More

McGraw-Hill Higher Education and Blackboard have teamed up. What does this mean for you?

1. **Your life, simplified.** Now you and your students can access McGraw-Hill's Connect™ and Create™ right from within your Blackboard course—all with one single sign-on. Say goodbye to the days of logging in to multiple applications.

2. **Deep integration of content and tools.** Not only do you get single sign-on with Connect™ and Create™, you also get deep integration of McGraw-Hill content and content engines right in Blackboard. Whether you're choosing a book for your course or building Connect™ assignments, all the tools you need are right where you want them—inside Blackboard.

3. **Seamless Gradebooks.** Are you tired of keeping multiple gradebooks and manually synchronizing grades into Blackboard? We thought so. When a student completes an integrated Connect™ assignment, the grade for that assignment automatically (and instantly) feeds your Blackboard grade center.

4. **A solution for everyone.** Whether your institution is already using Blackboard or you just want to try Blackboard on your own, we have a solution for you. McGraw-Hill and Blackboard can now offer you easy access to industry-leading technology and content, whether your campus hosts it, or we do. Be sure to ask your local McGraw-Hill representative for details.

Online Course Management

No matter what online course management system you use (WebCT, BlackBoard, or eCollege), we have a course content ePack available for Haddock, 2e. Our new ePacks are specifically designed to make it easy to navigate and access content online. They are easier than ever to install on the latest version of the course management system available today.

Don't forget that you can count on the highest level of service from McGraw-Hill. Our online course management specialists are ready to assist you with your online course needs. They provide training and will answer any questions you have throughout the life of your adoption. So try our new ePacks for Haddock, 2e, and make online course content delivery easy.

ALEKS®

Improve Student Learning Outcomes and Save Instructor Time with ALEKS®

Available online in partnership with McGraw-Hill/Irwin, **ALEKS** is a unique, Web-based program that provides individualized assessment and learning in accounting. ALEKS interacts with students much like a skilled human tutor by using artificial intelligence and adaptive questioning to assess precisely a student's knowledge and provide instruction on the exact topics the student is most **ready to learn.** By providing topics to meet individual students' needs, allowing students to move between explanation and practice, correcting and analyzing errors, and defining terms, ALEKS helps students master course content quickly and easily.

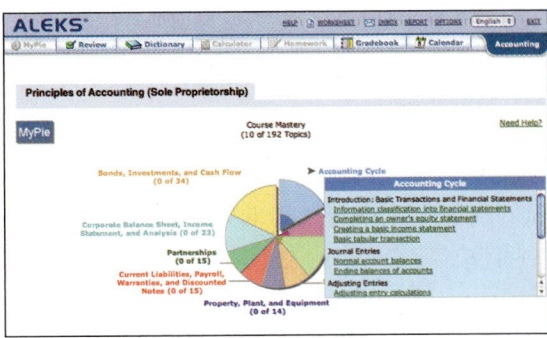

ALEKS also includes an Instructor Module with powerful, assignment-driven features and extensive content flexibility to simplify course management so instructors spend less time with administrative tasks and more time directing student learning. The complimentary Instructor Module provides a course calendar, a customizable gradebook with automatically graded assignments, textbook integration, and dynamic reports to monitor student and class progress.

To learn more about ALEKS, visit **www.aleks.com/highered/business.**

CourseSmart

Learn Smart. Choose Smart. CourseSmart is a new way for faculty to find and review eTextbooks. It's also a great option for students who are interested in accessing their course materials digitally and saving money.

CourseSmart offers thousands of the most commonly adopted textbooks across hundreds of courses from a wide variety of higher-education publishers. It is the only place for faculty to review and compare the full text of a textbook online, providing immediate access without the environmental impact of requesting a print exam copy.

With the CourseSmart eTextbook, students can save up to 45 percent off the cost of a print book, reduce their impact on the environment, and access powerful Web tools for learning. CourseSmart is an online eTextbook, which means users access and view their textbook online when connected to the Internet. Students can also print sections of the book for maximum portability. CourseSmart eTextbooks are available in one standard online reader with full text search, notes and highlighting, and e-mail tools for sharing notes between classmates.
http://www.coursesmart.com

McGraw-Hill Customer Care Contact Information

At McGraw-Hill, we understand that getting the most from new technology can be challenging. That's why our services don't stop after you purchase our products. You can e-mail our Product Specialists 24 hours a day to get product training online. Or you can search our knowledge bank of Frequently Asked Questions on our support Web site. For Customer Support, call **800-331-5094,** or visit **www.mhhe.com/support.** One of our Technical Support Analysts will be able to assist you in a timely fashion.

Instructor Supplements

Instructor CD-ROM

ISBN: 9780077520441 (MHID: 0077520440)

This all-in-one resource incorporates the Test Bank, PowerPoint® Slides, Instructor's Resource Guide, and Solutions Manual.

Online Learning Center (OLC)

www.mhhe.com/haddock2e

The Online Learning Center (OLC) that accompanies *College Accounting: A Contemporary Approach* provides a wealth of extra material for both instructors and students. With content specific to each chapter of the book, the Haddock OLC doesn't require any building or maintenance on your part.

A secure **Instructor Edition** stores your essential course materials to save you prep time before class. The **Instructor's Resource Guide, Solutions Manual, PowerPoint® Slides, Test Bank,** and **Computerized Test Bank** are now just a couple of clicks away.

The OLC Web site also serves as a doorway to McGraw-Hill's other technology solutions.

Instructor's Resource Guide

This supplement contains extensive chapter-by-chapter lecture notes, along with useful suggestions for presenting key concepts and ideas, to help with classroom presentation. The lecture notes coordinate closely with the PowerPoint® Slides, making lesson planning even easier.

Solutions Manual

This supplement contains completed step-by-step calculations to all assignment and Study Guide material, as well as a general discussion of the Thinking Critically questions that appear throughout the text.

Test Bank

This comprehensive Test Bank includes more than 2,000 true/false, multiple-choice, and completion questions and problems.

EZ Test

McGraw-Hill's EZ Test is a flexible and easy-to-use electronic testing program that allows instructors to create tests from book-specific items. EZ Test accommodates a wide range of question types and allows instructors to add their own questions. Multiple versions of the test can be created and any test  can be exported for use with course management systems such as BlackBoard/WebCT. EZ Test Online is a new service that gives instructors a place to easily administer EZ Test-created exams and quizzes online. The program is available for Windows and Macintosh environments.

Assurance of Learning Ready

Many educational institutions today are focused on the notion of assurance of learning, an important element of some accreditation standards. *College Accounting: A Contemporary Approach, 2e*, is designed specifically to support your assurance of learning initiatives with a simple, yet powerful, solution.

Each test bank question for *College Accounting: A Contemporary Approach*, 2e, maps to a specific chapter learning objective listed in the text. You can use our test bank software, *EZ Test, EZ Test Online*, or *Connect Accounting* to easily query for learning objectives that directly relate to the learning objectives for your course. You can then use the reporting features of *EZ Test* to aggregate student results in similar fashion, making the collection and presentation of assurance of learning data simple and easy.

AACSB Statement

McGraw-Hill Companies is a proud corporate member of AACSB International. Understanding the importance and value of AACSB accreditation, *College Accounting: A Contemporary Approach* recognizes the curricula guidelines detailed in AACSB standards for business accreditation by connecting selected questions in the test bank to the general knowledge and skill guidelines found in the AACSB standards.

The statements contained in *College Accounting: A Contemporary Approach*, 2e, are provided only as a guide for the users of this text. The AACSB leaves content coverage and assessment clearly within the realm and control of individual schools, the mission of the school, and the faculty. While *College Accounting: A Contemporary Approach*, 2e, and the teaching package make no claim of any specific AACSB qualification or evaluation, we have, within *College Accounting: A Contemporary Approach*, 2e, labeled selected questions according to the six general knowledge and skills areas.

Student Supplements

Study Guide/Working Papers

ISBN: 9780077430740 (MHID: 0077430743)

This study aid summarizes essential points in each chapter, tests students' knowledge using self test questions, and contains forms that help students organize their solutions to homework problems.

Action Video Practice Set

ISBN: 9780073365527 (MHID: 0073365521)

Action Video Productions is a sole proprietorship service business that uses source documents, a general journal, a general ledger, worksheets, and a filing system to provide students with a usable practice set. The strength of this set is the use of source documents in conjunction with the daily business activities. This set can be completed after Chapter 6 of *College Accounting: A Contemporary Approach*.

Student Guide for QuickBooks Accountant with QuickBooks Accountant Templates

ISBN: 9780077514532 (MHID: 007751453X)

To better prepare students for accounting in the real world, end-of-chapter material in Haddock is tied to QuickBooks Accountant 2011 software. The accompanying study guide provides a step-by-step walkthrough for students on how to complete the problem in the software.

Peachtree Templates

Available on the Online Learning Center. Selected problems in the text are tied to templates created in Peachtree 2011. Students use the accompanying guide to complete the problem in the software.

Microsoft Excel Templates

Available on the Online Learning Center. Prepared by Jack Terry of ComSource Associates, Inc., this spreadsheet-based software uses Excel to solve selected problems in the text, which are identified in the margins of the text with appropriate icons. The Student Excel Templates are available only on the text's Web site.

Online Learning Center (OLC)

www.mhhe.com/haddock2e

The Online Learning Center (OLC) is full of resources for students, including: Online Quizzing, PowerPoint Presentations, Excel Templates, Peachtree Templates, Internet Insights, Accounting on the Job, and McGraw-Hill *Connect Accounting*.

Acknowledgments

The authors are deeply grateful to the following accounting educators for their input during development of *College Accounting: A Contemporary Approach*, 2e. The feedback of these knowledgeable instructors provided the authors with valuable assistance in meeting the changing needs of the college accounting classroom.

Julia Angel,
North Arkansas College

Anna Beavers,
Laney College

Donald Benoit,
Mitchell College

George Bloom,
Santa Ana College

Steven Christian,
Jackson Community College

Joan Cook,
Milwaukee Area Technical College

Cheryl Corke,
Genesee Community College

Noel Craven,
El Camino College

John Daugherty,
Pitt Community College

Gisela Dicklin,
Edmonds Community College

Patti Fedjie,
Minot State University

John Forsythe,
Utah Career College

Regina Gainey,
Westwood College

Becky Hancock,
El Paso Community College

David Juriga,
St. Louis Community College

Norm Katz,
National College–Stow

Rosemary Keasey,
Butler County Community College

Christy Land,
Catawba Valley Community College

Leksell Lee,
Lake Superior College

Bruce Maule,
San Mateo County Community College

John Miller,
Metropolitan College–Elkhorn

Roger L. Moore,
Arizona State University–Beebe

Lisa Nash,
Vincennes University

Jon Nitschke,
Montana State University–Great Falls

Richard Pettit,
Mountain View College

Debra Schmidt,
Cerritos College

Nelda Shelton,
Tarrant County College–South Campus

Ski Vanderlaan,
Delta College

Andy Williams,
Edmonds Community College

Thank You . . .

WE ARE GRATEFUL for the outstanding support from McGraw-Hill/Irwin. In particular, we would like to thank Stewart Mattson, Editorial Director; Tim Vertovec, Publisher; Steve Schuetz, Executive Editor; Rebecca Mann, Developmental Editor; Michelle Heaster, Marketing Manager; Diane Nowaczyk, Senior Project Manager; Michael McCormick, Senior Buyer; Matt Baldwin, Senior Designer; Keri Johnson, Photo Research Coordinator; Bruce Gin, Senior Media Project Manager; and Ron Nelms, Media Project Manager.

Finally, we would like to thank Beth Woods and Helen Roybark for working so hard to ensure an error-free thirteenth edition as well as Joanne Butler for her contributions.

M. David Haddock • John Price • Michael Farina

College Accounting: A Contemporary Approach by Haddock, Price, and Farina is especially designed for first-time accounting students and is very easily read and understood by the student. The textbook is organized to give reinforcement and review of chapter concepts and content and to give students immediate feedback on their comprehension of the subject. Students are also pushed to apply chapter content to current business situations to help strengthen their decision-making skills.

—George Bloom
Santa Ana College

To the Student

Welcome to *College Accounting: A Contemporary Approach.* This book and the accompanying study materials will help you bridge the gap from your first course in accounting to your next business course . . . and beyond, to your career.

    Marginal Icons are used throughout the text to link content to support materials on the Web or via other media, or to highlight consistent elements throughout the text:

    This icon indicates that the content being discussed is related to internal control.

    Continuing problems build on one another from chapter to chapter, allowing you to use the concepts you've just been introduced to in a chapter to revisit and further reinforce material you've learned in previous chapters.

    This icon means that you have the option of working the problem you see at the end of a chapter in Excel, a tool you will use often in the real world, even if you do not go on to be an accountant! The excel templates are available on the text's Web site.

    The Quickbooks software grew out of the success of the personal finance software Quicken. Problems are pulled into Quickbooks, just as they are into Excel, giving you yet another way to practice using software that you are likely to run into in the business world. There is also a Student Guide for Quickbooks Pro available to you as a printed supplement that will assist you in working with Quickbooks.

    Peachtree is an accounting tool that you are likely to encounter if you decide to make accounting your career. This icon indicates that you can work the problem in Peachtree, gaining experience that will be invaluable once you graduate. The Peachtree templates are available on the Online Learning Center.

    McGraw-Hill's *Connect Accounting* system allows you to submit homework online if your professor chooses to utilize it in the classroom. Your professor will request that you obtain this software when you purchase your book if he/she plans to ask you to submit your homework online.

    Self Reviews are a great way to double-check that you've understood what you've just read in your book or what your professor has just covered in lecture. There is a Self Review at the end of every section. Answers to the self reviews can be found at the end of each chapter so you can check your work and make sure you understand a topic before moving on to the next section.

    Learning Objectives can be found at the beginning of each chapter as well as at the beginning of each section. The section opener objectives also contain a brief explanation for "Why It's Important" to study the concept presented.

Online Learning Center (www.mhhe.com/haddock2e) The Web site that accompanies Haddock/Price/Farina's *College Accounting: A Contemporary Approach,* 2e, is a great resource for you. Don't be afraid to use it! On the Online Learning Center (OLC), there are a lot of great materials that will help you not only get through your course, but also get a good grade and remember what you learned. You will find things like:

- Practice Quizzes
- PowerPoint® Slides
- International Insights
- Accounting on the Job Feature

To access the OLC, just go to the link above and look to the left. You'll see a link to the "Student Edition"—click on this and you will find a variety of Course-Wide Content in the top left corner, including accounting videos. Under this, you will see a drop-down menu from which you can choose whatever chapter you want and find additional resources.

Practice Set *College Accounting: A Contemporary Approach,* 2e, comes with a different full-length practice set (in addition to the Mini-Practice Sets included inside the textbook) that you can purchase to get additional practice applying the concepts you've learned in class. Your instructor can provide you with the answers so you can check your work.

Study Guide and Working Papers In addition to giving you a hard copy place to enter the answers to the questions, exercises, and problems your instructor assigns you in class, the Study Guide and Working Papers also include additional activities, exercises, true/false questions, and a demonstration problem that you can work—all of which give you more chances to practice what you're going to see on the test!

Our two main goals are to help you understand and apply accounting and prepare you for the future, whether that includes additional study or a new workplace. We hope the aids we've provided for you as listed above will help enhance your study and ultimately give you a greater understanding of accounting and how it applies in the real world.

Good luck with your studies. We think it will be well worth your efforts.

Brief Contents

Contents

College Accounting

Accounting: The Language of Business

LEARNING OBJECTIVES

1. Define accounting.
2. Identify and discuss career opportunities in accounting.
3. Identify the users of financial information.
4. Compare and contrast the three types of business entities.
5. Describe the process used to develop generally accepted accounting principles.
6. Define the accounting terms new to this chapter.

NEW TERMS

accounting
accounting system
auditing
auditor's report
certified public accountant (CPA)
corporation
creditor
discussion memorandum
economic entity
entity
exposure draft
financial statements
generally accepted accounting principles (GAAP)
governmental accounting
international accounting
management advisory services
managerial accounting
partnership
public accountants
separate entity assumption
social entity
sole proprietorship
Statements of Financial Accounting Standards
stock
stockholders
tax accounting

Google   www.google.com

Can you imagine looking up stock quotes, getting directions, or checking the local weather without help from google.com? Before the development of search engine technology, accessing information quickly was nearly impossible. Although the Internet had its origins in the 1950s, it wasn't until 1995, when Google's founders Larry Page and Sergey Brin developed a new approach to online search that revolutionized the Internet.

Google's features and performance have grown over the years and attracted new users at an astounding rate. By 2000, Google officially became the world's largest search engine with its introduction of a *billion-page index* – the first time so much of the Web's content had been made available in a searchable format. As a publicly owned global Internet communications, commerce, and media company, Google reports financial information to investors, owners, and managers every quarter. Revenues of $6.82 billion were reported for the quarter ended June 30, 2010, an increase of 24 percent compared to the second quarter of 2009.

thinking critically

If you were considering purchasing stock in Google Inc., how would a basic understanding of accounting assist you?

Section 1

SECTION OBJECTIVES	TERMS TO LEARN
>> 1. Define accounting. **WHY IT'S IMPORTANT** Business transactions affect many aspects of our lives. **>> 2. Identify and discuss career opportunities in accounting.** **WHY IT'S IMPORTANT** There's something for everyone in the field of accounting. Accounting professionals are found in every workplace from public accounting firms to government agencies, from corporations to nonprofit organizations. **>> 3. Identify the users of financial information.** **WHY IT'S IMPORTANT** A wide variety of individuals and businesses depend on financial information to make decisions.	accounting accounting system auditing certified public accountant (CPA) financial statements governmental accounting management advisory services managerial accounting public accountants tax accounting

What Is Accounting?

Accounting provides financial information about a business or a nonprofit organization. Owners, managers, investors, and other interested parties need financial information in order to make decisions. Because accounting is used to communicate financial information, it is often called the "language of business."

The Need for Financial Information

Suppose a relative leaves you a substantial sum of money and you decide to carry out your lifelong dream of opening a small sportswear shop. You rent space in a local shopping center, purchase fixtures and equipment, purchase goods to sell, hire salespeople, and open the store to customers. Before long you realize that, to run your business successfully, you need financial information about the business. You probably need information that provides answers to the following questions:

- How much cash does the business have?
- How much money do customers owe the business?
- What is the cost of the merchandise sold?
- What is the change in sales volume?
- How much money is owed to suppliers?
- What is the profit or loss?

As your business grows, you will need even more financial information to evaluate the firm's performance and make decisions about the future. An efficient accounting system allows owners and managers to quickly obtain a wide range of useful information. The need for timely information is one reason that businesses have an accounting system directed by a professional staff.

>> 1. OBJECTIVE

Define accounting.

Accounting Defined

Accounting is the process by which financial information about a business is recorded, classified, summarized, interpreted, and communicated to owners, managers, and other interested parties. An **accounting system** is designed to accumulate data about a firm's financial

4

affairs, classify the data in a meaningful way, and summarize it in periodic reports called **financial statements.** Owners and managers obtain a lot of information from financial statements. The accountant:

- establishes the records and procedures that make up the accounting system,
- supervises the operations of the system,
- interprets the resulting financial information.

Most owners and managers rely heavily on the accountant's judgment and knowledge when making financial decisions.

Accounting Careers

>> 2. OBJECTIVE
Identify and discuss career opportunities in accounting.

Many jobs are available in the accounting profession, and they require varying amounts of education and experience. Bookkeepers and accountants are responsible for keeping records and providing financial information about the business. Generally, bookkeepers are responsible for recording business transactions. In large firms, bookkeepers may also supervise the work of accounting clerks. Accounting clerks are responsible for recordkeeping for a part of the accounting system—perhaps payroll, accounts receivable, or accounts payable. Accountants usually supervise bookkeepers and prepare the financial statements and reports of the business.

Newspapers and Web sites often have job listings for accounting clerks, bookkeepers, and accountants:

- Accounting clerk positions usually require one to two accounting courses and little or no experience.
- Bookkeeper positions usually require one to two years of accounting education plus experience as an accounting clerk.
- Accountant positions usually require a bachelor's degree but are sometimes filled by experienced bookkeepers or individuals with a two-year college degree. Most entry-level accountant positions do not have an experience requirement. Both the education and experience requirements for accountant positions vary according to the size of the firm.

Accountants usually choose to practice in one of three areas:

- public accounting
- managerial accounting
- governmental accounting

PUBLIC ACCOUNTING

Public accountants work for public accounting firms. Public accounting firms provide accounting services for other companies. Usually they offer three services:

- auditing
- tax accounting
- management advisory services

The largest public accounting firms in the United States are called the "Big Four." The "Big Four" are Deloitte & Touche, Ernst & Young, KPMG, and PricewaterhouseCoopers.

Many public accountants are **certified public accountants (CPAs).** To become a CPA, an individual must have a certain number of college credits in accounting courses, demonstrate good personal character, pass the Uniform CPA Examination, and fulfill the experience requirements of the state of practice. CPAs must follow the professional code of ethics.

Auditing is the review of financial statements to assess their fairness and adherence to generally accepted accounting principles. Accountants who are CPAs perform financial audits.

Tax accounting involves tax compliance and tax planning. *Tax compliance* deals with the preparation of tax returns and the audit of those returns. *Tax planning* involves giving advice to clients on how to structure their financial affairs in order to reduce their tax liability.

Management advisory services involve helping clients improve their information systems or their business performance.

ABOUT
ACCOUNTING

Accounting Services
The role of the CPA is expanding. In the past, accounting firms handled audits and taxes. Today accountants provide a wide range of services, including financial planning, investment advice, accounting and tax software advice, and profitability consulting. Accountants provide clients with information and advice on electronic business, health care performance measurement, risk assessment, business performance measurement, and information system reliability.

MANAGERIAL ACCOUNTING

Managerial accounting, also referred to as *private accounting,* involves working for a single business in industry. Managerial accountants perform a wide range of activities, including:

- establishing accounting policies,
- managing the accounting system,
- preparing financial statements,
- interpreting financial information,
- providing financial advice to management,
- preparing tax forms,
- performing tax planning services,
- preparing internal reports for management.

GOVERNMENTAL ACCOUNTING

Governmental accounting involves keeping financial records and preparing financial reports as part of the staff of federal, state, or local governmental units. Governmental units do not earn profits. However, governmental units receive and pay out huge amounts of money and need procedures for recording and managing this money.

Some governmental agencies hire accountants to audit the financial statements and records of the businesses under their jurisdiction and to uncover possible violations of the law. The Securities and Exchange Commission, the Internal Revenue Service, the Federal Bureau of Investigation, and Homeland Security employ a large number of accountants.

>>3. OBJECTIVE

Identify the users of financial information.

Users of Financial Information

The results of the accounting process are communicated to many individuals and organizations. Who are these individuals and organizations, and why do they want financial information about a particular firm?

OWNERS AND MANAGERS

Assume your sportswear shop is in full operation. One user of financial information about the business is you, the owner. You need information that will help you evaluate the results of your operations and plan and make decisions for the future. Questions such as the following are difficult to answer without financial information:

- Should you drop the long-sleeved pullover that is not selling well from the product line, or should you just reduce the price?
- How much should you charge for the denim jacket that you are adding to the product line?
- How much should you spend on advertising?
- How does this month's profit compare with last month's profit?
- Should you open a new store?

SUPPLIERS

A number of other people are interested in the financial information about your business. For example, businesses that supply you with sportswear need to assess the ability of your firm to pay its bills. They also need to set a credit limit for your firm.

BANKS

What if you decide to ask your bank for a loan so that you can open a new store? The bank needs to be sure that your firm will repay the loan on time. The bank will ask for financial information prepared by your accountant. Based on this information, the bank will decide whether to make the loan and the terms of the loan.

TAX AUTHORITIES

The Internal Revenue Service (IRS) and other state and local tax authorities are interested in financial information about your firm. This information is used to determine the tax base:

- Income taxes are based on taxable income.
- Sales taxes are based on sales income.
- Property taxes are based on the assessed value of buildings, equipment, and inventory (the goods available for sale).

The accounting process provides all of this information.

REGULATORY AGENCIES AND INVESTORS

If an industry is regulated by a governmental agency, businesses in that industry have to supply financial information to the regulating agency. For example, the Federal Communications Commission receives financial information from radio and television stations. The Securities and Exchange Commission (SEC) oversees the financial information provided by publicly owned corporations to their investors and potential investors. Publicly owned corporations trade their shares on stock exchanges and in over-the-counter markets. Congress passed the Securities Act of 1933 and the Securities Exchange Act of 1934 in order to protect those who invest in publicly owned corporations.

The SEC is responsible for reviewing the accounting methods used by publicly owned corporations. The SEC has delegated this review to the accounting profession but still has the final say on any financial accounting issue faced by publicly owned corporations. If the SEC does not agree with the reporting that results from an accounting method, the SEC can suspend trading of a company's shares on the stock exchanges.

> Major changes were made to the regulatory environment in the accounting profession with the passage of the Public Company Accounting Reform and Investor Protection Act of 2002 (also known as the Sarbanes-Oxley Act) that was signed into law by President Bush on August 2, 2002. The Act was the most far-reaching regulatory crackdown on corporate fraud and corruption since the creation of the Securities and Exchange Commission in 1934.

The Sarbanes-Oxley Act was passed in response to the wave of corporate accounting scandals starting with the demise of Enron Corporation in 2001, the arrest of top executives at WorldCom and Adelphia Communications Corporation, and ultimately the demise of Arthur Andersen, an international public accounting firm formerly a member of the "Big Five." Arthur Andersen was found guilty of an obstruction of justice charge after admitting that the firm destroyed thousands of documents and electronic files related to the Enron audit engagement. Although on May 31, 2005, the Supreme Court of the United States reversed the Andersen guilty verdict, Arthur Andersen has not returned as a viable business. As a result of the demise of Arthur Andersen, the "Big Five" are now the "Big Four."

The Act significantly tightens regulation of financial reporting by publicly held companies and their accountants and auditors. The Sarbanes-Oxley Act creates a five-member Public Company Accounting Oversight Board. The Board will have investigative and enforcement powers to oversee the accounting profession and to discipline corrupt accountants and auditors. The Securities and Exchange Commission will oversee the Board. Two members of the Board will be certified public accountants, to regulate the accountants who audit public companies, and the remaining three must not be and cannot have been CPAs. The chair of the Board may be held by one of the CPA members, provided that the individual has not been engaged as a practicing CPA for five years.

Major provisions of the bill include rules on consulting services, auditor rotation, criminal penalties, corporate governance, and securities regulation. The Act prohibits accountants from offering a broad range of consulting services to publicly traded companies that they audit and requires accounting firms to change the lead audit or coordinating partner and the reviewing partner for a company every five years. Additionally, it is a felony to "knowingly" destroy or create documents to "impede, obstruct or influence" any existing or contemplated federal investigation. Auditors are also required to maintain all audit or review work papers for seven years. Criminal penalties, up to 20 years in prison, are imposed for obstruction of justice and the Act raises the maximum sentence for defrauding pension funds to 10 years.

Chief executives and chief financial officers of publicly traded corporations are now required to certify their financial statements and these executives will face up to 20 years in prison if they "knowingly or willfully" allow materially misleading information into their financial statements. Companies must also disclose, as quickly as possible, material changes in their financial position. Wall Street investment firms are prohibited from retaliating against analysts who criticize investment-banking clients of the firm. The Act contains a provision with broad new protection for whistle blowers and lengthens the time that investors have to file lawsuits against corporations for securities fraud.

By narrowing the type of consulting services that accountants can provide to companies that they audit, requiring auditor rotation, and imposing stiff criminal penalties for violation of the Act, it appears that this new legislation will significantly help to restore public confidence in financial statements and markets and change the regulatory environment in which accountants operate.

CUSTOMERS

Customers pay special attention to financial information about the firms with which they do business. For example, before a business spends a lot of money on a new computer system, the business wants to know that the computer manufacturer will be around for the next several years in order to service the computer, replace parts, and provide additional components. The business analyzes the financial information about the computer manufacturer in order to determine its economic health and the likelihood that it will remain in business.

FIGURE 1.1

Users of Financial Information

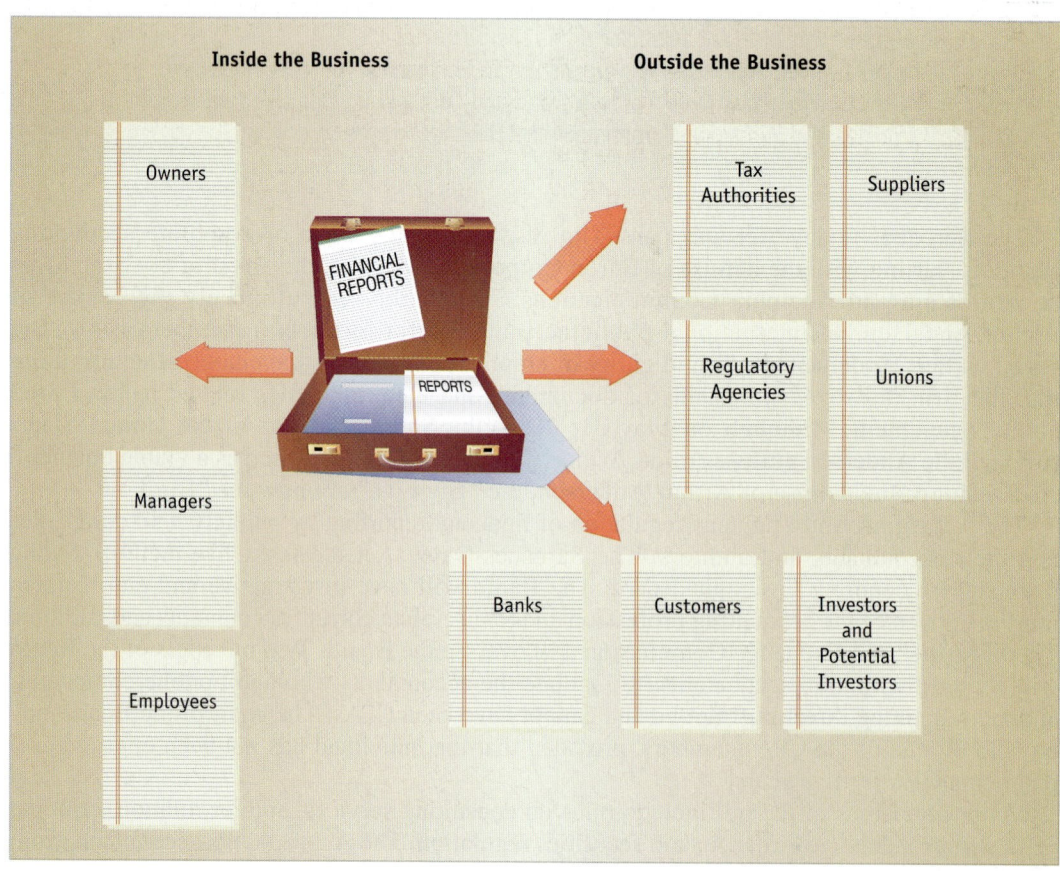

EMPLOYEES AND UNIONS

Often employees are interested in the financial information of the business that employs them. Employees who are members of a profit-sharing plan pay close attention to the financial results because they affect employee income. Employees who are members of a labor union use financial information about the firm to negotiate wages and benefits.

Figure 1.1 illustrates different financial information users. As you learn about the accounting process, you will appreciate why financial information is so important to these individuals and organizations. You will learn how financial information meets users' needs.

Section **1** Self Review

QUESTIONS

1. Why is accounting called the "language of business"?

2. What are financial statements?

3. What are the names of three accounting job positions?

EXERCISES

4. Which organization has the final say on financial accounting issues faced by publicly owned corporations?

   a. Securities and Exchange Commission

   b. Federal Trade Commission

   c. U.S. Treasury Department

   d. Internal Revenue Service

5. One requirement for becoming a CPA is to pass the:

   a. Final CPA Examination

   b. SEC Accounting Examination

   c. Uniform CPA Examination

   d. State Board Examination

ANALYSIS

6. The owner of the sporting goods store where you work has decided to expand the store. She has decided to apply for a loan. What type of information will she need to give to the bank?

(Answers to Section 1 Self Review are on page 19.)

Business and Accounting

The accounting process involves recording, classifying, summarizing, interpreting, and communicating financial information about an economic or social entity. An **entity** is recognized as having its own separate identity. An entity may be an individual, a town, a university, or a business. The term **economic entity** usually refers to a business or organization whose major purpose is to produce a profit for its owners. **Social entities** are nonprofit organizations, such as cities, public schools, and public hospitals. This book focuses on the accounting process for businesses, but keep in mind that nonprofit organizations also need financial information.

Types of Business Entities

The three major legal forms of business entity are the sole proprietorship, the partnership, and the corporation. In general, the accounting process is the same for all three forms of business. Later in the book you will study the different ways certain transactions are handled depending on the type of business entity. For now, however, you will learn about the different types of business entities.

SOLE PROPRIETORSHIPS

A **sole proprietorship** is a business entity owned by one person. The life of the business ends when the owner is no longer willing or able to keep the business going. Many small businesses are operated as sole proprietorships.

The owner of a sole proprietorship is legally responsible for the debts and taxes of the business. If the business is unable to pay its debts, the **creditors** (those people, companies, or government agencies to whom the business owes money) can turn to the owner for payment. The owner may have to pay the debts of the business from personal resources, including personal savings. When the time comes to pay income taxes, the owner's income and the income of the business are combined to compute the total tax responsibility of the owner.

It is important that the business transactions be kept separate from the owner's personal transactions. If the owner's personal transactions are mixed with those of the business, it will be difficult to measure the performance of the business. The term **separate entity assumption** describes the concept of keeping the firm's financial records separate from the owner's personal financial records.

PARTNERSHIPS

A **partnership** is a business entity owned by two or more people. The partnership structure is common in businesses that offer professional services, such as law firms, accounting firms, architectural firms, medical practices, and dental practices. At the beginning of the partnership, two or more individuals enter into a contract that details the rights, obligations, and limitations of each partner, including:

- the amount each partner will contribute to the business,
- each partner's percentage of ownership,
- each partner's share of the profits,
- the duties each partner will perform,
- the responsibility each partner has for the amounts owed by the business to creditors and tax authorities.

The partners choose how to share the ownership and profits of the business. They may share equally or in any proportion agreed upon in the contract. When a partner leaves, the partnership is dissolved and a new partnership may be formed with the remaining partners.

Partners are individually, and as a group, responsible for the debts and taxes of the partnership. If the partnership is unable to pay its debts or taxes, the partners' personal property, including personal bank accounts, may be used to provide payment. It is important that partnership transactions be kept separate from the personal financial transactions of the partners.

> Under the Limited Liability Partnership Act of most states, a Limited Liability Partnership (LLP) may be formed. An LLP is a general partnership that provides some limited liability for all partners. LLP partners are responsible and have liability for their own actions and the actions of those under their control or supervision. They are not liable for the actions or malfeasance of another partner. Except for the limited liability aspect, LLPs generally have the same characteristics, advantages, and disadvantages as any other partnership.

CORPORATIONS

A **corporation** is a business entity that is separate from its owners. A corporation has a legal right to own property and do business in its own name. Corporations are very different from sole proprietorships and partnerships.

Stock, issued in the form of stock certificates, represents the ownership of the corporation. Corporations may be *privately* or *publicly* owned. Privately owned corporations are also called *closely held* corporations. The ownership of privately owned corporations is limited to specific individuals, usually family members. Stock of closely held corporations is not traded on an exchange. In contrast, stock of publicly owned corporations is bought and sold on stock exchanges and in over-the-counter markets. Most large corporations have issued (sold) thousands of shares of stock.

An owner's share of the corporation is determined by the number of shares of stock held by the owner compared to the total number of shares issued by the corporation. Assume that Hector Flores owns 600 shares of Sample Corporation. If Sample Corporation has issued 2,000 shares of stock, Flores owns 30 percent of the corporation (600 shares ÷ 2,000 shares = 0.30 or 30%). Some corporate decisions require a vote by the

>> **4. OBJECTIVE**

Compare and contrast the three types of business entities.

important!

Separate Entity Assumption

For *accounting* purposes, all forms of business are considered separate entities from their owners. However, the corporation is the only form of business that is a separate *legal* entity.

owners. For Sample Corporation, Flores has 600 votes, one for each share of stock that he owns. The other owners have 1,400 votes.

> Subchapter S Corporations, also known as S corporations, are entities formed as corporations which meet the requirements of Subchapter S of the Internal Revenue Code to be treated essentially as a partnership so the corporation pays no income tax. Instead, shareholders include their share of corporate profits, and any items that require special tax treatment, on their individual income tax returns. Otherwise, S corporations have all of the characteristics of regular corporations. The advantage of the S corporation is that the owners have limited liability and avoid double taxation.

One of the advantages of the corporate form of business is the indefinite life of the corporation. A sole proprietorship ends when the owner dies or discontinues the business. A partnership ends on the death or withdrawal of a partner. In contrast, a corporation does not end when ownership changes. Some corporations have new owners daily because their shares are actively traded (sold) on stock exchanges.

Corporate owners, called **stockholders** or *shareholders,* are not personally responsible for the debts or taxes of the corporation. If the corporation is unable to pay its bills, the most stockholders can lose is their investment in the corporation. In other words, the stockholders will not lose more than the cost of the shares of stock.

The accounting process for the corporate entity, like that of the sole proprietorship and the partnership, is separate from the financial affairs of its owners. Usually this separation is easy to maintain. Most stockholders do not participate in the day-to-day operations of the business.

Table 1.1 summarizes the business characteristics for sole proprietorships, partnerships, and corporations.

Generally Accepted Accounting Principles

The Securities and Exchange Commission has the final say on matters of financial reporting by publicly owned corporations. The SEC has delegated the job of determining proper accounting standards to the accounting profession. However, the SEC sometimes overrides decisions the accounting profession makes. To fulfill its responsibility, the accounting profession has developed, and continues to develop, **generally accepted accounting principles (GAAP).** Generally accepted accounting principles must be followed by publicly owned companies unless they can show that doing so would produce information which is misleading.

TABLE 1.1

Major Characteristics of Business Entities

Characteristic	Type of Business Entity		
	Sole Proprietorship	**Partnership**	**Corporation**
Ownership	One owner	Two or more owners	One or more owners, even thousands
Life of the business	Ends when the owner dies, is unable to carry on operations, or decides to close the firm	Ends when one or more partners withdraw, when a partner dies, or when the partners decide to close the firm	Can continue indefinitely; ends only when the business goes bankrupt or when the stockholders vote to liquidate
Responsibility for debts of the business	Owner is responsible for firm's debt when the firm is unable to pay	Partners are responsible individually and jointly for firm's debts when the firm is unable to pay	Stockholders are not responsible for firm's debts; they can lose only the amount they invested

THE DEVELOPMENT OF GENERALLY ACCEPTED ACCOUNTING PRINCIPLES

Generally accepted accounting principles are developed by the Financial Accounting Standards Board (FASB), which is composed of five full-time members. The FASB issues **Statements of Financial Accounting Standards.** The FASB develops these statements and, before issuing them, obtains feedback from interested people and organizations.

First, the FASB writes a **discussion memorandum** to explain the topic being considered. Then public hearings are held where interested parties can express their opinions, either orally or in writing. The groups that consistently express opinions about proposed FASB statements are the SEC, the American Institute of Certified Public Accountants (AICPA), public accounting firms, the American Accounting Association (AAA), and businesses with a direct interest in a particular statement.

The AICPA is a national association for certified public accountants. The AAA is a group of accounting educators. AAA members research possible effects of a proposed FASB statement and offer their opinions to the FASB.

After public hearings, the FASB releases an **exposure draft,** which describes the proposed statement. Then the FASB receives and evaluates public comments about the exposure draft. Finally, FASB members vote on the statement. If at least four members approve, the statement is issued. The process used to develop GAAP is shown in Figure 1.2 on page 14.

Accounting principles vary from country to country. **International accounting** is the study of the accounting principles used by different countries. In 1973, the International Accounting Standards Committee (IASC) was formed. Recently, the IASC's name was changed to the International Accounting Standards Board (IASB). The IASB deals with issues caused by the lack of uniform accounting principles. The IASB also makes recommendations to enhance comparability of reporting practices.

THE USE OF GENERALLY ACCEPTED ACCOUNTING PRINCIPLES

Every year, publicly traded companies submit financial statements to the SEC. The financial statements are audited by independent certified public accountants (CPAs). The CPAs are called *independent* because they are not employees of the company being audited and they do not have a financial interest in the company. The financial statements include the auditor's report. The **auditor's report** contains the auditor's opinion about the fair presentation of the operating results and financial position of the business. The auditor's report also confirms that the financial information is prepared in conformity with generally accepted accounting principles. The financial statements and the auditor's report are made available to the public, including existing and potential stockholders.

important!

GAAP

The SEC requires all publicly owned companies to follow generally accepted accounting principles. As new standards are developed or refined, accountants interpret the standards and adapt accounting practices to the new standards.

>> **5. OBJECTIVE**

Describe the process used to develop generally accepted accounting principles.

MANAGERIAL IMPLICATIONS

FINANCIAL INFORMATION

- Managers of a business make sure that the firm's accounting system produces financial information that is timely, accurate, and fair.
- Financial statements should be based on generally accepted accounting principles.
- Each year a publicly traded company must submit financial statements, including an independent auditor's report, to the SEC.
- Internal reports for management need not follow generally accepted accounting principles but should provide

useful information that will aid in monitoring and controlling operations.

- Financial information can help managers to control present operations, make decisions, and plan for the future.
- The sound use of financial information is essential to good management.

THINKING CRITICALLY

If you were a manager, how would you use financial information to make decisions?

FIGURE 1.2   **The Process Used by the FASB to Develop Generally Accepted Accounting Principles**

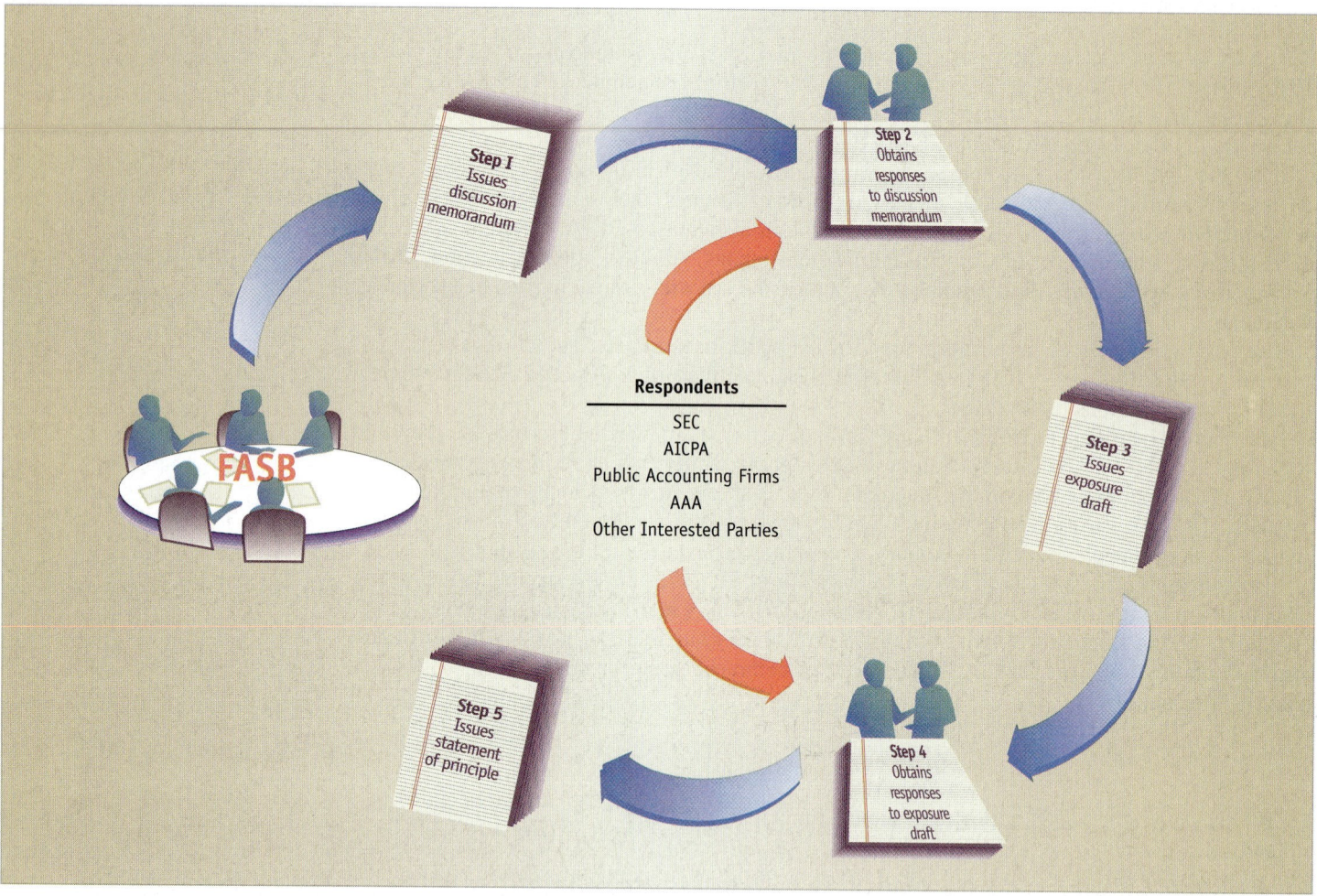

Businesses and the environment in which they operate are constantly changing. The economy, technology, and laws change. Generally accepted accounting principles are changed and refined as accountants respond to the changing environment.

Section 2 Self Review

QUESTIONS

1. Why are generally accepted accounting principles needed?

2. How are generally accepted accounting principles developed?

3. What are generally accepted accounting principles?

EXERCISES

4. A nonprofit organization such as a public school is a(n):

a. social unit
b. economic unit
c. social entity
d. economic entity

5. An organization that has two or more owners who are legally responsible for the debts and taxes of the business is a:

a. social entity
b. partnership

c. sole proprietorship
d. corporation

6. You plan to open a business with two of your friends. You would like to form a corporation, but your friends prefer the partnership form of business. What are some of the advantages of the corporate form of business?

(Answers to Section 2 Self Review are on page 19.)

REVIEW   Chapter Summary

Accounting is often called the "language of business." The financial information about a business is communicated to interested parties in financial statements.

Learning Objectives

1 Define accounting.

Accounting is the process by which financial information about a business is recorded, classified, summarized, interpreted, and communicated to owners, managers, and other interested parties. Accurate accounting information is essential for making business decisions.

2 Identify and discuss career opportunities in accounting.

- There are many job opportunities in accounting.
- Accounting clerk positions, such as accounts receivable clerk, accounts payable clerk, and payroll clerk, require the least education and experience.
- Bookkeepers usually have experience as accounting clerks and a minimum of one to two years of accounting education.
- Most entry-level accounting positions require a college degree or significant experience as a bookkeeper.
- Accountants usually specialize in one of three major areas: public, managerial, or governmental accounting.
  - Some accountants work for public accounting firms and perform auditing, tax accounting, or management advisory functions.
  - Other accountants work in private industry where they set up and supervise accounting systems, prepare financial reports, prepare internal reports, or assist in determining the prices to charge for the firm's products.
  - Still other accountants work for government agencies. They keep track of public funds and expenditures, or they audit the financial records of businesses and individuals to determine whether the records are in compliance with regulatory laws, tax laws, and other laws. The Securities and Exchange Commission, the Internal Revenue Service, the Federal Bureau of Investigation, and Homeland Security employ many accountants.

3 Identify the users of financial information.

All types of businesses need and use financial information. Users of financial information include owners and managers, employees, suppliers, banks, tax authorities, regulatory agencies, and investors. Nonprofit organizations need similar financial information.

4 Compare and contrast the three types of business entities.

- A sole proprietorship is owned by one person. The owner is legally responsible for the debts and taxes of the business.
- A partnership is owned by two or more people. The owners are legally responsible for the debts and taxes of the business.
- A corporation is a separate legal entity from its owners.
- Note that all three types of business entities are considered separate entities for accounting purposes.

5 Describe the process used to develop generally accepted accounting principles.

- The SEC has delegated the authority to develop generally accepted accounting principles to the accounting profession. The Financial Accounting Standards Board handles this task. A series of steps used by the FASB includes issuing a discussion memorandum, an exposure draft, and a statement of principle.
- The SEC oversees the Public Company Accounting Oversight Board that was created by the Sarbanes-Oxley Act. The Board regulates financial reporting by accountants and auditors of publicly held companies.
- Each year, firms that sell stock on stock exchanges or in over-the-counter markets must publish audited financial reports that follow generally accepted accounting principles. They must submit their reports to the Securities and Exchange Commission. They must also make the reports available to stockholders.

6 Define the accounting terms new to this chapter.

Glossary

Accounting (p. 4) The process by which financial information about a business is recorded, classified, summarized, interpreted, and communicated to owners, managers, and other interested parties

Accounting system (p. 4) A process designed to accumulate, classify, and summarize financial data

Auditing (p. 5) The review of financial statements to assess their fairness and adherence to generally accepted accounting principles

Auditor's report (p. 13) An independent accountant's review of a firm's financial statements

Certified public accountant (CPA) (p. 5) An independent accountant who provides accounting services to the public for a fee

Corporation (p. 11) A publicly or privately owned business entity that is separate from its owners and has a legal right to own property and do business in its own name; stockholders are not responsible for the debts or taxes of the business

Creditor (p. 10) One to whom money is owed

Discussion memorandum (p. 13) An explanation of a topic under consideration by the Financial Accounting Standards Board

Economic entity (p. 10) A business or organization whose major purpose is to produce a profit for its owners

Entity (p. 10) Anything having its own separate identity, such as an individual, a town, a university, or a business

Exposure draft (p. 13) A proposed solution to a problem being considered by the Financial Accounting Standards Board

Financial statements (p. 5) Periodic reports of a firm's financial position or operating results

Generally accepted accounting principles (GAAP) (p. 12) Accounting standards developed and applied by professional accountants

Governmental accounting (p. 6) Accounting work performed for a federal, state, or local governmental unit

International accounting (p. 13) The study of accounting principles used by different countries

Management advisory services (p. 5) Services designed to help clients improve their information systems or their business performance

Managerial accounting (p. 6) Accounting work carried on by an accountant employed by a single business in industry

Partnership (p. 11) A business entity owned by two or more people who are legally responsible for the debts and taxes of the business

Public accountants (p. 5) Members of firms that perform accounting services for other companies

Separate entity assumption (p. 11) The concept of keeping a firm's financial records separate from the owner's personal financial records

Social entity (p. 10) A nonprofit organization, such as a city, public school, or public hospital

Sole proprietorship (p. 10) A business entity owned by one person who is legally responsible for the debts and taxes of the business

Statements of Financial Accounting Standards (p. 13) Accounting principles established by the Financial Accounting Standards Board

Stock (p. 11) Certificates that represent ownership of a corporation

Stockholders (p. 12) The owners of a corporation; also called shareholders

Tax accounting (p. 5) A service that involves tax compliance and tax planning

Comprehensive Self Review

1. What is the purpose of accounting?
2. What is the purpose of the auditor's report?
3. What are the three types of business entities?
4. What does the accounting process involve?
5. How is the ownership of a corporation different from that of a sole proprietorship?

(Answers to Comprehensive Self Review are on page 19.)

Discussion Questions

1. What types of people or organizations are interested in financial information about a firm, and why are they interested in this information?
2. What is the function of the Securities and Exchange Commission?
3. What are the three types of business entities, and how do they differ?
4. Why is it important for business records to be separate from the records of the business's owner or owners? What is the term accountants use to describe this separation of personal and business records?
5. What is the purpose of the Financial Accounting Standards Board?
6. What groups consistently offer opinions about proposed FASB statements?
7. What are the three major areas of accounting?
8. What types of services do public accountants provide?
9. What is tax planning?
10. What are the major functions or activities performed by accountants in private industry?
11. What led to the passage of the Public Company Accounting Reform and Investor Protection Act of 2002?
12. What is the purpose of the Public Company Accounting Oversight Board?

PROBLEM

Critical Thinking Problem

Which Type of Business Entity?

Since graduating from college five years ago, Ned Turner has worked for a national chain of men's clothing stores. Ned has held several positions with the company and is currently manager of a local branch store.

Over the past three years, Ned has observed a pattern in men who purchase suits. He believes that the majority of men's suit purchases are black, brown, blue, gray, and olive. He also notices that French cuff shirts are quite fashionable, but few stores carry a wide color selection. Since he has always wanted to be in business for himself, Ned's idea is to open a shop that sells suits that are black, brown, blue, gray, and olive and to carry a wide array of colors of French cuff shirts. The store will also sell fashionable ties and cuff links. Ned already has a name for his store, The Three B's and Go Suit Shop. Ned has discussed his plan with a number of people in the industry and they believe his idea is a viable one.

A new upscale shopping mall is opening nearby and Ned has decided that now is the time to take the plunge and go into business for himself. Ned plans to open the Three B's and Go Suit Shop in the new mall.

One of the things Ned must decide in the process of transforming his idea to reality is the form of ownership for his new business. Should it be organized as a sole proprietorship, a partnership, or a corporation?

What advice would you give Ned? What advantages and disadvantages are there to each choice? The following diagram will help you organize your thoughts.

Business Entity	Advantages	Disadvantages
Sole Proprietorship		
Partnership		
Corporation		

BUSINESS CONNECTIONS

Managerial FOCUS

Know Accounting

1. Why is financial information important?

2. What is the role of the manager versus the accountant?

3. What would you tell a small business owner who says he does not see a need for an accounting system in his business because he closely supervises the day-to-day operations and knows exactly what is happening with the business?

4. As an owner or manager of a business, what questions would you ask to judge the firm's performance, control operations, make decisions, and plan for the future?

5. Besides earning a profit, what other objectives might a business have? Can financial information play an important role in these objectives?

6. What kind of problems can you foresee if a business owner and/or manager does not have a basic knowledge of accounting?

7. Why are international accounting standards important to management?

8. Does a business owner/manager need to worry about the separate entity assumption? Why or why not?

Ethical DILEMMA

To Tell or Not to Tell

You are employed as an accountant for ABC Computers. Your company is in the process of signing a large contract with an electronics components supplier. You have a personal friend that works for the electronics components supplier, and you have personal knowledge that they have trouble paying their bills. Should you report this to your employer before the purchase?

Financial Statement ANALYSIS

Notes to Financial Statements

Within a company's annual report, a section called "Notes to Consolidated Financial Statements" offers general information about the company along with detailed notes related to its financial statements.

Analyze Online: On the American Eagle Outfitters, Inc., Web site (www.ae.com), click on About AE located at the bottom of the page. Then click on AE Investment Information.

Analyze:

1. Would American Eagle Outfitters, Inc. be considered an economic entity or a social entity? Why?

2. What types of merchandise does this company sell?

3. Who are the potential users of the information presented? Why would this information be helpful to these users?

4. What age consumer does the company target?

TEAMWORK

Determining Information

Palfreyman Mattress Company is planning to expand into selling bedroom furniture. This expansion will require a loan from the bank. The bank has requested financial information. Discuss, in a group, the information the bank would require. What information, if any, would you not provide the bank?

FASB—What is it?

Go to the FASB Web site at www.FASB.org. The FASB pronouncements are listed. How many FASB pronouncements are currently listed? How are they listed?

Internet | CONNECTION

Answers to **Self Reviews**

Answers to Section 1 Self Review

1. The results of the accounting process—financial statements—communicate essential information about a business to concerned individuals and organizations.
2. Periodic reports that summarize the financial affairs of a business.
3. Clerk, bookkeeper, and accountant.
4. **a.** Securities and Exchange Commission
5. **c.** Uniform CPA Examination
6. Current sales and expenses figures, anticipated sales and expenses, and the cost of the expansion.

Answers to Section 2 Self Review

1. GAAP help to ensure that financial information fairly presents a firm's operating results and financial position.
2. The FASB develops proposed statements and solicits feedback from interested individuals, groups, and companies. The FASB evaluates the opinions received and votes on the statement.
3. Accounting standards that are changed and refined in response to changes in the environment in which businesses operate.
4. **c.** social entity
5. **b.** partnership
6. The shareholders are not responsible for the debts and taxes of the corporation. Corporations can continue in existence indefinitely.

Answers to Comprehensive Self Review

1. To gather and communicate financial information about a business.
2. To obtain the objective opinion of a professional accountant from outside the company that the statements fairly present the operating results and financial position of the business and that the information was prepared according to GAAP.
3. Sole proprietorship, partnership, and corporation.
4. Recording, classifying, summarizing, interpreting, and communicating financial information about a business.
5. A sole proprietorship is a business entity owned by one person. A corporation is a separate legal entity that has a legal right to own property and do business in its own name.

Analyzing Business Transactions

LEARNING OBJECTIVES

1. Record in equation form the financial effects of a business transaction.
2. Define, identify, and understand the relationship between asset, liability, and owner's equity accounts.
3. Analyze the effects of business transactions on a firm's assets, liabilities, and owner's equity and record these effects in accounting equation form.
4. Prepare an income statement.
5. Prepare a statement of owner's equity and a balance sheet.
6. Define the accounting terms new to this chapter.

NEW TERMS

accounts payable
accounts receivable
assets
balance sheet
break even
business transaction
capital
equity
expense
fair market value
fundamental accounting equation
income statement
liabilities
net income
net loss
on account
owner's equity
revenue
statement of owner's equity
withdrawals

www.southwest.com

Rollin King and Herb Kelleher had a simple notion when they got into the airline business: If you get your passengers to their destinations when they want to get there, on time, at the lowest possible fares, and make darn sure they have a good time doing it, people will fly your airline.

In an economy where airlines struggle to stay out of bankruptcy, Southwest has flourished. Southwest is one of the most profitable airlines—posting a profit for the 37th consecutive year in a row and reporting net profits of $99 million in 2009. How has Southwest differentiated itself? Every airline needs to be safe, reliable, and reasonable in terms of pricing. Southwest is all of these, but the airline has stood out with customers via its brand personality. Southwest is fun, quirky, and has a sense of humor. From chili cook-offs to paper airplane contests and dance competitions you never know what might happen when you board a Southwest flight but you know you'll have a good time.

thinking critically

How can a company's corporate culture affect net profits and the company's bottom line?

SECTION OBJECTIVES

>> 1. **Record in equation form the financial effects of a business transaction.**

   WHY IT'S IMPORTANT
   Learning the fundamental accounting equation is a basis for understanding business transactions.

>> 2. **Define, identify, and understand the relationship between asset, liability, and owner's equity accounts.**

   WHY IT'S IMPORTANT
   The relationship between assets, liabilities, and owner's equity is the basis for the entire accounting system.

TERMS TO LEARN

accounts payable
assets
balance sheet
business transaction
capital
equity
liabilities
on account
owner's equity

Property and Financial Interest

The accounting process starts with the analysis of business transactions. A **business transaction** is any financial event that changes the resources of a firm. For example, purchases, sales, payments, and receipts of cash are all business transactions. The accountant analyzes each business transaction to decide what information to record and where to record it.

>> 1. OBJECTIVE

Record in equation form the financial effects of a business transaction.

Beginning with Analysis

Let's analyze the transactions of Wells' Consulting Services, a firm that provides a wide range of accounting and consulting services. Carolyn Wells, CPA, has a master's degree in accounting. She is the sole proprietor of Wells' Consulting Services. Carlos Valdez, the office manager, has an associate's degree in business and has taken 12 semester hours of accounting. The firm is located in a large office complex.

Every month, Wells' Consulting Services bills clients for the accounting and consulting services provided that month. Customers can also pay in cash when the services are rendered.

STARTING A BUSINESS

Let's start from the beginning. Carolyn Wells obtained the funds to start the business by withdrawing $100,000 from her personal savings account. The first transaction of the new business was opening a checking account in the name of Wells' Consulting Services. The separate bank account helps Wells keep her financial interest in the business separate from her personal funds.

When a business transaction occurs, it is analyzed to identify how it affects the equation *property equals financial interest.* This equation reflects the fact that in a free enterprise system, all property is owned by someone. In this case, Wells owns the business because she supplied the property (cash).

Use these steps to analyze the effect of a business transaction:

1. Describe the financial event.
   - Identify the property.
   - Identify who owns the property.
   - Determine the amount of increase or decrease.

2. Make sure the equation is in balance.

Property	=	Financial Interest

BUSINESS TRANSACTION

Carolyn Wells withdrew $100,000 from personal savings and deposited it in a new checking account in the name of Wells' Consulting Services.

ANALYSIS

a. The business received $100,000 of *property* in the form of cash.

a. Wells had a $100,000 *financial interest* in the business.

Note that the equation *property equals financial interest* remains in balance. The total of one side of the equation must always equal the total of the other side.

Property		=	Financial Interest
	Cash	=	**Carolyn Wells, Capital**
(a) Invested cash	+**$100,000**		
(a) Increased equity			+**$100,000**
New balances	$100,000	=	$100,000

An owner's financial interest in the business is called **equity,** or **capital.** Carolyn Wells has $100,000 equity in Wells' Consulting Services.

PURCHASING EQUIPMENT FOR CASH

The first priority for office manager Carlos Valdez was to get the business ready for opening day on December 1.

BUSINESS TRANSACTION

Wells' Consulting Services issued a $5,000 check to purchase a computer and other equipment.

ANALYSIS

b. The firm purchased new property (equipment) for $5,000.

b. The firm paid out $5,000 in cash.

The equation remains in balance.

Property				=	Financial Interest
	Cash	**+**	**Equipment**	**=**	**Carolyn Wells, Capital**
Previous balances	$100,000			=	$100,000
(b) Purchased equipment		+	**$5,000**		
(b) Paid cash	**−5,000**				
New balances	$95,000	+	$5,000	=	$100,000

Notice that there is a change in the composition of the firm's property. Now the firm has cash and equipment. The equation shows that the total value of the property remains the same, $100,000. Carolyn Wells' financial interest, or equity, is also unchanged. Note that property (Cash and Equipment) is equal to financial interest (Carolyn Wells, Capital).

These activities are recorded for the business entity Wells' Consulting Services. Carolyn Wells' personal assets, such as her personal bank account, house, furniture, and automobile, are kept separate from the property of the firm. Nonbusiness property is not included in the accounting records of the business entity.

PURCHASING EQUIPMENT ON CREDIT

Valdez purchased additional office equipment. Office Plus, the store selling the equipment, allows Wells' Consulting Services 60 days to pay the bill. This arrangement is called buying **on account.** The business has a *charge account,* or *open-account credit,* with its suppliers. Amounts that a business must pay in the future are known as **accounts payable.** The companies or individuals to whom the amounts are owed are called *creditors.*

BUSINESS TRANSACTION

Wells' Consulting Services purchased office equipment on account from Office Plus for $6,000.

ANALYSIS

c. The firm purchased new property (equipment) that cost $6,000.

c. The firm owes $6,000 to Office Plus.

The equation remains in balance.

Property				=	Financial Interest		
	Cash	**+**	**Equipment**	**=**	**Accounts Payable**	**+**	**Carolyn Wells, Capital**
Previous balances	$95,000	+	$5,000	=			$100,000
(c) Purchased equip.		+	**6,000**	=			
(c) Incurred debt					**+$6,000**		
New balances	$95,000	+	$11,000	=	$6,000	+	$100,000

Office Plus is willing to accept a claim against Wells' Consulting Services until the bill is paid. Now there are two different financial interests or claims against the firm's property—the creditor's claim (Accounts Payable) and the owner's claim (Carolyn Wells, Capital). Notice that the total property increases to $106,000. Cash is $95,000 and equipment is $11,000. Carolyn Wells, Capital stays the same; but the creditor's claim increases to $6,000. After this transaction is recorded, the left side of the equation still equals the right side.

When Ben Cohen and Jerry Greenfield founded Ben & Jerry's Homemade Ice Cream, Inc., in 1978, they invested $8,000 of their own funds and borrowed funds of $4,000. The equation *property equals financial interest* is expressed as

Property	=	**Financial Interest**
cash	=	creditors' claims
		+ owners' claims
$12,000	=	$ 4,000
		+ 8,000
		$12,000

PURCHASING SUPPLIES

Valdez purchased supplies so that Wells' Consulting Services could start operations. The company that sold the items requires cash payments from companies that have been in business less than six months.

BUSINESS TRANSACTION

Wells' Consulting Services issued a check for $1,500 to Office Delux, Inc., to purchase office supplies.

ANALYSIS

d. The firm purchased office supplies that cost $1,500.

d. The firm paid $1,500 in cash.

The equation remains in balance.

	Property					=	**Financial Interest**		
	Cash	+	Supplies	+	Equipment	=	Accounts Payable	+	Carolyn Wells, Capital
Previous balances	$95,000			+	$11,000	=	$6,000	+	$100,000
(d) Purchased supplies		+	$1,500						
(d) Paid cash	−$1,500								
New balances	$93,500	+	$1,500	+	$11,000	=	$6,000	+	$100,000

Notice that total property remains the same, even though the form of the property has changed. Also note that all of the property (left side) equals all of the financial interests (right side).

PAYING A CREDITOR

Valdez decided to reduce the firm's debt to Office Plus by $2,500.

Wells' Consulting Services issued a check for $2,500 to Office Plus.

ANALYSIS

e. The firm paid $2,500 in cash.

e. The claim of Office Plus against the firm decreased by $2,500.

The equation remains in balance.

	Property					=	Financial Interest		
	Cash	+	Supplies	+	Equipment	=	Accounts Payable	+	Carolyn Wells, Capital
Previous balances	$93,500	+	$1,500	+	$11,000	=	$6,000	+	$100,000
(e) Paid cash	**−$2,500**								
(e) Decreased debt							**−$2,500**		
New balances	$91,000	+	$1,500	+	$11,000	=	$3,500	+	$100,000

RENTING FACILITIES

In November, Valdez arranged to rent facilities for $4,000 per month, beginning in December. The landlord required that rent for the first two months—December and January—be paid in advance. The firm prepaid (paid in advance) the rent for two months. As a result, the firm obtained the right to occupy facilities for a two-month period. In accounting, this right is considered a form of property.

Wells' Consulting Services issued a check for $8,000 to pay for rent for the months of December and January.

ANALYSIS

f. The firm prepaid the rent for the next two months in the amount of $8,000.

f. The firm decreased its cash balance by $8,000.

The equation remains in balance.

	Property							=	Financial Interest		
	Cash	+	Supplies	+	Prepaid Rent	+	Equipment	=	Accounts Payable	+	Carolyn Wells, Capital
Previous balances	$91,000	+	$1,500			+	$11,000	=	$3,500	+	$100,000
(f) Paid cash	**−$8,000**										
(f) Prepaid rent					**+$8,000**						
New balances	$83,000	+	$1,500	+	$8,000	+	$11,000	=	$3,500	+	$100,000

Notice that when property values and financial interests increase or decrease, the total of the items on one side of the equation still equals the total on the other side.

Property		=	Financial Interest	
Cash	$ 83,000		Accounts Payable	$ 3,500
Supplies	1,500		Carolyn Wells, Capital	100,000
Prepaid Rent	8,000			
Equipment	11,000			
Total	$103,500		Total	$103,500

> The balance sheet is also called the *statement of financial position*. Caterpillar Inc. reported assets of $60 billion, liabilities of $31.6 billion, and owners' equity of $28.4 billion on its statement of financial position at December 31, 2009.

Assets, Liabilities, and Owner's Equity

>> 2. OBJECTIVE
Define, identify, and understand the relationship between asset, liability, and owner's equity accounts.

Accountants use special accounting terms when they refer to property and financial interests. For example, they refer to the property that a business owns as **assets** and to the debts or obligations of the business as **liabilities.** The owner's financial interest is called **owner's equity.** (Sometimes owner's equity is called *proprietorship* or *net worth*. Owner's equity is the preferred term and is used throughout this book.) At regular intervals, Wells reviews the status of the firm's assets, liabilities, and owner's equity in a financial statement called a **balance sheet.** The balance sheet shows the firm's financial position on a given date. Figure 2.1 shows the firm's balance sheet on November 30, the day before the company opened for business.

The assets are listed on the left side of the balance sheet and the liabilities and owner's equity are on the right side. This arrangement is similar to the equation *property equals financial interest.* Property is shown on the left side of the equation, and financial interest appears on the right side.

The balance sheet in Figure 2.1 shows:

- the amount and types of property the business owns,
- the amount owed to creditors,
- the owner's interest.

This statement gives Carolyn Wells a complete picture of the financial position of her business on November 30.

FIGURE 2.1   Balance Sheet for Wells' Consulting Services

Wells' Consulting Services
Balance Sheet
November 30, 2013

Assets		Liabilities	
Cash	83 000 00	Accounts Payable	3 500 00
Supplies	1 500 00		
Prepaid Rent	8 000 00	Owner's Equity	
Equipment	11 000 00	Carolyn Wells, Capital	100 000 00
Total Assets	103 500 00	Total Liabilities and Owner's Equity	103 500 00

Section 1 Self Review

QUESTIONS

1. What is a business transaction?

2. Describe a transaction that increases an asset and the owner's equity.

3. What does the term "accounts payable" mean?

EXERCISES

4. Teresa Wells purchased a computer for $3,250 on account for her business. What is the effect of this transaction?

   a. Equipment increase of $3,250 and accounts payable increase of $3,250.

   b. Equipment decrease of $3,250 and accounts payable increase of $3,250.

   c. Equipment increase of $3,250 and cash increase of $3,250.

   d. Cash decrease of $3,250 and owner's equity increase of $3,250.

5. John Amos began a new business by depositing $75,000 in the business bank account. He wrote two checks from the business account: $12,000 for office furniture and $4,000 for office supplies. What is his financial interest in the company?

   a. $61,000

   b. $59,000

   c. $63,000

   d. $75,000

ANALYSIS

6. Specialty Import Co. has no liabilities. The asset and owner's equity balances are as follows. What is the balance of "Supplies"?

Cash	$25,000
Office Equipment	$15,000
Supplies	????
Jason Odgen, Capital	$50,000

   $ 10,000

(Answers to Section 1 Self Review are on page 50.)

SECTION OBJECTIVES

>> 3. Analyze the effects of business transactions on a firm's assets, liabilities, and owner's equity and record these effects in accounting equation form.

   WHY IT'S IMPORTANT
   Property will always equal financial interest.

>> 4. Prepare an income statement.

   WHY IT'S IMPORTANT
   The income statement shows the results of operations.

>> 5. Prepare a statement of owner's equity and a balance sheet.

   WHY IT'S IMPORTANT
   These financial statements show the financial condition of a business.

TERMS TO LEARN

accounts receivable
break even
expense
fair market value
fundamental accounting equation
income statement
net income
net loss
revenue
statement of owner's equity
withdrawals

The Accounting Equation and Financial Statements

The word *balance* in the title "balance sheet" has a special meaning. It emphasizes that the total on the left side of the report must equal, or balance, the total on the right side.

The Fundamental Accounting Equation

In accounting terms, the firm's assets must equal the total of its liabilities and owner's equity. This equality can be expressed in equation form, as illustrated here. The amounts are for Wells' Consulting Services on November 30.

Assets	=	Liabilities	+	Owner's Equity
$103,500	=	$3,500	+	$100,000

The relationship between assets and liabilities plus owner's equity is called the **fundamental accounting equation.** The entire accounting process of analyzing, recording, and reporting business transactions is based on the fundamental accounting equation.

If any two parts of the equation are known, the third part can be determined. For example, consider the basic accounting equation for Wells' Consulting Services on November 30, with some information missing.

	Assets	=	Liabilities	+	Owner's Equity
1.	?	=	$3,500	+	$100,000
2.	$103,500	=	?	+	$100,000
3.	$103,000	=	$3,500	+	?

In the first case, we can solve for assets by adding liabilities to owner's equity ($3,500 + $100,000) to determine that assets are $103,500. In the second case, we can solve for liabilities by subtracting owner's equity from assets ($103,500 − $100,000) to determine that liabilities are $3,500. In the third case, we can solve for owner's equity by subtracting liabilities from assets ($103,500 − $3,500) to determine that owner's equity is $100,000.

>> **3. OBJECTIVE**

Analyze the effects of business transactions on a firm's assets, liabilities, and owner's equity and record these effects in accounting equation form.

$$A = L + OE$$

important!

Revenues increase owner's equity.
Expenses decrease owner's equity.

29

EARNING REVENUE AND INCURRING EXPENSES

Wells' Consulting Services opened for business on December 1. Some of the other businesses in the office complex became the firm's first clients. Wells also used her contacts in the community to identify other clients. Providing services to clients started a stream of revenue for the business. **Revenue,** or *income,* is the inflow of money or other assets that results from the sales of goods or services or from the use of money or property. A sale on account does not increase money, but it does create a claim to money. When a sale occurs, the revenue increases assets and also increases owner's equity.

An **expense,** on the other hand, involves the outflow of money, the use of other assets, or the incurring of a liability. Expenses include the costs of any materials, labor, supplies, and services used to produce revenue. Expenses cause a decrease in owner's equity.

A firm's accounting records show increases and decreases in assets, liabilities, and owner's equity as well as details of all transactions involving revenue and expenses. Let's use the fundamental accounting equation to show how revenue and expenses affect the business.

SELLING SERVICES FOR CASH

During the month of December, Wells' Consulting Services earned a total of $36,000 in revenue from clients who paid cash for accounting and bookkeeping services. This involved several transactions throughout the month. The total effect of these transactions is analyzed below.

ANALYSIS

g. The firm received $36,000 in cash for services provided to clients.

g. Revenues increased by $36,000, which results in a $36,000 increase in owner's equity.

The fundamental accounting equation remains in balance.

	Assets								=	Liabilities	+	Owner's Equity		
	Cash	+	Supplies	+	Prepaid Rent	+	Equipment	=	Accounts Payable	+	Carolyn Wells, Capital	+	Revenue
Previous balances	$ 83,000	+	$1,500	+	$8,000	+	$11,000	=	$3,500	+	$100,000		
(g) Received cash	+$36,000												
(g) Increased owner's equity by earning revenue												+	$36,000
New balances	$119,000	+	$1,500	+	$8,000	+	$11,000	=	$3,500	+	$100,000	+	$36,000
				$139,500								$139,500		

Notice that revenue amounts are recorded in a separate column under owner's equity. Keeping revenue separate from the owner's equity will help the firm compute total revenue more easily when the financial statements are prepared.

SELLING SERVICES ON CREDIT

Wells' Consulting Services has some charge account clients. These clients are allowed 30 days to pay. Amounts owed by these clients are known as **accounts receivable.** This is a new form of asset for the firm—claims for future collection from customers. During December, Wells' Consulting Services earned $11,000 of revenue from charge account clients. The effect of these transactions is analyzed as follows:

ANALYSIS

h. The firm acquired a new asset, accounts receivable, of $11,000.

h. Revenues increased by $11,000, which results in an $11,000 increase in owner's equity.

The fundamental accounting equation remains in balance.

	Assets								=	Liab.	+	Owner's Equity		
	Cash	+	Accts. Rec.	+	Supp.	+	Prepaid Rent	+	Equip.	=	Accts. Pay.	+	Carolyn Wells, Capital	+	Rev.
Previous balances	$119,000			+	$1,500	+	$8,000	+	$11,000	=	$3,500	+	$100,000	+	$36,000
(h) Received new asset—accts. rec.			+$11,000												
(h) Increased owner's equity by earning revenue														+	$11,000
New balances	$119,000	+	$11,000	+	$1,500	+	$8,000	+	$11,000	=	$3,500	+	$100,000	+	$47,000

$150,500 $150,500

COLLECTING RECEIVABLES

During December, Wells' Consulting Services received $6,000 on account from clients who owed money for services previously billed. The effect of these transactions is analyzed below.

ANALYSIS

i. The firm received $6,000 in cash.

i. Accounts receivable decreased by $6,000.

The fundamental accounting equation remains in balance.

	Assets								=	Liab.	+	Owner's Equity		
	Cash	+	Accts. Rec.	+	Supp.	+	Prepaid Rent	+	Equip.	=	Accts. Pay.	+	Carolyn Wells, Capital	+	Rev.
Previous balances	$119,000	+	$11,000	+	$1,500	+	$8,000	+	$11,000	=	$3,500	+	$100,000	+	$47,000
(i) Received cash	+$6,000														
(i) Decreased accounts receivable			−$6,000												
New balances	$125,000	+	$5,000	+	$1,500	+	$8,000	+	$11,000	=	$3,500	+	$100,000	+	$47,000

$150,500 $150,500

In this type of transaction, one asset is changed for another asset (accounts receivable for cash). Notice that revenue is not increased when cash is collected from charge account clients. The revenue was recorded when the sale on account took place (see entry (**h**)). Notice that the fundamental accounting equation, *assets equal liabilities plus owner's equity,* stays in balance regardless of the changes arising from individual transactions.

PAYING EMPLOYEES' SALARIES

So far Wells has done very well. Her equity has increased by the revenues earned. However, running a business costs money, and these expenses reduce owner's equity.

During the first month of operations, Wells' Consulting Services hired an accounting clerk. The salaries for the new accounting clerk and the office manager are considered an expense to the firm.

BUSINESS TRANSACTION

In December, Wells' Consulting Services paid $8,000 in salaries for the accounting clerk and Carlos Valdez.

ANALYSIS

j. The firm decreased its cash balance by $8,000.

j. The firm paid salaries expense in the amount of $8,000, which decreased owner's equity.

The fundamental accounting equation remains in balance.

	Assets					=	Liab. +		Owner's Equity		
	Cash	+ Accts Rec.	+ Supp.	+ Prepaid Rent	+ Equip.	=	Accts. Pay.	+ Carolyn Wells, Capital	+ Rev.	− Exp.
Previous balances	$125,000	+ $5,000	+ $1,500	+ $8,000	+ $11,000	=	$3,500	+ $100,000	+ $47,000	
(j) Paid cash	**−$8,000**									
(j) Decreased owner's equity by incurring salaries exp.										**+ $8,000**
New balances	$117,000	+ $5,000	+ $1,500	+ $8,000	+ $11,000	=	$3,500	+ $100,000	+ $47,000	− $8,000
			$142,500						$142,500	

Notice that expenses are recorded in a separate column under owner's equity. The separate record of expenses is kept for the same reason that the separate record of revenue is kept—to analyze operations for the period.

PAYING UTILITIES EXPENSE

At the end of December, the firm received a $650 utilities bill.

BUSINESS TRANSACTION

Wells' Consulting Services issued a check for $650 to pay the utilities bill.

ANALYSIS

k. The firm decreased its cash balance by $650.

k. The firm paid utilities expense of $650, which decreased owner's equity.

The fundamental accounting equation remains in balance.

	Assets						=	Liab.	+	Owner's Equity			
	Cash	+	Accts. Rec.	+	Supp.	+	Prepaid Rent	+	Equip.	=	Accts. Pay.	+	C. Wells, Capital	+	Rev.	−	Exp.

	Cash	Accts. Rec.	Supp.	Prepaid Rent	Equip.		Accts. Pay.	C. Wells, Capital	Rev.	Exp.
Previous balances	$117,000 +	$5,000 +	$1,500 +	$8,000 +	$11,000 =		$3,500 +	$100,000 +	$47,000 −	$8,000
(k) Paid cash	−$650									
(k) Decreased owner's equity by utilities exp.										+ $650
New balances	$116,350 +	$5,000 +	$1,500 +	$8,000 +	$11,000 =		$3,500 +	$100,000 +	$47,000 −	$8,650

$141,850 $141,850

EFFECT OF OWNER'S WITHDRAWALS

On December 30, Wells withdrew $5,000 in cash for personal expenses. **Withdrawals** are funds taken from the business by the owner for personal use. Withdrawals are not a business expense but a decrease in the owner's equity.

BUSINESS TRANSACTION

Carolyn Wells wrote a check to withdraw $5,000 cash for personal use.

ANALYSIS

l. The firm decreased its cash balance by $5,000.

l. Owner's equity decreased by $5,000.

The fundamental accounting equation remains in balance.

	Assets						=	Liab.	+	Owner's Equity			
	Cash	+	Accts. Rec.	+	Supp.	+	Prepaid Rent	+	Equip.	=	Accts. Pay.	+	Carolyn Wells, Capital	+	Rev.	−	Exp.

	Cash	Accts. Rec.	Supp.	Prepaid Rent	Equip.		Accts. Pay.	Carolyn Wells, Capital	Rev.	Exp.
Previous balances	$116,350 +	$5,000 +	$1,500 +	$8,000 +	$11,000 =		$3,500 +	$100,000 +	$47,000 −	$8,650
(l) Withdrew cash	−$5,000									
(l) Decreased owner's equity								− $5,000		
New balances	$111,350 +	$5,000 +	$1,500 +	$8,000 +	$11,000 =		$3,500 +	$95,000 +	$47,000 −	$8,650

$136,850 $136,850

SUMMARY OF TRANSACTIONS

Figure 2.2 on page 34 summarizes the transactions of Wells' Consulting Services through December 31. Notice that after each transaction, the fundamental accounting equation is in balance. Test your understanding by describing the nature of each transaction. Then check your results by referring to the discussion of each transaction.

FIGURE 2.2   Transactions of Wells' Consulting Services Through December 31, 2013

	Cash	+ Accts. Rec.	+ Supp.	+ Prepaid Rent	+ Equip.	= Accts. Pay.	+ C. Wells, Capital	+ Rev.	− Exp.
(a)	+$100,000						+ $100,000		
Balances	100,000					=	100,000		
(b)	−5,000				+ $5,000				
Balances	95,000				+ 5,000	=	100,000		
(c)					+ 6,000	+ $6,000			
Balances	95,000				+ 11,000	= 6,000	+ 100,000		
(d)	−1,500		+ $1,500						
Balances	93,500		+ 1,500		+ 11,000	= 6,000	+ 100,000		
(e)	−2,500					−2,500			
Balances	91,000		+ 1,500		+ 11,000	= 3,500	+ 100,000		
(f)	−8,000			+ $8,000					
Balances	83,000		+ 1,500	+ 8,000	+ 11,000	= 3,500	+ 100,000		
(g)	+36,000							+ $36,000	
Balances	119,000		+ 1,500	+ 8,000	+ 11,000	= 3,500	+ 100,000	+ 36,000	
(h)		+ $11,000						+ 11,000	
Balances	119,000	+ 11,000	+ 1,500	+ 8,000	+ 11,000	= 3,500	+ 100,000	+ 47,000	
(i)	+6,000	− 6,000							
Balances	125,000	+ 5,000	+ 1,500	+ 8,000	+ 11,000	= 3,500	+ 100,000	+ 47,000	
(j)	−8,000								+ $8,000
Balances	117,000	+ 5,000	+ 1,500	+ 8,000	+ 11,000	= 3,500	+ 100,000	+ 47,000	− 8,000
(k)	−650								+ 650
Balances	116,350	+ 5,000	+ 1,500	+ 8,000	+ 11,000	= 3,500	+ 100,000	+ 47,000	− 8,650
(l)	−5,000						− 5,000		
Balances	$111,350	+ $5,000	+ $1,500	+ $8,000	+ $11,000	= $3,500	+ $95,000	+ $47,000	− $8,650

$136,850 $136,850

The Income Statement

To be meaningful to owners, managers, and other interested parties, financial statements should provide information about revenue and expenses, assets and claims on the assets, and owner's equity.

The **income statement** shows the results of business operations for a specific period of time such as a month, a quarter, or a year. The income statement shows the revenue earned and the expenses of doing business. (The income statement is sometimes called a *profit and loss statement* or a *statement of income and expenses.* The most common term, income statement, is used throughout this text.) Figure 2.3 shows the income statement for Wells' Consulting Services for its first month of operation.

The income statement shows the difference between income from services provided or goods sold and the amount spent to operate the business. **Net income** results when revenue is greater than the expenses for the period. When expenses are greater than revenue, the result is a **net loss.** In the rare case when revenue and expenses are equal, the firm is said to **break even.** The income statement in Figure 2.3 shows a net income; revenue is greater than expenses.

The three-line heading of the income statement shows *who, what,* and *when.*

■ Who—the business name appears on the first line.

>> **4. OBJECTIVE**

Prepare an income statement.

Financial Statements

Financial statements are reports that summarize a firm's financial affairs.

FIGURE 2.3

Income Statement for Wells'
Consulting Services

Wells' Consulting Services			
Income Statement			
Month Ended December 31, 2013			
Revenue			
Fees Income			47 000 00
Expenses			
Salaries Expense	8 000 00		
Utilities Expense	6 50 00		
Total Expenses		8 650 00	
Net Income		38 350 00	

- What—the report title appears on the second line.
- When—the period covered appears on the third line.

The third line of the income statement heading in Figure 2.3 indicates that the report covers operations for the "Month Ended December 31, 2013." Review how other time periods are reported on the third line of the income statement heading.

Period Covered	Third Line of Heading
Jan., Feb., Mar.	Three-Month Period Ended March 31, 2013
Jan. to Dec.	Year Ended December 31, 2013
July 1 to June 30	Fiscal Year Ended June 30, 2013

Note the use of single and double rules in amount columns. A single line is used to show that the amounts above it are being added or subtracted. Double lines are used under the final amount in a column or section of a report to show that the amount is complete. Nothing is added to or subtracted from an amount with a double line.

> Some companies refer to the income statement as the *statement of operations*. American Eagle Outfitters, Inc., reported $2.99 billion in sales on consolidated statements of operations for the fiscal year ended January 2010.

The income statement for Wells' Consulting Services does not have dollar signs because it was prepared on accounting paper with ruled columns. However, dollar signs are used on income statements that are prepared on plain paper, that is, not on a ruled form.

The Statement of Owner's Equity and the Balance Sheet

The **statement of owner's equity** reports the changes that occurred in the owner's financial interest during the reporting period. This statement is prepared before the balance sheet so that the amount of the ending capital balance is available for presentation on the balance sheet. Figure 2.4 on page 36 shows the statement of owner's equity for Wells' Consulting Services. Note that the statement of owner's equity has a three-line heading: *who, what,* and *when.*

- The first line of the statement of owner's equity is the capital balance at the beginning of the period.
- Net income is an increase to owner's equity; net loss is a decrease to owner's equity.
- Withdrawals by the owner are a decrease to owner's equity.

>> 5. OBJECTIVE

Prepare a statement of owner's equity and a balance sheet.

FIGURE 2.4

Statement of Owner's Equity for
Wells' Consulting Services

Wells' Consulting Services Statement of Owner's Equity Month Ended December 31, 2013			
Carolyn Wells, Capital, December 1, 2013			1 0 0 0 0 0 00
Net Income for December	3 8 3 5 0 00		
Less Withdrawals for December	5 0 0 0 00		
Increase in Capital			3 3 3 5 0 00
Carolyn Wells, Capital, December 31, 2013			1 3 3 3 5 0 00

- Additional investments by the owners are an increase to owner's equity.
- The total of changes in equity is reported on the line "Increase in Capital" (or "Decrease in Capital").
- The last line of the statement of owner's equity is the capital balance at the end of the period.

If Carolyn Wells had made any additional investments during December, this would appear as a separate line on Figure 2.4. Additional investments can be cash or other assets such as equipment. If an investment is made in a form other than cash, the investment is recorded at its fair market value. **Fair market value** is the current worth of an asset or the price the asset would bring if sold on the open market.

The ending balances in the asset and liability accounts are used to prepare the balance sheet.

	Assets					=	Liab.	+	Owner's Equity			
	Cash	+ Accts. Rec.	+ Supp.	+ Prepaid Rent	+ Equip.	=	Accts. Pay.	+	C. Wells, Capital	+ Rev.	− Exp.	
New balances	$111,350	+ $5,000	+ $1,500	+ $8,000	+ $11,000	=	$3,500	+	$95,000	+ $47,000	− $8,650	
			$136,850							$136,850		

important!

Financial Statements

The balance sheet is a snapshot of the firm's financial position on a specific date. The income statement, like a movie or video, shows the results of business operations over a period of time.

The ending capital balance from the statement of owner's equity is also used to prepare the balance sheet. Figure 2.5 shows the balance sheet for Wells' Consulting Services on December 31, 2013.

The balance sheet shows:

- Assets—the types and amounts of property that the business owns,
- Liabilities—the amounts owed to creditors,
- Owner's Equity—the owner's equity on the reporting date.

In preparing a balance sheet, remember the following:

- The three-line heading gives the firm's name (who), the title of the report (what), and the date of the report (when).
- Balance sheets prepared using the account form (as in Figure 2.5) show total assets on the same horizontal line as the total liabilities and owner's equity.
- Dollar signs are omitted when financial statements are prepared on paper with ruled columns. Statements that are prepared on plain paper, not ruled forms, show dollar signs with the first amount in each column and with each total.
- A single line shows that the amounts above it are being added or subtracted. Double lines indicate that the amount is the final amount in a column or section of a report.

Figure 2.6 shows the connections among the financial statements. Financial statements are prepared in a specific order:

- income statement
- statement of owner's equity
- balance sheet

FIGURE 2.5   Balance Sheet for Wells' Consulting Services

Wells' Consulting Services
Balance Sheet
December 31, 2013

Assets			Liabilities		
Cash	1 1 1 3 5 0	00	Accounts Payable	3 5 0 0	00
Accounts Receivables	5 0 0 0	00			
Supplies	1 5 0 0	00			
Prepaid Rent	8 0 0 0	00	Owner's Equity		
Equipment	1 1 0 0 0	00	Carolyn Wells, Capital	1 3 3 3 5 0	00
Total Assets	1 3 6 8 5 0	00	Total Liabilities and Owner's Equity	1 3 6 8 5 0	00

Step 1:   Prepare the Income Statement

Wells' Consulting Services
Income Statement
Month Ended December 31, 2013

Revenue				
Fees Income			4 7 0 0 0	00
Expenses				
Salaries Expense	8 0 0 0	00		
Utilities Expense	6 5 0	00		
Total Expenses			8 6 5 0	00
Net Income			3 8 3 5 0	00

Step 2: Prepare the Statement of Owner's Equity

Wells' Consulting Services
Statement of Owner's Equity
Month Ended December 31, 2013

Carolyn Wells, Capital, December 1, 2013			1 0 0 0 0 0	00
Net Income for December	3 8 3 5 0	00		
Less Withdrawals for December	5 0 0 0	00		
Increase in Capital			3 3 3 5 0	00
Carolyn Wells, Capital, December 31, 2013			1 3 3 3 5 0	00

Step 3: Prepare the Balance Sheet

Wells' Consulting Services
Balance Sheet
December 31, 2013

Assets			Liabilities		
Cash	1 1 1 3 5 0	00	Accounts Payable	3 5 0 0	00
Accounts Receivables	5 0 0 0	00			
Supplies	1 5 0 0	00			
Prepaid Rent	8 0 0 0	00	Owner's Equity		
Equipment	1 1 0 0 0	00	Carolyn Wells, Capital	1 3 3 3 5 0	00
Total Assets	1 3 6 8 5 0 0		Total Liabilities and Owner's Equity	1 3 6 8 5 0	00

FIGURE 2.6

Process for Preparing Financial Statements

Net income (or loss) is transferred to the statement of owner's equity.

The ending capital balance is transferred to the balance sheet.

MANAGERIAL IMPLICATIONS

ACCOUNTING SYSTEMS

- Sound financial records and statements are necessary so that businesspeople can make good decisions.
- Financial statements show:
  - the amount of profit or loss,
  - the assets on hand,
  - the amount owed to creditors,
  - the amount of owner's equity.

- Well-run and efficiently managed businesses have good accounting systems that provide timely and useful information.
- Transactions involving revenue and expenses are recorded separately from owner's equity in order to analyze operations for the period.

THINKING CRITICALLY

If you were buying a business, what would you look for in the company's financial statements?

Net income from the income statement is used to prepare the statement of owner's equity. The ending capital balance from the statement of owner's equity is used to prepare the balance sheet.

The Importance of Financial Statements

Preparing financial statements is one of the accountant's most important jobs. Each day millions of business decisions are made based on the information in financial statements.

Business managers and owners use the balance sheet and the income statement to control current operations and plan for the future. Creditors, prospective investors, governmental agencies, and others are interested in the profits of the business and in the asset and equity structure.

Section 2 Self Review

QUESTIONS

1. What are withdrawals and how do they affect the basic accounting equation?

2. If an owner gives personal tools to the business, how is the transaction recorded?

3. What information is included in the financial statement headings?

EXERCISES

4. What information is contained in the income statement?

     a. revenues and expenses for a period of time

     b. revenue and expenses on a specific date

     c. assets, liabilities, and owner's equity for a period of time

     d. assets, liabilities, and owner's equity on a specific date

5. Interior Designs has assets of $90,000 and liabilities of $35,000. What is the owner's equity?

     a. $25,000

     b. $15,000

     c. $80,000

     d. $55,000

ANALYSIS

6. Haden Hardware had revenues of $55,000 and expenses of $26,000. How does this affect owner's equity?

(Answers to Section 2 Self Review are on page 50.)

REVIEW   Chapter Summary

Accounting begins with the analysis of business transactions. Each transaction changes the financial position of a business. In this chapter, you have learned how to analyze business transactions and how they affect assets, liabilities, and owner's equity. After transactions are analyzed and recorded, financial statements reflect the summarized changes to and results of business operations.

Learning Objectives

1   **Record in equation form the financial effects of a business transaction.**

The equation *property equals financial interest* reflects the fact that in a free enterprise system all property is owned by someone. This equation remains in balance after each business transaction.

2   **Define, identify, and understand the relationship between asset, liability, and owner's equity accounts.**

The term *assets* refers to property. The terms *liabilities* and *owner's equity* refer to financial interest. The relationship between assets, liabilities, and owner's equity is shown in equation form.

Assets	=	Liabilities + Owner's Equity
Owner's Equity	=	Assets − Liabilities
Liabilities	=	Assets − Owner's Equity

3   **Analyze the effects of business transactions on a firm's assets, liabilities, and owner's equity and record these effects in accounting equation form.**

1. Describe the financial event.
   - Identify the property.
   - Identify who owns the property.
   - Determine the amount of the increase or decrease.
2. Make sure the equation is in balance.

4   **Prepare an income statement.**

The income statement summarizes changes in owner's equity that result from revenue and expenses. The difference between revenue and expenses is the net income or net loss of the business for the period.

An income statement has a three-line heading:
- who
- what
- when

For the income statement, "when" refers to a period of time.

5   **Prepare a statement of owner's equity and a balance sheet.**

Changes in owner's equity for the period are summarized on the statement of owner's equity.
- Net income increases owner's equity.
- Added investments increase owner's equity.
- A net loss for the period decreases owner's equity.
- Withdrawals by the owner decrease owner's equity.

A statement of owner's equity has a three-line heading:
- who
- what
- when

For the statement of owner's equity, "when" refers to a period of time.

The balance sheet shows the assets, liabilities, and owner's equity on a given date.

A balance sheet has a three-line heading:
- who
- what
- when

For the balance sheet, "when" refers to a single date.

The financial statements are prepared in the following order.

1. Income Statement   *P&L*
2. Statement of Owner's Equity
3. Balance Sheet

6   **Define the accounting terms new to this chapter.**

Glossary

Accounts payable (p. 24) Amounts a business must pay in the future

Accounts receivable (p. 30) Claims for future collection from customers

Assets (p. 27) Property owned by a business

Balance sheet (p. 27) A formal report of a business's financial condition on a certain date; reports the assets, liabilities, and owner's equity of the business

Break even (p. 34) A point at which revenue equals expenses

Business transaction (p. 22) A financial event that changes the resources of a firm

Capital (p. 23) Financial investment in a business; equity

Equity (p. 23) An owner's financial interest in a business

Expense (p. 30) An outflow of cash, use of other assets, or incurring of a liability

Fair market value (p. 36) The current worth of an asset or the price the asset would bring if sold on the open market

Fundamental accounting equation (p. 29) The relationship between assets and liabilities plus owner's equity

Income statement (p. 34) A formal report of business operations covering a specific period of time; also called a profit and loss statement or a statement of income and expenses

Liabilities (p. 27) Debts or obligations of a business

Net income (p. 34) The result of an excess of revenue over expenses

Net loss (p. 34) The result of an excess of expenses over revenue

On account (p. 24) An arrangement to allow payment at a later date; also called a charge account or open-account credit

Owner's equity (p. 27) The financial interest of the owner of a business; also called proprietorship or net worth

Revenue (p. 30) An inflow of money or other assets that results from the sales of goods or services or from the use of money or property; also called income

Statement of owner's equity (p. 35) A formal report of changes that occurred in the owner's financial interest during a reporting period

Withdrawals (p. 33) Funds taken from the business by the owner for personal use

Comprehensive **Self Review**

1. If one side of the fundamental accounting equation is decreased, what will happen to the other side? Why?
2. What is the difference between buying for cash and buying on account? *Paying Now or later*
3. In what order are the financial statements prepared? Why?
4. What effect do revenue and expenses have on owner's equity?
5. Describe a transaction that will cause Accounts Payable and Cash to decrease by $700.

(Answers to Comprehensive Self Review are on page 51.)

Discussion **Questions**

1. What is the fundamental accounting equation? *A = L + OE*
2. What are expenses? *$ spent*
3. What is revenue? *$ made*

4. Describe the effects of each of the following business transactions on assets, liabilities, and owner's equity.

   a. Sold services on credit.

   b. Bought furniture for cash.

   c. Paid cash to a creditor.

   d. Sold services for cash.

   e. Paid salaries to employees.

   f. Bought equipment on credit.

5. What information does the income statement contain?

6. How is net income determined?

7. What information is shown in the heading of a financial statement?

8. Why does the third line of the headings differ on the balance sheet and the income statement?

9. What information does the statement of owner's equity contain?

10. How does net income affect owner's equity?

11. What are assets, liabilities, and owner's equity?

12. What information does the balance sheet contain?

APPLICATIONS

Exercises

Determining accounting equation amounts.

◀ **Exercise 2.1**
Objectives 1, 2

Just before Anderson Laboratories opened for business, Roy Anderson, the owner, had the following assets and liabilities. Determine the totals that would appear in the firm's fundamental accounting equation (Assets = Liabilities + Owner's Equity).

Cash	$40,500
Laboratory Equipment	75,600
Laboratory Supplies	6,800
Loan Payable	15,100
Accounts Payable	9,875

$$\underset{122,900}{A} = \underset{24975}{L} \overset{+OE}{\ } 97925$$

Completing the accounting equation.

◀ **Exercise 2.2**
Objectives 1, 2

The fundamental accounting equation for several businesses follows. Supply the missing amounts.

	Assets	=	Liabilities	+	Owner's Equity
1.	$26,800	=	$5,060	+	$? 21,740
2.	$23,200	=	$4,680	+	$? 18,520
3.	$15,575	=	$? 5425	+	$10,150
4.	$? 35975	=	$3,900	+	$32,075
5.	$33,500	=	$? 8625	+	$24,875

Exercise 2.3

Objectives 1, 2, 3

▶ **Determining the effects of transactions on the accounting equation.**

Indicate the impact of each of the transactions below on the fundamental accounting equation (Assets = Liabilities + Owner's Equity) by placing a "+" to indicate an increase and a "−" to indicate a decrease. The first transaction is entered as an example.

	Assets	=	Liabilities	+	Owner's Equity
Transaction 1	+				+

TRANSACTIONS

1. Owner invested $90,000 in the business. +
2. Purchased $26,700 supplies on account. +
3. Purchased equipment for $21,000 cash. −
4. Paid $6,000 for rent (in advance). +
5. Performed services for $7,800 cash. +
6. Paid $2,160 for utilities. −
7. Performed services for $10,500 on account. +
8. Received $6,600 from charge customers. +
9. Paid salaries of $4,500 to employees. −
10. Paid $6,000 to a creditor on account. −

Exercise 2.4

Objectives 1, 2, 3

▶ **Determining balance sheet amounts.**

The following financial data are for the dental practice of Dr. Donna Wells when she began operations in July. Determine the amounts that would appear in Dr. Wells' balance sheet.

1. Owes $18,000 to the Jones Equipment Company.
2. Has cash balance of $12,500.
3. Has dental supplies of $3,150.
4. Owes $3,680 to Ace Furniture Supply.
5. Has dental equipment of $25,550.
6. Has office furniture of $7,000.

Exercise 2.5

Objectives 1, 2, 3

▶ **Determining the effects of transactions on the accounting equation.**

Quick Copy had the transactions listed below during the month of April. Show how each transaction would be recorded in the accounting equation. Compute the totals at the end of the month. The headings to be used in the equation follow.

Assets			=	Liabilities	+	Owner's Equity			
Cash	+ Accounts Receivable	+ Equipment	=	Accounts Payable	+	Amos Roberts, Capital	+ Revenue	− Expenses	

TRANSACTIONS

1. Amos Roberts started the business with a cash investment of $50,000.
2. Purchased equipment for $17,000 on credit.
3. Performed services for $2,100 in cash.

4. Purchased additional equipment for $3,600 in cash.

5. Performed services for $4,550 on credit.

6. Paid salaries of $3,950 to employees.

7. Received $2,200 cash from charge account customers.

8. Paid $9,000 to a creditor on account.

Computing net income or net loss.

◀ **Exercise 2.6**
Objective 4

Clark Computer Maintenance and Repair Shop had the following revenue and expenses during the month ended June 30. Did the firm earn a net income or incur a net loss for the period? What was the amount?

Fees for computer repairs	$39,600
Advertising expense	5,300
Salaries expense	18,100
Telephone expense	650
Fees for printer repairs	5,550
Utilities expense	1,100

Identifying transactions.

◀ **Exercise 2.7**
Objectives 1, 2, 3

The following equation shows the effects of a number of transactions that took place at Main Street Auto Repair Company during the month of August. Describe each transaction.

	Assets			=	Liabilities	+		Owner's Equity			
	Cash +	Accounts Receivable +	Equipment	=	Accounts Payable	+	Helen Rush, Capital	+	Revenue	−	Expenses
Bal.	$80,000 +	$6,000 +	$64,000	=	$38,000	+	$112,000	+	0	−	0
1.	+10,000								+$10,000		
2.	−7,600		+7,600								
3.	−3,800				−3,800						
4.	−6,700										−$6,700
5.	+1,500	− 1,500									
6.		+12,000							+12,000		
7.	−4,100										−4,100

Preparing an income statement.

◀ **Exercise 2.8**
Objective 4

At the beginning of September, Alexander Parker started Parker Investment Services, a firm that offers advice about investing and managing money. On September 30, the accounting records of the business showed the following information. Prepare an income statement for the month of September 2013.

Cash	$32,100	Fees Income	$72,800
Accounts Receivable	3,000	Advertising Expense	5,500
Office Supplies	2,400	Salaries Expense	15,000
Office Equipment	36,500	Telephone Expense	700
Accounts Payable	4,700	Withdrawals	8,000
Alexander Parker, Capital, September 1, 2013	25,700		

Computing net income or net loss.

◀ **Exercise 2.9**
Objective 4

On December 1, Doris Turner opened a speech and hearing clinic. During December, her firm had the following transactions involving revenue and expenses. Did the firm earn a net income or incur a net loss for the period? What was the amount?

Paid $2,600 for advertising.

Provided services for $2,300 in cash.

Paid $700 for telephone service.

Paid salaries of $2,100 to employees.

Provided services for $2,500 on credit.

Paid $350 for office cleaning service.

Exercise 2.10

Objective 5

 **>>>**
Problem

▶ **Preparing a statement of owner's equity and a balance sheet.**

Using the information provided in Exercise 2.8, prepare a statement of owner's equity for the month of September and a balance sheet for Parker Investment Services as of September 30, 2013.

PROBLEMS

Problem Set A 

Problem 2.1A

Objectives 1, 2, 3

▶ **Analyzing the effects of transactions on the accounting equation.**

On July 1, John Walker established Home Appraisal Services, a firm that provides expert residential appraisals and represents clients in home appraisal hearings.

INSTRUCTIONS

Analyze the following transactions. Record in equation form the changes that occur in assets, liabilities, and owner's equity. (Use plus, minus, and equals signs.)

TRANSACTIONS

1. The owner invested $92,000 in cash to begin the business.
2. Paid $18,750 in cash for the purchase of equipment.
3. Purchased additional equipment for $12,400 on credit.
4. Paid $10,800 in cash to creditors.
5. The owner made an additional investment of $25,000 in cash.
6. Performed services for $7,200 in cash.
7. Performed services for $4,300 on account.
8. Paid $3,000 for rent expense.
9. Received $2,500 in cash from credit clients.
10. Paid $5,460 in cash for office supplies.
11. The owner withdrew $8,000 in cash for personal expenses.

Analyze: What is the ending balance of cash after all transactions have been recorded?

Problem 2.2A

Objectives 1, 2, 3

▶ **Analyzing the effects of transactions on the accounting equation.**

Jim Jackson is a painting contractor who specializes in painting commercial buildings. At the beginning of June, his firm's financial records showed the following assets, liabilities, and owner's equity.

Cash	$60,000	Accounts Payable	$10,200
Accounts Receivable	15,600	Jim Jackson, Capital	90,500
Office Furniture	34,800	Revenue	55,600
Auto	22,500	Expenses	23,400

INSTRUCTIONS

Set up an accounting equation using the balances given above. Record the effects of the following transactions in the equation. (Use plus, minus, and equals signs.) Record new balances after each transaction has been entered. Prove the equality of the two sides of the final equation on a separate sheet of paper.

TRANSACTIONS

1. Performed services for $6,580 on credit.
2. Paid $1,600 in cash for new office chairs.
3. Received $10,200 in cash from credit clients.
4. Paid $780 in cash for telephone service.
5. Sent a check for $2,500 in partial payment of the amount due creditors.
6. Paid salaries of $8,700 in cash.
7. Sent a check for $1,020 to pay electric bill.
8. Performed services for $9,500 in cash.
9. Paid $2,250 in cash for auto repairs.
10. Performed services for $11,500 on account.

Analyze: What is the amount of total assets after all transactions have been recorded?

Preparing a balance sheet.

◀ **Problem 2.3A**

eXcel Objective 5

Valdez Equipment Repair Service is owned by Francisco Valdez.

INSTRUCTIONS

Use the following figures to prepare a balance sheet dated February 28, 2013. (You will need to compute the owner's equity.)

Cash	$33,300	Equipment	$77,000
Supplies	5,380	Accounts Payable	23,000
Accounts Receivable	12,200		

Analyze: What is the net worth, or owner's equity, at February 28, 2013 for Valdez Equipment Repair Service?

Preparing an income statement, a statement of owner's equity, and a balance sheet.

◀ **Problem 2.4A**

Objectives 4, 5

eXcel

The following equation shows the transactions of West Cleaning Service during May. The business is owned by Carol West.

	Assets				=	Liab. +		Owner's Equity		
	Cash +	Accts. Rec. +	Supp. +	Equip. =		Accts. Pay. +	C. West, Capital +	Rev.	−	Exp.
Balances, May 1	14,000 +	2,000 +	4,800 +	32,800 =		6,000 +	47,600 +	0	−	0
Paid for utilities	−880									+880
New balances	13,120 +	2,000 +	4,800 +	32,800 =		6,000 +	47,600 +	0	−	880
Sold services for cash	+4,880							+4,880		
New balances	18,000 +	2,000 +	4,800 +	32,800 =		6,000 +	47,600 +	4,880	−	880
Paid a creditor	−1,600					−1,600				
New balances	16,400 +	2,000 +	4,800 +	32,800 =		4,400 +	47,600 +	4,880	−	880
Sold services on credit		+2,400						+2,400		
New balances	16,400 +	4,400 +	4,800 +	32,800 =		4,400 +	47,600 +	7,280	−	880
Paid salaries	−8,400									+8,400
New balances	8,000 +	4,400 +	4,800 +	32,800 =		4,400 +	47,600 +	7,280	−	9,280
Paid telephone bill	−304									+304
New balances	7,696 +	4,400 +	4,800 +	32,800 =		4,400 +	47,600 +	7,280	−	9,584
Withdrew cash for personal expenses	−2,000						−2,000			
New balances	5,696 +	4,400 +	4,800 +	32,800 =		4,400 +	45,600 +	7,280	−	9,584

INSTRUCTIONS

Analyze each transaction carefully. Prepare an income statement and a statement of owner's equity for the month. Prepare a balance sheet for May 31, 2013. List the expenses in detail on the income statement.

Analyze: In order to complete the balance sheet, which amount was transferred from the statement of owner's equity?

Problem Set B

Problem 2.1B ▶ **Analyzing the effects of transactions on the accounting equation.**

Objectives 1, 2, 3

On September 1, Mireya Cortez opened Self Images Tutoring Service.

INSTRUCTIONS

Analyze the following transactions. Use the fundamental accounting equation form to record the changes in property, claims of creditors, and owner's equity. (Use plus, minus, and equals signs.)

TRANSACTIONS

1. The owner invested $36,000 in cash to begin the business.
2. Purchased equipment for $16,000 in cash.
3. Purchased $6,000 of additional equipment on credit.
4. Paid $3,000 in cash to creditors.
5. The owner made an additional investment of $6,000 in cash.
6. Performed services for $4,200 in cash.
7. Performed services for $3,650 on account.
8. Paid $2,600 for rent expense.
9. Received $2,500 in cash from credit clients.
10. Paid $3,150 in cash for office supplies.
11. The owner withdrew $5,000 in cash for personal expenses.

Analyze: Which transactions increased the company's debt? By what amount?

Problem 2.2B ▶ **Analyzing the effects of transactions on the accounting equation.**

Objectives 1, 2, 3

Rhonda Johnson owns Johnson's Consulting Service. At the beginning of September, her firm's financial records showed the following assets, liabilities, and owner's equity.

Cash	$19,000	Accounts Payable	$ 5,000
Accounts Receivable	6,000	Rhonda Johnson, Capital	24,900
Supplies	6,400	Revenue	26,000
Office Furniture	12,000	Expenses	12,500

INSTRUCTIONS

Set up an equation using the balances given above. Record the effects of the following transactions in the equation. (Use plus, minus, and equals signs.) Record new balances after each transaction has been entered. Prove the equality of the two sides of the final equation on a separate sheet of paper.

TRANSACTIONS

1. Performed services for $4,000 on credit.
2. Paid $1,440 in cash for utilities.
3. Performed services for $5,000 in cash.
4. Paid $800 in cash for office cleaning service.
5. Sent a check for $2,400 to a creditor.
6. Paid $960 in cash for the telephone bill.

7. Issued checks for $7,000 to pay salaries.

8. Performed services for $5,600 in cash.

9. Purchased additional supplies for $1,000 on credit.

10. Received $3,000 in cash from credit clients.

Analyze: What is the ending balance for owner's equity after all transactions have been recorded?

Preparing a balance sheet.

◀ **Problem 2.3B**
Objective 5

David Taylor is opening a tax preparation service on December 1, which will be called Taylor's Tax Service. David plans to open the business by depositing $24,000 cash into a business checking account. The following assets will also be owned by the business: furniture (fair market value of $8,000) and computers and printers (fair market value of $9,600). There are no outstanding debts of the business as it is formed.

INSTRUCTIONS

Prepare a balance sheet for December 1, 2013, for Taylor's Tax Service by entering the correct balances in the appropriate accounts. (You will need to use the accounting equation to compute owner's equity.)

Analyze: If Taylor's Tax Service had an outstanding debt of $8,000 when the business was formed, what amount should be reported on the balance sheet for owner's equity?

Preparing an income statement, a statement of owner's equity, and a balance sheet.

◀ **Problem 2.4B**
Objectives 4, 5

The equation below shows the transactions of Linda Carter, Attorney and Counselor of Law, during August. This law firm is owned by Linda Carter.

	Assets				=	Liab. +		Owner's Equity		
	Cash +	Accts. Rec. +	Supp. +	Equip. =		Accts. Pay. +	L. Carter, Capital +	Rev. −		Exp.
Balances, Aug. 1	7,200	1,800 +	5,400 +	10,000 =		1,200 +	23,200 +	0 −		0
Paid for utilities	−600									+600
New balances	6,600 +	1,800 +	5,400 +	10,000 =		1,200 +	23,200 +	0 −		600
Performed services for cash	+6,000							+6,000		
New balances	12,600 +	1,800 +	5,400 +	10,000 =		1,200 +	23,200 +	6,000 −		600
Paid a creditor	−600						−600			
New balances	12,000 +	1,800 +	5,400 +	10,000 =		600 +	23,200 +	6,000 −		600
Performed services on credit		+4,800						+4,800		
New balances	12,000 +	6,600 +	5,400 +	10,000 =		600 +	23,200 +	10,800 −		600
Paid salaries	−5,400									+5,400
New balances	6,600 +	6,600 +	5,400 +	10,000 =		600 +	23,200 +	10,800 −		6,000
Paid telephone bill	−600									+600
New balances	6,000 +	6,600 +	5,400 +	10,000 =		600 +	23,200 +	10,800 −		6,600
Withdrew cash for personal expenses	−1,200						−1,200			
New balances	4,800 +	6,600 +	5,400 +	10,000 =		600 +	22,000 +	10,800 −		6,600

INSTRUCTIONS

Analyze each transaction carefully. Prepare an income statement and a statement of owner's equity for the month. Prepare a balance sheet for August 31, 2013. List the expenses in detail on the income statement.

Analyze: In order to complete the statement of owner's equity, which amount was transferred from the income statement?

Critical Thinking Problem 2.1

Accounting for a New Company

James Mitchell opened a gym and fitness studio called Body Builders Fitness Center at the beginning of November of the current year. It is now the end of December, and James is trying to determine whether he made a profit during his first two months of operations. You offer to help him and ask to see his accounting records. He shows you a shoe box and tells you that every piece of paper pertaining to the business is in that box.

As you go through the material in the shoe box, you discover the following:

a.   A receipt from Clayton Properties for $8,000 for November's rent on the exercise studio.

b.   Bank deposit slips totaling $7,360 for money collected from customers who attended exercise classes.

c.   An invoice for $50,000 for exercise equipment. The first payment is not due until December 31.

d.   A bill for $2,100 from the maintenance service that cleans the studio. James has not yet paid this bill.

e.   A December 19 parking ticket for $200. James says he was in a hurry that morning to get to the Fitness Center on time and forgot to put money in the parking meter.

f.   A handwritten list of customers and fees for the classes they have taken. As the customers attend the classes, James writes their names and the amount of each customer's fee on the list. As customers pay, James crosses their names off the list. Fees not crossed off the list amount to $2,400.

g.   A credit card receipt for $800 for printing flyers advertising the grand opening of the studio. For convenience, James used his personal credit card.

h.   A credit card receipt for $800 for four warm-up suits James bought to wear at the studio. He also put this purchase on his personal credit card.

Use the concepts you have learned in this chapter to help James.

1.   Prepare an income statement for the first two months of operation of Body Builders Fitness Center.

2.   How would you evaluate the results of the first two months of operation?

3.   What advice would you give James concerning his system of accounting?

Critical Thinking Problem 2.2

Financial Statements

The following account balances are for Dolly Garcia, Certified Public Accountant, as of April 30, 2013.

Cash	$26,000
Accounts Receivable	10,800
Maintenance Expense	4,400
Advertising Expense	3,750
Fees Earned	23,800
Dolly Garcia, Capital, April 1	?
Salaries Expense	9,000
Machinery	19,000
Accounts Payable	12,800
Dolly Garcia, Drawing	5,200

INSTRUCTIONS

Using the accounting equation form, determine the balance for Dolly Garcia, Capital, April 1, 2013. Prepare an income statement for the month of April, a statement of owner's equity, and a balance sheet as of April 30, 2013. List the expenses on the income statement in alphabetical order.

Analyze: What net change in owner's equity occurred during the month of April?

BUSINESS CONNECTIONS

Interpreting Results

1. How does an accounting system help managers control operations and make sound decisions?
2. Why should managers be concerned with changes in the amount of creditors' claims against the business?
3. Is it reasonable to expect that all new businesses will have a net income from the first month's operations? From the first year's operations?
4. After examining financial data for a monthly period, the owner of a small business expressed surprise that the firm's cash balance had decreased during the month even though there was substantial net income. Do you think this owner is right to expect cash to increase because of a substantial net income? Why or why not?

To Record or Not to Record

You are Sarineh, a new Accounts Receivable Clerk for Robinson Paper Supply. Toward the end of the month, Joseph Lee, a very personable sales associate, tells you that the previous A/R clerk always recorded a Sales Invoice when he got a verbal agreement from a customer to buy paper supplies. He has a verbal order from his favorite customer for $5,000 of paper and wants you to create a Sales Invoice today. You know that in order to create a Sales Invoice you need a purchase order from the customer. You also know that Mr. Lee receives a monthly bonus based on the monthly sales. If his sales are above $10,000, he gets a 10 percent bonus. Would you agree to record the sales of products before receiving the purchase order from the customer? What effect would it have on the customer, on the Sales Associate, on the company, and on the job?

Income Statement

Financial Statement ANALYSIS

Review the following excerpt from the 2009 consolidated statement of income for Southwest Airlines Co. Answer the questions that follow.

SOUTHWEST

Southwest Airlines Co. Consolidated Statement of Income Years Ended December 31, 2007, 2008, and 2009			
	2009	*2008*	*2007*
Operating Revenues (in millions):			
Passenger	$9,892	$10,549	$9,457
Freight	118	145	130
Other	340	329	274
Total operating revenues	10,350	11,023	9,861
Net Income	$99	$178	$645

Analyze:

1. Although the format for the heading of an income statement can vary from company to company, the heading should contain the answers to who, what, and when. List the answers to each question for the statement presented above.

2. What three types of revenue are reflected on this statement?

3. The net income of $99,000,000 reflected on Southwest Airlines Co.'s consolidated statement of income for 2009 will be transferred to the next financial statement to be prepared. Net income is needed to complete which statement?

Analyze Online: Find the *Investor Relations* section of the Southwest Airlines Co. Web site (www.southwest.com) and answer the following questions.

4. What total operating revenues did Southwest Airlines Co. report for the most recent quarter?

5. Find the most recent press release posted on the Web site. Read the press release, and summarize the topic discussed. What effect, if any, do you think this will have on company earnings? Why?

Internet | CONNECTION

Selling on Internet

Go to the Federated Corporation Web site at www.federated-fds.com. What companies are included in this corporation? Can you see a link to purchase items on line? What transaction, if any, would you record when an item is ordered from the Internet? Does the Web site include job offerings? What jobs would be available in Finance (go to Support operations, finance to find the requirements for a job)?

TEAMWORK

Working to Provide Accurate Data

Christy's Fabrics is a large fabric provider to the general public. The accounting office has three employees: accounts receivable clerk, accounts payable clerk, and full charge bookkeeper. The accounts receivable clerk creates the sales invoices and records the cash receipts, the accounts payable clerk creates and pays the purchase orders, and the full charge bookkeeper reconciles the checking account. Assign each group member one of the three jobs. Identify the accounts and describe the transactions that would be recorded by that assigned job. What effect would each transaction have on each account? How would each member of the accounting department work together to present accurate information for the decision makers?

Answers to **Self Reviews**

Answers to Section 1 Self Review

1. A financial event that changes the resources of the firm.

2. An example is the initial investment of cash in a business by the owner.

3. Amounts that a company must pay to creditors in the future.

4. **a.** Equipment is increased by $3,250 and accounts payable is increased by $3,250.

5. **d.** $75,000

6. $10,000

Answers to Section 2 Self Review

1. Funds taken from the business to pay for personal expenses. They decrease the owner's equity in the business.

2. As an additional investment by the owner recorded on the basis of fair market value.

3. The firm's name (who), the title of the statement (what), and the time period covered by the report (when).

4. **a.** revenue and expenses for a period of time

5. **d.** $55,000

6. $29,000 increase

Answers to Comprehensive Self Review

1. The opposite side of the accounting equation will decrease because a decrease in assets results in a corresponding decrease in either a liability or the owner's equity.

2. Buying for cash results in an immediate decrease in cash; buying on account results in a liability recorded as accounts payable.

3. The income statement is prepared first because the net income or loss is needed to complete the statement of owner's equity. The statement of owner's equity is prepared next to update the change in owner's equity. The balance sheet is prepared last.

4. Revenue increases owner's equity. Expenses decrease owner's equity.

5. The payment of $700 to a creditor on account.

Analyzing Business Transactions Using T Accounts

LEARNING OBJECTIVES

1. Set up T accounts for assets, liabilities, and owner's equity.
2. Analyze business transactions and enter them in the accounts.
3. Determine the balance of an account.
4. Set up T accounts for revenue and expenses.
5. Prepare a trial balance from T accounts.
6. Prepare an income statement, a statement of owner's equity, and a balance sheet.
7. Develop a chart of accounts.
8. Define the accounting terms new to this chapter.

NEW TERMS

account balance
accounts
chart of accounts
classification
credit
debit
double-entry system
drawing account
footing
normal balance
permanent account
slide
T account
temporary account
transposition
trial balance

 www.att.com

In 1876, Alexander Graham Bell invented the telephone and gave birth to the company that would become AT&T. The Bell Telephone Company was formed by Gardiner Hubbard and Thomas Watson in 1877 and within a year the newly formed Bell company had 10,000 phones in service.

Over the past century the company has been in business, AT&T has broadened its offerings through new-product development and diversification. Recognized as one of the leading worldwide providers of IP-based communications services to business, AT&T also offers the greatest number of phones that work in most countries; the largest Wi-Fi network in the United States; and the largest number of high-speed Internet access subscribers in the United States. Worldwide revenues in 2009 reached $123 billion.

thinking critically

How might accountants in 1877 have recorded The Bell Telephone Company's first sales transaction? How did this transaction affect the fundamental accounting equation?

SECTION OBJECTIVES

>> 1. Set up T accounts for assets, liabilities, and owner's equity.

WHY IT'S IMPORTANT

The T account is an important visual tool used as an alternative to the fundamental accounting equation.

>> 2. Analyze business transactions and enter them in the accounts.

WHY IT'S IMPORTANT

Accountants often use T accounts to help analyze and classify business transactions.

>> 3. Determine the balance of an account.

WHY IT'S IMPORTANT

Accurate account balances contribute to a reliable accounting system.

TERMS TO LEARN

account balance

accounts

classification

footing

normal balance

T account

Transactions That Affect Assets, Liabilities, and Owner's Equity

In this chapter, you will learn how to record the changes caused by business transactions. This recordkeeping is a basic part of accounting systems.

Asset, Liability, and Owner's Equity Accounts

The accounting equation is one tool for analyzing the effects of business transactions. However, businesses do not record transactions in equation form. Instead, businesses establish separate records, called **accounts,** for assets, liabilities, and owner's equity. Use of accounts helps owners and staff analyze, record, classify, summarize, and report financial information. Accounts are recognized by their **classification** as assets, liabilities, or owner's equity. Asset accounts show the property a business owns. Liability accounts show the debts of the business. Owner's equity accounts show the owner's financial interest in the business. Each account has a name that describes the type of property, the debt, or the financial interest.

Accountants use T accounts to analyze transactions. A **T account** consists of a vertical line and a horizontal line that resemble the letter **T.** The name of the account is written on the horizontal (top) line. Increases and decreases in the account are entered on either side of the vertical line.

The following are T accounts for assets, liabilities, and owner's equity:

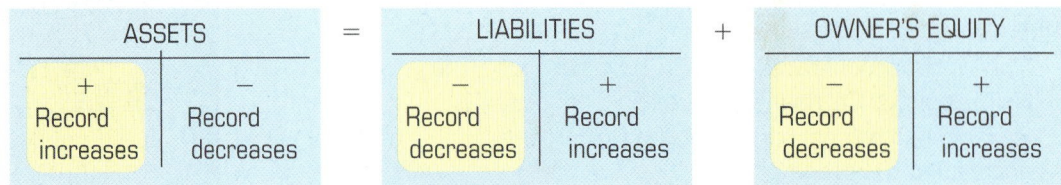

RECORDING A CASH INVESTMENT

Asset accounts show items of value owned by a business. Carolyn Wells invested $100,000 in the business. Carlos Valdez, the office manager for Wells' Consulting Services, set up a *Cash* account. Cash is an asset. Assets appear on the left side of the accounting equation. Cash increases appear on the left side of the *Cash* T account. Decreases are shown on the right side. Valdez entered the cash investment of $100,000 **(a)** on the left side of the *Cash* account.

T accounts normally do not have plus and minus signs. We show them to help you identify increases (+) and decreases (−) in accounts.

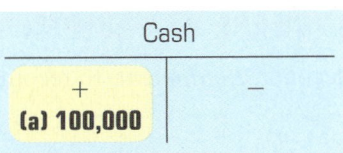

Carlos Valdez set up an account for owner's equity called *Carolyn Wells, Capital.* Owner's equity appears on the right side of the accounting equation (Assets = Liabilities + Owner's Equity). Increases in owner's equity appear on the right side of the T account. Decreases in owner's equity appear on the left side. Valdez entered the investment of $100,000 **(a)** on the right side of the *Carolyn Wells, Capital* account.

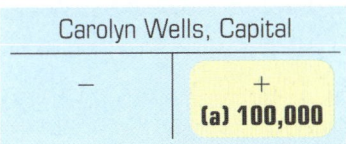

Use these steps to analyze the effects of the business transactions:

1. Analyze the financial event.
   - Identify the accounts affected.
   - Classify the accounts affected.
   - Determine the amount of increase or decrease for each account.
2. Apply the left-right rules for each account affected.
3. Make the entry in T-account form.

>>**1. OBJECTIVE**
Set up T accounts for assets, liabilities, and owner's equity.

recall

The Accounting Equation
Assets = Liabilities + Owner's Equity

>>**2. OBJECTIVE**
Analyze business transactions and enter them in the accounts.

BUSINESS TRANSACTION

Carolyn Wells withdrew $100,000 from personal savings and deposited it in the new business checking account for Wells' Consulting Services.

ANALYSIS
a. The asset account, *Cash,* is increased by $100,000.
a. The owner's equity account, *Carolyn Wells, Capital,* is increased by $100,000.

LEFT-RIGHT RULES
LEFT   Increases to asset accounts are recorded on the left side of the T account. Record $100,000 on the left side of the *Cash* T account.

RIGHT   Increases to owner's equity accounts are recorded on the right side of the T account. Record $100,000 on the right side of the *Carolyn Wells, Capital* T account.

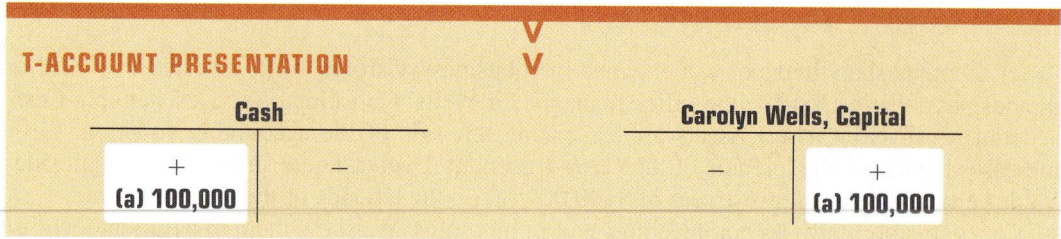

RECORDING A CASH PURCHASE OF EQUIPMENT

Carlos Valdez set up an asset account, *Equipment,* to record the purchase of a computer and other equipment.

BUSINESS TRANSACTION

Wells' Consulting Services issued a $5,000 check to purchase a computer and other equipment.

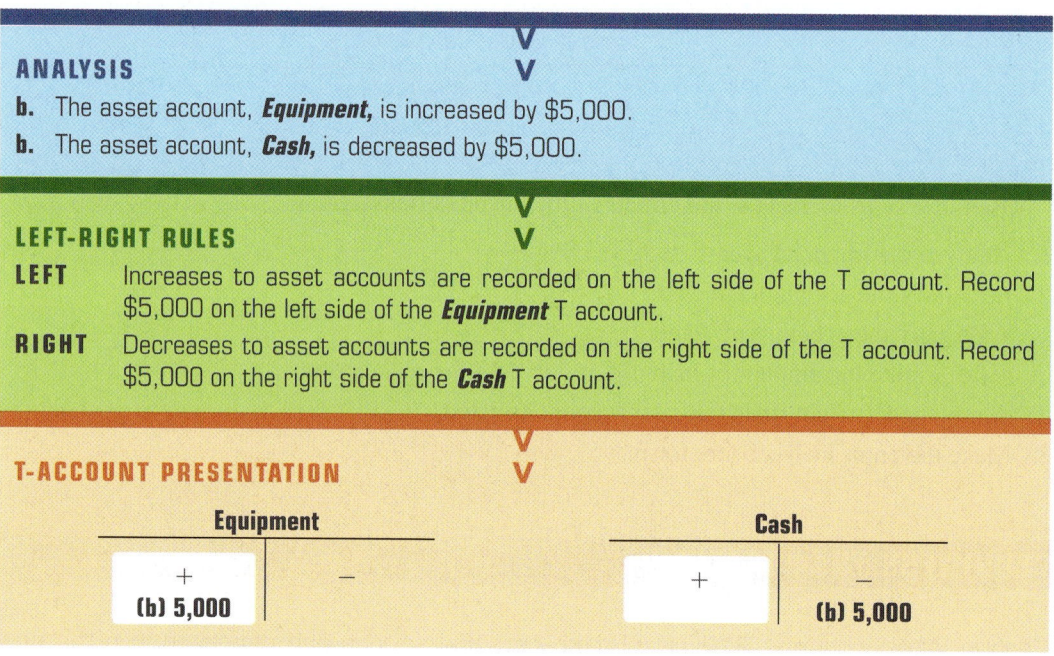

Let's look at the T accounts to review the effects of the transactions. Valdez entered $5,000 **(b)** on the left (increase) side of the *Equipment* account. He entered $5,000 **(b)** on the right (decrease) side of the *Cash* account. Notice that the *Cash* account shows the effects of two transactions.

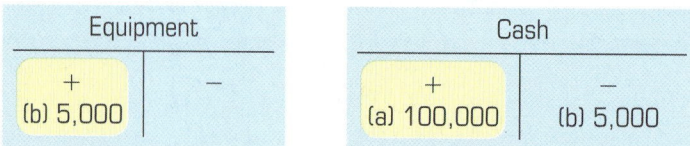

RECORDING A CREDIT PURCHASE OF EQUIPMENT

Liabilities are amounts a business owes its creditors. Liabilities appear on the right side of the accounting equation (Assets = Liabilities + Owner's Equity). Increases in liabilities are on the right side of liability T accounts. Decreases in liabilities are on the left side of liability T accounts.

BUSINESS TRANSACTION

The firm bought office equipment for $6,000 on account from Office Plus.

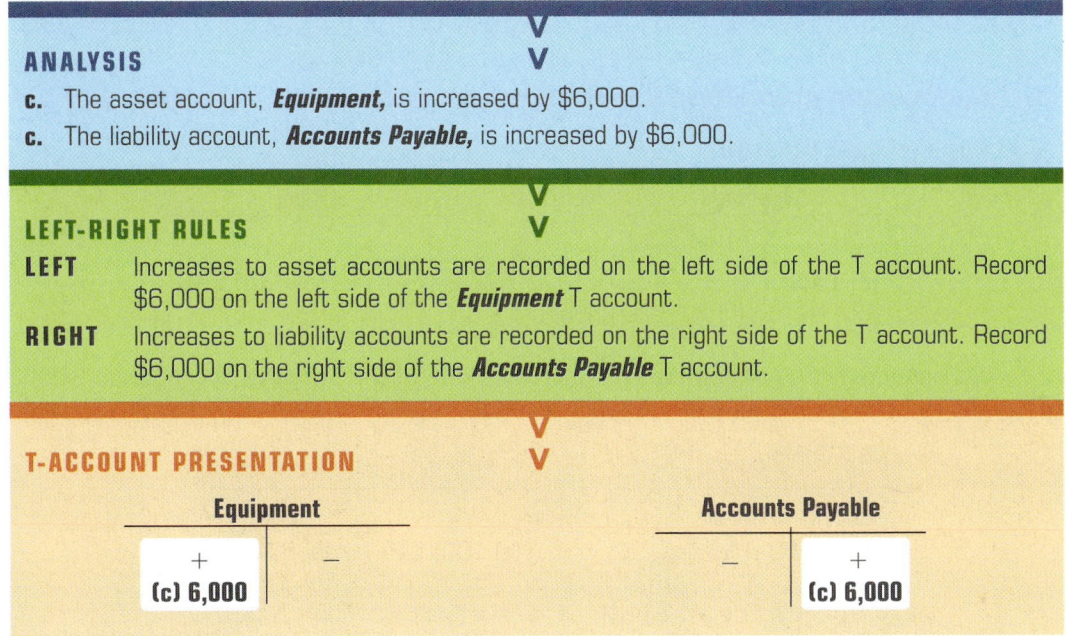

ANALYSIS

c. The asset account, *Equipment,* is increased by $6,000.

c. The liability account, *Accounts Payable,* is increased by $6,000.

LEFT-RIGHT RULES

LEFT Increases to asset accounts are recorded on the left side of the T account. Record $6,000 on the left side of the *Equipment* T account.

RIGHT Increases to liability accounts are recorded on the right side of the T account. Record $6,000 on the right side of the *Accounts Payable* T account.

T-ACCOUNT PRESENTATION

Equipment		Accounts Payable	
+	–	–	+
(c) 6,000			(c) 6,000

important!

For liability T accounts
- right side shows increases,
- left side shows decreases.

Let's look at the T accounts to review the effects of the transactions. Valdez entered $6,000 **(c)** on the left (increase) side of the *Equipment* account. It now shows two transactions. He entered $6,000 **(c)** on the right (increase) side of the *Accounts Payable* account.

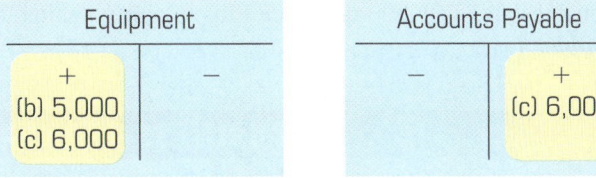

Equipment		Accounts Payable	
+	–	–	+
(b) 5,000			(c) 6,000
(c) 6,000			

> The balance sheet of Avery Dennison Corporation at January 1, 2009, showed machinery and equipment balances of $1.4 billion.

RECORDING A CASH PURCHASE OF SUPPLIES

Carlos Valdez set up an asset account called *Supplies.*

BUSINESS TRANSACTION

Wells' Consulting Services issued a check for $1,500 to Office Delux Inc. to purchase office supplies.

ANALYSIS

d. The asset account, *Supplies,* is increased by $1,500.

d. The asset account, *Cash,* is decreased by $1,500.

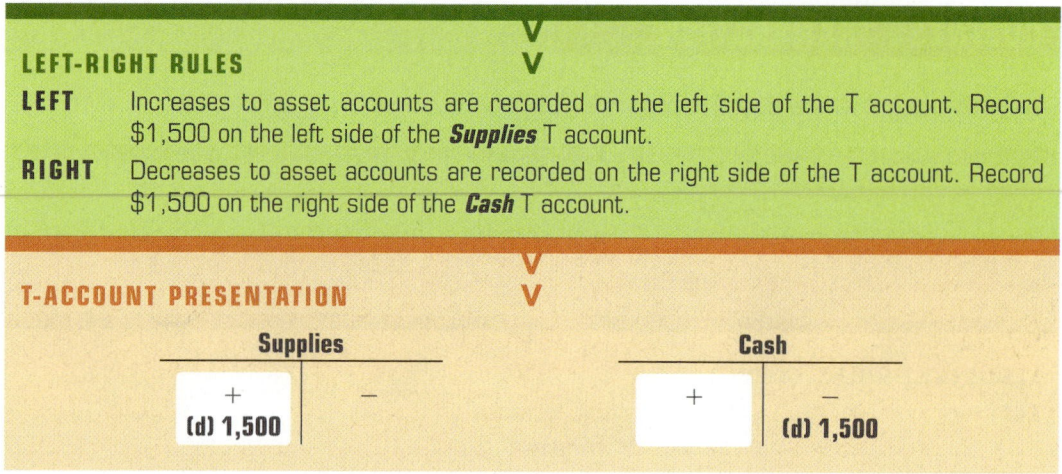

Valdez entered $1,500 (**d**) on the left (increase) side of the **Supplies** account and $1,500 (**d**) on the right (decrease) side of the **Cash** account.

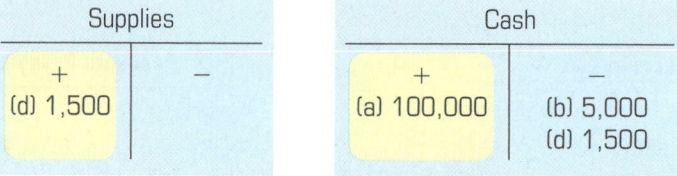

Notice that the **Cash** account now shows three transactions: the initial investment by the owner (**a**), the cash purchase of equipment (**b**), and the cash purchase of supplies (**d**).

RECORDING A PAYMENT TO A CREDITOR

On November 30, the business paid $2,500 to Office Plus to apply against the debt of $6,000 shown in *Accounts Payable.*

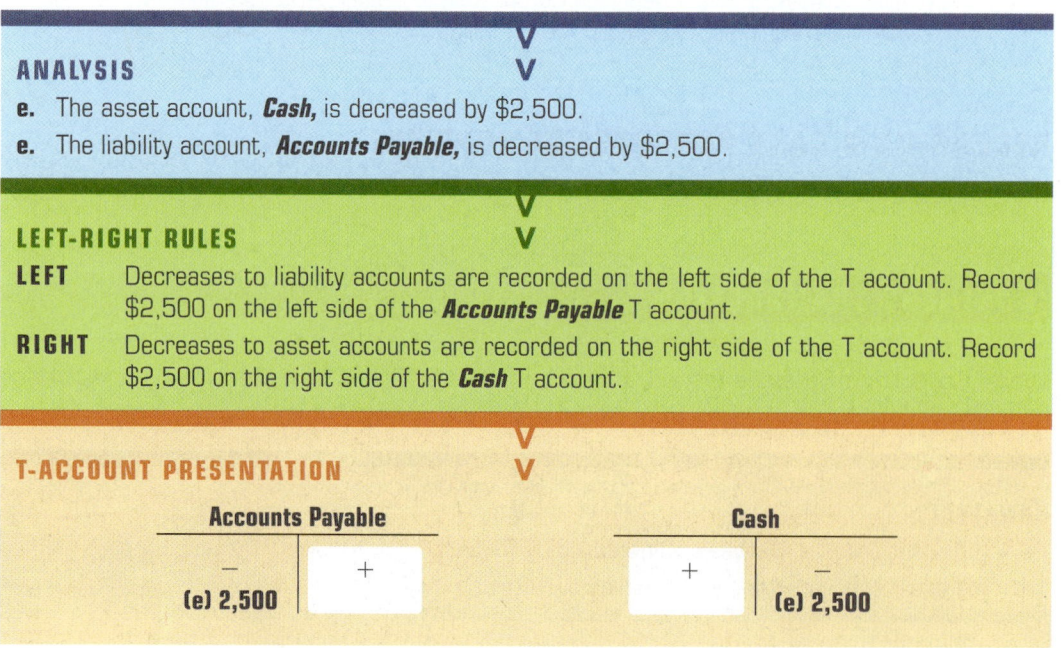

Let's look at the T accounts to review the effects of the transactions. Valdez entered $2,500 (**e**) on the right (decrease) side of the **Cash** account. He entered $2,500 (**e**) on the left (decrease) side of the **Accounts Payable** account. Notice that both accounts show the effects of several transactions.

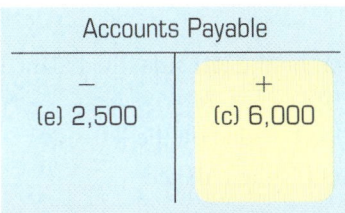
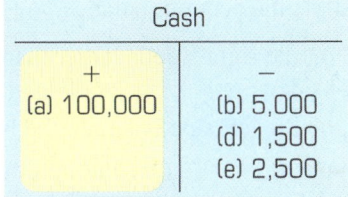

Accounts Payable	
−	+
(e) 2,500	(c) 6,000

Cash	
+	−
(a) 100,000	(b) 5,000
	(d) 1,500
	(e) 2,500

RECORDING PREPAID RENT

In November, Wells' Consulting Services was required to pay the December and January rent in advance. Valdez set up an asset account called **Prepaid Rent.**

BUSINESS TRANSACTION

Wells' Consulting Services issued a check for $8,000 to pay rent for the months of December and January.

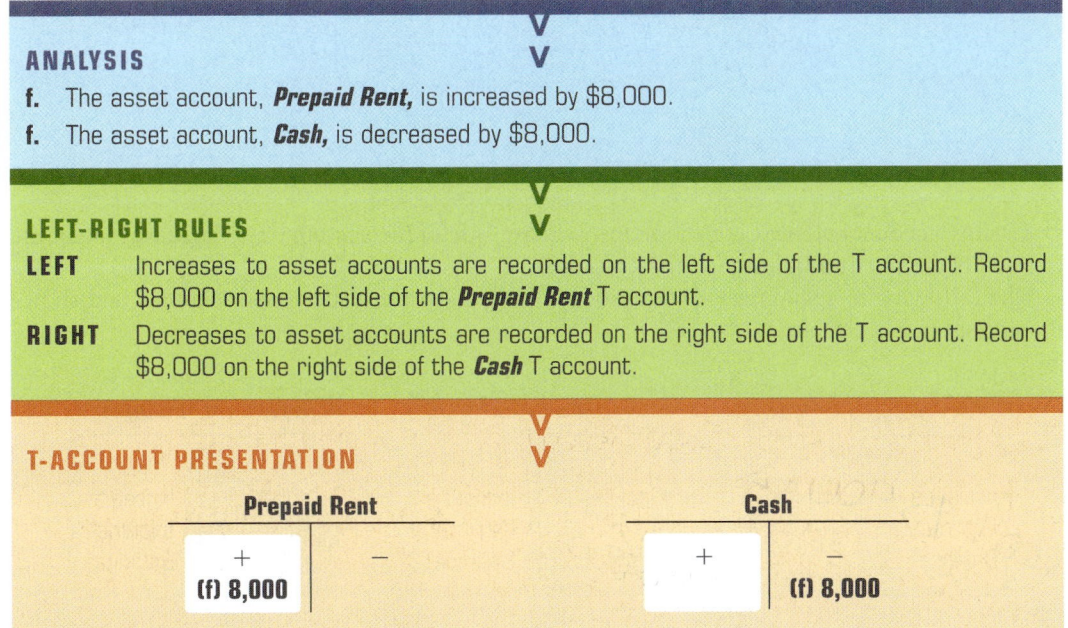

ANALYSIS

f. The asset account, **Prepaid Rent,** is increased by $8,000.

f. The asset account, **Cash,** is decreased by $8,000.

LEFT-RIGHT RULES

LEFT Increases to asset accounts are recorded on the left side of the T account. Record $8,000 on the left side of the **Prepaid Rent** T account.

RIGHT Decreases to asset accounts are recorded on the right side of the T account. Record $8,000 on the right side of the **Cash** T account.

T-ACCOUNT PRESENTATION

Prepaid Rent	
+	−
(f) 8,000	

Cash	
+	−
	(f) 8,000

Let's review the T accounts to see the effects of the transactions. Valdez entered $8,000 (**f**) on the left (increase) side of the **Prepaid Rent** account. He entered $8,000 (**f**) on the right (decrease) side of the **Cash** account.

Notice that the **Cash** account shows the effects of numerous transactions. It shows initial investment (**a**), equipment purchase (**b**), supplies purchase (**d**), payment on account (**e**), and advance rent payment (**f**).

Prepaid Rent	
+	−
(f) 8,000	

Cash	
+	−
(a) 100,000	(b) 5,000
	(d) 1,500
	(e) 2,500
	(f) 8,000

Account Balances

An **account balance** is the difference between the amounts on the two sides of the account. First add the figures on each side of the account. If the column has more than one figure, enter the total in small pencil figures called a **footing.** Then subtract the smaller total from the larger total. The result is the account balance.

- If the total on the right side is larger than the total on the left side, the balance is recorded on the right side.
- If the total on the left side is larger, the balance is recorded on the left side.
- If an account shows only one amount, that amount is the balance.
- If an account contains entries on only one side, the total of those entries is the account balance.

Let's look at the *Cash* account for Wells' Consulting Services. The left side shows $100,000. The total of the right side is $17,000. Subtract the footing of $17,000 from $100,000. The result is the account balance of $83,000. The account balance is shown on the left side of the account.

	Cash	
+		−
(a) 100,000		(b) 5,000
		(d) 1,500
		(e) 2,500
		(f) 8,000
		17,000 ← Footing
Bal. 83,000		

Usually account balances appear on the increase side of the account. The increase side of the account is the **normal balance** of the account.

The following is a summary of the procedures to increase or decrease accounts and shows the normal balance of accounts.

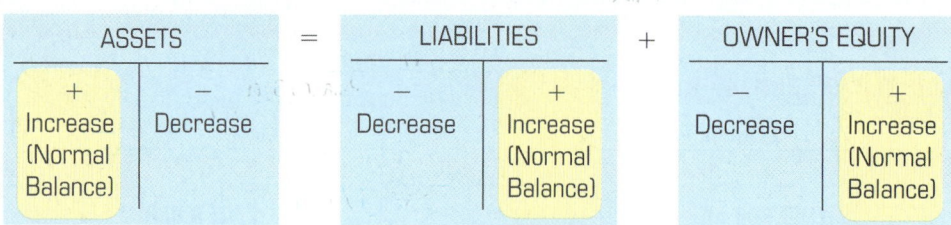

Figure 3.1 shows a summary of the account balances for Wells' Consulting Services.
Figure 3.2 shows a balance sheet prepared for November 30, 2013.
In equation form, the firm's position after these transactions is:

Assets									=	Liabilities	+	Owner's Equity
Cash	+	Supp.	+	Prepaid Rent	+		Equip.		=	Accounts Payable	+	Carolyn Wells, Capital
$83,000	+	$1,500	+	$8,000	+		$11,000		=	$3,500	+	$100,000

FIGURE 3.1

T-Account Balances for Wells'
Consulting Services

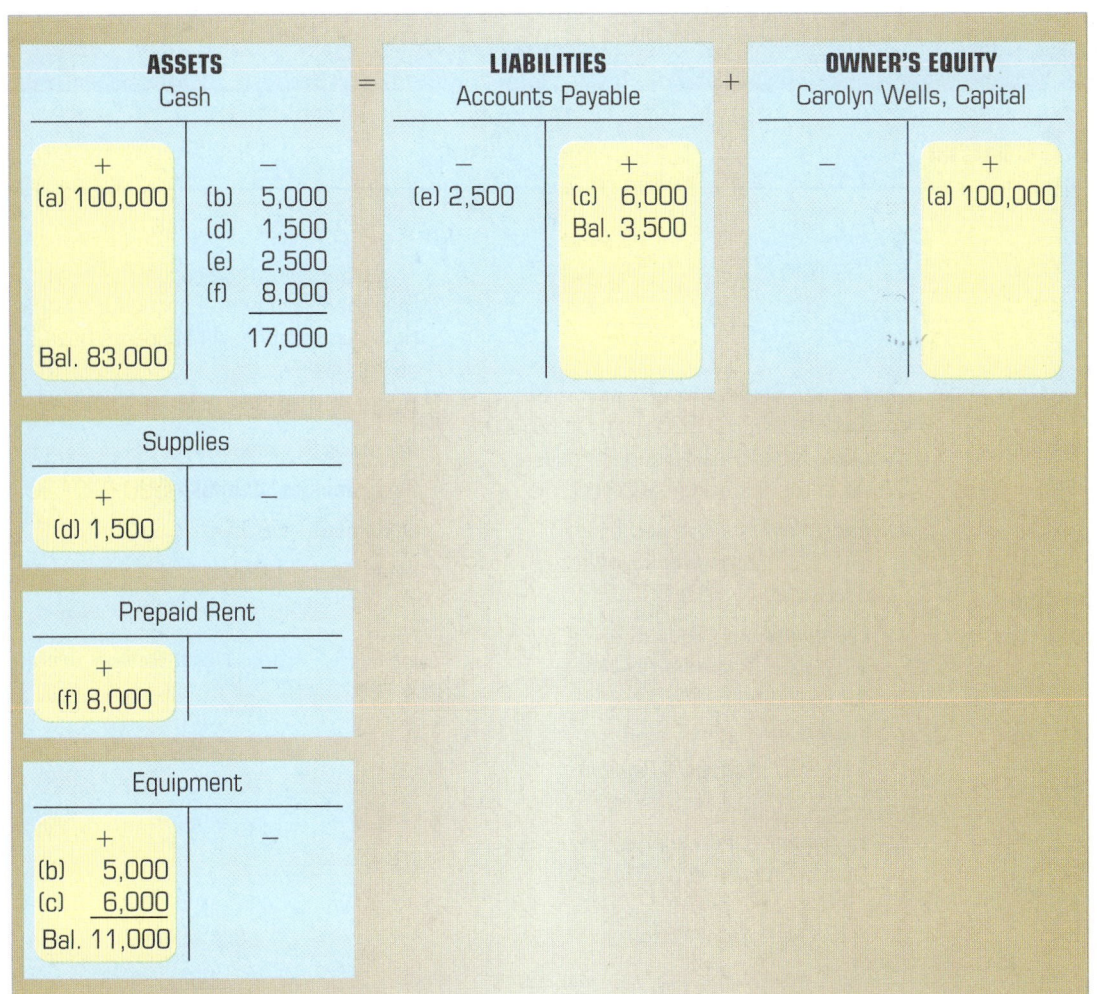

FIGURE 3.2   **Balance Sheet for Wells' Consulting Services**

Assets						Liabilities					
Cash		8 3 0 0 0	00		Accounts Payable		3 5 0 0	00			
Supplies		1 5 0 0	00								
Prepaid Rent		8 0 0 0	00		Owner's Equity						
Equipment		1 1 0 0 0	00		Carolyn Wells, Capital		100 0 0 0	00			
Total Assets		1 0 3 5 0 0	00		Total Liabilities and Owner's Equity		103 5 0 0	00			

Wells' Consulting Services
Balance Sheet
November 30, 2013

Notice how the balance sheet reflects the fundamental accounting equation.

Section 1 Self Review

QUESTIONS

1. Increases are recorded on which side of asset, liability, and owner's equity accounts?

2. What is a footing?

3. What is meant by the "normal balance" of an account? What is the normal balance side for asset, liability, and owner's equity accounts?

EXERCISES

4. Foot and find the balance of the **Cash** account.

Cash	
+	−
26,000	10,000
18,000	3,000
	2,500
	2,350

17,850

a. 44,000
b. 29,500
c. 26,150
d. 24,100

5. The Wilson Company purchased new computers for $10,800 from Office Supplies, Inc., to be paid in 30 days. Which of the following is correct?

a. **Equipment** is increased by $10,800. **Accounts Payable** is decreased by $10,800.

b. **Equipment** is increased by $10,800. **Accounts Payable** is increased by $10,800.

c. **Equipment** is decreased by $10,800. **Accounts Payable** is increased by $10,800.

d. **Equipment** is increased by $10,800. **Cash** is decreased by $10,800.

ANALYSIS

6. From the following accounts, show that the fundamental accounting equation is in balance. All accounts have normal balances.

Cash—$15,400

Accounts Payable—$10,000

David Jenkins, Capital—$30,000

Equipment—$20,000

Supplies—$4,600

(Answers to Section 1 Self Review are on pages 86–87.)

$4,600 + 15,400 + 20,000 = 10,000 + 30,000$
$+ 40,000$

SECTION OBJECTIVES

>> **4. Set up T accounts for revenue and expenses.**

WHY IT'S IMPORTANT

T accounts help you understand the effects of all business transactions.

>> **5. Prepare a trial balance from T accounts.**

WHY IT'S IMPORTANT

The trial balance is an important check of accuracy at the end of the accounting period.

>> **6. Prepare an income statement, a statement of owner's equity, and a balance sheet.**

WHY IT'S IMPORTANT

Financial statements summarize the financial activities and condition of the business.

>> **7. Develop a chart of accounts.**

WHY IT'S IMPORTANT

Businesses require a system that allows accounts to be easily identified and located.

TERMS TO LEARN

chart of accounts
credit
debit
double-entry system
drawing account
permanent account
slide
temporary account
transposition
trial balance

Transactions That Affect Revenue, Expenses, and Withdrawals

Let's examine the revenue and expense transactions of Wells' Consulting Services for December to see how they are recorded.

Revenue and Expense Accounts

Some owner's equity accounts are classified as revenue or expense accounts. Separate accounts are used to record revenue and expense transactions.

RECORDING REVENUE FROM SERVICES SOLD FOR CASH

During December, the business earned $36,000 in revenue from clients who paid cash for bookkeeping, accounting, and consulting services. This involved several transactions. Carlos Valdez entered $36,000 **(g)** on the left (increase) side of the asset account *Cash.*

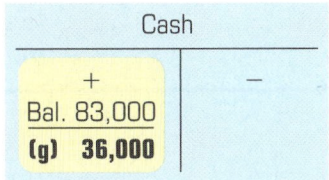

>> 4. OBJECTIVE

Set up T accounts for revenue and expenses.

How is the increase in owner's equity recorded? One way would be to record the $36,000 on the right side of the **Carolyn Wells, Capital** account. However, the preferred way is to keep revenue separate from the owner's investment until the end of the accounting period. Therefore, Valdez opened a revenue account for **Fees Income.**

Valdez entered $36,000 (**g**) on the right side of the **Fees Income** account. Revenues increase owner's equity. Increases in owner's equity appear on the right side of the T account. Therefore, increases in revenue appear on the right side of revenue T accounts.

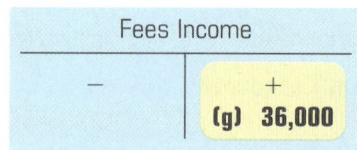

The right side of the revenue account shows increases and the left side shows decreases. Decreases in revenue accounts are rare but might occur because of corrections or transfers.

Let's review the effects of the transactions. Valdez entered $36,000 (**g**) on the left (increase) side of the **Cash** account and $36,000 (**g**) on the right (increase) side of the **Fees Income** account.

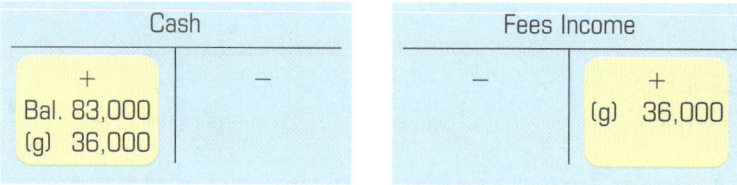

At this point, the firm needs just one revenue account. Most businesses have separate accounts for different types of revenue. For example, sales of goods such as clothes are recorded in the revenue account **Sales.**

RECORDING REVENUE FROM SERVICES SOLD ON CREDIT

In December, Wells' Consulting Services earned $11,000 from various charge account clients. Valdez set up an asset account, **Accounts Receivable.**

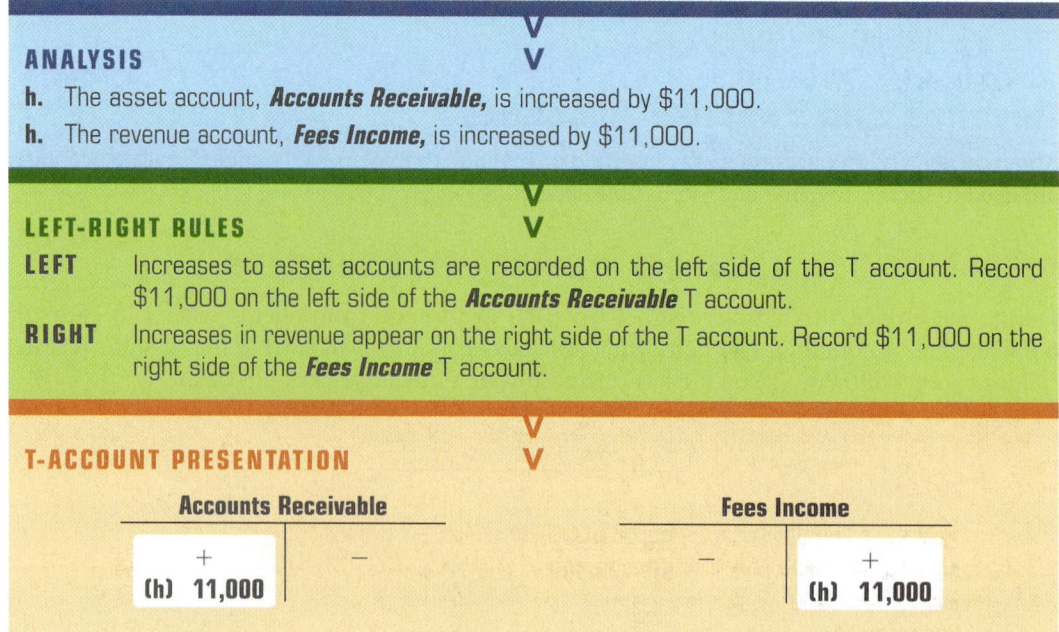

Let's review the effects of the transactions. Valdez entered $11,000 (**h**) on the left (increase) side of the *Accounts Receivable* account and $11,000 (**h**) on the right (increase) side of the *Fees Income* account.

Accounts Receivable		Fees Income	
+	−	−	+
(h) 11,000			(g) 36,000
			(h) 11,000

RECORDING COLLECTIONS FROM ACCOUNTS RECEIVABLE

Charge account clients paid $6,000, reducing the amount owed to Wells' Consulting Services.

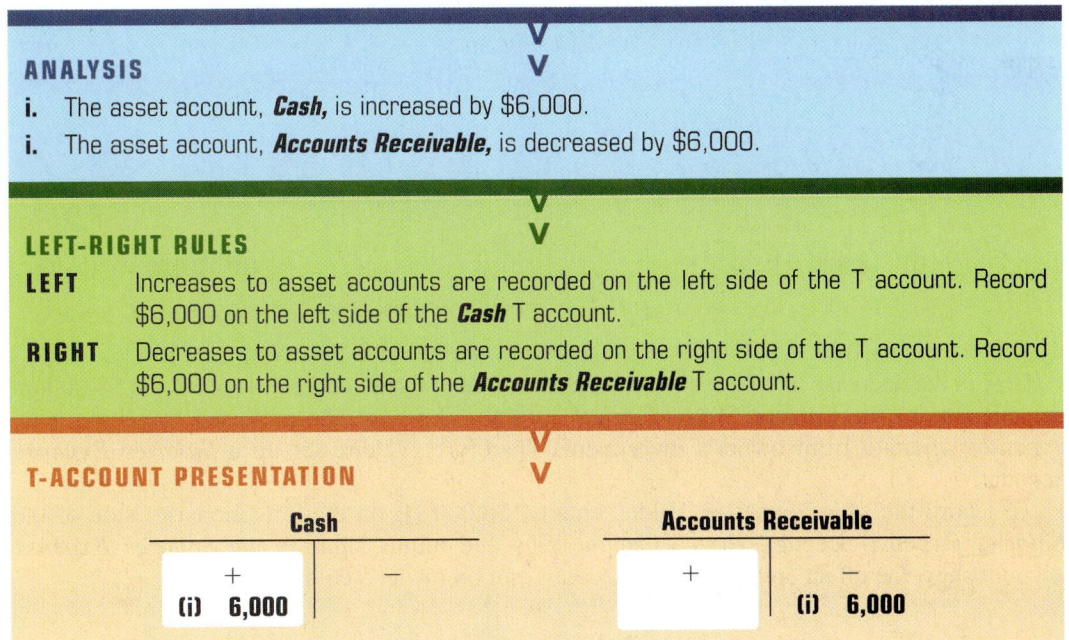

ANALYSIS

i.   The asset account, *Cash*, is increased by $6,000.

i.   The asset account, *Accounts Receivable*, is decreased by $6,000.

LEFT-RIGHT RULES

LEFT   Increases to asset accounts are recorded on the left side of the T account. Record $6,000 on the left side of the *Cash* T account.

RIGHT   Decreases to asset accounts are recorded on the right side of the T account. Record $6,000 on the right side of the *Accounts Receivable* T account.

T-ACCOUNT PRESENTATION

Cash		Accounts Receivable	
+	−	+	−
(i) 6,000			(i) 6,000

Let's review the effects of the transactions. Valdez entered $6,000 (**i**) on the left (increase) side of the *Cash* account and $6,000 (**i**) on the right (decrease) side of the *Accounts Receivable* account. Notice that revenue is not recorded when cash is collected from charge account clients. The revenue was recorded when the sales on credit were recorded (**h**).

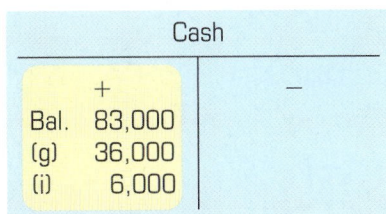

Cash		Accounts Receivable	
+	−	+	−
Bal. 83,000		(h) 11,000	(i) 6,000
(g) 36,000			
(i) 6,000			

RECORDING AN EXPENSE FOR SALARIES

Expenses decrease owner's equity. Decreases in owner's equity appear on the left side of the T account. Therefore, increases in expenses (which are decreases in owner's equity) are recorded on the left side of expense T accounts. Decreases in expenses are recorded on the right side of the T accounts. Decreases in expenses are rare but may result from corrections or transfers.

recall

Expense
An expense is an outflow of cash, the use of other assets, or the incurring of a liability.

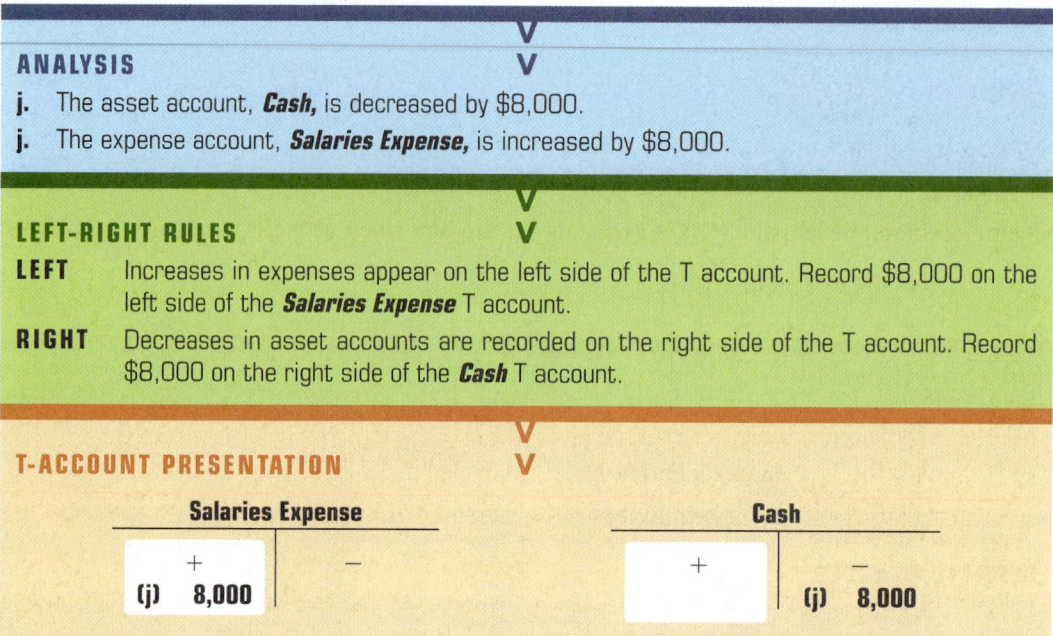

BUSINESS TRANSACTION

In December, Wells' Consulting Services paid $8,000 in salaries.

ANALYSIS

j. The asset account, **Cash**, is decreased by $8,000.

j. The expense account, **Salaries Expense**, is increased by $8,000.

LEFT-RIGHT RULES

LEFT Increases in expenses appear on the left side of the T account. Record $8,000 on the left side of the **Salaries Expense** T account.

RIGHT Decreases in asset accounts are recorded on the right side of the T account. Record $8,000 on the right side of the **Cash** T account.

T-ACCOUNT PRESENTATION

How is the decrease in owner's equity recorded? One way would be to record the $8,000 on the left side of the **Carolyn Wells, Capital** account. However, the preferred way is to keep expenses separate from owner's investment. Therefore, Valdez set up a **Salaries Expense** account.

To record the salary expense, Valdez entered $8,000 **(j)** on the left (increase) side of the **Salaries Expense** account. Notice that the plus and minus signs in the **Salaries Expense** account show the effect on the expense account, not on owner's equity.

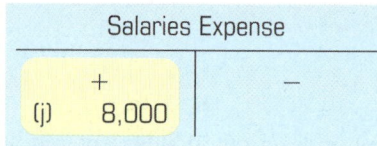

Valdez entered $8,000 **(j)** on the right (decrease) side of the **Cash** T account.

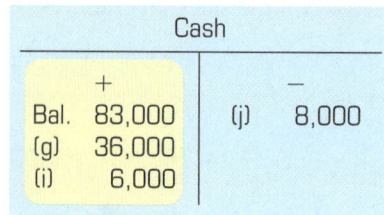

Most companies have numerous expense accounts. The various expense accounts appear in the Expenses section of the income statement.

RECORDING AN EXPENSE FOR UTILITIES

At the end of December, Wells' Consulting Services received a $650 bill for utilities. Valdez set up an account for **Utilities Expense.**

BUSINESS TRANSACTION

Wells' Consulting Services issued a check for $650 to pay the utilities bill.

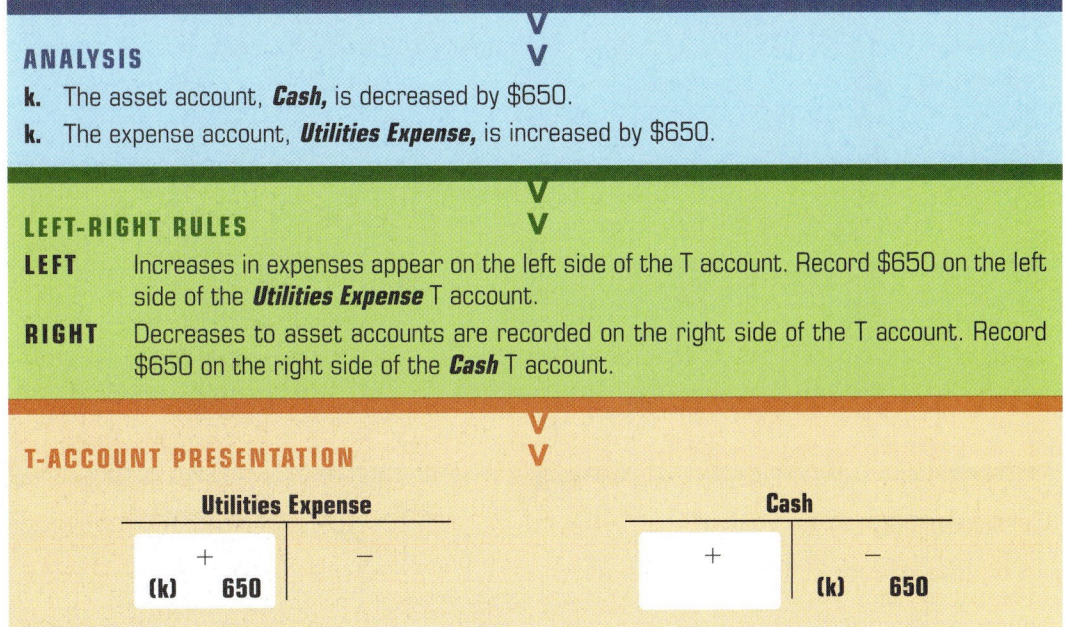

ANALYSIS

k. The asset account, *Cash,* is decreased by $650.

k. The expense account, *Utilities Expense,* is increased by $650.

LEFT-RIGHT RULES

LEFT Increases in expenses appear on the left side of the T account. Record $650 on the left side of the *Utilities Expense* T account.

RIGHT Decreases to asset accounts are recorded on the right side of the T account. Record $650 on the right side of the *Cash* T account.

T-ACCOUNT PRESENTATION

Utilities Expense			Cash		
+	–		+	–	
(k) 650				(k) 650	

Let's review the effects of the transactions.

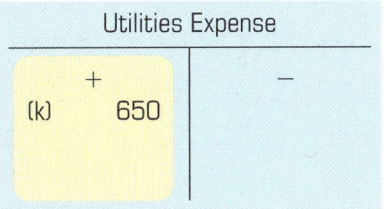

Utilities Expense			Cash		
+	–		+		–
(k) 650			Bal. 83,000	(j) 8,000	
			(g) 36,000	(k) 650	
			(i) 6,000		

The Drawing Account

In sole proprietorships and partnerships, the owners generally do not pay themselves salaries. To obtain funds for personal living expenses, owners make withdrawals of cash. The withdrawals are against previously earned profits that have become part of capital or against profits that are expected in the future.

Since withdrawals decrease owner's equity, withdrawals could be recorded on the left side of the capital account. However, the preferred way is to keep withdrawals separate from the owner's capital account until the end of the accounting period. An owner's equity account called a **drawing account** is set up to record withdrawals. Increases in the drawing account (which are decreases in owner's equity) are recorded on the left side of the drawing T accounts.

BUSINESS TRANSACTION

Carolyn Wells wrote a check to withdraw $5,000 cash for personal use.

ANALYSIS

l. The asset account, *Cash,* is decreased by $5,000.

l. The owner's equity account, *Carolyn Wells, Drawing,* is increased by $5,000.

FIGURE 3.3

The Relationship between Owner's Equity and Revenue, Expenses, and Withdrawals

important!

Normal Balances

Debit: Credit:

Asset   Liability

Expense Revenue

Drawing Capital

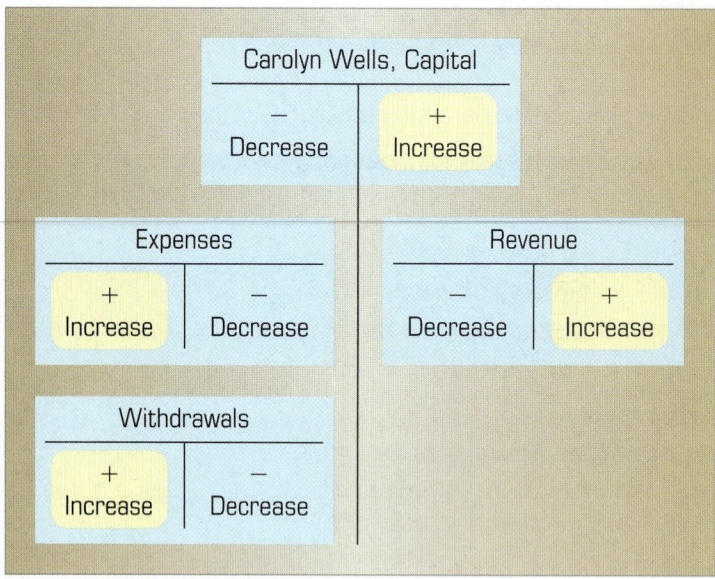

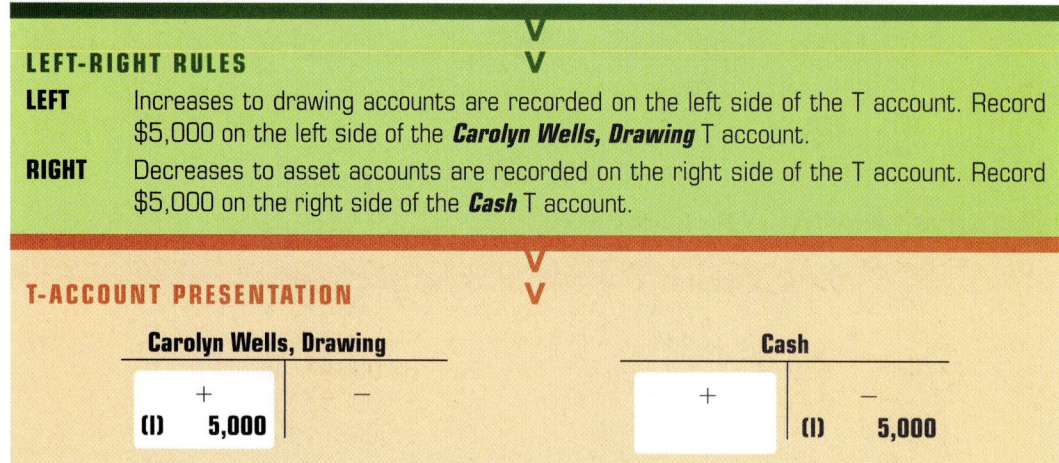

LEFT-RIGHT RULES

LEFT   Increases to drawing accounts are recorded on the left side of the T account. Record $5,000 on the left side of the **Carolyn Wells, Drawing** T account.

RIGHT   Decreases to asset accounts are recorded on the right side of the T account. Record $5,000 on the right side of the **Cash** T account.

T-ACCOUNT PRESENTATION

Carolyn Wells, Drawing		Cash	
+	−	+	−
(l) 5,000			(l) 5,000

Let's review the transactions. Valdez entered $5,000 **(l)** on the right (decrease) side of the asset account, **Cash,** and $5,000 **(l)** on the left (increase) side of **Carolyn Wells, Drawing.** Note that the plus and minus signs show the effect on the drawing account, not on owner's equity.

Figure 3.3 shows a summary of the relationship between the capital account and the revenue, expense, and drawing accounts.

The Rules of Debit and Credit

Accountants do not use the terms *left side* and *right side* when they talk about making entries in accounts. Instead, they use the term **debit** for an entry on the left side and **credit** for an entry on the right side. Figure 3.4 summarizes the rules for debits and credits. The accounting system is called the **double-entry system.** This is because each transaction has at least two entries—a debit and a credit.

FIGURE 3.4   Rules for Debits and Credits

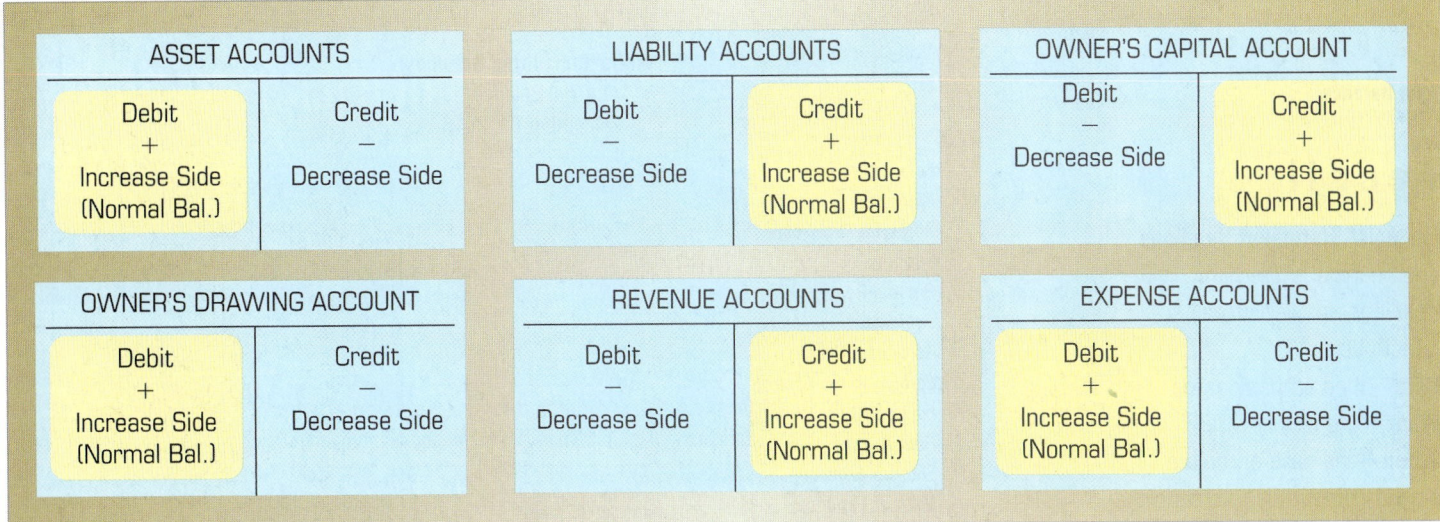

After the December transactions for Wells' Consulting Services are recorded, the account balances are calculated. Figure 3.5 below shows the account balances at the end of December. Notice that the fundamental accounting equation remains in balance (Assets = Liabilities + Owner's Equity).

The Trial Balance

Once the account balances are computed, a trial balance is prepared. The **trial balance** is a statement that tests the accuracy of total debits and credits after transactions have been

FIGURE 3.5

End-of-December 2013 Account Balances

ASSETS			=	LIABILITIES		+	OWNER'S EQUITY	
Cash				Accounts Payable			Carolyn Wells, Capital	

Bal.	83,000	(j)	8,000	
(g)	36,000	(k)	650	
(i)	6,000	(l)	5,000	
	125,000		13,650	
Bal.	111,350			

Accounts Payable

	Bal.	3,500

Carolyn Wells, Capital

	Bal.	100,000

Accounts Receivable

(h)	11,000	(i)	6,000
Bal.	5,000		

Carolyn Wells, Drawing

(l)	5,000

Supplies

Bal.	1,500

Fees Income

	(g)	36,000
	(h)	11,000
	Bal.	47,000

Prepaid Rent

Bal.	8,000

Salaries Expense

(j)	8,000

Equipment

Bal.	11,000

Utilities Expense

(k)	650

ACCOUNT NAME	DEBIT		CREDIT	
Cash	111 3 5 0 00			
Accounts Receivable	5 0 0 0 00			
Supplies	1 5 0 0 00			
Prepaid Rent	8 0 0 0 00			
Equipment	11 0 0 0 00			
Accounts Payable			3 5 0 0 00	
Carolyn Wells, Capital			100 0 0 0 00	
Carolyn Wells, Drawing	5 0 0 0 00			
Fees Income			47 0 0 0 00	
Salaries Expense	8 0 0 0 00			
Utilities Expense	6 5 0 00			
Totals	150 5 0 0 00		150 5 0 0 00	

Wells' Consulting Services
Trial Balance
December 31, 2013

recall

Financial Statement Headings

The financial statement headings answer three questions:

Who—the company name

What—the report title

When—the date of, or the period covered by, the report

recorded. If total debits do not equal total credits, there is an error. Figure 3.6 above shows the trial balance for Wells' Consulting Services. To prepare a trial balance, perform the following steps:

1. Enter the trial balance heading showing the company name, report title, and closing date for the accounting period.

2. List the account names in the same order as they appear on the financial statements.
   - Assets
   - Liabilities
   - Owner's Equity
   - Revenue
   - Expenses

3. Enter the ending balance of each account in the appropriate Debit or Credit column.

4. Total the Debit column.

5. Total the Credit column.

6. Compare the total debits with the total credits.

MANAGERIAL IMPLICATIONS

FINANCIAL STATEMENTS

- Recording entries into accounts provides an efficient method of gathering data about the financial affairs of a business.

- A chart of accounts is usually similar from company to company; balance sheet accounts are first, followed by income statement accounts.

- A trial balance proves the financial records are in balance.

- The income statement reports the revenue and expenses for the period and shows the net income or loss.

- The statement of owner's equity shows the change in owner's equity during the period.

- The balance sheet summarizes the assets, liabilities, and owner's equity of the business on a given date.

- Owners, managers, creditors, banks, and many others use financial statements to make decisions about the business.

THINKING CRITICALLY

What are some possible consequences of not recording financial data correctly?

UNDERSTANDING TRIAL BALANCE ERRORS

>>**5. OBJECTIVE**
Prepare a trial balance from
T accounts.

If the totals of the Debit and Credit columns are equal, the financial records are in balance. If the totals of the Debit and Credit columns are not equal, there is an error. The error may be in the trial balance, or it may be in the financial records. Some common errors are:

- adding trial balance columns incorrectly;
- recording only half a transaction—for example, recording a debit but not recording a credit, or vice versa;
- recording both halves of a transaction as debits or credits rather than recording one debit and one credit;
- recording an amount incorrectly from a transaction;
- recording a debit for one amount and a credit for a different amount;
- making an error when calculating the account balances.

FINDING TRIAL BALANCE ERRORS

If the trial balance does not balance, try the following procedures:

1. Check the arithmetic. If the columns were originally added from top to bottom, verify the total by adding from bottom to top.
2. Check that the correct account balances were transferred to the correct trial balance columns.
3. Check the arithmetic used to compute the account balances.
4. Check that each transaction was recorded correctly in the accounts by tracing the amounts to the analysis of the transaction.

Sometimes you can determine the type of the error by the amount of the difference. Compute the difference between the debit total and the credit total. If the difference is divisible by 2, a debit might be recorded as a credit, or a credit recorded as a debit.

If the difference is divisible by 9, there might be a transposition. A **transposition** occurs when the digits of a number are switched (357 for 375). The test for a transposition is:

$$375$$
$$-357 \qquad 18/9 = 2$$
$$18$$

Also check for slides. A **slide** occurs when the decimal point is misplaced (375 for 37.50). We can test for a slide in the following manner:

$$375.00$$
$$37.50 \qquad 337.50/9 = 37.50$$
$$337.50$$

Financial Statements

>>**6. OBJECTIVE**
Prepare an income state-
ment, a statement of owner's
equity, and a balance sheet.

After the trial balance is prepared, the financial statements are prepared. Figure 3.7 shows the financial statements for Wells' Consulting Services. The amounts are taken from the trial balance. As you study the financial statements, note that net income from the income statement is used on the statement of owner's equity. Also note that the ending balance of the *Carolyn Wells, Capital* account, computed on the statement of owner's equity, is used on the balance sheet.

Chart of Accounts

>>**7. OBJECTIVE**
Develop a chart of accounts.

A **chart of accounts** is a list of all the accounts used by a business. Figure 3.8 shows the chart of accounts for Wells' Consulting Services. Each account has a number and a name. The balance sheet accounts are listed first, followed by the income statement accounts. The account number is assigned based on the type of account.

FIGURE 3.7

Financial Statements for Wells'
Consulting Services

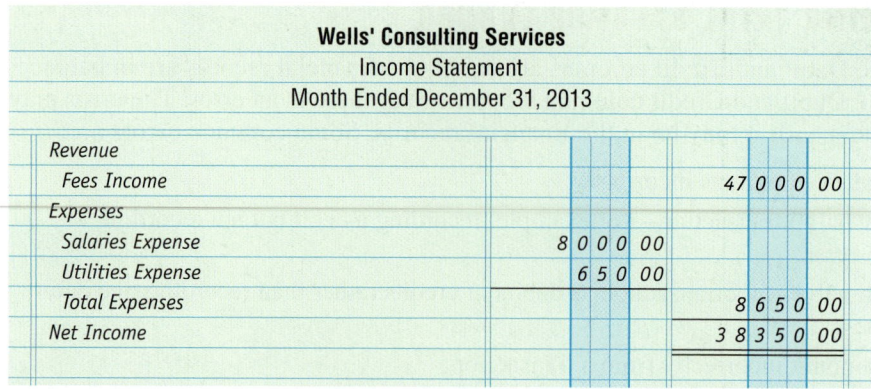

Wells' Consulting Services
Income Statement
Month Ended December 31, 2013

Revenue		
Fees Income		47 000 00
Expenses		
Salaries Expense	8 000 00	
Utilities Expense	650 00	
Total Expenses		8 650 00
Net Income		38 350 00

Wells' Consulting Services
Statement of Owner's Equity
Month Ended December 31, 2013

Carolyn Wells, Capital, December 1, 2013		100 000 00
Net Income for December	38 350 00	
Less Withdrawals for December	5 000 00	
Increase in Capital		33 350 00
Carolyn Wells, Capital, December 31, 2013		133 350 00

Wells' Consulting Services
Balance Sheet
December 31, 2013

Assets		Liabilities	
Cash	111 350 00	Accounts Payable	3 500 00
Accounts Receivable	5 000 00		
Supplies	1 500 00		
Prepaid Rent	8 000 00	Owner's Equity	
Equipment	11 000 00	Carolyn Wells, Capital	133 350 00
Total Assets	136 850 00	Total Liabilities and Owner's Equity	136 850 00

Asset Accounts	100–199	Revenue Accounts	400–499
Liability Accounts	200–299	Expense Accounts	500–599
Owner's Equity Accounts	300–399		

Notice that the accounts are not numbered consecutively. For example, asset account numbers jump from 101 to 111 and then to 121, 137, and 141. In each block of numbers, gaps are left so that additional accounts can be added when needed.

Permanent and Temporary Accounts

The asset, liability, and owner's equity accounts appear on the balance sheet at the end of an accounting period. The balances of these accounts are then carried forward to start the new period. Because they continue from one accounting period to the next, these accounts are called **permanent accounts** or *real accounts*.

Revenue and expense accounts appear on the income statement. The drawing account appears on the statement of owner's equity. These accounts classify and summarize changes in owner's equity during the period. They are called **temporary accounts** or *nominal accounts* because the balances in these accounts are transferred to the capital account at the end of the accounting period. In the next period, these accounts start with zero balances.

FIGURE 3.8

Chart of Accounts

Wells' Consulting Services Chart of Accounts	
Account Number	**Account Name**
Balance Sheet Accounts	
100–199	**ASSETS**
101	Cash
111	Accounts Receivable
121	Supplies
137	Prepaid Rent
141	Equipment
200–299	**LIABILITIES**
202	Accounts Payable
300–399	**OWNER'S EQUITY**
301	Carolyn Wells, Capital
Statement of Owner's Equity Account	
302	Carolyn Wells, Drawing
Income Statement Accounts	
400–499	**REVENUE**
401	Fees Income
500–599	**EXPENSES**
511	Salaries Expense
514	Utilities Expense

important!

Balance Sheet Accounts

The amounts on the balance sheet are carried forward to the next accounting period.

important!

Income Statement Accounts

The amounts on the income statement are transferred to the capital account at the end of the accounting period.

Section 2 Self Review

QUESTIONS

[handwritten: Credit Debit, Credit Credit]

1. What is the increase side for **Cash**; **Accounts Payable**; and **Carolyn Wells, Capital?**

2. What is a trial balance and what is its purpose?

3. What is a transposition? A slide?

EXERCISES

4. The company owner took $4,000 cash for personal use. What is the entry for this transaction?

   a. Debit **Cash** and credit **Jason Taylor, Drawing.**

   b. Debit **Jason Taylor, Drawing** and credit **Cash.** *[circled]*

   c. Debit **Jason Taylor, Capital** and credit **Cash.**

   d. Debit **Cash** and credit **Jason Taylor, Capital.**

5. Which account has a normal debit balance?

   a. Accounts Payable

   b. L. T., Capital

   c. L. T., Drawing *[circled]*

   d. Fees Income *[struck through]*

ANALYSIS

6. Describe the errors in the Tuttle Interiors trial balance.

[handwritten: Normal = increase]

[handwritten: Not Balanced]

Tuttle Interiors Trial Balance December 31, 2013				
	DEBIT		**CREDIT**	
Cash	30 0 0 0 00			
Accts. Rec.	20 0 0 0 00			
Equip.	14 0 0 0 00			
Accts. Pay.			30 0 0 0 00	
S. Tuttle, Capital			44 0 0 0 00	
S. Tuttle, Drawing			20 0 0 0 00	←
Fees Income	28 0 0 0 00 →			
Rent Exp.	4 0 0 0 00			
Supplies Exp.	4 0 0 0 00			
Telephone Exp.	10 0 0 0 00			
Totals	110 0 0 0 00		94 0 0 0 00	
✓	102,000.00		102,000.00	

(Answers to Section 2 Self Review are on page 87.)

3 Chapter REVIEW Chapter Summary

In this chapter, you have learned how to use T accounts to help analyze and record business transactions. A chart of accounts can be developed to easily identify all the accounts used by a business. After determining the balance for all accounts, the trial balance is prepared to ensure that all transactions have been recorded accurately.

Learning Objectives

1 Set up T accounts for assets, liabilities, and owner's equity.

T accounts consist of two lines, one vertical and one horizontal, that resemble the letter T. The account name is written on the top line. Increases and decreases to the account are entered on either the left side or the right side of the vertical line.

2 Analyze business transactions and enter them in the accounts.

Each business transaction is analyzed for its effects on the fundamental accounting equation, Assets = Liabilities + Owner's Equity. Then these effects are recorded in the proper accounts. Accounts are classified as assets, liabilities, or owner's equity.

- Increases in an asset account appear on the debit, or left, side because assets are on the left side of the accounting equation. The credit, or right, side records decreases.

- An increase in a liability account is recorded on the credit, or right, side. The left, or debit, side of a liability account is used for recording decreases.

- Increases in owner's equity are shown on the credit (right) side of an account. Decreases appear on the debit (left) side.

- The drawing account is used to record the withdrawal of cash from the business by the owner. The drawing account decreases owner's equity.

3 Determine the balance of an account.

The difference between the amounts recorded on the two sides of an account is known as the balance of the account.

4 Set up T accounts for revenue and expenses.

- Revenue accounts increase owner's equity; therefore, increases are recorded on the credit side of revenue accounts.

- Expenses are recorded on the debit side of the expense accounts because expenses decrease owner's equity.

5 Prepare a trial balance from T accounts.

The trial balance is a statement to test the accuracy of the financial records. Total debits should equal total credits.

6 Prepare an income statement, a statement of owner's equity, and a balance sheet.

The income statement is prepared to report the revenue and expenses for the period. The statement of owner's equity is prepared to analyze the change in owner's equity during the period. Then the balance sheet is prepared to summarize the assets, liabilities, and owner's equity of the business at a given point in time.

7 Develop a chart of accounts.

A firm's list of accounts is called its chart of accounts. Accounts are arranged in a predetermined order and are numbered for handy reference and quick identification. Typically, accounts are numbered in the order in which they appear on the financial statements. Balance sheet accounts come first, followed by income statement accounts.

8 Define the accounting terms new to this chapter.

Glossary

Account balance (p. 60) The difference between the amounts recorded on the two sides of an account

Accounts (p. 54) Written records of the assets, liabilities, and owner's equity of a business

Chart of accounts (p. 71) A list of the accounts used by a business to record its financial transactions

Classification (p. 54) A means of identifying each account as an asset, liability, or owner's equity

Credit (p. 68) An entry on the right side of an account

Debit (p. 68) An entry on the left side of an account

Double-entry system (p. 68) An accounting system that involves recording the effects of each transaction as debits and credits

Drawing account (p. 67) A special type of owner's equity account set up to record the owner's withdrawal of cash from the business

Footing (p. 60) A small pencil figure written at the base of an amount column showing the sum of the entries in the column

Normal balance (p. 60) The increase side of an account

Permanent account (p. 72) An account that is kept open from one accounting period to the next

Slide (p. 71) An accounting error involving a misplaced decimal point

T account (p. 54) A type of account, resembling a T, used to analyze the effects of a business transaction

Temporary account (p. 72) An account whose balance is transferred to another account at the end of an accounting period

Transposition (p. 71) An accounting error involving misplaced digits in a number

Trial balance (p. 69) A statement to test the accuracy of total debits and credits after transactions have been recorded

Comprehensive **Self Review**

1. Your friend has prepared financial statements for her business. She has asked you to review the statements for accuracy. The trial balance debit column totals $71,000 and the credit column totals $84,000. What steps would you take to find the error?

2. On which side of asset, liability, and owner's equity accounts are decreases recorded?

3. What type of accounts are found on the balance sheet?

4. What are withdrawals and how are they recorded?

5. What is a chart of accounts?

(Answers to Comprehensive Self Review are on page 87.)

Discussion Questions

1. Indicate whether each of the following types of accounts would normally have a debit balance or a credit balance:

    a. An asset account

    b. A liability account

    c. The owner's capital account

    d. A revenue account

    e. An expense account

2. What are accounts?

3. How is the balance of an account determined?

4. What is the purpose of a chart of accounts?

5. In what order do accounts appear in the chart of accounts?

6. When a chart of accounts is created, number gaps are left within groups of accounts. Why are these number gaps necessary?

7. Accounts are classified as permanent or temporary accounts. What do these classifications mean?

8. Why is *Prepaid Rent* considered an asset account?

9. Why is the modern system of accounting usually called the double-entry system?

10. The terms *debit* and *credit* are often used in describing the effects of transactions on different accounts. What do these terms mean?

11. Are the following accounts permanent or temporary accounts?

    a. Fees Income

    b. Johnny Jones, Drawing

    c. Accounts Payable

    d. Accounts Receivable

    e. Johnny Jones, Capital

    f. Prepaid Rent

    g. Cash

    h. Advertising Expense

    i. Utilities Expense

    j. Equipment

    k. Salaries Expense

    l. Prepaid Insurance

APPLICATIONS

Exercises

Exercise 3.1

Objective 1

▶ **Setting up T accounts.**

Williams Cleaning Service has the following account balances on December 31, 2013. Set up a T account for each account and enter the balance on the proper side of the account.

Cash	$18,000	Accounts Payable	$23,200
Equipment	$45,000	Wade Williams, Capital	$39,800

Exercise 3.2

Objective 2

▶ **Using T accounts to analyze transactions.**

Donna Wells decided to start a dental practice. The first five transactions for the business follow. For each transaction, (1) determine which two accounts are affected, (2) set up T accounts for the affected accounts, and (3) enter the debit and credit amounts in the T accounts.

1. Donna invested $80,000 cash in the business.

2. Paid $20,000 in cash for equipment.

3. Performed services for cash amounting to $8,000.

4. Paid $2,800 in cash for advertising expense.

5. Paid $2,000 in cash for supplies.

Exercise 3.3

Objective 3

▶ **Determining debit and credit balances.**

Indicate whether each of the following accounts normally has a debit balance or a credit balance:

1. Ted Wilson, Capital

2. Cash

3. Fees Income
4. Accounts Payable
5. Supplies
6. Salaries Expense
7. Accounts Receivable
8. Equipment

Identifying debits and credits.

◀ **Exercise 3.4**
Objective 3

In each of the following sentences, fill in the blanks with the word *debit* or *credit:*

1. Revenue accounts normally have ___?___ balances. These accounts increase on the ___?___ side and decrease on the ___?___ side.

2. Asset accounts normally have ___?___ balances. These accounts increase on the ___?___ side and decrease on the ___?___ side.

3. Liability accounts normally have ___?___ balances. These accounts increase on the ___?___ side and decrease on the ___?___ side.

4. Expense accounts normally have ___?___ balances. These accounts increase on the ___?___ side and decrease on the ___?___ side.

5. The owner's capital account normally has a ___?___ balance. This account increases on the ___?___ side and decreases on the ___?___ side.

Determining account balances.

◀ **Exercise 3.5**
Objective 3

The following T accounts show transactions that were recorded by Apartment Locators, a firm that specializes in local apartment renting. The entries for the first transaction are labeled with the letter (a), the entries for the second transaction with the letter (b), and so on. Determine the balance of each account.

Cash				
(a)	180,000	(b)	36,000	
(d)	20,000	(e)	600	
(g)	2,000	(h)	10,000	
		(i)	4,000	

Equipment	
(c)	70,000

Accounts Receivable			
(f)	8,000	(g)	2,000

Accounts Payable	
(c)	70,000

Supplies	
(b)	36,000

David Thomas, Capital	
(a)	180,000

Fees Income		
(d)	20,000
(f)	8,000

Telephone Expense	
(e)	600

David Thomas, Drawing	
(i)	4,000

Salaries Expense	
(h)	10,000

Preparing a trial balance and an income statement.

◀ **Exercise 3.6**
Objectives 5, 6

CONTINUING >>>
Problem

Using the account balances from Exercise 3.5, prepare a trial balance and an income statement for Apartment Locators. The trial balance is for December 31, 2013, and the income statement is for the month ended December 31, 2013.

Exercise 3.7

Objective 6

▶ **Preparing a statement of owner's equity and a balance sheet.**

From the trial balance and the net income or net loss determined in Exercise 3.6, prepare a statement of owner's equity and a balance sheet for Apartment Locators as of December 31, 2013.

Exercise 3.8

Objective 7

▶ **Preparing a chart of accounts.**

The accounts that will be used by Zant Moving Company follow. Prepare a chart of accounts for the firm. Classify the accounts by type, arrange them in an appropriate order, and assign suitable account numbers.

Sue Zant, Capital	Salaries Expense
Office Supplies	Prepaid Rent
Accounts Payable	Fees Income
Cash	Accounts Receivable
Utilities Expense	Telephone Expense
Office Equipment	Sue Zant, Drawing

PROBLEMS

Problem Set A

Problem 3.1A

Objectives 1

▶ **Using T accounts to record transactions involving assets, liabilities, and owner's equity.**

The following transactions occurred at several different businesses and are not related.

INSTRUCTIONS

Analyze each of the transactions. For each, decide what accounts are affected and set up T accounts. Record the effects of the transaction in the T accounts. Use plus and minus signs before the amounts to show the increases and decreases.

TRANSACTIONS

1. James Walker, an owner, made an additional investment of $16,000 in cash.
2. A firm purchased equipment for $9,000 in cash.
3. A firm sold some surplus office furniture for $1,200 in cash.
4. A firm purchased a computer for $2,700, to be paid in 60 days.
5. A firm purchased office equipment for $10,200 on credit. The amount is due in 60 days.
6. Carol Rose, owner of Rose Travel Agency, withdrew $5,000 of her original cash investment.
7. A firm bought a delivery truck for $32,000 on credit; payment is due in 90 days.
8. A firm issued a check for $2,500 to a supplier in partial payment of an open account balance.

Analyze: List the transactions that directly affected an owner's equity account.

Using T accounts to record transactions involving assets, liabilities, and owner's equity.

◄ **Problem 3.2A**

Objectives 1, 2

e**X**cel

The following transactions took place at Professional Counseling Services, a business established by Greta Davis.

INSTRUCTIONS

For each transaction, set up T accounts from this list: *Cash; Office Furniture; Office Equipment; Automobile; Accounts Payable; Greta Davis, Capital;* and *Greta Davis, Drawing.* Analyze each transaction. Record the amounts in the T accounts affected by that transaction. Use plus and minus signs to show increases and decreases in each account.

TRANSACTIONS

1. Greta Davis invested $60,000 cash in the business.
2. Purchased office furniture for $16,000 in cash.
3. Bought a fax machine for $950; payment is due in 30 days.
4. Purchased a used car for the firm for $16,000 in cash.
5. Davis invested an additional $10,000 cash in the business.
6. Bought a new computer for $3,000; payment is due in 60 days.
7. Paid $950 to settle the amount owed on the fax machine.
8. Davis withdrew $4,000 in cash for personal expenses.

Analyze: Which transactions affected asset accounts?

Using T accounts to record transactions involving revenues and expenses.

◄ **Problem 3.3A**

Objectives 2, 4

The following occurred during June at Carter's Professional Counseling.

INSTRUCTIONS

Analyze each transaction. Use T accounts to record these transactions and be sure to put the name of the account on the top of each account. Record the effects of the transaction in the T accounts. Use plus and minus signs before the amounts to show the increases and decreases.

TRANSACTIONS

1. Purchased office supplies for $2,000.
2. Delivered monthly statements, collected fee income of $21,000.
3. Paid the current month's office rent of $4,000.
4. Completed professional counseling, billed client for $3,000.
5. Client paid fee of $1,000 for weekly counseling, previously billed.
6. Paid office salary of $3,600.
7. Paid telephone bill of $480.
8. Billed client for $2,000 fee for preparing a counseling memorandum.

9. Purchased office supplies of $1,000 on account.

10. Paid office salary of $3,600.

11. Collected $2,000 from client who was billed.

12. Clients paid a total of $8,100 cash in fees.

Analyze: How much cash did the business spend during the month?

Problem 3.4A ▶ **Using T accounts to record all business transactions.**

Objectives 1, 2, 4

The following accounts and transactions are for John Wilson, Landscape Consultant.

 **INSTRUCTIONS**

Analyze the transactions. Record each in the appropriate T accounts. Use plus and minus signs in front of the amounts to show the increases and decreases. Identify each entry in the T accounts by writing the letter of the transaction next to the entry.

ASSETS
Cash
Accounts Receivable
Office Furniture
Office Equipment

LIABILITIES
Accounts Payable

OWNER'S EQUITY
John Wilson, Capital
John Wilson, Drawing

REVENUE
Fees Income

EXPENSES
Rent Expense
Utilities Expense
Salaries Expense
Telephone Expense
Miscellaneous Expense

TRANSACTIONS

a. Wilson invested $150,000 in cash to start the business.

b. Paid $5,000 for the current month's rent.

c. Bought office furniture for $15,720 in cash.

d. Performed services for $7,200 in cash.

e. Paid $1,150 for the monthly telephone bill.

f. Performed services for $13,000 on credit.

g. Purchased a computer and copier for $36,000, paid $12,000 in cash immediately with the balance due in 30 days.

h. Received $6,500 from credit clients.

i. Paid $3,000 in cash for office cleaning services for the month.

j. Purchased additional office chairs for $4,800; received credit terms of 30 days.

k. Purchased office equipment for $30,000 and paid half of this amount in cash immediately; the balance is due in 30 days.

l. Issued a check for $8,400 to pay salaries.

m. Performed services for $13,500 in cash.

n. Performed services for $15,000 on credit.

o. Collected $7,000 on accounts receivable from charge customers.

p. Issued a check for $2,400 in partial payment of the amount owed for office chairs.

q. Paid $600 to a duplicating company for photocopy work performed during the month.

r. Paid $1,120 for the monthly electric bill.

s. Wilson withdrew $8,000 in cash for personal expenses.

Analyze: What liabilities does the business have after all transactions have been recorded?

Preparing financial statements from T accounts.

◀ **Problem 3.5A**
Objectives 3, 5, 6
e**X**cel
CONTINUING >>>
Problem

The accountant for the firm owned by John Wilson prepares financial statements at the end of each month.

INSTRUCTIONS

Use the figures in the T accounts for Problem 3.4A to prepare a trial balance, an income statement, a statement of owner's equity, and a balance sheet. (The first line of the statement headings should read "John Wilson, Landscape Consultant.") Assume that the transactions took place during the month ended June 30, 2013. Determine the account balances before you start work on the financial statements.

Analyze: What is the change in owner's equity for the month of June?

Problem Set B

Using T accounts to record transactions involving assets, liabilities, and owner's equity.

◀ **Problem 3.1B**
Objectives 1, 2

The following transactions occurred at several different businesses and are not related.

INSTRUCTIONS

Analyze each of the transactions. For each transaction, set up T accounts. Record the effects of the transaction in the T accounts. Use plus and minus signs to show the increases and decreases.

TRANSACTIONS

1. A firm purchased equipment for $16,000 in cash.

2. The owner, Angie Carvajal, withdrew $4,000 cash.

3. A firm sold a piece of surplus equipment for $3,000 in cash.

4. A firm purchased a used delivery truck for $12,000 in cash.

5. A firm paid $3,600 in cash to apply against an account owed.

6. A firm purchased office equipment for $5,000. The amount is to be paid in 60 days.

7. Chuck Vinson, owner of the company, made an additional investment of $20,000 in cash.

8. A firm paid $1,500 by check for office equipment that it had previously purchased on credit.

Analyze: Which transactions affect liability accounts?

Problem 3.2B
Objectives 1, 2

▶ ## Using T accounts to record transactions involving assets, liabilities, and owner's equity.

The following transactions took place at Windmill Equipment Service.

INSTRUCTIONS

For each transaction, set up T accounts from the following list: *Cash*; *Shop Equipment; Store Equipment; Truck; Accounts Payable; Joseph Tejan, Capital;* and *Joseph Tejan, Drawing*. Analyze each transaction. Record the effects of the transactions in the T accounts. Use plus and minus signs before the amounts to show the increases and decreases.

TRANSACTIONS

1. Joseph Tejan invested $20,000 cash in the business.
2. Purchased shop equipment for $1,800 in cash.
3. Bought store fixtures for $1,200; payment is due in 30 days.
4. Purchased a used truck for $10,000 in cash.
5. Tejan gave the firm his personal tools that have a fair market value of $3,000.
6. Bought a used cash register for $2,500; payment is due in 30 days.
7. Paid $400 in cash to apply to the amount owed for store fixtures.
8. Tejan withdrew $1,600 in cash for personal expenses.

Analyze: Which transactions affect the *Cash* account?

Problem 3.3B
Objectives 2, 4

▶ ## Using T accounts to record transactions involving revenue and expenses.

The following transactions took place at China Express Laundry and Cleaners.

INSTRUCTIONS

Analyze each of the transactions. For each transaction, decide what accounts are affected and set up T accounts. Record the effects of the transaction in the T accounts. Use plus and minus signs before the amounts to show the increases and decreases.

TRANSACTIONS

1. Paid $3,800 for the current month's rent.
2. Performed services for $8,000 in cash.
3. Paid salaries of $5,600.
4. Performed additional services for $10,800 on credit.
5. Paid $1,200 for the monthly telephone bill.
6. Collected $4,000 from accounts receivable.
7. Received a $190 refund for an overcharge on the telephone bill.

8. Performed services for $5,200 on credit.

9. Paid $850 in cash for the monthly electric bill.

10. Paid $1,200 in cash for gasoline purchased for the firm's van during the month.

11. Received $4,200 from charge account customers.

12. Performed services for $8,600 in cash.

Analyze: What total cash was collected for Accounts Receivable during the month?

Using T accounts to record all business transactions.

The accounts and transactions of Kathryn Price, Counselor and Attorney at Law, follow.

◀ **Problem 3.4B**
Objectives 1, 2, 4

INSTRUCTIONS

Analyze the transactions. Record each in the appropriate T accounts. Use plus and minus signs in front of the amounts to show the increases and decreases. Identify each entry in the T accounts by writing the letter of the transaction next to the entry.

ASSETS
Cash
Accounts Receivable
Office Furniture
Office Equipment
Automobile

LIABILITIES
Accounts Payable

OWNER'S EQUITY
Kathryn Price, Capital
Kathryn Price, Drawing

REVENUE
Fees Income

EXPENSES
Automobile Expense
Rent Expense
Utilities Expense
Salaries Expense
Telephone Expense

TRANSACTIONS

a. Kathryn Price invested $120,000 in cash to start the business.

b. Paid $6,400 for the current month's rent.

c. Bought a used automobile for the firm for $36,000 in cash.

d. Performed services for $8,000 in cash.

e. Paid $1,600 for automobile repairs.

f. Performed services for $9,150 on credit.

g. Purchased office chairs for $5,600 on credit.

h. Received $4,500 from credit clients.

i. Paid $3,600 to reduce the amount owed for the office chairs.

j. Issued a check for $1,300 to pay the monthly utility bill.

k. Purchased office equipment for $19,600 and paid half of this amount in cash immediately; the balance is due in 30 days.

l. Issued a check for $13,700 to pay salaries.

m. Performed services for $4,750 in cash.

n. Performed services for $5,500 on credit.

o. Paid $796 for the monthly telephone bill.

p. Collected $3,800 on accounts receivable from charge customers.

q. Purchased additional office equipment and received a bill for $5,440 due in 30 days.

r. Paid $800 in cash for gasoline purchased for the automobile during the month.

s. Kathryn Price withdrew $6,000 in cash for personal expenses.

Analyze: What outstanding amount is owed to the company from its credit customers?

Problem 3.5B ▶

Objectives 3, 5, 6

CONTINUING >>>
Problem

Preparing financial statements from T accounts.

The accountant for the firm owned by Kathryn Price prepares financial statements at the end of each month.

INSTRUCTIONS

Use the figures in the T accounts for Problem 3.4B to prepare a trial balance, an income statement, a statement of owner's equity, and a balance sheet. (The first line of the statement headings should read "Kathryn Price, Counselor and Attorney at Law.") Assume that the transactions took place during the month ended April 30, 2013. Determine the account balances before you start work on the financial statements.

Analyze: What net change in owner's equity occurred during the month of April?

Critical Thinking Problem 3.1

Financial Condition

At the beginning of the summer, Ted Coe was looking for a way to earn money to pay for his college tuition in the fall. He decided to start a lawn service business in his neighborhood. To get the business started, Ted used $3,000 from his savings account to open a checking account for his new business, Elegant Lawn Care. He purchased two used power mowers and various lawn care tools for $1,000, and paid $1,800 for a second-hand truck to transport the mowers.

Several of his neighbors hired him to cut their grass on a weekly basis. He sent these customers monthly bills. By the end of the summer, they had paid him $600 in cash and owed him another $1,150. Ted also cut grass on an as-needed basis for other neighbors who paid him $500.

During the summer, Ted spent $200 for gasoline for the truck and mowers. He paid $500 to a friend who helped him on several occasions. An advertisement in the local paper cost $100. Now, at the end of the summer, Ted is concerned because he has only $500 left in his checking account. He says, "I worked hard all summer and have only $500 to show for it. It would have been better to leave the money in the bank."

Prepare an income statement, a statement of owner's equity, and a balance sheet for Elegant Lawn Care. Explain to Ted whether or not he is "better off" than he was at the beginning of the summer. (Hint: T accounts might be helpful in organizing the data.)

Critical Thinking Problem 3.2

Sole Proprietorship

Linda Carter is an architect who operates her own business. The accounts and transactions for the business follow.

INSTRUCTIONS

(1) Analyze the transactions for January 2013. Record each in the appropriate T accounts. Use plus and minus signs in front of the amounts to show the increases and decreases. Identify each entry in the T account by writing the letter of the transaction next to the entry.

(2) Determine the account balances. Prepare a trial balance, an income statement, a statement of owner's equity, and a balance sheet.

ASSETS
Cash
Accounts Receivable
Office Furniture
Office Equipment
LIABILITIES
Accounts Payable
OWNER'S EQUITY
Linda Carter, Capital
Linda Carter, Drawing
REVENUE
Fees Income
EXPENSES
Advertising Expense
Utilities Expense
Salaries Expense
Telephone Expense
Miscellaneous Expense

TRANSACTIONS

a. Linda Carter invested $20,000 in cash to start the business.

b. Paid $2,000 for advertisements in a design magazine.

c. Purchased office furniture for $3,600 in cash.

d. Performed services for $4,050 in cash.

e. Paid $210 for the monthly telephone bill.

f. Performed services for $1,560 on credit.

g. Purchased a fax machine for $475; paid $150 in cash with the balance due in 30 days.

h. Paid a bill for $550 from the office cleaning service.

i. Received $2,160 from clients on account.

j. Purchased additional office chairs for $590; received credit terms of 30 days.

k. Paid $4,000 for salaries.

l. Issued a check for $540 in partial payment of the amount owed for office chairs.

m. Received $2,800 in cash for services performed.

n. Issued a check for $460 for utilities expense.

o. Performed services for $3,200 on credit.

p. Collected $1,200 from clients on account.

q. Linda Carter withdrew $2,500 in cash for personal expenses.

r. Paid $600 to Quick Copy Service for photocopy work performed during the month.

Analyze: Using the basic accounting equation, what is the financial condition of Linda Carter's business at month-end?

BUSINESS CONNECTIONS

Informed Decisions

Managerial | FOCUS

1. How do the income statement and the balance sheet help management make sound decisions?

2. How can management find out, at any time, whether a firm can pay its bills as they become due?

3. If a firm's expenses equal or exceed its revenue, what actions might management take?

4. In discussing a firm's latest financial statements, a manager says that it is the "results on the bottom line" that really count. What does the manager mean?

To Open or Not to Open

As the full charge bookkeeper, you are responsible for keeping the chart of accounts up to date. At the end of each year, you analyze the accounts to verify that each account should be active for accumulation of costs, revenues, and expenses. In July, the accounts payable clerk has asked you to open an account named New Expenses. You know that an account name should be specific and well defined. You feel that the A/P clerk might want to charge some expenses to that account that would not be appropriate. Why do you think the A/P clerk needs this New Expenses account? Who needs to know this information and what action should you consider?

Management Letter and Annual Report

Annual reports released by publicly held companies include a letter to the stockholders written by the chief executive officer, chairman of the board, or president.

Analyze Online: Locate the Adobe Systems Incorporated Web site (www.adobe.com). Within *Investor Relations* in the *About Adobe* link, find the annual report for the current year. Read the letter to the stockholders within the annual report.

Analyze:

1. What types of information can a company's management deliver using the letter to stockholders?

2. What annual revenue did Adobe Systems Incorporated report for fiscal 2009?

3. What amount of cash, cash equivalents, and short term investments did Adobe have on hand at the end of 2009?

4. Are the financial results presented in the current year more or less favorable than those presented for fiscal 2008?

5. What is Adobe's targeted revenue for the first quarter of 2010?

Specific Chart of Accounts

A chart of accounts varies with each type of business as well as each company. In a group, compare and contrast the accounts that would appear in Jones Real Estate Office, Christy's Clothing Emporium, Lee's Grocery Store, and Sarkis' Plumbing Service. What accounts would appear in all companies? What accounts would be specific to each business?

10K Reports

Financial statements can reveal a great deal about a company. Corporations are required to produce a 10K report that includes the income statement and balance sheet. Go to the companies' Web sites listed below, select investor relations, annual report, and 10K report. From the income statement, decide the most profitable company. From the balance sheet, decide the company with the largest amount of cash available and the one with the most assets. (www.federated-fds.com) (www.jcpenny.com) (www.honeywell.com)

Answers to **Self Reviews**

Answers to Section 1 Self Review

1. Increases in asset accounts are recorded on the left side. Increases in liability and owner's equity accounts are recorded on the right side.

2. The sum of several entries on either side of an account that is entered in small pencil figures.

3. The increase side of an account. The normal balance of an asset account is on the left side. The normal balance of liability and owner's equity accounts is on the right side.

4. **c.** 26,150

5. **b.** *Equipment* is increased by $10,800. *Accounts Payable* is increased by $10,800.

6.

								David Jenkins,
Cash	+	Equipment	+	Supplies	=	Accounts Payable	+	Capital
$15,400	+	$20,000	+	$4,600	=	$10,000	+	$30,000
				$40,000	=	$40,000		

Answers to Section 2 Self Review

1. The increase side of *Cash* is the left, or debit, side. The increase side of *Accounts Payable* is the right, or credit, side. The increase side of *Carolyn Wells, Capital* is the right, or credit, side.

2. The trial balance is a list of all the accounts and their balances. Its purpose is to prove the equality of the total debits and credits.

3. A transposition is an error in which the digits of a number are switched, for example, when 517 is recorded as 571. A slide is an error in which the decimal point is misplaced, for example, when 317 is written as 3.17.

4. **b.** *Jason Taylor, Drawing* would be debited and *Cash* would be credited.

5. **c.** *L. T., Drawing*

6. *S. Tuttle, Drawing*—20,000 should be in the Debit column.

   Fees Income—28,000 should be in the Credit column.

   The new column totals will be 102,000.

Answers to Comprehensive Self Review

1. ■ Check the math by adding the columns again.

   ■ Determine whether the account balances are in the correct columns.

   ■ Check the accounts to see whether the balances in the accounts were computed correctly.

   ■ Check the accuracy of transactions recorded during the period.

2. Decreases in asset accounts are recorded on the credit side. Decreases in liability and owner's equity accounts are recorded on the debit side.

3. The asset, liability, and owner's equity accounts.

4. Cash taken from the business by the owner to obtain funds for personal living expenses. Withdrawals are recorded in a special type of owner's equity account called a drawing account.

5. A list of the numbers and names of the accounts of a business. It provides a system by which the accounts of the business can be easily identified and located.

The General Journal and the General Ledger

LEARNING OBJECTIVES

1. Record transactions in the general journal.
2. Prepare compound journal entries.
3. Post journal entries to general ledger accounts.
4. Correct errors made in the journal or ledger.
5. Define the accounting terms new to this chapter.

NEW TERMS

accounting cycle
audit trail
balance ledger form
chronological order
compound entry
correcting entry

general journal
general ledger
journal
journalizing
ledger
posting

Willamette Valley Vineyards   www.willamettevalleyvineyards.com

The Willamette Valley is the heart of Oregon's agriculture country. The valley is one of Oregon's major wine-growing regions and boasts over 200 wineries that produce a variety of vintages. Willamette Valley Vineyards is regarded as one of Oregon's top wineries. Started in 1983 with a small 50-acre vineyard, the company has carefully nurtured its growth, producing top-quality wines that have been served at the White House and consistently earn high marks from *Wine Spectator* and *Wine Enthusiast*.

The company pays alcohol excise taxes based on product sales to both the Oregon Liquor Control Commission and to the U.S. Department of the Treasury, Alcohol and Tobacco Tax and Trade Bureau. An audit by the Alcohol and Tobacco Tax Trade Board uncovered some reporting issues and though Willamette Valley disputed the findings, it eventually acknowledged that an expense of $80,000 claimed in 2003 should have recognized liability across three years rather than recognizing it all in 2003. The company had to restate its financial statements for the years ended 2003, 2002, and 2001 to reflect the correct excise tax for each of the periods and to record the estimated interest and penalties with respect to the related estimated excise tax liability.

thinking critically

Careful recordkeeping is critical to all business, large and small. How did Willamette Valley Vineyard's recordkeeping affect the outcome of the dispute described above?

SECTION OBJECTIVES

>> 1. **Record transactions in the general journal.**

   WHY IT'S IMPORTANT
   Written records for all business transactions are necessary. The general journal acts as the "diary" of the business.

>> 2. **Prepare compound journal entries.**

   WHY IT'S IMPORTANT
   Compound entries contain several debits or credits for a single business transaction, creating efficiencies in journalizing.

TERMS TO LEARN

accounting cycle
audit trail
chronological order
compound entry
general journal
journal
journalizing

The General Journal

The **accounting cycle** is a series of steps performed during each accounting period to classify, record, and summarize data for a business and to produce needed financial information. The first step in the accounting cycle is to analyze business transactions. You learned this skill in Chapter 3. The second step in the accounting cycle is to prepare a record of business transactions.

Journals

Business transactions are recorded in a **journal,** which is a diary of business activities. The journal lists transactions in **chronological order,** that is, in the order in which they occur. The journal is sometimes called the *record of original entry* because it is where transactions are first entered in the accounting records. There are different types of journals. This chapter will examine the general journal. You will become familiar with other journals in later chapters.

> Most corporations use accounting software to record business transactions. Industry-specific software is available for accounting firms, oil and gas companies, construction firms, medical firms, and any other industry-specific business enterprise.

The General Journal

>>1. OBJECTIVE

Record transactions in the general journal.

important!

The Diary of a Business

The general journal is similar to a diary. The general journal details, in chronological order, the economic events of the business.

The **general journal** is a financial record for entering all types of business transactions. **Journalizing** is the process of recording transactions in the general journal.

Figure 4.1 shows the general journal for Wells' Consulting Services. Notice that the general journal has a page number. To record a transaction, enter the year at the top of the Date column. In the Date column, write the month and day on the first line of the first entry. After the first entry, enter the year and month only when a new page is started or when the year or the month changes. In the Date column, write the day of each transaction on the first line of each transaction.

In the Description column, enter the account to be debited. Write the account name close to the left margin of the Description column, and enter the amount on the same line in the Debit column.

Enter the account to be credited on the line beneath the debit. Indent the account name about one-half inch from the left margin. Enter the amount on the same line in the Credit column.

Then enter a complete but concise description of the transaction in the Description column. Begin the description on the line following the credit. The description is indented about one inch from the left margin.

Write account names exactly as they appear in the chart of accounts. This will minimize errors when amounts are transferred from the general journal to the accounts.

FIGURE 4.1

General Journal Entry

GENERAL JOURNAL				PAGE _1_	
DATE	DESCRIPTION	POST. REF.	DEBIT	CREDIT	
1 2013					**1**
2 Nov. 6	Cash		100 00 0 00		**2**
3	Carolyn Wells, Capital			100 00 0 00	**3**
4	Investment by owner				**4**
5					**5**

— Record the year first, then the month and day.
— Record the debit first.
— Indent about one-half inch and record the credit.
— Indent again and write the description.

Leave a blank line between general journal entries. Some accountants use this blank line to number each general journal entry.

When possible, the journal entry description should refer to the source of the information. For example, the journal entry to record a payment should include the check number in the description. Document numbers are part of the audit trail. The **audit trail** is a chain of references that makes it possible to trace information, locate errors, and prevent fraud. The audit trail provides a means of checking the journal entry against the original data on the documents.

RECORDING NOVEMBER TRANSACTIONS IN THE GENERAL JOURNAL

In Chapters 2 and 3, you learned a step-by-step method for analyzing business transactions. In this chapter, you will learn how to complete the journal entry for a business transaction in the same manner. Review the following steps before you continue.

1. Analyze the financial event:
   - Identify the accounts affected.
   - Classify the accounts affected.
   - Determine the amount of increase or decrease for each account affected.
2. Apply the rules of debit and credit:
   a. Which account is debited? For what amount?
   b. Which account is credited? For what amount?
3. Make the entry in T-account form.
4. Record the complete entry in general journal form.

BUSINESS TRANSACTION

On November 6, Carolyn Wells withdrew $100,000 from personal savings and deposited it in a new business checking account for Wells' Consulting Services.

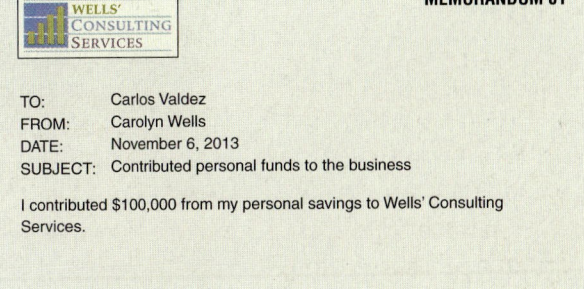

MEMORANDUM 01

WELLS' CONSULTING SERVICES

TO: Carlos Valdez
FROM: Carolyn Wells
DATE: November 6, 2013
SUBJECT: Contributed personal funds to the business

I contributed $100,000 from my personal savings to Wells' Consulting Services.

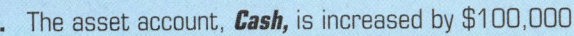

ANALYSIS
a. The asset account, **Cash,** is increased by $100,000.
a. The owner's equity account, **Carolyn Wells, Capital,** is increased by $100,000.

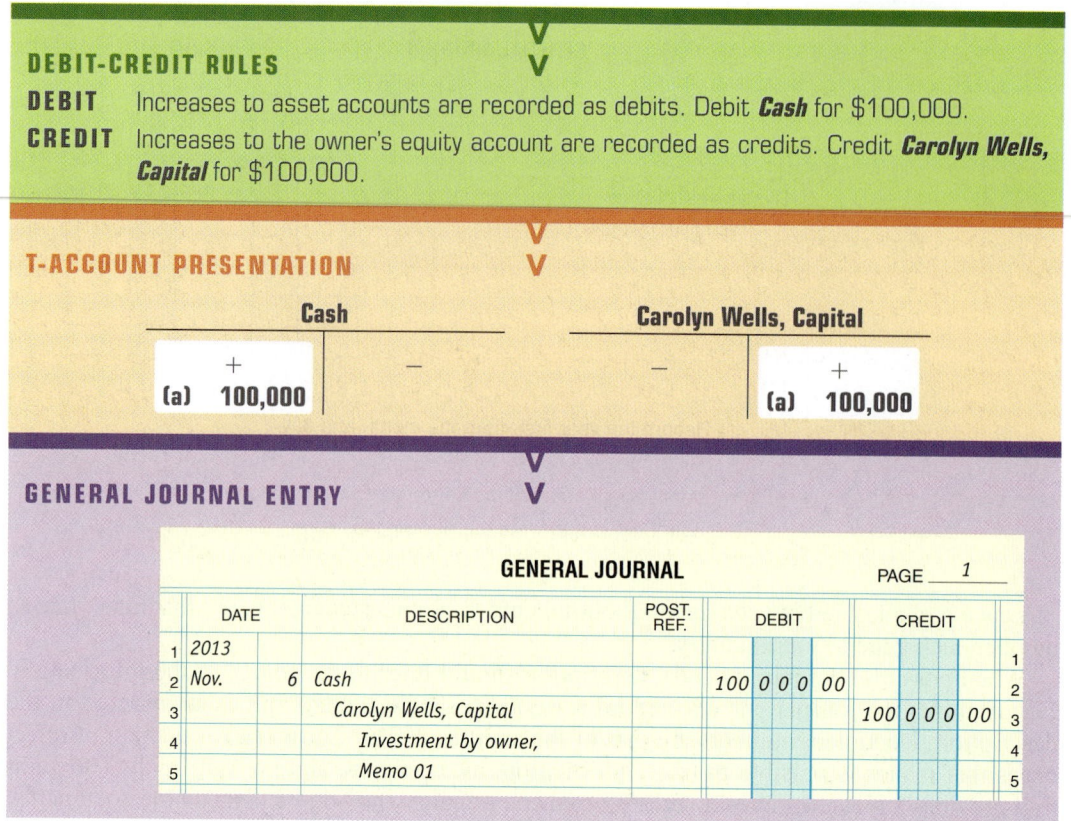

DEBIT-CREDIT RULES

DEBIT   Increases to asset accounts are recorded as debits. Debit *Cash* for $100,000.

CREDIT   Increases to the owner's equity account are recorded as credits. Credit *Carolyn Wells, Capital* for $100,000.

T-ACCOUNT PRESENTATION

Cash				Carolyn Wells, Capital	
+	–			–	+
(a) 100,000					(a) 100,000

GENERAL JOURNAL ENTRY

GENERAL JOURNAL   PAGE _____1_____

	DATE		DESCRIPTION	POST. REF.	DEBIT	CREDIT	
1	2013						1
2	Nov.	6	Cash		100 0 0 0 00		2
3			Carolyn Wells, Capital			100 0 0 0 00	3
4			Investment by owner,				4
5			Memo 01				5

BUSINESS TRANSACTION

On November 7, Wells' Consulting Services issued Check 1001 for $5,000 to purchase a computer and other equipment.

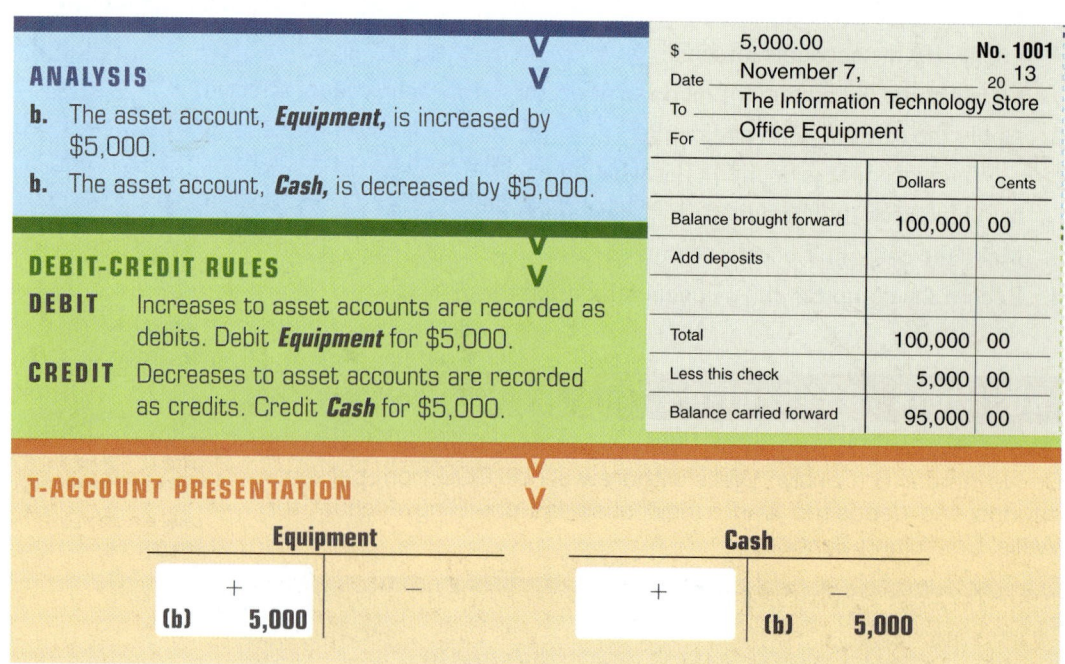

ANALYSIS

b. The asset account, *Equipment,* is increased by $5,000.

b. The asset account, *Cash,* is decreased by $5,000.

DEBIT-CREDIT RULES

DEBIT   Increases to asset accounts are recorded as debits. Debit *Equipment* for $5,000.

CREDIT   Decreases to asset accounts are recorded as credits. Credit *Cash* for $5,000.

$ 5,000.00		No. 1001
Date November 7,		20 13
To The Information Technology Store		
For Office Equipment		
	Dollars	Cents
Balance brought forward	100,000	00
Add deposits		
Total	100,000	00
Less this check	5,000	00
Balance carried forward	95,000	00

T-ACCOUNT PRESENTATION

Equipment			Cash	
+	–		+	–
(b) 5,000				(b) 5,000

GENERAL JOURNAL ENTRY

	DATE		DESCRIPTION	POST. REF.	DEBIT	CREDIT	
			GENERAL JOURNAL			PAGE ___1___	
6	Nov.	7	Equipment		5 0 0 0 00		6
7			Cash			5 0 0 0 00	7
8			Purchased equip., Check 1001				8

The check number appears in the description and forms part of the audit trail for the transaction.

BUSINESS TRANSACTION

On November 10, Wells' Consulting Services purchased office equipment on account for $6,000.

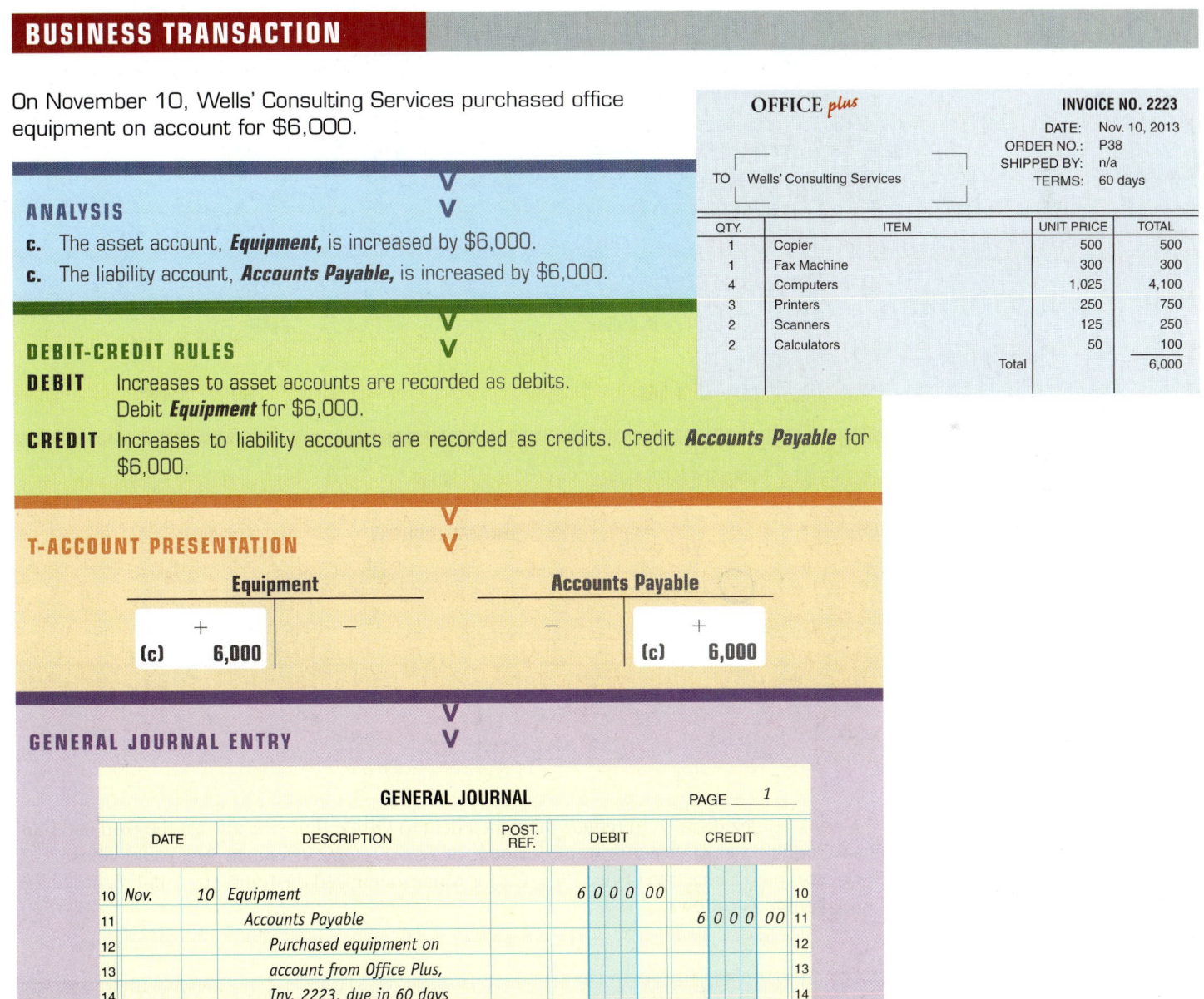

OFFICE *plus*

INVOICE NO. 2223

DATE: Nov. 10, 2013
ORDER NO.: P38
SHIPPED BY: n/a
TERMS: 60 days

TO   Wells' Consulting Services

QTY.	ITEM	UNIT PRICE	TOTAL
1	Copier	500	500
1	Fax Machine	300	300
4	Computers	1,025	4,100
3	Printers	250	750
2	Scanners	125	250
2	Calculators	50	100
	Total		6,000

ANALYSIS

c. The asset account, **Equipment**, is increased by $6,000.
c. The liability account, **Accounts Payable**, is increased by $6,000.

DEBIT-CREDIT RULES

DEBIT Increases to asset accounts are recorded as debits. Debit **Equipment** for $6,000.

CREDIT Increases to liability accounts are recorded as credits. Credit **Accounts Payable** for $6,000.

T-ACCOUNT PRESENTATION

Equipment			Accounts Payable	
+	−		−	+
(c) 6,000				(c) 6,000

GENERAL JOURNAL ENTRY

	DATE		DESCRIPTION	POST. REF.	DEBIT	CREDIT	
			GENERAL JOURNAL			PAGE ___1___	
10	Nov.	10	Equipment		6 0 0 0 00		10
11			Accounts Payable			6 0 0 0 00	11
12			Purchased equipment on				12
13			account from Office Plus,				13
14			Inv. 2223, due in 60 days				14

The supplier's name (Office Plus) and invoice number (2223) appear in the journal entry description and form part of the audit trail for the transaction. The journal entry can be checked against the data on the original document, Invoice 2223.

BUSINESS TRANSACTION

On November 28, Wells' Consulting Services purchased supplies for $1,500, Check 1002.

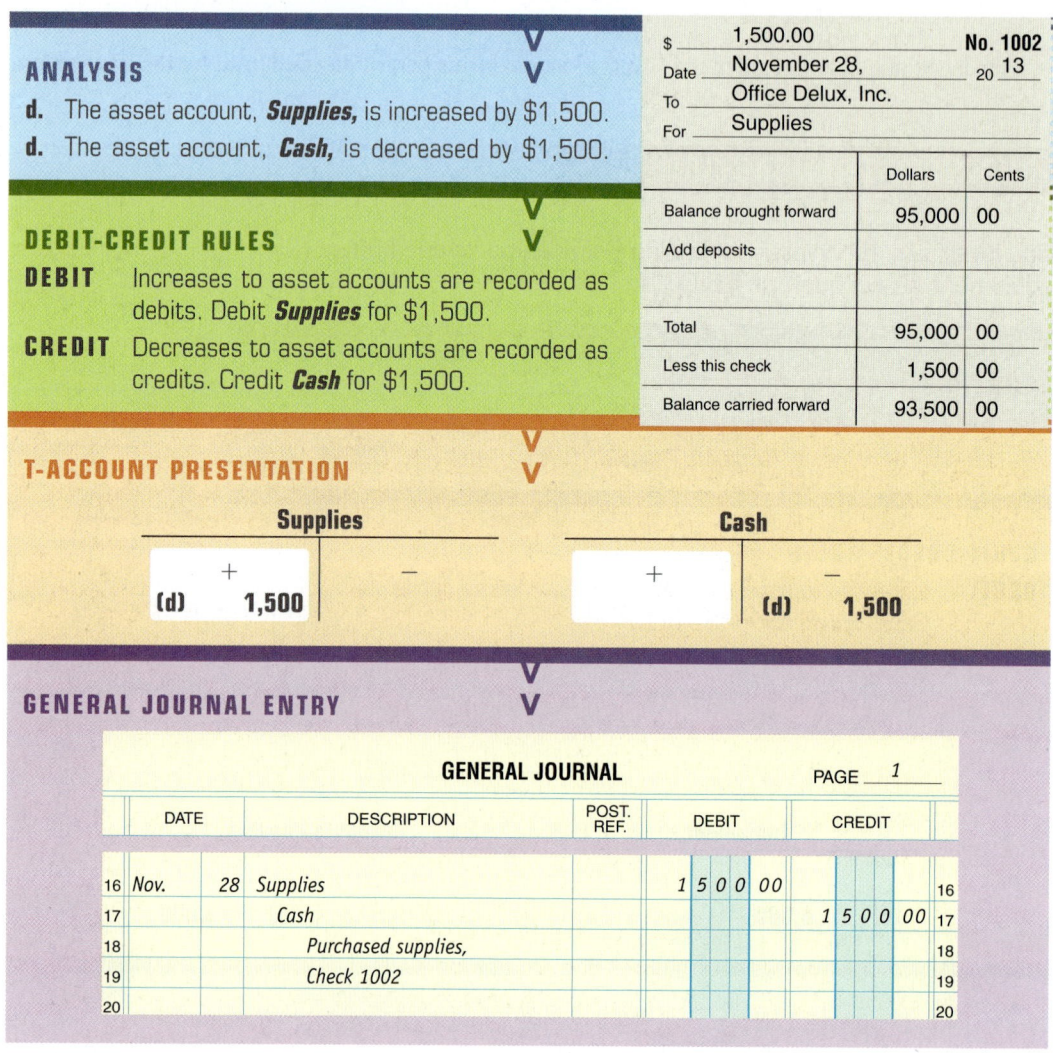

ANALYSIS

d. The asset account, **Supplies,** is increased by $1,500.

d. The asset account, **Cash,** is decreased by $1,500.

DEBIT-CREDIT RULES

DEBIT   Increases to asset accounts are recorded as debits. Debit **Supplies** for $1,500.

CREDIT Decreases to asset accounts are recorded as credits. Credit **Cash** for $1,500.

$ 1,500.00		No. 1002
Date November 28,		20 13
To Office Delux, Inc.		
For Supplies		

	Dollars	Cents
Balance brought forward	95,000	00
Add deposits		
Total	95,000	00
Less this check	1,500	00
Balance carried forward	93,500	00

T-ACCOUNT PRESENTATION

Supplies		Cash	
+	–	+	–
(d) 1,500			(d) 1,500

GENERAL JOURNAL ENTRY

GENERAL JOURNAL   PAGE 1

	DATE		DESCRIPTION	POST. REF.	DEBIT	CREDIT	
16	Nov.	28	Supplies		1 5 0 0 00		16
17			Cash			1 5 0 0 00	17
18			Purchased supplies,				18
19			Check 1002				19
20							20

Carlos Valdez decided to reduce the firm's debt to Office Plus. Recall that the firm had purchased equipment on account in the amount of $6,000. On November 30, Wells' Consulting Services issued a check to Office Plus. Carlos Valdez analyzed the transaction and recorded the journal entry as follows.

BUSINESS TRANSACTION

On November 30, Wells' Consulting Services paid Office Plus $2,500 in partial payment of Invoice 2223, Check 1003.

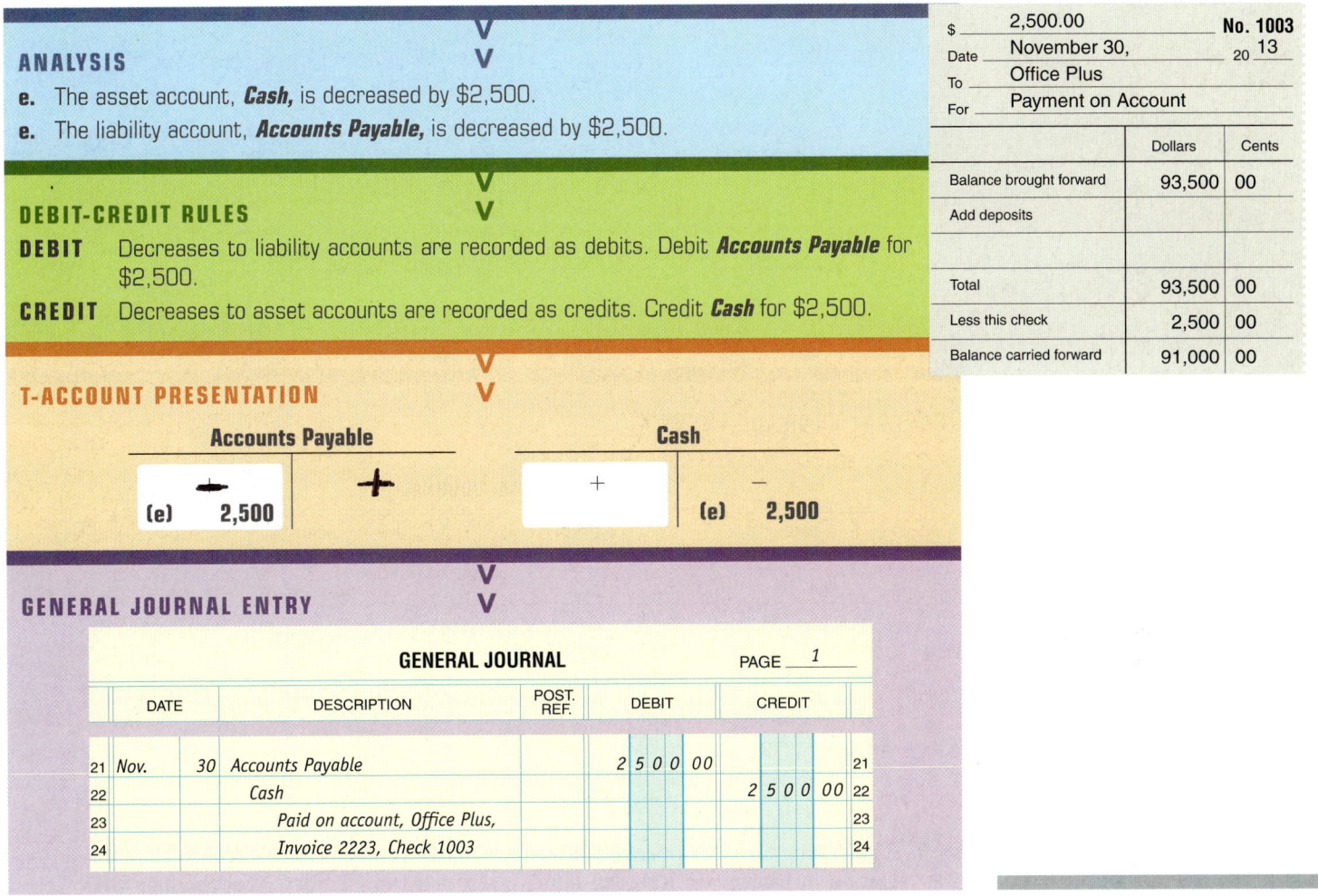

Notice that the general journal Description column includes three important items for the audit trail:

- the supplier name,
- the invoice number,
- the check number.

In the general journal, always enter debits before credits. This is the case even if the credit item is considered first when mentally analyzing the transaction.

Wells' Consulting Services issued a check in November to pay December and January rent in advance. Recall that the right to occupy facilities is considered a form of property. Carlos Valdez analyzed the transaction and recorded the journal entry as follows.

BUSINESS TRANSACTION

On November 30, Wells' Consulting Services wrote Check 1004 for $8,000 to prepay rent for December and January.

ANALYSIS

f. The asset account, **Prepaid Rent,** is increased by $8,000.

f. The asset account, **Cash,** is decreased by $8,000.

$	8,000.00		No. 1004
Date	November 30,		20 13
To	Davidson Properties		
For	Prepaid Rent		

	Dollars	Cents
Balance brought forward	91,000	00
Add deposits		
Total	91,000	00
Less this check	8,000	00
Balance carried forward	83,000	00

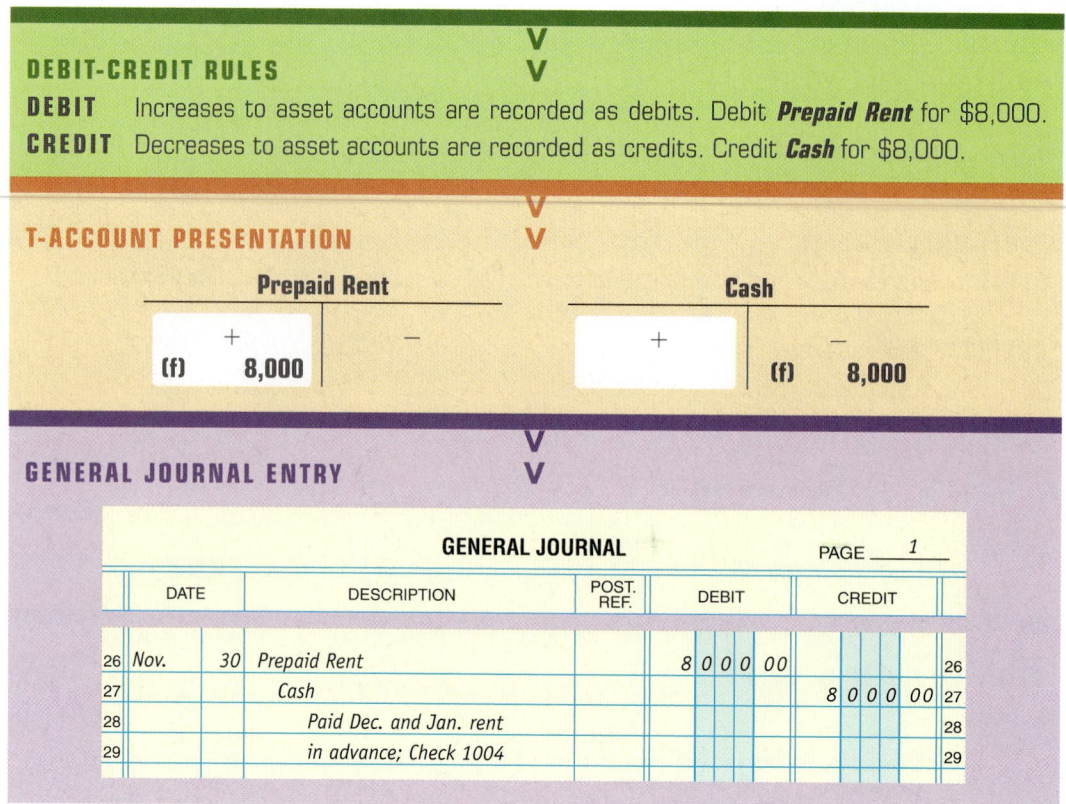

DEBIT-CREDIT RULES

DEBIT   Increases to asset accounts are recorded as debits. Debit *Prepaid Rent* for $8,000.

CREDIT   Decreases to asset accounts are recorded as credits. Credit *Cash* for $8,000.

T-ACCOUNT PRESENTATION

Prepaid Rent		Cash	
+	−	+	−
(f) 8,000			(f) 8,000

GENERAL JOURNAL ENTRY

GENERAL JOURNAL   PAGE ___1___

	DATE		DESCRIPTION	POST. REF.	DEBIT	CREDIT	
26	Nov.	30	Prepaid Rent		8 0 0 0 00		26
27			Cash			8 0 0 0 00	27
28			Paid Dec. and Jan. rent				28
29			in advance; Check 1004				29

RECORDING DECEMBER TRANSACTIONS IN THE GENERAL JOURNAL

Wells' Consulting Services opened for business on December 1. Let's review the transactions that occurred in December. Refer to items **g** through **l** in Chapter 3 for the analysis of each transaction.

1. Performed services for $36,000 in cash.
2. Performed services for $11,000 on credit.
3. Received $6,000 in cash from credit clients on their accounts.
4. Paid $8,000 for salaries.
5. Paid $650 for a utility bill.
6. The owner withdrew $5,000 for personal expenses.

Figure 4.2 shows the entries in the general journal. In an actual business, transactions involving fees income and accounts receivable occur throughout the month and are recorded when they take place. For the sake of simplicity, these transactions are summarized and recorded as of December 31 for Wells' Consulting Services.

>> 2.   OBJECTIVE

Prepare compound journal entries.

PREPARING COMPOUND ENTRIES

So far, each journal entry consists of one debit and one credit. Some transactions require a **compound entry**—a journal entry that contains more than one debit or credit. In a compound entry, record all debits first followed by the credits.

> When Allstate purchased an insurance division of CNA Financial Corporation, Allstate paid cash and issued a 10-year note payable (a promise to pay). Detailed accounting records are not available to the public, but a compound journal entry was probably used to record this transaction.

FIGURE 4.2

General Journal Entries
for December

	DATE		DESCRIPTION	POST. REF.	DEBIT	CREDIT	
1	2013						1
2	Dec.	31	Cash		36 000 00		2
3			Fees Income			36 000 00	3
4			Performed services for cash				4
5							5
6		31	Accounts Receivable		11 000 00		6
7			Fees Income			11 000 00	7
8			Performed services on credit				8
9							9
10		31	Cash		6 000 00		10
11			Accounts Receivable			6 000 00	11
12			Received cash from credit				12
13			clients on account				13
14							14
15		31	Salaries Expense		8 000 00		15
16			Cash			8 000 00	16
17			Paid monthly salaries to				17
18			employees, Checks				18
19			1005–1006				19
20							20
21		31	Utilities Expense		6 50 00		21
22			Cash			6 50 00	22
23			Paid monthly bill for utilities,				23
24			Check 1007				24
25							25
26		31	Carolyn Wells, Drawing		5 000 00		26
27			Cash			5 000 00	27
28			Owner withdrew cash for				28
29			personal expenses,				29
30			Check 1008				30
31							31
32							32
33							33
34							34
35							35

GENERAL JOURNAL   PAGE ___2___

Suppose that on November 7, when Wells' Consulting Services purchased the equipment for $5,000, Carolyn Wells paid $2,500 in cash and agreed to pay the balance in 30 days. This transaction is analyzed below and on the next page.

BUSINESS TRANSACTION

On November 7, the firm purchased equipment for $5,000, issued Check 1001 for $2,500, and agreed to pay the balance in 30 days.

ANALYSIS

The asset account, *Equipment*, is increased by $5,000. The asset account, *Cash*, is decreased by $2,500.
The liability account, *Accounts Payable*, is increased by $2,500.

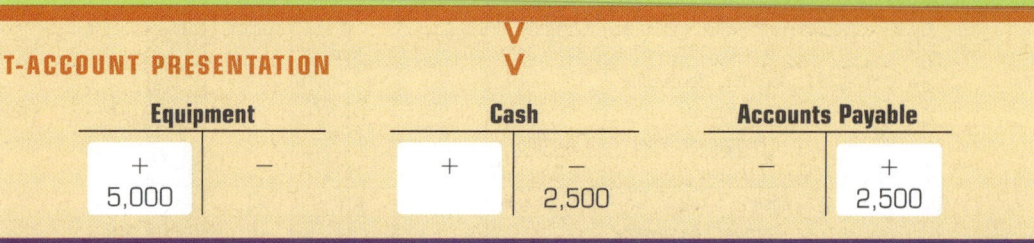

DEBIT-CREDIT RULES

DEBIT Increases to assets are recorded as debits. Debit *Equipment* for $5,000.

CREDIT Decreases to assets are credits. Credit *Cash* for $2,500. Increases to liabilities are credits. Credit *Accounts Payable* for $2,500.

T-ACCOUNT PRESENTATION

Equipment			Cash			Accounts Payable	
+	−		+	−		−	+
5,000				2,500			2,500

GENERAL JOURNAL ENTRY

GENERAL JOURNAL PAGE ___1___

	DATE		DESCRIPTION	POST. REF.	DEBIT	CREDIT	
6	Nov.	7	Equipment		5 0 0 0 00		6
7			Cash			2 5 0 0 00	7
8			Accounts Payable			2 5 0 0 00	8
9			Bought equip. from The				9
10			Information Technology Store,				10
11			Inv. 11, issued Ck. 1001 for				11
12			$2,500, bal. due in 30 days				12

recall

Debits = Credits

No matter how many accounts are affected by a transaction, total debits must equal total credits.

Section 1 Self Review

EXERCISES

1. The part of the journal entry to be recorded first is the:

   a. asset.

   b. credit.

   c. debit.

   d. liability.

2. A general journal is like a(n):

   a. address book.

   b. appointment calendar.

   c. diary.

   d. to-do list.

QUESTIONS

3. Why are check and invoice numbers included in the journal entry description?

Audit trail

4. Why is the journal referred to as the "record of original entry"?

5. In a compound journal entry, if two accounts are debited, must two accounts be credited?

No

ANALYSIS

6. The accountant for Quality Lawncare never includes descriptions when making journal entries. What effect will this have on the accounting system?

(Answers to Section 1 Self Review are on page 120.)

The General Ledger

You learned that a journal contains a chronological (day-by-day) record of a firm's transactions. Each journal entry shows the accounts and the amounts involved. Using the journal as a guide, you can enter transaction data in the accounts.

Ledgers

T accounts are used to analyze transactions quickly but are not used to maintain financial records. Instead, businesses keep account records on a special form that makes it possible to record all data efficiently. There is a separate form for each account. The account forms are kept in a book or binder called a **ledger.** The ledger is called the *record of final entry* because the ledger is the last place that accounting transactions are recorded.

The process of transferring data from the journal to the ledger is known as **posting.** Posting takes place after transactions are journalized. Posting is the third step of the accounting cycle.

THE GENERAL LEDGER

Every business has a general ledger. The **general ledger** is the master reference file for the accounting system. It provides a permanent, classified record of all accounts used in a firm's operations.

LEDGER ACCOUNT FORMS

There are different types of general ledger account forms. Carlos Valdez decided to use a balance ledger form. A **balance ledger form** shows the balance of the account after each entry is posted. Look at Figure 4.3 on page 100. It shows the first general journal entry, the investment by the owner. It also shows the general ledger forms for *Cash* and *Carolyn Wells, Capital.* On the ledger form, notice the:

- account name and number;
- columns for date, description, and posting reference (post. ref.);
- columns for debit, credit, balance debit, and balance credit.

> **important!**
>
> **General Journal and General Ledger**
> The general journal is the record of *original* entry. The general ledger is the record of *final* entry.

FIGURE 4.3

Posting from the General Journal to the General Ledger

GENERAL JOURNAL   PAGE ___1___

	DATE		DESCRIPTION	POST. REF.	DEBIT	CREDIT	
1	2013						1
2	Nov.	6	Cash	101	100 000 00		2
3			Carolyn Wells, Capital	301		100 000 00	3
4			Investment by owner				4
5							5
6							
7							

ACCOUNT __Cash__   ACCOUNT NO. __101__

DATE		DESCRIPTION	POST. REF.	DEBIT	CREDIT	BALANCE DEBIT	BALANCE CREDIT
2013							
Nov.	6		J1	100 000 00		100 000 00	

ACCOUNT __Carolyn Wells, Capital__   ACCOUNT NO. __301__

DATE		DESCRIPTION	POST. REF.	DEBIT	CREDIT	BALANCE DEBIT	BALANCE CREDIT
2013							
Nov.	6		J1		100 000 00		100 000 00

>> 3. OBJECTIVE

Post journal entries to general ledger accounts.

recall

Normal Balance

The normal balance of an account is its increase side.

POSTING TO THE GENERAL LEDGER

Examine Figure 4.4. On November 7, Carlos Valdez made a general journal entry to record the purchase of equipment. To post the data from the journal to the general ledger, Valdez entered the debit amount in the Debit column in the ***Equipment*** account and the credit amount in the Credit column in the ***Cash*** account.

In the general journal, identify the first account listed. In Figure 4.4, ***Equipment*** is the first account. In the general ledger, find the ledger form for the first account listed. In Figure 4.4, this is the ***Equipment*** ledger form.

The steps to post from the general journal to the general ledger follow:

1. On the ledger form, enter the date of the transaction. Enter a description of the entry, if necessary. Usually routine entries do not require descriptions.

2. On the ledger form, enter the general journal page in the Posting Reference column. On the ***Equipment*** ledger form, the **J1** in the Posting Reference column indicates that the journal entry is recorded on page 1 of the general journal. The letter **J** refers to the general journal.

3. On the ledger form, enter the debit amount in the Debit column or the credit amount in the Credit column. In Figure 4.4 on the ***Equipment*** ledger form, $5,000 is entered in the Debit column.

4. On the ledger form, compute the balance and enter it in the Debit Balance column or the Credit Balance column. In Figure 4.4, the balance in the ***Equipment*** account is a $5,000 debit.

5. On the general journal, enter the ledger account number in the Posting Reference column. In Figure 4.4, the account number 141 is entered in the Posting Reference column next to "Equipment."

Repeat the process for the next account in the general journal. In Figure 4.4, Valdez posted the credit amount from the general journal to the ***Cash*** ledger account. Notice on the ***Cash*** ledger form that he entered the credit of $5,000 and then computed the account balance. After the transaction is posted, the balance of the ***Cash*** account is $95,000.

Be sure to enter the numbers in the Posting Reference columns. This indicates that the entry was posted and ensures against posting the same entry twice. Posting references are part of the audit trail. They allow a transaction to be traced from the ledger to the journal entry, and then to the source document.

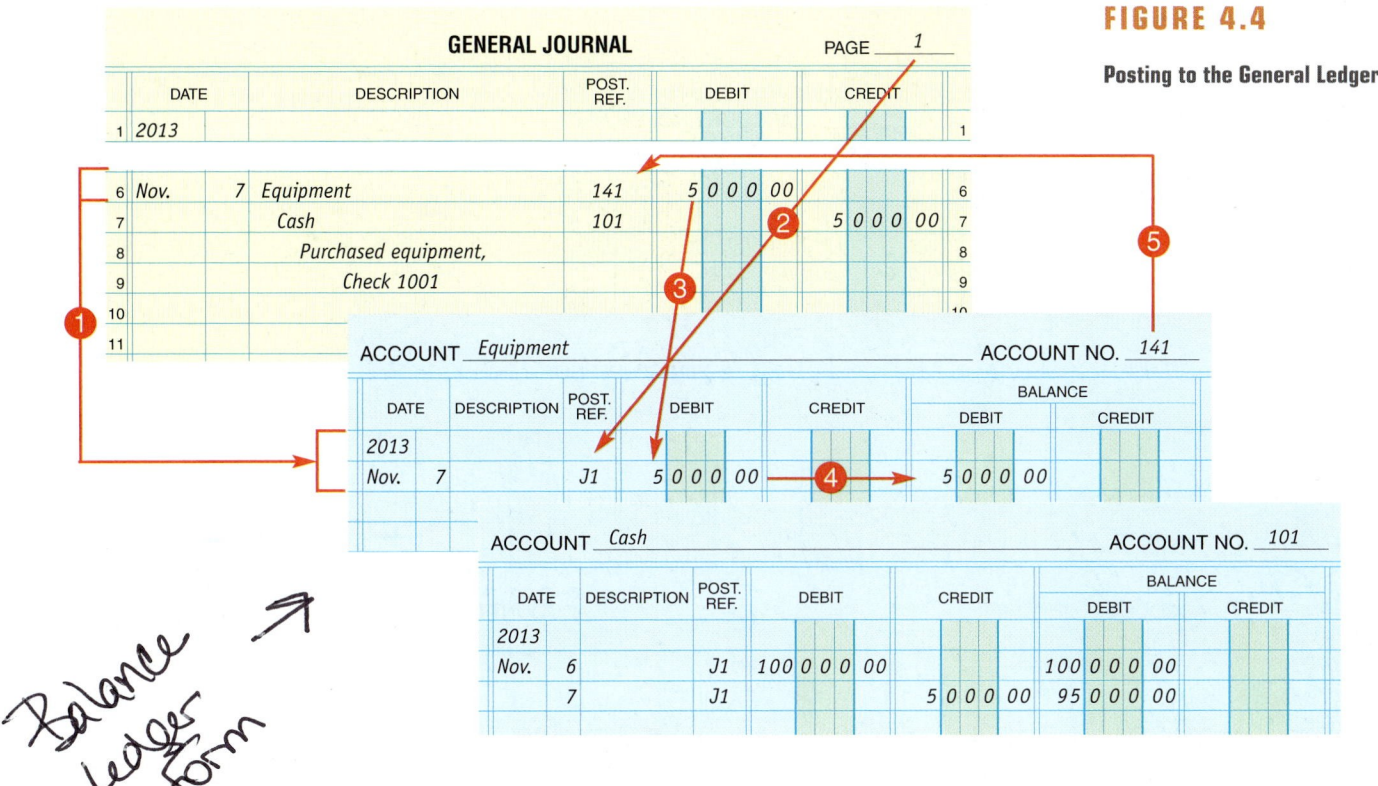

FIGURE 4.4

Posting to the General Ledger

Balance ledger form →

Figure 4.5 shows the general ledger after all the entries for November and December are posted.

Each ledger account provides a complete record of the increases and decreases to that account. The balance ledger form also shows the current balance for the account.

In the general ledger accounts, the balance sheet accounts appear first and are followed by the income statement accounts. The order is:

- assets
- liabilities
- owner's equity
- revenue
- expenses

This arrangement speeds the preparation of the trial balance and the financial statements.

FIGURE 4.5

Posted General Ledger Accounts

ACCOUNT _Cash_   ACCOUNT NO. _101_

DATE		DESCRIPTION	POST. REF.	DEBIT	CREDIT	BALANCE DEBIT	BALANCE CREDIT
2013							
Nov.	6		J1	100 000 00		100 000 00	
	7		J1		5 000 00	95 000 00	
	28		J1		1 500 00	93 500 00	
	30		J1		2 500 00	91 000 00	
	30		J1		8 000 00	83 000 00	
Dec.	31		J2	36 000 00		119 000 00	
	31		J2	6 000 00		125 000 00	
	31		J2		8 000 00	117 000 00	
	31		J2		650 00	116 350 00	
	31		J2		5 000 00	111 350 00	

(continued)

FIGURE 4.5 (continued)

ACCOUNT _Accounts Receivable_ ACCOUNT NO. _111_

DATE		DESCRIPTION	POST. REF.	DEBIT	CREDIT	BALANCE DEBIT	BALANCE CREDIT
2013							
Dec.	31		J2	11 000 00		11 000 00	
	31		J2		6 000 00	5 000 00	

ACCOUNT _Supplies_ ACCOUNT NO. _121_

DATE		DESCRIPTION	POST. REF.	DEBIT	CREDIT	BALANCE DEBIT	BALANCE CREDIT
2013							
Nov.	28		J1	1 500 00		1 500 00	

ACCOUNT _Prepaid Rent_ ACCOUNT NO. _137_

DATE		DESCRIPTION	POST. REF.	DEBIT	CREDIT	BALANCE DEBIT	BALANCE CREDIT
2013							
Nov.	30		J1	8 000 00		8 000 00	

ACCOUNT _Equipment_ ACCOUNT NO. _141_

DATE		DESCRIPTION	POST. REF.	DEBIT	CREDIT	BALANCE DEBIT	BALANCE CREDIT
2013							
Nov.	7		J1	5 000 00		5 000 00	
	10		J1	6 000 00		11 000 00	

ACCOUNT _Accounts Payable_ ACCOUNT NO. _202_

DATE		DESCRIPTION	POST. REF.	DEBIT	CREDIT	BALANCE DEBIT	BALANCE CREDIT
2013							
Nov.	10		J1		6 000 00		6 000 00
	30		J1	2 500 00			3 500 00

ACCOUNT _Carolyn Wells, Capital_ ACCOUNT NO. _301_

DATE		DESCRIPTION	POST. REF.	DEBIT	CREDIT	BALANCE DEBIT	BALANCE CREDIT
2013							
Nov.	6		J1		100 000 00		100 000 00

ACCOUNT _Carolyn Wells, Drawing_ ACCOUNT NO. _302_

DATE		DESCRIPTION	POST. REF.	DEBIT	CREDIT	BALANCE DEBIT	BALANCE CREDIT
2013							
Dec.	31		J2	5 000 00		5 000 00	

(continued)

FIGURE 4.5 (continued)

ACCOUNT _Fees Income_   ACCOUNT NO. _401_

DATE		DESCRIPTION	POST. REF.	DEBIT	CREDIT	BALANCE DEBIT	BALANCE CREDIT
2013							
Dec.	31		J2		36 000 00		36 000 00
	31		J2		11 000 00		47 000 00

ACCOUNT _Salaries Expense_   ACCOUNT NO. _511_

DATE		DESCRIPTION	POST. REF.	DEBIT	CREDIT	BALANCE DEBIT	BALANCE CREDIT
2013							
Dec.	31		J2	8 000 00		8 000 00	

ACCOUNT _Utilities Expense_   ACCOUNT NO. _514_

DATE		DESCRIPTION	POST. REF.	DEBIT	CREDIT	BALANCE DEBIT	BALANCE CREDIT
2013							
Dec.	31		J2	6 50 00		6 50 00	

Correcting Journal and Ledger Errors

Sometimes errors are made when recording transactions in the journal. For example, a journal entry may show the wrong account name or amount. The method used to correct an error depends on whether or not the journal entry has been posted to the ledger:

- If the error is discovered *before* the entry is posted, neatly cross out the incorrect item and write the correct data above it. Do not erase the error. To ensure honesty and provide a clear audit trail, erasures are not made in the journal.

- If the error is discovered *after* posting, a **correcting entry** —a journal entry made to correct the erroneous entry—is journalized and posted. Do not erase or change the journal entry or the postings in the ledger accounts.

Note that erasures are never permitted in the journal or ledger.

>> **4. OBJECTIVE**
Correct errors made in the journal or ledger.

recall

Order of Accounts
The general ledger lists accounts in the same order as they appear on the trial balance: assets, liabilities, owner's equity, revenue, and expenses.

MANAGERIAL IMPLICATIONS

ACCOUNTING SYSTEMS

- Business managers should be sure that their firms have efficient procedures for recording transactions.
- A well-designed accounting system allows timely and accurate posting of data to the ledger accounts.
- The information that appears in the financial statements is taken from the general ledger.
- Since management uses financial information for decision making, it is essential that the financial statements be prepared quickly at the end of each period and that they contain the correct amounts.

- The promptness and accuracy of the statements depend on the efficiency of the recording process.
- A well-designed accounting system has a strong audit trail.
- Every business should be able to trace amounts through the accounting records and back to the documents where the transactions were first recorded.

THINKING CRITICALLY
What are the consequences of not having a good audit trail?

Let's look at an example. On September 1, an automobile repair shop purchased some shop equipment for $18,000 in cash. By mistake, the journal entry debited the **Office Equipment** account rather than the **Shop Equipment** account, as follows.

	DATE		DESCRIPTION	POST. REF.	DEBIT	CREDIT	
1	2013						1
2	Sept.	1	Office Equipment	141	18 0 0 0 00		2
3			Cash	101		18 0 0 0 00	3
4			Purchased equipment,				4
5			Check 1104				5
6							6
7							7

GENERAL JOURNAL   PAGE 16

The error was discovered after the entry was posted to the ledger. To correct the error, a correcting journal entry was prepared and posted. The correcting entry debits **Shop Equipment** and credits **Office Equipment** for $18,000. This entry transfers $18,000 out of the **Office Equipment** account and into the **Shop Equipment** account.

GENERAL JOURNAL   PAGE 28

	DATE		DESCRIPTION	POST. REF.	DEBIT	CREDIT	
1	2013						1
2	Oct.	1	Shop Equipment	151	18 0 0 0 00		2
3			Office Equipment	141		18 0 0 0 00	3
4			To correct error made on				4
5			Sept. 1 when a purchase				5
6			of shop equipment was				6
7			recorded as office				7
8			equipment				8
9							9

Suppose that the error was discovered before the journal entry was posted to the ledger. In that case, the accountant would neatly cross out "Office Equipment" and write "Shop Equipment" above it. The correct account (**Shop Equipment**) would be posted to the ledger in the usual manner.

Section 2 Self Review

QUESTIONS

1. What is entered in the Posting Reference column of the general journal?

2. Why are posting references made in ledger accounts and in the journal?

3. Are the following statements true or false? Why?

   a. "If a journal entry that contains an error has been posted, erase the entry and change the posting in the ledger accounts."

   b. "Once an incorrect journal entry has been posted, the incorrect amounts remain in the general ledger accounts."

EXERCISES

4. The general journal organizes accounting information in:

   a. account order.

   b. alphabetical order.

   c. date order.

5. The general ledger organizes accounting information in:

   a. account order.

   b. alphabetical order.

   c. date order.

ANALYSIS

6. Draw a diagram of the first three steps of the accounting cycle.

(Answers to Section 2 Self Review are on page 120.)

REVIEW   Chapter Summary

In this chapter, you have studied the method for journalizing business transactions in the records of a company. The details of each transaction are then posted to the general ledger. A well-designed accounting system provides for prompt and accurate journalizing and posting of all transactions.

Learning Objectives

1 Record transactions in the general journal.

- Recording transactions in a journal is called journalizing, the second step in the accounting cycle.
  - A journal is a daily record of transactions.
  - A written analysis of each transaction is contained in a journal.
- The general journal is widely used in business. It can accommodate all kinds of business transactions. Use the following steps to record a transaction in the general journal:
  - Number each page in the general journal. The page number will be used as a posting reference.
  - Enter the year at the top of the Date column. After that, enter the year only when a new page is started or when the year changes.
  - Enter the month and day in the Date column of the first line of the first entry. After that, enter the month only when a new page is started or when the month changes. Always enter the day on the first line of a new entry.
  - Enter the name of the account to be debited in the Description column.
  - Enter the amount to be debited in the Debit column.
  - Enter the name of the account to be credited on the next line. Indent the account name about one-half inch.
  - Enter the amount to be credited in the Credit column.
  - Enter a complete but concise description on the next line. Indent the description about one inch.
- Note that the debit portion is always recorded first.
- If possible, include source document numbers in descriptions in order to create an audit trail.

2 Prepare compound journal entries.

A transaction might require a journal entry that contains several debits or credits. All debits are recorded first, followed by the credits.

3 Post journal entries to general ledger accounts.

- Posting to the general ledger is the third step in the accounting cycle. Posting is the transfer of data from journal entries to ledger accounts.
- The individual accounts together form a ledger. All the accounts needed to prepare financial statements are found in the general ledger.
- Use the following steps to post a transaction.
  - On the ledger form:
    1. Enter the date of the transaction. Enter the description, if necessary.
    2. Enter the posting reference in the Posting Reference column. When posting from the general journal, use the letter **J** followed by the general journal page number.
    3. Enter the amount in either the Debit column or the Credit column.
    4. Compute the new balance and enter it in either the Debit Balance column or the Credit Balance column.
  - On the general journal:
    5. Enter the ledger account number in the Posting Reference column.
- To summarize the steps of the accounting cycle discussed so far:
  1. Analyze transactions.
  2. Journalize transactions.
  3. Post transactions.

4 Correct errors made in the journal or ledger.

To ensure honesty and to provide a clear audit trail, erasures are not permitted in a journal. A correcting entry is journalized and posted to correct a previous mistake. Posting references in the journal and the ledger accounts cross reference the entries and form another part of the audit trail. They make it possible to trace or recheck any transaction.

5 Define the accounting terms new to this chapter.

1. Analyzing
2 Journalizing 3. Posting

Glossary

Accounting cycle (p. 90) A series of steps performed during each accounting period to classify, record, and summarize data for a business and to produce needed financial information

Audit trail (p. 91) A chain of references that makes it possible to trace information, locate errors, and prevent fraud

Balance ledger form (p. 99) A ledger account form that shows the balance of the account after each entry is posted

Chronological order (p. 90) Organized in the order in which the events occur

Compound entry (p. 96) A journal entry with more than one debit or credit

Correcting entry (p. 103) A journal entry made to correct an erroneous entry

General journal (p. 90) A financial record for entering all types of business transactions; a record of original entry

General ledger (p. 99) A permanent, classified record of all accounts used in a firm's operation; a record of final entry

Journal (p. 90) The record of original entry

Journalizing (p. 90) Recording transactions in a journal

Ledger (p. 99) The record of final entry

Posting (p. 99) Transferring data from a journal to a ledger

Comprehensive **Self Review**

1. How do you correct a journal entry that has not been posted?
2. What is recorded in the Posting Reference column of a general journal?
3. Why is the ledger called the "record of final entry"?
4. Which of the following shows both the debits and credits of the entire transaction?
    a. An entry in the general journal
    b. A posting to a general ledger account
5. Give examples of items that might appear in an audit trail.

(Answers to Comprehensive Self Review are on pages 120–121.)

Discussion Questions

1. In what order are accounts arranged in the general ledger? Why?
2. What are posting references? Why are they used?
3. What is an audit trail? Why is it desirable to have an audit trail?
4. How should corrections be made in the general journal?
5. What is the accounting cycle?
6. What is the purpose of a journal?
7. What procedure is used to record an entry in the general journal?
8. What is the value of having a description for each general journal entry?
9. What is a compound journal entry?
10. What is a ledger?
11. What is posting?

APPLICATIONS

Exercises

Analyzing transactions.

◄ Exercise 4.1
Objective 1

Selected accounts from the general ledger of the Taylor Shipping Service follow. Analyze the following transactions and indicate by number what accounts should be debited and credited for each transaction.

    101 Cash
    111 Accounts Receivable
    121 Supplies
    131 Equipment
    202 Accounts Payable
    301 Sam Taylor, Capital
    401 Fees Income
    511 Rent Expense
    514 Salaries Expense
    517 Utilities Expense

TRANSACTIONS

1. Gave a cash refund of $1,500 to a customer because of a lost package. (The customer had previously paid in cash.)   101 C   401 D
2. Sent a check for $2,100 to the utility company to pay the monthly bill.   101 C   517
3. Provided services for $15,600 on credit.
4. Purchased new equipment for $9,200 and paid for it immediately by check.
5. Issued a check for $7,000 to pay a creditor on account.
6. Performed services for $10,500 in cash.
7. Collected $12,500 from credit customers.
8. The owner made an additional investment of $50,000 in cash.
9. Purchased supplies for $6,500 on credit.
10. Issued a check for $7,500 to pay the monthly rent.

Recording transactions in the general journal.

◄ Exercise 4.2
Objective 1

Selected accounts from the general ledger of Vinzant Consulting Services follow. Record the general journal entries that would be made to record the following transactions. Be sure to include dates and descriptions in these entries.

    101 Cash
    111 Accounts Receivable
    121 Supplies
    131 Equipment
    141 Automobile
    202 Accounts Payable
    301 Mary Vinzant, Capital
    302 Mary Vinzant, Drawing
    401 Fees Income
    511 Rent Expense
    514 Salaries Expense
    517 Telephone Expense

DATE	TRANSACTIONS
2013	
Sept. 1	Mary Vinzant invested $50,000 in cash to start the firm.
4	Purchased office equipment for $5,500 on credit from Zen, Inc.; received Invoice 9823, payable in 30 days.
16	Purchased an automobile that will be used to visit clients; issued Check 1001 for $13,500 in full payment.
20	Purchased supplies for $420; paid immediately with Check 1002.
23	Returned damaged supplies for a cash refund of $120.
30	Issued Check 1003 for $3,200 to Zen, Inc., as payment on account for Invoice 9823.
30	Withdrew $2,000 in cash for personal expenses.
30	Issued Check 1004 for $1,200 to pay the rent for October.
30	Performed services for $2,250 in cash.
30	Paid $385 for monthly telephone bill, Check 1005.

Exercise 4.3

Objectives 1, 3

▶ **Posting to the general ledger.**

Post the journal entries that you prepared for Exercise 4.2 to the general ledger. Use the account names shown in Exercise 4.2.

Exercise 4.4

Objective 2

▶ **Compound journal entries.**

The following transactions took place at the Thomas Employment Agency during November 2013. Record the general journal entries that would be made for these transactions. Use a compound entry for each transaction.

DATE	TRANSACTIONS
Nov. 5	Performed services for Talent Search, Inc., for $30,000; received $14,000 in cash and the client promised to pay the balance in 60 days.
18	Purchased a graphing calculator for $375 and some supplies for $525 from Office Supply; issued Check 1008 for the total.
23	Received Invoice 1602 for $1,600 from Automotive Technicians Repair for repairs to the firm's automobile; issued Check 1009 for half the amount and arranged to pay the other half in 30 days.

Exercise 4.5

Objective 4

▶ **Recording a correcting entry.**

On July 9, 2013, an employee of Capital Corporation mistakenly debited *Utilities Expense* rather than *Telephone Expense* when recording a bill of $950 for the May telephone service. The error was discovered on July 30. Prepare a general journal entry to correct the error.

Exercise 4.6

Objective 4

▶ **Recording a correcting entry.**

On September 16, 2013, an employee of Carmel Company mistakenly debited the *Truck* account rather than the *Repair Expense* account when recording a bill of $750 for repairs. The error was discovered on October 1. Prepare a general journal entry to correct the error.

PROBLEMS

Problem Set A

Recording transactions in the general journal.

The transactions that follow took place at the Lancastor Sports Arena during September 2013. This firm has indoor courts where customers can play tennis for a fee. It also rents equipment and offers tennis lessons.

◄ **Problem 4.1A**
Objective 1

eXcel

INSTRUCTIONS

Record each transaction in the general journal, using the following chart of accounts. Be sure to number the journal page 1 and to write the year at the top of the Date column. Include a description for each entry.

ASSETS
101 Cash
111 Accounts Receivable
121 Supplies
141 Equipment

LIABILITIES
202 Accounts Payable

OWNER'S EQUITY
301 Patrice Rebello, Capital
302 Patrice Rebello, Drawing

REVENUE
401 Fees Income

EXPENSES
511 Equipment Repair Expense
512 Rent Expense
513 Salaries Expense
514 Telephone Expense
517 Utilities Expense

DATE	TRANSACTIONS
Sept. 1	Issued Check 1169 for $1,400 to pay the September rent.
5	Performed services for $2,500 in cash.
6	Performed services for $1,350 on credit.
10	Paid $600 for monthly telephone bill; issued Check 1170.
11	Paid for equipment repairs of $840 with Check 1171.
12	Received $3,200 on account from credit clients.
15	Issued Checks 1172–1177 for $4,200 for salaries.
18	Issued Check 1178 for $2,000 to purchase supplies.
19	Purchased new tennis rackets for $2,250 on credit from The Tennis Supply Shop; received Invoice 3108, payable in 30 days.
20	Issued Check 1179 for $2,760 to purchase new nets. (Equip.)
21	Received $950 on account from credit clients.
21	Returned a damaged net and received a cash refund of $450.
22	Performed services for $3,260 in cash.
23	Performed services for $4,850 on credit.
26	Issued Check 1180 for $460 to purchase supplies.
28	Paid the monthly electric bill of $2,250 with Check 1181.
30	Issued Checks 1182–1187 for $4,200 for salaries.
30	Issued Check 1188 for $4,200 cash to Patrice Rebello for personal expenses.

Analyze: If the company paid a bill for supplies on October 1, what check number would be included in the journal entry description?

Problem 4.2A ▶

Objectives 1, 2, 3

Journalizing and posting transactions.

On October 1, 2013, Wilson Adams opened an advertising agency. He plans to use the chart of accounts listed below.

INSTRUCTIONS

1. Journalize the transactions. Number the journal page 1, write the year at the top of the Date column, and include a description for each entry.

2. Post to the ledger accounts. Before you start the posting process, open accounts by entering account names and numbers in the headings. Follow the order of the accounts in the chart of accounts.

ASSETS
101 Cash
111 Accounts Receivable
121 Supplies
141 Office Equipment
151 Art Equipment

LIABILITIES
202 Accounts Payable

OWNER'S EQUITY
301 Wilson Adams, Capital
302 Wilson Adams, Drawing

REVENUE
401 Fees Income

EXPENSES
511 Office Cleaning Expense
514 Rent Expense
517 Salaries Expense
520 Telephone Expense
523 Utilities Expense

DATE		TRANSACTIONS
Oct.	1	Wilson Adams invested $50,000 cash in the business.
	2	Paid October office rent of $2,500; issued Check 1001.
	5	Purchased desks and other office furniture for $14,000 from Office Furniture Mart, Inc.; received Invoice 6704 payable in 60 days.
	6	Issued Check 1002 for $2,700 to purchase art equipment.
	7	Purchased supplies for $1,050; paid with Check 1003.
	10	Issued Check 1004 for $500 for office cleaning service.
	12	Performed services for $3,600 in cash and $1,400 on credit. (Use a compound entry.)
	15	Returned damaged supplies for a cash refund of $300.
	18	Purchased a computer for $2,500 from Office Furniture Mart, Inc., Invoice 7108; issued Check 1005 for a $1,500 down payment, with the balance payable in 30 days. (Use one compound entry.)
	20	Issued Check 1006 for $7,000 to Office Furniture Mart, Inc., as payment on account for Invoice 6704.
	26	Performed services for $3,900 on credit.
	27	Paid $275 for monthly telephone bill; issued Check 1007.
	30	Received $3,200 in cash from credit customers.
	30	Mailed Check 1008 to pay the monthly utility bill of $350.
	30	Issued Checks 1009–1011 for $7,500 for salaries.

Analyze: What is the balance of account 202 in the general ledger?

Recording correcting entries.

◀ **Problem 4.3A**
Objective 4

The following journal entries were prepared by an employee of Jupiter Company who does not have an adequate knowledge of accounting.

INSTRUCTIONS

Examine the journal entries carefully to locate the errors. Provide a brief written description of each error. Assume that *Office Equipment* and *Office Supplies* were recorded at the correct values.

	DATE		DESCRIPTION	POST. REF.	DEBIT	CREDIT	
1	2013						1
2	April	1	Accounts Payable		12 4 0 0 00		2
3			Fees Income			12 4 0 0 00	3
4			Performed services on credit				4
5							5
6		2	Cash		5 0 0 00		6
7			Telephone Expense			5 0 0 00	7
8			Paid for March telephone				8
9			service, Check 1917				9
10							10
11		3	Office Equipment		7 2 0 0 00		11
12			Office Supplies		8 0 0 00		12
13			Cash			8 4 0 0 00	13
14			Purchased file cabinet and				14
15			office supplies, Check 1918				15
16							16
17							17
18							18
19							19
20							20

GENERAL JOURNAL   PAGE ___3___

Analyze: After the correcting journal entries have been posted, what effect do the corrections have on the company's reported assets?

Problem 4.4A ▶

Objectives 1, 2, 3

Journalizing and posting transactions

Four transactions for Farm Supply & Repair that took place in November 2013 appear below, along with the general ledger accounts used by the company.

INSTRUCTIONS

Record the transactions in the general journal and post them to the appropriate ledger accounts. Be sure to number the journal page 1 and to write the year at the top of the Date column.

Cash	101	Equipment	151
Accounts Receivable	111	Accounts Payable	202
Office Supplies	121	Erwin Tobias, Capital	301
Tools	131	Fees Income	401
Machinery	141		

DATE	TRANSACTIONS
Nov. 1	Erwin Tobias invested $45,000 in cash plus tools with a fair market value of $1,000 to start the business.
2	Purchased equipment for $1,950 and supplies for $450 from Office Depot, Invoice 501; issued Check 100 for $600 as a down payment with the balance due in 30 days.
10	Performed services for James Wilson for $1,900, who paid $500 in cash with the balance due in 30 days.
20	Purchased machinery for $3,000 from Cottle Machinery, Inc., Invoice 709; issued Check 101 for $1,000 in cash as a down payment with the balance due in 30 days.

Analyze: What liabilities does the business owe as of November 30?

Problem Set B

Recording transactions in the general journal.

The transactions listed below took place at Cox Building Cleaning Service during September 2013. This firm cleans commercial buildings for a fee.

INSTRUCTIONS

Analyze and record each transaction in the general journal. Choose the account names from the chart of accounts shown below. Be sure to number the journal page 1 and to write the year at the top of the Date column.

ASSETS
101 Cash
111 Accounts Receivable
141 Equipment

LIABILITIES
202 Accounts Payable

OWNER'S EQUITY
301 Cathy Cox, Capital
302 Cathy Cox, Drawing

REVENUE
401 Fees Income

EXPENSES
501 Cleaning Supplies Expense
502 Equipment Repair Expense
503 Office Supplies Expense
511 Rent Expense
514 Salaries Expense
521 Telephone Expense
524 Utilities Expense

DATE	TRANSACTIONS
Sept. 1	Cathy Cox invested $25,000 in cash to start the business.
5	Performed services for $2,800 in cash.
6	Issued Check 1000 for $1,800 to pay the September rent.
7	Performed services for $3,600 on credit.
9	Paid $400 for monthly telephone bill; issued Check 1001.
10	Issued Check 1002 for $250 for equipment repairs.
12	Received $490 from credit clients.
14	Issued Checks 1003–1004 for $9,500 to pay salaries.
18	Issued Check 1005 for $700 for cleaning supplies.
19	Issued Check 1006 for $600 for office supplies.
20	Purchased equipment for $5,000 from Reese Equipment, Inc., Invoice 1012; issued Check 1007 for $2,000 with the balance due in 30 days.
22	Performed services for $2,950 in cash.
24	Issued Check 1008 for $450 for the monthly electric bill.
26	Performed services for $3,600 on account.
30	Issued Checks 1009–1010 for $9,500 to pay salaries.
30	Issued Check 1011 for $3,000 to Cathy Cox to pay for personal expenses.

Analyze: How many transactions affected expense accounts?

Problem 4.2B

Objectives 1, 2, 3

▶ **Journalizing and posting transactions.**

In June 2013, Wallace King opened a photography studio that provides services to public and private schools. His firm's financial activities for the first month of operations and the chart of accounts appear below.

INSTRUCTIONS

1. Journalize the transactions. Number the journal page 1 and write the year at the top of the Date column. Describe each entry.

2. Post to the ledger accounts. Before you start the posting process, open the accounts by entering the names and numbers in the headings. Follow the order of the accounts in the chart of accounts.

ASSETS
101 Cash
111 Accounts Receivable
121 Supplies
141 Office Equipment
151 Photographic Equipment

LIABILITIES
202 Accounts Payable

OWNER'S EQUITY
301 Wallace King, Capital
302 Wallace King, Drawing

REVENUE
401 Fees Income

EXPENSES
511 Office Cleaning Expense
514 Rent Expense
517 Salaries Expense
520 Telephone Expense
523 Utilities Expense

DATE		TRANSACTIONS
June	1	Wallace King invested $16,000 cash in the business.
	2	Issued Check 1001 for $900 to pay the June rent.
	5	Purchased desks and other office furniture for $3,750 from Brown, Inc., received Invoice 5312, payable in 60 days.
	6	Issued Check 1002 for $950 to purchase photographic equipment.
	7	Purchased supplies for $238; paid with Check 1003.
	10	Issued Check 1004 for $200 for office cleaning service.
	12	Performed services for $650 in cash and $650 on credit. (Use one compound entry.)
	15	Returned damaged supplies; received a $75 cash refund.
	18	Purchased a computer for $1,025 from Craft Office Supply, Invoice 304; issued Check 1005 for a $500 down payment. The balance is payable in 30 days. (Use one compound entry.)
	20	Issued Check 1006 for $2,100 to Brown, Inc., as payment on account for office furniture, Invoice 5312.
	26	Performed services for $1,000 on credit.
	27	Paid $290 for monthly telephone bill; issued Check 1007.
	30	Received $1,050 in cash from credit clients on account.
	30	Issued Check 1008 to pay the monthly utility bill of $275.
	30	Issued Checks 1009–1011 for $2,800 for salaries.

Analyze: What was the *Cash* account balance after the transaction of June 27 was recorded?

Recording correcting entries.

◄   **Problem 4.3B**
Objective 4

All the journal entries shown below contain errors. The entries were prepared by an employee of Texas Corporation who does not have an adequate knowledge of accounting.

INSTRUCTIONS

Examine the journal entries carefully to locate the errors. Provide a brief written description of each error. Assume that *Office Equipment* and *Office Supplies* were recorded at the correct values.

	GENERAL JOURNAL				PAGE ___1___		
DATE		DESCRIPTION	POST. REF.	DEBIT		CREDIT	
2013							1
Jan.	1	Accounts Payable		4 5 0 00			2
		Fees Income				4 5 0 00	3
		Performed services on credit					4
							5
	2	Cash		6 2 50			6
		Telephone Expense				6 2 50	7
		Paid for January telephone					8
		service, Check 1601					9
							10
	3	Office Equipment		3 7 5 00			11
		Office Supplies		9 5 00			12
		Cash				4 5 0 00	13
		Purchased file cabinet and					14
		office supplies, Check 1602					15
							16

Analyze: After the correcting journal entries have been posted, what effect do the corrections have on the reported assets of the company?

Problem 4.4B

Objectives 1, 2, 3

▶ **Journalizing and posting transactions.**

Several transactions that occurred during December 2013, the first month of operation for Boley's Accounting Services, follow. The company uses the general ledger accounts listed below.

INSTRUCTIONS

Record the transactions in the general journal (page 1) and post to the appropriate accounts.

Cash	101		Furniture & Fixtures	151
Accounts Receivable	111		Accounts Payable	202
Office Supplies	121		Richard Boley, Capital	301
Computers	131		Fees Income	401
Office Equipment	141			

DATE	TRANSACTIONS
Dec. 3	Richard Boley began business by depositing $15,000 cash into a business checking account.
4	Purchased a computer for $1,200 cash.
5	Purchased furniture and fixtures on account for $4,000.
6	Purchased office equipment for $1,095 cash.
10	Rendered services to client and sent bill for $1,300.
11	Purchased office supplies for $450.
15	Received invoice for furniture purchased on December 5 and paid it.

Analyze: Describe the activity for account 202 during the month.

Critical Thinking Problem 4.1

Financial Statements

Sherrye Cravens is a new staff accountant for Oxford Beauty Supply. She has asked you to review the financial statements prepared for April to find and correct any errors. Review the income statement and balance sheet that follow and identify the errors Cravens made (she did not prepare a statement of owner's equity). Prepare a corrected income statement and balance sheet, as well as a statement of owner's equity, for Oxford Beauty Supply.

Oxford Beauty Supply
Income Statement
April 30, 2013

Revenue		
Fees Income		18 3 0 0 00
Expenses		
Salaries Expense	4 5 0 0 00	
Rent Expense	9 0 0 00	
Repair Expense	1 5 0 00	
Utilities Expense	8 5 0 00	
Drawing	2 0 0 0 00	
Total Expenses		8 8 5 0 00
Net Income		10 7 0 0 00

Oxford Beauty Supply
Balance Sheet
Month Ended April 30, 2013

Assets		Liabilities	
Land	6 0 0 0 00	Accounts Receivable	3 5 0 0 00
Building	20 0 0 0 00		
Cash	7 5 0 0 00	Owner's Equity	
Accounts Payable	2 5 0 0 00	Ken Oxford, Capital, April 1, 2013	24 6 0 0 00
Total Assets	28 1 0 0 00	Total Liabilities and Owner's Equity	28 1 0 0 00

Critical Thinking Problem 4.2

Start-Up Business

On June 1, 2013, Wade Wilson opened the California Talent Agency. He plans to use the chart of accounts given below.

INSTRUCTIONS

1. Journalize the transactions. Be sure to number the journal pages and write the year at the top of the Date column. Include a description for each entry.

2. Post to the ledger accounts. Before you start the posting process, open the accounts by entering the account names and numbers in the headings. Using the list of accounts below, assign appropriate account numbers and place them in the correct order in the ledger.

3. Prepare a trial balance.

4. Prepare the income statement.

5. Prepare a statement of owner's equity.

6. Prepare the balance sheet.

ACCOUNTS

Accounts Payable	Wade Wilson, Drawing
Office Furniture	Recording Equipment
Accounts Receivable	Rent Expense
Advertising Expense	Salaries Expense
Cash	Supplies
Fees Income	Telephone Expense
Wade Wilson, Capital	Utilities Expense

DATE	TRANSACTIONS
June 1	Wade Wilson invested $15,000 cash to start the business.
2	Issued Check 201 for $900 to pay the June rent for the office.
3	Purchased desk and other office furniture for $6,000 from Davis Office Supply, Invoice 5103; issued Check 202 for a $2,000 down payment with the balance due in 30 days.
4	Issued Check 203 for $800 for supplies.
6	Performed services for $3,000 in cash.
7	Issued Check 204 for $1,000 to pay for advertising expense.
8	Purchased recording equipment for $7,500 from Rhythms & Moves, Inc., Invoice 2122; issued Check 205 for a down payment of $2,500 with the balance due in 30 days.
10	Performed services for $2,450 on account.
11	Issued Check 206 for $1,500 to Davis Office Supply as payment on account.
12	Performed services for $4,500 in cash.
15	Issued Check 207 for $2,500 to pay an employee's salary.
18	Received payments of $2,000 from credit clients on account.
20	Issued Check 208 for $3,000 to Rhythms & Moves, Inc. as payment on account.
25	Issued Check 209 in the amount of $175 for the monthly telephone bill.
27	Issued Check 210 in the amount of $400 for the monthly electric bill.
28	Issued Check 211 to Wade Wilson for $2,000 for personal living expenses.
30	Issued Check 212 for $2,500 to pay salary of an employee.

Analyze: How many postings were made to the **Cash** account?

BUSINESS CONNECTIONS

Business Records

1. The owner of a new business recently questioned the accountant about the value of having both a journal and a ledger. The owner believes that it is a waste of effort to enter data about transactions in two different records. How would you explain the value of having both records?

2. Why should management insist that a firm's accounting system have a strong audit trail?

3. Why should management be concerned about the efficiency of a firm's procedures for journalizing and posting transactions?

4. How might a poor set of recording procedures affect the flow of information to management?

Correcting Entries

As the full charge bookkeeper, your job is to make any corrections to the general ledger accounts. Each correction needs the reason for the change and the effect on each account, whether it is an increase or decrease.

Louisa has come to you for help. For the third time this month, she has recorded a cash receipt twice. She wants you to record a correcting entry that will reverse her mistakes. The correcting entry she wants you to make will record a credit to the Cash account and a debit to Sales. What should you investigate before making a decision about the correcting entry? What is happening to the cash account? Is this a continual problem for Louisa? Would you accept a dinner offer from Louisa if you fix her mistake?

Balance Sheet

Review the following excerpt taken from the Walmart consolidated balance sheet as of January 31, 2010.

Analyze:

(Amounts in millions) January 31, 2010	
Property, Plant, and Equipment at cost:	
Land	$22,591
Building and improvements	77,452
Fixtures and equipment	35,450
Transportation equipment	2,355

1. When the accountant for Walmart records a purchase of transportation equipment, what type of account is debited? If Walmart purchases transportation equipment on credit, what account might be credited?

2. What type of source document might be reflected in the journal entry to record the purchase of equipment?

3. If the accounting manager reviewed the *Transportation Equipment* account in the general ledger, what types of information might be listed there? What ending balance would be reflected at January 31, 2010?

Analyze Online: Locate the Web site for Walmart (www.walmartstores.com), which provides an online store for consumers as well as corporate information. Within the Web site, locate the consolidated balance sheet for the current year.

4. What kinds of property, plant, and equipment are listed on the balance sheet?

5. What is the balance reported for transportation equipment?

Audit Trail

An audit trail allows an individual to track a transaction from the journal entry to the general ledger through to the financial statements. The audit trail can also find all the transactions that comprise the dollar amount for each account listed on the income statement and balance sheet. Your team has been assigned the duty to diagram the audit trail for your company. In your diagram, show several transactions and how they would be tracked from the journal entry to the financial statement and back to the journal entry.

Accounting Careers

Enter "Accounting Careers" in a search tool like Google. Select a site that will provide the skills and talents required for an accountant. Also find the salaries for accountants in your local area. Note the amount of experience and education needed to receive the salary you want to be earning in the next five years.

Answers to **Self Reviews**

Answers to Section 1 Self Review

1. **c.** debit.
2. **c.** diary.
3. To provide an audit trail to trace information through the accounting system.
4. It is the first accounting record where transactions are entered.
5. No. The only requirement is that the total debits must equal the total credits.
6. The audit trail will be very difficult to follow.

Answers to Section 2 Self Review

1. The ledger account number.
2. They indicate that the entry has been posted and ensure against posting the same entry twice.
3. Both statements are false. If an incorrect journal entry was posted, a correcting entry should be journalized and posted. To ensure honesty and provide a clear audit trail, erasures are not permitted in the journal.
4. **c.** date order.
5. **a.** account order.
6.

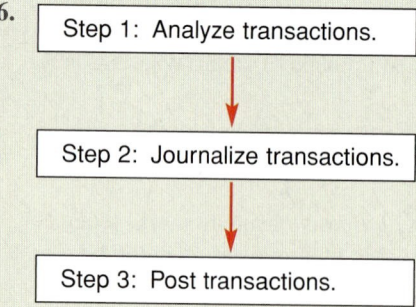

Answers to Comprehensive Self Review

1. Neatly cross out the incorrect item and write the correct data above it.
2. The general ledger account number.

3. It is the last accounting record in which a transaction is recorded.

4. **a.** An entry in the general journal.

5. Check number.

   Invoice number for goods purchased on credit from a vendor.

   Invoice number for services billed to a charge account customer.

   Memorandum number.

Adjustments and the Worksheet

Chapter 5

LEARNING OBJECTIVES

1. Complete a trial balance on a worksheet.
2. Prepare adjustments for unrecorded business transactions.
3. Complete the worksheet.
4. Prepare an income statement, statement of owner's equity, and balance sheet from the completed worksheet.
5. Journalize and post the adjusting entries.
6. Define the accounting terms new to this chapter.

NEW TERMS

account form balance sheet
adjusting entries
adjustments
book value
contra account
contra asset account
depreciation
prepaid expenses
report form balance sheet
salvage value
straight-line depreciation
worksheet

Boeing www.boeing.com

The International Space Station (ISS) is a truly global project, involving the scientific and technological resources of 16 countries and the efforts of more than 100,000 people throughout the world. As the prime contractor, Boeing has been responsible for design, development, construction, and integration of the ISS, as well as assistance to NASA with the operation of this orbital outpost.

The ISS is the largest, most complex international scientific project in history and our largest adventure into space to date. In 2010, Boeing officially turned over the U.S. on-orbit segment of the ISS to NASA. Often referred to as "handing over the keys," the DD-250 is equivalent to a final bill of sale that formally transfers ownership. Through the review board, NASA and Boeing verified the delivery, assembly, integration, and activation of all hardware and software required by contract. The success of the ISS has validated Boeing's position as a leader in the defense industry and has contributed to the company's overall revenue growth.

thinking critically

How do you think Boeing accounts for wear and tear of its equipment?

The Worksheet

Financial statements are completed as soon as possible in order to be useful. One way to speed the preparation of financial statements is to use a worksheet. A **worksheet** is a form used to gather all data needed at the end of an accounting period to prepare the financial statements. Preparation of the worksheet is the fourth step in the accounting cycle.

Figure 5.1 shows a common type of worksheet. The heading shows the company name, report title, and period covered. In addition to the Account Name column, this worksheet contains five sections: Trial Balance, Adjustments, Adjusted Trial Balance, Income Statement, and Balance Sheet. Each section includes a Debit column and a Credit column. The worksheet has 10 columns in which to enter dollar amounts.

>>**1. OBJECTIVE**

Complete a trial balance on a worksheet.

recall

Trial Balance

If total debits do not equal total credits, there is an error in the financial records. The error must be found and corrected.

The Trial Balance Section

Refer to Figure 5.2 as you read about how to prepare the Trial Balance section of the worksheet.

1. Enter the general ledger account names.
2. Transfer the general ledger account balances to the Debit and Credit columns of the Trial Balance section.
3. Total the Debit and Credit columns to prove that the trial balance is in balance.
4. Place a double rule under each Trial Balance column to show that the work in that column is complete.

FIGURE 5.1

Ten-Column Worksheet

Wells' Consulting Services
Worksheet
Month Ended December 31, 2013

ACCOUNT NAME	TRIAL BALANCE		ADJUSTMENTS	
	DEBIT	CREDIT	DEBIT	CREDIT
1				
2				
3				
4				
5				

FIGURE 5.2   **A Partial Worksheet**

Wells' Consulting Services
Worksheet
Month Ended December 31, 2013

	ACCOUNT NAME	TRIAL BALANCE DEBIT	TRIAL BALANCE CREDIT	ADJUSTMENTS DEBIT	ADJUSTMENTS CREDIT
1	Cash	111 350 00			
2	Accounts Receivable	5 000 00			
3	Supplies	1 500 00			(a) 500 00
4	Prepaid Rent	8 000 00			(b) 4 000 00
5	Equipment	11 000 00			
6	Accumulated Depreciation—Equipment				(c) 183 00
7	Accounts Payable		3 500 00		
8	Carolyn Wells, Capital		100 000 00		
9	Carolyn Wells, Drawing	5 000 00			
10	Fees Income		47 000 00		
11	Salaries Expense	8 000 00			
12	Utilities Expense	650 00			
13	Supplies Expense			(a) 500 00	
14	Rent Expense			(b) 4 000 00	
15	Depreciation Expense—Equipment			(c) 183 00	
16	Totals	150 500 00	150 500 00	4 683 00	4 683 00
17					
18					
19					

Notice that the trial balance has four new accounts: *Accumulated Depreciation—Equipment, Supplies Expense, Rent Expense,* and *Depreciation Expense—Equipment.* These accounts have zero balances now, but they will be needed later as the worksheet is completed.

The Adjustments Section

Usually, account balances change because of transactions with other businesses or individuals. For Wells' Consulting Services, the account changes recorded in Chapter 4 were caused by transactions with the firm's suppliers, customers, the landlord, and employees. It is easy to recognize, journalize, and post these transactions as they occur.

Some changes are not caused by transactions with other businesses or individuals. They arise from the internal operations of the firm during the accounting period. Journal entries made to update accounts for previously unrecorded items are called **adjustments** or **adjusting entries.** These changes are first entered on the worksheet at the end of each accounting period. The worksheet provides a convenient form for gathering the information and determining the effects of the changes. Let's look at the adjustments made by Wells' Consulting Services on December 31, 2013.

>>2. OBJECTIVE

Prepare adjustments for unrecorded business transactions.

ADJUSTED TRIAL BALANCE DEBIT	ADJUSTED TRIAL BALANCE CREDIT	INCOME STATEMENT DEBIT	INCOME STATEMENT CREDIT	BALANCE SHEET DEBIT	BALANCE SHEET CREDIT	
						1
						2
						3
						4
						5

recall

Trial Balance

On the trial balance, accounts are listed in this order: assets, liabilities, owner's equity, revenue, and expenses.

ADJUSTING FOR SUPPLIES USED

On November 28, 2013, Wells' Consulting Services purchased $1,500 of supplies. On December 31, the trial balance shows a $1,500 balance in the *Supplies* account. This amount is too high because some of the supplies were used during December.

An adjustment must be made for the supplies used. Otherwise, the asset account, *Supplies,* is overstated because fewer supplies are actually on hand. The expense account, *Supplies Expense,* is understated. The cost of the supplies used represents an operating expense that has not been recorded.

On December 31, Carlos Valdez counted the supplies. Remaining supplies totaled $1,000. This meant that supplies amounting to $500 were used during December ($1,500 − $1,000 = $500). At the end of December, an adjustment must be made to reflect the supplies used. The adjustment reduces the *Supplies* account to $1,000, the amount of supplies remaining. It increases the *Supplies Expense* account by $500 for the amount of supplies used. Notice that the adjustment for supplies is based on actual usage.

Refer to Figure 5.2 on page 125 to review the adjustment on the worksheet: a debit of $500 to *Supplies Expense* and a credit of $500 to *Supplies.* Both the debit and credit are labeled **(a)** to identify the two parts of the adjustment.

Supplies is a type of prepaid expense. **Prepaid expenses** are items that are acquired and paid for in advance of their use. Other common prepaid expenses are prepaid rent, prepaid insurance, and prepaid advertising. When cash is paid for these items, amounts are debited to *Prepaid Rent, Prepaid Insurance,* and *Prepaid Advertising;* all are asset accounts. As prepaid expenses are used, an adjustment is made to reduce the asset accounts and to increase the related expense accounts.

ADJUSTMENT

Record the adjustment for supplies.

ABOUT
ACCOUNTING

Accounting Software

The use of accounting software eliminates the need to prepare a worksheet. However, adjusting entries must always be made to properly reflect account balances at the end of a reporting period.

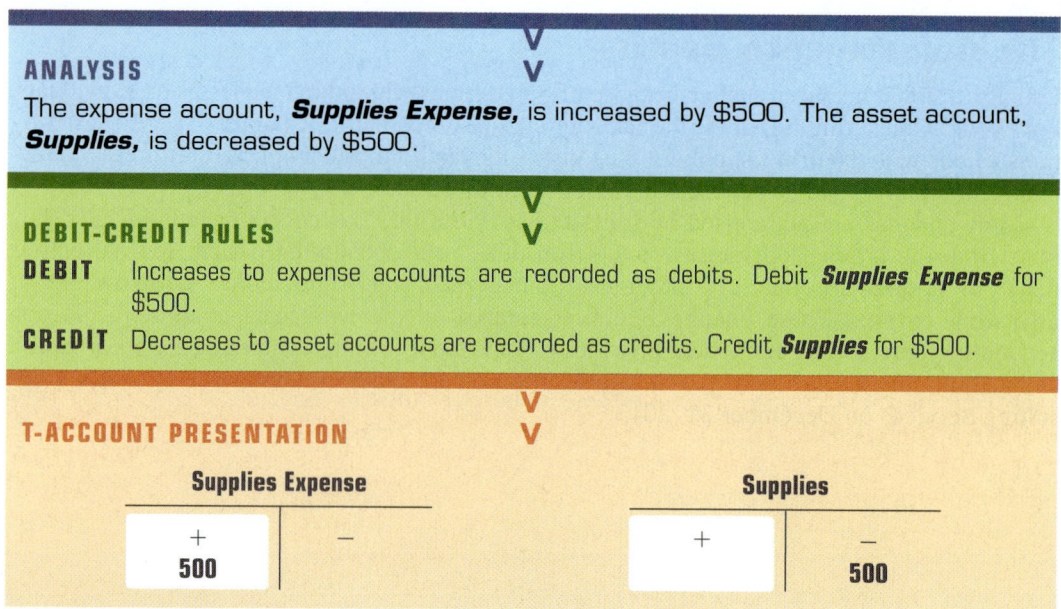

ANALYSIS

The expense account, **Supplies Expense,** is increased by $500. The asset account, **Supplies,** is decreased by $500.

DEBIT-CREDIT RULES

DEBIT   Increases to expense accounts are recorded as debits. Debit **Supplies Expense** for $500.

CREDIT   Decreases to asset accounts are recorded as credits. Credit **Supplies** for $500.

T-ACCOUNT PRESENTATION

Supplies Expense		Supplies	
+	−	+	−
500			500

Let's review the effect of the adjustment on the asset account, *Supplies.* Recall that the *Supplies* account already had a balance of $1,500. If no adjustment is made, the balance would remain at $1,500, even though only $1,000 of supplies are left.

Supplies

	+			−	
Bal.	1,500		Adj.	500	
Bal.	1,000				

ADJUSTING FOR EXPIRED RENT

On November 30, 2013, Wells' Consulting Services paid $8,000 rent for December and January. The right to occupy facilities for the specified period is an asset. The $8,000 was debited to **Prepaid Rent,** an asset account. On December 31, 2013, the **Prepaid Rent** balance is $8,000. This is too high because one month of rent has been used. The expired rent is $4,000 ($8,000 ÷ 2 months). At the end of December, an adjustment is made to reflect the expired rent.

ADJUSTMENT

Record the adjustment for expired rent.

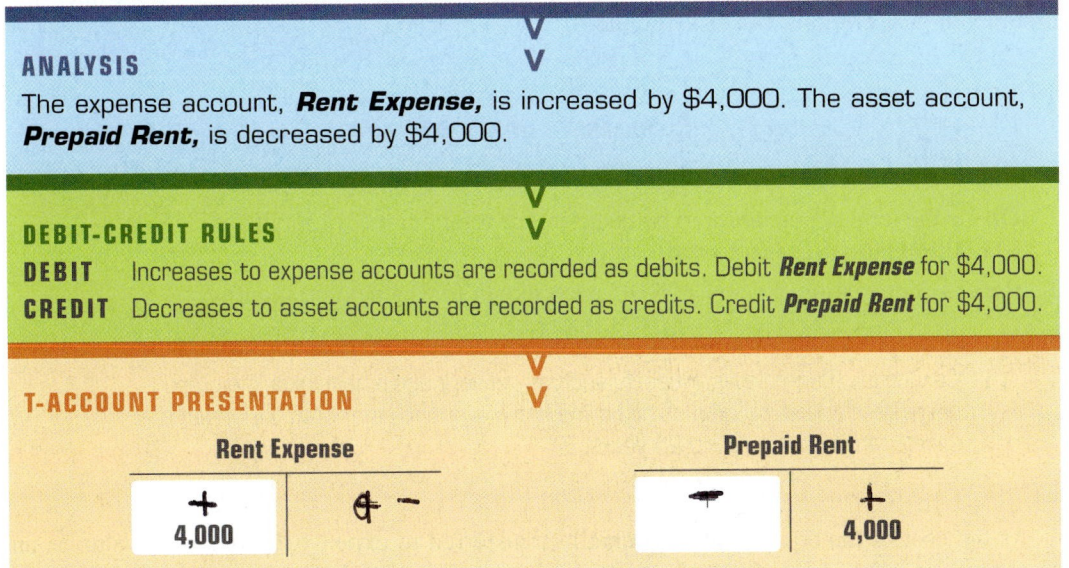

ANALYSIS

The expense account, **Rent Expense,** is increased by $4,000. The asset account, **Prepaid Rent,** is decreased by $4,000.

DEBIT-CREDIT RULES

DEBIT   Increases to expense accounts are recorded as debits. Debit **Rent Expense** for $4,000.

CREDIT Decreases to asset accounts are recorded as credits. Credit **Prepaid Rent** for $4,000.

T-ACCOUNT PRESENTATION

Rent Expense			Prepaid Rent	
+	−		−	+
4,000				4,000

Let's review the effect of the adjustment on the asset account, **Prepaid Rent.** The beginning balance of $8,000 represents prepaid rent for the months of December and January. By December 31, the prepaid rent for the month of December is "used up." The adjustment reducing **Prepaid Rent** recognizes the expense of occupying the facilities in December. The $4,000 ending balance represents prepaid rent for the month of January.

Prepaid Rent

	+			−	
Bal.	8,000		Adj.	4,000	
Bal.	4,000				

important!

Prepaid Expense

Prepaid rent is recorded as an asset at the time it is paid. As time elapses, the asset is used up. An adjustment is made to reduce the asset and to recognize rent expense.

Refer again to Figure 5.2 to review the adjustment on the worksheet: a debit of $4,000 to **Rent Expense** and a credit of $4,000 to **Prepaid Rent.** Both parts of the adjustment are labeled (**b**).

ADJUSTING FOR DEPRECIATION

There is one more adjustment to make at the end of December. It involves the equipment purchased in November. The cost of long-term assets such as equipment is not recorded as an expense when purchased. Instead, the cost is recorded as an asset and spread over the time the assets are used for the business. **Depreciation** is the process of allocating the cost of long-term assets over their expected useful lives. There are many ways to calculate depreciation. Wells' Consulting Services uses the straight-line depreciation method. This method results in an equal amount of depreciation being charged to each accounting period during the asset's useful life. The formula for straight-line depreciation is

$$\text{Depreciation} = \frac{\text{Cost} - \text{Salvage value}}{\text{Estimated useful life}}$$

Salvage value is an estimate of the amount that may be received by selling or disposing of an asset at the end of its useful life.

Wells' Consulting Services purchased $11,000 worth of equipment. The equipment has an estimated useful life of five years and no salvage value. The depreciation for December, the first month of operations, is $183 (rounded).

$$\frac{\$11,000 - \$0}{60 \text{ months}} = \$183 \text{ (rounded)}$$

1. Convert the asset's useful life from years to months: 5 years × 12 months = 60 months.
2. Divide the total depreciation to be taken by the total number of months:
   $11,000 ÷ 60 = $183 (rounded).
3. Record depreciation expense of $183 each month for the next 60 months.

> Conoco Inc. depreciates property such as refinery equipment, pipelines, and deepwater drill ships on a straight-line basis over the estimated life of each asset, ranging from 15 to 25 years.

As the cost of the equipment is gradually transferred to expense, its recorded value as an asset must be reduced. This procedure cannot be carried out by directly decreasing the balance in the asset account. Generally accepted accounting principles require that the original cost of a long-term asset continue to appear in the asset account until the firm has used up or disposed of the asset.

The adjustment for depreciation is recorded in a contra account entitled **Accumulated Depreciation—Equipment.** A contra account has a normal balance that is opposite that of a related account. For example, the **Equipment** account is an asset and has a normal debit balance. **Accumulated Depreciation—Equipment** is a contra asset account with a normal credit balance, which is opposite the normal balance of an asset account. The adjustment to reflect depreciation for December is a $183 debit to **Depreciation Expense—Equipment** and a $183 credit to **Accumulated Depreciation—Equipment.**

The **Accumulated Depreciation—Equipment** account is a record of all depreciation taken on the equipment. The financial records show the original cost of the equipment (**Equipment,**

$11,000) and all depreciation taken (*Accumulated Depreciation—Equipment,* $183). The difference between the two accounts is called book value. <mark>Book value</mark> is that portion of an asset's original cost that has not yet been depreciated. Three amounts are reported on the financial statements for equipment:

Equipment	$11,000
Less accumulated depreciation	− 183
Equipment at book value	$10,817

ADJUSTMENT

Record the adjustment for depreciation.

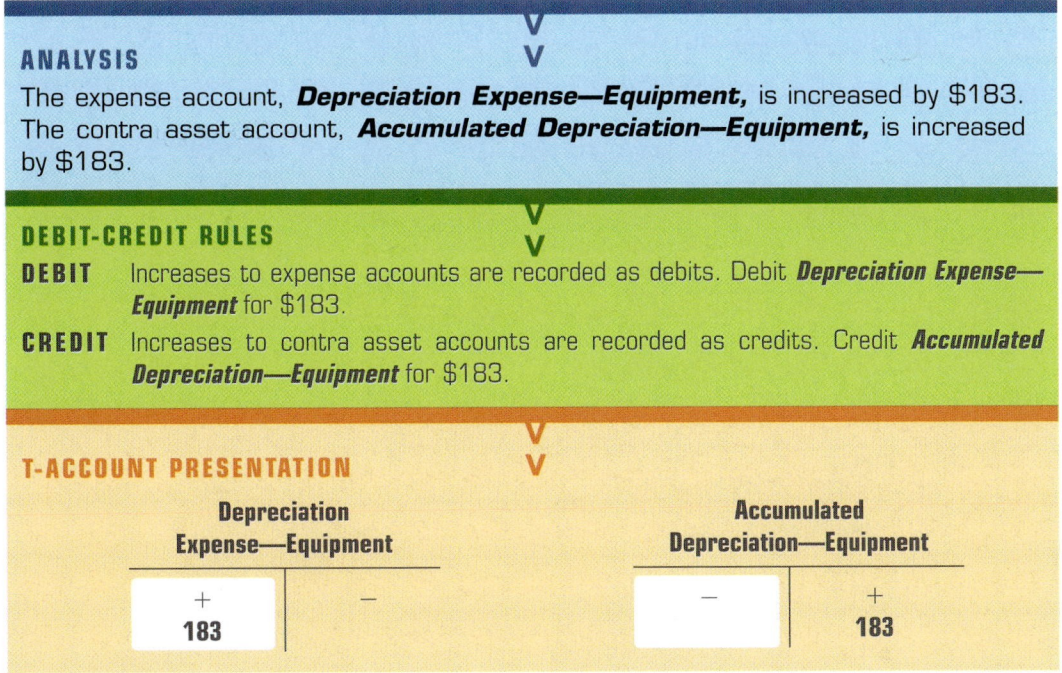

ANALYSIS

The expense account, *Depreciation Expense—Equipment,* is increased by $183. The contra asset account, *Accumulated Depreciation—Equipment,* is increased by $183.

DEBIT-CREDIT RULES

DEBIT   Increases to expense accounts are recorded as debits. Debit *Depreciation Expense—Equipment* for $183.

CREDIT   Increases to contra asset accounts are recorded as credits. Credit *Accumulated Depreciation—Equipment* for $183.

T-ACCOUNT PRESENTATION

Depreciation Expense—Equipment		Accumulated Depreciation—Equipment	
+	−	−	+
183			183

Refer to Figure 5.2 on page 125 to review the depreciation adjustment on the worksheet. The two parts of the adjustment are labeled **(c).**

If Wells' Consulting Services had other kinds of long-term tangible assets, an adjustment for depreciation would be made for each one. Long-term tangible assets include land, buildings, equipment, trucks, automobiles, furniture, and fixtures. Depreciation is calculated on all long-term tangible assets except land. Land is not depreciated.

Notice that each adjustment involved a balance sheet account (an asset or a contra asset) and an income statement account (an expense). When all adjustments have been entered, total and rule the Adjustments columns. Be sure that the totals of the Debit and Credit columns are equal. If they are not, locate and correct the error or errors before continuing. Figure 5.2 shows the completed Adjustments section.

Section 1 Self Review

QUESTIONS

1. What are adjustments?

2. Why is the worksheet prepared?

3. Why are prepaid expenses adjusted at the end of an accounting period?

EXERCISES

4. On January 1, a firm paid $21,600 for six months' rent, January through June. What is the adjustment for rent expense at the end of January?

   a. **Rent Expense** is debited for $21,600 and **Prepaid Rent** is credited for $21,600.

   b. **Rent Expense** is debited for $3,600 and **Prepaid Rent** is credited for $3,600.

   c. **Prepaid Rent** is debited for $3,600 and **Rent Expense** is credited for $3,600.

   d. No adjustment is made until the end of June.

5. A firm paid $1,200 for supplies during the accounting period. At the end of the accounting period, the firm had $300 of supplies on hand. What adjustment is entered on the worksheet?

   a. **Supplies Expense** is debited for $900 and **Supplies** is credited for $900.

   b. **Supplies** is debited for $300 and **Supplies Expense** is credited for $300.

   c. **Supplies Expense** is debited for $300 and **Supplies** is credited for $300.

   d. **Supplies** is debited for $900 and **Supplies Expense** is credited for $900.

ANALYSIS

6. Three years ago, HB Delivery bought a delivery truck for $70,000. The truck has no salvage value and a five-year useful life. What is the book value of the truck at the end of three years? $28,000

(Answers to Section 1 Self Review are on page 153.)

SECTION OBJECTIVES	TERMS TO LEARN
>> 3. **Complete the worksheet.**	account form balance sheet
WHY IT'S IMPORTANT	report form balance sheet
The worksheet summarizes both internal and external financial events of a period.	
>> 4. **Prepare an income statement, statement of owner's equity, and balance sheet from the completed worksheet.**	
WHY IT'S IMPORTANT	
Using a worksheet saves time in preparing the financial statements.	
>> 5. **Journalize and post the adjusting entries.**	
WHY IT'S IMPORTANT	
Adjusting entries update the financial records of the business.	

Financial Statements

The worksheet is used to prepare the financial statements. Preparing financial statements is the fifth step in the accounting cycle.

The Adjusted Trial Balance Section

The next task is to prepare the Adjusted Trial Balance section.

1. Combine the figures from the Trial Balance section and the Adjustments section of the worksheet. Record the computed results in the Adjusted Trial Balance columns.
2. Total the Debit and Credit columns in the Adjusted Trial Balance section. Confirm that debits equal credits.

Figure 5.3 on pages 132–133 shows the completed Adjusted Trial Balance section of the worksheet. The accounts that do not have adjustments are simply extended from the Trial Balance section to the Adjusted Trial Balance section. For example, the **Cash** account balance of $111,350 is recorded in the Debit column of the Adjusted Trial Balance section without change.

The balances of accounts that are affected by adjustments are recomputed. Look at the **Supplies** account. It has a $1,500 debit balance in the Trial Balance section and shows a $500 credit in the Adjustments section. The new balance is $1,000 ($1,500 − $500). It is recorded in the Debit column of the Adjusted Trial Balance section.

Use the following guidelines to compute the amounts for the Adjusted Trial Balance section.

■ If the account has a debit balance in the Trial Balance section and a debit entry in the Adjustments section, add the two amounts.

>>**3. OBJECTIVE**
Complete the worksheet.

If the Trial Balance section has a:	AND if the entry in the Adjustments section is a:	Then:
Debit balance	Debit	Add the amounts.
Debit balance	Credit	Subtract the credit amount.
Credit balance	Credit	Add the amounts.
Credit balance	Debit	Subtract the debit amount.

FIGURE 5.3   **A Partial Worksheet**

	ACCOUNT NAME	TRIAL BALANCE DEBIT	TRIAL BALANCE CREDIT	ADJUSTMENTS DEBIT	ADJUSTMENTS CREDIT	
1	Cash	111 350 00				
2	Accounts Receivable	5 000 00				
3	Supplies	1 500 00			(a)	500 00
4	Prepaid Rent	8 000 00			(b)	4 000 00
5	Equipment	11 000 00				
6	Accumulated Depreciation—Equipment				(c)	183 00
7	Accounts Payable		3 500 00			
8	Carolyn Wells, Capital		100 000 00			
9	Carolyn Wells, Drawing	5 000 00				
10	Fees Income		47 000 00			
11	Salaries Expense	8 000 00				
12	Utilities Expense	650 00				
13	Supplies Expense			(a)	500 00	
14	Rent Expense			(b)	4 000 00	
15	Depreciation Expense—Equipment			(c)	183 00	
16	Totals	150 500 00	150 500 00	4 683 00	4 683 00	
17	Net Income					

- If the account has a debit balance in the Trial Balance section and a credit entry in the Adjustments section, subtract the credit amount.

- If the account has a credit balance in the Trial Balance section and a credit entry in the Adjustments section, add the two amounts.

- If the account has a credit balance in the Trial Balance section and a debit entry in the Adjustments section, subtract the debit amount.

Prepaid Rent has a Trial Balance debit of $8,000 and an Adjustments credit of $4,000. Enter $4,000 ($8,000 − $4,000) in the Adjusted Trial Balance Debit column.

Four accounts that started with zero balances in the Trial Balance section are affected by adjustments. They are ***Accumulated Depreciation—Equipment, Supplies Expense, Rent Expense,*** and ***Depreciation Expense—Equipment.*** The figures in the Adjustments section are simply extended to the Adjusted Trial Balance section. For example, ***Accumulated Depreciation—Equipment*** has a zero balance in the Trial Balance section and a $183 credit in the Adjustments section. Extend the $183 to the Adjusted Trial Balance Credit column.

Once all account balances are recorded in the Adjusted Trial Balance section, total and rule the Debit and Credit columns. Be sure that total debits equal total credits. If they are not equal, find and correct the error or errors.

The Income Statement and Balance Sheet Sections

The Income Statement and Balance Sheet sections of the worksheet are used to separate the amounts needed for the balance sheet and the income statement. For example, to prepare an income statement, all revenue and expense account balances must be in one place.

Starting at the top of the Adjusted Trial Balance section, examine each general ledger account. For accounts that appear on the balance sheet, enter the amount in the appropriate column of the Balance Sheet section. For accounts that appear on the income statement, enter the amount in the appropriate column of the Income Statement section. Take care to enter debit amounts in the Debit column and credit amounts in the Credit column.

ADJUSTED TRIAL BALANCE		INCOME STATEMENT		BALANCE SHEET		
DEBIT	CREDIT	DEBIT	CREDIT	DEBIT	CREDIT	
111 3 5 0 00						1
5 0 0 0 00						2
1 0 0 0 00						3
4 0 0 0 00						4
11 0 0 0 00						5
	1 8 3 00					6
	3 5 0 0 00					7
	100 0 0 0 00					8
5 0 0 0 00						9
	47 0 0 0 00					10
8 0 0 0 00						11
6 5 0 00						12
5 0 0 00						13
4 0 0 0 00						14
1 8 3 00						15
150 6 8 3 00	150 6 8 3 00					16
						17

PREPARING THE BALANCE SHEET SECTION

Refer to Figure 5.4 on pages 134–135 as you learn how to complete the worksheet. Asset, liability, and owner's equity accounts appear on the balance sheet. The first five accounts that appear on the worksheet are assets. Extend the asset accounts to the Debit column of the Balance Sheet section. The next account, *Accumulated Depreciation—Equipment,* is a contra asset account. Extend it to the Credit column of the Balance Sheet section. Extend *Accounts Payable* and *Carolyn Wells, Capital* to the Credit column of the Balance Sheet section. Extend *Carolyn Wells, Drawing* to the Debit column of the Balance Sheet section.

PREPARING THE INCOME STATEMENT SECTION

Revenue and expense accounts appear on the income statement. Extend the *Fees Income* account to the Credit column of the Income Statement section. The last five accounts on the worksheet are expense accounts. Extend these accounts to the Debit column of the Income Statement section.

After all account balances are transferred from the Adjusted Trial Balance section of the worksheet to the financial statement sections, total the Debit and Credit columns in the Income Statement section. For Wells' Consulting Services, the debits (expenses) total $13,333 and the credits (revenue) total $47,000.

Next, total the columns in the Balance Sheet section. For Wells' Consulting Services, the debits (assets and drawing account) total $137,350 and the credits (contra asset, liabilities, and owner's equity) total $103,683.

Return to the Income Statement section. The totals of these columns are used to determine the net income or net loss. Subtract the smaller column total from the larger one. Enter the difference on the line below the smaller total. In the Account Name column, enter "Net Income" or "Net Loss."

In this case, the total of the Credit column, $47,000, exceeds the total of the Debit column, $13,333. The Credit column total represents revenue. The Debit column total represents expenses. The difference between the two amounts is a net income of $33,667. Enter $33,667 in the Debit column of the Income Statement section.

recall

Locating Errors

If total debits do not equal total credits, find the difference between total debits and total credits. If the difference is divisible by 9, there could be a transposition error. If the difference is divisible by 2, an amount could be entered in the wrong (Debit or Credit) column.

FIGURE 5.4   A Completed Worksheet

Wells' Consulting Services
Worksheet
Month Ended December 31, 2013

ACCOUNT NAME	TRIAL BALANCE DEBIT	TRIAL BALANCE CREDIT	ADJUSTMENTS DEBIT	ADJUSTMENTS CREDIT
1 Cash	111 3 5 0 00			
2 Accounts Receivable	5 0 0 0 00			
3 Supplies	1 5 0 0 00			(a) 5 0 0 00
4 Prepaid Rent	8 0 0 0 00			(b) 4 0 0 0 00
5 Equipment	11 0 0 0 00			
6 Accumulated Depreciation—Equipment				(c) 1 8 3 00
7 Accounts Payable		3 5 0 0 00		
8 Carolyn Wells, Capital		100 0 0 0 00		
9 Carolyn Wells, Drawing	5 0 0 0 00			
10 Fees Income		47 0 0 0 00		
11 Salaries Expense	8 0 0 0 00			
12 Utilities Expense	6 5 0 00			
13 Supplies Expense			(a) 5 0 0 00	
14 Rent Expense			(b) 4 0 0 0 00	
15 Depreciation Expense—Equipment			(c) 1 8 3 00	
16 Totals	150 5 0 0 00	150 5 0 0 00	4 6 8 3 00	4 6 8 3 00
17 Net Income				
18				

Net income causes a net increase in owner's equity. As a check on accuracy, the amount in the Balance Sheet Debit column is subtracted from the amount in the Credit column and compared to net income. In the Balance Sheet section, subtract the smaller column total from the larger one. The difference should equal the net income or net loss computed in the Income Statement section. Enter the difference on the line below the smaller total. For Wells' Consulting Services, enter $33,667 in the Credit column of the Balance Sheet section.

Total the Income Statement and Balance Sheet columns. Make sure that total debits equal total credits for each section.

Wells' Consulting Services had a net income. If it had a loss, the loss would be entered in the Credit column of the Income Statement section and the Debit column of the Balance Sheet section. "Net Loss" would be entered in the Account Name column on the worksheet.

Preparing Financial Statements

When the worksheet is complete, the next step is to prepare the financial statements, starting with the income statement. Preparation of the financial statements is the fifth step in the accounting cycle.

>>4.   OBJECTIVE

Prepare an income statement, statement of owner's equity, and balance sheet from the completed worksheet.

PREPARING THE INCOME STATEMENT

Use the Income Statement section of the worksheet to prepare the income statement. Figure 5.5 on page 136 shows the income statement for Wells' Consulting Services. Compare it to the worksheet in Figure 5.4.

If the firm had incurred a net loss, the final amount on the income statement would be labeled "Net Loss for the Month."

ADJUSTED TRIAL BALANCE		INCOME STATEMENT		BALANCE SHEET		
DEBIT	CREDIT	DEBIT	CREDIT	DEBIT	CREDIT	
111 350 00				111 350 00		1
5 000 00				5 000 00		2
1 000 00				1 000 00		3
4 000 00				4 000 00		4
11 000 00				11 000 00		5
	1 83 00				1 83 00	6
	3 500 00				3 500 00	7
	100 000 00				100 000 00	8
5 000 00				5 000 00		9
	47 000 00		47 000 00			10
8 000 00		8 000 00				11
650 00		650 00				12
500 00		500 00				13
4 000 00		4 000 00				14
1 83 00		1 83 00				15
150 683 00	150 683 00	13 333 00	47 000 00	137 350 00	103 683 00	16
		33 667 00			33 667 00	17
		47 000 00	47 000 00	137 350 00	137 350 00	18

PREPARING THE STATEMENT OF OWNER'S EQUITY

The statement of owner's equity reports the changes that have occurred in the owner's financial interest during the reporting period. Use the data in the Balance Sheet section of the worksheet, as well as the net income or net loss figure, to prepare the statement of owner's equity.

- From the Balance Sheet section of the worksheet, use the amounts for owner's capital; owner's withdrawals, if any; and owner's investments, if any.

- From the Income Statement section of the worksheet, use the amount calculated for net income or net loss.

The statement of owner's equity is prepared before the balance sheet because the ending capital balance is needed to prepare the balance sheet. The statement of owner's equity reports the change in owner's capital during the period ($28,667) as well as the ending capital ($128,667). Figure 5.6 on page 136 shows the statement of owner's equity for Wells' Consulting Services.

PREPARING THE BALANCE SHEET

The accounts listed on the balance sheet are taken directly from the Balance Sheet section of the worksheet. Figure 5.7 on page 136 shows the balance sheet for Wells' Consulting Services.

Note that the equipment's book value is reported on the balance sheet ($10,817). Do not confuse book value with market value. Book value is the portion of the original cost that has not been depreciated. *Market value* is what a willing buyer will pay a willing seller for the asset. Market value may be higher or lower than book value.

Notice that the amount for *Carolyn Wells, Capital,* $128,667, comes from the statement of owner's equity.

The balance sheet in Figure 5.7 is prepared using the report form. The **report form balance sheet** lists the asset accounts first, followed by liabilities and owner's equity. Chapters 2 and 3 illustrated the **account form balance sheet,** with assets on the left and liabilities and

FIGURE 5.5

Income Statement

Wells' Consulting Services					
Income Statement					
Month Ended December 31, 2013					
Revenue					
Fees Income				47 0 0 0	00
Expenses					
Salaries Expense	8 0 0 0	00			
Utilities Expense	6 5 0	00			
Supplies Expense	5 0 0	00			
Rent Expense	4 0 0 0	00			
Depreciation Expense—Equipment	1 8 3	00			
Total Expenses				13 3 3 3	00
Net Income for the Month				33 6 6 7	00

FIGURE 5.6

Statement of Owner's Equity

Wells' Consulting Services					
Statement of Owner's Equity					
Month Ended December 31, 2013					
Carolyn Wells, Capital, December 1, 2013				100 0 0 0	00
Net Income for December	33 6 6 7	00			
Less Withdrawals for December	5 0 0 0	00			
Increase in Capital				28 6 6 7	00
Carolyn Wells, Capital, December 31, 2013				128 6 6 7	00

FIGURE 5.7

Balance Sheet

Wells' Consulting Services					
Balance Sheet					
December 31, 2013					
Assets					
Cash				111 3 5 0	00
Accounts Receivable				5 0 0 0	00
Supplies				1 0 0 0	00
Prepaid Rent				4 0 0 0	00
Equipment	11 0 0 0	00			
Less Accumulated Depreciation	1 8 3	00		10 8 1 7	00
Total Assets				132 1 6 7	00
Liabilities and Owner's Equity					
Liabilities					
Accounts Payable				3 5 0 0	00
Owner's Equity					
Carolyn Wells, Capital				128 6 6 7	00
Total Liabilities and Owner's Equity				132 1 6 7	00

FIGURE 5.8A   Worksheet Summary

The worksheet is used to gather all the data needed at the end of an accounting period to prepare the financial statements. The worksheet heading contains the name of the company (WHO), the title of the statement being prepared (WHAT), and the period covered (WHEN). The worksheet contains 10 money columns that are arranged in five sections labeled Trial Balance, Adjustments, Adjusted Trial Balance, Income Statement, and Balance Sheet. Each section includes a Debit column and a Credit column.

The information reflected in the worksheet below is for Wells' Consulting Services for the period ending December 31, 2013. The illustrations that follow will highlight the preparation of each part of the worksheet.

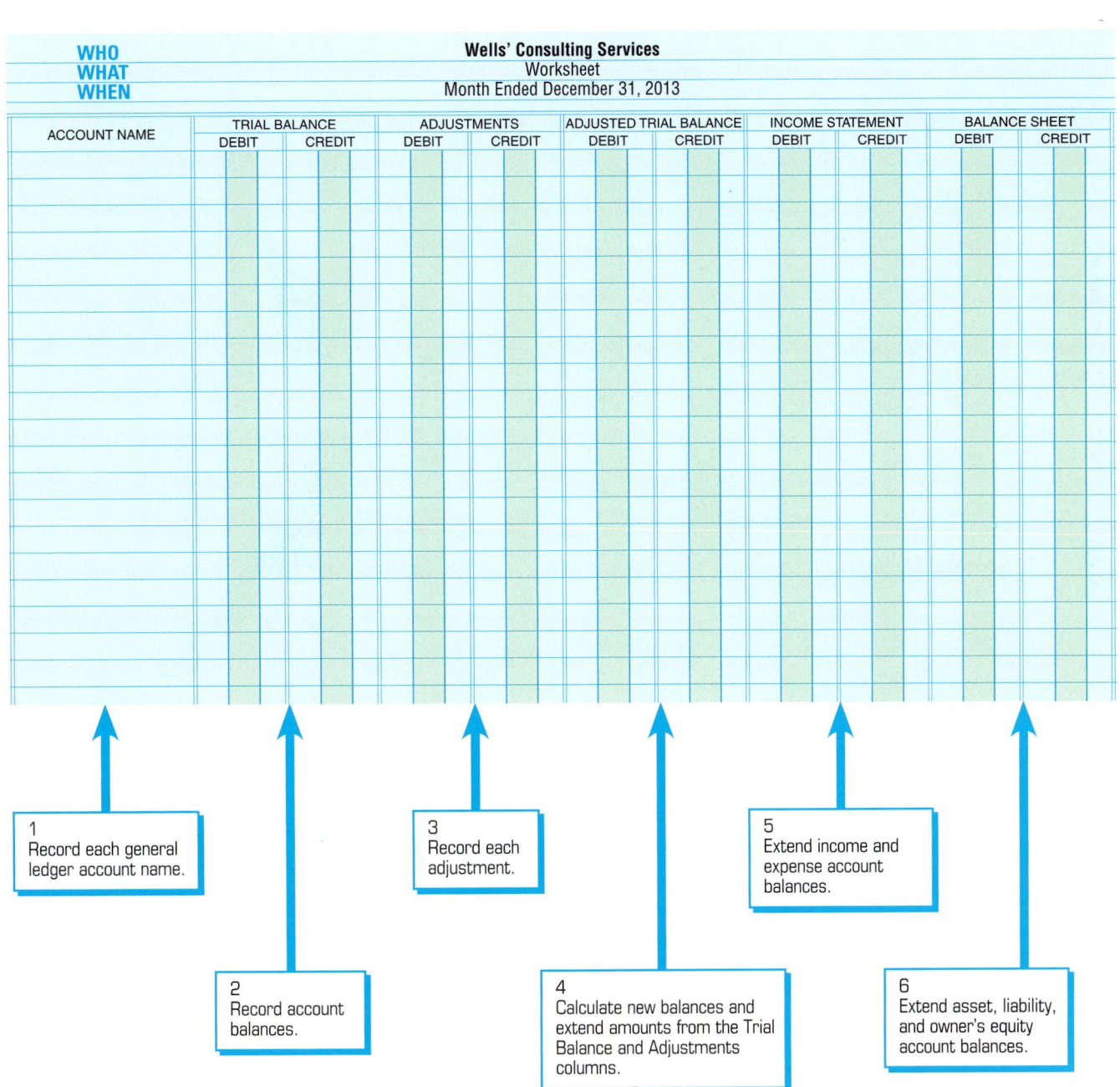

1 Record each general ledger account name.

2 Record account balances.

3 Record each adjustment.

4 Calculate new balances and extend amounts from the Trial Balance and Adjustments columns.

5 Extend income and expense account balances.

6 Extend asset, liability, and owner's equity account balances.

FIGURE 5.8B   The Trial Balance Columns

The first step in preparing the worksheet for Wells' Consulting Services is to list the general ledger accounts and their balances in the Account Name and Trial Balance sections of the worksheet. The equality of total debits and credits is proved by totaling the Debit and Credit columns.

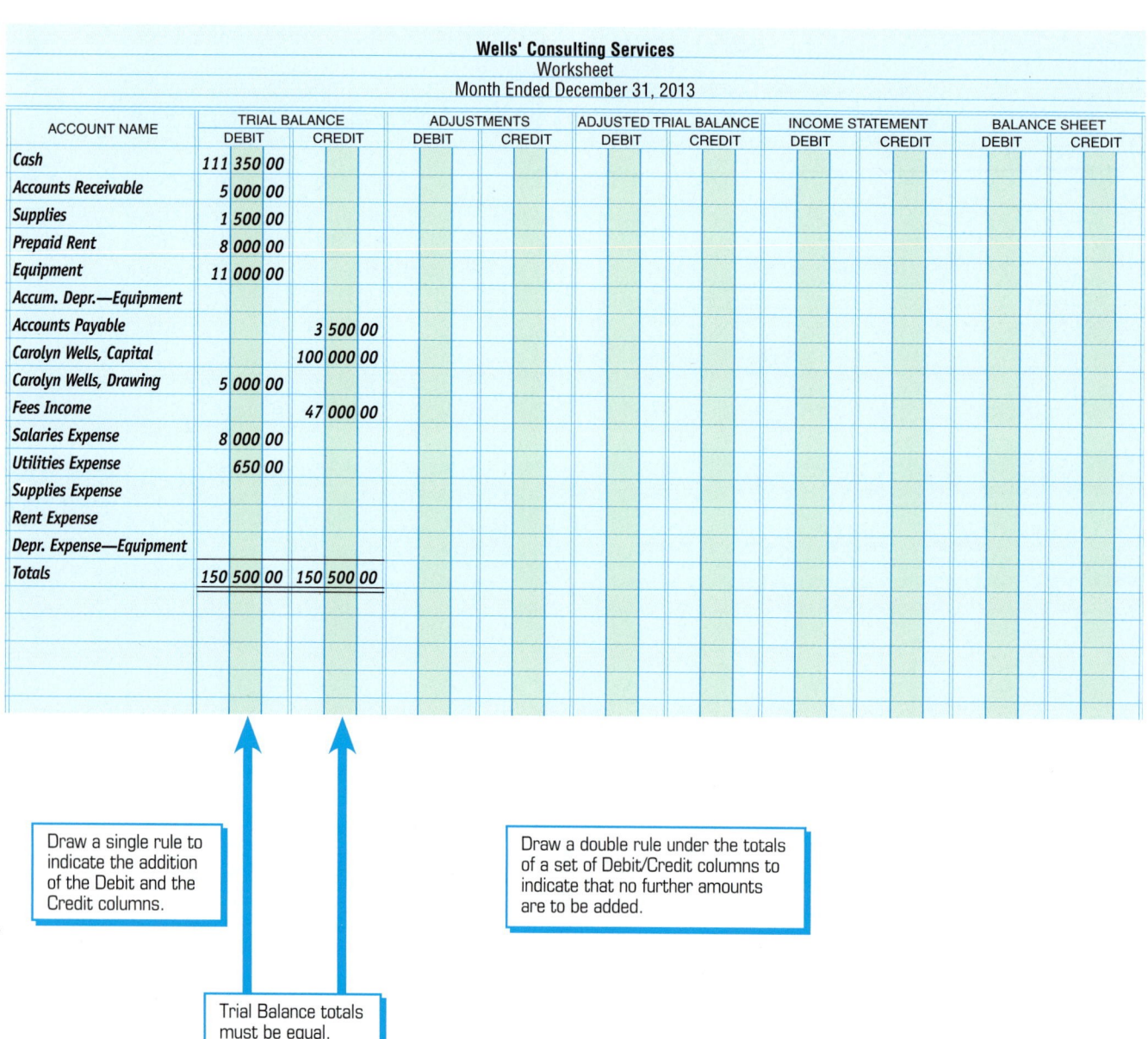

Wells' Consulting Services
Worksheet
Month Ended December 31, 2013

ACCOUNT NAME	TRIAL BALANCE		ADJUSTMENTS		ADJUSTED TRIAL BALANCE		INCOME STATEMENT		BALANCE SHEET	
	DEBIT	CREDIT	DEBIT	CREDIT	DEBIT	CREDIT	DEBIT	CREDIT	DEBIT	CREDIT
Cash	111 350 00									
Accounts Receivable	5 000 00									
Supplies	1 500 00									
Prepaid Rent	8 000 00									
Equipment	11 000 00									
Accum. Depr.—Equipment										
Accounts Payable		3 500 00								
Carolyn Wells, Capital		100 000 00								
Carolyn Wells, Drawing	5 000 00									
Fees Income		47 000 00								
Salaries Expense	8 000 00									
Utilities Expense	650 00									
Supplies Expense										
Rent Expense										
Depr. Expense—Equipment										
Totals	150 500 00	150 500 00								

Draw a single rule to indicate the addition of the Debit and the Credit columns.

Draw a double rule under the totals of a set of Debit/Credit columns to indicate that no further amounts are to be added.

Trial Balance totals must be equal.

FIGURE 5.8G Preparing the Financial Statements

The information needed to prepare the financial statements is obtained from the worksheet.

Wells' Consulting Services
Income Statement
Month Ended December 31, 2013

Revenue		
Fees Income		47 000 00
Expenses		
Salaries Expense	8 000 00	
Utilities Expense	650 00	
Supplies Expense	500 00	
Rent Expense	4 000 00	
Depreciation Expense—Equipment	183 00	
Total Expenses		13 333 00
Net Income for the Month		33 667 00

> When expenses for the period are less than revenue, a net income results. The net income is transferred to the statement of owner's equity.

Wells' Consulting Services
Statement of Owner's Equity
Month Ended December 31, 2013

Carolyn Wells, Capital, December 1, 2013		100 000 00
Net Income for December	33 667 00	
Less Withdrawals for December	5 000 00	
Increase in Capital		28 667 00
Carolyn Wells, Capital, December 31, 2013		128 667 00

> The withdrawals are subtracted from the net income for the period to determine the change in owner's equity.

Wells' Consulting Services
Balance Sheet
December 31, 2013

Assets		
Cash		111 350 00
Accounts Receivable		5 000 00
Supplies		1 000 00
Prepaid Rent		4 000 00
Equipment	11 000 00	
Less Accumulated Depreciation	183 00	10 817 00
Total Assets		132 167 00
Liabilities and Owner's Equity		
Liabilities		
Accounts Payable		3 500 00
Owner's Equity		
Carolyn Wells, Capital		128 667 00
Total Liabilities and Owner's Equity		132 167 00

> The ending capital balance is transferred from the statement of owner's equity to the balance sheet.

SUMMARY OF FINANCIAL STATEMENTS

THE INCOME STATEMENT

The income statement is prepared directly from the data in the Income Statement section of the worksheet. The heading of the income statement contains the name of the firm (WHO), the name of the statement (WHAT), and the period covered by the statement (WHEN). The revenue section of the statement is prepared first. The revenue account name is obtained from the Account Name column of the worksheet. The balance of the revenue account is obtained from the Credit column of the Income Statement section of the worksheet. The expenses section of the income statement is prepared next. The expense account titles are obtained from the Account Name column of the worksheet. The balance of each expense account is obtained from the Debit column of the Income Statement section of the worksheet.

Determining the net income or net loss for the period is the last step in preparing the income statement. If the firm has more revenue than expenses, a net income is reported for the period. If the firm has more expenses than revenue, a net loss is reported. The net income or net loss reported must agree with the amount calculated on the worksheet.

THE STATEMENT OF OWNER'S EQUITY

The statement of owner's equity is prepared from the data in the Balance Sheet section of the worksheet and the general ledger capital account. The statement of owner's equity is prepared before the balance sheet so that the amount of the ending capital balance is available for presentation on the balance sheet. The heading of the statement contains the name of the firm (WHO), the name of the statement (WHAT), and the date of the statement (WHEN).

The statement begins with the capital account balance at the beginning of the period. Next, the increase or decrease in the owner's capital account is determined. The increase or decrease is computed by adding the net income (or net loss) for the period to any additional investments made by the owner during the period and subtracting withdrawals for the period. The increase or decrease is added to the beginning capital balance to obtain the ending capital balance.

THE BALANCE SHEET

The balance sheet is prepared from the data in the Balance Sheet section of the worksheet and the statement of owner's equity. The balance sheet reflects the assets, liabilities, and owner's equity of the firm on the balance sheet date. The heading of the statement contains the name of the firm (WHO), the name of the statement (WHAT), and the date of the statement (WHEN).

The assets section of the statement is prepared first. The asset account titles are obtained from the Account Name column of the worksheet. The balance of each asset account is obtained from the Debit column of the Balance Sheet section of the worksheet. The liability and owner's equity section is prepared next. The liability and owner's equity account titles are obtained from the Account Name column of the worksheet. The balance of each liability account is obtained from the Credit column of the Balance Sheet section of the worksheet. The ending balance for the owner's capital account is obtained from the statement of owner's equity. Total liabilities and owner's equity must equal total assets.

owner's equity on the right. The report form is widely used because it provides more space for entering account names and its format is easier to prepare.

> Some companies show long-term assets at a net amount. "Net" means that accumulated depreciation has been subtracted from the original cost. For example, The Boeing Company's consolidated statement of financial position as of December 31, 2009, states:
>   Property, plant, and equipment, net: $8,784 million
> The accumulated depreciation amount does not appear on the balance sheet.

Figure 5.8A through 5.8G on the preceding pages provides a step-by-step demonstration of how to complete the worksheet and financial statements for Wells' Consulting Services.

Journalizing and Posting Adjusting Entries

The worksheet is a tool. It is used to determine the effects of adjustments on account balances. It is also used to prepare the financial statements. However, the worksheet is not part of the permanent accounting record.

After the financial statements are prepared, the adjustments shown on the worksheet must become part of the permanent accounting record. Each adjustment is journalized and posted to the general ledger accounts. Journalizing and posting adjusting entries is the sixth step in the accounting cycle.

>>5. OBJECTIVE
Journalize and post the adjusting entries.

For Wells' Consulting Services, three adjustments are needed to provide a complete picture of the firm's operating results and its financial position. Adjustments are needed for supplies expense, rent expense, and depreciation expense.

Refer to Figure 5.4 on pages 134–135 for data needed to record the adjustments. Enter the words "Adjusting Entries" in the Description column of the general journal. Some accountants prefer to start a new page when they record the adjusting entries. Then journalize the adjustments in the order in which they appear on the worksheet.

After journalizing the adjusting entries, post them to the general ledger accounts. Figure 5.9 on page 138 shows how the adjusting entries for Wells' Consulting Services on December 31, 2013, were journalized and posted. Account numbers appear in the general journal Posting Reference column because all entries have been posted. In each general ledger account, the word "Adjusting" appears in the Description column.

Remember that the worksheet is not part of the accounting records. Adjustments that are on the worksheet must be recorded in the general journal and posted to the general ledger in order to become part of the permanent accounting records.

FIGURE 5.9

Journalized and Posted
Adjusting Entries

GENERAL JOURNAL   PAGE ___3___

	DATE		DESCRIPTION	POST. REF.	DEBIT	CREDIT	
1	2013		*Adjusting Entries*				1
2	Dec.	31	Supplies Expense	517	5 0 0 00		2
3			Supplies	121		5 0 0 00	3
4							4
5		31	Rent Expense	520	4 0 0 0 00		5
6			Prepaid Rent	137		4 0 0 0 00	6
7							7
8		31	Depr. Expense—Equipment	523	1 8 3 00		8
9			Accum. Depr.—Equipment	142		1 8 3 00	9
10							10
11							

ACCOUNT Supplies   ACCOUNT NO. 121

DATE		DESCRIPTION	POST. REF.	DEBIT	CREDIT	BALANCE DEBIT	BALANCE CREDIT
2013							
Nov.	28		J1	1 5 0 0 00		1 5 0 0 00	
Dec.	31	Adjusting	J3		5 0 0 00	1 0 0 0 00	

ACCOUNT Prepaid Rent   ACCOUNT NO. 137

DATE		DESCRIPTION	POST. REF.	DEBIT	CREDIT	BALANCE DEBIT	BALANCE CREDIT
2013							
Nov.	30		J2	8 0 0 0 00		8 0 0 0 00	
Dec.	31	Adjusting	J3		4 0 0 0 00	4 0 0 0 00	

ACCOUNT Accumulated Depreciation—Equipment   ACCOUNT NO. 142

DATE		DESCRIPTION	POST. REF.	DEBIT	CREDIT	BALANCE DEBIT	BALANCE CREDIT
2013							
Dec.	31	Adjusting	J3		1 8 3 00		1 8 3 00

ACCOUNT Supplies Expense   ACCOUNT NO. 517

DATE		DESCRIPTION	POST. REF.	DEBIT	CREDIT	BALANCE DEBIT	BALANCE CREDIT
2013							
Dec.	31	Adjusting	J3	5 0 0 00		5 0 0 00	

ACCOUNT Rent Expense   ACCOUNT NO. 520

DATE		DESCRIPTION	POST. REF.	DEBIT	CREDIT	BALANCE DEBIT	BALANCE CREDIT
2013							
Dec.	31	Adjusting	J3	4 0 0 0 00		4 0 0 0 00	

ACCOUNT Depreciation Expense—Equipment   ACCOUNT NO. 523

DATE		DESCRIPTION	POST. REF.	DEBIT	CREDIT	BALANCE DEBIT	BALANCE CREDIT
2013							
Dec.	31	Adjusting	J3	1 8 3 00		1 8 3 00	

MANAGERIAL IMPLICATIONS   <<

WORKSHEETS

■ The worksheet permits quick preparation of the financial statements. Quick preparation of financial statements allows management to obtain timely information.

■ Timely information allows management to:
- ■ evaluate the results of operations,
- ■ evaluate the financial position of the business,
- ■ make decisions.

■ The worksheet provides a convenient form for gathering information and determining the effects of internal changes, such as:
- ■ recording an expense for the use of a long-term asset like equipment,
- ■ recording the actual use of prepaid items.

■ The more accounts that a firm has in its general ledger, the more useful the worksheet is in speeding the preparation of the financial statements.

■ It is important to management that the appropriate adjustments are recorded in order to present a complete and accurate picture of the firm's financial affairs.

THINKING CRITICALLY

Why is it necessary to record an adjustment for depreciation?

Section 2 Self Review

QUESTIONS

1. Why is it necessary to journalize and post adjusting entries even though the data are already recorded on the worksheet?

2. What amounts appear on the statement of owner's equity?

3. What is the difference between a report form balance sheet and an account form balance sheet?

EXERCISES

4. **Accumulated Depreciation—Equipment** is a(n):
   a. asset account.
   b. contra asset account.
   c. liability account.
   d. contra liability account.

5. On a worksheet, the adjusted balance of the **Supplies** account is extended to the:
   a. Income Statement Debit column.
   b. Balance Sheet Debit column.
   c. Income Statement Credit column.
   d. Balance Sheet Credit column.

ANALYSIS

6. Willis Repair Shop purchased equipment for $28,000. **Depreciation Expense** for the month is $500. What is the balance of the **Equipment** account after posting the depreciation entry? Why?

(Answers to Section 2 Self Review are on page 153.)

5 Chapter REVIEW   Chapter Summary

At the end of the operating period, adjustments for internal events are recorded to update the accounting records. In this chapter, you have learned how the accountant uses the worksheet and adjusting entries to accomplish this task.

Learning Objectives

1 Complete a trial balance on a worksheet.

A worksheet is normally used to save time in preparing the financial statements. Preparation of the worksheet is the fourth step in the accounting cycle. The trial balance is the first section of the worksheet to be prepared.

2 Prepare adjustments for unrecorded business transactions.

Some changes arise from the internal operations of the firm itself. Adjusting entries are made to record these changes. Any adjustments to account balances should be entered in the Adjustments section of the worksheet.

■ Prepaid expenses are expense items that are acquired and paid for in advance of their use. At the time of their acquisition, these items represent assets and are recorded in asset accounts. As they are used, their cost is transferred to expense by means of adjusting entries at the end of each accounting period.

Examples of general ledger asset accounts and the related expense accounts follow:

Asset Accounts	Expense Accounts
Supplies	Supplies Expense
Prepaid Rent	Rent Expense
Prepaid Insurance	Insurance Expense

■ Depreciation is the process of allocating the cost of a long-term tangible asset to operations over its expected useful life. Part of the asset's cost is charged off as an expense at the end of each accounting period during the asset's useful life. The straight-line method of depreciation is widely used. The formula for straight-line depreciation is:

$$\text{Depreciation} = \frac{\text{Cost} - \text{Salvage value}}{\text{Estimated useful life}}$$

3 Complete the worksheet.

An adjusted trial balance is prepared to prove the equality of the debits and credits after adjustments have been entered on the worksheet. Once the Debit and Credit columns have been totaled and ruled, the Income Statement and Balance Sheet columns of the worksheet are completed. The net income or net loss for the period is determined, and the worksheet is completed.

4 Prepare an income statement, statement of owner's equity, and balance sheet from the completed worksheet.

All figures needed to prepare the financial statements are properly reflected on the completed worksheet. The accounts are arranged in the order in which they must appear on the income statement and balance sheet. Preparation of the financial statements is the fifth step of the accounting cycle.

5 Journalize and post the adjusting entries.

After the financial statements have been prepared, the accountant must make permanent entries in the accounting records for the adjustments shown on the worksheet. The adjusting entries are then posted to the general ledger. Journalizing and posting the adjusting entries is the sixth step in the accounting cycle.

To summarize the steps of the accounting cycle discussed so far:

1. Analyze transactions.
2. Journalize transactions.
3. Post the journal entries.
4. Prepare a worksheet.
5. Prepare financial statements.
6. Record adjusting entries.

6 Define the accounting terms new to this chapter.

Glossary

Account form balance sheet (p. 135) A balance sheet that lists assets on the left and liabilities and owner's equity on the right (see Report form balance sheet)

Adjusting entries (p. 125) Journal entries made to update accounts for items that were not recorded during the accounting period

Adjustments (p. 125) See Adjusting entries

Book value (p. 129) That portion of an asset's original cost that has not yet been depreciated

Contra account (p. 128) An account with a normal balance that is opposite that of a related account

Contra asset account (p. 128) An asset account with a credit balance, which is contrary to the normal balance of an asset account

Depreciation (p. 128) Allocation of the cost of a long-term asset to operations during its expected useful life

Prepaid expenses (p. 126) Expense items acquired, recorded, and paid for in advance of their use

Report form balance sheet (p. 135) A balance sheet that lists the asset accounts first, followed by liabilities and owner's equity

Salvage value (p. 128) An estimate of the amount that could be received by selling or disposing of an asset at the end of its useful life

Straight-line depreciation (p. 128) Allocation of an asset's cost in equal amounts to each accounting period of the asset's useful life

Worksheet (p. 124) A form used to gather all data needed at the end of an accounting period to prepare financial statements

Comprehensive **Self Review**

1. The *Drawing* account is extended to which column of the worksheet?

2. Is the normal balance for *Accumulated Depreciation* a debit or credit balance?

3. Why is the net income for a period recorded in the Balance Sheet section of the worksheet as well as the Income Statement section?

4. The *Supplies* account has a debit balance of $6,000 in the Trial Balance column. The Credit column in the Adjustments section is $1,750. What is the new balance? The new balance will be extended to which column of the worksheet?

5. Why are assets depreciated?

(Answers to Comprehensive Self Review are on page 153.)

Discussion **Questions**

1. A firm purchases machinery, which has an estimated useful life of 10 years and no salvage value, for $30,000 at the beginning of the accounting period. What is the adjusting entry for depreciation at the end of one month if the firm uses the straight-line method of depreciation?

2. What adjustment would be recorded for expired insurance?

3. What are prepaid expenses? Give four examples.

4. Why is it necessary to make an adjustment for supplies used?

5. Are the following assets depreciated? Why or why not?

    a. Prepaid Insurance

    b. Delivery Truck

    c. Land

    d. Manufacturing Equipment

    e. Prepaid Rent

    f. Furniture

    g. Store Equipment

    h. Prepaid Advertising

    i. Computers

6. What effect does each of the following items have on net income?

    a. The owner withdrew cash from the business.

    b. Credit customers paid $1,000 on outstanding balances that were past due.

    c. The business bought equipment on account that cost $10,000.

    d. The business journalized and posted an adjustment for depreciation of equipment.

7. What effect does each item in Question 6 have on owner's equity?

8. Why is it necessary to journalize and post adjusting entries?

9. What three amounts are reported on the balance sheet for a long-term asset such as equipment?

10. How does a contra asset account differ from a regular asset account?

11. What is book value?

12. Why is an accumulated depreciation account used in making the adjustment for depreciation?

13. How does the straight-line method of depreciation work?

14. Give three examples of assets that are subject to depreciation.

APPLICATIONS

Exercises

Exercise 5.1

Objective 2

▶ **Calculating adjustments.**

Determine the necessary end-of-June adjustments for Anderson Company.

1. On June 1, 2013, Anderson Company, a new firm, paid $5,400 rent in advance for a six-month period. The $5,400 was debited to the ***Prepaid Rent*** account.

2. On June 1, 2013, the firm bought supplies for $7,450. The $7,450 was debited to the ***Supplies*** account. An inventory of supplies at the end of June showed that items costing $3,050 were on hand.

3. On June 1, 2013, the firm bought equipment costing $60,000. The equipment has an expected useful life of 10 years and no salvage value. The firm will use the straight-line method of depreciation.

Exercise 5.2

Objective 2

▶ **Calculating adjustments.**

For each of the following situations, determine the necessary adjustments.

1. A firm purchased a two-year insurance policy for $6,000 on July 1, 2013. The $6,000 was debited to the ***Prepaid Insurance*** account. What adjustment should be made to record expired insurance on the firm's July 31, 2013, worksheet?

2. On December 1, 2013, a firm signed a contract with a local radio station for advertising that will extend over a one-year period. The firm paid $15,000 in advance and debited the amount to *Prepaid Advertising.* What adjustment should be made to record expired advertising on the firm's December 31, 2013, worksheet?

Worksheet through Adjusted Trial Balance.

◄ **Exercise 5.3**
Objectives 1, 2

On January 31, 2013, the general ledger of Herron Company showed the following account balances. Prepare the worksheet through the Adjusted Trial Balance section. Assume that every account has the normal debit or credit balance. The worksheet covers the month of January.

ACCOUNTS
Cash	62,000
Accounts Receivable	21,500
Supplies	8,000
Prepaid Insurance	7,200
Equipment	90,500
Accum. Depr.—Equip.	0
Accounts Payable	15,700
Alfred Herron, Capital	80,950
Fees Income	112,000
Depreciation Exp.—Equip.	0
Insurance Expense	0
Rent Expense	9,600
Salaries Expense	9,850
Supplies Expense	0

Additional information:

a. Supplies used during January totaled $5,200.
b. Expired insurance totaled $1,800.
c. Depreciation expense for the month was $1,575.

Correcting net income.

◄ **Exercise 5.4**
Objectives 2, 3

Assume that a firm reports net income of $80,000 prior to making adjusting entries for the following items: expired rent, $6,000; depreciation expense, $7,200; and supplies used, $2,600.
  Assume that the required adjusting entries have not been made. What effect do these errors have on the reported net income?

Journalizing and posting adjustments.

◄ **Exercise 5.5**
Objective 5

Wade Company must make three adjusting entries on December 31, 2013.

a. Supplies used, $10,000; (supplies totaling $16,000 were purchased on December 1, 2013, and debited to the *Supplies* account).
b. Expired insurance, $7,200 on December 1, 2013; the firm paid $43,200 for six months' insurance coverage in advance and debited *Prepaid Insurance* for this amount.
c. Depreciation expense for equipment, $4,800.

Make the journal entries for these adjustments and post the entries to the general ledger accounts: Use page 3 of the general journal for the adjusting entries. Use the following accounts and numbers.

Supplies	121
Prepaid Insurance	131
Accum. Depr.—Equip.	142
Depreciation Exp.—Equip.	517
Insurance Expense	521
Supplies Expense	523

PROBLEMS

Problem Set A

Problem 5.1A ▶ **Completing the worksheet.**

Objectives 1, 2, 3

The trial balance of Dumas Company as of January 31, 2013, after the company completed the first month of operations, is shown in the partial worksheet below.

INSTRUCTIONS

1. Record the trial balance in the Trial Balance section of the worksheet.
2. Complete the worksheet by making the following adjustments: supplies on hand at the end of the month, $6,400; expired insurance, $10,000; depreciation expense for the period, $2,200.

Analyze: How does the insurance adjustment affect **Prepaid Insurance?**

Dumas Company
Worksheet (Partial)
Month Ended January 31, 2013

	ACCOUNT NAME	TRIAL BALANCE DEBIT	TRIAL BALANCE CREDIT	ADJUSTMENTS DEBIT	ADJUSTMENTS CREDIT
1	Cash	104 0 0 0 00			
2	Accounts Receivable	20 8 0 0 00			
3	Supplies	38 4 0 0 00			
4	Prepaid Insurance	60 0 0 0 00			
5	Equipment	108 0 0 0 00			
6	Accumulated Depreciation—Equipment				
7	Accounts Payable		24 8 0 0 00		
8	John Dumas, Capital		252 0 0 0 00		
9	John Dumas, Drawing	14 4 0 0 00			
10	Fees Income		103 2 0 0 00		
11	Depreciation Expense—Equipment				
12	Insurance Expense				
13	Salaries Expense	31 2 0 0 00			
14	Supplies Expense				
15	Utilities Expense	3 2 0 0 00			
16	Totals	380 0 0 0 00	380 0 0 0 00		

Problem 5.2A ▶ **Reconstructing a partial worksheet.**

Objectives 1, 2, 3

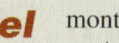

The adjusted trial balance of University Book Store as of November 30, 2013, after the firm's first month of operations, appears on the next page.
Appropriate adjustments have been made for the following items:

a. Supplies used during the month, $4,800.
b. Expired rent for the month, $6,000.
c. Depreciation expense for the month, $1,400.

INSTRUCTIONS

1. Record the Adjusted Trial Balance in the Adjusted Trial Balance columns of the worksheet.
2. Prepare the adjusting entries in the Adjustments columns.
3. Complete the Trial Balance columns of the worksheet prior to making the adjusting entries.

Analyze: What was the balance of **Prepaid Rent** prior to the adjusting entry for expired rent?

University Book Store Adjusted Trial Balance November 30, 2013		
Account Name	**Debit**	**Credit**
Cash	45,150	
Accounts Receivable	6,624	
Supplies	7,200	
Prepaid Rent	36,000	
Equipment	54,000	
Accumulated Depreciation—Equipment		1,400
Accounts Payable		16,000
Julie Acker, Capital		81,674
Julie Acker, Drawing	6,000	
Fees Income		84,000
Depreciation Expense—Equipment	1,400	
Rent Expense	6,000	
Salaries Expense	15,000	
Supplies Expense	4,800	
Utilities Expense	900	
Totals	183,074	183,074

Preparing financial statements from the worksheet.

◄ **Problem 5.3A**
Objective 4

The completed worksheet for Orange Corporation as of December 31, 2013, after the company had completed the first month of operation, appears across the tops of pages 146–147.

INSTRUCTIONS

1. Prepare an income statement.
2. Prepare a statement of owner's equity. The owner made no additional investments during the month.
3. Prepare a balance sheet (use the report form).

Analyze: If the adjustment to *Prepaid Advertising* had been $4,800 instead of $2,400, what net income would have resulted?

Preparing a worksheet and financial statements, journalizing adjusting entries, and posting to ledger accounts.

◄ **Problem 5.4A**
Objectives
1, 2, 3, 4, 5

Sadie Palmer owns Palmer Creative Designs. The trial balance of the firm for January 31, 2013, the first month of operations, is shown on the bottom of page 146.

INSTRUCTIONS

1. Complete the worksheet for the month.
2. Prepare an income statement, statement of owner's equity, and balance sheet. No additional investments were made by the owner during the month.
3. Journalize and post the adjusting entries. Use 3 for the journal page number. Use the following account numbers: Supplies, 121; Prepaid Advertising, 130; Prepaid Rent, 131; Accumulated Depreciation—Equipment, 142; Supplies Expense, 517; Advertising Expense, 519; Rent Expense, 520; Depreciation Expense, 523.

End-of-the-month adjustments must account for the following items:

a. Supplies were purchased on January 1, 2013; inventory of supplies on January 31, 2013, is $1,100.
b. The prepaid advertising contract was signed on January 1, 2013, and covers a four-month period.

Orange Corporation
Worksheet
Month Ended December 31, 2013

ACCOUNT NAME	TRIAL BALANCE DEBIT	TRIAL BALANCE CREDIT	ADJUSTMENTS DEBIT	ADJUSTMENTS CREDIT
1 Cash	77 2 0 0 00			
2 Accounts Receivable	12 0 0 0 00			
3 Supplies	10 1 0 0 00			(a) 6 0 0 0 00
4 Prepaid Advertising	14 4 0 0 00			(b) 2 4 0 0 00
5 Equipment	60 0 0 0 00			
6 Accumulated Depreciation—Equipment				(c) 1 2 0 0 00
7 Accounts Payable		12 0 0 0 00		
8 Ted Coe, Capital		108 0 0 0 00		
9 Ted Coe, Drawing	7 2 0 0 00			
10 Fees Income		79 5 0 0 00		
11 Advertising Expense			(b) 2 4 0 0 00	
12 Depreciation Expense—Equipment			(c) 1 2 0 0 00	
13 Salaries Expense	16 8 0 0 00			
14 Supplies Expense			(a) 6 0 0 0 00	
15 Utilities Expense	1 8 0 0 00			
16 Totals	199 5 0 0 00	199 5 0 0 00	9 6 0 0 00	9 6 0 0 00
17 Net Income				
18				
19				

c. Rent of $1,600 expired during the month.

d. Depreciation is computed using the straight-line method. The equipment has an estimated useful life of 10 years with no salvage value.

Analyze: If the adjusting entries had not been made for the month, would net income be overstated or understated?

Palmer Creative Designs
Worksheet (Partial)
Month Ended January 31, 2013

ACCOUNT NAME	TRIAL BALANCE DEBIT	TRIAL BALANCE CREDIT
1 Cash	35 5 0 0 00	
2 Accounts Receivable	12 6 0 0 00	
3 Supplies	7 7 5 0 00	
4 Prepaid Advertising	8 4 0 0 00	
5 Prepaid Rent	19 2 0 0 00	
6 Equipment	21 6 0 0 00	
7 Accumulated Depreciation—Equipment		
8 Accounts Payable		15 5 5 0 00
9 Sadie Palmer, Capital		60 0 0 0 00
10 Sadie Palmer, Drawing	7 0 0 0 00	
11 Fees Income		47 6 0 0 00
12 Advertising Expense		
13 Depreciation Expense—Equipment		
14 Rent Expense		
15 Salaries Expense	9 7 0 0 00	
16 Supplies Expense		
17 Utilities Expense	1 4 0 0 00	
18 Totals	123 1 5 0 00	123 1 5 0 00
19		

	ADJUSTED TRIAL BALANCE		INCOME STATEMENT		BALANCE SHEET		
	DEBIT	CREDIT	DEBIT	CREDIT	DEBIT	CREDIT	
1	77 200 00				77 200 00		
2	12 000 00				12 000 00		
3	4 100 00				4 100 00		
4	12 000 00				12 000 00		
5	60 000 00				60 000 00		
6		1 200 00				1 200 00	
7		12 000 00				12 000 00	
8		108 000 00				108 000 00	
9	7 200 00				7 200 00		
10		79 500 00		79 500 00			
11	2 400 00		2 400 00				
12	1 200 00		1 200 00				
13	16 800 00		16 800 00				
14	6 000 00		6 000 00				
15	1 800 00		1 800 00				
16	200 700 00	200 700 00	28 200 00	79 500 00	172 500 00	121 200 00	
17			51 300 00			51 300 00	
18			79 500 00	79 500 00	172 500 00	172 500 00	
19							

Problem Set B

Completing the worksheet.

The trial balance of Torres Company as of February 28, 2013, appears below.

◀   **Problem 5.1B**
Objectives 1, 2, 3

Torres Company
Worksheet (Partial)
Month Ended February 28, 2013

	ACCOUNT NAME	TRIAL BALANCE		ADJUSTMENTS	
		DEBIT	CREDIT	DEBIT	CREDIT
1	Cash	36 500 00			
2	Accounts Receivable	3 200 00			
3	Supplies	2 100 00			
4	Prepaid Rent	12 000 00			
5	Equipment	23 000 00			
6	Accumulated Depreciation—Equipment				
7	Accounts Payable		6 000 00		
8	Paul Torres, Capital		49 250 00		
9	Paul Torres, Drawing	1 500 00			
10	Fees Income		27 000 00		
11	Depreciation Expense—Equipment				
12	Rent Expense				
13	Salaries Expense	3 150 00			
14	Supplies Expense				
15	Utilities Expense	800 00			
16	Totals	82 250 00	82 250 00		
17					

INSTRUCTIONS

1. Record the trial balance in the Trial Balance section of the worksheet.

2. Complete the worksheet by making the following adjustments: supplies on hand at the end of the month, $1,100; expired rent, $1,000; depreciation expense for the period, $500.

Analyze: Why do you think the account *Accumulated Depreciation—Equipment* has a zero balance on the trial balance shown?

Problem 5.2B ▶ **Reconstructing a partial worksheet.**

Objectives 1, 2, 3

The adjusted trial balance of Glenn Brantley, Attorney-at-Law, as of November 30, 2013, after the company had completed the first month of operations, appears below.
    Appropriate adjustments have been made for the following items:

a. Supplies used during the month, $7,200.

b. Expired rent for the month, $6,800.

c. Depreciation expense for the month, $1,100.

Glenn Brantley, Attorney-at-Law Adjusted Trial Balance Month Ended November 30, 2013		
Account Name	**Debit**	**Credit**
Cash	70,100	
Accounts Receivable	17,000	
Supplies	13,600	
Prepaid Rent	81,600	
Equipment	132,000	
Accumulated Depreciation—Equipment		1,100
Accounts Payable		34,000
Glenn Brantley, Capital		160,000
Glenn Brantley, Drawing	12,000	
Fees Income		171,400
Depreciation Expense—Equipment	1,100	
Rent Expense	6,800	
Salaries Expense	21,600	
Supplies Expense	7,200	
Utilities Expense	3,500	
Totals	366,500	366,500

INSTRUCTIONS

1. Record the adjusted trial balance in the Adjusted Trial Balance columns of the worksheet.

2. Prepare the adjusting entries in the Adjustments columns.

3. Complete the Trial Balance columns of the worksheet prior to making the adjusting entries.

Analyze: Which contra asset account is on the adjusted trial balance?

Problem 5.3B ▶ **Preparing financial statements from the worksheet.**

Objective 4

The completed worksheet for JT's Accounting Services for the month ended December 31, 2013, appears on pages 150–151.

INSTRUCTIONS

1. Prepare an income statement.

2. Prepare a statement of owner's equity. The owner made no additional investments during the month.

3. Prepare a balance sheet.

Analyze: By what total amount did the value of assets reported on the balance sheet decrease due to the adjusting entries?

Preparing a worksheet and financial statements, journalizing adjusting entries, and posting to ledger accounts.

◀ **Problem 5.4B**

**Objectives
1, 2, 3, 4, 5**

Raul Rojas owns Rojas Estate Planning and Investments. The trial balance of the firm for June 30, 2013, the first month of operations, is shown below.

	Rojas Estate Planning and Investments					
	Worksheet (Partial)					
	Month Ended June 30, 2013					
ACCOUNT NAME	TRIAL BALANCE		ADJUSTMENTS			
	DEBIT	CREDIT	DEBIT		CREDIT	
1 Cash	19 7 0 0 00					
2 Accounts Receivable	6 1 0 0 00					
3 Supplies	7 6 0 0 00					
4 Prepaid Advertising	14 4 0 0 00					
5 Prepaid Rent	36 0 0 0 00					
6 Equipment	48 0 0 0 00					
7 Accumulated Depreciation—Equipment						
8 Accounts Payable		10 8 0 0 00				
9 Paul Rojas, Capital		60 1 0 0 00				
10 Paul Rojas, Drawing	4 0 0 0 00					
11 Fees Income		73 8 0 0 00				
12 Advertising Expense						
13 Depreciation Expense—Equipment						
14 Rent Expense						
15 Salaries Expense	7 6 0 0 00					
16 Supplies Expense						
17 Utilities Expense	1 3 0 0 00					
18 Totals	144 7 0 0 00	144 7 0 0 00				
19						

INSTRUCTIONS

1. Complete the worksheet for the month.

2. Prepare an income statement, statement of owner's equity, and balance sheet. No additional investments were made by the owner during the month.

3. Journalize and post the adjusting entries. Use 3 for the journal page number. Use the account numbers provided in Problem 5.4A.

End-of-month adjustments must account for the following:

a. The supplies were purchased on June 1, 2013; inventory of supplies on June 30, 2013, showed a value of $3,000.

b. The prepaid advertising contract was signed on June 1, 2013, and covers a four-month period.

c. Rent of $3,000 expired during the month.

d. Depreciation is computed using the straight-line method. The equipment has an estimated useful life of five years with no salvage value.

Analyze: Why are the costs that reduce the value of equipment not directly posted to the asset account Equipment?

JT's Accounting Services
Worksheet
Month Ended December 31, 2013

	ACCOUNT NAME	TRIAL BALANCE DEBIT	TRIAL BALANCE CREDIT	ADJUSTMENTS DEBIT	ADJUSTMENTS CREDIT	
1	Cash	33 9 0 0 00				
2	Accounts Receivable	4 4 0 0 00				
3	Supplies	3 0 0 0 00			(a) 1 2 0 0 00	
4	Prepaid Advertising	8 0 0 0 00			(b) 1 6 0 0 00	
5	Fixtures	36 0 0 0 00				
6	Accumulated Depreciation—Fixtures				(c) 6 0 0 00	
7	Accounts Payable		15 0 0 0 00			
8	Jason Taylor, Capital		60 0 0 0 00			
9	Jason Taylor, Drawing	6 0 0 0 00				
10	Fees Income		62 6 6 0 00			
11	Advertising Expense			(b) 1 6 0 0 00		
12	Depreciation Expense—Fixtures			(c) 6 0 0 00		
13	Rent Expense	7 0 0 0 00				
14	Salaries Expense	37 2 0 0 00				
15	Supplies Expense			(a) 1 2 0 0 00		
16	Utilities Expense	2 1 6 0 00				
17	Totals	137 6 6 0 00	137 6 6 0 00	3 4 0 0 00	3 4 0 0 00	
18	Net Income					
19						
20						

Critical Thinking Problem 5.1

The Effect of Adjustments

Assume you are the accountant for Thompson Industries. Robert Thompson, the owner of the company, is in a hurry to receive the financial statements for the year ended December 31, 2013, and asks you how soon they will be ready. You tell him you have just completed the trial balance and are getting ready to prepare the adjusting entries. Mr. Thompson tells you not to waste time preparing adjusting entries but to complete the worksheet without them and prepare the financial statements based on the data in the trial balance. According to him, the adjusting entries will not make that much difference. The trial balance shows the following account balances:

Prepaid Rent	$ 42,000
Supplies	18,000
Building	420,000
Accumulated Depreciation—Building	33,600

If the income statement were prepared using trial balance amounts, the net income would be $165,500.

A review of the company's records reveals the following information:

1. Rent of $42,000 was paid on July 1, 2013, for 12 months.

2. Purchases of supplies during the year totaled $18,000. An inventory of supplies taken at year-end showed supplies on hand of $3,500.

3. The building was purchased three years ago and has an estimated life of 25 years.

4. No adjustments have been made to any of the accounts during the year.

Write a memo to Mr. Thompson explaining the effect on the financial statements of omitting the adjustments. Indicate the change to net income that results from the adjusting entries.

ADJUSTED TRIAL BALANCE		INCOME STATEMENT		BALANCE SHEET		
DEBIT	CREDIT	DEBIT	CREDIT	DEBIT	CREDIT	
33 9 0 0 00				33 9 0 0 00		1
4 4 0 0 00				4 4 0 0 00		2
1 8 0 0 00				1 8 0 0 00		3
6 4 0 0 00				6 4 0 0 00		4
36 0 0 0 00				36 0 0 0 00		5
	6 0 0 00				6 0 0 00	6
	15 0 0 0 00				15 0 0 0 00	7
	60 0 0 0 00				60 0 0 0 00	8
6 0 0 0 00				6 0 0 0 00		9
	62 6 6 0 00		62 6 6 0 00			10
1 6 0 0 00		1 6 0 0 00				11
6 0 0 00		6 0 0 00				12
7 0 0 0 00		7 0 0 0 00				13
37 2 0 0 00		37 2 0 0 00				14
1 2 0 0 00		1 2 0 0 00				15
2 1 6 0 00		2 1 6 0 00				16
138 2 6 0 00	138 2 6 0 00	49 7 6 0 00	62 6 6 0 00	88 5 0 0 00	75 6 0 0 00	17
		12 9 0 0 00			12 9 0 0 00	18
		62 6 6 0 00	62 6 6 0 00	88 5 0 0 00	88 5 0 0 00	19
						20

Critical Thinking Problem 5.2

Worksheet and Financial Statements

The account balances for the Thatcher International Company on January 31, 2013, follow. The balances shown are after the first month of operations.

101	Cash	$36,950	401	Fees Income	$61,850
111	Accounts Receivable	6,800	511	Advertising Expense	3,000
121	Supplies	4,300	514	Depr. Expense—Equip.	0
131	Prepaid Insurance	30,000	517	Insurance Expense	0
141	Equipment	48,000	518	Rent Expense	5,000
142	Accum. Depr.—Equip.	0	519	Salaries Expense	13,400
202	Accounts Payable	12,000	520	Supplies Expense	0
301	Maggie Thatcher, Capital	80,000	523	Telephone Expense	700
302	Maggie Thatcher, Drawing	4,000	524	Utilities Expense	1,700

INSTRUCTIONS

1. Prepare the Trial Balance section of the worksheet.
2. Record the following adjustments in the Adjustments section of the worksheet:
   a. Supplies used during the month amounted to $2,100.
   b. The amount in the *Prepaid Insurance* account represents a payment made on January 1, 2013, for six months of insurance coverage.
   c. The equipment, purchased on January 1, 2013, has an estimated useful life of 10 years with no salvage value. The firm uses the straight-line method of depreciation.

3. Complete the worksheet.

4. Prepare an income statement, statement of owner's equity, and balance sheet (use the report form).

5. Record the balances in the general ledger accounts, then journalize and post the adjusting entries. Use 3 for the journal page number.

Analyze: If the useful life of the equipment had been 12 years instead of 10 years, how would net income have been affected?

BUSINESS CONNECTIONS

Understanding Adjustments

Managerial | FOCUS

1. A building owned by Amos Company was recently valued at $425,000 by a real estate expert. The president of the company is questioning the accuracy of the firm's latest balance sheet because it shows a book value of $275,000 for the building. How would you explain this situation to the president?

2. At the beginning of the year, Wilson Company purchased a new building and some expensive new machinery. An officer of the firm has asked you whether this purchase will affect the firm's year-end income statement. What answer would you give?

3. Suppose the president of a company where you work as an accountant questions whether it is worthwhile for you to spend time making adjustments at the end of each accounting period. How would you explain the value of the adjustments?

4. How does the worksheet help provide vital information to management?

Adjustments

Ethical | DILEMMA

The supplies adjustment records the supplies used for the month from a cupboard that is filled at various times of the month. Sally asks you to record a larger supplies adjustment than is indicated from the ending balance in the supplies cupboard. Sally wants to use these supplies at the nonprofit organization she attends. Would you record a higher supplies expense so Sally could take these extra supplies to her charitable organization?

Depreciation

Financial Statement | ANALYSIS

DuPont reported depreciation expense of $1,251 million on its consolidated financial statements for the period ended December 31, 2009. The following excerpt is taken from the company's consolidated balance sheet for the same year:

(Dollars in millions, except per share) December 31, 2009

Property, Plant and Equipment	$28,915
Less: Accumulated depreciation	17,821
Net property, plant, and equipment	11,094

Analyze:

1. What percentage of the original cost of property, plant, and equipment was depreciated *during* 2009?

2. What percentage of property, plant, and equipment cost was depreciated *as of* December 31, 2009?

3. If the company continued to record depreciation expense at this level each year, how many years remain until all assets would be fully depreciated? (Assume no salvage values.)

Analyze Online: Connect to the DuPont Web Site (www.dupont.com). Click on the *Investor Center* link to find information on quarterly earnings.

4. What is the most recent quarterly earnings statement presented? What period does the statement cover?

5. For the most recent quarter, what depreciation expense was reported?

Matching Expenses with Revenues

Mike Mincks is a building contractor. He and his customer have agreed that he will submit a bill to them when he is 25 percent complete, 50 percent complete, 75 percent complete, and 100 percent complete. For example, he has a $100,000 room addition. When he has completed 25 percent, he will bill his customer $25,000. The problem occurs when he is 40 percent complete, has incurred expenses but cannot yet bill his customer. How can his revenue and expenses match? Discuss in a group several ways that Mike's accountant could solve this problem. What accounts would be used?

Prepaid Insurance

Prepaid insurance is the most common adjusting entry for a company. Use google.com to do a search of the various insurance companies that provide a variety of insurances to business. Try business insurance companies. Which type of insurances do they offer a business?

Answers to **Self Reviews**

Answers to Section 1 Self Review

1. Entries made to update accounts at the end of an accounting period to include previously unrecorded items that belong to the period.
2. So that the financial statements can be prepared more efficiently.
3. To properly reflect the remaining cost to be used by the business (asset) and the amount already used by the business (expense).
4. b. *Rent Expense* is debited for $3,600. *Prepaid Rent* is credited for $3,600.
5. a. *Supplies Expense* is debited for $900. *Supplies* is credited for $900.
6. $28,000.

Answers to Section 2 Self Review

1. The worksheet is only a tool that aids in the preparation of financial statements. Any changes in account balances recorded on the worksheet are not shown in the general journal and the general ledger until the adjusting entries have been journalized and posted.
2. (a) Beginning owner's equity.
   (b) Net income or net loss for the period.
   (c) Additional investments by the owner for the period.
   (d) Withdrawals by the owner for the period.
   (e) Ending balance of owner's equity.
3. On a report form balance sheet, the liabilities and owner's equity are listed under the assets. On the account form, they are listed to the right of the assets.
4. b. contra asset account.
5. b. Balance Sheet Debit column.
6. $28,000. The adjustment for equipment depreciation is a debit to *Depreciation Expense* and a credit to *Accumulated Depreciation—Equipment.* The *Equipment* account is not changed.

Answers to Comprehensive Self Review

1. Debit column of the Balance Sheet section.
2. Credit balance.
3. Net income causes a net increase in owner's equity.
4. $4,250. Debit column of the Balance Sheet section.
5. To allocate the cost of the asset to operations during its expected useful life.

Closing Entries and the Postclosing Trial Balance

LEARNING OBJECTIVES

1. Journalize and post closing entries.
2. Prepare a postclosing trial balance.
3. Interpret financial statements.
4. Review the steps in the accounting cycle.
5. Define the accounting terms new to this chapter.

NEW TERMS

closing entries
income summary account

interpret
postclosing trial balance

www.carnival.com

The folks at Carnival Cruise Lines have made it their business to help people enjoy their leisure time. For nearly 40 years Carnival has made luxurious ocean cruising a reasonable vacation option for many individuals. Often, for under $100 per person per day (about the cost 25 years ago), passengers can enjoy a seven-day Caribbean cruise on a ship with soaring atriums, expansive spas, children's facilities, and double promenades offering a myriad of entertainment venues.

Since the TSS *Mardi Gras* made its first voyage in 1972, Carnival Corporation has grown to become the most popular cruise line in the world, attracting four million guests annually. Carnival Cruise Lines is the flagship company of Carnival Corporation & plc, the largest cruise vacation group in the world, with a portfolio of cruise brands in North America, Europe, Australia, and Asia. Headquartered in Miami, Florida, and London, England, Carnival Corporation & plc generated $13.2 billion in revenues in 2009 and realized a total net income of over $1.8 billion.

thinking critically

How do Carnival's managers use financial statements to evaluate performance? How might these evaluations affect business policies or strategies?

SECTION OBJECTIVE

>> 1. **Journalize and post closing entries.**

WHY IT'S IMPORTANT
A business ends its accounting cycle at a given point in time. The closing process prepares the accounting records for the beginning of a new accounting cycle.

TERMS TO LEARN

closing entries
Income Summary account

Closing Entries

In Chapter 5, we discussed the worksheet and the adjusting entries. In this chapter, you will learn about closing entries.

The Closing Process

The seventh step in the accounting cycle is to journalize and post closing entries. **Closing entries** are journal entries that:

- transfer the results of operations (net income or net loss) to owner's equity,
- reduce revenue, expense, and drawing account balances to zero.

THE INCOME SUMMARY ACCOUNT

The **Income Summary account** is a special owner's equity account that is used only in the closing process to summarize results of operations. *Income Summary* has a zero balance after the closing process, and it remains with a zero balance until after the closing procedure for the next period.

FIGURE 6.1 Worksheet for Wells' Consulting Services

		Wells' Consulting Services				
		Worksheet				
		Month Ended December 31, 2013				
	ACCOUNT NAME	TRIAL BALANCE		ADJUSTMENTS		
		DEBIT	CREDIT	DEBIT		CREDIT
1	Cash	111 350 00				
2	Accounts Receivable	5 000 00				
3	Supplies	1 500 00			(a)	500 00
4	Prepaid Rent	8 000 00			(b)	4 000 00
5	Equipment	11 000 00				
6	Accum. Dep.—Equipment				(c)	1 83 00
7	Accounts Payable		3 500 00			
8	Carolyn Wells, Capital		100 000 00			
9	Carolyn Wells, Drawing	5 000 00				
10	Fees Income		47 000 00			
11	Salaries Expense	8 000 00				
12	Utilities Expense	650 00				
13	Supplies Expense			(a) 500 00		
14	Rent Expense			(b) 4 000 00		
15	Dep. Expense—Equipment			(c) 1 83 00		
16						
17	Totals	150 500 00	150 500 00	4 683 00		4 683 00
18	Net Income					
19						

Income Summary is classified as a temporary owner's equity account. Other names for this account are *Revenue and Expense Summary* and *Income and Expense Summary*.

STEPS IN THE CLOSING PROCESS

>>1. OBJECTIVE
Journalize and post closing entries.

There are four steps in the closing process:

1. Transfer the balance of the revenue account to the *Income Summary* account.
2. Transfer the expense account balances to the *Income Summary* account.
3. Transfer the balance of the *Income Summary* account to the owner's capital account.
4. Transfer the balance of the drawing account to the owner's capital account.

The worksheet contains the data necessary to make the closing entries. Refer to Figure 6.1 as you study each closing entry.

STEP 1: TRANSFER REVENUE ACCOUNT BALANCES

On December 31, the worksheet for Wells' Consulting Services shows one revenue account, *Fees Income.* It has a credit balance of $47,000. To *close* an account means to reduce its balance to zero. In the general journal, enter a debit of $47,000 to close the *Fees Income* account. To balance the journal entry, enter a credit of $47,000 to the *Income Summary* account. This closing entry transfers the total revenue for the period to the *Income Summary* account and reduces the balance of the revenue account to zero.

The analysis of this closing entry is shown on the next page. In this chapter, the visual analyses will show the beginning balances in all T accounts in order to illustrate closing entries.

ADJUSTED TRIAL BALANCE		INCOME STATEMENT		BALANCE SHEET		
DEBIT	CREDIT	DEBIT	CREDIT	DEBIT	CREDIT	
111 3 5 0 00				111 3 5 0 00		1
5 0 0 0 00				5 0 0 0 00		2
1 0 0 0 00				1 0 0 0 00		3
4 0 0 0 00				4 0 0 0 00		4
11 0 0 0 00				11 0 0 0 00		5
	1 8 3 00				1 8 3 00	6
	3 5 0 0 00				3 5 0 0 00	7
	100 0 0 0 00				100 0 0 0 00	8
5 0 0 0 00				5 0 0 0 00		9
	47 0 0 0 00		47 0 0 0 00			10
8 0 0 0 00		8 0 0 0 00				11
6 5 0 00		6 5 0 00				12
5 0 0 00		5 0 0 00				13
4 0 0 0 00		4 0 0 0 00				14
1 8 3 00		1 8 3 00				15
						16
150 6 8 3 00	150 6 8 3 00	13 3 3 3 00	47 0 0 0 00	137 3 5 0 00	103 6 8 3 00	17
		33 6 6 7 00			33 6 6 7 00	18
		47 0 0 0 00	47 0 0 0 00	137 3 5 0 00	137 3 5 0 00	19

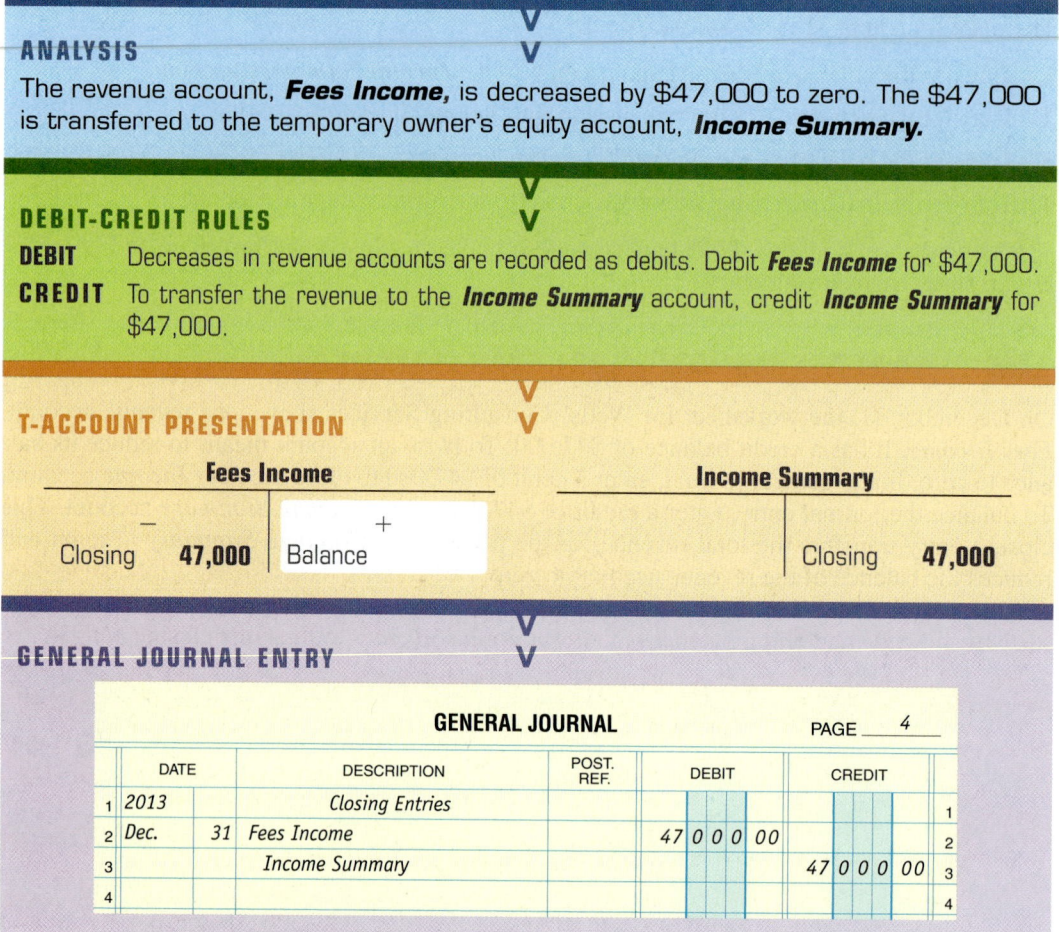

CLOSING ENTRY

First Closing Entry—Close Revenue to Income Summary

ANALYSIS

The revenue account, *Fees Income*, is decreased by $47,000 to zero. The $47,000 is transferred to the temporary owner's equity account, *Income Summary.*

DEBIT-CREDIT RULES

DEBIT   Decreases in revenue accounts are recorded as debits. Debit *Fees Income* for $47,000.

CREDIT   To transfer the revenue to the *Income Summary* account, credit *Income Summary* for $47,000.

T-ACCOUNT PRESENTATION

Fees Income		Income Summary
− +		
Closing **47,000** Balance		Closing **47,000**

GENERAL JOURNAL ENTRY

GENERAL JOURNAL   PAGE ___4___

	DATE	DESCRIPTION	POST. REF.	DEBIT	CREDIT	
1	2013	Closing Entries				1
2	Dec. 31	Fees Income		47 0 0 0 00		2
3		Income Summary			47 0 0 0 00	3
4						4

Write "Closing Entries" in the Description column of the general journal on the line above the first closing entry.

> Safeway Inc. reported sales of $40.8 billion for the fiscal year ended December 31, 2009. To close the revenue, the company would debit the *Sales* account and credit the *Income Summary* account.

STEP 2: TRANSFER EXPENSE ACCOUNT BALANCES

The Income Statement section of the worksheet for Wells' Consulting Services lists five expense accounts. Since expense accounts have debit balances, enter a credit in each account to reduce its balance to zero. Debit the total of the expenses, $13,333, to the *Income Summary* account. This closing entry transfers total expenses to the *Income Summary* account and reduces the balances of the expense accounts to zero. This is a compound journal entry; it has more than one credit.

CLOSING ENTRY

Second Closing Entry—Close Expenses to Income Summary

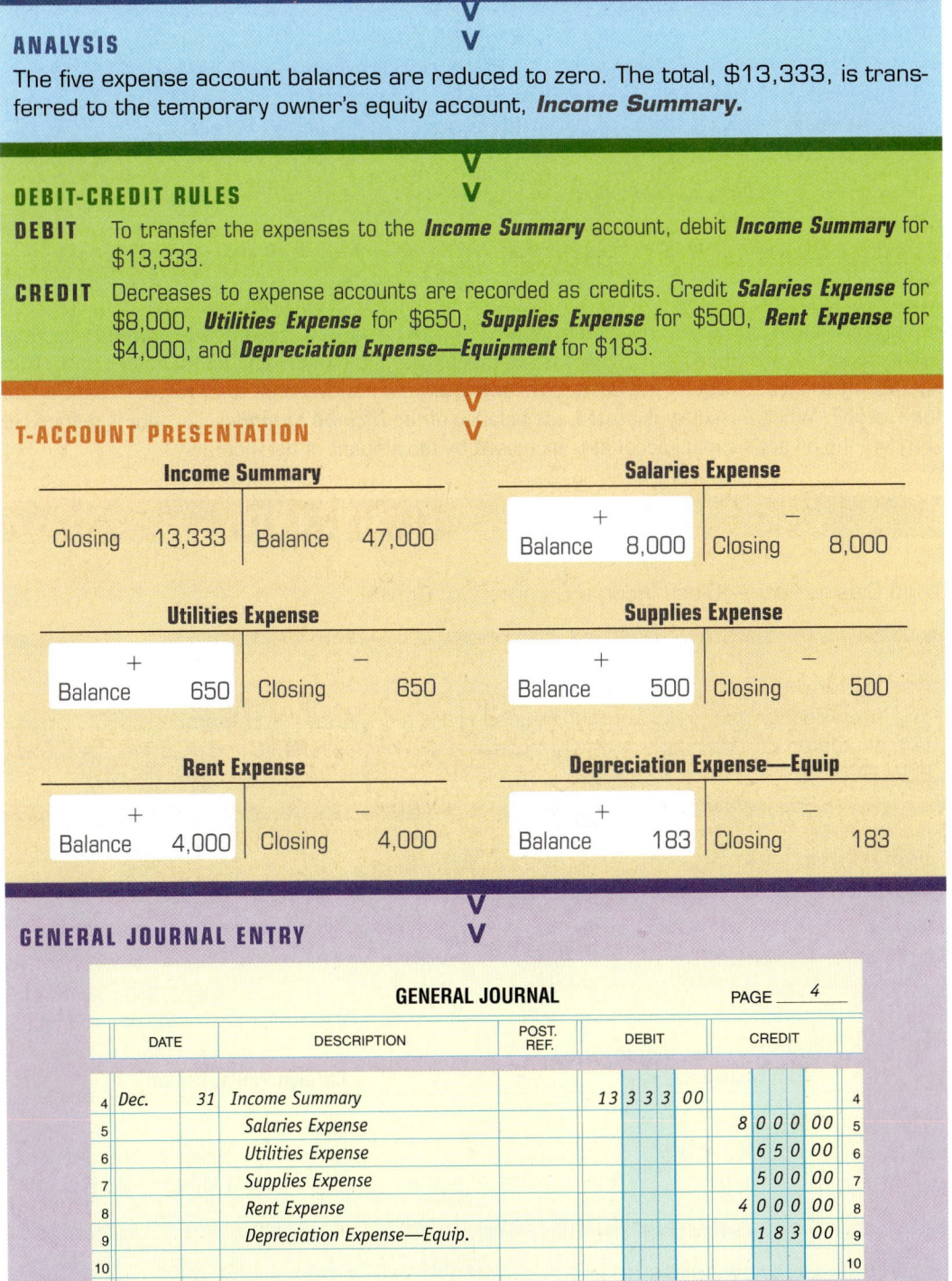

ANALYSIS

The five expense account balances are reduced to zero. The total, $13,333, is transferred to the temporary owner's equity account, **Income Summary.**

DEBIT-CREDIT RULES

DEBIT   To transfer the expenses to the **Income Summary** account, debit **Income Summary** for $13,333.

CREDIT   Decreases to expense accounts are recorded as credits. Credit **Salaries Expense** for $8,000, **Utilities Expense** for $650, **Supplies Expense** for $500, **Rent Expense** for $4,000, and **Depreciation Expense—Equipment** for $183.

T-ACCOUNT PRESENTATION

Income Summary	
Closing 13,333	Balance 47,000

Salaries Expense	
+	−
Balance 8,000	Closing 8,000

Utilities Expense	
+	−
Balance 650	Closing 650

Supplies Expense	
+	−
Balance 500	Closing 500

Rent Expense	
+	−
Balance 4,000	Closing 4,000

Depreciation Expense—Equip	
+	−
Balance 183	Closing 183

GENERAL JOURNAL ENTRY

GENERAL JOURNAL   PAGE ___4___

	DATE		DESCRIPTION	POST. REF.	DEBIT	CREDIT	
4	Dec.	31	Income Summary		13 3 3 3 00		4
5			Salaries Expense			8 0 0 0 00	5
6			Utilities Expense			6 5 0 00	6
7			Supplies Expense			5 0 0 00	7
8			Rent Expense			4 0 0 0 00	8
9			Depreciation Expense—Equip.			1 8 3 00	9
10							10

recall

Revenue
Revenue increases owner's equity.

recall

Expenses
Expenses decrease owner's equity.

After the second closing entry, the **Income Summary** account reflects all of the entries in the Income Statement columns of the worksheet.

	Income Summary	
Dr.		**Cr.**
Closing 13,333		Closing 47,000
		Balance 33,667

For the year ended December 31, 2009, operating expenses for Safeway, Inc., totaled $10.3 million. At the end of the year, accountants for Safeway, Inc. transferred the balances of all expense accounts to the *Income Summary* account.

STEP 3: TRANSFER NET INCOME OR NET LOSS TO OWNER'S EQUITY

The next step in the closing process is to transfer the balance of *Income Summary* to the owner's capital account. After the revenue and expense accounts are closed, the *Income Summary* account has a credit balance of $33,667, which is net income for the month. The journal entry to transfer net income to owner's equity is a debit to *Income Summary* and a credit to *Carolyn Wells, Capital* for $33,667. When this entry is posted, the balance of the *Income Summary* account is reduced to zero and the owner's capital account is increased by the amount of net income.

CLOSING ENTRY

Third Closing Entry—Close Income Summary to Capital

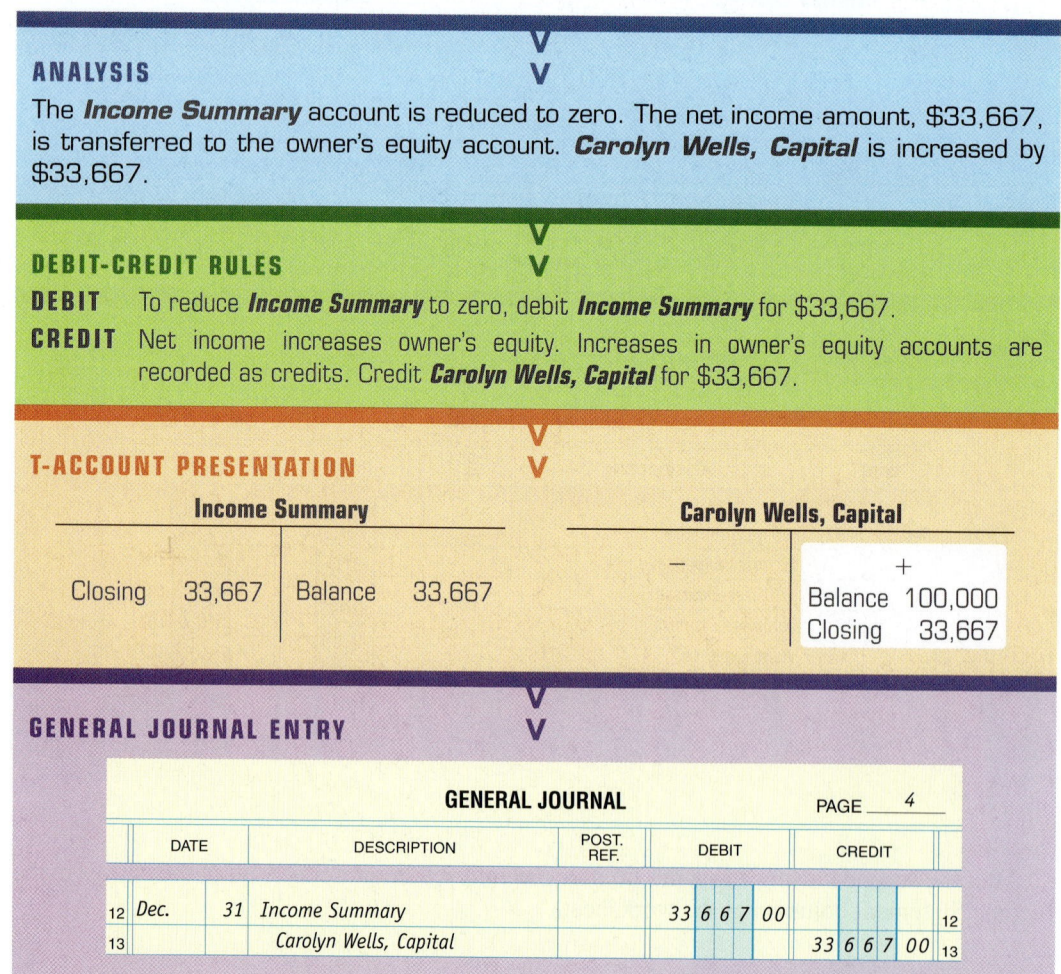

ANALYSIS

The *Income Summary* account is reduced to zero. The net income amount, $33,667, is transferred to the owner's equity account. *Carolyn Wells, Capital* is increased by $33,667.

DEBIT-CREDIT RULES

DEBIT To reduce *Income Summary* to zero, debit *Income Summary* for $33,667.

CREDIT Net income increases owner's equity. Increases in owner's equity accounts are recorded as credits. Credit *Carolyn Wells, Capital* for $33,667.

T-ACCOUNT PRESENTATION

Income Summary			
Closing 33,667		Balance 33,667	

Carolyn Wells, Capital	
−	+
	Balance 100,000
	Closing 33,667

GENERAL JOURNAL ENTRY

		GENERAL JOURNAL			PAGE ___4___
	DATE	DESCRIPTION	POST. REF.	DEBIT	CREDIT
12	Dec. 31	Income Summary		33 6 6 7 00		12
13		Carolyn Wells, Capital			33 6 6 7 00	13

After the third closing entry, the *Income Summary* account has a zero balance. The summarized expenses ($13,333) and revenue ($47,000) have been transferred to the owner's equity account ($33,667 net income).

Income Summary			Carolyn Wells, Capital	
Dr.	**Cr.**		**Dr.**	**Cr.**
			−	+
Expenses 13,333	Revenue 47,000			Balance 100,000
Closing 33,667				Net Inc. 33,667
Balance 0				Balance 133,667

STEP 4: TRANSFER THE DRAWING ACCOUNT BALANCE TO CAPITAL

You will recall that withdrawals are funds taken from the business by the owner for personal use. Withdrawals are recorded in the drawing account. Withdrawals are not expenses of the business. They do not affect net income or net loss.

Withdrawals appear in the statement of owner's equity as a deduction from capital. Therefore, the drawing account is closed directly to the capital account.

When this entry is posted, the balance of the drawing account is reduced to zero and the owner's capital account is decreased by the amount of the withdrawals.

recall

Withdrawals
Withdrawals decrease owner's equity.

CLOSING ENTRY

Fourth Closing Entry—Close Withdrawals to Capital

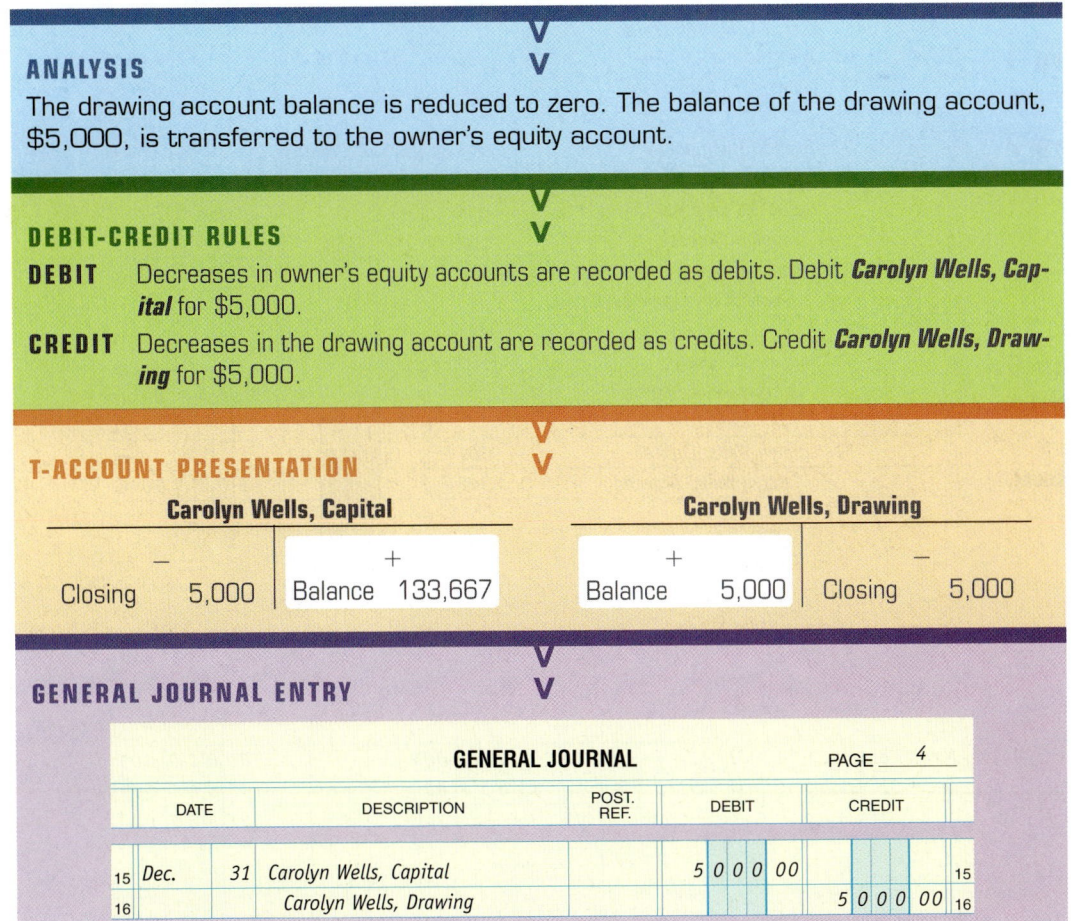

ANALYSIS
The drawing account balance is reduced to zero. The balance of the drawing account, $5,000, is transferred to the owner's equity account.

DEBIT-CREDIT RULES

DEBIT   Decreases in owner's equity accounts are recorded as debits. Debit *Carolyn Wells, Capital* for $5,000.

CREDIT   Decreases in the drawing account are recorded as credits. Credit *Carolyn Wells, Drawing* for $5,000.

T-ACCOUNT PRESENTATION

Carolyn Wells, Capital			Carolyn Wells, Drawing	
−	+		+	−
Closing 5,000	Balance 133,667		Balance 5,000	Closing 5,000

GENERAL JOURNAL ENTRY

	GENERAL JOURNAL			PAGE 4

DATE		DESCRIPTION	POST. REF.	DEBIT	CREDIT
15	Dec. 31	Carolyn Wells, Capital		5 0 0 0 00	
16		Carolyn Wells, Drawing			5 0 0 0 00

The new balance of the *Carolyn Wells, Capital* account agrees with the amount listed in the Owner's Equity section of the balance sheet.

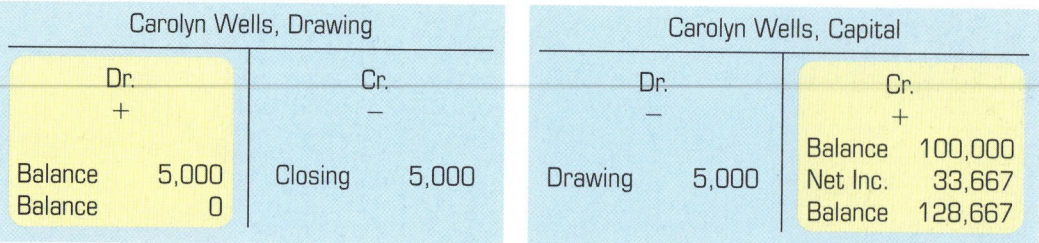

Carolyn Wells, Drawing				Carolyn Wells, Capital			
Dr.		**Cr.**		**Dr.**		**Cr.**	
+		**−**		**−**		**+**	
						Balance	100,000
Balance	5,000	Closing	5,000	Drawing	5,000	Net Inc.	33,667
Balance	0					Balance	128,667

Figure 6.2 shows the general journal and general ledger for Wells' Consulting Services after the closing entries are recorded and posted. Note that:

■ "Closing" is entered in the Description column of the ledger accounts;

■ the balance of *Carolyn Wells, Capital* agrees with the amount shown on the balance sheet for December 31;

■ the ending balances of the drawing, revenue, and expense accounts are zero.

This example shows the closing process at the end of one month. Usually businesses make closing entries at the end of the fiscal year only.

FIGURE 6.2

Closing Process Completed: General Journal and General Ledger

GENERAL JOURNAL   PAGE ___4___

	DATE		DESCRIPTION	POST. REF.	DEBIT	CREDIT	
1	2013		*Closing Entries*				1
2	Dec.	31	Fees Income	401	47 0 0 0 00		2
3			Income Summary	309		47 0 0 0 00	3
4							4
5		31	Income Summary	309	13 3 3 3 00		5
6			Salaries Expense	511		8 0 0 0 00	6
7			Utilities Expense	514		6 5 0 00	7
8			Supplies Expense	517		5 0 0 00	8
9			Rent Expense	520		4 0 0 0 00	9
10			Depreciation Expense—Equip.	523		1 8 3 00	10
11							11
12		31	Income Summary	309	33 6 6 7 00		12
13			Carolyn Wells, Capital	301		33 6 6 7 00	13
14							14
15		31	Carolyn Wells, Capital	301	5 0 0 0 00		15
16			Carolyn Wells, Drawing	302		5 0 0 0 00	16
17							17

Step 1 Close revenue.

Step 2 Close expense accounts.

Step 3 Close Income Summary.

Step 4 Close Drawing account.

ACCOUNT _Carolyn Wells, Capital_   ACCOUNT NO. _301_

DATE		DESCRIPTION	POST. REF.	DEBIT	CREDIT	BALANCE DEBIT	BALANCE CREDIT
2013							
Nov.	6		J1		100 0 0 0 00		100 0 0 0 00
Dec.	31	Closing	J4		33 6 6 7 00		133 6 6 7 00
	31	Closing	J4	5 0 0 0 00			128 6 6 7 00

ACCOUNT Carolyn Wells, Drawing **ACCOUNT NO.** 302

DATE		DESCRIPTION	POST. REF.	DEBIT	CREDIT	BALANCE DEBIT	BALANCE CREDIT
2013							
Dec.	31		J2	5 000 00		5 000 00	
	31	Closing	J4		5 000 00	– 0 –	

ACCOUNT Income Summary **ACCOUNT NO.** 309

DATE		DESCRIPTION	POST. REF.	DEBIT	CREDIT	BALANCE DEBIT	BALANCE CREDIT
2013							
Dec.	31	Closing	J4		47 000 00		47 000 00
	31	Closing	J4	13 333 00			33 667 00
	31	Closing	J4	33 667 00			– 0 –

ACCOUNT Fees Income **ACCOUNT NO.** 401

DATE		DESCRIPTION	POST. REF.	DEBIT	CREDIT	BALANCE DEBIT	BALANCE CREDIT
2013							
Dec.	31		J2		36 000 00		36 000 00
	31		J2		11 000 00		47 000 00
	31	Closing	J4	47 000 00			– 0 –

ACCOUNT Salaries Expense **ACCOUNT NO.** 511

DATE		DESCRIPTION	POST. REF.	DEBIT	CREDIT	BALANCE DEBIT	BALANCE CREDIT
2013							
Dec.	31		J2	8 000 00		8 000 00	
	31	Closing	J4		8 000 00	– 0 –	

ACCOUNT Utilities Expense **ACCOUNT NO.** 514

DATE		DESCRIPTION	POST. REF.	DEBIT	CREDIT	BALANCE DEBIT	BALANCE CREDIT
2013							
Dec.	31		J2	650 00		650 00	
	31	Closing	J4		650 00	– 0 –	

ACCOUNT Supplies Expense **ACCOUNT NO.** 517

DATE		DESCRIPTION	POST. REF.	DEBIT	CREDIT	BALANCE DEBIT	BALANCE CREDIT
2013							
Dec.	31	Adjusting	J3	500 00		500 00	
	31	Closing	J4		500 00	– 0 –	

ACCOUNT _Rent Expense_   **ACCOUNT NO.** _520_

DATE		DESCRIPTION	POST. REF.	DEBIT	CREDIT	BALANCE DEBIT	BALANCE CREDIT
2013							
Dec.	31	Adjusting	J3	4 0 0 0 00		4 0 0 0 00	
	31	Closing	J4		4 0 0 0 00	– 0 –	

ACCOUNT _Depreciation Expense—Equipment_   **ACCOUNT NO.** _523_

DATE		DESCRIPTION	POST. REF.	DEBIT	CREDIT	BALANCE DEBIT	BALANCE CREDIT
2013							
Dec.	31	Adjusting	J3	1 8 3 00		1 8 3 00	
	31	Closing	J4		1 8 3 00	– 0 –	

You have now seen seven steps of the accounting cycle. The steps we have discussed are (1) analyze transactions, (2) journalize the transactions, (3) post the transactions, (4) prepare a worksheet, (5) prepare financial statements, (6) record adjusting entries, and (7) record closing entries. Two steps remain. They are (8) prepare a postclosing trial balance, and (9) interpret the financial information.

Section **1** Self Review

QUESTIONS

1. What are the four steps in the closing process?

2. What is the journal entry to close the drawing account?

3. How is the **Income Summary** account classified?

EXERCISES

4. After the closing entries are posted, which account normally has a balance other than zero?

 a. _Capital_

 b. _Fees Income_

 c. _Income Summary_

 d. _Rent Expense_

5. After closing, which accounts have zero balances?

 a. asset and liability accounts

 b. liability and capital accounts

 c. liability, drawing, and expense accounts

 d. revenue, drawing, and expense accounts

ANALYSIS

6. The business owner removes supplies that are worth $450 from the company stockroom. She intends to take them home for personal use. What effect will this have on the company's net income?

(Answers to Section 1 Self Review are on page 184.)

>> 2. **Prepare a postclosing trial balance.**

WHY IT'S IMPORTANT

The postclosing trial balance helps the accountant identify any errors in the closing process.

>> 3. **Interpret financial statements.**

WHY IT'S IMPORTANT

Financial statements contain information that can impact and drive operating decisions and plans for the future of the company.

>> 4. **Review the steps in the accounting cycle.**

WHY IT'S IMPORTANT

Proper treatment of data as it flows through the accounting system ensures reliable financial reports.

TERMS TO LEARN

interpret
postclosing trial balance

Using Accounting Information

In this section, we will complete the accounting cycle for Wells' Consulting Services.

Preparing the Postclosing Trial Balance

The eighth step in the accounting cycle is to prepare the postclosing trial balance, or *after-closing trial balance*. The **postclosing trial balance** is a statement that is prepared to prove the equality of total debits and credits. It is the last step in the end-of-period routine. The postclosing trial balance verifies that:

■ total debits equal total credits;

■ revenue, expense, and drawing accounts have zero balances.

On the postclosing trial balance, the only accounts with balances are the permanent accounts:

■ assets

■ liabilities

■ owner's equity

Figure 6.3 shows the postclosing trial balance for Wells' Consulting Services.

FIGURE 6.3

Postclosing Trial Balance

Wells' Consulting Services Postclosing Trial Balance December 31, 2013		
ACCOUNT NAME	DEBIT	CREDIT
Cash	111 350 00	
Accounts Receivable	5 000 00	
Supplies	1 000 00	
Prepaid Rent	4 000 00	
Equipment	11 000 00	
Accumulated Depreciation—Equipment		183 00
Accounts Payable		3 500 00
Carolyn Wells, Capital		128 667 00
Totals	132 350 00	132 350 00

>>2. OBJECTIVE

Prepare a postclosing trial balance.

FINDING AND CORRECTING ERRORS

If the postclosing trial balance does not balance, there are errors in the accounting records. Find and correct the errors before continuing. Refer to Chapter 3 for tips on how to find common errors. Also use the audit trail to trace data through the accounting records to find errors.

>>3. OBJECTIVE

Interpret financial statements.

Interpreting the Financial Statements

The ninth and last step in the accounting cycle is interpreting the financial statements. Management needs timely and accurate financial information to operate the business successfully. To **interpret** the financial statements means to understand and explain the meaning and importance of information in accounting reports. Information in the financial statements provides answers to many questions:

- What is the cash balance?
- How much do customers owe the business?
- How much does the business owe suppliers?
- What is the profit or loss?

> Managers of The Home Depot, Inc., use the corporation's financial statements to answer questions about the business. How much cash does our business have? What net earnings did our company report this year? For the fiscal year ended January 31, 2010, The Home Depot, Inc., reported an ending cash balance of $1.4 billion and net earnings of $2.7 billion.

Figure 6.4 shows the financial statements for Wells' Consulting Services at the end of its first accounting period. By interpreting these statements, management learns that:

- the cash balance is $111,350,
- customers owe $5,000 to the business,
- the business owes $3,500 to its suppliers,
- the profit was $33,667.

FIGURE 6.4

End-of-Month Financial
Statements

Wells' Consulting Services
Income Statement
Month Ended December 31, 2013

Revenue		
Fees Income		47 000 00
Expenses		
Salaries Expense	8 000 00	
Utilities Expense	650 00	
Supplies Expense	500 00	
Rent Expense	4 000 00	
Depreciation Expense—Equipment	183 00	
Total Expenses		13 333 00
Net Income for the Month		33 667 00

Wells' Consulting Services
Statement of Owner's Equity
Month Ended December 31, 2013

Carolyn Wells, Capital, December 1, 2013		100 000 00
Net Income for December	33 667 00	
Less Withdrawals for December	5 000 00	
Increase in Capital		28 667 00
Carolyn Wells, Capital, December 31, 2013		128 667 00

Wells' Consulting Services
Balance Sheet
December 31, 2013

Assets		
Cash		111 350 00
Accounts Receivable		5 000 00
Supplies		1 000 00
Prepaid Rent		4 000 00
Equipment	11 000 00	
Less Accumulated Depreciation	183 00	10 817 00
Total Assets		132 167 00
Liabilities and Owner's Equity		
Liabilities		
Accounts Payable		3 500 00
Owner's Equity		
Carolyn Wells, Capital		128 667 00
Total Liabilities and Owner's Equity		132 167 00

ABOUT
ACCOUNTING

Professional Consultants
Professionals in the
consulting field, such as
accountants and lawyers,
need to understand
accounting so they can bill
for services performed.
Because clients have
different billing rates
depending on the service
performed, specialized
software is used to manage
the paperwork and keep
track of the billings and
payments.

>>4. OBJECTIVE

Review the steps in the accounting cycle.

The Accounting Cycle

You have learned about the entire accounting cycle as you studied the financial affairs of Wells' Consulting Services during its first month of operations. Figure 6.5 summarizes the steps in the accounting cycle.

Step 1.   **Analyze transactions.** Analyze source documents to determine their effects on the basic accounting equation. The data about transactions appears on a variety of source documents such as:

- sales slips,
- purchase invoices,
- credit memorandums,
- check stubs.

Step 2.   **Journalize the transactions.** Record the effects of the transactions in a journal.

Step 3.   **Post the journal entries.** Transfer data from the journal to the general ledger accounts.

Step 4.   **Prepare a worksheet.** At the end of each period, prepare a worksheet.

- Use the Trial Balance section to prove the equality of debits and credits in the general ledger.
- Use the Adjustments section to enter changes in account balances that are needed to present an accurate and complete picture of the financial affairs of the business.
- Use the Adjusted Trial Balance section to verify the equality of debits and credits after the adjustments. Extend the amounts from the Adjusted Trial Balance section to the Income Statement and Balance Sheet sections.
- Use the Income Statement and Balance Sheet sections to prepare the financial statements.

Step 5.   **Prepare financial statements.** Prepare financial statements to report information to owners, managers, and other interested parties.

- The income statement shows the results of operations for the period.
- The statement of owner's equity reports the changes in the owner's financial interest during the period.
- The balance sheet shows the financial position of the business at the end of the period.

recall

The Accounting Cycle

The accounting cycle is a series of steps performed during each period to classify, record, and summarize data to produce needed financial information.

FIGURE 6.5

The Accounting Cycle

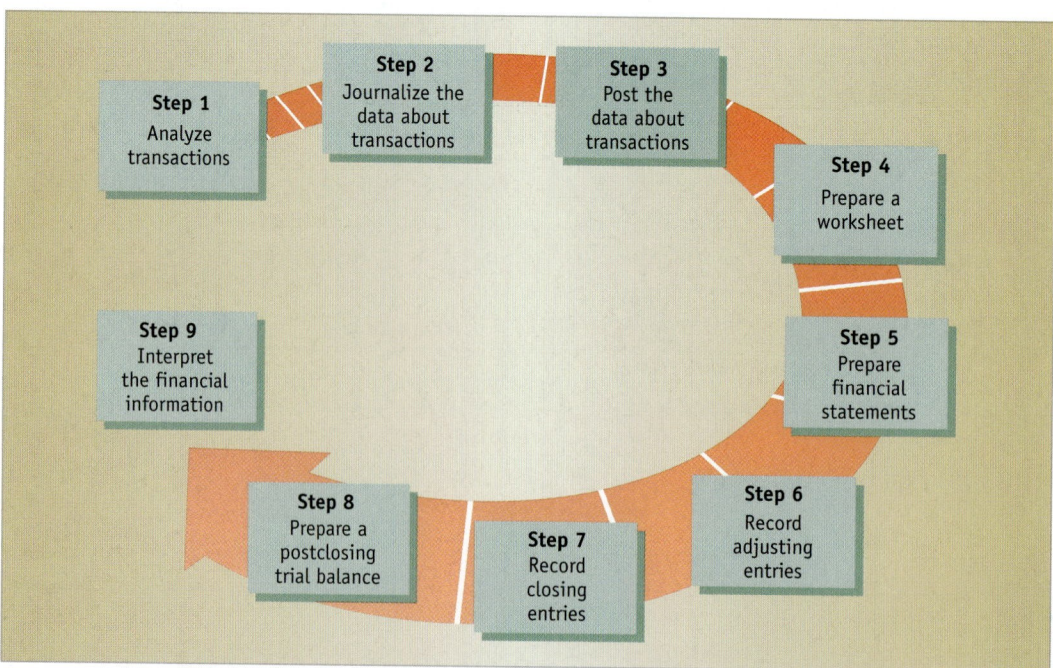

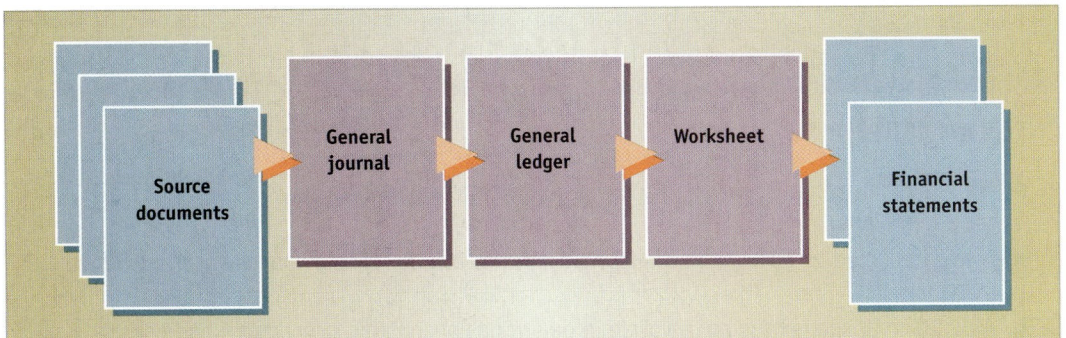

FIGURE 6.6

Flow of Data through a Simple
Accounting System

Step 6. **Record adjusting entries.** Use the worksheet to journalize and post adjusting entries. The adjusting entries are a permanent record of the changes in account balances shown on the worksheet.

Step 7. **Record closing entries.** Journalize and post the closing entries to:
- transfer net income or net loss to owner's equity;
- reduce the balances of the revenue, expense, and drawing accounts to zero.

Step 8. **Prepare a postclosing trial balance.** The postclosing trial balance shows that the general ledger is in balance after the closing entries are posted. It is also used to verify that there are zero balances in revenue, expense, and drawing accounts.

Step 9. **Interpret the financial information.** Use financial statements to understand and communicate financial information and to make decisions. Accountants, owners, managers, and other interested parties interpret financial statements by comparing such things as profit, revenue, and expenses from one accounting period to the next.

> In addition to financial statements, Adobe Systems Incorporated prepares a Financial Highlights report. This report lists total assets, revenue, net income, and the number of worldwide employees for the past five years.

After studying the accounting cycle of Wells' Consulting Services, you have an understanding of how data flows through a simple accounting system for a small business:

- Source documents are analyzed.
- Transactions are recorded in the general journal.
- Transactions are posted from the general journal to the general ledger.
- Financial information is proved, adjusted, and summarized on the worksheet.
- Financial information is reported on financial statements.

Figure 6.6 illustrates this data flow.

As you will learn in later chapters, some accounting systems have more complex records, procedures, and financial statements. However, the steps of the accounting cycle and the underlying accounting principles remain the same.

MANAGERIAL IMPLICATIONS

FINANCIAL INFORMATION

- Management needs timely and accurate financial information to control operations and make decisions.
- A well-designed and well-run accounting system provides reliable financial statements to management.
- Although management is not involved in day-to-day accounting procedures and end-of-period processes, the efficiency of the procedures affects the quality and promptness of the financial information that management receives.

THINKING CRITICALLY

If you owned or managed a business, how often would you want financial statements prepared? Why?

Monthly make changes needed in timely manner

Section **2** Self Review

QUESTIONS

1. What accounts appear on the postclosing trial balance?

2. What are the last three steps in the accounting cycle?

3. Why is a postclosing trial balance prepared?

EXERCISES

4. After the revenue and expense accounts are closed, *Income Summary* has a debit balance of $60,000. What does this figure represent?

   a. net profit of $60,000
   (b) net loss of $60,000
   c. owner's withdrawals of $60,000
   (d) increase in owner's equity of $60,000

5. Which of the following accounts will not appear on the postclosing trial balance?

   (a.) *J. T. Amos, Drawing*
   b. *Cash*
   c. *J. T. Amos, Capital*
   d. *Accounts Payable*

ANALYSIS

6. On which financial statement would you find the answer to each question?

   - What were the total fees earned this month? *Net Income Statement*
   - How much money is owed to suppliers? *Balance*

- Did the business make a profit? *Income*
- Is there enough cash to purchase new equipment? *Balance*
- What were the expenses? *Income*
- Do customers owe money to the business? *Balance*

(Answers to Section 2 Self Review are on page 185.)

REVIEW   Chapter Summary

After the worksheet and financial statements have been completed and adjusting entries have been journalized and posted, the closing entries are recorded and a postclosing trial balance is prepared.

Learning Objectives

1   Journalize and post closing entries.

Journalizing and posting the closing entries is the seventh step in the accounting cycle. Closing entries transfer the results of operations to owner's equity and reduce the balances of the revenue and expense accounts to zero. The worksheet provides the data necessary for the closing entries. A temporary owner's equity account, *Income Summary,* is used. There are four steps in the closing process:

1. The balance of the revenue account is transferred to the *Income Summary* account.

Debit *Revenue*

Credit *Income Summary*

2. The balances of the expense accounts are transferred to the *Income Summary* account.

Debit *Income Summary*

Credit *Expenses*

3. The balance of the *Income Summary* account—net income or net loss—is transferred to the owner's capital account.

If *Income Summary* has a credit balance:

Debit *Income Summary*

Credit *Owner's Capital*

If *Income Summary* has a debit balance:

Debit *Owner's Capital*

Credit *Income Summary*

4. The drawing account is closed to the owner's capital account.

Debit *Owner's Capital*

Credit *Drawing*

After the closing entries have been posted, the capital account reflects the results of operations for the period. The revenue and expense accounts, with zero balances, are ready to accumulate data for the next period.

2   Prepare a postclosing trial balance.

Preparing the postclosing trial balance is the eighth step in the accounting cycle. A postclosing trial balance is prepared to test the equality of total debit and credit balances in the general ledger after the adjusting and closing entries have been recorded. This report lists only permanent accounts open at the end of the period—asset, liability, and the owner's capital accounts. The temporary accounts—revenue, expenses, drawing, and *Income Summary*—apply only to one accounting period and do not appear on the postclosing trial balance.

3   Interpret financial statements.

The ninth step in the accounting cycle is interpreting the financial statements. Business decisions must be based on accurate and timely financial information.

4   Review the steps in the accounting cycle.

The accounting cycle consists of a series of steps that are repeated in each fiscal period. These steps are designed to classify, record, and summarize the data needed to produce financial information.

The steps of the accounting cycle are:

1. Analyze transactions.
2. Journalize the transactions.
3. Post the journal entries.
4. Prepare a worksheet.
5. Prepare financial statements.
6. Record adjusting entries.
7. Record closing entries.
8. Prepare a postclosing trial balance.
9. Interpret the financial information.

5   Define the accounting terms new to this chapter.

Glossary

Closing entries (p. 156) Journal entries that transfer the results of operations (net income or net loss) to owner's equity and reduce the revenue, expense, and drawing account balances to zero

Income Summary account (p. 156) A special owner's equity account that is used only in the closing process to summarize the results of operations

Interpret (p. 166) To understand and explain the meaning and importance of something (such as financial statements)

Postclosing trial balance (p. 165) A statement that is prepared to prove the equality of total debits and credits after the closing process is completed

Comprehensive **Self Review**

1. Is the following statement true or false? Why? "All owner's equity accounts appear on the postclosing trial balance."

2. What is the last step in the accounting cycle?

3. What three financial statements are prepared during the accounting cycle?

4. A firm has $56,000 in revenue for the period. Give the entry to close the **Fees Income** account.

5. A firm has the following expenses: **Rent Expense,** $3,600; **Salaries Expense,** $7,000; **Supplies Expense,** $1,500. Give the entry to close the expense accounts.

(Answers to Comprehensive Self Review are on page 185.)

Discussion Questions

1. Where does the accountant obtain the data needed for the closing entries?

2. How is the **Income Summary** account used in the closing procedure?

3. Why does the accountant record closing entries at the end of a period?

4. Where does the accountant obtain the data needed for the adjusting entries?

5. What three procedures are performed at the end of each accounting period before the financial information is interpreted?

6. Briefly describe the flow of data through a simple accounting system.

7. Name the steps of the accounting cycle.

8. What is the accounting cycle?

9. What accounts appear on a postclosing trial balance?

10. Why is a postclosing trial balance prepared?

APPLICATIONS

Exercises

Exercise 6.1    **Journalize closing entries.**

Objective 1

On December 31, 2013, the ledger of Davis Company contained the following account balances:

Cash	$32,000	Mesia Davis, Drawing	$25,000
Accounts Receivable	2,400	Fees Income	48,750
Supplies	1,600	Depreciation Expense	2,250

Equipment	25,000	Salaries Expense	16,000
Accumulated Depreciation	2,000	Supplies Expense	2,500
Accounts Payable	2,500	Telephone Expense	2,100
Mesia Davis, Capital	47,250	Utilities Expense	4,150

All the accounts have normal balances. Journalize the closing entries. Use 4 as the general journal page number.

Accounting cycle.

Following are the steps in the accounting cycle. Arrange the steps in the proper sequence.

1. Record closing entries.
2. Interpret the financial information.
3. Prepare a postclosing trial balance.
4. Prepare financial statements.
5. Prepare a worksheet.
6. Record adjusting entries.
7. Analyze transactions.
8. Journalize the transactions.
9. Post the journal entries.

◄ **Exercise 6.2**
Objective 4

Postclosing trial balance.

From the following list, identify the accounts that will appear on the postclosing trial balance.

◄ **Exercise 6.3**
Objective 2

ACCOUNTS

1. Cash
2. Accounts Receivable
3. Supplies
4. Equipment
5. Accumulated Depreciation
6. Accounts Payable
7. John Martin, Capital
8. John Martin, Drawing
9. Fees Income
10. Depreciation Expense
11. Salaries Expense
12. Supplies Expense
13. Utilities Expense

Financial statements.

◄ **Exercise 6.4**
Objective 3

Managers often consult financial statements for specific types of information. Indicate whether each of the following items would appear on the income statement, statement of owner's equity, or the balance sheet. Use *I* for the income statement, *E* for the statement of owner's equity, and *B* for the balance sheet. If an item appears on more than one statement, use all letters that apply to that item.

1. Accumulated depreciation on the firm's equipment
2. Amount of depreciation charged off on the firm's equipment during the period
3. Original cost of the firm's equipment
4. Book value of the firm's equipment
5. Total expenses for the period
6. Accounts payable of the business
7. Owner's withdrawals for the period
8. Cash on hand

9. Revenue earned during the period

10. Total assets of the business

11. Net income for the period

12. Owner's capital at the end of the period

13. Supplies on hand

14. Cost of supplies used during the period

15. Accounts receivable of the business

Exercise 6.5

Objective 1

▶ **Closing entries.**

The *Income Summary* and *Harold Gibson, Capital* accounts for Gibson Production Company at the end of its accounting period follow.

ACCOUNT __Income Summary__   ACCOUNT NO. __399__

DATE		DESCRIPTION	POST. REF.	DEBIT	CREDIT	BALANCE	
						DEBIT	CREDIT
2013							
Dec.	31	Closing	J4		65 0 0 0 00		65 0 0 0 00
	31	Closing	J4	34 9 0 0 00			30 1 0 0 00
	31	Closing	J4	30 1 0 0 00			– 0 –

ACCOUNT __Harold Gibson, Capital__   ACCOUNT NO. __301__

DATE		DESCRIPTION	POST. REF.	DEBIT	CREDIT	BALANCE	
						DEBIT	CREDIT
2013							
Dec.	1		J1		110 0 0 0 00		110 0 0 0 00
	31	Closing	J4		30 1 0 0 00		140 1 0 0 00
	31	Closing	J4	10 0 0 0 00			130 1 0 0 00

Complete the following statements:

1. Total revenue for the period is _____.

2. Total expenses for the period are _____.

3. Net income for the period is _____.

4. Owner's withdrawals for the period are _____.

Exercise 6.6

Objective 1

▶ **Closing entries.**

The ledger accounts of Rapid Speed Internet Company appear as follows on March 31, 2013:

ACCOUNT NO.	ACCOUNT	BALANCE
101	Cash	$70,000
111	Accounts Receivable	15,000
121	Supplies	9,600
131	Prepaid Insurance	24,000
141	Equipment	108,000
142	Accumulated Depreciation—Equipment	40,320
202	Accounts Payable	12,000
301	Gloria Bahamon, Capital	120,000
302	Gloria Bahamon, Drawing	12,000
401	Fees Income	325,000
510	Depreciation Expense—Equipment	20,160

511	Insurance Expense	10,400
514	Rent Expense	32,000
517	Salaries Expense	156,000
518	Supplies Expense	4,600
519	Telephone Expense	5,800
523	Utilities Expense	8,400

All accounts have normal balances. Journalize and post the closing entries. Use 4 as the page number for the general journal in journalizing the closing entries. Use account number 399 for the Income Summary Account.

Closing entries.

◄ **Exercise 6.7**
Objective 1

On December 31, the *Income Summary* account of Escobedo Company has a debit balance of $27,000 after revenue of $29,000 and expenses of $56,000 were closed to the account. *Rosa Escobedo, Drawing* has a debit balance of $3,000 and *Rosa Escobedo, Capital* has a credit balance of $48,000. Record the journal entries necessary to complete closing the accounts. What is the new balance of *Rosa Escobedo, Capital?*

Accounting cycle.

◄ **Exercise 6.8**
Objective 4

Complete a chart of the accounting cycle by writing the steps of the cycle in their proper sequence.

PROBLEMS

Problem Set A

Adjusting and closing entries.

◄ **Problem 6.1A**
Objective 1

Economic Research Associates, owned by Paul Harris, is retained by large companies to test consumer reaction to new products. On January 31, 2013, the firm's worksheet showed the following adjustments data: (a) supplies used, $2,240; (b) expired rent, $12,000; and (c) depreciation on office equipment, $4,480. The balances of the revenue and expense accounts listed in the Income Statement section of the worksheet and the drawing account listed in the Balance Sheet section of the worksheet are given below:

REVENUE AND EXPENSE ACCOUNTS

401 Fees Income	$90,000 Cr.
511 Depr. Expense—Office Equipment	4,480 Dr.
514 Rent Expense	12,000 Dr.
517 Salaries Expense	48,500 Dr.
520 Supplies Expense	2,240 Dr.
523 Telephone Expense	1,250 Dr.
526 Travel Expense	10,290 Dr.
529 Utilities Expense	1,150 Dr.

DRAWING ACCOUNT

| 302 Paul Harris, Drawing | 10,000 Dr. |

INSTRUCTIONS

1. Record the adjusting entries in the general journal, page 3.

2. Record the closing entries in the general journal, page 4.

Analyze: What closing entry is required to close a drawing account?

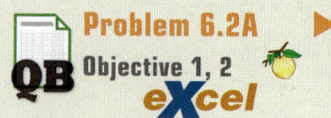

Problem 6.2A

QB Objective 1, 2

e**X**cel

▶ **Journalizing and posting adjusting and closing entries and preparing a postclosing trial balance.**

A completed worksheet for The Warrior Group is shown on the bottom of these two pages.

INSTRUCTIONS

1. Record balances as of December 31, 2013, in the ledger accounts.

2. Journalize (use 3 as the page number) and post the adjusting entries. Use account number 131 for Prepaid Advertising and the same account numbers for all other accounts shown on page 186 for Wells' Consulting Services chart of accounts.

3. Journalize (use 4 as the page number) and post the closing entries.

4. Prepare a postclosing trial balance.

Analyze: How many accounts are listed in the Adjusted Trial Balance section? How many accounts are listed on the postclosing trial balance?

Problem 6.3A

Objective 1   e**X**cel

▶ **Journalizing and posting closing entries.**

On December 31, after adjustments, Cavazos Company's ledger contains the following account balances:

101 Cash	$37,200 Dr.
111 Accounts Receivable	16,800 Dr.
121 Supplies	3,000 Dr.
131 Prepaid Rent	39,600 Dr.
141 Equipment	54,000 Dr.
142 Accumulated Depreciation—Equip.	1,500 Cr.
202 Accounts Payable	7,500 Cr.
301 Monica Cavazos, Capital (12/1/2013)	55,620 Cr.
302 Monica Cavazos, Drawing	7,200 Dr.

The Warrior Group

Worksheet

Month Ended December 31, 2013

	ACCOUNT NAME	TRIAL BALANCE		ADJUSTMENTS	
		DEBIT	CREDIT	DEBIT	CREDIT
1	Cash	92 4 0 0 00			
2	Accounts Receivable	12 0 0 0 00			
3	Supplies	6 0 0 0 00			(a) 2 4 0 0 00
4	Prepaid Advertising	24 0 0 0 00			(b) 3 0 0 0 00
5	Equipment	60 0 0 0 00			
6	Accumulated Depreciation—Equipment				(c) 2 4 0 0 00
7	Accounts Payable		12 0 0 0 00		
8	Gayle Warrior, Capital		132 0 0 0 00		
9	Gayle Warrior, Drawing	8 4 0 0 00			
10	Fees Income		75 0 0 0 00		
11	Supplies Expense			(a) 2 4 0 0 00	
12	Advertising Expense			(b) 3 0 0 0 00	
13	Depreciation Expense—Equipment			(c) 2 4 0 0 00	
14	Salaries Expense	14 4 0 0 00			
15	Utilities Expense	1 8 0 0 00			
16	Totals	219 0 0 0 00	219 0 0 0 00	7 8 0 0 00	7 8 0 0 00
17	Net Income				
18					
19					

401 Fees Income	138,000 Cr.
511 Advertising Expense	4,800 Dr.
514 Depreciation Expense—Equip.	900 Dr.
517 Rent Expense	3,600 Dr.
519 Salaries Expense	28,800 Dr.
523 Utilities Expense	6,720 Dr.

INSTRUCTIONS

1. Record the balances in the ledger accounts as of December 31.
2. Journalize the closing entries in the general journal, page 4. Use account number 399 for the Income Summary Account.
3. Post the closing entries to the general ledger accounts.

Analyze: What is the balance of the *Salaries Expense* account after closing entries are posted?

Worksheet, journalizing and posting adjusting and closing entries, and the postclosing trial balance.

◄ **Problem 6.4A**
Objective 1, 2
e**X**cel

A partially completed worksheet for Nationwide Auto Detailing Service, a firm that details cars and vans, follows on page 178.

INSTRUCTIONS

1. Record balances as of December 31 in the ledger accounts.
2. Prepare the worksheet.
3. Journalize (use 3 as the journal page number) and post the adjusting entries. Use account number 131 for Prepaid Advertising and the same account numbers for all other accounts shown on page 186 for Wells' Consulting Services chart of accounts.
4. Journalize (use 4 as the journal page number) and post the closing entries.
5. Prepare a postclosing trial balance.

ADJUSTED TRIAL BALANCE		INCOME STATEMENT		BALANCE SHEET		
DEBIT	CREDIT	DEBIT	CREDIT	DEBIT	CREDIT	
92 400 00				92 400 00		1
12 000 00				12 000 00		2
3 600 00				3 600 00		3
21 000 00				21 000 00		4
60 000 00				60 000 00		5
	2 400 00				2 400 00	6
	12 000 00				12 000 00	7
	132 000 00				132 000 00	8
8 400 00				8 400 00		9
	75 000 00		75 000 00			10
2 400 00		2 400 00				11
3 000 00		3 000 00				12
2 400 00		2 400 00				13
14 400 00		14 400 00				14
1 800 00		1 800 00				15
221 400 00	221 400 00	24 000 00	75 000 00	197 400 00	146 400 00	16
		51 000 00			51 000 00	17
		75 000 00	75 000 00	197 400 00	197 400 00	18
						19

Nationwide Auto Detailing Service
Worksheet
Month Ended December 31, 2013

	ACCOUNT NAME	TRIAL BALANCE		ADJUSTMENTS	
		DEBIT	CREDIT	DEBIT	CREDIT
1	Cash	31 0 5 0 00			
2	Accounts Receivable	4 9 5 0 00			
3	Supplies	4 0 0 0 00			(a) 1 6 0 0 00
4	Prepaid Advertising	3 0 0 0 00			(b) 1 4 0 0 00
5	Equipment	20 0 0 0 00			
6	Accumulated Depreciation—Equipment				(c) 4 8 0 00
7	Accounts Payable		5 0 0 0 00		
8	Richard Harris, Capital		35 5 0 0 00		
9	Richard Harris, Drawing	2 0 0 0 00			
10	Fees Income		30 0 0 0 00		
11	Salaries Expense	4 8 0 0 00			
12	Utilities Expense	7 0 0 00			
13	Supplies Expense			(a) 1 6 0 0 00	
14	Advertising Expense			(b) 1 4 0 0 00	
15	Depreciation Expense—Equipment			(c) 4 8 0 00	
16	Totals	70 5 0 0 00	70 5 0 0 00	3 4 8 0 00	3 4 8 0 00
17					
18					
19					

Analyze: What total debits were posted to the general ledger to complete all closing entries for the month of December?

Problem Set B

Problem 6.1B

Objective 1

▶ **Adjusting and closing entries.**

Williams Cleaning and Maintenance, owned by Jay Williams, provides cleaning services to hotels, motels, and hospitals. On January 31, 2013, the firm's worksheet showed the following adjustment data. The balances of the revenue and expense accounts listed in the Income Statement section of the worksheet and the drawing account listed in the Balance Sheet section of the worksheet are also given.

ADJUSTMENTS

a. Supplies used, $8,580

b. Expired insurance, $4,440

c. Depreciation on machinery, $3,360

REVENUE AND EXPENSE ACCOUNTS

401 Fees Income	$98,400 Cr.
511 Depreciation Expense—Machinery	3,360 Dr.
514 Insurance Expense	4,440 Dr.
517 Rent Expense	9,000 Dr.
520 Salaries Expense	48,000 Dr.
523 Supplies Expense	8,580 Dr.
526 Telephone Expense	630 Dr.

529 Utilities Expense	1,920 Dr.
DRAWING ACCOUNT	
302 Jay Williams, Drawing	7,200 Dr.

INSTRUCTIONS

1. Record the adjusting entries in the general journal, page 3.

2. Record the closing entries in the general journal, page 4. Use account numbers provided on page 186 for any account number not given.

Analyze: What effect did the adjusting entry for expired insurance have on the *Insurance Expense* account?

Journalizing and posting adjusting and closing entries and preparing a postclosing trial balance.

◄ **Problem 6.2B**
Objectives 1, 2

A completed worksheet for Cedar Canyon Nursery and Landscape is shown on pages 180–181.

INSTRUCTIONS

1. Record the balances as of December 31 in the ledger accounts.

2. Journalize (use 3 as the page number) and post the adjusting entries. Use account number 131 for Prepaid Advertising and the same account numbers for all other accounts as shown on page 186 for Wells' Consulting Services chart of accounts.

3. Journalize (use 4 as the page number) and post the closing entries.

4. Prepare a postclosing trial balance.

Analyze: What total credits were posted to the general ledger to complete the closing entries?

Journalizing and posting closing entries.

◄ **Problem 6.3B**
Objective 1

On December 31, after adjustments, The Taylor Family Farm's ledger contains the following account balances.

101 Cash	$171,000 Dr.
111 Accounts Receivable	43,200 Dr.
121 Supplies	18,000 Dr.
131 Prepaid Rent	138,600 Dr.
141 Equipment	216,000 Dr.
142 Accumulated Depreciation—Equip.	5,400 Cr.
202 Accounts Payable	58,500 Cr.
301 James Taylor, Capital (12/1/2013)	344,700 Cr.
302 James Taylor, Drawing	21,600 Dr.
401 Fees Income	324,000 Cr.
511 Advertising Expense	19,800 Dr.
514 Depreciation Expense—Equip.	5,400 Dr.
517 Rent Expense	12,600 Dr.
519 Salaries Expense	64,800 Dr.
523 Utilities Expense	21,600 Dr.

INSTRUCTIONS

1. Record the balances in the ledger accounts as of December 31.

2. Journalize the closing entries in the general journal, page 4. Use account number 399 for the Income Summary Account

3. Post the closing entries to the general ledger accounts.

Analyze: List the accounts affected by closing entries for the month of December.

Cedar Canyon Nursery and Landscape
Worksheet
Month Ended December 31, 2013

	ACCOUNT NAME	TRIAL BALANCE		ADJUSTMENTS		
		DEBIT	CREDIT	DEBIT	CREDIT	
1	Cash	64 8 0 0 00				
2	Accounts Receivable	12 0 0 0 00				
3	Supplies	12 0 0 0 00			(a) 6 0 0 0 00	
4	Prepaid Advertising	18 0 0 0 00			(b) 2 4 0 0 00	
5	Equipment	120 0 0 0 00				
6	Accumulated Depreciation—Equipment				(c) 3 0 0 0 00	
7	Accounts Payable		18 0 0 0 00			
8	Randy Scott, Capital		164 4 0 0 00			
9	Randy Scott, Drawing	16 8 0 0 00				
10	Fees Income		93 6 0 0 00			
11	Supplies Expense			(a) 6 0 0 0 00		
12	Advertising Expense			(b) 2 4 0 0 00		
13	Depreciation Expense—Equipment			(c) 3 0 0 0 00		
14	Salaries Expense	28 8 0 0 00				
15	Utilities Expense	3 6 0 0 00				
16	Totals	276 0 0 0 00	276 0 0 0 00	11 4 0 0 00	11 4 0 0 00	
17	Net Income					
18						
19						
20						

Problem 6.4B
Objectives 1, 2, 4

▶ **Worksheet, journalizing and posting adjusting and closing entries, and the postclosing trial balance.**

A partially completed worksheet for Scott Wilson, CPA, for the month ending June 30, 2013, is shown below.

Scott Wilson, CPA
Worksheet
Month Ended June 30, 2013

	ACCOUNT NAME	TRIAL BALANCE		ADJUSTMENTS		
		DEBIT	CREDIT	DEBIT	CREDIT	
1	Cash	31 9 5 0 00				
2	Accounts Receivable	11 3 4 0 00				
3	Supplies	15 7 5 0 00			(a) 2 7 0 0 00	
4	Computers	28 8 0 0 00				
5	Accumulated Depreciation—Computers		2 8 8 0 00		(b) 2 4 0 00	
6	Accounts Payable		12 6 0 0 00			
7	Scott Wilson, Capital		62 2 3 5 00			
8	Scott Wilson, Drawing	12 0 0 0 00				
9	Fees Income		67 9 5 0 00			
10	Salaries Expense	37 7 2 5 00				
11	Supplies Expense			(a) 2 7 0 0 00		
12	Depreciation Expense—Computers			(b) 2 4 0 00		
13	Travel Expense	5 4 0 0 00				
14	Utilities Expense	2 7 0 0 00				
15	Totals	145 6 6 5 00	145 6 6 5 00	2 9 4 0 00	2 9 4 0 00	
16						
17						

| ADJUSTED TRIAL BALANCE | | INCOME STATEMENT | | BALANCE SHEET | | |
DEBIT	CREDIT	DEBIT	CREDIT	DEBIT	CREDIT	
64 800 00				64 800 00		1
12 000 00				12 000 00		2
6 000 00				6 000 00		3
15 600 00				15 600 00		4
120 000 00				120 000 00		5
	3 000 00				3 000 00	6
	18 000 00				18 000 00	7
	164 400 00				164 400 00	8
16 800 00				16 800 00		9
	93 600 00		93 600 00			10
6 000 00		6 000 00				11
2 400 00		2 400 00				12
3 000 00		3 000 00				13
28 800 00		28 800 00				14
3 600 00		3 600 00				15
279 000 00	279 000 00	43 800 00	93 600 00	235 200 00	185 400 00	16
		49 800 00			49 800 00	17
		93 600 00	93 600 00	235 200 00	235 200 00	18
						19
						20

INSTRUCTIONS

1. Record the balances as of June 30 in the ledger accounts.

2. Prepare the worksheet.

3. Journalize (use 3 as the journal page number) and post the adjusting entries. Use account number 121 for Supplies; 131 for Computers; 142 for the Accumulated Depreciation account; 309 for Income Summary; 517 for Supplies Expense; 519 for Travel Expense; and 523 for Depreciation Expense.

4. Journalize (use 4 as the journal page number) and post the closing entries.

5. Prepare a postclosing trial balance.

Analyze: What is the reported net income for the month of June for Scott Wilson, CPA?

Critical Thinking Problem 6.1

The Closing Process

The Trial Balance section of the worksheet for Contemporary Fashions for the period ended December 31, 2013, appears on the next page. Adjustments data are also given.

    ADJUSTMENTS
    a. Supplies used, $14,400
    b. Expired insurance, $9,600
    c. Depreciation expense for machinery, $4,800

INSTRUCTIONS

1. Complete the worksheet.

2. Prepare an income statement.

3. Prepare a statement of owner's equity.

Contemporary Fashions
Worksheet
Month Ended December 31, 2013

	ACCOUNT NAME	TRIAL BALANCE		ADJUSTMENTS	
		DEBIT	CREDIT	DEBIT	CREDIT
1	Cash	163 2 0 0 00			
2	Accounts Receivable	36 0 0 0 00			
3	Supplies	28 8 0 0 00			(a) 14 4 0 0 00
4	Prepaid Insurance	43 2 0 0 00			(b) 9 6 0 0 00
5	Machinery	336 0 0 0 00			
6	Accumulated Depreciation—Machinery				(c) 4 8 0 0 00
7	Accounts Payable		54 0 0 0 00		
8	Jada McBride, Capital		298 3 2 0 00		
9	Jada McBride, Drawing	24 0 0 0 00			
10	Fees Income		330 0 0 0 00		
11	Supplies Expense			(a) 14 4 0 0 00	
12	Insurance Expense			(b) 9 6 0 0 00	
13	Salaries Expense	44 4 0 0 00			
14	Depreciation Expense—Machinery			(c) 4 8 0 0 00	
15	Utilities Expense	6 7 2 0 00			
16	Totals	682 3 2 0 00	682 3 2 0 00	28 8 0 0 00	28 8 0 0 00
17					
18					
19					

4. Prepare a balance sheet.

5. Journalize the adjusting entries in the general journal, page 3.

6. Journalize the closing entries in the general journal, page 4.

7. Prepare a postclosing trial balance.

Analyze: If the adjusting entry for expired insurance had been recorded in error as a credit to *Insurance Expense* and a debit to *Prepaid Insurance* for $9,600, what reported net income would have resulted?

Critical Thinking Problem 6.2

Owner's Equity

Wilson Reed, the bookkeeper for Home Interior Improvements and Designs Company, has just finished posting the closing entries for the year to the ledger. He is concerned about the following balances:

Capital account balance in the general ledger:	$48,550
Ending capital balance on the statement of owner's equity:	27,800

Wilson knows that these amounts should agree and asks for your assistance in reviewing his work.

Your review of the general ledger of Home Interior Improvements and Designs Company reveals a beginning capital balance of $25,000. You also review the general journal for the accounting period and find the closing entries shown on the next page.

1. What errors did Mr. Reed make in preparing the closing entries for the period?

2. Prepare a general journal entry to correct the errors made.

3. Explain why the balance of the capital account in the ledger after closing entries have been posted will be the same as the ending capital balance on the statement of owner's equity.

	DATE		DESCRIPTION	POST. REF.	DEBIT	CREDIT	
1	2013		Closing Entries				1
2	Dec.	31	Fees Income		49 0 0 0 00		2
3			Accumulated Depreciation		4 2 5 0 00		3
4			Accounts Payable		16 5 0 0 00		4
5			Income Summary			69 7 5 0 00	5
6							6
7		31	Income Summary		46 2 0 0 00		7
8			Salaries Expense			39 0 0 0 00	8
9			Supplies Expense			2 5 0 0 00	9
10			Depreciation Expense			1 2 0 0 00	10
11			James Walker, Drawing			3 5 0 0 00	11
12							12
13							13
14							14

GENERAL JOURNAL   PAGE __15__

BUSINESS CONNECTIONS

Interpreting Financial Statements

1. An officer of Carson Company recently commented that when he receives the firm's financial statements, he looks at just the bottom line of the income statement—the line that shows the net income or net loss for the period. He said that he does not bother with the rest of the income statement because "it's only the bottom line that counts." He also does not read the balance sheet. Do you think this manager is correct in the way he uses the financial statements? Why or why not?

2. The president of Henderson Corporation is concerned about the firm's ability to pay its debts on time. What items on the balance sheet would help her to assess the firm's debt-paying ability?

3. Why is it important that a firm's financial records be kept up-to-date and that management receive the financial statements promptly after the end of each accounting period?

4. What kinds of operating and general policy decisions might be influenced by data on the financial statements?

Timing of a Check

On the last day of the fiscal year, Gevok Means comes to you for a favor. He asks that you enter a check for $1,000 to GM Company for Miscellaneous Expense. You notice the invoice looks a little different from other invoices that are processed. Gevok needs the check immediately to get supplies today to complete the project for a favorite customer. You know that by preparing the closing entries tomorrow, Miscellaneous Expense will be set to zero for the beginning of the new year. Should you write this check and record the expense or find an excuse to write the check tomorrow? What would be the effect if the invoice to GM Company was erroneous and you had written the check?

Income Statement

In 2009, CSX Corporation, which operates under the name Surface Transportation, reported operating expenses of $6,756 million. A partial list of the company's operating expenses follows. CSX Corporation reported revenues from external customers to be $9,041 million for the year. These revenues are divided among two operations: intermodal and rail.

Revenue from External Customers

(Dollars in millions)

Intermodal	$1,204
Rail	7,837

Operating Expenses

(Dollars in millions)

Labor and Fringe Benefits	$2,629
Materials, Supplies, and Other	1,715
Inland Transportation	264
Depreciation	908
Fuel	849
Equipment and Other Rents	391

Analyze:

1. If the given categories represent the related general ledger accounts, what journal entry would be made to close the expense accounts at year-end?

2. What journal entry would be made to close the revenue accounts?

Analyze Online: Locate the Web site for CSX Corporation (www.csx.com). Click on *CSX Corporation* and then click on *Investor Relations*. Within the *Financial Information* link, find the most recent annual report.

3. On the consolidated statement of earnings, what was the amount reported for operating expenses?

4. What percentage increase or decrease does this figure represent from the operating expenses reported in 2009 of $6,756 million?

TEAMWORK

Accounting Cycle

Understanding the steps in the accounting cycle is important to get accurate information about the condition of your company. In teams, make strips of paper with the nine steps of the accounting cycle. Give two or three strips to each member of the group. Each team member needs to put his or her strips in the proper order of the nine steps.

Internet | CONNECTION

Certified Bookkeeper

Certification in your field indicates you have a certain level of education and training. Go to the American Institute of Professional Bookkeepers Web site at www.aipb.com. From the certification program icon, determine the three requirements to become a certified bookkeeper.

Answers to **Self Reviews**

Answers to Section 1 Self Review

1. Close the revenue account to *Income Summary.*
   Close the expense accounts to *Income Summary.*
   Close the *Income Summary* account to the capital account.
   Close the drawing account to the capital account.

2. Debit *Capital* and credit *Drawing.*

3. A temporary owner's equity account.

4. **a.** *Capital*

5. **d.** revenue, drawing, and expense accounts

6. No effect on net income.

Answers to Section 2 Self Review

1. Asset, liability, and the owner's capital accounts.
2. (7) Record closing entries, (8) prepare a postclosing trial balance, (9) interpret the financial statements.
3. To make sure the general ledger is in balance after the adjusting and closing entries are posted.
4. **b.** net loss of $60,000
5. **a.** *J. T. Amos, Drawing*
6. The income statement will answer questions about fees earned, expenses incurred, and profit. The balance sheet will answer questions about the cash balance, the amount owed by customers, and the amount owed to suppliers.

Answers to Comprehensive Self Review

1. False. The *temporary* owner's equity accounts do not appear on the postclosing trial balance. The temporary owner's equity accounts are the drawing account and *Income Summary.*
2. Interpret the financial statements.
3. Income statement, statement of owner's equity, and balance sheet.
4. Fees Income   56,000
      Income Summary   56,000
5. Income Summary   12,100
      Rent Expense   3,600
      Salaries Expense   7,000
      Supplies Expense   1,500

Mini-Practice Set 1

Service Business Accounting Cycle

Wells' Consulting Services

This project will give you an opportunity to apply your knowledge of accounting principles and proce-dures by handling all the accounting work of Wells' Consulting Services for the month of January 2014.

INTRODUCTION

Assume that you are the chief accountant for Wells' Consulting Services. During January, the business will use the same types of records and procedures that you learned about in Chapters 1 through 6. The chart of accounts for Wells' Consulting Services has been expanded to include a few new accounts. Follow the instructions to complete the accounting records for the month of January.

Wells' Consulting Services
Chart of Accounts

Assets	**Revenue**
101 Cash	401 Fees Income
111 Accounts Receivable	
121 Supplies	**Expenses**
134 Prepaid Insurance	511 Salaries Expense
137 Prepaid Rent	514 Utilities Expense
141 Equipment	517 Supplies Expense
142 Accumulated Depreciation—Equipment	520 Rent Expense
	523 Depreciation Expense—Equipment
Liabilities	526 Advertising Expense
202 Accounts Payable	529 Maintenance Expense
	532 Telephone Expense
Owner's Equity	535 Insurance Expense
301 Carolyn Wells, Capital	
302 Carolyn Wells, Drawing	
309 Income Summary	

INSTRUCTIONS

1. Open the general ledger accounts and enter the balances for January 1, 2014. Obtain the necessary figures from the postclosing trial balance prepared on December 31, 2013, which appears on page 166.

2. Analyze each transaction and record it in the general journal. Use page 3 to begin January's transactions.

3. Post the transactions to the general ledger accounts.

4. Prepare the Trial Balance section of the worksheet.

5. Prepare the Adjustments section of the worksheet.
   a. Compute and record the adjustment for supplies used during the month. An inventory taken on January 31 showed supplies of $3,050 on hand.
   b. Compute and record the adjustment for expired insurance for the month.
   c. Record the adjustment for one month of expired rent of $4,000.
   d. Record the adjustment for depreciation of $183 on the old equipment for the month. The first adjustment for depreciation for the new equipment will be recorded in February.

6. Complete the worksheet.

7. Prepare an income statement for the month.

8. Prepare a statement of owner's equity.

9. Prepare a balance sheet using the report form.

10. Journalize and post the adjusting entries.

11. Journalize and post the closing entries.

12. Prepare a postclosing trial balance.

Analyze: Compare the January 31 balance sheet you prepared with the December 31 balance sheet shown on page 167.

a. What changes occurred in total assets, liabilities, and the owner's ending capital?

b. What changes occurred in *Cash* and *Accounts Receivable* accounts?

c. Has there been an improvement in the firm's financial position? Why or why not?

DATE	TRANSACTIONS
Jan. 2	Purchased supplies for $4,000; issued Check 1015.
2	Purchased a one-year insurance policy for $6,000; issued Check 1016.
7	Sold services for $18,000 in cash and $2,000 on credit during the first week of January.
12	Collected a total of $3,000 on account from credit customers during the first week of January.
12	Issued Check 1017 for $2,800 to pay for special promotional advertising to new businesses on the local radio station during the month.
13	Collected a total of $2,500 on account from credit customers during the second week of January.
14	Returned supplies that were damaged for a cash refund of $550.
15	Sold services for $19,500 in cash and $2,500 on credit during the second week of January.
20	Purchased supplies for $3,600 from White's, Inc.; received Invoice 2384 payable in 30 days.
20	Sold services for $10,500 in cash and $2,250 on credit during the third week of January.
20	Collected a total of $3,200 on account from credit customers during the third week of January.
21	Issued Check 1018 for $5,025 to pay for maintenance work on the office equipment.
22	Issued Check 1019 for $2,800 to pay for special promotional advertising to new businesses in the local newspaper.
23	Received the monthly telephone bill for $875 and paid it with Check 1020.
26	Collected a total of $2,800 on account from credit customers during the fourth week of January.
27	Issued Check 1021 for $3,000 to Office Plus, as payment on account for Invoice 2223.
28	Sent Check 1022 for $2,175 in payment of the monthly bill for utilities.
29	Sold services for $16,500 in cash and $3,500 on credit during the fourth week of January.
31	Issued Checks 1023–1027 for $20,500 to pay the monthly salaries of the regular employees and three part-time workers.
31	Issued Check 1028 for $12,000 for personal use.
31	Issued Check 1029 for $3,050 to pay for maintenance services for the month.
31	Purchased additional equipment for $12,800 from Contemporary Equipment Company; issued Check 1030 for $10,000 and bought the rest on credit. The equipment has a five-year life and no salvage value.
31	Sold services for $4,250 in cash and $1,450 on credit on January 31.

Accounting for Sales, Accounts Receivable, and Cash Receipts

Chapter 7

LEARNING OBJECTIVES

1. Record sales on account, credit card sales, sales returns, and cash receipt transactions in a general journal.
2. Compute trade discounts.
3. Compute and record cash discounts on sales.
4. Post from the general journal to the general ledger accounts and to the subsidiary ledger.
5. Prepare a schedule of accounts receivable.
6. Record the payment of sales taxes.
7. Define the accounting terms new to this chapter.

NEW TERMS

accounts receivable ledger
contra revenue account
control account
credit memorandum
credit terms
list price
manufacturing business
merchandise inventory
merchandising business
net sales
open-account credit
retail business
sales allowance
sales discounts
sales return
Sales Returns and Allowances
schedule of accounts receivable
service business
subsidiary ledger
trade discount
wholesale business

indi

www.indicustom.com

indi was launched in 2008 with a mission to completely revolutionize the way apparel is sold. The company uses state-of-the-art mass customization technologies to provide customers with the perfect pair of jeans. By using a unique fit technology program, customers answer questions about their body and generate customized patterns. The patterns are sent to manufacturing partners where fabric is cut and sewn, washed, packaged, and then shipped directly to customers. As a direct merchant, indi works directly with manufacturers, eliminating wholesalers. Customers shop directly with indi via phone or Web site.

The firm aims to provide customers with:

Custom Fit—indi jeans are made to fit each customer's unique body measurements.
One of a Kind Style—Customers use the firm's cutting-edge technology to personally select fabric, wash, rise, leg shape, and finish.
Online Digital Closet—Each customer's pattern and order history is stored in a personalized Digital Closet to allow for easy reorders or adjustments.

thinking critically

What other factors besides a perfect fit are important to the success of a company like indi?

SECTION OBJECTIVES

>> 1. **Record sales on account, credit card sales, sales returns, and cash receipt transactions in a general journal.**

WHY IT'S IMPORTANT

Credit sales are a major source of revenue for many businesses.

TERMS TO LEARN

contra revenue account

credit memorandum

manufacturing business

merchandise inventory

merchandising business

open-account credit

retail business

sales allowance

sales return

service business

subsidiary ledger

Understanding Merchandising Companies

When a chart of accounts is developed for a firm, one important consideration is the nature of the firm's operations. The three basic types of businesses are a **service business,** which sells services; a **merchandising business,** which sells goods that it purchases for resale; and a **manufacturing business,** which sells goods that it produces. Each of these businesses would require a different chart of accounts.

Merchandising companies sell products, not services. Their accounting practices are different than service companies. We will focus on these differences and explain the general ledger accounts used by merchandising companies.

This chapter focuses on recording transactions executed by merchandising companies when they sell goods. In the next chapter, we will learn to record transactions of merchandising companies when they buy goods.

The distribution channel is the means that manufacturers of products use to sell their products to consumers. A common example of the distribution channel is:

Manufacturer sells to *Wholesaler* who sells to *Retailer* who sells to *Consumer.*

In this section, we learn to record transactions for a retailer. We will use a general journal to record transactions. Later, we will learn to post transactions from the general journal to the general ledger and the **subsidiary ledger.** A subsidiary ledger is a ledger that contains accounts of a single type, such as customers or vendors. Finally, we will focus on recording transactions for a wholesaler.

Wells' Consulting Services, the firm that was described in Chapters 2 through 6, is a service business. The firm we will examine next, Maxx-Out Sporting Goods, is a merchandising business that sells the latest sporting goods and sportswear for men, women, and children. It is a **retail business.** It sells goods and services directly to individual customers. Maxx-Out Sporting Goods is a sole proprietorship owned and managed by Max Ferraro, who was formerly a sales manager for a major retailing chain.

Maxx-Out Sporting Goods must account for purchases and sales of goods, and for **merchandise inventory**—the stock of goods kept on hand. The new accounts we will be using in this chapter are summarized at the top of the next page.

important!

Business Classifications

The term *merchandising* refers to the type of business operation, not the type of legal entity. Maxx-Out Sporting Goods could have been a partnership or a corporation instead of a sole proprietorship.

Name of Account	Type of Account	Normal Balance	Used to Record
Sales	Revenue	CR	Sales of merchandise inventory
Sales Tax Payable	Liability	CR	Sales tax charged to customers
Sales Discounts	Contra revenue	DR	Early payment discounts given to buyer by seller
Sales Returns and Allowances	Contra revenue	DR	Products returned by buyer on the seller's books
Credit Card Expense	Expense	DR	Fees charged by credit card companies to seller

Contra revenue accounts are discussed on page 193.

Recording Sales for Cash and On Account

The *Sales* account is the primary revenue account for a merchandising company. Let's suppose Maxx-Out Sporting Goods sells merchandise for cash and on account. The journal entry to record a sale of $500 for cash on January 2 follows:

>> 1. OBJECTIVE

Record sales on account, credit card sales, sales returns, and cash receipt transactions in a general journal.

		GENERAL JOURNAL			PAGE 2	
	DATE	DESCRIPTION	POST. REF.	DEBIT	CREDIT	
1	2013					1
2	Jan. 2	Cash		500 00		2
3		Sales			500 00	3
4		Record cash sales				4
5						5

Maxx-Out Sporting Goods also grants credit terms to certain customers. One of those customers is Roy Anderson. On January 3, Maxx-Out Sporting Goods sold merchandise on credit to Roy Anderson, issuing Sales Slip 1101 for $400. The journal entry to record that sale follows:

		GENERAL JOURNAL			PAGE 2	
	DATE	DESCRIPTION	POST. REF.	DEBIT	CREDIT	
1	2013					1
2	Jan. 3	Accounts Receivable		400 00		2
3		Sales			400 00	3
4		Sold merchandise on credit to				4
5		Roy Anderson, Sales Slip 1101				5

The following journal entry records Roy Anderson's payment of the amount due on January 31:

		GENERAL JOURNAL			PAGE 2	
	DATE	DESCRIPTION	POST. REF.	DEBIT	CREDIT	
1	2013					1
2	Jan. 31	Cash		400 00		2
3		Accounts Receivable			400 00	3
4		Received cash from Roy Anderson				4
5		on account				5

Recording Sales with Sales Tax Payable for Cash and On Account

Most state and many local governments impose a sales tax on the sale of certain goods and services. Businesses are required to collect this tax from their customers and pay it to the proper tax agency at regular intervals. When taxable goods and services are sold on credit, the sales tax is usually recorded at time of sale, even though it will be collected from the customer later. A liability account called Sales Tax Payable is credited for the sales tax charged.

If Maxx-Out Sporting Goods was required to charge its customers an 8 percent sales tax, the amount collected for the sales tax on a $500 sale for cash would be $40 ($500 × 8% = $40). The amount collected from the customer would be $540 ($500 for the merchandise, plus $40 for the sales tax). The journal entry to record a sale of $500 plus tax for cash follows:

GENERAL JOURNAL PAGE __2__

	DATE		DESCRIPTION	POST. REF.	DEBIT	CREDIT	
1	2013						1
2	Jan.	2	Cash		5 4 0 00		2
3			Sales Tax Payable			4 0 00	3
4			Sales			5 0 0 00	4
5			Record cash sales				5

If Maxx-Out Sporting Goods sold merchandise on credit to Ann Anh on January 8 for $600 plus tax, it would bill Ann Anh for $600 plus tax of $48 ($600 × 8% = $48). See Figure 7.1. The total amount billed would be $648 ($600 for the merchandise, plus $48 for the sales tax). The journal entry to record that sale follows:

GENERAL JOURNAL PAGE __2__

	DATE		DESCRIPTION	POST. REF.	DEBIT	CREDIT	
1	2013						1
2	Jan.	8	Accounts Receivable		6 4 8 00		2
3			Sales Tax Payable			4 8 00	3
4			Sales			6 0 0 00	4
5			Sold merchandise on credit to				5
6			Ann Anh, Sales Slip 1102				6
7							7

FIGURE 7.1

Customer's Sales Slip

Ann Anh's payment on account received February 1 is illustrated in the following entry:

	DATE		DESCRIPTION	POST. REF.	DEBIT	CREDIT	
1	2013						1
2	Feb.	1	Cash		6 4 8 00		2
3			Accounts Receivable			6 4 8 00	3
4			Received cash from Ann Anh				4
5			on account				5
6							6

GENERAL JOURNAL   PAGE 2

Recording Sales Returns and Sales Allowances

If something is wrong with the goods sold, the firm may take back the goods, resulting in a **sales return.** Or, they may negotiate a reduction in the sales price, resulting in a **sales allowance.**

If the goods returned were initially paid for with cash, the customer will receive a cash refund. When a return or allowance is related to a credit sale, the normal practice is to issue a document called a **credit memorandum** to the customer instead of giving a cash refund. The credit memorandum documents the reduction in the customer's account balance by the amount of the return or allowance. If the sale was made with sales tax added, the sales tax paid on the goods returned will also be credited to the customer's account.

The **Sales Returns and Allowances** account is debited to record returns and allowances. By debiting Sales Returns and Allowances instead of debiting the Sales account, management can monitor the balance of the Sales Returns and Allowances account and see if product returns or allowances increase. Business managers use this record as a measure of operating efficiency. The Sales Returns and Allowances account is a **contra revenue account** because it has a debit balance, which is contrary, or the opposite of, the normal balance for revenue accounts.

The journal entry to record a cash refund for a return on January 2 of $100 merchandise sold for cash, plus sales tax of $8, follows.

GENERAL JOURNAL   PAGE 2

	DATE		DESCRIPTION	POST. REF.	DEBIT	CREDIT	
1	2013						1
2	Jan.	2	Sales Returns and Allowances		1 0 0 00		2
3			Sales Tax Payable		8 00		3
4			Cash			1 0 8 00	4
5			Refund to customer for returned				5
6			merchandise and sales tax paid				6

Let's revisit the sale on account to Ann Anh of $600 plus sales tax of $48 recorded January 8. If Maxx-Out Sporting Goods issued Credit Memorandum 101 on January 20 for a return of $200 merchandise purchased on account by Ann Anh, plus 8 percent sales tax, the credit memorandum would total $216 ($200 for the merchandise returned, plus $16 sales tax previously billed to Ann Anh). See Figure 7.2. The issuance of the credit memorandum would be analyzed and recorded in the following manner:

FIGURE 7.2

Credit Memorandum

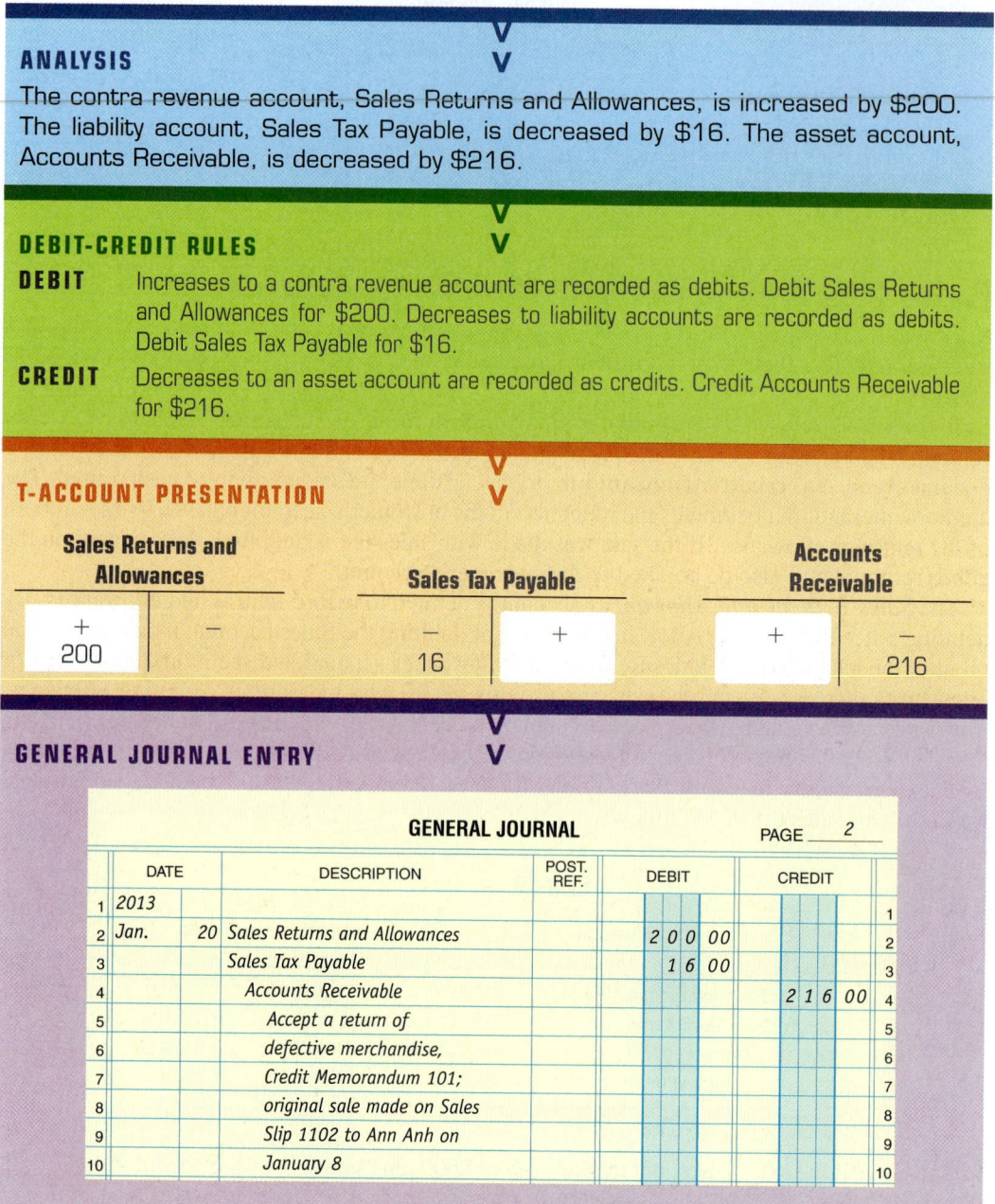

ANALYSIS

The contra revenue account, Sales Returns and Allowances, is increased by $200. The liability account, Sales Tax Payable, is decreased by $16. The asset account, Accounts Receivable, is decreased by $216.

DEBIT-CREDIT RULES

DEBIT Increases to a contra revenue account are recorded as debits. Debit Sales Returns and Allowances for $200. Decreases to liability accounts are recorded as debits. Debit Sales Tax Payable for $16.

CREDIT Decreases to an asset account are recorded as credits. Credit Accounts Receivable for $216.

T-ACCOUNT PRESENTATION

Sales Returns and Allowances		Sales Tax Payable		Accounts Receivable	
+	−	−	+	+	−
200		16			216

GENERAL JOURNAL ENTRY

GENERAL JOURNAL   PAGE ___2___

	DATE		DESCRIPTION	POST. REF.	DEBIT	CREDIT	
1	2013						1
2	Jan.	20	Sales Returns and Allowances		2 0 0 00		2
3			Sales Tax Payable		1 6 00		3
4			Accounts Receivable			2 1 6 00	4
5			Accept a return of				5
6			defective merchandise,				6
7			Credit Memorandum 101;				7
8			original sale made on Sales				8
9			Slip 1102 to Ann Anh on				9
10			January 8				10

Ann Anh paid the amount due of $432 on January 31. The amount due was calculated by subtracting the amount of Credit Memorandum 101 ($216) from the original amount on Sales Slip 1102 ($648). The journal entry to record her payment follows:

GENERAL JOURNAL   PAGE ___2___

	DATE		DESCRIPTION	POST. REF.	DEBIT	CREDIT	
1	2013						1
2	Jan.	31	Cash		4 3 2 00		2
3			Accounts Receivable			4 3 2 00	3
4			Received cash from Ann Anh				4
5			on account after deducting				5
6			Credit Memorandum 101				6
7							7

Credit Policies

The use of credit is considered to be one of the most important factors in the rapid growth of modern economic systems. Sales on credit are made by large numbers of wholesalers and retailers of goods and by many professional people and service businesses. The assumption is that the volume of both sales and profits will increase if buyers are given a period of a month or more to pay for the goods or services they purchase.

However, the increase in profits a business expects when it grants credit will be realized only if each customer completes the transaction by paying for the goods or services purchased. If payment is not received, the expected profits become actual losses and the purpose for granting credit is defeated. Business firms try to protect against the possibility of such losses by investigating a customer's credit record and ability to pay for purchases before allowing any credit to the customer.

Professional people, such as doctors, lawyers, architects, and owners of small businesses like Maxx-Out Sporting Goods, usually make their own decisions about granting credit. Such decisions may be based on personal judgment or on reports available from credit bureaus, information supplied by other creditors, and credit ratings supplied by national firms such as Dun & Bradstreet.

> Equifax, a leader in providing consumer and commercial credit information, was founded in Atlanta in 1899. For the fiscal year ended December 2009, the company reported revenues of $1.82 billion.

Larger businesses maintain a credit department to determine the amounts and types of credit that should be granted to customers. In addition to using credit data supplied by institutions, the credit department may obtain financial statements and related reports from customers who have applied for credit. This information is analyzed to help determine the maximum amount of credit that may be granted and suitable credit terms for the customer. Financial statements that have been audited by certified public accountants are used extensively by credit departments.

Even though the credit investigation is thorough, some accounts receivable become uncollectible. Unexpected business developments, errors of judgment, incorrect financial data, and many other causes may lead to defaults in payments by customers. Experienced managers know that some uncollectible accounts are to be expected in normal business operations and that limited losses indicate that a firm's credit policies are sound. Provisions for such limited losses from uncollectible accounts are usually made in budgets and other financial projections.

Each business must develop credit policies that achieve maximum sales with minimum losses from uncollectible accounts:

- A credit policy that is too tight results in a low level of losses at the expense of increases in sales volume.

- A credit policy that is too lenient may result in increased sales volume accompanied by a high level of losses.

Good judgment based on knowledge and experience must be used to achieve a well-balanced credit policy.

Different types of credit have evolved with the growing economy and changing technology. The different types of credit require different account treatments.

Accounting for Different Types of Credit Sales

The most common types of credit sales are:

- Open-account credit
- Business credit cards
- Bank credit cards
- Cards issued by credit card companies

Open-account credit sales and business credit card sales are accounted for as sales on credit. Sales to customers using bank credit cards, and cards issued by credit card companies, require special accounting procedures and are discussed below.

Accounting for Credit Card Sales

Sales made to customers paying with bank credit cards, such as MasterCard and VISA, are treated as cash sales. In most cases, the amount processed on the card is transferred to the seller's bank account the same day. Fees charged by the credit card company for processing these sales are debited to an account called **Credit Card Expense.** It is important to note these fees are charged on the total amount of the sale plus any sales tax.

For example, assume Maxx-Out Sporting Goods sells merchandise on January 15 totaling $900 to customers using bank credit cards, plus 8 percent sales tax. The bank credit card company charges a 3 percent discount fee. Cash would be debited for $942.84, computed as follows:

Merchandise sales	$900.00
Plus sales tax ($900.00 × 8%)	72.00
	$972.00
Less: bank fee ($972.00 × 3%)	−29.16
Debit to Cash	$942.84

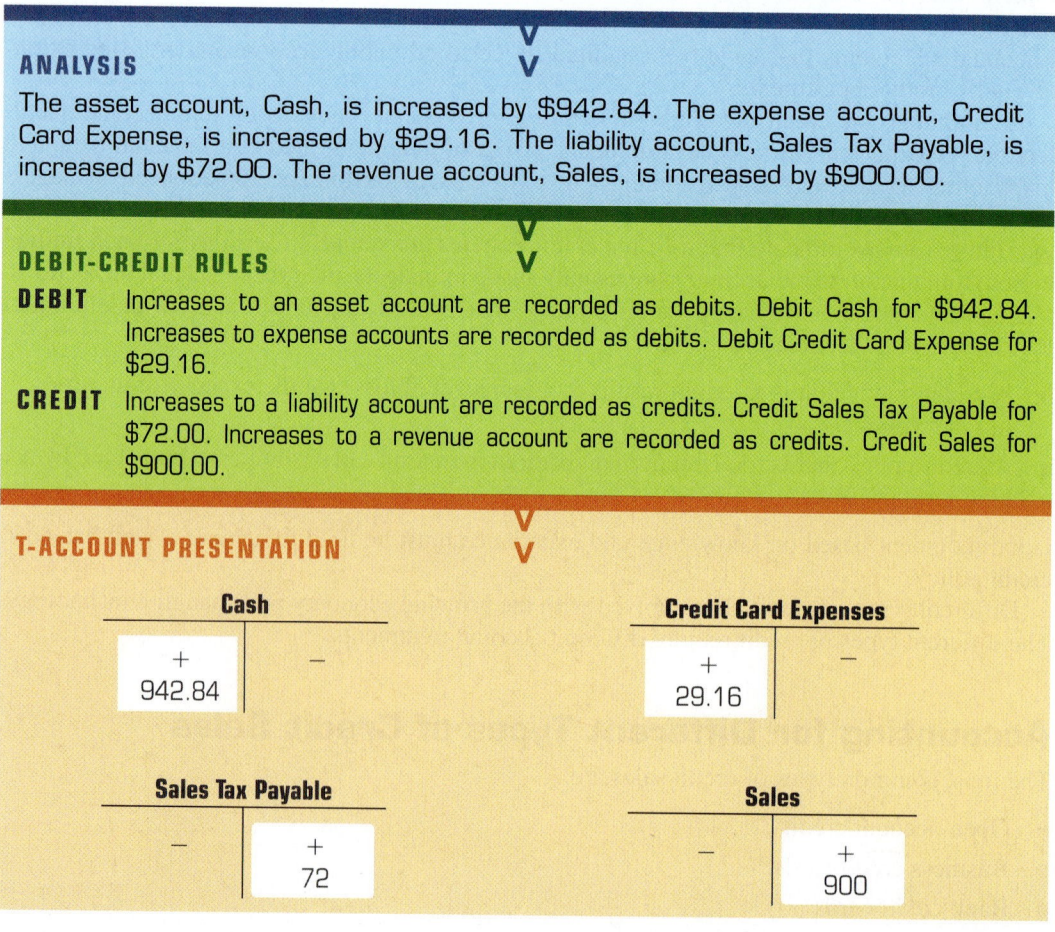

BUSINESS TRANSACTION

ANALYSIS

The asset account, Cash, is increased by $942.84. The expense account, Credit Card Expense, is increased by $29.16. The liability account, Sales Tax Payable, is increased by $72.00. The revenue account, Sales, is increased by $900.00.

DEBIT-CREDIT RULES

DEBIT   Increases to an asset account are recorded as debits. Debit Cash for $942.84. Increases to expense accounts are recorded as debits. Debit Credit Card Expense for $29.16.

CREDIT   Increases to a liability account are recorded as credits. Credit Sales Tax Payable for $72.00. Increases to a revenue account are recorded as credits. Credit Sales for $900.00.

T-ACCOUNT PRESENTATION

Cash		Credit Card Expenses	
+	−	+	−
942.84		29.16	

Sales Tax Payable		Sales	
−	+	−	+
	72		900

GENERAL JOURNAL ENTRY

The following journal entry records the sales made to customers using bank credit cards on January 15.

	DATE		DESCRIPTION	POST. REF.	DEBIT	CREDIT	
1	2013						1
2	Jan.	15	Cash		9 4 2 84		2
3			Credit Card Expense		2 9 16		3
4			Sales			9 0 0 00	4
5			Sales Tax Payable			7 2 00	5
6			Record sales to customers using				6
7			bank credit cards				7

GENERAL JOURNAL — PAGE 2

Credit Card Companies   Credit cards such as American Express and Diners Club are issued by business firms or subsidiaries of business firms that are operated for the special purpose of handling credit card transactions. The potential cardholder must submit an application and pay an annual fee to the credit card company. If the credit references are satisfactory, the credit card is issued. It is normally reissued at one-year intervals so long as the company's credit experience with the cardholder remains satisfactory. These types of credit cards are also called *nonbank* credit cards.

Hotels, restaurants, airline companies, many types of retail stores, and a wide variety of other businesses accept these credit cards. When making sales to cardholders, sellers usually prepare their own sales slip or bill and then complete a special sales slip required by the credit card company. As with the sales slips for bank credit cards, the forms must be imprinted with the identifying data on the customer's card and signed by the customer. Such sales slips are sometimes referred to as *sales invoices, sales drafts,* or *sales vouchers.* The term used varies from one credit card company to another.

Sales to customers using nonbank credit cards such as American Express and Diners Club are accounted for as sales on account. These nonbank credit cards usually take a few days to pay the seller. The amount remitted to the seller is net of the discount fee.

For example, Maxx-Out Sporting Goods sells merchandise on January 16 totaling $1,000 to customers paying with American Express, plus 8 percent sales tax. Assume American Express charges a 7 percent discount fee. The discount withheld by American Express would be $75.60 ($1,080.00 × 7%). The journal entries to record the sales on January 16 and the subsequent payment on January 23 by American Express are illustrated below:

	DATE		DESCRIPTION	POST. REF.	DEBIT	CREDIT	
1	2013						1
2	Jan.	16	Accounts Receivable		1 0 8 0 00		2
3			Sales			1 0 0 0 00	3
4			Sales Tax Payable			8 0 00	4
5			Record sales to customers using				5
6			American Express				6
7							7
8		23	Credit Card Expense		7 5 60		8
9			Cash		1 0 0 4 40		9
10			Accounts Receivable			1 0 8 0 00	10
11			Record payment received from				11
12			American Express				12

GENERAL JOURNAL — PAGE 2

Section 1 Self Review

QUESTIONS

1. What are net sales?

2. What is a sales return? What is a sales allowance?

3. What account is used to record sales tax owed by a business to a city or state?

EXERCISES

4. Where would you report net sales?

   a. general journal

   b. general ledger

   c. income statement

   d. accounts receivable subsidiary ledger

5. Types of business operations are:

   a. service, merchandising, corporation

   b. sole proprietorship, merchandising, manufacturing

   c. service, merchandising, manufacturing

ANALYSIS

6. A company made a sale of $900 on credit to Wells Company. The sales tax rate is 8 percent. The company's accountant prepared the following journal entry to record the transaction (ignore posting references):

	Debit	Credit
Accounts Receivable/ Wells Company	828.00	
Sales Tax Payable	72.00	
Sales		900.00

What entry should have been made to record the transaction?

(Answers to Section 1 Self Review are on pages 224–225.)

SECTION OBJECTIVES	TERMS TO LEARN
>> 2. **Compute trade discounts.** **WHY IT'S IMPORTANT** Trade discounts allow for flexible pricing structures.	accounts receivable ledger control account credit terms list price net sales *Sales Discounts* schedule of accounts receivable trade discount wholesale business
>> 3. **Compute and record cash discounts on sales.** **WHY IT'S IMPORTANT** It is common practice for wholesale businesses to offer discounts to their customers for early payment of invoices.	
>> 4. **Post from the general journal to the general ledger accounts and to the subsidiary ledger.** **WHY IT'S IMPORTANT** A well-designed accounting system provides useful information to management.	
>> 5. **Prepare a schedule of accounts receivable.** **WHY IT'S IMPORTANT** This schedule provides a snapshot of amounts due from customers.	
>> 6. **Record the payment of sales taxes.** **WHY IT'S IMPORTANT** Businesses are legally responsible for accurately reporting and paying sales taxes.	

Special Topics in Merchandising

The operations of Maxx-Out Sporting Goods are typical of those of many retail businesses—businesses that sell goods and services directly to individual customers. In contrast, a **wholesale business** is a manufacturer or distributor of goods that sells to retailers or large customers such as hotels and hospitals. The basic procedures used by wholesalers to handle sales and accounts receivable are the same as those used by retailers. However, many wholesalers offer trade discounts, which are not commonly found in retail operations.

Computing Trade Discounts

A wholesale business offers goods to trade customers at less than retail prices. This price adjustment is based on the volume purchased by trade customers and takes the form of a **trade discount,** which is a reduction from the **list price**—the established retail price. There may be a single trade discount or a series of discounts for each type of goods. The net price (list price less all trade discounts) is the amount the wholesaler records as sales.

The same goods may be offered to different customers at different trade discounts, depending on the size of the order and the costs of selling to the various types of customers.

If the list price of the goods is $1,500 and the trade discount is quoted in a series such as 25 and 15 percent, a different net price will result:

>> 2. OBJECTIVE
Compute trade discounts.

199

important!

Trade Discounts

The amount of sales revenue recorded is the list price minus the trade discount.

List price	$1,500.00
Less first discount ($1,500 × 25%)	375.00
Difference	$1,125.00
Less second discount ($1,125 × 15%)	168.75
Invoice price	$ 956.25

>> **3. OBJECTIVE**

Compute and record cash discounts on sales.

Cash Discounts on Sales

Maxx-Out Sporting Goods, like most retail businesses, does not offer cash discounts. However, many wholesale businesses offer cash discounts to customers who pay within a certain time period. These are known as **credit terms.** For example, a wholesaler may offer a 1 percent discount if the customer pays within 10 days of the invoice; otherwise, the amount is due in whole in 30 days. This credit term would be expressed on the invoice as 1/10, n/30. To the wholesaler this is a *sales discount.* Sales discounts are recorded when the payment is received. Sales discounts are recorded in a contra revenue account, *Sales Discounts.*

Modern Sportsman, a wholesaler, offers credit terms of 1/10, n/30 to its customers. On January 20, Modern Sportsman sold merchandise for $2,000 on account to Maxx-Out Sporting Goods, issuing Invoice 909. Modern Sportsman received payment for Invoice 909, less the cash discount of $20 ($2,000 × 1%), on January 29. The journal entries to record the sale and subsequent payment received follow:

		GENERAL JOURNAL			PAGE 2
	DATE	DESCRIPTION	POST. REF.	DEBIT	CREDIT
1	2013				1
2	Jan. 20	Accounts Receivable		2 0 0 0 00	2
3		Sales			2 0 0 0 00 3
4		Sold merchandise on credit to			4
5		Maxx-Out Sporting Goods,			5
6		Invoice 909, 1/10, n/30			6
7					7
8	29	Sales Discounts		2 0 00	8
9		Cash		1 9 8 0 00	9
10		Accounts Receivable			2 0 0 0 00 10
11		Received payments on account			11
12		from Maxx-Out Sporting Goods,			12
13		Invoice 909			13

Cash Discounts on Sales, with Sales Returns

A customer returning merchandise and paying within the discount period is only entitled to a cash discount on the balance owed after the return. For example, Modern Sportsman sells merchandise for $1,000 on account to Maxx-Out Sporting Goods on January 21, terms 1/10, n/30, Invoice 910. Maxx-Out Sporting Goods returned $100 of the merchandise on January 23, receiving credit memorandum 120 from Modern Sportsman. Maxx-Out Sporting Goods paid the balance owed, less a 1 percent discount, on January 30. The amount received by Modern Sportsman on January 30 would be $891, calculated as follows:

Original sale	$1,000.00
Less return	100.00
Balance	900.00
Less 1% discount ($900.00 × 1%)	9.00
Amount received	$ 891.00

The journal entries for Modern Sportsman to record the sale, return, and payment received follow:

GENERAL JOURNAL   PAGE ___2___

	DATE		DESCRIPTION	POST. REF.	DEBIT	CREDIT	
1	2013						1
2	Jan.	21	Accounts Receivable		1 0 0 0 00		2
3			Sales			1 0 0 0 00	3
4			Sold merchandise on cerdit to				4
5			Maxx-Out Sporting Goods,				5
6			Invoice 910, 1/10, n/30.				6

GENERAL JOURNAL   PAGE ___2___

	DATE		DESCRIPTION	POST. REF.	DEBIT	CREDIT	
1	2013						1
2	Jan.	23	Sales Returns and Allowances		1 0 0 00		2
3			Accounts Receivable			1 0 0 00	3
4			Accept a return of defective				4
5			merchandise, Credit				5
6			Memorandum 120, original sale				6
7			made on Invoice 910,				7
8			January 21, to Maxx-Out				8
9			Sporting Goods				9
10							10
11		30	Cash		8 9 1 00		11
12			Sales Discounts		9 00		12
13			Accounts Receivable			9 0 0 00	13
14			Received payment on account				14
15			from Maxx-Out Sporting Goods,				15
16			Invoice 910				16

Reporting Net Sales

At the end of each accounting period, the balance of the **Sales Returns and Allowances** account and the **Sales Discount** account is subtracted from the balance of the **Sales** account in the Revenue section of the income statement. The resulting figure is the **net sales** for the period.

For example, the **Sales Returns and Allowances** account contains a balance of $600 at the end of January. The **Sales Discount** account balance is $100 at the end of January. The **Sales** account has a balance of $25,700 at the end of January. The Revenue section of the firm's income statement will appear as follows:

Maxx-Out Sporting Goods
Income Statement (Partial)
Month Ended January 31, 2013

Revenue		
Sales		$ 2 5 7 0 0 00
Less: Sales Returns and Allowances	$ 6 0 0 00	
Sales Discounts	1 0 0 00	7 0 0 00
Net Sales		$ 2 5 0 0 0 00

The Accounts Receivable Ledger

A business that extends credit to customers must manage its accounts receivable carefully. Accounts receivable represents a substantial asset for many businesses, and this asset must be converted to cash in a timely manner. Otherwise, a firm may not be able to pay its bills even though it has a large volume of sales and earns a satisfactory profit.

The accountant needs detailed information about the transactions with credit customers at all times. This information is provided by an **accounts receivable ledger** with individual accounts for all credit customers. The accounts receivable ledger is referred to as a subsidiary ledger because it is separate from and subordinate to the general ledger. The accounts receivable account in the general ledger is referred to as the **control account,** since its balance summarizes the total amount due from customers.

Management uses the accounts receivable ledger to verify that customers are paying their balances on time and that they are within their credit limits. The accounts receivable ledger also provides a convenient way to answer questions from credit customers. Customers may ask about current balances or about a possible billing error.

The accounts for credit customers are maintained in a balance ledger form with three money columns, as illustrated below:

NAME	_Ann Anh_					
ADDRESS	_7517 Woodrow Wilson Lane, Dallas, Texas 75267-6205_					

DATE	DESCRIPTION	POST. REF.	DEBIT	CREDIT	BALANCE

Notice that this form does not contain a column for whether the account has a debit or credit balance. The balances in the customer accounts are presumed to be debit balances since asset accounts normally have debit balances. However, occasionally there is a credit balance because a customer has overpaid an amount owed. In this case, the balance owed may be placed inside parentheses, or circled, to show that it is a credit amount owed to the customer.

For a small business such as Maxx-Out Sporting Goods, customer accounts are alphabetized in the accounts receivable ledger. Larger firms and firms that use computers assign an account number to each customer's account and arrange the customer accounts in numeric order. Postings to the accounts receivable ledger should be made daily so that the customer accounts can be kept up to date at all times.

Posting transactions from the general journal to the general ledger is done in the same way discussed in Chapter 4. Firms using an accounts receivable ledger need to add the customer's name after "Accounts Receivable" in the "Description" portion of the general journal. The posting to the customer's account in the accounts receivable ledger is signified by entering a "/", followed by a check mark (✔), after the account number for accounts receivable in the chart of accounts.

To illustrate posting from a general journal to the accounts receivable ledger, let's see how the original sale, sales return, and subsequent payment from Ann Anh would look in both the general journal and accounts receivable ledger, after postings are complete:

GENERAL JOURNAL   PAGE ___2___

	DATE		DESCRIPTION	POST. REF.	DEBIT	CREDIT	
1	2013						1
2	Jan.	8	Accounts Receivable/Ann Anh	111/✓	6 4 8 00		2
3			Sales	401		6 0 0 00	3
4			Sales Tax Payable	231		4 8 00	4
5			Sold merchandise on account				5
6			to Ann Anh, Sales Slip 1102				6
7							7
8		20	Sales Returns and Allowances	451	2 0 0 00		8
9			Sales Tax Payable	231	1 6 00		9
10			Accounts Receivable/Ann Anh	111/✓		2 1 6 00	10
11			Accept return of defective				11
12			merchandise, Credit				12
13			Memorandum 101; original				13
14			sales made on Sale Slip 1102				14
15			of January 8				15
16							16
17		31	Cash	101	4 3 2 00		17
18			Accounts Receivable/Ann Anh	111/✓		4 3 2 00	18
19			Received cash on account from				19
20			Ann Anh, after deducting				20
21			credit Memorandum 101				21

NAME   Ann Anh

ADDRESS   7517 Woodrow Wilson Lane, Dallas, Texas 75267-6205

DATE		DESCRIPTION	POST. REF.	DEBIT	CREDIT	BALANCE
2013						
Jan.	8	Sales Slip 1102	J1	6 4 8 00		6 4 8 00
	20	CM 101	J1		2 1 6 00	4 3 2 00
	31		J1		4 3 2 00	- 0 -

Schedule of Accounts Receivable

At the end of each month, after all the postings have been made, the balances in the accounts receivable ledger must be proved against the balance of the *Accounts Receivable* general ledger account. First a **schedule of accounts receivable,** which lists the subsidiary ledger accounts balances, is prepared. The total of the schedule is compared with the balance of the *Accounts Receivable* account. If the two figures are not equal, errors must be located and corrected.

On January 31, the accounts receivable ledger at Maxx-Out Sporting Goods contains the accounts shown on the next page. To prepare a schedule of accounts receivable, the names of all customers with account balances are listed with the amount of their unpaid balances. The customer balances are added to find the total owed to Maxx-Out Sporting Goods by its credit customers. Any discrepancies between the total of the schedule of accounts receivable and the control account would be investigated.

>> **5. OBJECTIVE**

Prepare a schedule of accounts receivable.

NAME   _Roy Anderson_

ADDRESS   _8913 South Hampton Road, Dallas, Texas 75232-6002_

DATE		DESCRIPTION	POST. REF.	DEBIT	CREDIT	BALANCE
2013						
Jan.	1	Balance	✓			432 00
	3	Sales Slip 1101	J1	432 00		864 00
	7		J1		432 00	432 00
	31	Sales Slip 1105	J1	270 00		702 00

NAME   _Ann Anh_

ADDRESS   _7517 Woodrow Wilson Lane, Dallas, Texas 75267-6205_

DATE		DESCRIPTION	POST. REF.	DEBIT	CREDIT	BALANCE
2013						
Jan.	8	Sales Slip 1102	J1	648 00		648 00
	20	CM 101	J1		216 00	432 00
	31		J1		432 00	- 0 -

NAME   _Vickie Bowman_

ADDRESS   _1712 Red Bird Lane, Dallas, Texas 75267-6502_

DATE		DESCRIPTION	POST. REF.	DEBIT	CREDIT	BALANCE
2013						
Jan.	1	Balance	✓			270 00
	11		J1		270 00	- 0 -

NAME   _Linda Carter_

ADDRESS   _1819 Belt Line Road, Dallas, Texas 75267-6318_

DATE		DESCRIPTION	POST. REF.	DEBIT	CREDIT	BALANCE
2013						
Jan.	1	Balance	✓			54 00
	21	Sales Slip 1104	J1	486 00		540 00
	25	CM 102	J1		486 00	54 00

Maxx-Out Sporting Goods

Schedule of Accounts Receivable

January 31, 2013

Roy Anderson	702 00
Ann Anh	- 0 -
Vickie Bowman	- 0 -
Linda Carter	54 00
Total	756 00

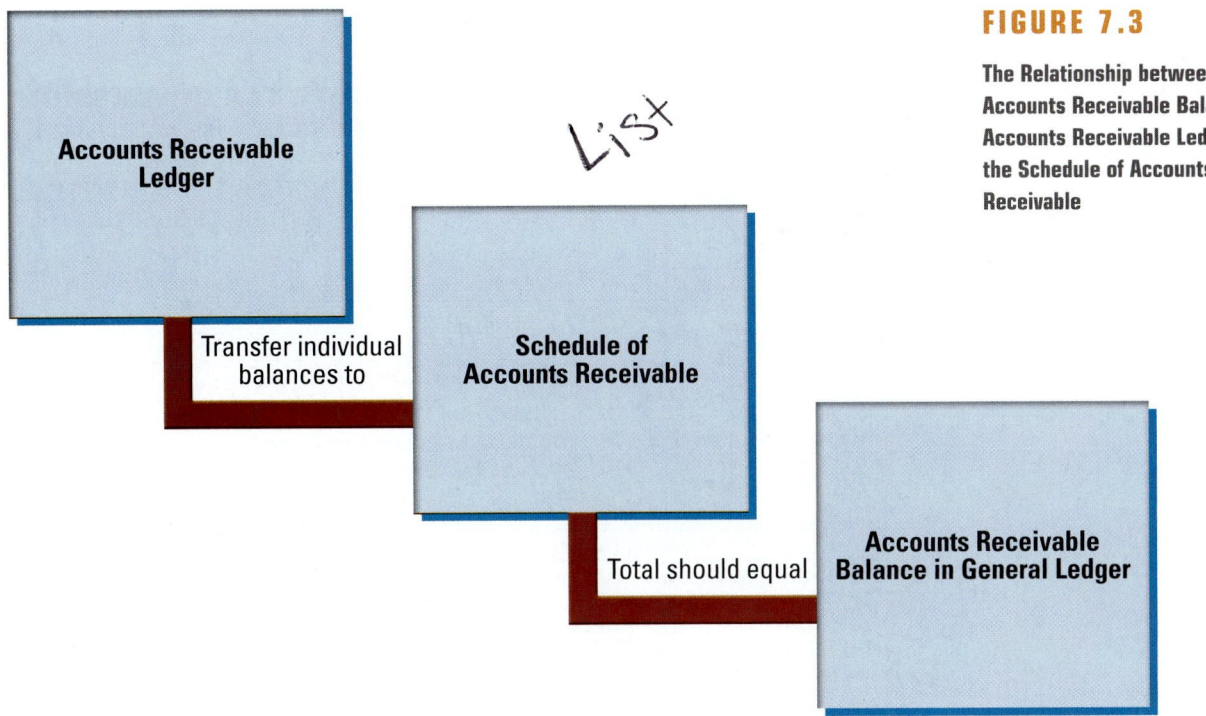

FIGURE 7.3

The Relationship between the
Accounts Receivable Balance, the
Accounts Receivable Ledger, and
the Schedule of Accounts
Receivable

The relationship between the Accounts Receivable balance in the general ledger, the Accounts Receivable ledger, and the Schedule of Accounts Receivable is illustrated in Figure 7.3.

Sales Taxes

>> **6. OBJECTIVE**
Record the payment of sales taxes.

Many cities and states impose a tax on retail sales. Sales tax rates by city and state governments vary. However, the procedures used to account for these taxes are similar.

A sales tax may be levied on all retail sales, but often certain items are exempt. In most cases the amount of the sales tax is stated separately and then added to the retail price of the merchandise.

The retailer is required to collect sales tax from customers, make periodic payments to the taxing authority (usually monthly), and pay the taxes due when the reports are filed. In some states, the government may allow the retailer to retain part of the sales tax owed as compensation for collecting it.

The sales tax return for Maxx-Out Sporting Goods for the month ended January 31, 2013, is shown in Figure 7.4. As shown on Line 7 of the return, Maxx-Out Sporting Goods collected $2,000 in sales taxes from customers in January 2013. Maxx-Out Sporting Goods is allowed to keep 1 percent of the sales taxes collected, or $20 (1% × $2,000) as a discount. The net amount owed, as per Line 14 of the sales tax return, is $1,980.

The journal entry to record the payment of the amount due would debit *Sales Tax Payable* for $1,980 and credit *Cash* for $1,980. The journal entry to record the discount kept by Maxx-Out Sporting Goods would debit *Sales Tax Payable* for $20 and credit *Miscellaneous Income* for $20.

SALES TAX RETURN

ALWAYS REFER TO THIS NUMBER WHEN WRITING THE DIVISION →	**LICENSE NUMBER** 217539

—IMPORTANT—
ANY CHANGE IN OWNERSHIP REQUIRES A NEW LICENSE: NOTIFY THIS DIVISION IMMEDIATELY.

This return DUE on the 1st day of month following period covered by the return, and becomes DELINQUENT on the 21st day.

37-9462315
FED. E.I. NO. OR S.S NO.

STATE TAX COMMISSION
SALES AND USE TAX DIVISION
DRAWER 20
CAPITAL CITY, STATE 78711
RETURN REQUESTED

January 31, 2013
—Sales for period ending—

MAKE ALL REMITTANCES
PAYABLE TO
STATE TAX COMMISSIOIN
DO NOT SEND CASH
STAMPS NOT ACCEPTED

OWNER'S NAME AND LOCATION

Maxx-Out Sporting Goods
2007 Trendsetter Lane
Dallas, Texas 75268-0967

COMPUTATION OF SALES TAX	For Taxpayer's Use	Do Not Use This Column
1. TOTAL Gross proceeds of sales or Gross Receipts (to include rentals)	25,000.00	
2. Add cost of personal property purchased on a RETAIL LICENSE FOR RESALE but USED BY YOU or YOUR EMPLOYEES, including GIFTS and PREMIUMS	–0–	
3. USE TAX—Add cost of personal property purchased outside of STATE for your use, storage, or consumption	–0–	
4. Total (Lines 1, 2, and 3)	25,000.00	
5. LESS ALLOWABLE DEDUCTIONS (Must be itemized on reverse side)	–0–	
6. Net taxable total (Line 4 minus Line 5)	25,000.00	
7. Sales and Use Tax Due (8% of Line 6)	2,000.00	
8. LESS TAXPAYER'S DISCOUNT—(Deductible only when amount of TAX due is not delinquent at time of payment) →	20.00	
IF LINE 7 IS LESS THAN $100.00 —DEDUCT 3% IF LINE 7 IS $100 BUT LESS THAN $1,000.00 —DEDUCT 2% IF LINE 7 IS $1,000.00 OR MORE —DEDUCT 1%		
9. NET AMOUNT OF TAX PAYABLE (Line 7 minus Line 8)	1,980.00	
Add the following penalty and interest if return or remittance is late. 10. Specific Penalty: 25% of tax _ _ _ _ _ _ _ _ _ _ _ _ _ _ _ _ _ $_____ 11. Interest: 1/2 of 1% per month from due date until paid. $_____ TOTAL PENALTY AND INTEREST →		
12. TOTAL TAX, PENALTY AND INTEREST	1,980.00	
13. Subtract credit memo No.		
14. TOTAL AMOUNT DUE (IF NO SALES MADE SO STATE)	1,980.00	

I certify that this return, including the accompanying schedules or statements, has been examined by me and to the best of my knowledge and belief, a true and complete return, made in good faith, for the period stated, pursuant to the provisions of the Code of Laws, 20--, and Acts Amendatory Thereto.

URGENT—SEE THAT LICENSE NUMBER IS ON RETURN

Max Ferraro
SIGNATURE

		Division Use Only
Owner	February 7, 2013	
Owner, partner or title	Date	

Return must be signed by owner or if corporation, authorized person.

Section **2** Self Review

QUESTIONS

1. Which accounts are kept in the accounts receivable ledger?

2. What is the difference between list price and net price?

3. What is a wholesale business?

EXERCISES

4. A company that buys $5,000 of goods from a wholesaler offering trade discounts of 20 and 10 percent will pay what amount for the goods?
   a. $2,200
   b. $3,500
   c. $3,475
   d. $3,600

5. A wholesale business offers a trade discount of 35 percent on a list price of $3,600. At what amount should the wholesale business record the sale?
   a. $2,340
   b. $3,600
   c. $4,860

ANALYSIS

6. International Furniture, Inc., sells merchandise for $2,500 on account to Smith Furniture Shop on February 15, terms 1/10, n/30. Smith Furniture Shop returned $200 of the merchandise on February 20, and received a credit memorandum from International Furniture, Inc. What amount should Smith Furniture Shop pay to International Furniture, Inc., on February 24, less applicable cash discount?

(Answers to Section 2 Self Review are on page 225.)

7 Chapter **REVIEW**   **Chapter Summary**

It has been said that sales are the lifeblood of a business. In this chapter, you have learned to record various sales and cash receipts transactions for a merchandising business. You also used new accounts to record sales and cash receipts transactions of merchandising companies. Additionally, you learned to calculate amounts owed by individual credit customers using the accounts receivable ledger.

Learning Objectives

1   Record sales on account, credit card sales, sales returns, and cash receipt transactions in a general journal.

Companies sell products in many different ways—for cash, on account, and to customers paying with credit cards. Companies may also allow customers to return products for credit or for a cash refund. These transactions are recorded in the general journal. For transactions including sales tax, the sales tax liability is recorded at the time of the sale; this ensures company records reflect the appropriate amount of sales tax liability.

2   Compute trade discounts.

Wholesale businesses often offer goods to trade customers at less than retail prices. Trade discounts are expressed as a percentage off the list price. Multiply the list price by the percentage trade discount offered to compute the dollar amount.

3   Compute and record cash discounts on sales.

Many businesses offer discounts to customers for early payment of invoices. These are known as credit terms.

4   Post from the general journal to the general ledger accounts and to the subsidiary ledger.

Transactions are posted from the general journal to the general ledger accounts as discussed in Chapter 4. The accounts of individual credit customers are kept in a subsidiary ledger called the accounts receivable ledger. Daily postings are made to this ledger from the general journal. The balance of each customer's account is computed after each posting so that the amount owed is known at all times.

5   Prepare a schedule of accounts receivable.

Each month a schedule of accounts receivable is prepared. It is used to prove the subsidiary ledger totals match the Accounts Receivable account in the general ledger.

6   Record the payment of sales taxes.

Every business that collects sales taxes from its customers is responsible for accurately reporting and paying the amount of sales taxes collected to the appropriate government agency.

7   Define the accounting terms new to this chapter.

Glossary

Accounts receivable ledger (p. 202) A subsidiary ledger that contains credit customer accounts

Contra revenue account (p. 193) An account with a debit balance, which is contrary to the normal balance for a revenue account

Control account (p. 202) An account that links a subsidiary ledger and the general ledger since its balance summarizes the balances of the accounts in the subsidiary ledger

Credit memorandum (p. 193) A note verifying that a customer's account is being reduced by the amount of a sales return or sales allowance plus any sales tax that may have been involved

Credit terms (p. 200) Terms for payment on credit by buyer to seller

List price (p. 199) An established retail price

Manufacturing business (p. 190) A business that sells goods that it has produced

Merchandise inventory (p. 190) The stock of goods a merchandising business keeps on hand

Merchandising business (p. 190) A business that sells goods purchased for resale

Net sales (p. 201) The difference between the balance in the **Sales** account and the balance in the *Sales Returns and Allowances* account and the *Sales Discount* account

Open-account credit (p. 196) A system that allows the sale of services or goods with the understanding that payment will be made at a later date

Retail business (p. 190) A business that sells directly to individual consumers

Sales allowance (p. 193) A reduction in the price originally charged to customers for goods or services

Sales Discounts (p. 200) A contra revenue account where early payment discounts are recorded

Sales return (p. 193) A firm's acceptance of a return of goods from a customer

Sales Returns and Allowances (p. 193) A contra revenue account where sales returns and sales allowances are recorded; see definitions of sales return and sales allowance

Schedule of accounts receivable (p. 203) A listing of all balances of the accounts in the accounts receivable subsidiary ledger

Service business (p. 190) A business that sells services

Subsidiary ledger (p. 190) A ledger dedicated to accounts of a single type and showing details to support a general ledger account

Trade discount (p. 199) A reduction from list price

Wholesale business (p. 199) A business that manufactures goods for or distributes goods to retail businesses or large consumers such as hotels and hospitals

Comprehensive **Self Review**

1. A company offers a 2 percent discount if the customer pays within 10 days of the invoice. Otherwise, the amount is due in whole in 30 days. How would this company express these credit terms on its sales invoice?

2. What is a control account?

3. Why does a small merchandising business usually need a more complex set of financial records and statements than a small service business?

4. Why is it useful for a firm to have an accounts receivable ledger?

5. Explain how service, merchandising, and manufacturing businesses differ from one another.

(Answers to Comprehensive Self Review are on page 225.)

Discussion Questions

1. How do retail and wholesale businesses differ?

2. What purposes does the schedule of accounts receivable serve?

3. How are the net sales for an accounting period determined?

4. Why is a sales return or allowance usually recorded in a special Sales Returns and Allowances account rather than being debited to the Sales account?

5. What kind of account is Sales Returns and Allowances?

6. What kind of account is Sales Discounts?

7. The sales tax on a credit sale is not collected from the customer immediately. When is this tax usually entered in a firm's accounting records? What account is used to record this tax?

8. In a particular state, the sales tax rate is 5 percent of sales. The retailer is allowed to record both the selling price and the tax in the same account. Explain how to compute the sales tax due when this method is used.

9. What two methods are commonly used to record sales involving credit cards issued by credit card companies?

10. What procedure does a business use to collect amounts owed to it for sales on credit cards issued by credit card companies?

11. When a firm makes a sale involving a credit card issued by a credit card company, does the firm have an account receivable with the cardholder or with the credit card company?

12. What type of account is used to record the fees charged by the credit card company to the seller?

13. Why are bank credit card sales similar to cash sales for a business?

14. What is open-account credit?

15. What is a trade discount? Why do some firms offer trade discounts to their customers?

APPLICATIONS

Exercises

Exercise 7.1
Objective 1

▶ **Normal balances.**

Identify the normal balance of the following accounts. Use "dr" for debit or "cr" for credit.

Cr Dr Sales
Dr Sales Returns and Allowances
Dr Sales Discounts
Dr Credit Card Expense
Cr Sales Tax Payable

Exercise 7.2
Objective 1

▶ **Recording sales made for cash and on account.**

Hartoto Corporation operates in a state with no sales tax. Record the following transactions in a general journal:

DATE	TRANSACTIONS
2013 June 5	Sold merchandise on account to Mahonga Company; issued Sales Slip 1200 for $875, terms n/30.
15	Recorded cash sales, $1,840.
30	Received payment on account due from Mahonga Company for the sale on June 5.

Exercise 7.3
Objective 1

▶ **Recording sales made for cash and on account, with 8 percent sales tax.**

The following transactions took place at Hanson's Wildlife Resort during May. Hanson's Wildlife Resort must charge 8 percent sales tax on all sales:

DATE	TRANSACTIONS
2013 May 1	Sold merchandise on account to Bill Walker; issued Sales Slip 1015 for $1,500 plus 8 percent sales tax, terms n/30.
15	Recorded cash sales, $3,800 plus 8 percent sales tax.
31	Received payment on account due from Bill Walker for the sale on May 1.

Recording sales made for cash and on account, with 8 percent sales tax, and sales returns.

◀ **Exercise 7.4**
Objective 1

Record the following transactions of Fashion Designs in a general journal:

DATE	TRANSACTIONS
2013	
April 2	Sold merchandise for cash, $1,000 plus sales tax.
3	The customer purchasing merchandise for cash on April 2 returned $100 of the merchandise; provided a cash refund to the customer.
4	Sold merchandise on credit to Tisha Lee; issued Sales Slip 908 for $550 plus tax, terms n/30.
6	Accepted return of damaged merchandise from Tisha Lee; issued Credit Memorandum 302 for $50 plus tax. The original sale was made on Sales Slip 908 of April 4.
30	Received payment on account from Tisha Lee in payment of her purchase of April 4, less the return on April 6.

Recording sales made with bank credit cards and American Express, with 8 percent sales tax.

◀ **Exercise 7.5**
Objective 1

Record the following transactions of Ann's Fashion Boutique in a general journal:

DATE	TRANSACTIONS
2013	
Feb. 2	Sold merchandise totaling $2,800 to customers using bank credit cards. Record the 3 percent discount on credit card sales at time of sale.
15	Sold merchandise totaling $1,600 to customers using American Express.
20	Received amount due from American Express, less their 4 percent discount, for sales made by customers using American Express on February 15.

Computing a trade discount.

◀ **Exercise 7.6**
Objective 2

Amara Company made sales using the following list prices and trade discounts. What amount should be recorded for each sale?

1. List price of $540 and trade discount of 30 percent.
2. List price of $640 and trade discount of 20 percent.
3. List price of $220 and trade discount of 40 percent.

Computing a series of trade discounts.

◀ **Exercise 7.7**
Objective 2

Norville Distributors, a wholesale firm, made sales using the following list prices and trade discounts. What amount should be recorded for each sale?

1. List price of $3,500 and trade discounts of 25 percent and 15 percent.
2. List price of $4,200 and trade discounts of 25 percent and 15 percent.
3. List price of $2,550 and trade discounts of 20 percent and 10 percent.

Recording a sale made on account, with a sales discount.

◀ **Exercise 7.8**
Objective 3

On April 1, Moloney Meat Distributors sold merchandise on account to Fronke's Franks for $2,000 on Invoice 1001, terms 2/10, n/30. Payment was received in full from Fronke's Franks, less discount, on April 10.

Required: Record the transactions on April 1 and April 10. Use 14 as the journal page number.

Exercise 7.9

Objective 4

▶ **Posting to the general ledger and the accounts receivable ledger.**

Post the entries in the general journal below to the accounts receivable account in the general ledger and to the appropriate accounts in the accounts receivable ledger for Calderone Company.

Assume the following account balances at January 1, 2013:

Accounts Receivable (control account)	$8,640
Accounts Receivable—John Gibrone	5,400
Accounts Receivable—Jim Garcia	2,160
Accounts Receivable—June Lin	1,080

Use 111 as the account number for Accounts Receivable in the general ledger.

	GENERAL JOURNAL				PAGE 40	
	DATE	DESCRIPTION	POST. REF.	DEBIT	CREDIT	
1	2013					1
2	Jan. 8	Cash		5 4 0 00		2
3		Accounts Receivable/John Gibrone			5 4 0 00	3
4		Received partial payment on				4
5		account from John Gibrone				5
6						6
7	20	Sales Returns and Allowances		1 0 0 00		7
8		Sales Tax Payable		8 00		8
9		Accounts Receivable/Jim Garcia			1 0 8 00	9
10		Accept return of defective				10
11		merchandise, Credit				11
12		Mermorandun 121; original sale				12
13		made on Sales Slip 11102 of				13
14		December 27, 2012				14

Exercise 7.10

Objective 5

▶ **Preparing a schedule of accounts receivable.**

1. Use the final balances of the customer accounts after completing Exercise 7.9 to prepare a schedule of accounts receivable for Calderone Company at January 31, 2013.

2. Should the total of your accounts receivable schedule agree with the balance of the accounts receivable account in the general ledger at January 31, 2013?

PROBLEMS

Problem Set A

Problem 7.1A

Objectives 1, 4

▶ **Recording sales and cash receipts for a retail store.**

Amanda's Appliances began operations March 1, 2013. The firm sells its merchandise for cash and on open account. Sales are subject to a 6 percent sales tax. During March, Amanda's Appliances engaged in the following transactions:

DATE	TRANSACTIONS
2013 March 1	Sold merchandise on credit to Dave Allen; issued Sales Slip 101 for $550 plus sales tax of $33.
4	Sold merchandise on credit to Castor Phan; issued Sales Slip 102 for $900 plus sales tax of $54.
12	Sold merchandise on credit to Chris Hughes; issued Sales Slip 103 for $1,090 plus sales tax of $65.40.
15	Recorded cash sales for the period from March 1 to March 15 of $6,600 plus sales tax of $396.
25	Sold merchandise on credit to Brian Cooley; issued Sales Slip 104 for $850 plus sales tax of $51.
28	Received a check from Castor Phan of $120 to apply toward his account.
31	Recorded cash sales for the period from March 16 to March 31 of $3,500 plus sales tax of $210.
31	Received payment in full from Dave Allen for the sale of March 1.

INSTRUCTIONS

1. Open the general ledger accounts indicated below.
2. Record the transactions in a general journal. Use 1 as the journal page number.
3. Post the entries from the general journal to the appropriate general ledger accounts.

GENERAL LEDGER ACCOUNTS

101	Cash	221	Sales Tax Payable
111	Accounts Receivable	401	Sales

Analyze: What were the total cash receipts during March?

Recording sales, sales returns, and cash receipts for a retail store. ◀   Problem 7.2A
           Objective 1

Eddie's Electronics began operations September 1, 2013. The firm sells its merchandise for cash and on open account. Sales are subject to a 7 percent sales tax. During September, Eddie's Electronics engaged in the following transactions:

DATE	TRANSACTIONS
2013 Sept. 1	Sold a high-definition television set on credit to Candy Cho; issued Sales Slip 101 for $1,400 plus sales tax of $98.
3	Sold stereo equipment on credit to Jim Peterson; issued Sales Slip 102 for $925 plus sales tax of $64.75.
7	Sold a microwave oven on credit to Bridgette Huffman; issued Sales Slip 103 for $320 plus sales tax of $22.40.
12	Accepted return of defective stereo equipment from Jim Peterson; issued Credit Memorandum 101 for $125 plus sales tax of $8.75. The stereo equipment was sold on September 3.
15	Recorded cash sales for the period from September 1 to September 15 of $9,800 plus sales tax of $686.

(continued)

DATE	7.2A (cont.) TRANSACTIONS
16	Sold a gas dryer on credit to Kathy Sundstrand; issued Sales Slip 104 for $650 plus sales tax of $45.50.
17	Sold a home entertainment system on credit to Mark Navalta; issued Sales Slip 105 for $1,550 plus sales tax of $108.50.
18	Received $600 from Candy Cho on account.
20	Received payment in full from Jim Peterson for the sale of September 3, less the return of September 12.
25	Gave Mark Navalta an allowance because of scratches on his home entertainment system sold on September 17, Sales Slip 105; issued Credit Memorandum 102 for $100 plus sales tax of $7.
27	Received payment in full from Bridgette Huffman for the sale of September 7.
29	Sold a dishwasher on credit to Mark Navalta; issued Sales Slip 106 for $450 plus sales tax of $31.50.
30	Recorded cash sales for the period from September 16 to September 30 of $10,250 plus sales tax of $717.50.

INSTRUCTIONS

Record the transactions in a general journal. Use 1 as the page number.

Analyze: What portion of the sales during September were for entertainment items? (Hint: Do not forget to reduce sales by any sales returns or allowances.)

Problem 7.3A
Objectives 4 and 5

▶ **Posting transactions to the general ledger and accounts receivable ledger.**

INSTRUCTIONS

1. Open the general ledger accounts and accounts receivable ledger accounts indicated below.
2. Post the entries from the general journal in Problem 7.2A to the appropriate accounts in the general ledger and in the accounts receivable ledger.
3. Prepare a schedule of accounts receivable. Compare the balance of the Accounts Receivable control account with the total of the schedule.

GENERAL LEDGER ACCOUNTS

101	Cash	401	Sales
111	Accounts Receivable	421	Sales Returns and Allowances
221	Sales Tax Payable		

ACCOUNTS RECEIVABLE LEDGER ACCOUNTS

Candy Cho	Mark Navalta	Kathy Sundstrand
Bridgette Huffman	Jim Peterson	

Analyze: What is the amount of sales tax owed at September 30, 2013?

Problem 7.4A
Objectives 1 and 3

▶ **Recording sales, sales returns, cash discounts, and cash receipts for a wholesale business.**

Best Sounds is a wholesale business that sells musical instruments. Transactions involving sales and cash receipts for the firm during April 2013 follow. The firm sells its merchandise for cash and on open account. During April, Best Sounds engaged in the following transactions:

DATE	TRANSACTIONS
2013	
April 1	Sold merchandise for $3,500 to Alto Music Center; issued Invoice 3912 with terms of 2/10, n/30.
3	Received a check for $1,470 from Music Supply Store in payment of Invoice 2718 of March 25 ($1,500), less cash discount ($30).
5	Sold merchandise totaling $1,475 in cash to a new customer who has not yet established credit.
7	Merchandise of $75 sold on April 5 is returned for a cash refund.
8	Sold merchandise for $5,500 to Music Warehouse, issued Invoice 3913 with terms of 2/10, n/30.
10	Received payment from Alto Music Center in payment of Invoice 3912, less cash discount.
15	Accepted a return of damaged merchandise from Music Warehouse; issued Credit Memorandum 105 for $1,800. The original sale was made on Invoice 3913 on April 8.
17	Received payment from Music Warehouse for the sale of April 8, less the return on April 15; Music Warehouse deducted the appropriate cash discount from their payment.
19	Received a check for $1,800 as payment in full from Oldies Sounds for Invoice 3850 dated March 20.
20	Sold merchandise for $10,200 to Hawk Music Center; issued Invoice 3914 with terms of 2/10, n/30.
25	Sold merchandise for $9,800 to Modern Sounds; issued Invoice 3915 with terms of 2/10, n/30.
26	Sold merchandise for $7,600 to Country Tunes; issued Invoice 3916 with terms of 2/10, n/30.
27	Accepted a return of damaged merchandise from Modern Sounds; issued Credit Memorandum 106 for $400. The original sale was made on Invoice 3915 on April 25.
29	Received payment from Hawk Music Center for the sale of April 20, less cash discount.
30	Sold merchandise for $2,200 to Oldies Sounds; issued Invoice 3917 with terms of 2/10, n/30.

INSTRUCTIONS

Record the transactions in a general journal. Use 11 as the page number.

Analyze: What was the amount of the cash discount taken by Hawk Music Center on April 29?

Posting transactions to the general ledger and accounts receivable ledger.

◄ **Problem 7.5A**
Objectives 4 and 5

INSTRUCTIONS

1. Open the general ledger accounts and accounts receivable ledger accounts shown at the top of the next page. Enter the balances as of April 1, 2013.

2. Post the entries from the general journal in Problem 7.4A to the appropriate accounts in the general ledger and in the accounts receivable ledger.

3. Prepare a schedule of accounts receivable. Compare the balance of the Accounts Receivable control account with the total of the schedule.

GENERAL LEDGER ACCOUNTS

101	Cash, $26,400 Dr.		451	Sales Returns and Allowances
111	Accounts Receivable, $3,300 Dr.		452	Sales Discounts
401	Sales			

ACCOUNTS RECEIVABLE LEDGER ACCOUNTS

Alto Music Center	Music Supply Store	$1,500
Country Tunes	Music Warehouse	
Hawk Music Center	Oldies Sounds	$1,800
Modern Sounds		

Analyze: What were the total sales on account in April, prior to any returns, allowances, or discounts?

Problem 7.6A
Objectives 1, 2, 4

▶ **Recording sales made for cash, open account, and with credit cards.**

Unmatched Elegance Gift Shop sells cards, supplies, and various holiday greeting cards. Sales to retail customers are subject to an 8 percent sales tax. The firm sells its merchandise for cash; to customers using bank credit cards, such as MasterCard and VISA; and to customers using American Express. The bank credit cards charge a 2 percent fee. American Express charges a 3 percent fee. Unmatched Elegance Gift Shop also grants trade discounts to certain wholesale customers who place large orders. These orders are not subject to sales tax. During February 2013, Unmatched Elegance Gift Shop engaged in the following transactions:

DATE	TRANSACTIONS
2013 Feb. 1	Sold crystal goods to Beautiful Kitchens, a wholesale customer. The list price is $4,000, with a 25 percent trade discount. This sale is not subject to sales tax. Issued Invoice 5950 with terms of n/15.
15	Recorded cash sales for the period from February 1 to February 15 of $8,500 plus sales tax of $680.
15	Recorded sales for the period from February 1 to February 15 to customers using bank credit cards of $12,000 plus sales tax of $960. (Record the 2 percent credit card expense at this time.)
16	Received a check from Beautiful Kitchens in payment of Invoice 5950 dated February 1.
16	Sold merchandise to customers using American Express for $8,000 plus sales tax of $640.
17	Sold a set of Roman statues to Incredible Bedrooms, a wholesale customer. The list price is $8,000, with a 30 percent trade discount. This sale is not subject to sales tax. Issued Invoice 5951 with terms of n/15.
20	Received payment from American Express for amount billed on February 16, less a 3 percent credit card expense.
27	Received a check from Incredible Bedrooms in payment of Invoice 5951 dated February 17.
28	Recorded cash sales for the period from February 16 to February 28 of $7,250 plus sales tax of $580.
28	Recorded sales for the period from February 16 to February 28 to customers using bank credit cards of $10,000 plus sales tax of $800. (Record the 2 percent credit card expense at this time.)
28	Sold merchandise to customers using American Express for $9,200 plus sales tax of $736.

INSTRUCTIONS

1. Open the general ledger accounts indicated below and enter the balances as of February 1, 2013.

2. Record the transactions in a general journal. Use 10 as the journal page number.

3. Post the entries from the general journal to the appropriate accounts in the general ledger.

GENERAL LEDGER ACCOUNTS

101	Cash, $22,230 Dr.		401	Sales
121	Accounts Receivable		521	Credit Card Expense
222	Sales Tax Payable			

Analyze: What was the total credit card expense incurred in February?

Problem Set B

Recording sales and cash receipts for a retail store.   ◀   Problem 7.1B
Objectives 1, 4

Venus Office Supplies began operations October 1, 2013. The firm sells its merchandise for cash and on open account. Sales are subject to a 5 percent sales tax. During October, Venus Office Supplies engaged in the following transactions:

DATE	TRANSACTIONS
2013 Oct. 1	Sold merchandise on credit to Luis Beltazar, CPA; issued Sales Slip 101 for $600 plus sales tax of $30.
4	Sold merchandise on credit to Cervantes Consulting; issued Sales Slip 102 for $360 plus sales tax of $18.
12	Sold merchandise on credit to Andrew Mitchell, Attorney at Law; issued Sales Slip 103 for $450 plus sales tax of $22.50.
15	Recorded cash sales for the period from October 1 to October 15 of $3,825 plus sales tax of $191.25.
25	Sold merchandise on credit to A.D. & M. Escrow; issued Sales Slip 104 for $980 plus sales tax of $49.
28	Received a check from Cervantes Consulting of $175 to apply on account.
31	Recorded cash sales for the period from October 16 to October 31 of $4,350 plus sales tax of $217.50.
31	Received payment in full from Luis Beltazar, CPA for the sale of October 1.

INSTRUCTIONS

1. Open the general ledger accounts indicated below.

2. Record the transactions in a general journal. Use 1 as the journal page number.

3. Post the entries from the general journal to the appropriate general ledger accounts.

GENERAL LEDGER ACCOUNTS

101	Cash		221	Sales Tax Payable
111	Accounts Receivable		401	Sales

Analyze: How much is owed for sales taxes collected at October 31?

Problem 7.2B

Objective 1

▶ **Recording sales, sales returns, and cash receipts for a retail store.**

The Appliance Discounter began operations November 1, 2013. The firm sells its merchandise for cash and on open account. Sales are subject to a 6 percent sales tax. During November, The Appliance Discounter engaged in the following transactions:

DATE	TRANSACTIONS
2013 Nov. 1	Sold a dishwasher on credit to Andy Chin; issued Sales Slip 101 for $650 plus sales tax of $39.
2	Sold stereo equipment on credit to Jane Peters; issued Sales Slip 102 for $825 plus sales tax of $49.50.
7	Sold a trash compactor on credit to Bob Huffington; issued Sales Slip 103 for $410 plus sales tax of $24.60.
12	Accepted return of defective stereo equipment from Jane Peters; issued Credit Memorandum 101 for $95 plus sales tax of $5.70. The stereo equipment was sold on November 2.
15	Recorded cash sales for the period from November 1 to November 15 of $8,900 plus sales tax of $534.
16	Sold a microwave oven on credit to Gina Silvestri; issued Sales Slip 104 for $550 plus sales tax of $33.
17	Sold a home entertainment system on credit to Dennis Newcombe; issued Sales Slip 105 for $1,375 plus sales tax of $82.50.
18	Received $300 from Andy Chin on account.
20	Received payment in full from Jane Peters for the sale of November 2, less the return of November 12.
24	Gave Dennis Newcombe an allowance because of scratches on his home entertainment system sold on November 17, Sales Slip 105; issued Credit Memorandum 102 for $125 plus sales tax of $7.50.
28	Received payment in full from Bob Huffington for the sale of November 7.
29	Sold a gas stove on credit to Bob Huffington; issued Sales Slip 106 for $675 plus sales tax of $40.50.
30	Recorded cash sales for the period from November 16 to November 30 of $10,250 plus sales tax of $615.

INSTRUCTIONS

Record the transactions in a general journal. Use 1 as the journal page number.

Analyze: What is the total amount due from Bob Huffington for the November 29 sale?

Problem 7.3B

Objective 4 and 5

▶ **Posting transactions to the general ledger and accounts receivable ledger.**

INSTRUCTIONS

1. Open the general ledger accounts and accounts receivable ledger accounts indicated on the next page.

2. Post the entries from the general journal in Problem 7.2B to the appropriate accounts in the general ledger and in the accounts receivable ledger.

3. Prepare a schedule of accounts receivable. Compare the balance of the Accounts Receivable control account with the total of the schedule.

GENERAL LEDGER ACCOUNTS

101	Cash	401	Sales
111	Accounts Receivable	421	Sales Returns and Allowances
221	Sales Tax Payable		

ACCOUNTS RECEIVABLE LEDGER ACCOUNTS

Andy Chin   Jane Peters

Bob Huffington   Gina Silvestri

Dennis Newcombe

Analyze: Damaged or defective goods decreased sales by what dollar amount? By what percentage?

Recording sales, sales returns, cash discounts, and cash receipts for a wholesale business.

◄   **Problem 7.4B**
Objectives 1 and 3

The Urban Florist is a wholesale shop that sells flowers, plants, and plant supplies. Transactions involving sales and cash receipts for the firm during May 2013 follow. The firm sells its merchandise for cash and on open account. During May, The Urban Florist engaged in the following transactions:

DATE	TRANSACTIONS
2013	
May 1	Sold floral arrangements for $450 to Annie's Flowers; issued Invoice 9312 with terms of 2/10, n/30.
4	Received a check for $1,176 from Orange County Florist in payment of Invoice 9299 of April 25 ($1,200), less cash discount ($24).
6	Sold merchandise totaling $925 in cash to a new customer who has not yet established credit.
7	$25 of merchandise sold on May 6 is returned for a cash refund.
8	Sold floral arrangements for $1,500 to Rosa's Flowers and Gifts; issued Invoice 9313 with terms of 2/10, n/30.
10	Received payment from Annie's Flowers in payment of Invoice 9312, less cash discount.
14	Gave Rosa's Flowers and Gifts an allowance because of withered flowers discovered in one of the floral arrangements sold on May 8, Invoice 9313; issued Credit Memorandum 109 for $200.
17	Received payment from Rosa's Flowers and Gifts for the sale of May 8, less the return on May 14; Rosa's Flowers and Gifts deducted the appropriate cash discount from their payment.
19	Received a check for $2,900 as payment in full from White Lily Florists, Inc. Invoice 9279 dated April 20.
20	Sold table arrangements to Grand Party Supply; issued Invoice 9314 for $580 with terms of 2/10, n/30.
24	Sold roses to Miyata Floral Designs for $480; issued Invoice 9315 with terms of 2/10, n/30.
26	Sold potted plants to Cancino's Flower Shop for $850; issued Invoice 9316 with terms of 2/10, n/30.
27	Accepted a return of damaged roses from Miyata Floral Designs; issued Credit Memorandum 110 for $48. The original sale was made on Invoice 9315 on May 24.
29	Received payment from Grand Party Supply for the sale of May 20, less cash discount.
30	Sold plants for $1,200 to White Lily Flowers, Inc.; issued Invoice 9317 with terms of 2/10, n/30.

INSTRUCTIONS

Record the transactions in a general journal. Use 12 as the page number.

Analyze: What was the amount of the cash discount taken by Annie's Flowers on May 10?

Problem 7.5B ▶
Objectives 4 and 5

Posting transactions to the general ledger and accounts receivable ledger.

INSTRUCTIONS

1. Open the general ledger accounts and accounts receivable ledger accounts indicated below. Enter the balances as of May 1, 2013.

2. Post the entries from the general journal in Problem 7.4B to the appropriate accounts in the general ledger and in the accounts receivable ledger.

3. Prepare a schedule of accounts receivable. Compare the balance of the Accounts Receivable control account with the total of the schedule.

GENERAL LEDGER ACCOUNTS

101	Cash, $25,800 Dr.		451	Sales Returns and Allowances
111	Accounts Receivable, $4,100 Dr.		452	Sales Discounts
401	Sales			

ACCOUNTS RECEIVABLE LEDGER ACCOUNTS

Annie's Flowers	Orange County Florist	$1,200
Cancino's Flower Shop	Rosa's Flowers and Gifts	
Grand Party Supply	White Lily Florists, Inc.	$2,900
Miyata Floral Designs		

Analyze: What were total sales on account in May, prior to any returns, allowances, or discounts?

Problem 7.6B ▶
Objectives 1, 2, 4

Recording sales made for cash, open account, and with credit cards.

The Victorian Elegance China Shop sells china, stemware, and other gift items. Sales to retail customers are subject to an 8 percent sales tax. The firm sells its merchandise for cash; to customers using bank credit cards, such as MasterCard and VISA; and, to customers using American Express. The bank credit cards charge a 3 percent fee. American Express charges a 4 percent fee. The Victorian Elegance China Shop also grants trade discounts to certain wholesale customers who place large orders. These orders are not subject to sales tax. During June 2013, The Victorian Elegance China Shop engaged in the following transactions:

DATE	TRANSACTIONS
2013 June 1	Sold crystal goods to Wine Country Kitchens, a wholesale customer. The list price is $6,000, with a 30 percent trade discount. This sale is not subject to sales tax. Issued Invoice 6920 with terms of n/15.
15	Recorded cash sales for the period from June 1 to June 15 of $10,200 plus sales tax of $816.
15	Recorded sales for the period from June 1 to June 15 to customers using bank credit cards of $14,200 plus sales tax of $1,136. (Record the 3 percent credit card expense at this time.)
16	Received a check from Wine Country Kitchens in payment of Invoice 6920 dated June 1.
16	Sold merchandise to customers using American Express for $9,000 plus sales tax of $720.

(continued)

DATE	(7.4B cont) TRANSACTIONS
17	Sold a case of brass serving trays to Victorian Decadence, a wholesale customer. The list price is $18,000, with a 40 percent trade discount. This sale is not subject to sales tax. Issued Invoice 6921 with terms of n/15.
19	Received payment from American Express for amount billed on June 16, less a 4 percent credit card expense.
29	Received a check from Victorian Decadence in payment of Invoice 6921 dated June 17.
30	Recorded cash sales for the period from June 16 to June 30 of $9,550 plus sales tax of $764.
30	Recorded sales for the period from June 16 to June 30 to customers using bank credit cards of $11,700 plus sales tax of $936. (Record the 3 percent credit card expense at this time.)
30	Sold merchandise to customers using American Express for $8,200 plus sales tax of $656.

INSTRUCTIONS

1. Open the general ledger accounts indicated below and enter the balances as of June 1, 2013.

2. Record the transactions in a general journal. Use 15 as the journal page number.

3. Post the entries from the general journal to the appropriate accounts in the general ledger.

GENERAL LEDGER ACCOUNTS

101	Cash, $30,155 Dr.	401	Sales
121	Accounts Receivable	521	Credit Card Expense
222	Sales Tax Payable		

Analyze: What was the total credit card expense incurred in June?

Critical Thinking Problem 7.1

Recording sales, sales returns, and cash receipts for a retail store

Athletic X-Press Sporting Goods began operations March 1, 2013. The firm sells its merchandise for cash; on open account; to customers using bank credit cards, such as MasterCard and VISA; and, to customers using American Express. Merchandise sales are subject to an 8 percent sales tax. The bank credit cards charge a 3 percent fee. American Express charges a 4 percent fee. During March, Athletic X-Press Sporting Goods engaged in the following transactions:

DATE	TRANSACTIONS
2013 March 1	Sold merchandise on credit to Mark Everest; issued Sales Slip 101 for $700 plus sales tax of $56.
3	Sold merchandise on credit to Emily Ancheta; issued Sales Slip 102 for $300 plus sales tax of $24.
8	Accepted a return of merchandise from Mark Everest; the merchandise was originally sold on Sales Slip 101 of March 1; issued Credit Memorandum 1 for $108, which included sales tax of $8.

(continued)

DATE	RECORDING SALES, SALES RETURNS, AND CASH RECEIPTS FOR A RETAIL STORE (cont.) TRANSACTIONS
10	Received payment from Mark Everest in payment of his balance owed for merchandise sold on March 1, less the return of merchandise on March 8.
12	Sold merchandise on credit to Annie Han; issued Sales Slip 103 for $450 plus sales tax of $36.
15	Recorded cash sales for the period from March 1 to March 15 of $5,000 plus sales tax of $400.
15	Recorded sales for the period from March 1 to March 15 to customers using bank credit cards of $7,000 plus sales tax of $560. (Record the 3% credit card expense at this time.)
25	Sold merchandise on credit to Jason Cataldo; issued Sales Slip 104 for $300 plus sales tax of $24.
26	Sold merchandise to customers using American Express for $3,000 plus sales tax of $240.
28	Received a check from Annie Han of $100 to apply toward her account.
31	Recorded cash sales for the period from March 16 to March 31 of $5,500 plus sales tax of $440.
31	Received payment from American Express for amount billed on March 26, less a 4% fee.
31	Recorded sales for the period from March 16 to March 31 to customers using bank credit cards of $4,000 plus sales tax of $320. (Record the 3% credit card expense at this time.)

INSTRUCTIONS

1. Open the general ledger account and accounts receivable ledger accounts indicated below.
2. Record the transactions in a general journal. Use 1 as the journal page number.
3. Post the entries from the general journal to the appropriate account in the general ledger and in the accounts receivable ledger.
4. Prepare a schedule of accounts receivable. Compare the balance of the Accounts Receivable control account with the total of the schedule.

GENERAL LEDGER ACCOUNTS

111   Accounts Receivable

ACCOUNTS RECEIVABLE LEDGER ACCOUNTS

Emily Ancheta   Mark Everest

American Express   Annie Han

Jason Cataldo

Critical Thinking Problem 7.2

Retail Store

Carlos Zayas is the owner of The Home Pantry, a housewares store that sells a wide variety of items for the kitchen, bathroom, and home. The Home Pantry offers a company credit card to its customers.

The company has experienced an increase in sales since the credit card was introduced. Carlos is considering replacing his manual system of recording sales with electronic point-of-sale cash registers that are linked to a computer.

Cash sales are now rung up by the salesclerks on a cash register that generates a tape listing total cash sales at the end of the day. For credit sales, salesclerks prepare handwritten sales slips that are forwarded to the accountant for manual entry into the general journal and accounts receivable ledger.

The electronic register system Carlos is considering would use an optical scanner to read coded labels attached to the merchandise. As the merchandise is passed over the scanner, the code is sent to the computer. The computer is programmed to read the code and identify the item being sold, record the amount of the sale, maintain a record of total sales, update the inventory record, and keep a record of cash received.

If the sale is a credit transaction, the customer's company credit card number is entered into the register. The computer updates the customer's account in the accounts receivable ledger stored in computer memory.

If this system is used, many of the accounting functions are done automatically as sales are entered into the register. At the end of the day, the computer prints a complete listing of sales made, along with up-to-date balances for the general ledger and the accounts receivable ledger accounts related to sales transactions.

Listed below are four situations that Carlos is eager to eliminate. Would use of an electronic point-of-sale system as described above reduce or prevent these problems? Why or why not?

1. The accountant did not post a sale to the customer's subsidiary ledger account.

2. The salesclerk did not charge a customer for an item.

3. The customer purchased merchandise using a stolen credit card.

4. The salesclerk was not aware that the item purchased was on sale and did not give the customer the sale price.

BUSINESS CONNECTIONS

Retail Sales

1. How does the *Sales Returns and Allowances* account provide management with a measure of operating efficiency? What problems might be indicated by a high level of returns and allowances?

2. Suppose you are the accountant for a small chain of clothing stores. Up to now, the firm has offered open-account credit to qualified customers but has not allowed them to use bank credit cards. The president of the chain has asked your advice about changing the firm's credit policy. What advantages might there be in eliminating the open-account credit and accepting bank credit cards instead? Do you see any disadvantages?

3. During the past year, Cravens Company has had a substantial increase in its losses from uncollectible accounts. Assume that you are the newly hired controller of this firm and that you have been asked to find the reason for the increase. What policies and procedures would you investigate?

4. Suppose a manager in your company has suggested that the firm not hire an accountant to advise it on tax matters and to file tax returns. He states that tax matters are merely procedural in nature and that anyone who can read the tax form instructions can do the necessary work. Comment on this idea.

5. Why is it usually worthwhile for a business to sell on credit even though it will have some losses from uncollectible accounts?

6. How can a firm's credit policy affect its profitability?

7. Why should management insist that all sales on credit and other transactions affecting the firm's accounts receivable be journalized and posted promptly?

8. How can efficient accounting records help management maintain sound credit and collection policies?

Sales Return and Allowances

Credit memos are created when a product is returned. A debit to Sales Returns and Allowances and a credit to A/R is recorded when a credit memo is created. A credit memo will reduce A/R and write off the invoice. You have noticed that the A/R clerk, Margarita, has created an abnormally high number of credit memos. You notice the inventory does not reflect the additional inventory resulting from the Sales Returns and Allowances. What would you do and how would you document this decision?

Financial Statement ANALYSIS

Income Statement

An excerpt from the Consolidated Statements of Earnings for The Home Depot, Inc., is presented below. Review the financial data and answer the following analysis questions:

(Amounts in millions except per share data) Fiscal Year Ended January 31,	2010	2009	2008
Revenues:			
Net Sales	$66,176	$71,288	$77,349

Analyze:

1. Based on the financial statement presented above, what is The Home Depot, Inc.'s fiscal year period?

2. The Home Depot, Inc.'s statement reports one figure for net sales. Name one account whose balance may have been deducted from the *Sales* account balance to determine a net sales amount.

3. The data presented demonstrate a steady decrease in net sales over the three-year period. By what percentage have net sales of 2010 decreased from sales of 2008?

Analyze Online: Find the most recent consolidated statements of income on The Home Depot, Inc., Web site (www.homedepot.com). Click on *Investor Relations* then *Financial Reports* then *Annual Reports,* then select the link for the most recent annual report.

4. What dollar amount is reported for net sales for the most recent year?
5. What is the trend in net sales over the last three years?
6. What are some possible reasons for this trend?

TEAMWORK

Customer to Vendor

Divide into groups of four individuals. Your company is named Cole's Cooking Supplies. Assign one person as Cole's sales associate; one as the company's A/R clerk; one as the customer Louisa's Cooking School; and one as Louisa's A/P clerk. Record the transaction each individual would record from a sale of $50,000 for cooking supplies.

Internet CONNECTION

Accounting General Ledger Packages

Go to the QuickBooks and Peachtree Web sites at quickbooks.com and peachtree.com. Compare products at each site. What are some activities that each program can facilitate?

Answers to **Self Reviews**

Answers to Section 1 Self Review

1. Sales, less sales returns and allowances and less sales discounts.
2. A sales return results when a customer returns goods and the firm takes them back. A sales allowance results when the firm gives a customer a reduction in the sales price.

3. **Sales Tax Payable** is used to record sales taxes owed. It is classified as a liability.

4. **c.** income statement

5. **c.** service, merchandising, manufacturing

6. The entry that should have been made is:

	Debit	Credit
Accounts Receivable/Wells Company	972.00	
Sales Tax Payable		72.00
Sales		900.00

Answers to Section 2 Self Review

1. Individual accounts for all credit customers.

2. List price is the established retail price of an item. The net price is the amount left after all trade discounts are subtracted from the list price.

3. A wholesale business is a manufacturer or distributor of goods that sells to retailers or large customers such as hotels and hospitals.

4. **d.** $3,600

5. **a.** $2,340

6. $2,277

Answers to Comprehensive Self Review

1. 2/10, n/30

2. A control account is an account that serves as a link between a subsidiary ledger and the general ledger because its balance summarizes the balances of the accounts in the subsidiary ledger.

3. A merchandising business must account for the purchase and sale of goods and for its merchandise inventory.

4. It contains detailed information about the transactions with credit customers and shows the balances owed by credit customers at all times.

5. A service business sells services; a merchandising business sells goods that it has purchased for resale; and a manufacturing business sells goods that it has produced.

Accounting for Purchases, Accounts Payable, and Cash Payments

Chapter 8

LEARNING OBJECTIVES

1. Record purchases of merchandise on credit in a general journal.
2. Compute the net delivered cost of purchases.
3. Post from the general journal to the general ledger accounts.
4. Post transactions to the accounts payable subsidiary ledger.
5. Prepare a schedule of accounts payable.
6. Demonstrate a knowledge of the procedures for effective internal control of purchases.
7. Define the accounting terms new to this chapter.

NEW TERMS

accounts payable ledger
cash discount
cost of goods sold
Freight In account
purchase allowance
purchase invoice
purchase order
purchase requisition
purchase return
Purchases account
purchases discount
Purchases Returns and Allowances
receiving report
sales discount
sales invoice
schedule of accounts payable
Transportation In account

Williams-Sonoma   www.williams-sonoma.com

Williams-Sonoma began in 1956, when Chuck Williams opened a small specialty cookware shop in Sonoma, California. By offering French kitchen equipment most Americans had never seen before, the store gained popularity among home cooks and professional chefs from across the country. Since its humble beginnings in the late 1950s, Williams-Sonoma has evolved into a multibillion-dollar corporation.

To combat challenging economic conditions, Williams-Sonoma recently lowered prices on some of its high-ticket items to generate more sales and boost revenues. The company has also been ramping up its e-mail marketing efforts and stepping up its focus on new product lines and exclusive merchandise as a means of gaining new customers. These strategies seem to be paying off—the company recently reported that net profit rose to $30.8 million, or 28 cents a share.

thinking critically

How do you think Williams-Sonoma buyers determined the types of new products that might appeal to loyal customers or gain new customers?

Merchandising Purchases

In this chapter you will learn how Maxx-Out Sporting Goods manages its purchases of goods for resale and its accounts payable.

Accounting for Purchases

Most merchandising businesses purchase goods on credit under open-account arrangements. A large firm usually has a centralized purchasing department that is responsible for locating suppliers, obtaining price quotations, negotiating credit terms, and placing orders. In small firms, purchasing activities are handled by a single individual, usually the owner or manager.

PURCHASING PROCEDURES

When a sales department needs goods, it sends the purchasing department a purchase requisition. A **purchase requisition** lists the items to be ordered (Figure 8.1). It is signed by someone with the authority to approve requests for merchandise, usually the manager of the sales department. The purchasing department selects a supplier who can furnish the goods at a competitive price and then issues a purchase order (Figure 8.2). The **purchase order** specifies the exact items, quantity, price, and credit terms. It is signed by someone with authority to approve purchases, usually the purchasing agent.

When the goods arrive at the business, they are inspected. A **receiving report** is prepared to show the quantity and condition of the goods received. The purchasing department receives a copy of the receiving report and compares it to the purchase order.

If defective goods or the wrong quantity of goods are received, the purchasing department contacts the supplier and settles the problem.

Figure 8.3 shows the invoice for items ordered and shipped. The customer then receives an invoice, or bill, for items ordered and shipped. The customer, Maxx-Out Sporting Goods, calls it a **purchase invoice.** The seller calls it a **sales invoice.** The customer's accounting

FIGURE 8.1

Purchase Requisition

Maxx-Out Sporting Goods
2007 Trendsetter Lane
Dallas, TX 75268-0967

PURCHASE REQUISITION

No. 325

DEPARTMENT Men's   DATE OF REQUEST January 2, 2013

ADVISE ON DELIVERY John Amos   DATE REQUIRED January 25, 2013

QUANTITY	DESCRIPTION
10	Assorted colors men's sweat suits

APPROVED BY _____   REQUESTED BY _____

FOR PURCHASING DEPARTMENT USE ONLY

PURCHASE ORDER 9001   ISSUED TO: Modern Sportsman
DATE January 5, 2013   1718 Sherry Lane
Dallas, TX 75267-6205

FIGURE 8.2

Purchase Order

Maxx-Out Sporting Goods
2007 Trendsetter Lane
Dallas, TX 75268-0967

PURCHASE ORDER

To Modern Sportsman
1718 Sherry Lane
Dallas, TX 75267-6205

Date: January 5, 2013
Order No: 9001
Terms: n/30

QUANTITY	ITEM	UNIT PRICE	TOTAL
10	Assorted colors men's sweat suits	476.00	4,760.00

APPROVED BY Max Ferraro

FIGURE 8.3

Invoice

Modern Sportsman   INVOICE NO. 1100
1718 Sherry Lane
Dallas, TX 75267-6205

SOLD TO: Maxx-Out Sporting Goods
2007 Trendsetter Lane
Dallas, TX 75268-0967

DATE: January 15, 2013
ORDER NO.: 9001
SHIPPED BY: Metroplex Express
TERMS: n/30

YOUR ORDER NO.	SALESPERSON		TERMS
9001			n/30
DATE SHIPPED	SHIPPED BY		FOB
January 14, 2013	Metroplex Express		Dallas

QUANTITY	DESCRIPTION	UNIT PRICE	TOTAL
10	Assorted colors men's suits	476 00	4,760 00
	Freight		360 00
	Total		5,120 00

department compares the invoice to copies of the purchase order and receiving report. The accounting department checks the quantities, prices, and math on the invoice and then records the purchase. It is important to record purchases in the accounting records as soon as the invoice is verified. Shortly before the due date of the invoice, the accounting department issues a check to the supplier and records the payment.

> The purchasing department for The Home Depot, Inc., purchases 30,000 to 40,000 different kinds of home improvement supplies, building materials, and lawn and garden products.

In Chapter 7, we learned to account for the various sales and sales-related transactions typically engaged in by merchandising firms. In this chapter, we will learn to account for purchases and purchase-related transactions. The new accounts we will be using in this chapter are summarized below:

Name of Account	Type of Account	Normal Balance	Used to Record
Purchases	Expense	DR	Purchases of merchandise inventory
Purchases Returns and Allowances	Contra expense	CR	Returns of merchandise inventory to seller on the buyer's books
Purchases Discounts	Contra expense	CR	Record cash discounts taken for early payments to the seller by the buyer
Freight In or Transportation In	Expense	DR	Record payment of transportation costs on merchandise inventory purchased

THE PURCHASES ACCOUNT

The purchase of merchandise for resale is a cost of doing business. The purchase of merchandise is debited to the **Purchases account.** Purchases is a temporary expense account classified as cost of goods sold. The **cost of goods sold** is the actual cost to the business of the merchandise sold to customers.

Cost of goods sold accounts follow the debit and credit rules of expense accounts. The Purchases account is increased by debits and decreased by credits. Its normal balance is a debit. In the chart of accounts, the cost of goods sold accounts appear just before the expense accounts.

> Walmart purchases private-label products from suppliers and markets these as Walmart brands. Products such as Ol'Roy™ dog food and Spring Valley® vitamins are purchased at lower costs than nationally known brands. Thus, Walmart can sell these items at a lower price to its customers.

Due to the relatively small size of its operations, Maxx-Out Sporting Goods does not keep track of its inventory daily. Maxx-Out Sporting Goods uses a periodic inventory system. In a periodic inventory system, the amount of inventory on hand must be determined by counting merchandise inventory in stock.

Larger businesses need to know the number of units and the unit cost for inventory on hand at all times. These businesses use a perpetual inventory system. In a perpetual inventory system, the amount of inventory on hand is adjusted for each sale, purchase, or return. Electronic equipment, such as point-of-sale cash registers and scanners, help track inventory balances. The accounting for a perpetual system is not covered in this chapter.

PURCHASES AND CASH PAYMENTS WITH FREIGHT CHARGES

If the freight terms are free on board (FOB) shipping point, the buyer pays the freight charge—the cost of shipping the goods from the seller's warehouse to the buyer's location. If the freight terms are FOB destination, the seller pays the freight charges. There are two ways to handle the freight charges paid by the buyer:

- The buyer is billed directly by the transportation company for the freight charge. The buyer issues a check directly to the freight company.
- The seller pays the freight charge and includes it on the invoice. The invoice includes the price of the goods and the freight charge.

The freight charge is debited to the **Freight In** or **Transportation In account.** This is an expense account, included in cost of goods sold, showing transportation charges for merchandise purchased.

Maxx-Out Sporting Goods purchased merchandise from Modern Sportsman on January 15. Modern Sportsman paid the freight charge and included it on their invoice 1100. Maxx-Out Sporting Goods enters three elements in the accounting records:

Price of goods (debit **Purchases**)	$4,760.00
Freight charge (debit **Freight In**)	360.00
Total invoice (credit **Accounts Payable**)	$5,120.00

>>**1. OBJECTIVE**

Record purchases of merchandise on credit in a general journal.

Purchases		Freight In		Accounts Payable	
+	–	+	–	–	+
4,760		360			5,120

The journal entry to record the purchase follows:

GENERAL JOURNAL   PAGE 2

	DATE		DESCRIPTION	POST. REF.	DEBIT	CREDIT	
1	2013						1
2	Jan.	15	Purchases		4 7 6 0 00		2
3			Freight In		3 6 0 00		3
4			Accounts Payable			5 1 2 0 00	4
5			Purchased merchandise from				5
6			Modern Sportsman, Invoice 1100				6

The journal entry to record payment of this invoice on January 30 using check number 152 appears below:

GENERAL JOURNAL   PAGE 2

	DATE		DESCRIPTION	POST. REF.	DEBIT	CREDIT	
1	2013						1
2	Jan.	30	Accounts Payable		5 1 2 0 00		2
3			Cash			5 1 2 0 00	3
4			Paid Modern Sportsman				4
5			Invoice 1100, Check 152				5

Purchase Returns and Allowances

When merchandise arrives, it is examined to confirm that it is satisfactory. Occasionally, the wrong goods are shipped, or items are damaged or defective. A **purchase return** is when the business returns the goods. A **purchase allowance** is when the purchaser keeps the goods but receives a reduction in the price of the goods. The supplier issues a credit memorandum for the return or allowance. The credit memorandum reduces the amount that the purchaser owes.

Purchases returns and allowances are entered in the ***Purchases Returns and Allowances*** account, not in the ***Purchases*** account. The ***Purchases Returns and Allowances*** account is a complete record of returns and allowances. Business managers analyze this account to identify problem suppliers. ***Purchases Returns and Allowances*** is a contra expense under cost of goods sold. The normal balance of cost of goods sold accounts is a debit. The ***Purchases Returns and Allowances*** account has a normal credit balance.

RECORDING PURCHASES RETURNS AND ALLOWANCES

Maxx-Out Sporting Goods received merchandise costing $4,760 from Modern Sportsman on January 15, Invoice 1100, with freight charges of $360 paid by Modern Sportsman and added to the invoice. Maxx-Out Sporting Goods recorded the purchase as shown below:

	DATE		DESCRIPTION	POST. REF.	DEBIT	CREDIT	
1	2013						1
2	Jan.	15	Purchases		4 7 6 0 00		2
3			Freight In		3 6 0 00		3
4			Accounts Payable			5 1 2 0 00	4
5			Purchased merchandise from				5
6			Modern Sportsman, Invoice 1100				6

GENERAL JOURNAL   PAGE ___2___

Some goods were damaged, and the supplier granted a $476 purchase allowance on their credit memo 103 of January 27.

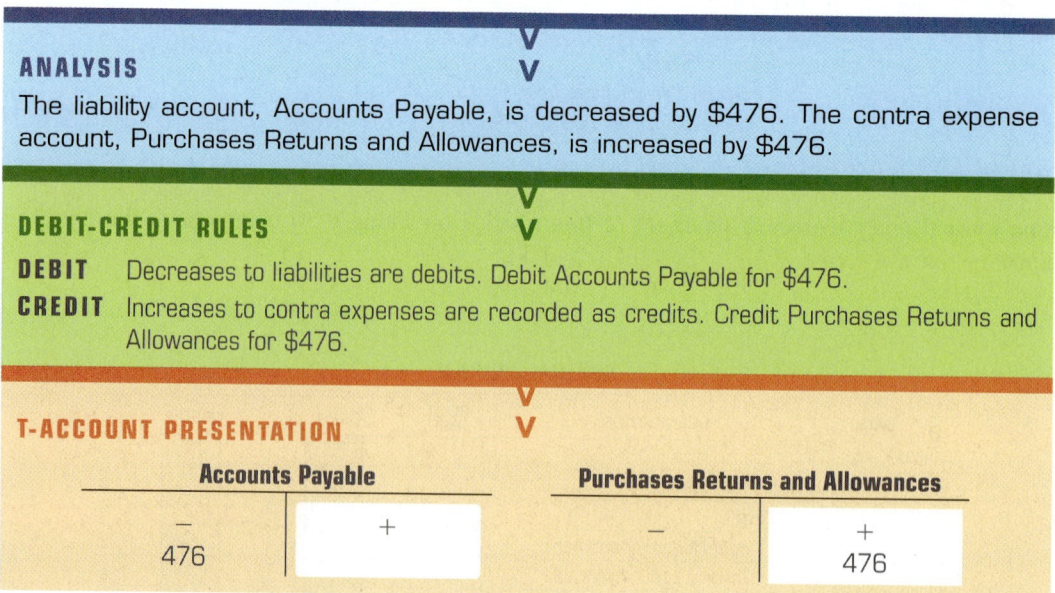

BUSINESS TRANSACTION

ANALYSIS

The liability account, Accounts Payable, is decreased by $476. The contra expense account, Purchases Returns and Allowances, is increased by $476.

DEBIT-CREDIT RULES

DEBIT   Decreases to liabilities are debits. Debit Accounts Payable for $476.

CREDIT   Increases to contra expenses are recorded as credits. Credit Purchases Returns and Allowances for $476.

T-ACCOUNT PRESENTATION

Accounts Payable		Purchases Returns and Allowances	
−	+	−	+
476			476

GENERAL JOURNAL ENTRY

	GENERAL JOURNAL				PAGE 2
	DATE	DESCRIPTION	POST. REF.	DEBIT	CREDIT
1	2013				
2	Jan. 27	Accounts Payable		4 7 6 00	
3		Purchases Returns and Allowances			4 7 6 00
4		Received Credit Memo 103			
5		for an allowance for damaged			
6		merchandise; original Invoice			
7		1100, January 15, 2013			

Notice the entry to record the receipt of the credit memorandum from Modern Sportsman reduces Accounts Payable by debiting it for $476. The amount owed to Modern Sportsman, after the purchase allowance, is $4,644 ($5,120 − $476 = $4,644). The entry to pay the amount owed to Modern Sportsman on January 31 with check number 153 is presented below.

	GENERAL JOURNAL				PAGE 2
	DATE	DESCRIPTION	POST. REF.	DEBIT	CREDIT
1	2013				
2	Jan. 31	Accounts Payable		4 6 4 4 00	
3		Cash			4 6 4 4 00
4		Paid amount due on			
5		Invoice 1100 to Modern			
6		Sportsman after receipt of			
7		Cerdit Memo 103, Check 153			

RECORDING PURCHASES DISCOUNTS

The invoice date and credit terms determine when payment is due. The following credit terms often appear on invoices:

- *Net 30 days* or *n/30* means that payment in full is due 30 days after the date of the invoice.
- *Net 10 days EOM,* or *n/10 EOM,* means that payment in full is due 10 days after the end of the month in which the invoice was issued.
- *2 percent 10 days, net 30 days,* or *2/10, n/30* means that if payment is made within 10 days of the invoice date, the customer can take a 2 percent discount. Otherwise, payment in full is due in 30 days. Note that discounts are not allowed on any freight portion of the invoice.

The 2 percent discount is a **cash discount;** it is a discount offered by suppliers to encourage quick payment by customers. To the customer it is known as a **purchases discount.** As discussed in Chapter 7 it is known as a **sales discount** to the seller/supplier.

The 2 percent discount does not apply to freight prepaid by the supplier and added to the invoice. For example, assume Maxx-Out Sporting Goods received merchandise costing $3,000 from Modern Sportsman on January 10, Invoice 880, terms 2/10, n/30, with freight charges of $200 paid by Modern Sportsman and added to the invoice. Maxx-Out Sporting Goods recorded the purchase as shown on the next page:

	GENERAL JOURNAL				PAGE 2	
	DATE	DESCRIPTION	POST. REF.	DEBIT	CREDIT	
1	2013					1
2	Jan. 10	Purchases		3 0 0 0 00		2
3		Freight In		2 0 0 00		3
4		Accounts Payable			3 2 0 0 00	4
5		Purchased merchandise from				5
6		Modern Sportsman, Invoice 880,				6
7		terms 2/10, n/30				7

Maxx-Out Sporting Goods paid the amount due, after deducting the 2 percent discount, on January 19 with check number 150. The amount due is $3,140, computed as follows:

Balance due	$3,200.00
Less: discount ($3,000 × 2%)	60.00
Amount due	$3,140.00

The journal entry to record the payment appears below:

	GENERAL JOURNAL				PAGE 2	
	DATE	DESCRIPTION	POST. REF.	DEBIT	CREDIT	
1	2013					1
2	Jan. 19	Accounts Payable		3 2 0 0 00		2
3		Purchases Discounts			6 0 00	3
4		Cash			3 1 4 0 00	4
5		Paid balance owed to				5
6		Modern Sportsman, Invoice 880,				6
7		Check 150				7

If there is a purchase return processed within the discount period, the buyer is entitled to take the cash discount only on the balance owed after the return. The following entries illustrate a purchase of $500 from Modern Sportsman on January 11, terms 2/10, n/30, with freight of $25 added, Invoice 910; a return of $100 on January 12, credit memorandum 112; and the final payment on January 20, check 149.

The merchandise purchase of $500, with freight of $25 added to the invoice, is recorded as follows:

	GENERAL JOURNAL				PAGE 2	
	DATE	DESCRIPTION	POST. REF.	DEBIT	CREDIT	
1	2013					1
2	Jan. 11	Purchases		5 0 0 00		2
3		Freight In		2 5 00		3
4		Accounts Payable			5 2 5 00	4
5		Purchased merchandise from				5
6		Modern Sportsman, Invoice 910,				6
7		term 2/10, n/30				7

The purchase return on January 12 is journalized below:

	DATE		DESCRIPTION	POST. REF.	DEBIT	CREDIT	
1	2013						1
2	Jan.	12	Accounts Payable		1 0 0 00		2
3			Purchases Returns and Allowances			1 0 0 00	3
4			Received Credit Memo 112				4
5			from Modern Sportsman for				5
6			return of product; original				6
7			Invoice 910, January 11, 2013				7

GENERAL JOURNAL   PAGE 2

The amount to be paid on January 20 is $417, calculated as follows:

Original amount owed	$ 525.00
Less: purchase return	100.00
Difference	425.00
Less: discount ($400 X 2%)	8.00
Amount paid	$ 417.00

Note that the discount is calculated on the original merchandise purchase of $500 less the purchase return of $100. Remember, no discount is allowed on freight.

The entry to record the payment follows:

	DATE		DESCRIPTION	POST. REF.	DEBIT	CREDIT	
1	2013						1
2	Jan.	20	Accounts Payable		4 2 5 00		2
3			Purchases Discounts			8 00	3
4			Cash			4 1 7 00	4
5			Paid amount owed to Modern				5
6			Sportsman, Invoice 910,				6
7			Check 149				7

GENERAL JOURNAL   PAGE 2

Determining the Net Delivered Cost of Purchases

>> 2. OBJECTIVE
Compute the net delivered cost of purchases.

The *Purchases* account accumulates the cost of merchandise bought for resale. The income statement of a merchandising business contains a section showing the total cost of purchases. This section combines information about the cost of the purchases, freight in, purchases returns and allowances, and purchases discounts for the period. Assume Maxx-Out Sporting Goods has the following general ledger account balances at January 31:

Purchases	$23,315
Freight In	1,565
Purchases Returns and Allowances	476
Purchases Discounts	124

The net delivered cost of purchases for Maxx-Out Sporting Goods in January is calculated as follows:

Purchases	$23,315
Freight In	1,565
Delivered Cost of Purchases	$24,880
Less Purchases Returns and Allowances	476
Less Purchases Discounts	124
Net Delivered Cost of Purchases	$24,280

In Chapter 13, you will see how the complete income statement for a merchandising business is prepared. You will learn about the Cost of Goods Sold section and how the net delivered cost of purchases is used in calculating the results of operations.

Section 1 Self Review

QUESTIONS

1. What is the name of the account used to record purchases of merchandise inventory? *Purchases*

2. What are net delivered cost of purchases? *Purchase + Freight*

3. What does "FOB shipping point" mean? *Seller pays*

EXERCISES

4. What form is sent to the supplier to order goods?
   a. Purchase invoice
   b. Purchase order
   c. Purchase requisition
   d. Sales invoice

5. The customer's accounting department should compare the purchase invoice from the supplier to:
   a. the purchases account and the sales invoice.
   b. the purchases account and the purchase order.
   c. the receiving report and the purchases account.
   d. the receiving report and the purchase order.

ANALYSIS

6. A company purchased merchandise of $600 on account from Fashion World, a supplier. Fashion World prepaid freight charges of $50, and added them to the invoice. The company's accountant prepared the following journal entry to record the transaction (ignore posting references):

	Debit	Credit
Purchases *Freight*	600.00 *50.00*	
Accounts Payable / Fashion World		650.00

What entry should have been made to record the transaction?

(Answers to Section 1 Self Review are on page 259.)

600
50

SECTION OBJECTIVES	TERMS TO LEARN
	accounts payable ledger schedule of accounts payable

>> **3. Post from the general journal to the general ledger accounts.**

WHY IT'S IMPORTANT

Accurate accounting gives management much needed information concerning purchases.

>> **4. Post transactions to the accounts payable subsidiary ledger.**

WHY IT'S IMPORTANT

Up-to-date records allow prompt payment of invoices.

>> **5. Prepare a schedule of accounts payable.**

WHY IT'S IMPORTANT

This schedule provides a snapshot of amounts owed to suppliers.

>> **6. Demonstrate a knowledge of the procedures for effective internal control of purchases.**

WHY IT'S IMPORTANT

Businesses try to prevent fraud, errors, and holding excess inventory.

Accounts Payable

Businesses that buy merchandise on credit can conduct more extensive operations and use financial resources more effectively than if they paid cash for all purchases. It is important to pay invoices on time so that the business maintains a good credit reputation with its suppliers.

RECORDING MERCHANDISE PURCHASED WITH A TRADE DISCOUNT

Recall from Chapter 7 that certain wholesale businesses offer goods to trade customers with the price computed using trade discounts. International Sportsman offers merchandise for sale with a list price of $1,000, with trade discounts of 20 percent and 10 percent, terms 2/10, n/30. Maxx-Out Sporting Goods purchases merchandise with a list price of $1,000 from International Sportsman, Invoice 5201. The amount owed for the purchase is computed as follows:

List price	$1,000.00
Less first discount ($1,000 × 20%)	200.00
Difference	$ 800.00
Less second discount ($800 × 10%)	80.00
Invoice price	$ 720.00

The journal entry to record the purchase on January 20 follows:

		GENERAL JOURNAL		PAGE ___2___		
	DATE	DESCRIPTION	POST. REF.	DEBIT	CREDIT	
1	2013					1
2	Jan. 20	Purchases		720 00		2
3		Accounts Payable			720 00	3
4		Purchased merchandise on credit				4
5		from International Sportsman,				5
6		Invoice 5201, 2/10, n/30				6
7						7

If Maxx-Out Sporting Goods pays the invoice within 10 days, it will be entitled to a $14.40 discount (2% × $720). The amount paid will be $705.60 ($720 − $14.40 = $705.60). The journal entry to record the payment on January 29 with check number 151 follows:

	DATE		DESCRIPTION	POST. REF.	DEBIT	CREDIT	
1	2013						1
2	Jan.	29	Accounts Payable		7 2 0 00		2
3			Purchases Discounts			1 4 40	3
4			Cash			7 0 5 60	4
5			Paid balance owed to				5
6			International Sportsman,				6
7			Invoice 5201, Check 151				7

GENERAL JOURNAL PAGE __2__

>> 3. OBJECTIVE
Post from the general journal to the general ledger accounts.

>> 4. OBJECTIVE
Post transactions to the accounts payable subsidiary ledger.

POSTING TO THE GENERAL LEDGER

Posting to the general ledger is done in the same manner as demonstrated in Chapter 4.

The Accounts Payable Ledger

Businesses need detailed records in order to pay invoices promptly. The **accounts payable ledger** provides information about the individual accounts for all creditors. The accounts payable ledger is a subsidiary ledger; it is separate from and subordinate to the general ledger. The accounts payable ledger contains a separate account for each creditor. Each account shows purchases, payments, and returns and allowances. The balance of the account shows the amount owed to the creditor.

Below is the accounts payable ledger account for International Sportsman. Notice that the Balance column does not indicate whether the balance is a debit or a credit. The form assumes that the balance will be a credit because the normal balance of liability accounts is a credit. A debit balance may exist if more than the amount owed was paid to the creditor or if returned goods were already paid for. If the balance is a debit, circle the amount to show that the account does not have the normal balance, or place parentheses ( ) around the amount.

NAME _International Sportsman_   TERMS _n/30_
ADDRESS _1718 Sherry Lane, Dallas, Texas 75267-6205_

DATE		DESCRIPTION	POST. REF.	DEBIT	CREDIT	BALANCE
2013						
Jan.	1	Balance	✓			1 6 0 0 00
	20	Invoice 5201	J2		7 2 0 00	2 3 2 0 00

Posting from the general journal to the accounts payable ledger is similar to posting the accounts receivable subsidiary ledger. The posting to the vendor's account in the accounts payable subsidiary ledger is signified by entering a "/", followed by a check mark, after the account number for accounts payable in the chart of accounts.

To illustrate posting from a general journal, let's see how the payment on account to International Sportsman above would look in the general journal, after it is posted:

		GENERAL JOURNAL				PAGE ___2___		
	DATE	DESCRIPTION	POST. REF.	DEBIT		CREDIT		
1	2013							1
2	Jan. 29	Accounts Payable/International	205/✓					2
3		Sportsman		7 2 0 00				3
4		Purchases Discounts	504			1 4 40		4
5		Cash	101			7 0 5 60		5
6		Paid balance owed to						6
7		International Sportsman,						7
8		Invoice 5201, Check 151						8
9								9

Small businesses like Maxx-Out Sporting Goods arrange the accounts payable ledger in alphabetical order. Large businesses and businesses that use computerized accounting systems assign an account number to each creditor and arrange the accounts payable ledger in numeric order.

Schedule of Accounts Payable

The total of the individual creditor accounts in the subsidiary ledger must equal the balance of the *Accounts Payable* control account. To prove that the control account and the subsidiary ledger are equal, businesses prepare a **schedule of accounts payable**—a list of all balances owed to creditors.

Below we will find the accounts payable subsidiary ledger for Maxx-Out Sporting Goods on January 31, followed by the schedule of accounts payable.

The total on the schedule of accounts payable should equal the balance of the control account, Accounts Payable, in the general ledger. If the amounts are not equal, it is essential to locate and correct the errors.

>> **5. OBJECTIVE**

Prepare a schedule of accounts payable.

NAME   Active Designs
ADDRESS   2313 Belt Line Road, Dallas, TX 75267-6205

DATE		DESCRIPTION	POST. REF.	DEBIT	CREDIT	BALANCE
2013						
Jan.	1	Balance	✓			2 2 0 0 00
	3	Invoice 5879	J1		2 8 6 5 00	5 0 6 5 00
	13		J2	3 2 0 0 00		1 8 6 5 00

NAME   Athletic Equipment, Inc.
ADDRESS   1027 St. James Avenue, Dallas, TX 75267-67205

DATE		DESCRIPTION	POST. REF.	DEBIT	CREDIT	BALANCE
2013						
Jan.	8	Invoice 8897	J1		4 2 0 0 00	4 2 0 0 00

NAME	International Sportsman					
ADDRESS	1718 Sherry Lane, Dallas, TX 75267-6205					

DATE		DESCRIPTION	POST. REF.	DEBIT	CREDIT	BALANCE
2013						
Jan.	1	Balance	✓			1 6 0 0 00
	20	Invoice 5201	J1		7 2 0 00	2 3 2 0 00
	29		J2	7 2 0 00		1 6 0 0 00

Maxx-Out Sporting Goods
Schedule of Accounts Payable
January 31, 2013

Active Designs	1 8 6 5 00
Athletic Equipment, Inc.	4 2 0 0 00
International Sportsman	1 6 0 0 00
Total	7 6 6 5 00

>> 6. OBJECTIVE

Demonstrate a knowledge of the procedures for effective internal control of purchases.

*inte*rnal **CONTROL**

ABOUT
ACCOUNTING

Employee Fraud

The Association of certified Fraud Examiners states that small businesses are especially vulnerable to occupational fraud. Lack of adequate internal controls was most commonly cited as the factor that allowed fraud to occur.

Internal Control of Purchases

Because of the large amount of money spent to buy goods, most businesses develop careful procedures for the control of purchases and payments. Some firms have a *voucher system,* a special system used to achieve internal control. Whether the voucher system is used or not, a business should be sure that its control process includes sufficient safeguards. The objectives of the controls are to:

- create written proof that purchases and payments are authorized;
- ensure that different people are involved in the process of buying goods, receiving goods, and making payments.

Separating duties among employees provides a system of checks and balances. In a small business with just a few employees, it might be difficult or impossible to separate duties. However, the business should design as effective a set of control procedures as the company's resources will allow. Effective systems have the following controls in place:

1. All purchases should be made only after proper authorization has been given in writing.
2. Goods should be carefully checked when they are received. They should then be compared with the purchase order and with the invoice received from the supplier.
3. The purchase order, receiving report, and invoice should be checked to confirm that the information on the documents is in agreement.
4. The computations on the invoice should be checked for accuracy.
5. Authorization for payment should be made by someone other than the person who ordered the goods, and this authorization should be given only after all the verifications have been made.
6. Another person should write the check for payment.
7. Prenumbered forms should be used for purchase requisitions, purchase orders, and checks. The numbers of the documents issued should be verified periodically to make sure that all forms can be accounted for.

MANAGERIAL IMPLICATIONS <<

ACCOUNTING FOR PURCHASES

- Management and the accounting staff need to work together to make sure that there are good internal controls over purchasing.
- A carefully designed system of checks and balances protects the business against fraud, errors, and excessive investment in merchandise.
- The accounting staff needs to record transactions efficiently so that up-to-date information about creditors is available.
- Using the accounts payable subsidiary ledger improves efficiency.
- To maintain a good credit reputation with suppliers, it is important to have an accounting system that ensures prompt payment of invoices.
- A well-run accounting system provides management with information about cash: cash required to pay suppliers, short-term loans needed to cover temporary cash shortages, and cash available for short-term investments.
- Separate accounts for recording purchases, freight charges, and purchases returns and allowances make it easy to analyze the elements in the cost of purchases.

THINKING CRITICALLY
As a manager, what internal controls would you put in your accounting system?

Section 2 Self Review

QUESTIONS

1. Which accounts are kept in the accounts payable ledger? *Creditors*

2. What is the purpose of the schedule of accounts payable? *Lists of A/P money owed*

3. The total of the schedule of accounts payable should equal the balance of which general ledger account? *A/P*

EXERCISES

4. In the accounts payable ledger, a supplier's account has a beginning balance of $4,800. Subsequently, a purchase of $1,600 from this supplier is journalized and then posted. What is the balance of the supplier's account?

   a. $3,200 debit
   b. $3,200 credit
   c. $6,400 credit
   d. $6,400 debit

5. Which of the following is not evidence of effective internal controls of purchases?

   a. All purchases should be made only after proper authorization is given in writing.

   b. The computations on the purchase invoice should be checked for accuracy.

   c. Prenumbered forms should be used for purchase requisitions, purchase orders, and checks.

   d. The same employee that issues the purchase order should also check the purchase invoice and write the check for payment.

ANALYSIS

6. Amber's Garden Supplies purchases merchandise on account from Lawn Supplies, Inc. The list is $1,000, with trade discounts of 25 percent and 10 percent, terms n/30. What amount should Amber's Garden Supplies pay to Lawn Supplies, Inc.?

   $675

   (Answers to Section 2 Self Review are on page 259.)

Review and Applications

8 Chapter **REVIEW**   **Chapter Summary**

In this chapter, you have learned to record various purchases and cash payment transactions for a merchandising business. Businesses with strong internal controls establish and follow procedures for approving requests for merchandise, choosing suppliers, placing orders with suppliers, checking goods after they arrive, identifying invoices, and approving payments.

Learning Objectives

1 Record purchases of merchandise on credit in a general journal.

Purchases on account must be entered in the firm's accounting records promptly and accurately. Most merchandising businesses normally purchase goods on credit.

2 Compute the net delivered cost of purchases.

The net delivered cost of purchases is computed by adding the cost of purchases and freight in, then subtracting any purchases returns and allowances and any purchases discounts. Net delivered cost of purchases is reported in the Cost of Goods Sold section of the income statement. Income statements for merchandising companies will be covered in Chapter 13.

3 Post from the general journal to the general ledger accounts.

Posting from the general journal to the general ledger is performed in the same manner described in Chapter 4.

4 Post transactions to the accounts payable subsidiary ledger.

An accounts payable subsidiary ledger helps a firm keep track of the amounts it owes to creditors. Postings are made to this ledger daily.

5 Prepare a schedule of accounts payable.

At month's end, a schedule of accounts payable is prepared. The schedule lists the balances owed to the firm's creditors. It is used to prove the subsidiary ledger totals match the Accounts Payable.

6 Demonstrate a knowledge of the procedures for effective internal control of purchases.

Purchases and payments should be properly authorized and processed with appropriate documentation to provide a system of checks and balances. A division of responsibilities within the purchasing process ensures strong internal controls.

7 Define the accounting terms new to this chapter.

Glossary

Accounts payable ledger (p. 238) A subsidiary ledger that contains a separate account for each creditor

Cash discount (p. 233) A discount offered by suppliers for payment received within a specified period of time

Cost of goods sold (p. 230) The actual cost to the business of the merchandise sold to customers

Freight In account (p. 231) An account showing transportation charges for items purchased

Purchase allowance (p. 232) A price reduction from the amount originally billed

Purchase invoice (p. 228) A bill received for goods purchased

Purchase order (p. 228) An order to the supplier of goods specifying items needed, quantity, price, and credit terms

Purchase requisition (p. 228) A list sent to the purchasing department showing the items to be ordered

Purchase return (p. 232) Return of unsatisfactory goods

Purchases account (p. 230) An account used to record cost of goods bought for resale during a period

Purchases discount (p. 233) A cash discount offered to the customer for payment within a specified period

Purchases Returns and Allowances (p. 232) A contra expense account where purchases returns and purchases allowances are recorded; see definitions of purchase allowance and purchase return

Receiving report (p. 228) A form showing quantity and condition of goods received

Sales discount (p. 233) A cash discount offered by the supplier for payment within a specified period

Sales invoice (p. 228) A supplier's billing document

Schedule of accounts payable (p. 239) A list of all balances owed to creditors

Transportation In account (p. 231) See Freight In account

Comprehensive **Self Review**

1. What is the name of the account used to record purchases of merchandise inventory?
2. What type of account is *Purchases Returns and Allowances?*
3. What is the purpose of the *Freight In* account?
4. What is the purpose of a purchase requisition? A purchase order?
5. What is the difference between a receiving report and an invoice?

(Answers to Comprehensive Self Review are on page 259.)

Discussion Questions

1. What major safeguards should be built into a system of internal control for purchases of goods?
2. What is the purpose of a credit memorandum?
3. What is a purchase allowance?
4. What is a purchase return?
5. What is a schedule of accounts payable? Why is it prepared?
6. What is the relationship of the *Accounts Payable* account in the general ledger to the accounts payable subsidiary ledger?
7. What type of accounts are kept in the accounts payable ledger?
8. Why is it useful for a business to have an accounts payable ledger?
9. How is the net delivered cost of purchases computed?
10. What journals can be used to enter various merchandise purchase transactions?
11. What is the difference between a purchase invoice and a sales invoice?
12. What is the normal balance of the *Purchases* accounts?
13. On what financial statement do the accounts related to purchases of merchandise appear? In which section of this statement are they reported?
14. Why is the use of a *Purchases Returns and Allowances* account preferred to crediting these transactions to *Purchases?*
15. What do the following credit terms means?
    a. n/30
    b. 2/10, n/30
    c. n/10 EOM
    d. n/20
    e. 1/10, n/20
    f. 3/5, n/30
    g. n/15 EOM

APPLICATIONS

Exercises

Exercise 8.1

Objective 1

▶ **Normal balances.**

Identify the normal balance of the following accounts. Use "Dr." for debit or "Cr." for credit.

_____ Purchases
_____ Purchases Returns and Allowances
_____ Purchases Discounts
_____ Freight In

Exercise 8.2

Objective 1

▶ **Recording purchases made for cash and on account.**

Jacob Corporation engaged in the following transactions during June. Record these transactions in a general journal.

DATE	TRANSACTIONS
2013 June 4	Purchased merchandise on account from Schmidt Company; Invoice 100 for $955; terms n/30.
15	Recorded purchases for cash, $1,440.
30	Paid amount due to Schmidt Company for the purchase on June 4.

Exercise 8.3

Objective 1

▶ **Recording purchases made for cash and on account, with purchases returns.**

Record the following transactions of Fronke's Fashions in a general journal:

DATE	TRANSACTIONS
2013 April 1	Purchased merchandise for cash, $1,210.
2	Returned merchandise for cash purchased on April 1; received a cash refund of $108.
4	Purchased merchandise on credit from Stein Distributors, Invoice 125, $661, terms n/30; freight of $36 prepaid by Stein and added to the invoice.
7	Returned damaged merchandise purchased on April 4 from Stein Distributors; received Credit Memorandum 202 for $43.
30	Paid the amount due to Stein Distributors for the purchase of April 4, less the return on April 7, Check 1458.

Recording purchases with purchases discounts.

◀ **Exercise 8.4**
Objective 1

Record the following transactions of Duong Designs in a general journal:

DATE	TRANSACTIONS
2013 April 1	Purchased merchandise on credit from O'Rourke Fabricators, Invoice 885, $1,000, terms 2/10, n/30; freight of $20 added paid by O'Rourke Fabricators and added to the invoice (total invoice amount, $1,020).
9	Paid amount due to O'Rourke Fabricators for the purchase of April 1, less the 2 percent discount, Check 457.
15	Purchased merchandise on credit from Kroll Company, Invoice 145, $750, terms 2/10, n/30; freight of $25 prepaid by Kroll and added to the invoice.
17	Returned damaged merchandise purchased on April 15 from Kroll Company; received Credit Memorandum 332 for $50.
24	Paid the amount due to Kroll Company for the purchase of April 15, less the return on April 17, taking the 2 percent discount, Check 470.

Recording purchases made with trade discounts.

◀ **Exercise 8.5**
Objective 1

Record the following transactions of Alenikov Design Warehouse:

DATE	TRANSACTIONS
2013 March 8	Purchased merchandise on credit from Classy Accessories, Invoice 1091, list price $4,000, trade discounts of 20% and 10%; terms 1/10, n/30.
17	Paid the amount owed on the purchase of March 8 from Classy Accessories, less the 1 percent discount, Check 185.

Journalizing merchandising transactions for buyer and seller.

◀ **Exercise 8.6**
Objective 1

Bryant Company (buyer) and Schmidt, Inc. (seller) engaged in the following transactions during February 2013:

Bryant Company

DATE	TRANSACTIONS
2013 Feb. 10	Purchased merchandise for $2,000 from Schmidt, Inc., Invoice 1980, terms 2/10, n/30.
13	Received Credit Memorandum 230 from Schmidt, Inc., for damaged merchandise totaling $100 that was returned; the goods were purchased on Invoice 1980, dated February 10.
19	Paid amount due to Schmidt, Inc., for Invoice 1980 of February 10, less the return of February 13 and less the cash discount, Check 2010.

Schmidt, Inc.

DATE	TRANSACTIONS
2013	
Feb. 10	Sold merchandise for $2,000 on account to Bryant Company, Invoice 1980, terms 2/10, n/30.
13	Issued Credit Memorandum 230 to Bryant Company for damaged merchandise totaling $100 that was returned; the goods were purchased on Invoice 1980, dated February 10.
19	Received payment from Bryant Company for Invoice 1980 of February 10, less the return of February 13 and less the cash discount, Check 2010.

Journalize the transactions above in a general journal for both Bryant Company and Schmidt, Inc. Use 20 as the journal page for both companies.

Exercise 8.7

Objective 2

▶ **Computing the net delivered cost of purchases.**

On June 30 the general ledger of Kisling, Inc., had the following balances:

Purchases	$40,795	Dr.
Freight In	2,226	Dr.
Purchases Returns and Allowances	2,810	Cr.
Purchases Discounts	2,050	Cr.

Compute the net delivered cost of purchases for Kisling, Inc.

Exercise 8.8

Objective 3, 4

▶ **Posting to the general ledger and the accounts payable ledger.**

Post the entries in the general journal below to the accounts payable account in the general ledger and to the appropriate accounts in the accounts payable ledger.

Assume the following account balances at January 1, 2013, for Trends, Inc.:

Accounts Payable (control account)	$5,100
Accounts Payable—Evans Enterprises	1,100
Accounts Payable—Stamos Distributors	2,600
Accounts Payable—Tonetta Company	1,400

Use 202 as the account number for accounts payable in the general ledger.

	GENERAL JOURNAL				PAGE _40_	
	DATE	DESCRIPTION	POST. REF.	DEBIT	CREDIT	
1	2013					1
2	Jan. 8	Accounts Payable/Stamos Distributors		200 00		2
3		Cash			200 00	3
4		Made partial payment				4
5		on account, Check 1240				5
6						6
7		10 Accounts Payable/Evans Enterprises		100 00		7
8		Purchases Returns and Allowances			100 00	8
9		Received Credit Memorandum				9
10		123 as allowance for				10
11		discolored merchandise				11
12						12
13						13

Preparing a schedule of accounts payable.

◀ **Exercise 8.9**
Objective 5

1. Use the final balances of the vendor accounts after completing Exercise 8.8 to prepare a schedule of accounts payable for Trends, Inc., as of January 31, 2013.

2. Does the total of your accounts payable schedule agree with the balance of the accounts payable account in the general ledger at January 31, 2013?

PROBLEMS

Problem Set A

Recording purchases and cash payments.

◀ **Problem 8.1A**
Objectives 1, 3

Ann's Photo Shop is a retail store that sells cameras and photography supplies. Ann's Photo Shop began operations April 1, 2013. The firm purchases its merchandise for cash and on open account. During April, Ann's Photo Shop engaged in the following transactions:

DATE	TRANSACTIONS
2013 April 1	Purchased camera film on credit from Camera & Film Products, Invoice 825, $965, terms n/30; freight of $11 prepaid by Camera & Film Products and added to the invoice (total amount due, $976).
3	Purchased lenses on credit for $810 from Vision Supplies, Inc., Invoice 998, terms n/30.
11	Purchased DVD camcorders on credit for $4,700 from Optical Products, Invoice 4101, terms n/30.
15	Recorded various purchases of merchandise for cash from April 1 to April 15, $2,100.
26	Purchased lighting equipment on credit from Myers Brothers Camera Supplies, Invoice 9288, $5,500, terms n/30; freight of $218 prepaid by Myers Brothers Camera Supplies and added to the invoice (total amount due, $5,718).
27	Issued Check 102 for $540 to Vision Supplies, Inc., in partial payment of Invoice 998 dated April 3.
30	Recorded various purchases of merchandise for cash from April 16 to April 30, $2,570.
30	Issued Check 103 to Camera & Film Products in payment of the total amount due on Invoice 825 dated April 1.

INSTRUCTIONS

1. Open the general ledger accounts indicated below. Enter the balance of cash as of April 1, 2013.

2. Record the transactions in a general journal. Use 1 as the journal page number.

3. Post the entries from the general journal to the appropriate general ledger accounts.

GENERAL LEDGER ACCOUNTS

101 Cash, $10,900 Dr.

205 Accounts Payable

501 Purchases

502 Freight In

Analyze: What were the total cash payments on account during April?

Problem 8.2A

Objective 1

▶ **Recording purchases, purchases returns, purchases discounts, and cash payments for a merchandising firm.**

Big Elk Ski Shop is a retail store that sells ski equipment and clothing. Big Elk Ski Shop commenced business on September 1, 2013. The firm purchases merchandise on open account. The firm's purchases, purchases returns and allowances, and cash payments on account during September 2013 follow:

DATE	TRANSACTIONS
2013	
Sept. 2	Purchased ski boots for $5,600 plus a freight charge of $210 from Colorado Ski Shop, Invoice 6672, terms n/30.
3	Purchased skis for $11,200 from Alaska Supply Company, Invoice 5916; terms 1/10, n/30.
7	Received Credit Memorandum 165 for $900 from Colorado Ski Shop for return of damaged ski boots; the boots were originally purchased September 2 on Invoice 6672.
11	Purchased ski jackets for $4,000 from Cold Mountain Clothing Company, Invoice 4091, terms n/30.
12	Issued Check 104 to Alaska Supply Company in payment of Invoice 5916, dated September 3, less the cash discount.
22	Purchased ski poles for $3,760 plus a freight charge of $120 from Alaska Supply Company, Invoice 5950, terms 1/10, n/30.
23	Purchased ski pants for $2,250 from Swenson Ski Goods, Invoice 528, terms n/30.
25	Received Credit Memorandum 245 for $300 from Swenson Ski Goods for return of defective ski pants; the pants were originally purchased September 23 on Invoice 528.
27	Purchased ski sweaters for $2,600 plus a freight charge of $100 from Colorado Ski Shop, Invoice 6722, terms n/30.
30	Issued Check 110 to Colorado Ski Shop in payment of Invoice 6672, dated September 2, less the return of September 7.

INSTRUCTIONS

Record the transactions in a general journal. Use 1 as the journal page number.

Analyze: What was the amount of the cash discount on September 12?

Problem 8.3A

Objectives 3, 4, 5

▶ **Posting purchases and cash payment transactions.**

INSTRUCTIONS

1. Open the general ledger accounts and accounts payable ledger accounts indicated on the next page. Enter the balance of Cash as of September 1, 2013.

2. Post the entries in Problem 8.2A from the general journal to the appropriate accounts in the general ledger and in the accounts payable ledger.

3. Prepare a schedule of accounts payable. Compare the balance of the Accounts Payable control account with the total of the schedule.

GENERAL LEDGER ACCOUNTS

101 Cash, $25,000 Dr.

201 Accounts Payable

501 Purchases

502 Freight In

503 Purchases Returns and Allowances

504 Purchases Discounts

ACCOUNTS PAYABLE LEDGER ACCOUNTS

Alaska Supply Company

Cold Mountain Clothing Company

Colorado Ski Shop

Swenson Ski Goods

Analyze: What portion of the purchases in September, before purchases returns and allowances and before purchases discounts, were for clothing items? Include ski boots as a clothing item.

Journalizing and posting purchases and cash payment transactions.

◀   **Problem 8.4A**
Objective 1

Maggiore Medical Devices is a medical devices wholesaler that commenced business on June 1, 2013. Maggiore Medical Devices purchases merchandise for cash and on open account. In June 2013, Maggiore Medical Devices engaged in the following purchasing and cash payment activities:

DATE	TRANSACTIONS
2013 June 1	Issued Check 101 to purchase merchandise, $3,500.
3	Purchased merchandise for $1,200 from BioCenter Inc., Invoice 606; terms 1/10, n/30.
5	Purchased merchandise for $4,850, plus a freight charge of $100 from New Concepts Corporation, Invoice 1011, terms 2/10, n/30.
9	Paid amount due to BioCenter Inc. for purchase of June 3, less discount, Check 102.
10	Received Credit Memorandum 227 from New Concepts Corporation for damaged merchandise totaling $200 that was returned; the goods were purchased on Invoice 1011, dated June 5.
11	Purchased merchandise for $1,580 from BioCenter Inc., Invoice 612; terms 1/10, n/30.
14	Paid amount due to New Concepts Corporation for Invoice 1011 of June 5, less the return of June 10 and less the cash discount, Check 103.
15	Purchased merchandise with a list price of $8,200 and trade discounts of 15 percent and 10 percent from Park Research, Invoice 1029, terms n/30.
20	Issued Check 104 to purchase merchandise, $2,000.
25	Returned merchandise purchased on June 20 as defective, receiving a cash refund of $180.
30	Purchased merchandise for $2,200, plus a freight charge of $75 from New Concepts Corporation, Invoice 1080; terms 2/10, n/30.

INSTRUCTIONS

Journalize the transactions on the previous page in a general journal. Use 1 as the journal page number.

Analyze: What was the amount of trade discounts received on the June 15 purchase from Park Research?

Problem 8.5A ▶ **Posting purchases and cash payment transactions.**

Objectives 3, 4, 5

INSTRUCTIONS

1. Open the general ledger accounts and accounts payable ledger accounts indicated below. Enter the balances as of June 1, 2013.

2. Post the transactions in Problem 8.4A to the appropriate accounts in the general ledger and the Accounts Payable subsidiary ledger.

3. Prepare a schedule of accounts payable at June 30, 2013.

GENERAL LEDGER ACCOUNTS

101 Cash, $36,400 Dr.

201 Accounts Payable

501 Purchases

502 Purchases Returns and Allowances

503 Purchases Discounts

504 Freight In

ACCOUNTS PAYABLE LEDGER ACCOUNTS

BioCenter Inc.

New Concepts Corporation

Park Research

Analyze: What was the amount of merchandise returned to vendors by Maggiore Medical Devices in June?

Problem 8.6A ▶ **Journalizing and posting merchandising transactions for buyer and seller.**

Objectives 1, 3, 4

Brown Company (buyer) and Smith, Inc. (seller), engaged in the following transactions during January 2013:

Brown Company

DATE	TRANSACTIONS
2013 Jan. 8	Issued Check 2101 for $1,960 on account to Smith, Inc., in payment of Invoice 1885 dated December 30, 2012, less cash discount of $40.
10	Purchased merchandise for $1,500 from Smith, Inc., Invoice 1920; terms 2/10, n/30.
15	Received Credit Memorandum 320 from Smith, Inc., for damaged merchandise totaling $100 that was returned; the goods were purchased on Invoice 1920, dated January 10.
19	Paid amount due to Smith, Inc., for Invoice 1920 of January 10, less the return of January 15 and less the cash discount, Check 2130.
30	Purchased merchandise for $3,200 from Smith, Inc., Invoice 1950; terms 2/10, n/30.

Smith, Inc.

DATE	TRANSACTIONS
2013 Jan. 8	Received payment of $1,960 on account from Brown Company in payment of Invoice 1885 dated December 30, 2012, less cash discount of $40.
10	Sold merchandise for $1,500 on account to Brown Company, Invoice 1920, terms 2/10, n/30.
15	Issued Credit Memorandum 320 to Brown Company for damaged merchandise totaling $100 that was returned; the goods were purchased on Invoice 1920, dated January 10.
19	Received payment from Brown Company for Invoice 1920 of January 10, less the return of January 15 and less the cash discount.
30	Sold merchandise for $3,200 to Brown Company, Invoice 1950; terms 2/10, n/30.

INSTRUCTIONS

1. Open the accounts payable ledger account and accounts receivable ledger account indicated below for both Brown Company and Smith, Inc. Enter the balances as of January 1, 2013.

2. Journalize the transactions above in a general journal for both Brown Company and Smith, Inc. Begin the journals for both companies with page 21.

3. Post the transactions to the appropriate accounts in the general ledger and the Accounts Payable subsidiary ledger for Brown Company.

4. Post the transactions to the appropriate accounts in the general ledger and the Accounts Receivable subsidiary ledger for Smith, Inc.

GENERAL LEDGER ACCOUNTS—BROWN COMPANY

201 Accounts Payable, $2,000 Cr.

ACCOUNTS PAYABLE LEDGER ACCOUNT—BROWN COMPANY

Smith, Inc., $2,000

GENERAL LEDGER ACCOUNTS—SMITH, INC.

111 Accounts Receivable, $2,000 Dr.

ACCOUNTS RECEIVABLE LEDGER ACCOUNT—SMITH, INC.

Brown Company, $2,000

Analyze: What is the balance of the accounts payable for Smith, Inc., in the Brown Company accounts payable subsidiary ledger? What is the balance of the accounts receivable for Brown Company in the Smith, Inc., accounts receivable subsidiary ledger?

Problem Set B

Recording purchases and cash payments.

◀ **Problem 8.1B**
Objectives 1, 3

The Garden Center is a retail store that sells garden equipment, furniture, and supplies. The Garden Center began operations June 1, 2013. The firm purchases its merchandise for cash and on open account. During June, The Garden Center engaged in the following transactions:

DATE	TRANSACTIONS
2013 June 1	Purchased lawn mowers on credit from Mow Down Corporation, Invoice 925, $5,025, terms n/30; freight of $125 prepaid by Mow Down Corporation and added to the invoice (total amount due, $5,150).
5	Purchased outdoor chairs and tables on credit for $6,760 from Patio Furniture, Inc., Invoice 992, terms n/30.
9	Purchased grass seed for $948 on credit from Summer Lawn Center, Invoice 4001, terms n/30.
15	Recorded various purchases of merchandise for cash from June 1 to June 15, $2,900.
20	Purchased lawn sprinkler systems on credit from Mason Industries, Invoice 9228, $7,250, terms n/30; freight of $320 prepaid by Mason Industries and added to the invoice (total amount due, $7,570).
27	Issued Check 104 for $3,000 to Patio Furniture, Inc., in partial payment of Invoice 992 dated June 5.
30	Recorded various purchases of merchandise for cash from June 16 to June 30, $2,650.
30	Issued Check 105 to Mow Down Corporation in payment of the total amount due on Invoice 925 dated June 1.

INSTRUCTIONS

1. Open the general ledger accounts indicated below. Enter the balance of cash as of June 1, 2013.

2. Record the transactions in a general journal. Use 1 as the journal page number.

3. Post the entries from the general journal to the appropriate general ledger accounts.

GENERAL LEDGER ACCOUNTS

101 Cash, $20,000 Dr.

205 Accounts Payable

501 Purchases

502 Freight In

Analyze: What were the total freight costs incurred during June?

Problem 8.2B
Objective 1

▶ **Recording purchases, purchases returns, purchase discounts, and cash payments for a merchandising firm.**

Tiffany's Card and Novelty Shop is a retail card, novelty, and business supply store. Tiffany's Card and Novelty Shop commenced business on April 1, 2013. The firm purchases merchandise on open account. The firm's purchases, purchases returns and allowances, and cash payments on account during April 2013 follow:

DATE	TRANSACTIONS
2013 April 2	Purchased copy paper for $2,200 plus a freight charge of $210 from Mailing and Packing Center, Invoice 3772, terms n/30.
8	Purchased assorted holiday gift cards for $1,900 from Special Occasion Cards, Invoice 9516; terms 1/10, n/30.

(continued)

DATE	(cont.) TRANSACTIONS
9	Received Credit Memorandum 155 for $200 from Mailing and Packing Center for return of copy paper that was water damaged. The copy paper was originally purchased April 2 on Invoice 3772.
12	Purchased five boxes of novelty items for $1,000 from Specialty Cards, Invoice 4901, terms n/30.
17	Issued Check 105 to Special Occasion Cards in payment of Invoice 9516, dated April 8, less the cash discount.
22	Purchased tray of cards for $900 from Specialty Cards, Invoice 4921, terms n/30.
23	Purchased supply of forms from Business Forms, Inc., for $1,980 plus shipping charges of $70 on Invoice 2020, terms n/30.
25	Received Credit Memorandum 225 for $100 from Specialty Cards for return of defective cards; the cards were originally purchased April 22 on Invoice 4921.
27	Purchased toner supplies for $2,900 plus a freight charge of $75 from Business Forms, Inc., Invoice 2029, terms n/30.
30	Issued Check 111 to Mailing and Packing Center in payment of Invoice 3772, April 2, less the return of April 9.

INSTRUCTIONS

Record the transactions in a general journal. Use 1 as the journal page number.

Analyze: Assume 600 cards were received from Specialty Cards on April 22. What was the cost per card?

Posting purchases and cash payments transactions.

◀   **Problem 8.3B**
Objectives 3, 4, 5

INSTRUCTIONS

1. Open the general ledger accounts and accounts payable ledger accounts indicated below. Enter the balance of Cash as of April 1, 2013.
2. Post the entries in Problem 8.2B from the general journal to the appropriate accounts in the general ledger and in the accounts payable ledger.
3. Prepare a schedule of accounts payable. Compare the balance of the Accounts Payable control account with the total of the schedule.

GENERAL LEDGER ACCOUNTS

101 Cash, $12,500 Dr.

201 Accounts Payable

501 Purchases

502 Freight In

503 Purchases Returns and Allowances

504 Purchases Discounts

ACCOUNTS PAYABLE LEDGER ACCOUNTS

Business Forms, Inc.

Mailing and Packing Center

Special Occasion Cards

Specialty Cards

Analyze: What was the amount of purchase discounts in April?

Problem 8.4B
Objective 1

▶ **Journalizing purchases and cash payment transactions.**

Dental Supplies, Inc., is a wholesale supplier of dental supplies and materials. Dental Supplies, Inc., commenced business on August 1, 2013. Dental Supplies, Inc., purchases merchandise for cash and on open account. In August 2013, Dental Supplies, Inc., engaged in the following purchasing and cash payment activities:

DATE	TRANSACTIONS
2013	
Aug. 1	Issued Check 101 to purchase merchandise, $2,500.
2	Purchased merchandise for $2,200 from Brown Dental Corporation, Invoice 866, terms 1/10, n/30.
5	Purchased merchandise for $3,900, plus a freight charge of $100 from Dental Concepts, Invoice 2111, terms 2/10, n/30.
10	Paid amount due to Brown Dental Corporation for purchase of August 2, less discount, Check 102.
10	Received Credit Memorandum 272 from Dental Concepts for damaged merchandise totaling $300 that was returned; the goods were purchased on Invoice 2111, dated August 5.
11	Purchased merchandise for $1,700 from Brown Dental Corporation, Invoice 898, terms 1/10, n/30.
14	Paid amount due to Dental Concepts for Invoice 2111 of April 5, less the return of August 10 and less the cash discount, Check 103.
15	Purchased merchandise with a list price of $4,000 and trade discounts of 20 percent and 10 percent from Surgical Supplies, Invoice 1902, terms n/30.
20	Issued Check 104 to purchase merchandise, $1,900.
24	Returned merchandise purchased on August 20 as defective, receiving a cash refund of $175.
30	Purchased merchandise for $2,125, plus a freight charge of $75 from Dental Concepts, Invoice 2285, terms 2/10, n/30.

INSTRUCTIONS

Journalize the transactions above in a general journal. Use 1 as the journal page number.

Analyze: What percentage of the total amount due Dental Concepts for the August 5 transaction is due to the freight charge?

Problem 8.5B
Objectives 3, 4, 5

▶ **Posting purchases and cash payment transactions.**

INSTRUCTIONS

1. Open the general ledger accounts and accounts payable ledger accounts indicated below. Enter the balances as of August 1, 2013.

2. Post the entries in Problem 8.4B to the appropriate accounts in the general ledger and the Accounts Payable subsidiary ledger.

3. Prepare a schedule of accounts payable at August 31, 2013.

GENERAL LEDGER ACCOUNTS

101 Cash, $39,700 Dr.

201 Accounts Payable

501 Purchases

502 Purchases Returns and Allowances

503 Purchases Discounts

504 Freight In

ACCOUNTS PAYABLE LEDGER ACCOUNTS

Brown Dental Corporation

Dental Concepts

Surgical Supplies

Analyze: What amount did Dental Supplies, Inc., owe to its supplier, Dental Concepts, on August 31?

Journalizing and posting merchandising transactions for buyer and seller.

◀   **Problem 8.6B**

Objectives 1, 3, 4

Banh Company (buyer) and Santoni, Inc. (seller), engaged in the following transactions during February 2013:

Banh Company

DATE	TRANSACTIONS
2013 Feb. 8	Issued Check 2001 for $5,880 on account to Santoni, Inc., in payment of Invoice 1985 dated January 30, 2013, less cash discount of $120.
9	Purchased merchandise for $3,800 from Santoni, Inc., Invoice 1990; terms 2/10, n/30.
15	Received Credit Memorandum 220 from Santoni, Inc., for damaged merchandise totaling $400 that was returned; the goods were purchased on Invoice 1990, dated February 9.
18	Paid amount due to Santoni, Inc., for Invoice 1990 of February 9, less the return of February 15 and less the cash discount, Check 2009.
28	Purchased merchandise for $6,200 from Santoni, Inc., Invoice 2008; terms 2/10, n/30.

Santoni, Inc.

DATE	TRANSACTIONS
2013 Feb. 8	Received payment of $5,880 on account from Banh Company in payment of Invoice 1985 dated January 30, 2013, less cash discount of $120.
9	Sold merchandise for $3,800 on account to Banh Company, Invoice 1990, terms 2/10, n/30.
15	Issued Credit Memorandum 220 to Banh Company for damaged merchandise totaling $400 that was returned; the goods were purchased on Invoice 1990, dated February 9.
18	Received payment from Banh Company for Invoice 1990 of February 9, less the return of February 15 and less the cash discount.
28	Sold merchandise for $6,200 to Banh Company, Invoice 2008; terms 2/10, n/30.

INSTRUCTIONS

1. Open the accounts payable ledger account and accounts receivable ledger account indicated on the next page for both Banh Company and Santoni, Inc. Enter the balances as of February 1, 2013.

2. Journalize the transactions above in a general journal for both Banh Company and Santoni, Inc. Begin the journals for both companies with page 12.

3. Post the transactions to the appropriate accounts in the general ledger and the Accounts Payable subsidiary ledger for Banh Company.

4. Post the transactions to the appropriate accounts in the general ledger and the Accounts Receivable subsidiary ledger for Santoni, Inc.

GENERAL LEDGER ACCOUNTS—BANH COMPANY

201 Accounts Payable, $6,000 Cr.

ACCOUNTS PAYABLE LEDGER ACCOUNT—BANH COMPANY

Santoni, Inc., $6,000

GENERAL LEDGER ACCOUNTS—SANTONI, INC.

111 Accounts Receivable, $6,000 Dr.

ACCOUNTS RECEIVABLE LEDGER ACCOUNT—SANTONI, INC.

Banh Company, $6,000

Analyze: What is the balance of the accounts payable for Santoni, Inc., in the Banh Company accounts payable subsidiary ledger? What is the balance of the accounts receivable for Banh Company in the Santoni, Inc., accounts receivable subsidiary ledger?

Critical Thinking Problem 8.1

Journalizing Merchandising Transactions

William Evans began Evans Distributors, a sporting goods distribution company, in January 2013, and engaged in the transactions below. Assume Evans Distributors and its customers take advantage of all cash discounts.

DATE	TRANSACTIONS
2013	
Jan. 1	William Evans started Evans Distributors with an investment of $49,000. He also invested personal business supplies worth $1,000.
2	Sold merchandise on account to Chu Corporation, $750, terms 2/10, n/30, Invoice 1001.
4	Purchased merchandise on account from Whitson Company, $1,600, terms 1/10, n/30, Invoice 1125.
5	Received and paid freight charges related to January 4 purchase of merchandise from Whitson Company, $100.
10	Chu Corporation returned merchandise purchased on January 2; issued credit memo #101 for $100.
11	Received payment in full from Chu Corporation.
13	Paid amount due to Whitson Company for purchase of January 4, Check 100.
15	Recorded cash sales for the two-week period ended Jan. 15 of $5,500.
15	Recorded sales on credit cards for the two-week period ended Jan. 15, $1,200; the bank charges a 3% fee on all credit card sales.
15	Paid wages, $1,400, Check 101.
16	Purchased equipment (not for resale), $1,750, Check 102.

(continued)

DATE	JOURNALIZING MERCHANDISING TRANSACTIONS (cont.) TRANSACTIONS
17	Paid freight for delivery of equipment purchased on January 16, $250, Check 103. (Note: freight charges for purchase of equipment should be debited to the Equipment account.)
18	Purchased merchandise on account from Terri Manufacturing for $4,000, subject to trade discount of 20%, terms 1/10, n/30, Invoice 2078.
20	Sold merchandise on account to Moloney Corp., $2,500, terms 1/10, n/30, Invoice 1002.
21	Purchased merchandise on account from Schmidt Company, $3,000, terms 1/10, n/30, Invoice 3204; freight prepaid by Schmidt Company and added to invoice, $70. (Total invoice amount, $3,070).
27	Paid amount owed to Terri Manufacturing for purchase of January 18, Check 104.
29	Received amount due from Moloney Corp. for the sale of January 20.
30	Paid amount due to Schmidt Company for purchase of January 21, Check 105.
31	Recorded cash sales for the period from January 16–31, $6,000.
31	Recorded sales on the credit cards for the period from January 16–31, $2,200; the bank charges a 3% fee on all credit card sales.

INSTRUCTIONS

Record the transactions in a general journal. Number the first journal as page 1. Provide brief explanations after each journal entry.

Critical Thinking Problem 8.2

Internal Control

Dora Alexander, owner of Passions Linen Shop, was preparing checks for payment of the current month's purchase invoices when she realized that there were two invoices from Sensuous Linen Company, each for the purchase of 100 red, heart-imprinted king size linen sets. Alexander thinks that Sensuous Linen Company must have billed Passions Linen Shop twice for the same shipment because she knows the shop would not have needed two orders for 100 red linen sets within a month.

1. How can Alexander determine whether Sensuous Linen Company billed Passions Linen Shop in error or whether Passions Linen Shop placed two identical orders for red, heart-imprinted linen sets?

2. If two orders were placed, how can Alexander prevent duplicate purchases from happening in the future?

BUSINESS CONNECTIONS

Cash Management

Managerial | FOCUS

1. Why should management be concerned about the timely payment of invoices?

2. Why is it important for a firm to maintain a satisfactory credit rating?

3. Suppose you are the new controller of a small but growing company and you find that the firm has a policy of paying cash for all purchases of goods even though it could obtain credit. The president of the company does not like the idea of having debts, but the vice president thinks

this is a poor business policy that will hurt the firm in the future. The president has asked your opinion. Would you agree with the president or the vice president? Why?

4. Why should management be concerned about the internal control of purchases?

5. How can good internal control of purchases protect a firm from fraud and errors and from excessive investment in merchandise?

6. In what way would excessive investment in merchandise harm a business?

Adding New Vendors

Ethical DILEMMA

Anait Artununian is the accounts payable clerk for Jiffy Delivery Service. This company runs 10 branches in the San Diego area. The company pays for a variety of expenses. Anait writes the checks for each of the vendors and the controller signs the checks. Anait has decided she needs a raise and the controller has told her to wait for six months. Anait has devised a plan to get a raise on her own. She creates a new vendor for her friend's business with the name Gevok Car Detailing. She also creates two purchase orders for car detailing service from Gevok's for $75 and $70. She writes checks to Gevok Car Detailing to pay these invoices. She knows the controller will sign all checks only looking at the checks over $100. She delivers the checks to Gevok who will deposit the checks in his bank account. Gevok then writes a check to her for $145. Is this a good way for Anait to obtain a raise? Is it an ethical practice? Eventually, what will be the effect of Anait's actions? What can the company do to prevent this type of behavior?

Income Statement

Financial Statement ANALYSIS

The following financial statement excerpt is taken from the *2009 Annual Report (for the fiscal year ended January 31, 2010)* for The Home Depot, Inc.:

Consolidated Statements of Earnings		
	For the year ended	
	January 31, 2010	*February 1, 2009*
(In millions)		
Net Sales	$ 66,176	$ 71,288
Cost of Sales	43,764	47,298
Gross Profit	$ 22,412	$ 23,990

1. The Cost of Sales amount on The Home Depot, Inc., consolidated statements of earnings represents the net cost of the goods that were sold for the period. For 2010, what percentage of net sales was the cost of sales? For fiscal 2009?

2. What factors might affect a merchandising company's cost of sales from one period to another?

Analyze Online: On the The Home Depot, Inc., Web site (www.homedepot.com), locate the Investor Relations' section.

3. Review the consolidated statements of operations found in the current year's annual report.

4. What amount is reported for cost of sales?

5. What amount is reported for net sales?

Payment Terms

TEAMWORK

A company is developing objectives for paying bills on account. Some possible objectives follow:

■ Stretch cash flow as much as possible.

■ Develop a good reputation as a company that always pays bills on time.

■ Do not pay vendors until payment is received from our customers.

In a group, discuss which payment terms best fit each objective. Additionally, discuss how each objective might impact the company.

Computer Check Format

Internet | CONNECTION

Go to the QuickBooks and Peachtree Web sites at quickbooks.com and peachtree.com. Select product overview and more information. You want to be sure to see a copy of a check and purchase order. Compare and contrast the information contained on each check and purchase order. How many copies can you get of the check and purchase order? How is the form different? How is it the same? What information should be included on a company's check and purchase invoice?

Answers to **Self Reviews**

Answers to Section 1 Self Review

1. Purchases.
2. Purchases plus freight in, less purchases returns and allowances less purchases discounts.
3. The buyer pays the freight charge.
4. **b.** Purchase order
5. **d.** the receiving report and the purchase order.
6. The entry that should have been made is:

	Debit	Credit
Purchases	600.00	
Freight-in	50.00	
Accounts Payable/Fashion World		650.00

Answers to Section 2 Self Review

1. Individual accounts for all suppliers.
2. It lists all of the creditors to whom money is owed.
3. Accounts payable.
4. **c.** $6,400 credit
5. **d.** The same employee that issues the purchase order should also check the purchase invoice and write the check for payment.
6. $675

Answers to Comprehensive Self Review

1. Purchases.
2. A contra expense account.
3. To record freight charges paid for purchases of merchandise inventory.
4. The purchase requisition is used by a sales department to notify the purchasing department of the items wanted. The purchase order is prepared by the purchasing department to order the necessary goods at an appropriate price from the selected supplier.
5. The receiving report shows the quantity of goods received and the condition of the goods. The invoice shows quantities and prices. The accounts payable clerk should compare the quantities per the invoice to the receiving report in order to ensure the firm is billed only for goods received. The accounts payable clerk should also compare the prices per the invoice to the purchase order to ensure the firm has not been overcharged. Checks written to pay for purchases are based on the invoice.

Cash

Chapter 9

LEARNING OBJECTIVES

1. Account for cash short or over.
2. Demonstrate a knowledge of procedures for a petty cash fund.
3. Demonstrate a knowledge of internal control routines for cash.
4. Write a check, endorse checks, prepare a bank deposit slip, and maintain a checkbook balance.
5. Reconcile the monthly bank statement.
6. Record any adjusting entries required from the bank reconciliation.
7. Understand how businesses use online banking to manage cash activities.
8. Define the accounting terms new to this chapter.

NEW TERMS

bank reconciliation statement
blank endorsement
bonding
canceled check
cash
Cash Short or Over account
check
credit memorandum
debit memorandum
deposit in transit
deposit slip
dishonored (NSF) check
drawee
drawer
electronic funds transfer (EFT)
endorsement
full endorsement
negotiable
outstanding checks
payee
petty cash analysis sheet
petty cash voucher
postdated check
promissory note
restrictive endorsement
service charge
statement of account

 H&R BLOCK®   www.hrblock.com | In the 1940s, Henry, Leon, and Richard Bloch borrowed $5,000 from a relative and founded United Business Company, an accounting services firm. By the mid-1950s they had 12 employees and were keeping books for various small local businesses in the Kansas City area. Things would change quickly, however. In 1954, on the basis of a recommendation from a client, the Blochs ran an ad for their tax preparation services and the small office was flooded with calls. It seems just as the IRS was phasing out its free tax preparation services and turning taxpayers away, the Bloch brothers were advertising their services.

United Business Company changed its name to H&R Block and shifted its focus from general accounting services to tax preparation. Within a year, business tripled and has kept growing ever since. The largest consumer tax services company in the United States, H&R Block has filed over 500 million tax returns since 1955. It earned $4.1 billion in revenues in 2009 with in-person and digital tax solutions.

thinking critically

What types of daily receipts and payments occur in a local H&R Block office?

SECTION OBJECTIVES	TERMS TO LEARN
>> 1. **Account for cash short or over.**	cash
WHY IT'S IMPORTANT	Cash Short or Over account
Discrepancies in cash are a possible indication that cash is mismanaged.	promissory note
	statement of account

Cash Receipts

Cash is the business asset that is most easily lost, mishandled, or even stolen. A well-managed business has careful procedures for controlling cash and recording cash transactions.

Cash Transactions

In accounting, the term **cash** is used for currency, coins, checks, money orders, and funds on deposit in a bank. Most cash transactions involve checks.

CASH RECEIPTS

The type of cash receipts depends on the nature of the business. Supermarkets receive checks as well as currency and coins. Department stores receive checks in the mail from charge account customers. Cash received by wholesalers is usually in the form of checks.

Maxx-Out Sporting Goods uses a cash register to record cash sales and to store currency and coin. As a transaction is entered, the cash register displays the amount of the transaction and prints a receipt for the customer. It also records the transaction in a cash register tape inside the machine.

Each cash register clerk is given a cash drawer with a set amount of cash. The cash is for giving change to customers. This cash is called a change fund. If there are more than one work shifts during the day, the store manager and the cash register clerk should both count the cash in the clerk's cash drawer at the end of each shift.

At the end of the day, the store manager prints transaction totals from the cash register. The store manager and the cash register clerk should both count the cash in that clerk's cash drawer. The store manager should prepare a cash proof. The cash proof verifies that the amount in the cash register, less the change fund, equals the amount shown on the cash register transaction totals.

Cash Sales and Cash Short or Over Occasionally, errors occur when making change. When errors happen, the cash in the cash register is either more than or less than the cash listed on the cash register tape. When cash receipts are more than the sales per the cash register tape, cash is *over*. When cash receipts are less than the sales per the cash register tape, cash is *short*. Cash tends to be short more often than over because customers are more likely to notice and complain if they receive too little change.

Record short or over amounts in the **Cash Short or Over account.** If the account has a credit balance, there is an overage, which is treated as revenue. If the account has a debit balance, there is a shortage, which is treated as an expense.

For example, Royal Jewelry Store, a retail business, keeps a $200 change fund in its cash register. Royal Jewelry Store started business on September 29. The cash sales per the cash register tape on September 29 were $2,200. The cash count was $2,397. The cash register was short by $3, calculated as follows:

>> **1. OBJECTIVE**

Account for cash short or over.

Cash count	$2,397
Less change fund	200
Bank deposit	$2,197
Sales per cash register tape	2,200
Amount short	$ (3)

The journal entry to record the sales and cash shortage for September 29 follows:

GENERAL JOURNAL   PAGE 1

	DATE	DESCRIPTION	POST. REF.	DEBIT	CREDIT	
1	2013					1
2	Sept. 29	Cash		2 197 00		2
3		Cash Short and Over		3 00		3
4		Sales			2 200 00	4
5		Record sales and cash shortage				5

The cash sales per the cash register tape on September 30 were $2,100. The cash count was $2,301. The cash register was over by $1, calculated as follows:

Cash count	$2,301
Less change fund	200
Bank deposit	$2,101
Sales per cash register tape	2,100
Amount over	$ 1

The journal entry to record the sales and cash overage for September 30 follows:

GENERAL JOURNAL   PAGE 2

	DATE	DESCRIPTION	POST. REF.	DEBIT	CREDIT	
1	2013					1
2	Sept. 30	Cash		2 101 00		2
3		Cash Short and Over			1 00	3
4		Sales			2 100 00	4
5		Record sales and cash overage				5

After these journal entries have been posted, the balance in the Cash Short and Over account on September 30 is $2 debit. This will be reported as an expense on the income statement for the period ended September 30.

GENERAL LEDGER

ACCOUNT Cash Short and Over   ACCOUNT NO. 620

DATE	DESCRIPTION	POST. REF.	DEBIT	CREDIT	BALANCE DEBIT	BALANCE CREDIT
2013						
Sept. 29		J1	3 00		3 00	
30		J2		1 00	2 00	

FIGURE 9.1

A Promissory Note

$ 800.00		July 31, 2012
Six Months	AFTER DATE _I_	PROMISE TO PAY
TO THE ORDER OF	Maxx-Out Sporting Goods	
Eight Hundred and no/100		DOLLARS
PAYABLE AT First Texas Bank		
VALUE RECEIVED with interest at 9%		
NO. _30_ DUE January 31, 2013		Stacee Fairley

Cash Received on Account Maxx-Out Sporting Goods makes sales on account and bills customers once a month. It sends a ==statement of account== that shows the transactions during the month and the balance owed. Customers are asked to pay within 30 days of receiving the statement. Checks from credit customers are journalized and posted, and then the checks are deposited in the bank.

Receipt of a Cash Refund Sometimes a business receives a cash refund for supplies, equipment, or other assets that are returned to the supplier. On January 17, Maxx-Out Sporting Goods received a $75 cash refund for supplies that were returned to the seller. The journal entry to record the refund debits cash for $75 and credits supplies for $75.

Collection of a Promissory Note and Interest A ==promissory note== is a written promise to pay a specified amount of money on a certain date. Most notes require that interest is paid at a specified rate. Businesses use promissory notes to extend credit for some sales transactions.

Sometimes promissory notes are used to replace an accounts receivable balance when the account is overdue. For example, on July 31 Maxx-Out Sporting Goods accepted a six-month promissory note from Stacee Fairley, who owed $800 on account (see Figure 9.1). Fairley had asked for more time to pay his balance. Maxx-Out Sporting Goods agreed to grant more time if Fairley signed a promissory note with 9 percent annual interest. The note provides more legal protection than an account receivable. The interest is compensation for the delay in receiving payment.

On the date of the transaction, July 31, Maxx-Out Sporting Goods recorded a general journal entry to increase notes receivable and to decrease accounts receivable for $800. The asset account, *Notes Receivable,* was debited and *Accounts Receivable* was credited.

	DATE		DESCRIPTION	POST. REF.	DEBIT	CREDIT	
			GENERAL JOURNAL		PAGE _16_		
1	2012						1
2	July	31	Notes Receivable	109	8 0 0 00		2
3			Accounts Receivable/Stacee Fairley	111 ✓		8 0 0 00	3
4			Received a 6-month, 9% note from				4
5			Stacee Fairley to replace open account				5

On January 31, 2013, the due date of the note, Maxx-Out Sporting Goods received a check for $836 from Fairley. This sum covered the amount of the note ($800) and the interest owed for the six-month period ($36). The journal entry to record receipt of this check follows:

GENERAL JOURNAL		PAGE	18		
DATE	DESCRIPTION	POST. REF.	DEBIT	CREDIT	
1	2013					1
2	Jan. 31	Cash		836 00		2
3		Interest Income			36 00	3
4		Notes Receivable			800 00	4
5		Payment from Stacee Fairly on note dated				5
6		July 31, 2012				6

Section 1 Self Review

QUESTIONS

1. What is a promissory note? In what situation would a business accept a promissory note?

2. What is a cash shortage? How is it recorded?

EXERCISES

3. How would the receipt of a $50 refund for supplies returned be recorded in a general journal?

4. Angela's Beauty Salon keeps a $100 change fund. At the end of the day, sales per the register tape were $795, and the cash count was $892. What is the amount of the cash shortage or overage?

   a. $3 over

   b. $3 short

   c. $97 over

   d. $97 short

5. Which items are considered cash?

   a. Currency

   b. Funds on deposit in the bank

   c. Money orders

   d. All of the above

ANALYSIS

6. You notice that the **Cash Short or Over** account has 15 entries during the month. The ending balance is a $10 shortage for the month. Is this a problem? Why or why not?

(Answers to Section 1 Self Review are on page 298.)

792

SECTION OBJECTIVES

>> **2. Demonstrate a knowledge of procedures for a petty cash fund.**

WHY IT'S IMPORTANT

Businesses use the petty cash fund to pay for small operating expenditures.

>> **3. Demonstrate a knowledge of internal control routines for cash.**

WHY IT'S IMPORTANT

Internal controls safeguard business assets.

TERMS TO LEARN

bonding
petty cash analysis sheet
petty cash voucher

Petty Cash and Internal Controls for Cash

A good system of internal control requires that payments be made by check. In a good internal control system one employee approves payments, another employee prepares the checks, and another employee records the transactions.

>> **2. OBJECTIVE**

Demonstrate a knowledge of procedures for a petty cash fund.

The Petty Cash Fund

In a well-managed business, most bills are paid by check. However, there are times when small expenditures are made with currency and coins. Most businesses use a petty cash fund to pay for small expenditures. Suppose that in the next two hours the office manager needs a $4 folder for a customer. It is not practical to obtain an approval and write a check for $4 in the time available. Instead, the office manager takes $4 from the petty cash fund to purchase the folder.

ESTABLISHING THE FUND

important!

Petty Cash

Only one person controls the petty cash fund. That person keeps receipts for all expenditures.

The amount of the petty cash fund depends on the needs of the business. Usually the office manager, cashier, or assistant is in charge of the petty cash fund. The cashier is responsible for petty cash. To set up the petty cash fund, Maxx-Out Sporting Goods wrote a $175 check to the cashier on February 1, using check number 160. She cashed the check and put the currency in a locked cash box.

The establishment of the petty cash fund should be recorded as follows:

	DATE		DESCRIPTION	POST. REF.	DEBIT	CREDIT	
1	2013						1
2	Feb.	1	Petty Cash		175 00		2
3			Cash			175 00	3
4			Establish petty cash fund, Check No. 160				4
5							5

GENERAL JOURNAL PAGE ___8___

MAKING PAYMENTS FROM THE FUND

Petty cash fund payments are limited to small amounts. A **petty cash voucher** is used to record the payments made from the petty cash fund. The petty cash voucher shows the voucher number,

FIGURE 9.2

Petty Cash Voucher

PETTY CASH VOUCHER 1

NOTE: This form must be computer processed or filled out in black ink.

DESCRIPTION OF EXPENDITURE	ACCOUNTS TO BE CHARGED	AMOUNT
Office supplies	Supplies 129	16 25
	Total	16 25

RECEIVED
THE SUM OF _Sixteen_ -- DOLLARS AND __25/100__ CENTS
SIGNED _L.T. Green_ ____ DATE _2/3/13_ ____ APPROVED BY __M.F.__ DATE _2/3/13_
        Metroplex Office Supply Co.

amount, purpose of the expenditure, and account to debit. The person receiving the funds signs the voucher, and the person who controls the petty cash fund initials the voucher. Figure 9.2 shows a petty cash voucher for $16.25 for office supplies.

THE PETTY CASH ANALYSIS SHEET

Most businesses use a **petty cash analysis sheet** to record transactions involving petty cash. The Receipts column shows cash put in the fund, and the Payments column shows the cash paid out. There are special columns for accounts that are used frequently, such as *Supplies, Freight In,* and *Miscellaneous Expense.* There is an Other Accounts Debit column for entries that do not fit in a special column. Figure 9.3 shows the petty cash analysis sheet for Maxx-Out Sporting Goods for February.

Replenishing the Fund The total vouchers plus the cash on hand should always equal the amount of the fund—$175 for Maxx-Out Sporting Goods. Replenish the petty cash fund at the end of each month or sooner if the fund is low. Refer to Figure 9.3 and note that the amount in the petty cash fund on February 28 is $15.25:

1. Total the columns on the petty cash analysis sheet.
2. Prove the petty cash fund by adding cash on hand and total payments. This should equal the petty cash fund balance ($15.25 + $159.75 = $175.00).

FIGURE 9.3 **Petty Cash Analysis Sheet**

								OTHER ACCOUNTS DEBIT	
DATE	VOU. NO.	DESCRIPTION	RECEIPTS	PAYMENTS	SUPPLIES DEBIT	DELIVERY EXPENSE DEBIT	MISC. EXPENSE DEBIT	ACCOUNT TITLE	AMOUNT
2013									
Feb. 1		Establish fund	175 00						
3	1	Office supplies		16 25	16 25				
6	2	Delivery service		24 00		24 00			
11	3	Withdrawal		25 00				M. Ferraro, Drawing	25 00
15	4	Postage stamps		37 00			37 00		
20	5	Delivery service		17 50		17 50			
26	6	Window washing		26 00			26 00		
28	7	Store supplies		14 00	14 00				
28		Totals	175 00	159 75	30 25	41 50	63 00		25 00
28		Balance on hand		15 25					
			175 00	175 00					
28		Balance on hand	15 25						
28		Replenish fund	159 75						
28		Carried forward	175 00						

Caption: **PETTY CASH ANALYSIS**   PAGE __1__

3. Write a check to restore the petty cash fund to its original balance.

4. Prepare the journal entry to record the check.

The journal entry to record the replenishment of the petty cash fund at February 28, using check number 191, is below:

	DATE		DESCRIPTION	POST. REF.	DEBIT	CREDIT	
1	2013						1
2	Feb.	28	Supplies		30 25		2
3			Delivery Expense		41 50		3
4			Miscellaneous Expense		63 00		4
5			Max Ferraro, Drawing		25 00		5
6			Cash			159 75	6
7			Replenish petty cash fund, Check No. 191				7

GENERAL JOURNAL   PAGE _9_

INTERNAL CONTROL OF THE PETTY CASH FUND

Whenever there is valuable property or cash to protect, appropriate safeguards must be established. Petty cash is no exception. The following internal control procedures apply to petty cash:

1. Use the petty cash fund only for small payments that cannot conveniently be made by check.

2. Limit the amount set aside for petty cash to the approximate amount needed to cover one month's payments from the fund.

3. Write petty cash fund checks to the person in charge of the fund, not to the order of "Cash."

4. Assign one person to control the petty cash fund. This person has sole control of the money and is the only one authorized to make payments from the fund.

5. Keep petty cash in a safe, a locked cash box, or a locked drawer.

6. Obtain a petty cash voucher for each payment. The voucher should be signed by the person who receives the money and should show the payment details. This provides an audit trail for the fund.

>>3. OBJECTIVE

Demonstrate a knowledge of internal control routines for cash.

Internal Control over Cash

In a well-managed business, there are internal control procedures for handling and recording cash receipts and cash payments. The internal control over cash should be tailored to the needs of the business. Accountants play a vital role in designing, establishing, and monitoring the cash control system. In developing internal control procedures for cash, certain basic principles must be followed.

CONTROL OF CASH RECEIPTS

As noted already, cash is the asset that is most easily stolen, lost, or mishandled. Yet cash is essential to carrying on business operations. It is important to protect all cash receipts to make sure that funds are available to pay expenses and take care of other business obligations. The following are essential cash receipt controls:

1. Have only designated employees receive and handle cash whether it consists of checks and money orders, or currency and coins. These employees should be carefully chosen for reliability and accuracy and should be carefully trained. In some businesses employees who handle cash are bonded. **Bonding** is the process by which employees are investigated by an insurance company. Employees who pass the background check can be bonded; that

is, the employer can purchase insurance on the employees. If the bonded employees steal or mishandle cash, the business is insured against the loss.

2. Keep cash receipts in a cash register, a locked cash drawer, or a safe while they are on the premises.

3. Make a record of all cash receipts as the funds come into the business. For currency and coins, this record is the audit tape in a cash register or duplicate copies of numbered sales slips. The use of a cash register provides an especially effective means of control because the machine automatically produces a tape showing the amounts entered. This tape is locked inside the cash register until it is removed by a supervisor.

4. Before a bank deposit is made, check the funds to be deposited against the record made when the cash was received. The employee who checks the deposit is someone other than the one who receives or records the cash.

5. Deposit cash receipts in the bank promptly—every day or several times a day. Deposit the funds intact—do not make payments directly from the cash receipts. The person who makes the bank deposit is someone other than the one who receives and records the funds.

6. Enter cash receipts transactions in the accounting records promptly. The person who records cash receipts is not the one who receives or deposits the funds.

7. Have the monthly bank statement sent to and reconciled by someone other than the employees who handle, record, and deposit the funds.

One of the advantages of efficient procedures for handling and recording cash receipts is that the funds reach the bank sooner. Cash receipts are not kept on the premises for more than a short time, which means that the funds are safer and are readily available for paying bills owed by the firm.

CONTROL OF CASH PAYMENTS

It is important to control cash payments so that the payments are made only for authorized business purposes. The following are essential cash payment controls:

1. Make all payments by check except for payments from special-purpose cash funds such as a petty cash fund or a travel and entertainment fund.

2. Issue checks only with an approved bill, invoice, or other document that describes the reason for the payment.

3. Have only designated personnel, who are experienced and reliable, approve bills and invoices.

4. Have checks prepared and recorded in the checkbook or check register by someone other than the person who approves the payments.

5. Have still another person sign and mail the checks to creditors. Consider requiring that two people sign all checks greater than a predesignated amount.

6. Use prenumbered check forms. Periodically, the numbers of the checks that were issued and the numbers of the blank check forms remaining should be verified to make sure that all check numbers are accounted for.

7. During the bank reconciliation process, compare the canceled checks to the checkbook or check register. The person who does the bank reconciliation should be someone other than the person who prepares or records the checks.

8. Enter promptly in the accounting records all cash payment transactions. The person who records cash payments should not be the one who approves payments or the one who writes the checks.

Small businesses usually cannot achieve the division of responsibility recommended for cash receipts and cash payments. However, no matter what size the firm, efforts should be made to set up effective control procedures for cash.

Section 2 Self Review

 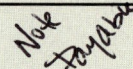
QUESTIONS

1. What account would be *credited* in the issuance of a promissory note to purchase store equipment?

2. Why does a business use a petty cash fund?

3. What journal entry records the establishment of a petty cash fund?

EXERCISES

4. Which journal entry could be used to record the replenishment of the petty cash fund?

   a. Debit Petty Cash Fund, credit Cash

   b. Debit Supplies, debit Delivery Expense, credit Cash

   c. Debit Supplies, debit Delivery Expense, credit Petty Cash Fund

   d. Debit Cash, credit Petty Cash Fund

5. Which of the following is not an example of good internal control over cash payments?

   a. Make all payments with currency rather than by check.

   b. Issue checks only with an approved bill.

   c. Have checks prepared and recorded in the accounting records by someone other than the person approving payments.

   d. Use prenumbered checks.

ANALYSIS

6. Your employer keeps a $75 petty cash fund. She asked you to replenish the fund. She is missing a receipt for $7.40, which she says she spent on postage. How should you handle this?

(Answers to Section 2 Self Review are on page 298.)

SECTION OBJECTIVES

>> **4.** **Write a check, endorse checks, prepare a bank deposit slip, and maintain a checkbook balance.**

WHY IT'S IMPORTANT

Banking tasks are basic practices in every business.

>> **5.** **Reconcile the monthly bank statement.**

WHY IT'S IMPORTANT

Reconciliation of the bank statement provides a good control of cash.

>> **6.** **Record any adjusting entries required from the bank reconciliation.**

WHY IT'S IMPORTANT

Certain items are not recorded in the accounting records during the month.

>> **7.** **Understand how businesses use online banking to manage cash activities.**

WHY IT'S IMPORTANT

Many businesses use online banking to manage a significant portion of cash activities.

TERMS TO LEARN

bank reconciliation statement
blank endorsement
canceled check
check
credit memorandum
debit memorandum
deposit in transit
deposit slip
dishonored (NSF) check
drawee
drawer
electronic funds transfer (EFT)
endorsement
full endorsement
negotiable
outstanding checks
payee
postdated check
restrictive endorsement
service charge

Banking Procedures

Businesses with good internal control systems safeguard cash. Many businesses make a daily bank deposit, and some make two or three deposits a day. Keeping excess cash is a dangerous practice. Also, frequent bank deposits provide a steady flow of funds for the payment of expenses.

Writing Checks

A **check** is a written order signed by an authorized person, the **drawer,** instructing a bank, the **drawee,** to pay a specific sum of money to a designated person or business, the **payee.** The checks in Figure 9.4 on the next page are **negotiable,** which means that ownership of the checks can be transferred to another person or business.

Before writing the check, complete the check stub. In Figure 9.4, the check stub for Check 111 shows:

- Balance brought forward: $12,025.50
- Check amount: $1,500.00
- Balance: $10,525.50
- Date: January 3, 2013
- Payee: Carter Real Estate Group
- Purpose: January rent

Once the stub has been completed, fill in the check. Carefully enter the date, the payee, and the amount in figures and words. Draw a line to fill any empty space after the payee's name and

>>4. OBJECTIVE

Write a check, endorse checks, prepare a bank deposit slip, and maintain a checkbook balance.

FIGURE 9.4   **Checks and Check Stubs**

No. 111	BAL BRO'T FOR'D	12,025	50
January 3 20 13			
Carter Real Estate Group			
TO ORDER OF			
January rent			
FOR			
	TOTAL	12,025	50
	AMOUNT THIS CHECK	1,500	00
	BALANCE	10,525	50

Maxx-Out Sporting Goods   **No. 111**
2007 Trendsetter Lane
Dallas, TX 75268-0967   11-8640
                                              1210

DATE __January 3__ 20 _13_

PAY TO THE ORDER OF __Carter Real Estate Group__ $ _1,500.00_

__One thousand five hundred__ ⁰⁰/100 _____ DOLLARS

FIRST TEXAS NATIONAL BANK
Dallas, TX 75267-6205

MEMO __Rent for January__   __Max Ferraro__

⑆1210⑈8640⑆ ⑈38⑈ 149886 7⑈

No. 112	BAL BRO'T FOR'D	10,525	50
January 10 20 13			
The Retail Equip. Ctr.			
TO ORDER OF			
store fixtures			
FOR			
	TOTAL	10,525	50
	AMOUNT THIS CHECK	2,400	00
	BALANCE	8,125	50

Maxx-Out Sporting Goods   **No. 112**
2007 Trendsetter Lane
Dallas, TX 75268-0967   11-8640
                                              1210

DATE __January 10__ 20 _13_

PAY TO THE ORDER OF __The Retail Equipment Center__ $ _2,400.00_

__Two thousand four hundred__ ⁰⁰/100 _____ DOLLARS

FIRST TEXAS NATIONAL BANK
Dallas, TX 75267-6205

MEMO __store fixtures__   __Max Ferraro__

⑆1210⑈8640⑆ ⑈38⑈ 149886 7⑈

after the amount in words. To be valid, checks need an authorized signature. For Maxx-Out Sporting Goods only Max Ferraro, the owner, is authorized to sign checks.

Figure 9.4 also shows the check stub for Check 112, a cash purchase from The Retail Equipment Center for $2,400. After Check 112, the account balance is $8,125.50 ($10,525.50 − $2,400.00).

DEBIT CARDS

Debit cards (also called check cards) look like credit cards or ATM (automated teller machine) cards, but operate like cash or a personal check. In this context, debit means "subtract," so when you use your debit card, you are subtracting your money from your bank account. Funds on deposit with a bank represent a liability to the bank. By debiting accounts when depositors use their debit cards, the bank reduces the depositors' account balances, thus reducing the bank's liabilities to depositors. Debit cards are accepted almost everywhere including grocery stores, retail stores, gasoline stations, and restaurants. Debit cards are popular because they offer an alternative to carrying checks or cash. Transactions that are completed with the debit card will appear on your bank statement.

Endorsing Checks

Each check needs an endorsement to be deposited. The **endorsement** is a written authorization that transfers ownership of a check. After the payee transfers ownership to the bank by an endorsement, the bank has a legal right to collect payment from the drawer, the person or business that issued the check. If the check cannot be collected, the payee guarantees payment to all subsequent holders.

Several forms of endorsement are shown in Figure 9.5. Endorsements are placed on the back of the check, on the left, near the perforated edge where the check was separated from the stub.

FIGURE 9.5

Types of Check Endorsement

Full Endorsement

PAY TO THE ORDER OF
FIRST TEXAS NATIONAL BANK
Maxx-Out Sporting Goods
38-14-98867

Blank Endorsement

Max Ferraro
38-14-98867

Restrictive Endorsement

PAY TO THE ORDER OF
FIRST TEXAS NATIONAL BANK
FOR DEPOSIT ONLY
Maxx-Out Sporting Goods
38-14-98867

FIGURE 9.6

Deposit Slip

CHECKING ACCOUNT DEPOSIT

DATE *January 8, 2013*

MAXX-OUT SPORTING GOODS
2007 Trendsetter Lane
Dallas, TX 75268-0967

FIRST TEXAS NATIONAL BANK
Dallas, TX 75267-6205

		DOLLARS	CENTS
CURRENCY		1810	00
COIN		219	80
1	11-2818	260	75
2	11-2818	290	18
3	11-1652	180	65
4	11-1652	598	32
5	11-5074	800	30
6	11-5074	700	00
7			
8			
9			
10			
11			
12			
TOTAL FROM OTHER SIDE OR ATTACHED LIST			
TOTAL		4,860.00	

ENTER ADDITIONAL CHECKS ON OTHER SIDE

Checks and other items are received for deposit subject to the terms and conditions of this bank's collection agreement.

⑆1210⑈8640⑆ ⑈38⑊ 1498867⑈

A **blank endorsement** is the signature of the payee that transfers ownership of the check without specifying to whom or for what purpose. Checks with a blank endorsement can be further endorsed by anyone who has the check, even if the check is lost or stolen.

A **full endorsement** is a signature transferring a check to a specific person, business, or bank. Only the person, business, or bank named in the full endorsement can transfer it to someone else.

The safest endorsement is the **restrictive endorsement.** A restrictive endorsement is a signature that transfers the check to a specific party for a specific purpose, usually for deposit to a bank account. Most businesses restrictively endorse the checks they receive using a rubber stamp.

Preparing the Deposit Slip

Businesses prepare a **deposit slip** to record each deposit of cash or checks to a bank account. Usually the bank provides deposit slips preprinted with the account name and number. Figure 9.6 shows the deposit slip for the January 8 deposit for Maxx-Out Sporting Goods.

Notice the printed numbers on the lower edge of the deposit slip. These are the same numbers on the bottom of the checks, Figure 9.4. The numbers are printed using a special *magnetic ink character recognition (MICR)* type that can be "read" by machine. Deposit slips and checks encoded with MICR are rapidly and efficiently processed by machine.

■ The 12 indicates that the bank is in the 12th Federal Reserve District.

■ The 10 is the routing number used in processing the document.

- The 8640 identifies First Texas National Bank.
- The 38 14 98867 is Maxx-Out Sporting Goods account number.

The deposit slip for Maxx-Out Sporting Goods shows the date, January 8. *Currency* is the paper money, $1,810.00. *Coin* is the amount in coins, $219.80. The checks and money orders are individually listed. Some banks ask that the *American Bankers Association (ABA) transit number* for each check be entered on the deposit slip. The transit number appears on the top part of the fraction that appears in the upper right corner of the check. In Figure 9.4, the transit number is 11-8640.

Many banks now allow businesses to deposit checks to an ATM without using deposit slips. The ATM receipt provides the depositor with images of the checks deposited as well as the toal amount of the deposit.

Handling Postdated Checks

Occasionally a business will receive a postdated check. A **postdated check** is dated some time in the future. If the business receives a postdated check, it should not deposit it before the date on the check. Otherwise, the check could be refused by the drawer's bank. Postdated checks are written by drawers who do not have sufficient funds to cover the check. The drawer expects to have adequate funds in the bank by the date on the check. Issuing or accepting postdated checks is not a proper business practice.

>>**5. OBJECTIVE**

Reconcile the monthly bank statement.

Reconciling the Bank Statement

Once a month, the bank sends a statement of the deposits received and the checks paid for each account. Figure 9.7 shows the bank statement for Maxx-Out Sporting Goods. It shows a day-

FIGURE 9.7

Bank Statement

FIRST TEXAS NATIONAL BANK

MAXX-OUT SPORTING GOODS
2007 Trendsetter Lane
Dallas, TX 75268-0967

Account Number: 38-14-98867

Period Ending   January, 31, 2013

CHECKS		DEPOSITS	DATE	BALANCE
Beginning Balance			December 31, 2012	$12,025.50
1,500.00-		702.00+	January 7	11,227.50
2,400.00-		4,860.00+	January 8	13,687.50
756.00-		270.00+	January 11	13,201.50
3,856.30-		15,000.00+	January 12	24,345.20
2,807.70-		540.00+	January 13	22,077.50
900.00-		5,166.00+	January 15	26,343.50
3,000.00-	318.00-	108.00+	January 17	23,133.50
276.00-	4,250.00-	75.00+	January 18	18,682.50
840.00-	1,000.00-	400.00+	January 22	17,242.50
1,600.00-		5,400.00+	January 22	21,042.50
525.00- DM		2,932.00+	January 29	23,449.50
25.00- SC		108.00+	January 31	23,532.50
1,135.00-		275.00+	January 31	22,672.50
		836.00+	January 31	23,508.50

LAST AMOUNT IN THIS
COLUMN IS YOUR BALANCE

Codes:	CC	Certified Check	EC	Error Correction
	CM	Credit Memorandum	OD	Overdrawn
	DM	Debit Memorandum	SC	Service Charge

PLEASE EXAMINE THIS STATEMENT UPON RECEIPT AND REPORT ANY ERRORS WITHIN TEN DAYS.

to-day listing of all transactions during the month. A code, explained at the bottom, identifies transactions that do not involve checks or deposits. For example, SC indicates a service charge. The last column of the bank statement shows the account balance at the beginning of the period, after each day's transactions, and at the end of the period.

Often the bank encloses canceled checks with the bank statement. **Canceled checks** are checks paid by the bank during the month. Canceled checks are proof of payment. They are filed after the bank reconciliation is complete.

Usually there is a difference between the ending balance shown on the bank statement and the balance shown in the checkbook. A bank reconciliation determines why the difference exists and brings the records into agreement.

CHANGES IN THE CHECKING ACCOUNT BALANCE

A **credit memorandum** explains any addition, other than a deposit, to the checking account. For example, when a note receivable is due, the bank may collect the note from the maker and place the proceeds in the checking account. The amount collected appears on the bank statement, and the credit memorandum showing the details of the transaction is enclosed with the bank statement.

A **debit memorandum** explains any deduction, other than a check, to the checking account. Service charges and dishonored checks appear as debit memorandums.

Bank **service charges** are fees charged by banks to cover the costs of maintaining accounts and providing services, such as the use of the night deposit box and the collection of promissory notes. The debit memorandum shows the type and amount of each service charge.

Figure 9.8 shows a debit memorandum for a $525.00 dishonored check. A **dishonored check** is one that is returned to the depositor unpaid. Normally, checks are dishonored because there are insufficient funds in the drawer's account to cover the check. The bank usually stamps the letters *NSF* for *Not Sufficient Funds* on the check. The business records a journal entry to debit Accounts Receivable and credit Cash for the amount of the dishonored check.

When a check is dishonored, the business contacts the drawer to arrange for collection. The drawer can ask the business to redeposit the check because the funds are now in the account. If so, the business records the check deposit again. Sometimes, the business requests a cash payment.

THE BANK RECONCILIATION PROCESS: AN ILLUSTRATION

When the bank statement is received, it is reconciled with the financial records of the business. On February 5 Maxx-Out Sporting Goods received the bank statement shown in Figure 9.7. The ending cash balance according to the bank is $23,508.50. On January 31 the *Cash* account, called the *book balance of cash,* is $16,060.70. The same amount appears on the check stub at the end of January.

Sometimes the difference between the bank balance and the book balance is due to errors. The bank might make an arithmetic error, give credit to the wrong depositor, or charge a check against the wrong account. Some banks require that errors in the bank statement be reported within a short period of time. The errors made by businesses include not recording a check or deposit, or recording a check or deposit for the wrong amount.

FIGURE 9.8

Debit Memorandum

```
┌─────────────────────────────────────────────────────────────────┐
│ DEBIT: MAXX-OUT SPORTING GOODS    FIRST TEXAS NATIONAL BANK       │
│        2007 Trendsetter Lane                                      │
│        Dallas, TX 75268-0967                                      │
│                                                                   │
│        38-14-98867              DATE: January 31, 2013            │
│                                                                   │
│  ┌──────────────────────────────────────────────┬─────────┐      │
│  │ NSF Check - David Newhouse                     │ 525 00  │      │
│  │                                                │         │      │
│  └──────────────────────────────────────────────┴─────────┘      │
│                                                                   │
│  APPROVED:  Max Ferraro                                           │
└─────────────────────────────────────────────────────────────────┘
```

FIGURE 9.9

Bank Reconciliation Statement

Maxx-Out Sporting Goods			
Bank Reconciliation Statement			
January 31, 2013			
Balance on Bank Statement			23 5 0 8 50
Additions:			
Deposits of January 31 in transit	5 9 4 0 00		
Check incorrectly charged to account	1 6 0 0 00	7 5 4 0 00	
		31 0 4 8 50	
Deductions for outstanding checks:			
Check 124 of January 31	5 6 5 00		
Check 125 of January 31	4 9 5 0 00		
Check 126 of January 31	3 2 0 0 00		
Check 127 of January 31	1 7 5 00		
Check 128 of January 31	1 7 2 80		
Check 129 of January 31	6 3 0 0 00		
Check 130 of January 31	1 7 5 00		
Total Checks Outstanding		15 5 3 7 80	
Adjusted Bank Balance		15 5 1 0 70	
Balance in Books		16 0 6 0 70	
Deductions:			
NSF Check	5 2 5 00		
Bank Service Charge	2 5 00	5 5 0 00	
Adjusted Book Balance		15 5 1 0 70	

Other than errors, there are four reasons why the book balance of cash may not agree with the balance on the bank statement:

1. **Outstanding checks** are checks that are recorded in the general journal but have not been paid by the bank.
2. **Deposit in transit** is a deposit that is recorded in the general journal but that reaches the bank too late to be shown on the monthly bank statement.
3. Service charges and other deductions are not recorded in the business records.
4. Deposits, such as the collection of promissory notes, are not recorded in the business records.

Figure 9.9 shows a **bank reconciliation statement** that accounts for the differences between the balance on the bank statement and the book balance of cash. The bank reconciliation statement format is:

First Section		**Second Section**	
	Bank statement balance		Book balance
+	deposits in transit	+	deposits not recorded
−	outstanding checks	−	deductions
+ or −	bank errors	+ or −	errors in the books
	Adjusted bank balance		Adjusted book balance

When the bank reconciliation statement is complete, the adjusted bank balance must equal the adjusted book balance.

Use the following steps to prepare the bank reconciliation statement:

First Section

1. Enter the balance on the bank statement, $23,508.50.
2. Compare the deposits in the checkbook with the deposits on the bank statement. Maxx-Out Sporting Goods had one deposit in transit. On January 31 receipts of $5,940.00 were placed in the bank's night deposit box. The bank recorded the deposit on February 1. The deposit will appear on the February bank statement.

3. List the outstanding checks:
   - Put the canceled checks in numeric order.
   - Compare the canceled checks to the check stubs, verifying the check numbers and amounts.
   - Examine the endorsements to make sure that they agree with the names of the payees.
   - List the checks that have not cleared the bank.
   - Maxx-Out Sporting Goods has seven outstanding checks totaling $15,537.80.

4. While reviewing the canceled checks for Maxx-Out Sporting Goods, Max Ferraro found a $1,600 check issued by The Dress Barn. The $1,600 was deducted from Maxx-Out Sporting Goods' account; it should have been deducted from the account for The Dress Barn. This is a bank error. Max Ferraro contacted the bank about the error. The correction will appear on the next bank statement. The bank error amount is added to the bank statement balance on the bank reconciliation statement.

5. The adjusted bank balance is $15,510.70.

Second Section

1. Enter the balance in books from the *Cash* account, $16,060.70.
2. Record any deposits made by the bank that have not been recorded in the accounting records. Maxx-Out Sporting Goods did not have any.
3. Record deductions made by the bank. There are two items:
   - the NSF check for $525,
   - the bank service charge for $25.
4. Record any errors in the accounting records that were discovered during the reconciliation process. Maxx-Out Sporting Goods did not have any errors in January.
5. The adjusted book balance is $15,510.70.

Notice that the adjusted bank balance and the adjusted book balance agree.

Adjusting the Financial Records

Items in the second section of the bank reconciliation statement include additions and deductions made by the bank that do not appear in the accounting records. Businesses prepare journal entries to record these items in the books.

For Maxx-Out Sporting Goods, two entries must be made. The first entry is for the NSF check from David Newhouse, a credit customer. The second entry is for the bank service charge. The effect of the two items is a decrease in the *Cash* account balance.

important!

Adjusted Book Balance
Make journal entries to record additions and deductions that appear on the bank statement but that have not been recorded in the general ledger.

>>6. OBJECTIVE
Record any adjusting entries required from the bank reconciliation.

MANAGERIAL IMPLICATIONS   <<

CASH

- It is important to safeguard cash against loss and theft.
- Management and the accountant need to work together:
  - to make sure that there are effective controls for cash receipts and cash payments,
  - to monitor the internal control system to make sure that it functions properly,
  - to develop procedures that ensure the quick and efficient recording of cash transactions.
- To make decisions, management needs up-to-date information about the cash position so that it can anticipate cash shortages and arrange loans or arrange for the temporary investment of excess funds.
- Management and the accountant need to establish controls over the banking activities—depositing funds, issuing checks, recording checking account transactions, and reconciling the monthly bank statement.

THINKING CRITICALLY

How would you determine how much cash to keep in the business checking account, as opposed to in a short-term investment?

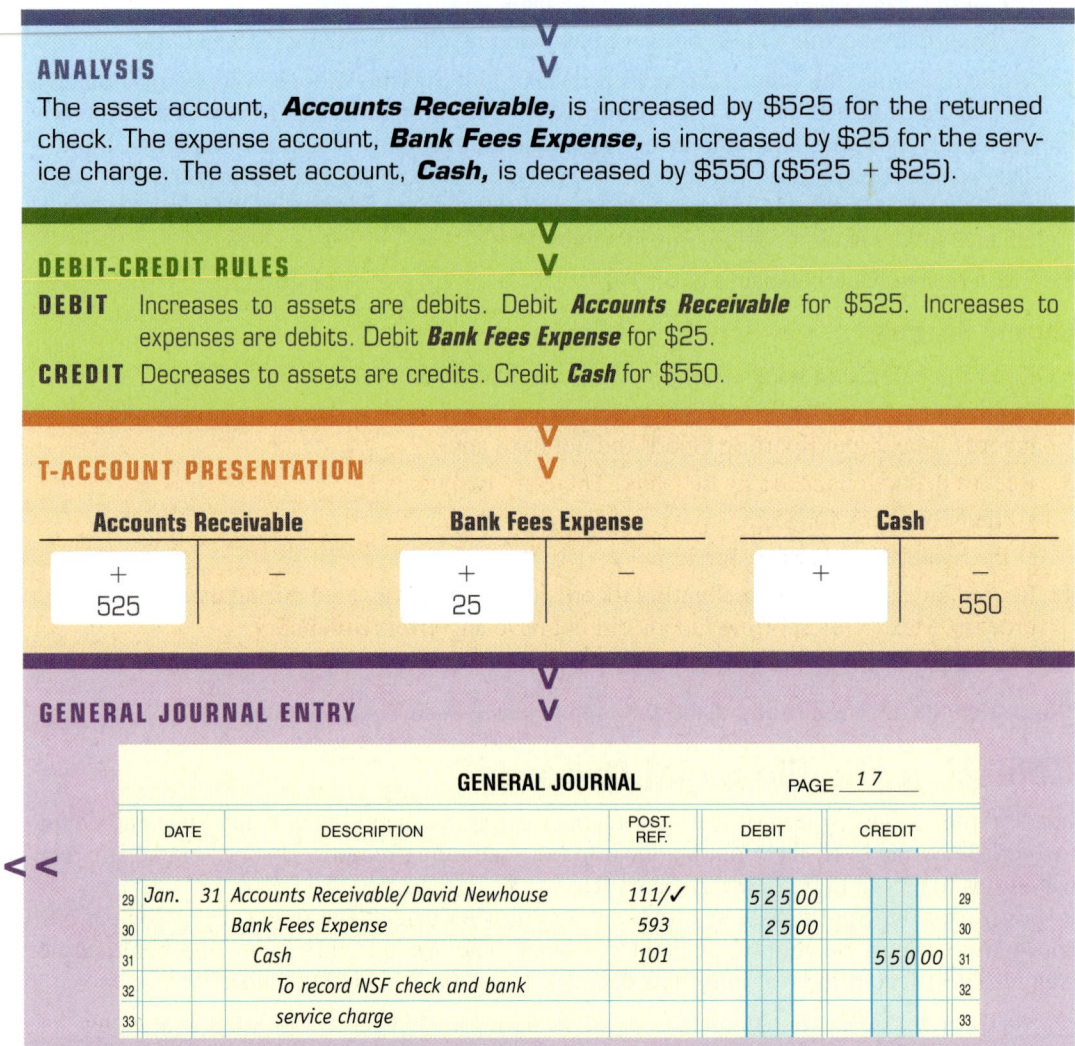

The January bank reconciliation statement (Figure 9.9 on page 276) shows an NSF check of $525 and a bank service charge of $25.

ANALYSIS

The asset account, **Accounts Receivable,** is increased by $525 for the returned check. The expense account, **Bank Fees Expense,** is increased by $25 for the service charge. The asset account, **Cash,** is decreased by $550 ($525 + $25).

DEBIT-CREDIT RULES

DEBIT   Increases to assets are debits. Debit **Accounts Receivable** for $525. Increases to expenses are debits. Debit **Bank Fees Expense** for $25.

CREDIT   Decreases to assets are credits. Credit **Cash** for $550.

T-ACCOUNT PRESENTATION

Accounts Receivable		Bank Fees Expense		Cash	
+	–	+	–	+	–
525		25			550

THE BOTTOM LINE

Adjusting Entries

Income Statement

Expenses	↑ 25
Net Income	↓ 25

Balance Sheet

Assets	↓ 25
Equity	↓ 25

GENERAL JOURNAL ENTRY

GENERAL JOURNAL   PAGE _17_

	DATE	DESCRIPTION	POST. REF.	DEBIT	CREDIT	
29	Jan. 31	Accounts Receivable/ David Newhouse	111/✓	525 00		29
30		Bank Fees Expense	593	25 00		30
31		Cash	101		550 00	31
32		To record NSF check and bank				32
33		service charge				33

After these entries are posted, the **Cash** account appears as follows:

ACCOUNT _Cash_   ACCOUNT NO. _101_

DATE	DESCRIPTION	POST. REF.	DEBIT	CREDIT	BALANCE DEBIT	BALANCE CREDIT
2013						
Jan. 1	Balance	✓			12 025 50	
31		J17		550 00	15 510 70	

Notice that $15,510.70 is the adjusted bank balance, the adjusted book balance, and the general ledger **Cash** balance. A notation is made on the latest check stub to deduct the amounts ($525 and $25). The notation includes the reasons for the deductions.

Sometimes the bank reconciliation reveals an error in the firm's financial records. For example, the February bank reconciliation for Maxx-Out Sporting Goods found that Check 151 was written for $465. The amount on the bank statement is $465. However, the check was recorded in the accounting records as $445. The business made a $20 error when recording the check.

Maxx-Out Sporting Goods prepared the following journal entry to correct the error. The $20 is also deducted on the check stub.

		GENERAL JOURNAL		PAGE 18			
	DATE	DESCRIPTION	POST. REF.	DEBIT	CREDIT		
1	2013					1
2						2
29	Feb. 28	Advertising Expense	514	20 00		29
30		Cash	101		20 00	30
31		To correct error for check				31
32		151 of February 22				32

Internal Control of Banking Activities

Well-run businesses put the following internal controls in place:

1. Limit access to the checkbook to designated employees. When the checkbook is not in use, keep it in a locked drawer or cabinet.

2. Use prenumbered check forms. Periodically, verify and account for all checks. Examine checks before signing them. Match each check to an approved invoice or other payment authorization.

3. Separate duties:
   - The person who writes the check should not sign or mail the check.
   - The person who performs the bank reconciliation should not handle or deposit cash receipts or write, record, sign, or mail checks.

4. File all deposit receipts, canceled checks, voided checks, and bank statements for future reference. These documents provide a strong audit trail for the checking account.

internal CONTROL

Using Online Banking

Many businesses now manage a significant portion of their cash activities using online banking. Online banking offers many features to make businesses more efficient. These features include:

- Businesses can initiate **electronic funds transfers (EFT)** to vendors from a computer instead of writing checks.

- Payments to government agencies for taxes can be submitted online, using the government agency Web site, to avoid late payment penalties.

- Businesses can receive EFT from customers, rather than receiving checks in the mail. This is especially important in transacting cash receipts from foreign customers. Routine payments, such as those for utilities expenses and loan payments can be automatically deducted from the company's bank account.

- Many banks offer security alerts for such instances as changes in mailing addresses and ATM and automatic payment withdrawals that exceed specified limits. Such alerts are often sent to the resposible company official via email or phone text messages. When an alert is received, the company should view account activity online to ensure cash transactions are legitimate.

There are usually no source documents for the transactions listed above. The accountant should check bank activity online frequently to ensure all EFT and other transactions initiated electronically are recorded in the accounting records.

For example, the online account activity of Western Imports and Exports for July 29, 30, and 31, 2013, is shown in Figure 9.10. The company's accountant was out of town during that period.

>>7. OBJECTIVE
Understand how businesses use online banking to manage cash activities.

FIGURE 9.10   **Online Account Activity**

Business Checking		Account #987-654321				
Date	**Type**	**Description**	**Additions**	**Payments**	**Balance**
7/31/2013	ATM	ATM withdrawal		$200.00	$27,819.91
7/31/2013	Check	Check #1421 (view)		$1,225.95	$28,019.91
7/30/2013	Bill payment	Online payment		$248.52	$29,245.86
7/30/2013	Check	Check #1420 (view)		$428.20	$29,494.38
7/30/2013	ACH credit	Baden Holding	$10,200.00		$29,922.58
7/30/2013	Deposit	Deposit ID #8989	$5,400.00		$19,722.58
7/30/2013	Loan payment	Online transfer to WE XXX		$3,900.00	$14,322.58
7/29/2013	Check	Check #1422 (view)		$850.00	$18,222.58

In matching these transactions to the company's **Cash** account in the general ledger, the accountant identified the following unrecorded transactions:

1. The loan payment on 7/30/2013 was an automatic debit by Western Equipment for the company's monthly payment on an equipment loan. The loan does not bear interest.
2. The ACH credit on 7/30/2013 was an EFT payment sent by Baden Holding, a German customer, on account.
3. The bill payment of 7/30/2013 was an automatic debit by West Communications (telephone).
4. The ATM withdrawal of 7/31/2013 was for personal use by the owner, Susan De Angelis.

The Accountant recorded these transations in the general journal, as follows:

	DATE		DESCRIPTION	POST. REF.	DEBIT	CREDIT	
1	2013						1
2	July	30	Notes Payable		3 9 0 0 00		2
3			Cash			3 9 0 0 00	3
4			To record loan payment to Western				4
5			Equipment				5
6							6
7		30	Cash		10 2 0 0 00		7
8			Accounts Receivable/Baden Holding			10 2 0 0 00	8
9			To record EFT received on account				9
10			from Baden Holding				10
11							11
12		30	Telephone Expense		2 4 8 52		12
13			Cash			2 4 8 52	13
14			To record online payment to				14
15			West Communications				15
16							16
17		31	Susan De Angelis, Drawing		2 0 0 00		17
18			Cash			2 0 0 00	18
19			To record ATM withdrawal by				19
20			Susan De Angelis for personal use				20

GENERAL JOURNAL   PAGE ___10___

In addition to the internal controls over banking activities discussed on page 279, companies using online banking should allow only authorized check signers access to the company's online account. Additionally, log-in information, such as user identification and passwords, should be changed frequently.

Section 3 Self Review

QUESTIONS

1. Which bank reconciliation items require journal entries?

2. Why does a payee endorse a check before depositing it?

3. What is a postdated check? When should postdated checks be deposited?

EXERCISES

4. Which of the following does not require an adjustment to the financial records?
   a. NSF check
   b. Bank service charge
   c. Check that was incorrectly recorded at $85, but was written and paid by the bank as $58
   d. Deposits in transit

5. On the bank reconciliation statement, you would not find a list of:
   a. canceled checks.
   b. deposits in transit.
   c. outstanding checks.
   d. NSF checks.

ANALYSIS

6. James is one of several accounting clerks at Uptown Beverage Company. His job duties include recording invoices as they are received, filing the invoices, and writing the checks for accounts payable. He is a fast and efficient clerk and usually has some time available each day to help other clerks. It has been suggested that reconciling the bank statement should be added to his job duties. Do you agree or disagree? Why or why not?

(Answers to Section 3 Self Review are on page 298.)

9 Chapter REVIEW   Chapter Summary

In this chapter, you have learned the basic principles of accounting for cash payments and cash receipts.

Learning Objectives

1 Account for cash short or over.

Errors can occur when making change. Cash register discrepancies should be recorded using the expense account **Cash Short or Over.**

2 Demonstrate a knowledge of procedures for a petty cash fund.

Although most payments are made by check, small payments are often made through a petty cash fund. A petty cash voucher is prepared for each payment and signed by the person receiving the money. The person in charge of the fund records expenditures on a petty cash analysis sheet. The fund is replenished with a check for the sum spent. An entry is made in the cash payments journal to debit the accounts involved.

3 Demonstrate a knowledge of internal control routines for cash.

All businesses need a system of internal controls to protect cash from theft and mishandling and to ensure accurate records of cash transactions. A checking account is essential to store cash safely and to make cash payments efficiently. For maximum control over outgoing cash, all payments should be made by check except those from carefully controlled special-purpose cash funds such as a petty cash fund.

4 Write a check, endorse checks, prepare a bank deposit slip, and maintain a checkbook balance.

Check writing requires careful attention to details. If a standard checkbook is used, the stub should be completed before the check so that it will not be forgotten. The stub gives the data needed to journalize the payment.

5 Reconcile the monthly bank statement.

A bank statement should be immediately reconciled with the cash balance in the firm's financial records. Usually, differences are due to deposits in transit, outstanding checks, and bank service charges, but many factors can cause lack of agreement between the bank balance and the book balance.

6 Record any adjusting entries required from the bank reconciliation.

Some differences between the bank balance and the book balance may require that the firm's records be adjusted after the bank statement is reconciled. Journal entries are recorded and then posted to correct the *Cash* account balance and the checkbook balance.

7 Understand how businesses use online banking to manage cash activities.

Many businesses now use online banking to receive cash payments from customers and to initiate cash payments.

8 Define the accounting terms new to this chapter.

Glossary

Bank reconciliation statement (p. 276) A statement that accounts for all differences between the balance on the bank statement and the book balance of cash

Blank endorsement (p. 273) A signature of the payee written on the back of the check that transfers ownership of the check without specifying to whom or for what purpose

Bonding (p. 268) The process by which employees are investigated by an insurance company that will insure the business against losses through employee theft or mishandling of funds

Canceled check (p. 275) A check paid by the bank on which it was drawn

Cash (p. 262) In accounting, currency, coins, checks, money orders, and funds on deposit in a bank

Cash Short or Over account (p. 262) An account used to record any discrepancies between the amount of currency and coins in the cash register and the amount shown on the audit tape

Check (p. 271) A written order signed by an authorized person instructing a bank to pay a specific sum of money to a designated person or business

Credit memorandum (p. 275) A form that explains any addition, other than a deposit, to a checking account

Debit memorandum (p. 275) A form that explains any deduction, other than a check, from a checking account

Deposit in transit (p. 276) A deposit that is recorded in the general journal but that reaches the bank too late to be shown on the monthly bank statement

Deposit slip (p. 273) A form prepared to record the deposit of cash or checks to a bank account

Dishonored (NSF) check (p. 275) A check returned to the depositor unpaid because of insufficient funds in the drawer's account; also called an NSF check

Drawee (p. 271) The bank on which a check is written

Drawer (p. 271) The person or firm issuing a check

Electronic funds transfer (EFT) (p. 279) An electronic transfer of money from one account to another

Endorsement (p. 272) A written authorization that transfers ownership of a check

Full endorsement (p. 273) A signature transferring a check to a specific person, firm, or bank

Negotiable (p. 271) A financial instrument whose ownership can be transferred to another person or business

Outstanding checks (p. 276) Checks that have been recorded in the general journal but have not yet been paid by the bank

Payee (p. 271) The person or firm to whom a check is payable

Petty cash analysis sheet (p. 267) A form used to record transactions involving petty cash

Petty cash voucher (p. 266) A form used to record the payments made from a petty cash fund

Postdated check (p. 274) A check dated some time in the future

Promissory note (p. 264) A written promise to pay a specified amount of money on a specific date

Restrictive endorsement (p. 273) A signature that transfers a check to a specific party for a stated purpose

Service charge (p. 275) A fee charged by a bank to cover the costs of maintaining accounts and providing services

Statement of account (p. 264) A form sent to a firm's customers showing transactions during the month and the balance owed

Comprehensive **Self Review**

1. Describe a full endorsement.
2. What is a petty cash voucher?
3. When is the petty cash fund replenished?
4. What is the classification of the Notes Payable account?
5. What does the term *cash* mean in business?

(Answers to Comprehensive Self Review are on page 298.)

Discussion Questions

1. What procedures are used to achieve internal control over banking activities?
2. Why are journal entries sometimes needed after the bank reconciliation statement is prepared?
3. Give some reasons why the bank balance and the book balance of cash might differ.

4. What is the book balance of cash?

5. Why is a bank reconciliation prepared?

6. What information is shown on the bank statement?

7. What type of information is entered on a check stub? Why should a check stub be prepared before the check is written?

8. What is a check?

9. Why are MICR numbers printed on deposit slips and checks?

10. Which type of endorsement is most appropriate for a business to use?

11. How are cash shortages and overages recorded?

12. Describe the major controls for petty cash.

13. When are petty cash expenditures entered in a firm's accounting records?

14. What is a promissory note? What entry is made to record the collection of a promissory note and interest?

15. Describe the major controls for cash payments.

16. Explain what *bonding* means. How does bonding relate to safeguarding cash?

17. Describe the major controls for cash receipts.

18. Explain the meaning of the following terms:
   a. Canceled check
   b. Outstanding check
   c. Deposit in transit
   d. Debit memorandum
   e. Credit memorandum
   f. Dishonored check
   g. Blank endorsement
   h. Deposit slip
   i. Drawee
   j. Restrictive endorsement
   k. Payee
   l. Drawer
   m. Service charge

APPLICATIONS

Exercises

Exercise 9.1

Objective 1

▶ **Journalizing cash receipts.**

Southern Gift Shop, a retail business, started business on April 29, 2013. It keeps a $300 change fund in its cash register. The cash receipts for the period from April 29 to April 30, 2013, are shown below. Record the cash receipts on April 29 and April 30, 2013, in a general journal. Start the general journal with page 1.

DATE	TRANSACTIONS
April 29	Cash sales per the cash register tape, $1,510. Cash count, $1,804.
30	Cash sales per the cash register tape, $1,420. Cash count, $1,722.

Recording the establishment of a petty cash fund.

◄ Exercise 9.2
Objective 2

On January 2, Westminister Legal Clinic issued Check 2108 for $350 to establish a petty cash fund. Indicate how this transaction would be recorded in a general journal. Use 1 as the journal page number.

Recording the replenishment of a petty cash fund.

◄ Exercise 9.3
Objective 2

On January 31, Chloe Inc. issued Check 3159 to replenish its petty cash fund. An analysis of payments from the fund showed these totals: *Supplies, $48; Delivery Expense, $89;* and *Miscellaneous Expense, $24.* Indicate how this transaction would be recorded in a general journal. Use 3 as the journal page number.

Determining an adjusted bank balance.

◄ Exercise 9.4
Objectives 5, 6

Chin Corporation received a bank statement showing a balance of $14,700 as of October 31, 2013. The firm's records showed a book balance of $14,262 on October 31. The difference between the two balances was caused by the following items. Prepare the adjusted bank balance section and the adjusted book balance section of the bank reconciliation statement. Also prepare the necessary journal entry:

1. A debit memorandum for an NSF check from James Dear for $424.
2. Three outstanding checks: Check 7017 for $124, Check 7098 for $55, and Check 7107 for $1,560.
3. A bank service charge of $20.
4. A deposit in transit of $857.

Analyzing bank reconciliation items.

◄ Exercise 9.5
Objectives 5, 6

At Thompson Delivery and Courier Service the following items were found to cause a difference between the bank statement and the firm's records. Indicate whether each item will affect the bank balance or the book balance when the bank reconciliation statement is prepared. Also indicate which items will require an accounting entry after the bank reconciliation is completed:

1. A deposit in transit.
2. A debit memorandum for a dishonored check.
3. A credit memorandum for a promissory note that the bank collected for Thompson.
4. An error found in Thompson's records, which involves the amount of a check. The firm's checkbook and general journal indicate $808 as the amount, but the canceled check itself and the listing on the bank statement show that $880 was the actual sum.
5. An outstanding check.
6. A bank service charge.
7. A check issued by another firm that was charged to Thompson's account by mistake.

Preparing a bank reconciliation statement.

◄ Exercise 9.6
Objectives 5, 6

Cantu Office Supply Company received a bank statement showing a balance of $68,005 as of March 31, 2013. The firm's records showed a book balance of $69,487 on March 31. The difference between the two balances was caused by the following items. Prepare a bank reconciliation statement for the firm as of March 31 and the necessary journal entries from the statement:

1. A debit memorandum for $50, which covers the bank's collection fee for the note.
2. A deposit in transit of $3,700.
3. A check for $248 issued by another firm that was mistakenly charged to Cantu's account.
4. A debit memorandum for an NSF check of $6,135 issued by Wilson Construction Company, a credit customer.
5. Outstanding checks: Check 3782 for $2,200; Check 3840 for $151.
6. A credit memorandum for a $6,300 noninterest-bearing note receivable that the bank collected for the firm.

Exercise 9.7

Objective 5

▶ **Determining the adjusted bank balance.**

Fierro Company received a bank statement showing a balance of $12,800 on November 30, 2013. During the bank reconciliation process, Fierro's accountant noted the following bank errors:

1. A check for $151 issued by Ferro, Inc., was mistakenly charged to Fierro Company's account.
2. Check 2782 was written for $200 but was paid by the bank as $1,200.
3. Check 2920 for $85 was paid by the bank twice.
4. A deposit for $580 on November 22 was credited by the bank for $850.

Assuming outstanding checks total $2,150, prepare the adjusted bank balance section of the November 30, 2013, bank reconciliation.

Exercise 9.8

Objective 7

▶ **Journalizing electronic transactions**

After returning from a three-day business trip, the accountant for Hunter Sales, Johanna Estrada, checked bank activity in the company's checking account online. The activity for the last three days follows:

Business Checking		Account #123456-987			
Date	**Type**	**Description**	**Additions**	**Payments**	**Balance**
09/24/2013	Loan payment	Online transfer to HMG XXXX		$4,000.00	$15,167.06
09/24/2013	Deposit	Deposit ID number 8888	$2,269.60		$19,167.06
09/23/2013	Check	Check #1554 (view)		$3,500.00	$16,897.46
09/23/2013	Bill payment	Online payment		$26.05	$20,397.46
09/22/2013	Check	Check #1553 (view)		$240.00	$20,423.51
09/22/2013	Check	Check #1551 (view)		$1,750.00	$20,663.51
09/22/2013	ACH credit	Edwards UK AP payment	$8,900.00		$22,413.51
09/22/2013	ATM	ATM withdrawal		$240.00	$13,513.51

After matching these transactions to the company's *Cash* account in the general ledger, Johanna noted the following unrecorded transactions:

1. The ATM withdrawal on 9/22/2013 was for personal use by the owner, Ronnie Hunter.
2. The ACH credit on 9/22/2013 was an electronic funds payment received on account from Edwards UK, a credit customer located in Great Britain.
3. The bill payment made 9/23/2013 was to Orange Trash Services (utilities).
4. The loan payment on 9/24/2013 was a automatic debit by Central Motors for the company's monthly payment on a loan for its automobiles. The loan does not bear interest.

Prepare the journal entries in a general journal to record the four transactions above. Use 21 as the page number.

PROBLEMS

Problem Set A

◄   **Problem 9.1A**

Objectives 1

Journalizing cash receipts, cash short and over, and posting to the general ledger.

Royalty Jewelry Store, a retail business, started business on June 25, 2013. It keeps a $300 change fund in its cash register. The cash receipts for the period from June 25 to June 30, 2013 are below:

INSTRUCTIONS

1. Open the general ledger account for Cash Short and Over, account number 620.

2. Record the cash receipts from June 25 to June 30, 2013, in a general journal. Start the general journal with page 1.

3. Post the amounts for Cash Short and Over in the journal entries to the general ledger.

DATE	TRANSACTIONS
June 25	Cash sales per the cash register tape, $1,220.
	Cash count, $1,511.
26	Cash sales per the cash register tape, $1,330.
	Cash count, $1,622.
27	Cash sales per the cash register tape, $1,342.
	Cash count, $1,643.
28	Cash sales per the cash register tape, $1,272.
	Cash count, $1,564.
29	Cash sales per the cash register tape, $1,119.
	Cash count, $1,421.
30	Cash sales per the cash register tape, $1,358.
	Cash count, $1,650.

Analyze: How will the balance in Cash Short and Over on June 30 be reported in the financial statements?

◄   **Problem 9.2A**

Objectives 2

Journalizing cash payments and recording petty cash transactions.

Rosa's Floral Arrangements, a retail business, started a $300 petty cash fund on June 1. Below are descriptions of the transactions to establish the petty cash fund, disburse petty cash during June, and replenish the petty cash fund on June 30:

INSTRUCTIONS

1. Record the transaction to establish the petty cash fund on June 1 in a general journal. Use 8 as the page number.

2. Record all transactions on a petty cash analysis sheet. Use 1 as the page number.

3. Record the transaction to replenish the petty cash fund on June 30 in the general journal.

DATE	TRANSACTIONS
June 1	Issued Check 550 for $300 to establish a petty cash fund.
5	Paid $40 from the petty cash fund for office supplies, Petty Cash Voucher 1.
8	Paid $41 from the petty cash fund for postage stamps, Petty Cash Voucher 2.
15	Paid $28 from the petty cash fund for delivery service, Petty Cash Voucher 3.
22	Paid $50 from the petty cash fund to the owner, Rosa Calderon, for her personal use, Petty Cash Voucher 4.
25	Paid $40 from the petty cash fund to have the store windows washed, Petty Cash Voucher 5.
29	Paid $57 from the petty cash fund for delivery service, Petty Cash Voucher 6.
30	Issued Check 590 for $256 to replenish the petty cash fund.
	(Foot the columns of the petty cash analysis sheet in order to determine the accounts that should be debited and the amounts involved.)

Analyze: What were the total payments from the petty cash fund in June?

Problem 9.3A
Objectives 5, 6

Preparing a bank reconciliation statement and journalizing entries to adjust the cash balance.

On May 2, 2013, Vacation Paradise received its April bank statement from First City Bank and Trust. Enclosed with the bank statement, which appears below, was a debit memorandum for $160 that covered an NSF check issued by Doris Fisher, a credit customer. The firm's checkbook contained the following information about deposits made and checks issued during April. The balance of the *Cash* account and the checkbook on April 30, 2013, was $3,972:

DATE	TRANSACTIONS	
April 1	Balance	$6,089
1	Check 1207	100
3	Check 1208	300
5	Deposit	350
5	Check 1209	275
10	Check 1210	2,000
17	Check 1211	50
19	Deposit	150
22	Check 1212	9
23	Deposit	150
26	Check 1213	200
28	Check 1214	18
30	Check 1215	15
30	Deposit	200

FIRST CITY BANK AND TRUST

Vacation Paradise   Account Number: 23-11070-08
1718 Jade Lane
San Diego, CA 92111-4998   Period Ending April 30, 2013

CHECKS	DEPOSITS	DATE	BALANCE
		Beginning Balance	
		March 31	6,089.00
100.00−	350.00+	April 6	6,339.00
275.00−	300.00−	April 10	5,764.00
2,000.00−		April 13	3,764.00
6.00− SC		April 14	3,758.00
	150.00+	April 20	3,908.00
50.00−		April 22	3,858.00
	150.00+	April 25	4,008.00
9.00−		April 26	3,999.00
200.00−	160.00− DM	April 29	3,639.00

INSTRUCTIONS

1. Prepare a bank reconciliation statement for the firm as of April 30, 2013.
2. Record general journal entries for any items on the bank reconciliation statement that must be journalized. Date the entries April 30, 2013.

Analyze: What checks remain outstanding after the bank statement has been reconciled?

Preparing a bank reconciliation statement and journalizing entries to adjust the cash balance.

◄ **Problem 9.4A**
Objectives 5, 6

On August 31, 2013, the balance in the checkbook and the *Cash* account of the Sunoma Inn was $12,281. The balance shown on the bank statement on the same date was $13,197.

Notes

a. The firm's records indicate that a $1,450 deposit dated August 30 and a $701 deposit dated August 31 do not appear on the bank statement.

b. A service charge of $8 and a debit memorandum of $320 covering an NSF check have not yet been entered in the firm's records. (The check was issued by Art Corts, a credit customer.)

c. The following checks were issued but have not yet been paid by the bank:

    Check 712, $110
    Check 713, $125
    Check 716, $238
    Check 736, $577
    Check 739, $78
    Check 741, $120

d. A credit memorandum shows that the bank collected a $2,084 note receivable and interest of $63 for the firm. These amounts have not yet been entered in the firm's records.

INSTRUCTIONS

1. Prepare a bank reconciliation statement for the firm as of August 31.
2. Record general journal entries for items on the bank reconciliation statement that must be journalized. Date the entries August 31, 2013.

Analyze: What effect did the journal entries recorded as a result of the bank reconciliation have on the fundamental accounting equation?

Problem 9.5A ▶
Objectives 5, 6

eXcel

Correcting errors revealed by a bank reconciliation.

During the bank reconciliation process at Fontes Company on May 2, 2013, the following two errors were discovered in the firm's records.

a. The checkbook and the general journal indicated that Check 2206 dated April 17 was issued for $695 to make a cash purchase of supplies. However, examination of the canceled check and the listing on the bank statement showed that the actual amount of the check was $14.

b. The checkbook and the general journal indicated that Check 2247 dated April 20 was issued for $130 to pay a utility bill. However, examination of the canceled check and the listing on the bank statement showed that the actual amount of the check was $164.

INSTRUCTIONS

1. Prepare the adjusted book balance section of the firm's bank reconciliation statement. The book balance as of April 30 was $20,275. The errors listed above are the only two items that affect the book balance.

2. Prepare general journal entries to correct the errors. Use page 11 and date the entries April 30, 2013. Check 2206 was correctly debited to *Supplies* on April 17, and Check 2247 was debited to *Utilities Expense* on April 20.

Analyze: If the errors described had not been corrected, would net income for the period be overstated or understated? By what amount?

Problem 9.6A ▶
Objectives 5, 6, and 7

Preparing a bank reconciliation statement and journalizing entries to adjust the cash balance.

On August 1, 2013, the accountant for Far West Imports downloaded the company's July 31, 2013, bank statement from the bank's Web site. The balance shown on the bank statement was $28,760. The July 31, 2013, balance in the *Cash* account in the general ledger was $14,242.

Jenny Irvine, the accountant for Far West Imports, noted the following differences between the bank's records and the company's *Cash* account in the general ledger:

a. An electronic funds transfer for $14,400 from Foncier Ricard, a customer located in France, was received by the bank on July 31.

b. Check 1422 was correctly written and recorded for $1,200. The bank mistakenly paid the check for $1,280.

c. The accounting records indicate that Check 1425 was issued for $60 to make a purchase of supplies. However, examination of the check online showed that the actual amount of the check was for $90.

d. A deposit of $900 made after banking hours on July 31 did not appear on the July 31 bank statement.

e. The following checks were outstanding: Check 1429 for $1,249, and Check 1430 for $141.

f. An automatic debit of $262 on July 31 from CentralComm for telephone service appeared on the bank statement but had not been recorded in the company's accounting records.

INSTRUCTIONS

1. Prepare a bank reconciliation for the firm as of July 31.

2. Record general journal entries for the items on the bank reconiliation that must be journalized. Date the entries July 31, 2013. Use 19 as the page number.

Analyze: What effect on total expenses occurred as a result of the general journal entries recorded?

Problem Set B

Journalizing cash receipts, cash short and over, and posting to the general ledger.

◀   **Problem 9.1B**
Objective 1

Western Gift Shop, a retail business, started business on April 25, 2013. It keeps a $225 change fund in its cash register. The cash receipts for the period from April 25 to April 30, 2013, are below:

INSTRUCTIONS

1. Open the general ledger account for Cash Short and Over, account number 620.
2. Record the cash receipts from April 25 to April 30, 2013, in a general journal. Start the general journal with page 1.
3. Post the amounts for Cash Short and Over in the journal entries to the general ledger.

DATE	TRANSACTIONS
April 25	Cash sales per the cash register tape, $1,300.
	Cash count, $1,524.
26	Cash sales per the cash register tape, $1,050.
	Cash count, $1,276.
27	Cash sales per the cash register tape, $1,230.
	Cash count, $1,452.
28	Cash sales per the cash register tape, $1,182.
	Cash count, $1,411.
29	Cash sales per the cash register tape, $1,082.
	Cash count, $1,308.
30	Cash sales per the cash register tape, $1,217.
	Cash count, $1,444.

Analyze: How will the balance in Cash Short and Over on April 30 be reported in the financial statements?

Journalizing cash payments and recording petty cash transactions.

◀   **Problem 9.2B**
Objective 2

The Asian Tales Gift Shop, a retail business, started a $250 petty cash fund on September 4. Below are descriptions of the transactions to establish the petty cash fund, disburse petty cash during September, and replenish the petty cash fund on September 30:

INSTRUCTIONS

1. Record the transaction on September 4 to establish the petty cash fund in a general journal. Use 7 as the page number.
2. Record all transactions on a petty cash analysis sheet. Use 1 as the page number.
3. Record the transaction on September 4 to replenish the petty cash fund in the general journal.

DATE	TRANSACTIONS
Sept. 4	Issued Check 910 for $250 to establish a petty cash fund.
6	Paid $22 from the petty cash fund for delivery service, Petty Cash Voucher 1.
12	Paid $32 from the petty cash fund for office supplies, Petty Cash Voucher 2.
18	Paid $75 from the petty cash fund to the owner, Fred Chin, for his personal use, Petty Cash Voucher 3.
24	Paid $30 from the petty cash fund for postage stamps, Petty Cash Voucher 4.
28	Paid $32 from the petty cash fund for delivery service, Petty Cash Voucher 5.
30	Issued Check 950 for $191 to replenish the petty cash fund.
	(Foot the columns of the petty cash analysis sheet in order to determine the accounts that should be debited and the amounts involved.)

Analyze: What is the balance of the Petty Cash Fund on September 30, after replenishment?

Problem 9.3B
Objectives 5, 6

▶ **Preparing a bank reconciliation statement and journalizing entries to adjust the cash balance.**

On October 7, 2013, Peter Chen, attorney-at-law, received his September bank statement from First Texas National Bank. Enclosed with the bank statement, which appears on the next page, was a debit memorandum for $118 that covered an NSF check issued by Annette Cole, a credit customer. The firm's checkbook contained the following information about deposits made and checks issued during September. The balance of the *Cash* account and the checkbook on September 30 was $8,134.

INSTRUCTIONS

1. Prepare a bank reconciliation statement for the firm as of September 30, 2013.
2. Record general journal entries for any items on the bank reconciliation statement that must be journalized. Date the entries September 30, 2013.

DATE	TRANSACTIONS	
Sept. 1	Balance	$6,500
1	Check 104	100
3	Check 105	10
3	Deposit	500
6	Check 106	225
10	Deposit	410
11	Check 107	200
15	Check 108	75
21	Check 109	60
22	Deposit	730
25	Check 110	16
25	Check 111	80
27	Check 112	140
28	Deposit	900

FIRST TEXAS NATIONAL BANK

Peter Chen, Attorney-at-Law
3510 North Central Expressway
Dallas, TX 75232-2709

Account Number: 22-8654-30

Period Ending September 30, 2013

CHECKS		DEPOSITS	DATE	BALANCE
Beginning Balance			August 31	6,500.00
		500.00+	September 3	7,000.00
100.00−			September 6	6,900.00
200.00−	10.00−	410.00+	September 11	7,100.00
225.00−			September 15	6,875.00
60.00−			September 19	6,815.00
		730.00+	September 23	7,545.00
80.00−	16.00−		September 25	7,449.00
7.50− SC	118.00− DM		September 28	7,323.50

Analyze: How many checks were paid (cleared the bank) according to the September 30 bank statement?

Preparing a bank reconciliation statement and journalizing entries to adjust the cash balance.

◀ **Problem 9.4B**
Objectives 5, 6

On July 31, 2013, the balance in Stacked Stone Masonry's checkbook and *Cash* account was $7,318.59. The balance shown on the bank statement on the same date was $8,442.03.

Notes

a. The following checks were issued but have not yet been paid by the bank: Check 533 for $148.95, Check 535 for $122.50, and Check 537 for $425.40.

b. A credit memorandum shows that the bank has collected a $1,550 note receivable and interest of $30 for the firm. These amounts have not yet been entered in the firm's records.

c. The firm's records indicate that a deposit of $994.07 made on July 31 does not appear on the bank statement.

d. A service charge of $14.34 and a debit memorandum of $145 covering an NSF check have not yet been entered in the firm's records. (The check was issued by Robert Briggs, a credit customer.)

INSTRUCTIONS

1. Prepare a bank reconciliation statement for the firm as of July 31, 2013.

2. Record general journal entries for any items on the bank reconciliation statement that must be journalized. Date the entries July 31, 2013.

Analyze: After all journal entries have been recorded and posted, what is the balance in the *Cash* account?

Correcting errors revealed by a bank reconciliation.

◀ **Problem 9.5B**
Objectives 5, 6

During the bank reconciliation process at Big Guy Movers Corporation on March 3, 2013, the following errors were discovered in the firm's records:

a. The checkbook and the general journal indicated that Check 1301 dated February 18 was issued for $361 to pay for hauling expenses. However, examination of the canceled check and the listing on the bank statement showed that the actual amount of the check was $316.

b. The checkbook and the general journal indicated that Check 1322 dated February 24 was issued for $404 to pay a telephone bill. However, examination of the canceled check and the listing on the bank statement showed that the actual amount of the check was $440.

INSTRUCTIONS

1. Prepare the adjusted book balance section of the firm's bank reconciliation statement. The book balance as of February 28, 2013, was $19,451. The errors listed are the only two items that affect the book balance.

2. Prepare general journal entries to correct the errors. Date the entries February 28, 2013. Check 1301 was debited to *Hauling Expense* on February 18, and Check 1322 was debited to *Telephone Expense* on February 24.

Analyze: What net change to the *Cash* account occurred as a result of the correcting journal entries?

Problem 9.6B
Objectives 5, 6, and 7

▶ **Preparing a bank reconciliation statement and journalizing entries to adjust the cash balance.**

On December 1, 2013, the accountant for Euro Specialty Products downloaded the company's November 30, 2013, bank statement from the bank's Web site. The balance shown on the bank statement was $29,734. The November 30, 2013, balance in the *Cash* account in the general ledger was $16,630.

Robert Kang, the accountant for Euro Specialty Products, noted the following differences between the bank's records and the company's *Cash* account in the general ledger.

a. The following checks were outstanding: Check 4129 for $1,322, and Check 4130 for $239.

b. A deposit of $1,224 made after banking hours on November 30 did not appear on the November 30 bank statement.

c. An automatic debit of $323 on November 30 from ClearComm for telephone service appeared on the bank statement but had not been recorded in the company's accounting records.

d. An electronic funds transfer for $12,800 from Cantori Cucine, a customer located in Italy, was received by the bank on November 30.

e. Check 4122 was correctly written and recorded for $1,200. The bank mistakenly paid the check for $1,000.

f. The accounting records indicate that Check 4125 was issued for $980 to make a purchase of equipment. However, examination of the check online showed that the actual amount of the check was for $890.

INSTRUCTIONS

1. Prepare a bank reconciliation for the firm as of November 30.

2. Record general journal entries for the items on the bank reconciliation that must be journalized. Date the entries November 30, 2013. Use 44 as the page number.

Analyze: What effect did the journal entries recorded as a result of the bank reconciliation have on total assets?

Critical Thinking Problem 9.1

Jim Springs is the owner and manager of California Car Wash. California Car Wash provides various car wash and car detailing services. California Car Wash also sells snacks and gift items in its waiting area.

California Car Wash has one cash register, where all payments from customers are received. There is a $400 change fund in the cash register at the beginning of each day. There are two cash register clerks, George and Alice, who work two different shifts during the day. Jim is quite busy as an owner and operator of the car wash, and trusts George and Alice completely. Jim does not see the need to count out the cash register drawers with George or Alice after their shifts are ended. Additionally, Jim prints out a cash register tape at the end of the day, but does not compare it to the deposit.

During the first week of August, Jim noticed an increase in business. However, the cash deposits to the bank were less than Jim thought they should be. He has contacted you for advice. You have compiled the sales per the cash register tapes, and the cash counts, for the period from August 1 to August 7. These amounts are as follows:

Date	Sales, per the cash register tape	Cash count
August 1	$2,222.50	$2,496.20
August 2	$2,135.90	$2,352.80
August 3	$2,303.45	$2,451.45
August 4	$2,287.30	$2,597.20
August 5	$2,335.45	$2,644.05
August 6	$2,155.50	$2,460.10
August 7	$2,255.90	$2,592.40

1. Calculate the total amount of cash sales and cash shortages for the period August 1 to August 7.
2. Prepare a journal entry dated August 7 that summarise the cash sales and cash shortages from August 1 to August 7. Use 56 as the page number.
3. What changes in procedures would you recommend to provide better control over cash receipts?

Critical Thinking Problem 9.2

Cash Controls

Tony Scavone is the owner of Scavone Builders, a successful small construction company. He spends most of his time out of the office supervising work at various construction sites, leaving the operation of the office to the company's cashier/bookkeeper, Gloria Smith. Gloria makes bank deposits, pays the company's bills, maintains the accounting records, and prepares monthly bank reconciliations.

Recently a friend told Tony that while he was at a party he overheard Gloria bragging that she paid for her new clothes with money from the company's cash receipts. She said her boss would never know because he never checks the cash records.

Tony admits that he does not check on Gloria's work. He now wants to know if Gloria is stealing from him. He asks you to examine the company's cash records to determine whether Gloria has stolen cash from the business and, if so, how much.

Your examination of the company's cash records reveals the following information:

1. Gloria prepared the following August 31, 2013, bank reconciliation.

Balance in books, August 31, 2013		$18,796
Additions:		
Outstanding checks		
Check 1780	$ 792	
Check 1784	1,819	
Check 1806	484	2,795
		$21,591
Deductions:		
Deposit in transit, August 28, 2013	$4,992	
Bank service charge	10	5,002
Balance on bank statement, July 31, 2013		$16,589

2. An examination of the general ledger shows the *Cash* account with a balance of $18,796 on August 31, 2013.
3. The August 31 bank statement shows a balance of $16,589.
4. The August 28 deposit of $4,992 does not appear on the August 31 bank statement.

5. A comparison of canceled checks returned with the August 31 bank statement with the cash payments journal reveals the following checks as outstanding:

Check 1590	$263
Check 1680	1,918
Check 1724	486
Check 1780	792
Check 1784	1,819
Check 1806	484

Prepare a bank statement using the format presented in this chapter for the month of August. Assume there were no bank or bookkeeping errors in August. Did Gloria take cash from the company? If so, how much and how did she try to conceal the theft? What changes would you recommend to Tony to provide better internal control over cash?

BUSINESS CONNECTIONS

Cash Management

Managerial FOCUS

1. The new accountant for Asheville Hardware Center, a large retail store, found the following weaknesses in the firm's cash-handling procedures. How would you explain to management why each of these procedures should be changed?

   a. No cash register proof is prepared at the end of each day. The amount of money in the register is considered the amount of cash sales for the day.

   b. Small payments are sometimes made from the currency and coins in the cash register. (The store has no petty cash fund.)

   c. During busy periods for the firm, cash receipts are sometimes kept on the premises for several days before a bank deposit is made.

   d. When funds are removed from the cash register at the end of each day, they are placed in an unlocked office cabinet until they are deposited.

   e. The person who makes the bank deposits also records them in the checkbook, journalizes cash receipts, and reconciles the bank statement.

2. Why should management be concerned about having accurate information about the firm's cash position available at all times?

3. Many banks now offer a variety of computer services to clients. Why is it not advisable for a firm to pay its bank to complete the reconciliation procedure at the end of each month?

4. Assume that you are the newly hired controller at Norton Company and that you have observed the following banking procedures in use at the firm. Would you change any of these procedures? Why or why not?

   a. A blank endorsement is made on all checks to be deposited.

   b. The checkbook is kept on the top of a desk so that it will be handy.

   c. The same person prepares bank deposits, issues checks, and reconciles the bank statement.

   d. The reconciliation process usually takes place two or three weeks after the bank statement is received.

   e. The bank statement and the canceled checks are thrown away after the reconciliation process is completed.

   f. As a shortcut in the reconciliation process, there is no attempt to compare the endorsements on the back of the canceled checks with the names of the payees shown on the face of these checks.

5. Why should management be concerned about achieving effective internal control over cash receipts and cash payments?

6. How does management benefit when cash transactions are recorded quickly and efficiently?

7. Why do some companies require that all employees who handle cash be bonded?

8. Why is it a good practice for a business to make all payments by check except for minor payments from a petty cash fund?

Borrowing from Petty Cash

Ethical DILEMMA

Daniel Garcia is in charge of the $100 petty cash for Garcia's Auto Repair service. When an employee needs a special part that is not in inventory, Daniel takes money from petty cash to buy the part. One day Daniel is short of cash and needs some lunch money. He decides to borrow $10 that he will pay back on payday in three days. Daniel continues this practice for three days for a total of $30. He does not have enough to pay the petty cash back. When he reconciles the petty cash, he records this $30 as Cash short/over expense. This is the first time he has done it. Is this an ethical action? What should Daniel do to fix this problem if there is one?

Balance Sheet

Financial Statement
ANALYSIS

The following excerpt was taken from The Home Depot, Inc. 2009 *Annual Report (for the fiscal year ended January 31, 2010):*

The Home Depot, Inc. Consolidated Balance Sheets		
	As of	
Millions except for numbers of shares and per-share data	*Jan. 31, 2010*	*Feb. 1, 2009*
ASSETS		
Current Assets:		
Cash and cash equivalents*	*$ 1,421*	*$ 519*
Total current assets	*$13,900*	*$13,362*
* Cash and Cash Equivalents: Short-term investments that have maturities of three months or less when purchased are considered to be cash equivalents.		

Analyze:

1. What percentage of total current assets is made up of cash and cash equivalents at January 31, 2010?

2. Cash receipt and cash payment transactions affect the total value of a company's assets. By what amount did the category "Cash and cash equivalents" change from February 1, 2009, to January 31, 2010?

3. If accountants at The Home Depot, Inc. failed to record cash receipts of $125,000 on January 31, 2010, what impact would this error have on the balance sheet category "Cash and cash equivalents"?

Internal Controls of Cash

TEAMWORK

You and four friends have decided to create a new service company called Unpacking for You. Your company unpacks for families once they have moved into a new house. Your business is primarily a cash business. Each family will pay you $100 for each room that is unpacked on the same day you finish the service. How will your business make sure that the payment from the customer is valid? How will you ensure that you will receive the cash when the customer pays the employee in cash?

Bank Charges

Internet CONNECTION

Many times a negative cash flow is a potential problem in a business. Go to the Web site for the local banks in your community. Check the requirements for a line of credit or mortgage in case your company needs cash quickly to buy a product you know you will sell for a large profit. Some bank Web sites could be: www.bankofamerica.com www.wellsfargo.com www.chasebank.com

Answers to **Self Reviews**

Answers to Section 1 Self Review

1. A written promise to pay a specified amount of money on a specified date. To grant credit in certain sales transactions or to replace open-account credit when a customer has an overdue balance.

2. A cash shortage occurs when cash in the register, less the change fund, is less than the sales per the cash register tape. The cash shortage is debited to Cash Short and Over.

3. Debit cash for $50, credit supplies for $50.

4. **b.** $3 short

5. **d.** All of the above

6. The frequency of cash discrepancies indicates that a problem may exist in the handling of the cash (depending on the size of the business and the number of registers, 15 entries may not be unusual).

Answers to Section 2 Self Review

1. Notes Payable

2. To make small expenditures that require currency and coins.

3. Debit Petty Cash Fund, credit Cash

4. **b.** Debit Supplies, debit Delivery Expense, credit Cash

5. **a.** Make all payments with currency rather than by check

6. You should explain to your employer that she must keep all receipts regardless of the amount. Ask your employer to complete a voucher for that amount, then record the entry in the proper account.

Answers to Section 3 Self Review

1. Items in the second section of the bank reconciliation statement require entries in the firm's financial records to correct the *Cash* account balance and make it equal to the checkbook balance. These may include bank fees, debit memorandums, NSF checks, and interest income.

2. Endorsement is the legal process by which the payee transfers ownership of the check to the bank.

3. A check that is dated in the future. It should not be deposited before its date because the drawer of the check may not have sufficient funds in the bank to cover the check at the current time.

4. **d.** Deposits in transit

5. **a.** canceled checks

6. Disagree. Good internal control requires separation of duties.

Answers to Comprehensive Self Review

1. A full endorsement contains the name of the payee plus the name of the firm or bank to whom the check is payable.

2. A record of when a payment is made from petty cash, the amount and purpose of the expenditure, and the account to be charged.

3. Petty cash can be replenished at any time if the fund runs low, but it should be replenished at the end of each month so that all expenses for the month are recorded.

4. Liability.

5. Checks, money orders, and funds on deposit in a bank as well as currency and coins.

Payroll Computations, Records, and Payment

LEARNING OBJECTIVES

1. Explain the major federal laws relating to employee earnings and withholding.
2. Compute gross earnings of employees.
3. Determine employee deductions for social security tax.
4. Determine employee deductions for Medicare tax.
5. Determine employee deductions for income tax.
6. Enter gross earnings, deductions, and net pay in the payroll register.
7. Journalize payroll transactions in the general journal.
8. Maintain an earnings record for each employee.
9. Define the accounting terms new to this chapter.

NEW TERMS

commission basis
compensation record
employee
Employee's Withholding Allowance Certificate (Form W-4)
exempt employees
federal unemployment taxes
hourly rate basis
independent contractor
individual earnings record
Medicare tax

payroll register
piece-rate basis
salary basis
Social Security Act
social security (FICA) tax
state unemployment taxes
tax-exempt wages
time and a half
wage-bracket table method
workers' compensation insurance

 www.clifbar.com

Gary Erickson has never been motivated much by money. An avid cyclist, he was inspired to create a better-tasting energy bar while forcing down a less-than-delicious snack on a 175-mile bike ride. With help from his mom, Gary concocted a better-tasting alternative, and the CLIF® Bar was introduced in 1992. The LUNA® Bar, the CLIF® Builder's Bar, and most recently, CLIF® Crunch (an all-natural granola bar) have joined the original CLIF® Bar and Gary's idea for a better energy bar evolved into a $200 million business. Though a financial success, Gary and his employees are proudest of their success as a "green" company. The company's aspirations are clearly stated on its Web site:

- Sustaining our Planet
- Sustaining our Community
- Sustaining our People
- Sustaining our Business
- Sustaining our Brands

Clif Bar is dedicated to the health and welfare of its employees. It is an unusual work environment filled with climbing walls, dogs, yoga classes, and employees running out to volunteer, but it works.

thinking critically

What types of benefits do you think are important to people working at a place like Clif Bar? What would be important to you?

Payroll Laws and Taxes

A large component of the activity of any business is concerned with payroll work. Payroll accounting is so important that it requires special consideration.

Who Is an Employee?

Payroll accounting relates only to earnings of those individuals classified as employees. An **employee** is hired by and works under the control and direction of the employer. Usually the employer provides the tools or equipment used by the employee, sets the employee's working hours, and determines how the employee completes the job. Examples of employees are the company president, the bookkeeper, the sales clerk, and the warehouse worker.

In contrast to an employee, an **independent contractor** is paid by the company to carry out a specific task or job, but is not under the direct supervision or control of the company. The independent contractor is told what needs to be done, but the means of doing the job are left to the independent contractor. Examples of independent contractors are the accountant who performs the independent audit, the outside attorney who renders legal advice, and the consultant who installs a new accounting system.

This text addresses issues related to employees but not to independent contractors. When dealing with independent contractors, businesses do not have to follow federal labor laws regulating minimum rates of pay and maximum hours of employment. The business is not required to withhold or match payroll taxes on amounts paid to independent contractors.

>> **1. OBJECTIVE**

Explain the major federal laws relating to employee earnings and withholding.

Federal Employee Earnings and Withholding Laws

Since the 1930s, many federal and state laws have affected the relationship between employers and employees. Some of these laws deal with working conditions, including hours and earnings. Others relate to income tax withholding. Some concern taxes that are levied against the employer to provide specific employee benefits.

THE FAIR LABOR STANDARDS ACT

The *Fair Labor Standards Act* of 1938, often referred to as the Wage and Hour Law, applies only to firms engaged directly or indirectly in interstate commerce. It sets a minimum hourly rate of pay and maximum hours of work per week to be performed at the regular rate of pay. When this book was printed, the minimum hourly rate of pay was $7.25, and the maximum number of hours at the regular pay rate was 40 hours per week. When an employee works more than 40 hours in a week, the employee earns at least one and one-half times the regular hourly rate of pay for the extra hours. This overtime rate is called **time and a half.** Even if the federal law does not apply to them, many employers pay time and a half for overtime because of union contracts or simply as good business practice.

SOCIAL SECURITY TAX

The *Federal Insurance Contributions Act (FICA)* is commonly referred to as the **Social Security Act.** The act, first passed in the 1930s, has been amended frequently. The Social Security Act provides the following benefits:

- Retirement benefits, or pension, when a worker reaches age 62.
- Benefits for the dependents of the retired worker.
- Benefits for the worker and the worker's dependents when the worker is disabled.
- Survivors benefits for the worker's minor dependent children and spouse when the worker dies.

These retirement and disability benefits are paid by the **social security tax,** sometimes called the **FICA tax.** Both the employer and the employee pay an equal amount of social security tax. The employer is required to withhold social security tax from the employee's pay. Periodically the employer sends the social security tax withheld to the federal government.

The rate of the social security tax and the calendar year earnings base to which it applies are frequently changed by Congress. In recent years, the social security tax rate has remained constant at 6.2 percent. The earnings base to which the tax applies has increased yearly. In 2011, the social security tax rate was 6.2 percent of the first $106,800 of salary or wages paid to each employee. In examples and problems, this text uses a social security tax rate of 6.2 percent of the first $106,800 of salary or wages.

MEDICARE TAX

The Medicare tax is closely related to the social security tax. Prior to 1992, it was a part of the social security tax. The **Medicare tax** is a tax levied equally on employees and employers to provide medical care for the employee and the employee's spouse after each has reached age 65.

In recent years, the Medicare tax rate has remained constant at 1.45 percent. The Medicare tax applies to all salaries and wages paid during the year. The employer is required to withhold the Medicare tax from the employee's pay and periodically send it to the federal government.

Note that the social security tax has an earnings base limit. The Medicare tax does not have an earnings base limit. The Medicare tax applies to *all* earnings paid during the year.

FEDERAL INCOME TAX

Employers are required to withhold from employees' earnings an estimated amount of income tax that will be payable by the employee on the earnings. The amount depends on several factors. Later in this chapter you will learn how to determine the amount to withhold from an employee's paycheck.

State and Local Taxes

Most states, and many local governments, require employers to withhold income taxes from employees' earnings to prepay the employees' state and local income taxes. These rules are generally almost identical to those governing federal income tax withholding, but they require separate general ledger accounts in the firm's accounting system.

Employer's Payroll Taxes and Insurance Costs

Remember that employers withhold social security and Medicare taxes from employees' earnings. In addition, employers pay social security and Medicare taxes on their employees'

important!

Wage Base Limit
The social security tax has a wage base limit. There is no wage base limit for the Medicare tax. All salaries and wages are subject to the Medicare tax.

earnings. Employers are also required to pay federal and state taxes for unemployment benefits and to carry workers' compensation insurance.

SOCIAL SECURITY TAX

The employer's share of the social security tax is 6.2 percent up to the earnings base. (In this text, the social security tax is 6.2 percent of the first $106,800 of earnings.) Periodically the employer pays to the federal government the social security tax withheld plus the employer's share of the social security tax.

	FICA
Employee (withheld)	6.2%
Employer (match)	6.2
Total	12.4%

MEDICARE TAX

The employer's share of Medicare tax is 1.45 percent of earnings. Periodically the employer pays to the federal government the Medicare tax withheld plus the employer's share of the Medicare tax.

The Medicare taxes the employer remits to the federal government are shown below:

	Medicare
Employee (withheld)	1.45%
Employer (match)	1.45
Total	2.90%

FEDERAL UNEMPLOYMENT TAX

The *Federal Unemployment Tax Act (FUTA)* provides benefits for employees who become unemployed. Taxes levied by the federal government against employers to benefit unemployed workers are called **federal unemployment taxes (FUTA).** Employers pay the entire amount of these taxes. In this text, we assume that the taxable earnings base is $7,000. That is, the tax applies to the first $7,000 of each employee's earnings for the year. In 2010, the FUTA tax rate was 6.2 percent, but can be reduced by the state unemployment tax rate. In examples and problems, this text uses a FUTA tax rate of 6.2%.

STATE UNEMPLOYMENT TAX

The federal and state unemployment programs work together to provide benefits for employees who become unemployed. Employers pay all of the **state unemployment taxes (SUTA).** Usually the earnings base for the federal and state unemployment taxes are the same, the first $7,000 of each employee's earnings for the year. For many states the SUTA tax rate is 5.4 percent.

The federal unemployment tax rate (6.2 percent) can be reduced by the rate charged by the state (5.4 percent in this example), so the FUTA rate can be as low as 0.8 percent (6.2% − 5.4%).

SUTA tax		5.4%
FUTA tax rate	6.2%	
Less SUTA tax	(5.4)	
Net FUTA tax		0.8
Total federal and state unemployment tax		6.2%

WORKERS' COMPENSATION INSURANCE

Workers' compensation insurance is not a tax, but insurance that protects employees against losses from job-related injuries or illnesses, or compensates their families if death occurs in the course of the employment. Workers' compensation requirements are defined by each state. Most states mandate workers' compensation insurance.

Employee Records Required by Law

> Many companies outsource payroll duties to professional payroll companies. ADP, Inc., is the world's largest provider of payroll services and employee information systems.

Federal laws require that certain payroll records be maintained. For each employee the employer must keep a record of:

- the employee's name, address, social security number, and date of birth;
- hours worked each day and week, and wages paid at the regular and overtime rates (certain exceptions exist for employees who earn salaries);
- cumulative wages paid throughout the year;
- amount of income tax, social security tax, and Medicare tax withheld for each pay period;
- proof that the employee is a United States citizen or has a valid work permit.

Section 1 Self Review

QUESTIONS

1. How are social security benefits financed?

2. How are unemployment insurance benefits financed?

3. What is "time and a half"?

EXERCISES

4. The purpose of FUTA is to provide benefits for:
   a. employees who become unemployed.
   b. employees who become injured while on the job.
   c. retired workers.
   d. disabled employees.

5. The earnings base limit for Medicare:
   a. is the same as the earnings base limit for social security.
   b. is lower than the earnings base limit for social security.
   c. is higher than the earnings base limit for social security.
   d. does not exist.

ANALYSIS

6. Susan Kennedy was hired by Harvey Architects to create three oil paintings for the president's office. Is Kennedy an employee? Why or why not?

(Answers to Section 1 Self Review are on pages 332–333.)

>> 2. **Compute gross earnings of employees.**

WHY IT'S IMPORTANT

Payroll is a large part of business activity.

>> 3. **Determine employee deductions for social security tax.**

WHY IT'S IMPORTANT

Employers are legally responsible for collecting and remitting this tax.

>> 4. **Determine employee deductions for Medicare tax.**

WHY IT'S IMPORTANT

Employers have legal responsibility.

>> 5. **Determine employee deductions for income tax.**

WHY IT'S IMPORTANT

Employers are legally responsible.

>> 6. **Enter gross earnings, deductions, and net pay in the payroll register.**

WHY IT'S IMPORTANT

The payroll register provides information needed to prepare paychecks.

TERMS TO LEARN

commission basis

Employee's Withholding Allowance Certificate (Form W-4)

exempt employees

hourly rate basis

payroll register

piece-rate basis

salary basis

tax-exempt wages

wage-bracket table method

Calculating Earnings and Taxes

Sanchez Furniture Company is a sole proprietorship owned and managed by Sarah Sanchez. Sanchez Furniture Company imports furniture and novelty items to sell over the Internet. It has five employees. The three shipping clerks and the shipping supervisor are paid on an hourly basis. The office clerk is paid a weekly salary. Payday is each Monday; it covers the wages and salaries earned the previous week. The employees are subject to withholding of social security, Medicare, and federal income taxes. The business pays social security and Medicare taxes, and federal and state unemployment insurance taxes. The business is required by state law to carry workers' compensation insurance. Since it is involved in interstate commerce, Sanchez Furniture Company is subject to the Fair Labor Standards Act.

From time to time, Sarah Sanchez, the owner, makes cash withdrawals to cover her personal expenses. The withdrawals of the owner of a sole proprietorship are not treated as salaries or wages.

Computing Total Earnings of Employees

The first step in preparing payroll is to compute the gross wages or salary for each employee. There are several ways to compute earnings:

Hourly rate basis workers earn a stated rate per hour. Gross pay depends on the number of hours worked.

Salary basis workers earn an agreed-upon amount for each week, month, or other period.

Commission basis workers, usually salespeople, earn a percentage of net sales.

Piece-rate basis manufacturing workers are paid based on the number of units produced.

Walmart has approximately 2 million employees in its worldwide operations, which include Walmart discount stores, Sam's Clubs, the distribution centers, and the home office. Fifty-one percent of its stores are in the United States. It is the number 1 retailer in Canada and Mexico. It also has operations in Asia, the United Kingdom, Central America, and South America.

Determining Pay for Hourly Employees

Two pieces of data are needed to compute gross pay for hourly rate basis employees: the number of hours worked during the payroll period, and the rate of pay.

HOURS WORKED

At Sanchez Furniture Company, the shipping supervisor keeps a weekly time sheet. Each day she enters the hours worked by each shipping clerk. At the end of the week, the office clerk uses the time sheet to compute the total hours worked and to prepare the payroll.

Many businesses use time clocks for hourly employees. Each employee has a time card and inserts it in the time clock to record the times of arrival and departure. The payroll clerk collects the cards at the end of the week, determines the hours worked by each employee, and multiplies the number of hours by the pay rate to compute the *gross pay*. Some time cards are machine readable. A computer determines the hours worked and makes the earnings calculations.

GROSS PAY

Alicia Martinez, Jorge Rodriguez, and George Dunlap are shipping clerks at Sanchez Furniture Company. They are hourly employees. Their gross pay for the week ended January 6 is determined as follows:

- Martinez worked 40 hours. She earns $10 an hour. Her gross pay is $400 (40 hours × $10).

- Rodriguez worked 40 hours. He earns $9.50 an hour. His gross pay is $380 (40 × $9.50).

- Dunlap earns $9 per hour. He worked 45 hours. He is paid 40 hours at regular pay and 5 hours at time and a half. There are two ways to compute Dunlap's gross pay:

  1. The Wage and Hour Law method identifies the *overtime premium,* the amount the firm could have saved if all the hours were paid at the regular rate. The overtime premium rate is $4.50, one-half of the regular rate ($9 × 1/2 = $4.50).

Total hours × regular rate:	
45 hours × $9	$405.00
Overtime premium:	
5 hours × $4.50	22.50
Gross pay	$427.50

>>**2. OBJECTIVE**
Compute gross earnings of employees.

recall

Owner Withdrawals
Withdrawals by the owner of a sole proprietorship are debited to a temporary owner's equity account (in this case, *Sarah Sanchez, Drawing*). Withdrawals are not treated as salary or wages.

2. The second method identifies how much the employee earned by working overtime.

Regular earnings:	
40 hours × $9	$360.00
Overtime earnings:	
5 hours × $13.50 ($9 × 1 1/2)	67.50
Gross pay	$427.50

Cecilia Wu is the shipping supervisor at Sanchez Furniture Company. She is an hourly employee. She earns $14 an hour, and she worked 40 hours. Her gross pay is $560 (40 × $14).

WITHHOLDINGS FOR HOURLY EMPLOYEES REQUIRED BY LAW

Recall that three deductions from employees' gross pay are required by federal law. They are FICA (social security) tax, Medicare tax, and federal income tax withholding.

>>**3. OBJECTIVE**

Determine employee deductions for social security tax.

Social Security Tax The social security tax is levied on both the employer and the employee. This text calculates social security tax using a 6.2 percent tax rate on the first $106,800 of wages paid during the calendar year. **Tax-exempt wages** are earnings in excess of the base amount set by the Social Security Act ($106,800). Tax-exempt wages are not subject to FICA withholding.

If an employee works for more than one employer during the year, the FICA tax is deducted and matched by each employer. When the employee files a federal income tax return, any excess FICA tax withheld from the employee's earnings is refunded by the government or applied to payment of the employee's federal income taxes.

To determine the amount of social security tax to withhold from an employee's pay, multiply the taxable wages by the social security tax rate. Round the result to the nearest cent.

The following shows the social security tax deductions for Sanchez Furniture Company's hourly employees.

Employee	Gross Pay	Tax Rate	Tax
Alicia Martinez	$400.00	6.2%	$ 24.80
Jorge Rodriguez	380.00	6.2	23.56
George Dunlap	427.50	6.2	26.51
Cecilia Wu	560.00	6.2	34.72
Total social security tax			$109.59

>>**4. OBJECTIVE**

Determine employee deductions for Medicare tax.

Medicare Tax The Medicare tax is levied on both the employee and the employer. To compute the Medicare tax to withhold from the employee's paycheck, multiply the wages by the Medicare tax rate, 1.45 percent. The following shows the Medicare tax deduction for hourly employees.

Employee	Gross Pay	Tax Rate	Tax
Alicia Martinez	$400.00	1.45%	$ 5.80
Jorge Rodriguez	380.00	1.45	5.51
George Dunlap	427.50	1.45	6.20
Cecilia Wu	560.00	1.45	8.12
Total Medicare tax			$25.63

Federal Income Tax A substantial portion of the federal government's revenue comes from the income tax on individuals. Employers are required to withhold federal income tax from employees' pay. Periodically the employer pays the federal income tax withheld to the federal government. After the end of the year, the employee files an income tax return. If the amount of federal income tax withheld does not cover the amount of income tax due, the employee pays the balance. If too much federal income tax has been withheld, the employee receives a refund.

Withholding Allowances The amount of federal income tax to withhold from an employee's earnings depends on the:

- earnings during the pay period,
- length of the pay period,
- marital status,
- number of withholding allowances.

Determining the number of withholding allowances for some taxpayers is complex. In the simplest circumstances, a taxpayer claims a withholding allowance for:

- the taxpayer,
- a spouse who does not also claim an allowance,
- each dependent for whom the taxpayer provides more than half the support during the year.

As the number of withholding allowances increases, the amount of federal income tax withheld decreases. The goal is to claim the number of withholding allowances so that the federal income tax withheld is about the same as the employee's tax liability.

To claim withholding allowances, employees complete **Employee's Withholding Allowance Certificate, Form W-4.** The employee gives the completed Form W-4 to the employer. If the number of exemption allowances decreases, the employee must file a new Form W-4 within 10 days. If the number of exemption allowances increases, the employee may, but is not required to, file another Form W-4. If an employee does not file a Form W-4, the employer withholds federal income tax based on zero withholding allowances.

Figure 10.1 shows Form W-4 for Alicia Martinez. Notice that on Line 5, Martinez claims one withholding allowance.

Computing Federal Income Tax Withholding Although there are several ways to compute the federal income tax to withhold from an employee's earnings, the **wage-bracket table method** is almost universally used. The wage-bracket tables are in *Publication 15, Circular E.* This publication contains withholding tables for weekly, biweekly, semimonthly, monthly, and daily or miscellaneous payroll periods for single and married persons. Figure 10.2 on pages 309–310 shows partial tables for single and married persons who are paid weekly.

Use the following steps to determine the amount to withhold:

1. Choose the table for the pay period and the employee's marital status.
2. Find the row in the table that matches the wages earned. Find the column that matches the number of withholding allowances claimed on Form W-4. The income tax to withhold is the intersection of the row and the column.

>>**5. OBJECTIVE**
Determine employee deductions for income tax.

important!

Pay-As-You-Go
Employee income tax withholding is designed to place employees on a pay-as-you-go basis in paying their federal income tax.

important!

Get It in Writing
Employers need a signed Form W-4 in order to change the employee's federal income tax withholding.

Employee	Gross Pay	Marital Status	Withholding Allowances	Income Tax Withholding
Alicia Martinez	$400.00	Married	1	$ 19.00
Jorge Rodriguez	380.00	Single	1	34.00
George Dunlap	427.50	Single	3	23.00
Cecilia Wu	560.00	Married	2	30.00
				$106.00

As an example, let's determine the amount to withhold from Cecilia Wu's gross pay. Wu is married, claims two withholding allowances, and earned $560 for the week:

1. Go to the table for married persons paid weekly, Figure 10.2B.
2. Find the line covering wages between $560 and $570. Find the column for two withholding allowances. The tax to withhold is $30; this is where the row and the column intersect.

Using the wage-bracket tables, can you find the federal income tax amounts to withhold for Martinez, Rodriguez, and Dunlap?

Other Deductions Required by Law Most states and some local governments require employers to withhold state and local income taxes from earnings. In some states, employers are also required to withhold disability or other taxes. The procedures are similar to those for federal income tax withholding. Apply the tax rate to the earnings, or use withholding tables.

FIGURE 10.1 Form W-4 (Partial)

------- Cut here and give Form W-4 to your employer. Keep the top part for your records. -------

Form **W-4**

Department of the Treasury
Internal Revenue Service

Employee's Withholding Allowance Certificate

► Whether you are entitled to claim a certain number of allowances or exemption from withholding is subject to review by the IRS. Your employer may be required to send a copy of this form to the IRS.

OMB No. 1545-0010

2013

1 Type or print your first name and middle initial	Last name	2 Your social security number
Alicia	**Martinez**	123 : 45 : 6789

Home address (number and street or rural route)
1712 Windmill Hill Lane

City or town, state, and ZIP code
Dallas, TX 75232-6002

3 ☐ Single ☑ Married ☐ Married, but withhold at higher Single rate.
Note. If married, but legally separated, or spouse is a nonresident alien, check the "Single" box.

4 If your last name differs from that shown on your social security card, check here. You must call 1-800-772-1213 for a new card. ► ☐

5	Total number of allowances you are claiming (from line H above or from the applicable worksheet on page 2)	5	1
6	Additional amount, if any, you want withheld from each paycheck	6	$

7 I claim exemption from withholding for 2010, and I certify that I meet **both** of the following conditions for exemption.
  • Last year I had a right to a refund of **all** federal income tax withheld because I had **no** tax liability **and**
  • This year I expect a refund of **all** federal income tax withheld because I expect to have **no** tax liability.
  If you meet both conditions, write "Exempt" here . . . . ► | 7 |

Under penalties of perjury, I declare that I have examined this certificate and to the best of my knowledge and belief, it is true, correct, and complete.
Employee's signature
(Form is not valid unless you sign it.) ► *Alicia Martinez*

Date ► *November 5, 2013*

8 Employer's name and address (Employer: Complete lines 8 and 10 only if sending to the IRS.)	9 Office code (optional)	10 Employer identification number (EIN)
Sanchez Furniture Co. 5910 Lake June Road, Dallas, TX 75232-6017		75 : 1234567

For Privacy Act and Paperwork Reduction Act Notice, see page 2.

Cat. No. 220Q

Form **W-4** (2010)

SINGLE Persons—WEEKLY Payroll Period   (For Wages Paid Through December 2013)

If the wages are –		And the number of withholding allowances claimed is –										
At least	But less than	0	1	2	3	4	5	6	7	8	9	10
		The amount of income tax to be withheld is –										
$0	$55	$0	$0	$0	$0	$0	$0	$0	$0	$0	$0	$0
55	60	1	0	0	0	0	0	0	0	0	0	0
60	65	1	0	0	0	0	0	0	0	0	0	0
65	70	2	0	0	0	0	0	0	0	0	0	0
70	75	2	0	0	0	0	0	0	0	0	0	0
75	80	3	0	0	0	0	0	0	0	0	0	0
80	85	3	0	0	0	0	0	0	0	0	0	0
85	90	4	0	0	0	0	0	0	0	0	0	0
90	95	4	0	0	0	0	0	0	0	0	0	0
95	100	5	0	0	0	0	0	0	0	0	0	0
100	105	5	0	0	0	0	0	0	0	0	0	0
105	110	6	0	0	0	0	0	0	0	0	0	0
110	115	6	0	0	0	0	0	0	0	0	0	0
115	120	7	1	0	0	0	0	0	0	0	0	0
120	125	7	1	0	0	0	0	0	0	0	0	0
125	130	8	2	0	0	0	0	0	0	0	0	0
130	135	8	2	0	0	0	0	0	0	0	0	0
135	140	9	3	0	0	0	0	0	0	0	0	0
140	145	9	3	0	0	0	0	0	0	0	0	0
145	150	10	4	0	0	0	0	0	0	0	0	0
150	155	10	4	0	0	0	0	0	0	0	0	0
155	160	11	5	0	0	0	0	0	0	0	0	0
160	165	11	5	0	0	0	0	0	0	0	0	0
165	170	12	6	0	0	0	0	0	0	0	0	0
170	175	12	6	0	0	0	0	0	0	0	0	0
175	180	13	7	1	0	0	0	0	0	0	0	0
180	185	13	7	1	0	0	0	0	0	0	0	0
185	190	14	8	2	0	0	0	0	0	0	0	0
190	195	14	8	2	0	0	0	0	0	0	0	0
195	200	15	9	3	0	0	0	0	0	0	0	0
200	210	16	9	3	0	0	0	0	0	0	0	0
210	220	18	10	4	0	0	0	0	0	0	0	0
220	230	19	11	5	0	0	0	0	0	0	0	0
230	240	21	12	6	1	0	0	0	0	0	0	0
240	250	22	13	7	2	0	0	0	0	0	0	0
250	260	24	15	8	3	0	0	0	0	0	0	0
260	270	25	16	9	4	0	0	0	0	0	0	0
270	280	27	18	10	5	0	0	0	0	0	0	0
280	290	28	19	11	6	0	0	0	0	0	0	0
290	300	30	21	12	7	1	0	0	0	0	0	0
300	310	31	22	13	8	2	0	0	0	0	0	0
310	320	33	24	15	9	3	0	0	0	0	0	0
320	330	34	25	16	10	4	0	0	0	0	0	0
330	340	36	27	18	11	5	0	0	0	0	0	0
340	350	37	28	19	12	6	0	0	0	0	0	0
350	360	39	30	21	13	7	1	0	0	0	0	0
360	370	40	31	22	14	8	2	0	0	0	0	0
370	380	42	33	24	15	9	3	0	0	0	0	0
380	390	43	34	25	17	10	4	0	0	0	0	0
390	400	45	36	27	18	11	5	0	0	0	0	0
400	410	46	37	28	20	12	6	0	0	0	0	0
410	420	48	39	30	21	13	7	1	0	0	0	0
420	430	49	40	31	23	14	8	2	0	0	0	0
430	440	51	42	33	24	15	9	3	0	0	0	0
440	450	52	43	34	26	17	10	4	0	0	0	0
450	460	54	45	36	27	18	11	5	0	0	0	0
460	470	55	46	37	29	20	12	6	0	0	0	0
470	480	57	48	39	30	21	13	7	1	0	0	0
480	490	58	49	40	32	23	14	8	2	0	0	0
490	500	60	51	42	33	24	15	9	3	0	0	0
500	510	61	52	43	35	26	17	10	4	0	0	0
510	520	63	54	45	36	27	18	11	5	0	0	0
520	530	64	55	46	38	29	20	12	6	0	0	0
530	540	66	57	48	39	30	21	13	7	1	0	0
540	550	67	58	49	41	32	23	14	8	2	0	0
550	560	69	60	51	42	33	24	15	9	3	0	0
560	570	70	61	52	44	35	26	17	10	4	0	0
570	580	72	63	54	45	36	27	18	11	5	0	0
580	590	73	64	55	47	38	29	20	12	6	0	0
590	600	75	66	57	48	39	30	21	13	7	1	0

FIGURE 10.2A

Sample Federal Withholding Tax Tables (Partial) Single Persons—Weekly Payroll Period

This table does not contain actual withholding amounts for the year 2013, and should not be used to determine payroll withholdings for 2013.

FIGURE 10.2B

Sample Federal Withholding Tax Tables (Partial) Married Persons—Weekly Payroll Period

MARRIED Persons—WEEKLY Payroll Period (For Wages Paid Through December 2013)

If the wages are –		And the number of withholding allowances claimed is –										
At least	But less than	0	1	2	3	4	5	6	7	8	9	10
		The amount of income tax to be withheld is –										
$0	$125	$0	$0	$0	$0	$0	$0	$0	$0	$0	$0	$0
125	130	0	0	0	0	0	0	0	0	0	0	0
130	135	0	0	0	0	0	0	0	0	0	0	0
135	140	0	0	0	0	0	0	0	0	0	0	0
140	145	0	0	0	0	0	0	0	0	0	0	0
145	150	0	0	0	0	0	0	0	0	0	0	0
150	155	0	0	0	0	0	0	0	0	0	0	0
155	160	0	0	0	0	0	0	0	0	0	0	0
160	165	1	0	0	0	0	0	0	0	0	0	0
165	170	1	0	0	0	0	0	0	0	0	0	0
170	175	2	0	0	0	0	0	0	0	0	0	0
175	180	2	0	0	0	0	0	0	0	0	0	0
180	185	3	0	0	0	0	0	0	0	0	0	0
185	190	3	0	0	0	0	0	0	0	0	0	0
190	195	4	0	0	0	0	0	0	0	0	0	0
195	200	4	0	0	0	0	0	0	0	0	0	0
200	210	5	0	0	0	0	0	0	0	0	0	0
210	220	6	0	0	0	0	0	0	0	0	0	0
220	230	7	1	0	0	0	0	0	0	0	0	0
230	240	8	2	0	0	0	0	0	0	0	0	0
240	250	9	3	0	0	0	0	0	0	0	0	0
250	260	10	4	0	0	0	0	0	0	0	0	0
260	270	11	5	0	0	0	0	0	0	0	0	0
270	280	12	6	0	0	0	0	0	0	0	0	0
280	290	13	7	1	0	0	0	0	0	0	0	0
290	300	14	8	2	0	0	0	0	0	0	0	0
300	310	15	9	3	0	0	0	0	0	0	0	0
310	320	16	10	4	0	0	0	0	0	0	0	0
320	330	17	11	5	0	0	0	0	0	0	0	0
330	340	18	12	6	0	0	0	0	0	0	0	0
340	350	19	13	7	1	0	0	0	0	0	0	0
350	360	20	14	8	2	0	0	0	0	0	0	0
360	370	21	15	9	3	0	0	0	0	0	0	0
370	380	22	16	10	4	0	0	0	0	0	0	0
380	390	23	17	11	5	0	0	0	0	0	0	0
390	400	24	18	12	6	0	0	0	0	0	0	0
400	410	25	19	13	7	1	0	0	0	0	0	0
410	420	26	20	14	8	2	0	0	0	0	0	0
420	430	27	21	15	9	3	0	0	0	0	0	0
430	440	28	22	16	10	4	0	0	0	0	0	0
440	450	30	23	17	11	5	0	0	0	0	0	0
450	460	31	24	18	12	6	0	0	0	0	0	0
460	470	33	25	19	13	7	1	0	0	0	0	0
470	480	34	26	20	14	8	2	0	0	0	0	0
480	490	36	27	21	15	9	3	0	0	0	0	0
490	500	37	28	22	16	10	4	0	0	0	0	0
500	510	39	30	23	17	11	5	0	0	0	0	0
510	520	40	31	24	18	12	6	0	0	0	0	0
520	530	42	33	25	19	13	7	1	0	0	0	0
530	540	43	34	26	20	14	8	2	0	0	0	0
540	550	45	36	27	21	15	9	3	0	0	0	0
550	560	46	37	29	22	16	10	4	0	0	0	0
560	570	48	39	30	23	17	11	5	0	0	0	0
570	580	49	40	32	24	18	12	6	0	0	0	0
580	590	51	42	33	25	19	13	7	1	0	0	0
590	600	52	43	35	26	20	14	8	2	0	0	0
600	610	54	45	36	27	21	15	9	3	0	0	0
610	620	55	46	38	29	22	16	10	4	0	0	0
620	630	57	48	39	30	23	17	11	5	0	0	0
630	640	58	49	41	32	24	18	12	6	0	0	0
640	650	60	51	42	33	25	19	13	7	1	0	0
650	660	61	52	44	35	26	20	14	8	2	0	0
660	670	63	54	45	36	27	21	15	9	3	0	0
670	680	64	55	47	38	29	22	16	10	4	0	0
680	690	66	57	48	39	30	23	17	11	5	0	0
690	700	67	58	50	41	32	24	18	12	6	0	0
700	710	69	60	51	42	33	25	19	13	7	1	0
710	720	70	61	53	44	35	26	20	14	8	2	0
720	730	72	63	54	45	36	27	21	15	9	3	0
730	740	73	64	56	47	38	29	22	16	10	4	0

This table does not contain actual withholding amounts for the year 2013, and should not be used to determine payroll withholdings for 2013.

WITHHOLDINGS NOT REQUIRED BY LAW

There are many payroll deductions not required by law but made by agreement between the employee and the employer. Some examples are:

- group life insurance,
- group medical insurance,

- company retirement plans,
- bank or credit union savings plans or loan repayments,
- United States saving bonds purchase plans,
- stocks and other investment purchase plans,
- employer loan repayments,
- union dues.

These and other payroll deductions increase the payroll recordkeeping work but do not involve any new principles or procedures. They are handled in the same way as the deductions for social security, Medicare, and federal income taxes.

Sanchez Furniture Company pays all medical insurance premiums for each employee. If the employee chooses to have medical coverage for a spouse or dependent, Sanchez Furniture Company deducts $40 per week for coverage for the spouse and each dependent. Dunlap and Wu each have $40 per week deducted to obtain the medical coverage.

Determining Pay for Salaried Employees

A salaried employee earns a specific sum of money for each payroll period. The office clerk at Sanchez Furniture Company earns a weekly salary.

HOURS WORKED

Salaried workers who do not hold supervisory jobs are covered by the provisions of the Wage and Hour Law that deal with maximum hours and overtime premium pay. Employers keep time records for all nonsupervisory salaried workers to make sure that their hourly earnings meet the legal requirements.

Salaried employees who hold supervisory or managerial positions are called **exempt employees.** They are not subject to the maximum hour and overtime premium pay provisions of the Wage and Hour Law.

GROSS EARNINGS

Cynthia Booker is the office clerk at Sanchez Furniture Company. During the first week of January, she worked 40 hours, her regular schedule. There are no overtime earnings because she did not work more than 40 hours during the week. Her salary of $480 is her gross pay for the week.

WITHHOLDINGS FOR SALARIED EMPLOYEES REQUIRED BY LAW

The procedures for withholding taxes for salaried employees is the same as withholding for hourly rate employees. Apply the tax rate to the earnings, or use withholding tables.

Recording Payroll Information for Employees

A payroll register is prepared for each pay period. The **payroll register** shows all the payroll information for the pay period.

THE PAYROLL REGISTER

Figure 10.3 on pages 312–313 shows the payroll register for Sanchez Furniture Company for the week ended January 6. Note that all employees were paid for eight hours on January 1, a holiday. To learn how to complete the payroll register, refer to Figure 10.3 and follow these steps:

1. *Columns A, B, and E.* Enter the employee's name (Column A), number of withholding allowances and marital status (Column B), and rate of pay (Column E). In a computerized payroll system, this information is entered once and is automatically retrieved each time payroll is prepared.

2. *Column C.* The Cumulative Earnings column (Column C) shows the total earnings for the calendar year before the current pay period. This figure is needed to determine

>>6. OBJECTIVE

Enter gross earnings, deductions, and net pay in the payroll register.

FIGURE 10.3 **Payroll Register**

PAYROLL REGISTER   WEEK BEGINNING _January 1, 2013_

NAME	NO. OF ALLOW.	MARITAL STATUS	CUMULATIVE EARNINGS	NO. OF HRS.	RATE/ SALARY	EARNINGS REGULAR	EARNINGS OVERTIME	GROSS AMOUNT	CUMULATIVE EARNINGS	
Martinez, Alicia	1	M		40	10.00	400 00		400 00	400 00	
Rodriguez, Jorge	1	S		40	9.50	380 00		380 00	380 00	
Dunlap, George	3	S		45	9.00	360 00	67 50	427 50	427 50	
Wu, Cecilia	2	M		40	14.00	560 00		560 00	560 00	
Booker, Cynthia	1	S		40	480.00	480 00		480 00	480 00	
			0 00			2 180 00	67 50	2 247 50	2 247 50	
(A)	(B)		(C)	(D)	(E)	(F)	(G)	(H)	(I)	

whether the employee has exceeded the earnings limit for the FICA and FUTA taxes. Since this is the first payroll period of the year, there are no cumulative earnings prior to the current pay period.

3. *Column D.* In Column D, enter the total number of hours worked in the current period. This data comes from the weekly time sheet.

4. *Columns F, G, and H.* Using the hours worked and the pay rate, calculate regular pay (Column F), the overtime earnings (Column G), and gross pay (Column H).

5. *Column I.* Calculate the cumulative earnings after this pay period (Column I) by adding the beginning cumulative earnings (Column C) and the current period's gross pay (Column H).

6. *Columns J, K, and L.* The Taxable Wages columns show the earnings subject to taxes for social security (Column J), Medicare (Column K), and FUTA (Column L). Only the earnings at or under the earnings limit are included in these columns.

7. *Columns M, N, O, and P.* The Deductions columns show the withholding for social security tax (Column M), Medicare tax (Column N), federal income tax (Column O), and medical insurance (Column P).

8. *Column Q.* Subtract the deductions (Columns M, N, O, and P) from the gross earnings (Column H). Enter the results in the Net Amount column (Column Q). This is the amount paid to each employee.

9. *Column R.* Enter the check number in Column R.

10. *Columns S and T.* The payroll register's last two columns classify employee earnings as office salaries (Column S) or shipping wages (Column T).

When the payroll data for all employees has been entered in the payroll register, total the columns. Check the balances of the following columns:

■ Total regular earnings plus total overtime earnings must equal the gross amount (Columns F + G = Column H).

■ The total gross amount less total deductions must equal the total net amount.

Gross amount		$2,247.50
Less deductions:		
Social security tax	$139.35	
Medicare tax	32.59	
Income tax	155.00	
Health insurance	80.00	
Total deductions		406.94
Net amount		$1,840.56

AND ENDING January 6, 2013   **PAID** January 8, 2013

TAXABLE WAGES			DEDUCTIONS				DISTRIBUTION			
SOCIAL SECURITY	MEDICARE	FUTA	SOCIAL SECURITY	MEDICARE	INCOME TAX	HEALTH INSURANCE	NET AMOUNT	CHECK NO.	OFFICE SALARIES	SHIPPING WAGES
400 00	400 00	400 00	24 80	5 80	19 00		350 40	1601		400 00
380 00	380 00	380 00	23 56	5 51	34 00		316 93	1602		380 00
427 50	427 50	427 50	26 51	6 20	23 00	40 00	331 79	1603		427 50
560 00	560 00	560 00	34 72	8 12	30 00	40 00	447 16	1604		560 00
480 00	480 00	480 00	29 76	6 96	49 00		394 28	1605	480 00	
2 247 50	2 247 50	2 247 50	139 35	32 59	155 00	80 00	1 840 56		480 00	1 767 50
(J)	(K)	(L)	(M)	(N)	(O)	(P)	(Q)	(R)	(S)	(T)

■ The office salaries and the shipping wages must equal gross earnings (Columns S + T = Column H).

The payroll register supplies all the information to make the journal entry to record the payroll. Journalizing the payroll is discussed in Section 3.

Section 2 Self Review

QUESTIONS

1. List four payroll deductions that are not required by law but can be made by agreement between the employee and the employer.

2. What factors determine the amount of federal income tax to be withheld from an employee's earnings?

3. What three payroll deductions does federal law require?

EXERCISES

4. Which of the following affects the amount of Medicare tax to be withheld from an hourly rate employee's pay?

   a. medical insurance premium
   b. marital status
   c. withholding allowances claimed on Form W-4
   d. hours worked

5. Stacy Anderson worked 48 hours during the week ending November 17. Her regular rate is $9 per hour. Calculate her gross earnings for the week.

   a. $432
   b. $492
   c. $468
   d. $444

ANALYSIS

6. Rosie Perez left a voice mail asking you to withhold an additional $40 of federal income tax from her wages each pay period, starting June 1. When should you begin withholding the extra amount?

(Answers to Section 2 Self Review are on page 333.)

SECTION OBJECTIVES

>> **7.** **Journalize payroll transactions in the general journal.**

WHY IT'S IMPORTANT
Payroll cost is an operating expense.

>> **8.** **Maintain an earnings record for each employee.**

WHY IT'S IMPORTANT
Federal law requires that employers maintain records.

TERMS TO LEARN

compensation record
individual earnings record

Recording Payroll Information

In this section you will learn how to prepare paychecks and journalize and post payroll transactions by following the January payroll activity for Sanchez Furniture Company.

>>**7. OBJECTIVE**

Journalize payroll transactions in the general journal.

Recording Payroll

Recording payroll involves two separate entries: one to record the payroll expense and another to pay the employees. The general journal entry to record the payroll expense is based on the payroll register. The gross pay is debited to **Shipping Wages Expense** for the shipping clerks and supervisor and to **Office Salaries Expense** for the office clerk. Each type of deduction is credited to a separate liability account (**Social Security Tax Payable, Medicare Tax Payable, Employee Income Tax Payable, Health Insurance Premiums Payable**). Net pay is credited to the liability account, **Salaries and Wages Payable.**

Refer to Figure 10.3 on pages 312–313 to see how the data on the payroll register is used to prepare the January 8 payroll journal entry for Sanchez Furniture Company. Following is an analysis of the entry.

BUSINESS TRANSACTION

The information in the payroll register (Figure 10.3) is used to record the payroll expense.

ANALYSIS

The expense account, **Office Salaries Expense,** is increased by $480.00. The expense account, **Shipping Wages Expense,** is increased by $1,767.50. The liability account for each deduction is increased: **Social Security Tax Payable,** $139.35; **Medicare Tax Payable,** $32.59; **Employee Income Tax Payable,** $155.00; **Health Insurance Premiums Payable,** $80.00. The liability account, **Salaries and Wages Payable,** is increased by the net amount of the payroll, $1,840.56.

DEBIT-CREDIT RULES

DEBIT Increases in expenses are recorded as debits. Debit *Office Salaries Expense* for $480.00. Debit *Shipping Wages Expense* for $1,767.50.

CREDIT Increases in liability accounts are recorded as credits. Credit *Social Security Tax Payable* for $139.35. Credit *Medicare Tax Payable* for $32.59. Credit *Employee Income Tax Payable* for $155.00. Credit *Health Insurance Premiums Payable* for $80.00. Credit *Salaries and Wages Payable* for $1,840.56

T-ACCOUNT PRESENTATION

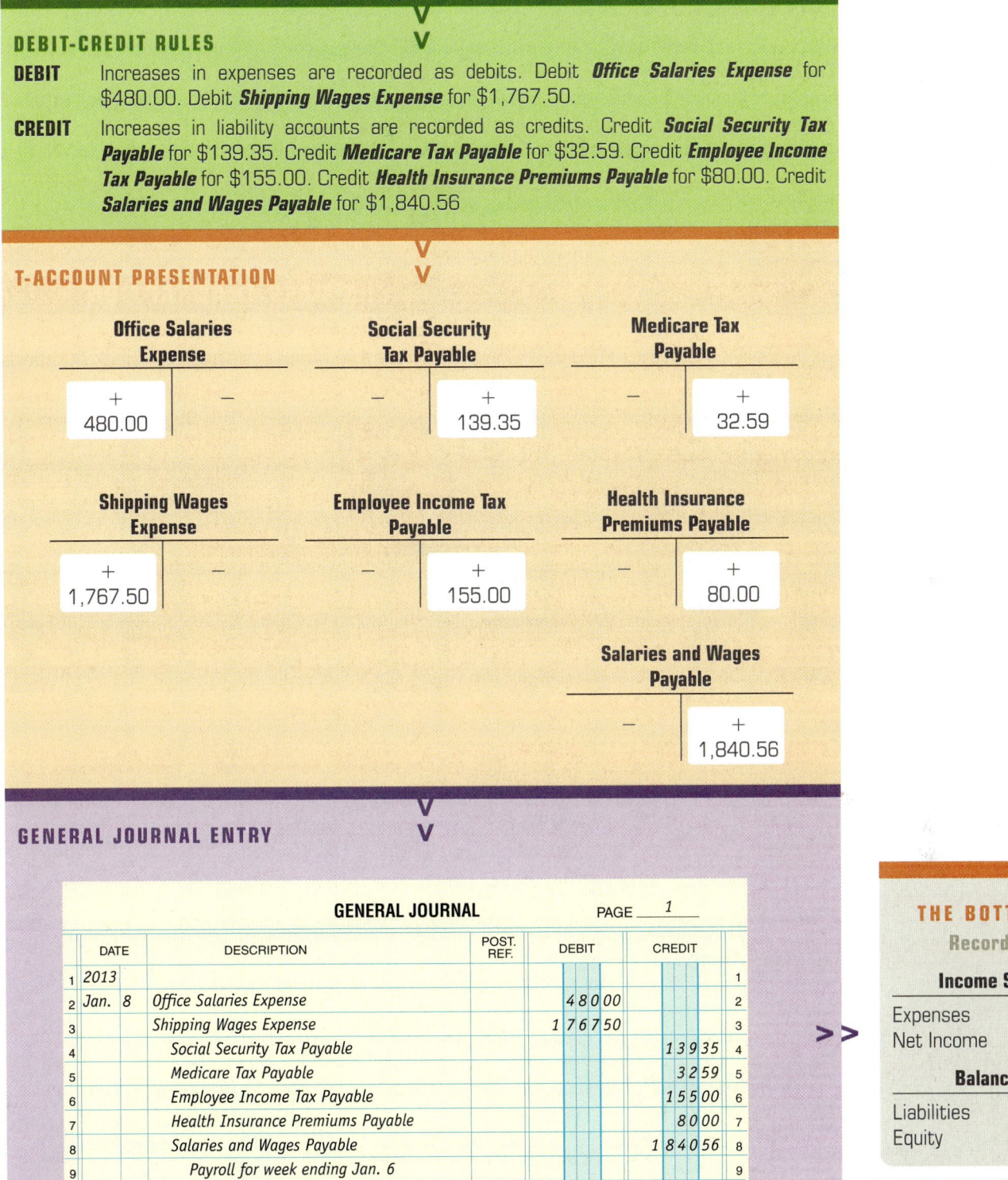

Office Salaries Expense		Social Security Tax Payable		Medicare Tax Payable	
+	–	–	+	–	+
480.00			139.35		32.59

Shipping Wages Expense		Employee Income Tax Payable		Health Insurance Premiums Payable	
+	–	–	+	–	+
1,767.50			155.00		80.00

Salaries and Wages Payable	
–	+
	1,840.56

GENERAL JOURNAL ENTRY

GENERAL JOURNAL   PAGE ___1___

	DATE		DESCRIPTION	POST. REF.	DEBIT	CREDIT	
1	2013						1
2	Jan.	8	Office Salaries Expense		480 00		2
3			Shipping Wages Expense		1767 50		3
4			Social Security Tax Payable			139 35	4
5			Medicare Tax Payable			32 59	5
6			Employee Income Tax Payable			155 00	6
7			Health Insurance Premiums Payable			80 00	7
8			Salaries and Wages Payable			1840 56	8
9			*Payroll for week ending Jan. 6*				9

>>

THE BOTTOM LINE
Record Payroll

Income Statement

Expenses	↑ 2,247.50
Net Income	↓ 2,247.50

Balance Sheet

Liabilities	↑ 2,247.50
Equity	↓ 2,247.50

> Southwest Airlines Co. recorded salaries, wages, and benefits of more than $3.45 billion for the year ended December 31, 2009.

Paying Employees

Most businesses pay their employees by check or by direct deposit. By using these methods, the business avoids the inconvenience and risk involved in dealing with currency.

PAYING BY CHECK

Paychecks may be written on the firm's regular checking account or on a payroll bank account. The check stub shows information about the employee's gross earnings, deductions, and net pay. Employees detach the stubs and keep them as a record of their payroll data. The check number is entered in the Check Number column of the payroll register (Figure 10.3, Column R). The canceled check provides a record of the payment, and the employee's endorsement serves as a receipt. Following is an analysis of the transaction to pay Sanchez Furniture Company's employees.

BUSINESS TRANSACTION

On January 8, Sanchez Furniture Company wrote five checks for payroll, check numbers 1601–1605.

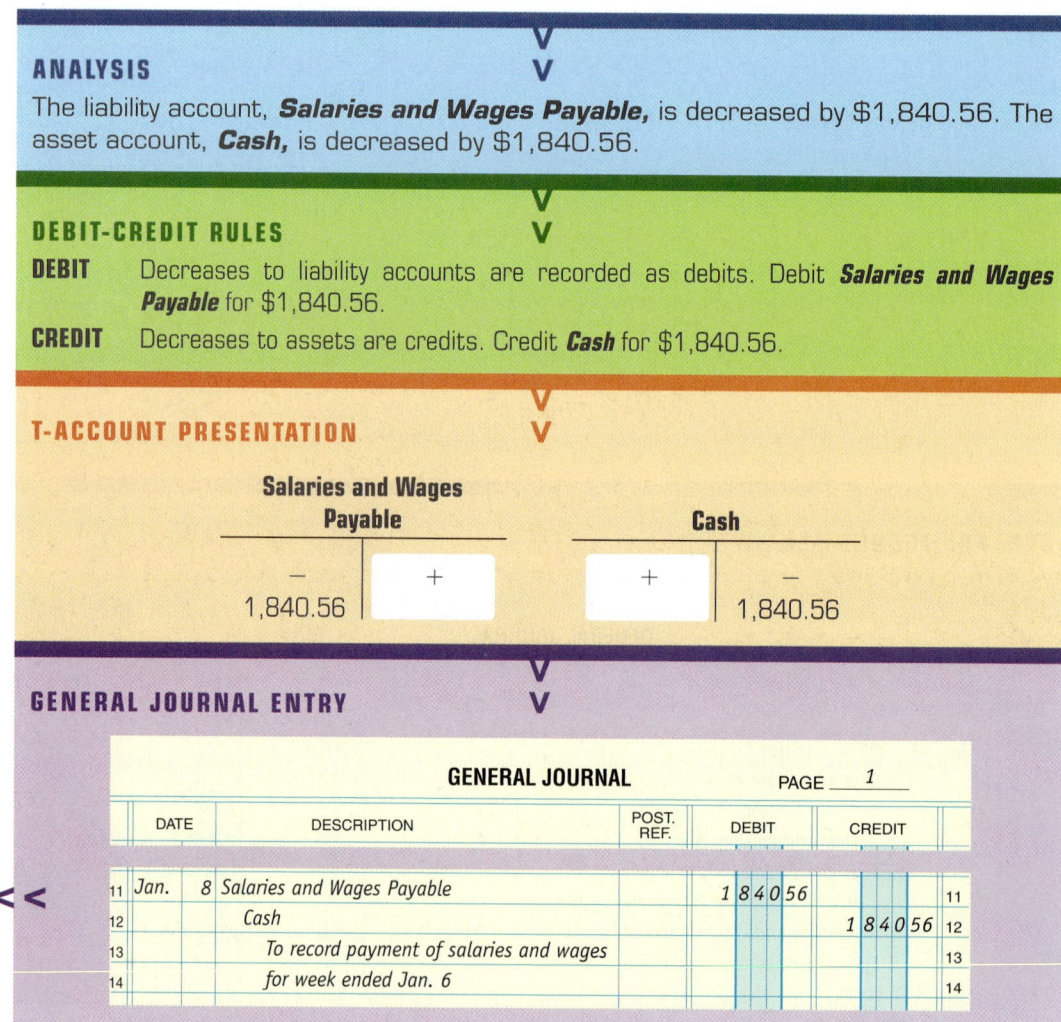

ANALYSIS

The liability account, **Salaries and Wages Payable,** is decreased by $1,840.56. The asset account, **Cash,** is decreased by $1,840.56.

DEBIT-CREDIT RULES

DEBIT   Decreases to liability accounts are recorded as debits. Debit **Salaries and Wages Payable** for $1,840.56.

CREDIT   Decreases to assets are credits. Credit **Cash** for $1,840.56.

T-ACCOUNT PRESENTATION

Salaries and Wages Payable		Cash	
−	+	+	−
1,840.56			1,840.56

GENERAL JOURNAL ENTRY

GENERAL JOURNAL   PAGE ___1___

	DATE	DESCRIPTION	POST. REF.	DEBIT	CREDIT	
11	Jan. 8	Salaries and Wages Payable		1 8 4 0 56		11
12		Cash			1 8 4 0 56	12
13		To record payment of salaries and wages				13
14		for week ended Jan. 6				14

Checks Written on a Separate Payroll Account   Many businesses write payroll checks from a separate payroll bank account. This is a two-step process:

1. A check is drawn on the regular bank account for the total amount of net pay and deposited in the payroll bank account.
2. Individual payroll checks are issued from the payroll bank account.

MANAGERIAL IMPLICATIONS   <<

LAWS AND CONTROLS

- It is management's responsibility to ensure that the payroll procedures and records comply with federal, state, and local laws.

- For most businesses, wages and salaries are a large part of operating expenses. Payroll records help management to keep track of and control expenses.

- Management should investigate large or frequent overtime expenditures.

- To prevent errors and fraud, management periodically should have the payroll records audited and payroll procedures evaluated.

- Two common payroll frauds are the overstatement of hours worked and the issuance of checks to nonexistent employees.

THINKING CRITICALLY

What controls would you put in place to prevent payroll fraud?

Using a separate payroll account simplifies the bank reconciliation of the regular checking account and makes it easier to identify outstanding payroll checks.

PAYING BY DIRECT DEPOSIT

A popular method of paying employees is the direct deposit method. The bank electronically transfers net pay from the employer's account to the personal account of the employee. On payday, the employee receives a statement showing gross earnings, deductions, and net pay.

Individual Earnings Records

An **individual earnings record,** also called a **compensation record,** is created for each employee. This record contains the employee's name, address, social security number, date of birth, number of withholding allowances claimed, rate of pay, and any other information needed to compute earnings and complete tax reports.

The payroll register provides the details that are entered on the employee's individual earnings record for each pay period. Figure 10.4 shows the earnings record for Alicia Martinez.

The earnings record shows the payroll period, the date paid, the regular and overtime hours, the regular and overtime earnings, the deductions, and the net pay. The cumulative earnings on the earnings record agrees with Column I of the payroll register (Figure 10.3). The earnings records are totaled monthly and at the end of each calendar quarter. This provides information needed to make tax payments and file tax returns.

>>8. OBJECTIVE

Maintain an earnings record for each employee.

FIGURE 10.4   An Individual Earnings Record

EARNINGS RECORD FOR _2013_

NAME _Alicia Martinez_   **RATE** _$10 per hour_   **SOCIAL SECURITY NO.** _123-45-6789_

ADDRESS _1712 Windmill Hill Lane, Dallas, TX 75232-6002_   **DATE OF BIRTH** _November 23, 1979_

WITHHOLDING ALLOWANCES _1_   **MARITAL STATUS** _M_

PAYROLL NO.	DATE WK. END.	DATE PAID	HOURS RG	HOURS OT	EARNINGS REGULAR	EARNINGS OVERTIME	EARNINGS TOTAL	EARNINGS CUMULATIVE	DEDUCTIONS SOCIAL SECURITY	DEDUCTIONS MEDICARE	DEDUCTIONS INCOME TAX	DEDUCTIONS OTHER	NET PAY
1	1/06	1/08	40		400 00		400 00	400 00	24 80	5 80	19 00		350 40
2	1/13	1/15	40		400 00		400 00	800 00	24 80	5 80	19 00		350 40
3	1/20	1/22	40		400 00		400 00	1200 00	24 80	5 80	19 00		350 40
4	1/27	1/29	40		400 00		400 00	1600 00	24 80	5 80	19 00		350 40
	January				1600 00		1600 00		99 20	23 20	76 00		1401 60

Completing January Payrolls

Figure 10.5 shows the entire cycle of computing, paying, journalizing, and posting payroll data. In order to complete the January payroll for Sanchez Furniture Company, assume that all employees worked the same number of hours each week of the month as they did the first week. Thus, they had the same earnings, deductions, and net pay each week.

ENTRY TO RECORD PAYROLL

As illustrated earlier in this section, one general journal entry is made to record the weekly payroll for all employees of Sanchez Furniture Company. This general journal entry records the payroll expense and liability, but not the payments to employees. Since we are assuming an identical payroll for each week of the month, each of the four weekly payrolls requires general journal entries identical to the one shown in Figure 10.5. Notice how the payroll register column totals are recorded in the general journal.

ENTRY TO RECORD PAYMENT OF PAYROLL

The weekly entries in the general journal to record payments to employees debit Salaries and Wages Payable and credit Cash.

POSTINGS TO LEDGER ACCOUNTS

The entries to record the weekly payroll expense and liability amounts are posted from the general journal to the accounts in the general ledger. The total of the Salaries and Wages Payable Debit column in the cash payments journal is posted to the *Salaries and Wages Payable* general ledger account.

FIGURE 10.5 **Journalizing and Posting Payroll Data**

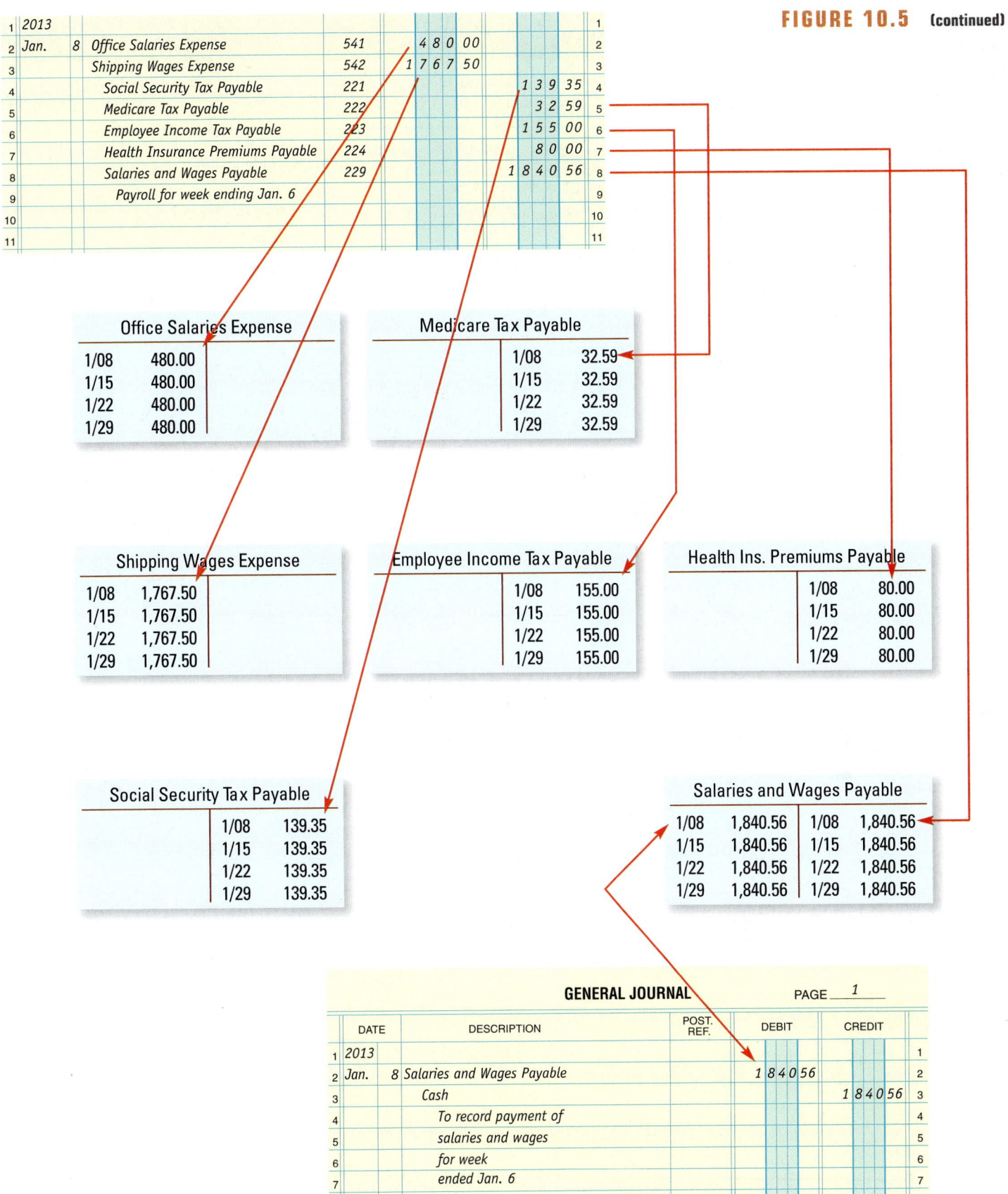

FIGURE 10.5 (continued)

Section 3 Self Review

(Answers to Section 3 Self Review are on page 333.)

QUESTIONS

1. What is the purpose of a payroll bank account?

2. What appears on an individual earnings record?

3. What accounts are debited and credited when individual payroll checks are written on the regular checking account?

EXERCISES

4. Details related to all employees' gross earnings, deductions, and net pay for a period are found in the:

   a. payroll register.

   b. individual earnings record.

   c. general journal.

   d. cash payments journal.

5. Payroll deductions are recorded in a separate:

   a. asset account.

   b. expense account.

   c. liability account.

   d. revenue account.

ANALYSIS

6. This general journal entry was made to record the payroll liability.

   Ofc. Salaries Exp. 600.00

   Shipping Wages
   Exp.   2,586.00

   Health Ins. Prem.
   Exp.   40.00

   Soc. Sec. Taxes
   Exp.   197.41

   Medicare Taxes
   Pay.   48.17

   Employee Income
   Tax Payable   266.00

   Cash   2,634.42

   What corrections should be made to this journal entry?

REVIEW   Chapter Summary

The main goal of payroll work is to compute the gross wages or salaries earned by each employee, the amounts to be deducted for various taxes and other purposes, and the net amount payable.

Learning Objectives

1 Explain the major federal laws relating to employee earnings and withholding.

Several federal laws affect payroll.

- The federal Wage and Hour Law limits to 40 the number of hours per week an employee can work at the regular rate of pay. For more than 40 hours of work a week, an employer involved in interstate commerce must pay one and one-half times the regular rate.

- Federal laws require that the employer withhold at least three taxes from the employee's pay: the employee's share of social security tax, the employee's share of Medicare tax, and federal income tax. Instructions for computing these taxes are provided by the government.

- If required, state disability and other income taxes can also be deducted.

- Voluntary deductions can also be made.

2 Compute gross earnings of employees.

To compute gross earnings for an employee, it is necessary to know whether the employee is paid using an hourly rate basis, a salary basis, a commission basis, or a piece-rate basis.

3 Determine employee deductions for social security tax.

The social security tax is levied in an equal amount on both the employer and the employee. The tax is a percentage of the employee's gross wages during a calendar year up to a wage base limit.

4 Determine employee deductions for Medicare tax.

The Medicare tax is levied in an equal amount on both the employer and the employee. There is no wage base limit for Medicare taxes.

5 Determine employee deductions for income tax.

Income taxes are deducted from an employee's paycheck by the employer and then are paid to the government periodically. Although several methods can be used to compute the amount of federal income tax to be withheld from employee earnings, the wage-bracket table method is most often used. The wage-bracket tables are in *Publication 15, Circular E, Employer's Tax Guide*. Withholding tables for various pay periods for single and married persons are contained in *Circular E*.

6 Enter gross earnings, deductions, and net pay in the payroll register.

Daily records of the hours worked by each nonsupervisory employee are kept. Using these hourly time sheets, the payroll clerk computes the employees' earnings, deductions, and net pay for each payroll period and records the data in a payroll register.

7 Journalize payroll transactions in the general journal.

The payroll register is used to prepare a general journal entry to record payroll expense and liability amounts. A separate journal entry is made to record payments to employees.

8 Maintain an earnings record for each employee.

At the beginning of each year, the employer sets up an individual earnings record for each employee. The amounts in the payroll register are posted to the individual earnings records throughout the year so that the firm has detailed payroll information for each employee. At the end of the year, employers provide reports that show gross earnings and total deductions to each employee.

9 Define the accounting terms new to this chapter.

Glossary

Commission basis (p. 305) A method of paying employees according to a percentage of net sales

Compensation record (p. 317) See Individual earnings record

Employee (p. 300) A person who is hired by and works under the control and direction of the employer

Employee's Withholding Allowance Certificate, Form W-4 (p. 307) A form used to claim exemption (withholding) allowances

Exempt employees (p. 311) Salaried employees who hold supervisory or managerial positions who are not subject to the maximum hour and overtime pay provisions of the Wage and Hour Law

Federal unemployment taxes (FUTA) (p. 302) Taxes levied by the federal government against employers to benefit unemployed workers

Hourly rate basis (p. 304) A method of paying employees according to a stated rate per hour

Independent contractor (p. 300) One who is paid by a company to carry out a specific task or job but is not under the direct supervision or control of the company

Individual earnings record (p. 317) An employee record that contains information needed to compute earnings and complete tax reports

Medicare tax (p. 301) A tax levied on employees and employers to provide medical care for the employee and the employee's spouse after each has reached age 65

Payroll register (p. 311) A record of payroll information for each employee for the pay period

Piece-rate basis (p. 305) A method of paying employees according to the number of units produced

Salary basis (p. 305) A method of paying employees according to an agreed-upon amount for each week or month

Social Security Act (p. 301) A federal act providing certain benefits for employees and their families; officially the Federal Insurance Contributions Act

Social security (FICA) tax (p. 301) A tax imposed by the Federal Insurance Contributions Act and collected on employee earnings to provide retirement and disability benefits

State unemployment taxes (SUTA) (p. 302) Taxes levied by a state government against employers to benefit unemployed workers

Tax-exempt wages (p. 306) Earnings in excess of the base amount set by the Social Security Act

Time and a half (p. 301) Rate of pay for an employee's work in excess of 40 hours a week

Wage-bracket table method (p. 307) A simple method to determine the amount of federal income tax to be withheld using a table provided by the government

Workers' compensation insurance (p. 303) Insurance that protects employees against losses from job-related injuries or illnesses, or compensates their families if death occurs in the course of the employment

Comprehensive **Self Review**

1. How does an independent contractor differ from an employee?
2. What is the purpose of the payroll register?
3. From an accounting and internal control viewpoint, would it be preferable to pay employees by check or cash? Explain.
4. How is the amount of social security tax to be withheld from an employee's earnings determined?
5. What is the purpose of workers' compensation insurance?

(Answers to Comprehensive Self Review are on page 333.)

Discussion **Questions**

1. What factors affect how much federal income tax must be withheld from an employee's earnings?
2. How does the Fair Labor Standards Act affect the wages paid by many firms? What types of firms are regulated by the act?

3. What aspects of employment are regulated by the Fair Labor Standards Act? What is another commonly used name for this act?

4. Give two examples of common payroll fraud.

5. What is an exempt employee?

6. How are the federal and state unemployment taxes related?

7. Does the employee bear any part of the SUTA tax? Explain.

8. How are earnings determined when employees are paid on the hourly rate basis?

9. What is the purpose of the Medicare tax?

10. What is the purpose of the social security tax?

11. How does the direct deposit method of paying employees operate?

12. What are the four bases for determining employee gross earnings?

13. What is the simplest method for finding the amount of federal income tax to be deducted from an employee's gross pay?

14. What publication of the Internal Revenue Service provides information about the current federal income tax rates and the procedures that employers should use to withhold federal income tax from an employee's earnings?

15. How does the salary basis differ from the hourly rate basis of paying employees?

APPLICATIONS

Exercises

Computing gross earnings.

◀ **Exercise 10.1**
Objective 2

The hourly rates of four employees of Johnson Enterprises follow, along with the hours that these employees worked during one week. Determine the gross earnings of each employee.

Employee No.	Hourly Rate	Hours Worked
1	$9.21	39
2	8.75	31
3	9.42	34
4	8.63	33

Computing regular earnings, overtime earnings, and gross pay.

◀ **Exercise 10.2**
Objective 2

During one week, four production employees of Martinez Manufacturing Company worked the hours shown below. All these employees receive overtime pay at one and one-half times their regular hourly rate for any hours worked beyond 40 in a week. Determine the regular earnings, overtime earnings, and gross earnings for each employee.

Employee No.	Hourly Rate	Hours Worked
1	$10.00	45
2	9.71	46
3	9.55	39
4	9.80	47

Exercise 10.3

Objective 3

▶ **Determining social security withholding.**

The monthly salaries for December and the year-to-date earnings of the employees of Canzano Consulting Company as of November 30 follow.

Employee No.	December Salary	Year-to-Date Earnings through November 30
1	$8,900	$97,900
2	9,000	72,000
3	9,709	106,800
4	9,000	99,000

Determine the amount of social security tax to be withheld from each employee's gross pay for December. Assume a 6.2 percent social security tax rate and an earnings base of $106,800 for the calendar year.

Exercise 10.4

Objective 4

CONTINUING >>>
Problem

▶ **Determining deduction for Medicare tax.**

Using the earnings data given in Exercise 10.3, determine the amount of Medicare tax to be withheld from each employee's gross pay for December. Assume a 1.45 percent Medicare tax rate and that all salaries and wages are subject to the tax.

Exercise 10.5

Objective 5

▶ **Determining federal income tax withholding.**

Data about the marital status, withholding allowances, and weekly salaries of the four office workers at Amos Publishing Company follow. Use the tax tables in Figure 10.2 on pages 309–310 to find the amount of federal income tax to be deducted from each employee's gross pay.

Employee No.	Marital Status	Withholding Allowances	Weekly Salary
1	M	1	$650
2	S	2	595
3	M	3	735
4	S	2	590

Exercise 10.6

Objective 7

▶ **Recording payroll transactions in the general journal.**

Excalibur Publishing has two office employees. A summary of their earnings and the related taxes withheld from their pay for the week ending August 7, 2013, follows.

	Ann Chen	David Kendrick
Gross earnings	$1,320.00	$1,190.00
Social security deduction	(81.84)	(73.78)
Medicare deduction	(19.14)	(17.26)
Income tax withholding	(353.36)	(214.32)
Net pay for week	$ 865.66	$ 884.64

1. Prepare the general journal entry to record the company's payroll for the week. Use the account names given in this chapter. Use 16 as the page number for the general journal.

2. Prepare the general journal entry to summarize the checks to pay the weekly payroll.

◄ Exercise 10.7
Objective 7

Journalizing payroll transactions.

On July 31, 2013, the payroll register of Reed Wholesale Company showed the following totals for the month: gross earnings, $38,600; social security tax, $2,393.20; Medicare tax, $559.70; income tax, $3,055.96; and net amount due, $32,591.14. Of the total earnings, $30,558.46 was for sales salaries and $8,041.54 was for office salaries. Prepare a general journal entry to record the monthly payroll of the firm on July 31, 2013. Use 20 as the page number for the general journal.

PROBLEMS

Problem Set A

◄ Problem 10.1A
Objectives
eXcel 2, 3, 4, 5, 7

Computing gross earnings, determining deductions, journalizing payroll transactions.

Kathy Burnett works for Trinity Industries. Her pay rate is $12.84 per hour and she receives overtime pay at one and one-half times her regular hourly rate for any hours worked beyond 40 in a week. During the pay period that ended December 31, 2013, Kathy worked 48 hours. Kathy is married and claims three withholding allowances on her W-4 form. Kathy's cumulative earnings prior to this pay period total $28,000. Kathy's wages are subject to the following deductions:

1. Social Security tax at 6.2 percent
2. Medicare tax at 1.45 percent
3. Federal income tax (use the withholding table shown in Figure 10.2B on page 310)
4. Health and disability insurance premiums, $151
5. Charitable contribution, $18
6. United States Savings Bond, $100

INSTRUCTIONS

1. Compute Kathy's regular, overtime, gross, and net pay.
2. Assuming the weekly payroll has been recorded, journalize the payment of her wages for the week ended December 31, 2013. Use 54 as the page number for the general journal.

Analyze: Based on Kathy's cumulative earnings through December 31, how much overtime pay did she earn this year?

Computing gross earnings, determining deductions, preparing payroll register, journalizing payroll transactions.

◄ Problem 10.2A
Objectives 2, 3, 4, 5
eXcel

City Place Movie Theaters has four employees and pays them on an hourly basis. During the week beginning June 24 and ending June 30, 2013, these employees worked the hours shown below. Information about hourly rates, marital status, withholding allowances, and cumulative earnings prior to the current pay period also appears below.

Employee	Regular Hours Worked	Hourly Rate	Marital Status	Withholding Allowances	Cumulative Earnings
Nelda Anderson	48	$11.75	M	1	$17,540
Earl Benson	49	10.50	M	4	16,875
Frank Cortez	40	10.25	M	1	15,980
Winnie Wu	52	9.75	S	2	14,560

INSTRUCTIONS

1. Enter the basic payroll information for each employee in a payroll register. Record the employee's name, number of withholding allowances, marital status, total and overtime hours, and regular hourly rate. Consider any hours worked beyond 40 in the week as overtime hours.

2. Compute the regular, overtime, and gross earnings for each employee. Enter the figures in the payroll register.

3. Compute the amount of social security tax to be withheld from each employee's earnings. Assume a 6.2 percent social security rate on the first $106,800 earned by the employee during the year. Enter the figures in the payroll register.

4. Compute the amount of Medicare tax to be withheld from each employee's earnings. Assume a 1.45 percent Medicare tax rate on all salaries and wages earned by the employee during the year. Enter the figures in the payroll register.

5. Determine the amount of federal income tax to be withheld from each employee's total earnings. Use the tax tables in Figure 10.2 on pages 309–310. Enter the figures in the payroll register.

6. Compute the net pay of each employee and enter the figures in the payroll register.

7. Total and prove the payroll register.

8. Prepare a general journal entry to record the payroll for the week ended June 30, 2013. Use 15 as the page number for the general journal.

9. Record the general journal entry to summarize payment of the payroll on July 3, 2013.

Analyze: What are Nelda Anderson's cumulative earnings on June 30, 2013?

Problem 10.3A ▶
Objectives 2, 3, 4, 5

Computing gross earnings, determining deductions, preparing payroll register, journalizing payroll transactions.

Alexander Wilson operates Metroplex Courier and Delivery Service. He has four employees who are paid on an hourly basis. During the work week beginning December 15 and ending December 21, 2013, his employees worked the number of hours shown below. Information about their hourly rates, marital status, and withholding allowances also appears below, along with their cumulative earnings for the year prior to the December 15–21 payroll period.

Employee	Hours Worked	Regular Hourly Rate	Marital Status	Withholding Allowances	Cumulative Earnings
Gloria Bahamon	46	$15.75	M	4	$32,760
Alex Garcia	42	27.50	S	1	57,200
Ron Price	48	25.90	M	3	53,872
Sara Russell	40	12.75	S	0	26,520

INSTRUCTIONS

1. Enter the basic payroll information for each employee in a payroll register. Record the employee's name, number of withholding allowances, marital status, total and overtime hours, and regular hourly rate. Consider any hours worked beyond 40 in the week as overtime hours.

2. Compute the regular, overtime, and gross earnings for each employee. Enter the figures in the payroll register.

3. Compute the amount of social security tax to be withheld from each employee's gross earnings. Assume a 6.2 percent social security rate on the first $106,800 earned by the employee during the year. Enter the figures in the payroll register.

4. Compute the amount of Medicare tax to be withheld from each employee's gross earnings. Assume a 1.45 percent Medicare tax rate on all salaries and wages earned by the employee during the year. Enter the figures in the payroll register.

5. Determine the amount of federal income tax to be withheld from each employee's total earnings. Use the tax tables in Figure 10.2 on pages 309–310 to determine the withholding for Russell. Withholdings for Bahamon is $103.00, $299.00 for Garcia, and $241 for Price. Enter the figures in the payroll register.

6. Compute the net amount due each employee and enter the figures in the payroll register.

7. Total and prove the payroll register. Bahamon and Russell are office workers. Garcia and Price are delivery workers.

8. Prepare a general journal entry to record the payroll for the week ended December 21, 2013. Use 32 as the page number for the general journal.

9. Prepare a general journal entry on December 23 to summarize payment of wages for the week.

Analyze: What percentage of total taxable wages was delivery wages?

Computing gross earnings, determining deduction and net amount due, journalizing payroll transactions.

◄ **Problem 10.4A**
Objectives
2, 3, 4, 5, 6, 7

e**X**cel

Nature's Best Publishing Company pays its employees monthly. Payments made by the company on October 31, 2013, follow. Cumulative amounts paid to the persons named prior to October 31 are also given.

1. Sara Parker, president, gross monthly salary of $19,400; gross earnings prior to October 31, $170,700.

2. Carolyn Wells, vice president, gross monthly salary of $15,600; gross earnings paid prior to October 31, $151,700.

3. Michelle Clark, independent accountant who audits the company's accounts and performs consulting services, $15,500; gross amounts paid prior to October 31, $43,900.

4. James Wu, treasurer, gross monthly salary of $5,000; gross earnings prior to October 31, $51,800.

5. Payment to Editorial Publishing Services for monthly services of Betty Jo Bradley, an editorial expert, $5,000; amount paid to Editorial Publishing Services prior to October 31, 2013, $33,100.

INSTRUCTIONS

1. Use an earnings ceiling of $106,800 for social security taxes and a tax rate of 6.2 percent and a tax rate of 1.45 percent on all earnings for Medicare taxes. Prepare a schedule showing the following information:

   a. Each employee's cumulative earnings prior to October 31.

   b. Each employee's gross earnings for October.

   c. The amounts to be withheld for each payroll tax from each employee's earnings; the employee's income tax withholdings are Sara Parker, $5,088; Carolyn Wells, $4,388; James Wu, $1,147.

   d. The net amount due each employee.

   e. The total gross earnings, the total of each payroll tax deduction, and the total net amount payable to employees.

2. Prepare the general journal entry to record the company's payroll on October 31. Use journal page 22. Omit explanations.

3. Prepare the general journal entry to record payments to employees on October 31.

Analyze: What distinguishes an employee from an independent contractor?

Problem Set B

Computing gross earnings, determining deductions, journalizing payroll transactions.

◄ **Problem 10.1B**
Objectives
2, 3, 4, 5, 7

Jacob Sandoval works for Alexander Valley Builders, Inc. His pay rate is $12.70 per hour and he receives overtime pay at one and one-half times his regular hourly rate for any hours worked beyond

40 in a week. During the pay period ended December 31, 2013, Jacob worked 48 hours. Jacob is married and claims three withholding allowances on his W-4 form. Jacob's cumulative earnings prior to this pay period total $28,000. Jacob's wages are subject to the following deductions:

1. Social security tax at 6.2 percent

2. Medicare tax at 1.45 percent

3. Federal income tax (use the withholding table shown in Figure 10.2B on page 310)

4. Health insurance premiums, $165

5. Charitable contribution, $519

6. Credit Union Savings, $75

INSTRUCTIONS

1. Compute Jacob's regular, overtime, gross, and net pay.

2. Assuming the weekly payroll has been recorded, journalize the payment of his wages for the week ended December 31, 2013. Use journal page 18.

Analyze: Based on Jacob's cumulative earnings through December 31, how much overtime pay did he earn this year?

Problem 10.2B ▶
Objectives 2, 3, 4, 5

Computing earnings, determining deductions and net amount due, preparing payroll register, journalizing payroll transactions.

The four employees for Cotton Cleaners are paid on an hourly basis. During the week of December 25–31, 2013, these employees worked the hours indicated. Information about their hourly rates, marital status, withholding allowances, and cumulative earnings prior to the current pay period also appears below.

Employee	Hours Worked	Regular Hourly Rate	Marital Status	Withholding Allowances	Cumulative Earnings
Barbara Brooks	47	$12.75	M	3	$ 44,179.00
Cynthia Carter	48	13.25	M	2	53,015.00
Mabel Easley	44	29.50	M	4	82,748.00
James Periot	28	37.25	S	2	104,486.00

INSTRUCTIONS

1. Enter the basic payroll information for each employee in a payroll register. Record the employee's name, number of withholding allowances, marital status, total hours, overtime hours, and regular hourly rate. Consider any hours worked beyond 40 in the week as overtime hours.

2. Compute the regular earnings, overtime premium, and gross earnings for each employee. Enter the figures in the payroll register.

3. Compute the amount of social security tax to be withheld from each employee's gross earnings. Assume a 6.2 percent social security tax rate on the first $106,800 earned by each employee during the year. Enter the figures in the payroll register.

4. Compute the amount of Medicare tax to be withheld from each employee's gross earnings. Assume a 1.45 percent Medicare tax rate on all earnings for each employee during the year. Enter the figure on the payroll register.

5. Determine the amount of federal income tax to be withheld from each employee's gross earnings. Income tax withholdings for Easley is $235 and $238 for Periot. Enter these figures in the payroll register.

6. Compute the net amount due each employee and enter the figures in the payroll register.

7. Complete the payroll register for the store employees.

8. Prepare a general journal entry to record the payroll for the week ended December 31, 2013. Use page 18 for the journal.

9. Record the general journal entry to summarize the payment on December 31, 2013, of the net amount due employees.

Analyze: What is the difference between the amount credited to the *Cash* account on December 31, 2013, for the payroll week ended December 31 and the amount debited to *Wages Expense* for the same payroll period? What causes the difference between the two figures?

Computing earnings, determining deductions and net amount due, preparing payroll register, journalizing payroll transactions.

◀ **Problem 10.3B**
Objectives 2, 3, 4, 5

Barbara Merino operates Merino Consulting Services. She has four employees and pays them on an hourly basis. During the week ended November 12, 2013, her employees worked the number of hours shown below. Information about their hourly rates, marital status, withholding allowances, and cumulative earnings for the year prior to the current pay period also appears below.

Employee	Hours Worked	Regular Hourly Rate	Marital Status	Withholding Allowances	Cumulative Earnings
Kathryn Allen	43	$10.50	M	3	$26,565
Calvin Cooke	36	10.25	S	2	25,933
Maria Vasquez	45	29.75	M	4	75,268
Hollie Visage	41	32.75	S	2	82,858

INSTRUCTIONS

1. Enter the basic payroll information for each employee in a payroll register. Record the employee's name, number of withholding allowances, marital status, total hours, overtime hours, and regular hourly rate. Consider any hours worked beyond 40 in the week as overtime hours.

2. Compute the regular earnings, overtime premium, and gross earnings for each employee. Enter the figures in the payroll register.

3. Compute the amount of social security tax to be withheld from each employee's gross earnings. Assume a 6.2 percent social security rate on the first $106,800 earned by the employee during the year. Enter the figures in the payroll register.

4. Compute the amount of Medicare tax to be withheld from each employee's gross earnings. Assume a 1.45 percent Medicare tax rate on all earning paid during the year. Enter the figures in the payroll register.

5. Use the tax tables in Figure 10.2 on pages 309–310 to determine the federal income tax to be withheld. Federal income tax to be withheld from Vasquez's pay is $192 and from Visage's pay is $267. Enter the figures in the payroll register.

6. Compute the net amount due each employee and enter the figures in the payroll register.

7. Complete the payroll register. Allen and Cooke are office workers. Earnings for Vasquez and Visage are charged to consulting wages.

8. Prepare a general journal entry to record the payroll for the week ended November 12, 2013. Use the account titles given in this chapter. Use journal page 32.

9. Prepare the general journal entry to summarize payment of amounts due employees on November 15, 2013.

Analyze: What total deductions were taken from employee paychecks for the pay period ended November 12?

Computing gross earnings, determining deduction and net amount due, journalizing payroll transactions.

◀ **Problem 10.4B**
Objectives
2, 3, 4, 5, 6, 7

Constantino Public Relations pays its employees monthly. Payments made by the company on November 30, 2013, follow. Cumulative amounts paid to the persons named prior to November 30 are also given.

1. Tony Constantino, president, gross monthly salary of $18,000; gross earnings prior to November 30, $180,000.

2. Chris Stamos, vice president, gross monthly salary of $15,000; gross earnings paid prior to November 30, $150,000.

3. Brenda Cates, independent media buyer who purchases media contracts for companies and performs other public relations consulting services, $15,650; gross amounts paid prior to November 30, $52,850.

4. Elaine Hayakawa, treasurer, gross monthly salary of $6,400; gross earnings prior to November 30, $64,000.

5. Payment to the Queen Marketing Group for monthly services of Cheryl Queen, a marketing and public relations expert, $15,500; amount paid to the Queen Marketing Group prior to November 30, $46,500.

INSTRUCTIONS

1. Use an earnings ceiling of $106,800 and a tax rate of 6.2 percent for social security taxes and a tax rate of 1.45 percent on all earnings for Medicare taxes. Prepare a schedule showing the following information:

   a. Each employee's cumulative earnings prior to November 30.

   b. Each employee's gross earnings for November.

   c. The amounts to be withheld for each payroll tax from each employee's earnings; the employee's income tax withholdings are Tony Constantino, $5,110; Chris Stamos, $3,700; Elaine Hayakawa, $1,200.

   d. The net amount due each employee.

   e. The total gross earnings, the total of each payroll tax deduction, and the total net amount payable to employees.

2. Give the general journal entry to record the company's payroll on November 30. Use journal page 24. Omit explanations.

3. Give the general journal entry to record payments to employees on November 30.

Analyze: What month in 2013 did Chris Stamos reach the withholding limit for social security?

Critical Thinking Problem 10.1

Payroll Accounting

Colorado Company pays salaries and wages on the last day of each month. Payments made on December 31, 2013, for amounts incurred during December are shown below. Cumulative amounts paid prior to December 31 to the persons named are also shown.

a. Mark Arnold, president, gross monthly salary $14,000; gross earnings paid prior to December 31, $154,000.

b. Heather Anthony, vice president, gross monthly salary $12,000; gross earnings paid prior to December 31, $72,000.

c. Jenny Rios, independent accountant who audits the company's accounts and performs certain consulting services, $13,000; gross amount paid prior to December 31, $35,000.

d. Vlade Tepic, treasurer, gross monthly salary $6,500; gross earnings paid prior to December 31, $71,500.

e. Payment to Wright Security Services for Eddie Wright, a security guard who is on duty on Saturdays and Sundays, $1,000; amount paid to Wright Security Services prior to December 31, $11,000.

INSTRUCTIONS

1. Using the tax rates and earnings ceilings given in this chapter, prepare a schedule showing the following information:

   a. Each employee's cumulative earnings prior to December 31.

   b. Each employee's gross earnings for December.

c. The amounts to be withheld for each payroll tax from each employee's earnings (employee income tax withholdings for Arnold are $3,216; for Anthony, $2,646; and for Tepic, $1,244).

d. The net amount due each employee.

e. The total gross earnings, the total of each payroll tax deduction, and the total net amount payable to employees.

2. Record the general journal entry for the company's payroll on December 31. Use journal page 32.

3. Record the general journal entry for payments to employees on December 31.

Analyze: What is the balance of the *Salaries Payable* account after all payroll entries have been posted for the month?

Critical Thinking Problem 10.2

Payroll Internal Controls

Several years ago, Paul Rivera opened Tito's Tacos, a restaurant specializing in homemade tacos. The restaurant was so successful that Rivera was able to expand, and his company now operates eight restaurants in the local area.

Rivera tells you that when he first started, he handled all aspects of the business himself. Now that there are eight Tito's Tacos, he depends on the managers of each restaurant to make decisions and oversee day-to-day operations. Paul oversees operations at the company's headquarters, which is located at the first Tito's Tacos.

Each manager interviews and hires new employees for a restaurant. The new employee is required to complete a W-4, which is sent by the manager to the headquarters office. Each restaurant has a time clock and employees are required to clock in as they arrive or depart. Blank time cards are kept in a box under the time clock. At the beginning of each week, employees complete the top of the card they will use during the week. The manager collects the cards at the end of the week and sends them to headquarters.

Paul hired his cousin Anna to prepare the payroll instead of assigning this task to the accounting staff. Because she is a relative, Paul trusts her and has confidence that confidential payroll information will not be divulged to other employees.

When Anna receives a W-4 for a new employee, she sets up an individual earnings record for the employee. Each week, using the time cards sent by each restaurant's manager, she computes the gross pay, deductions, and net pay for all the employees. She then posts details to the employees' earnings records and prepares and signs the payroll checks. The checks are sent to the managers, who distribute them to the employees.

As long as Anna receives a time card for an employee, she prepares a paycheck. If she fails to get a time card for an employee, she checks with the manager to see if the employee was terminated or has quit. At the end of the month, Anna reconciles the payroll bank account and prepares quarterly and annual payroll tax returns.

1. Identify any weaknesses in Tito's Tacos's payroll system.

2. Identify one way a manager could defraud Tito's Tacos under the present payroll system.

3. What internal control procedures would you recommend to Paul to protect against the fraud you identified above?

BUSINESS CONNECTIONS

Cash Management

1. Why should managers check the amount spent for overtime?

2. The new controller for Ellis Company, a manufacturing firm, has suggested to management that the business change from paying the factory employees in cash to paying them by check. What reasons would you offer to support this suggestion?

3. Why should management make sure that a firm has an adequate set of payroll records?

4. How can detailed payroll records help managers control expenses?

Salary vs. Hourly

Jeremy's Sweater Factory employs two managers for the factory. These managers work 12 hours per day at $15 per hour. After eight hours, they receive overtime pay. Management is trying to cut costs. They have decided to promote the managers to a salary position. The managers will be offered a daily salary of $200. Since they would be promoted to a salary position they will not receive overtime. The company has required they accept the promotion or find employment elsewhere. Is it ethical for the company to offer the managers a salary position? Is it ethical to require the employee to accept the promotion? Should the managers accept the promotion?

Balance Sheet

The Home Depot, Inc. reported the following data in its *2009 Annual Report (for the fiscal year ended January 31, 2010)*:

The Home Depot, Inc. and Subsidiaries		
Consolidated Balance Sheets		
(in millions except per share amounts)		
	Jan. 31, 2010	**Feb. 1, 2009**
Current liabilities:		
Accrued salaries and related expenses	*1,263*	*1,129*
Total current liabilities	*10,363*	*11,153*

Analyze:

1. What percentage of total current liabilities is made up of accrued salaries and related expenses at January 31, 2010?

2. By what amount did accrued salaries and related expenses change from fiscal 2009 to fiscal 2010?

Cycle to Pay Employee

There are many approvals needed to create a paycheck for an employee. Divide into groups of five to identify the jobs necessary to create a paycheck for an employee. Describe the function and, if necessary, the journal entry for each job.

Certified Payroll Professional

Log onto the Certified Payroll Professional (CPP) Web site at www.americanpayroll.org. Find the requirements to become a CPP. How many years of experience are required? What is the fee to take the exam? Describe the testing procedure.

Answers to **Self Reviews**

Answers to Section 1 Self Review

1. By a tax levied equally on both employers and employees. The tax amount is based on the earnings.

2. By state and federal taxes levied on the employer.

3. The federal requirement that covered employees be paid at a rate equal to one and one-half times their normal hourly rate for each hour worked in excess of 40 hours per week.

4. a. employees who become unemployed

5. **d.** does not exist

6. She is not an employee. She is an independent contractor because she has been hired to complete a specific job and is not under the control of the employer.

Answers to Section 2 Self Review

1. Health insurance premiums, life insurance premiums, union dues, retirement plans.

2. Amount of earnings, period covered by the payment, employee's marital status, and the number of withholding allowances.

3. Social security tax, Medicare tax, and federal income tax.

4. **d.** hours worked

5. **c.** $468

6. When you receive a signed Form W-4 for the change in withholding.

Answers to Section 3 Self Review

1. Using a separate payroll account simplifies the bank reconciliation procedure and makes it easier to identify outstanding payroll checks.

2. Employee's name, address, social security number, date of birth, number of withholding allowances claimed, marital status, rate of pay, and any other information needed to compute earnings and complete tax reports.

3. Debit *Salaries and Wages Payable* and credit *Cash.*

4. **a.** payroll register

5. **c.** liability account

6. *Health Insurance Premiums Expense* Dr. 40.00 should be *Health Insurance Premiums Payable* Cr. 40.00; *Social Security Taxes Expense* Cr. 197.41 should be *Social Security Tax Payable* Cr. 197.41; *Cash* Cr. 2,634.42 should be *Salaries and Wages Payable* Cr. 2,634.42

Answers to Comprehensive Self Review

1. An employee is one who is hired by the employer and who is under the control and direction of the employer. An independent contractor is paid by the company to carry out a specific task or job and is not under the direct supervision and control of the employer.

2. To record in one place all information about an employee's earnings and withholdings for the period.

3. By check because there is far less possibility of mistake, lost money, or fraud. The check serves as a receipt and permanent record of the transaction.

4. Social security taxes are determined by multiplying the amount of taxable earnings by the social security tax rate.

5. To compensate workers for losses suffered from job-related injuries or to compensate their families if the employee's death occurs in the course of employment.

Payroll Taxes, Deposits, and Reports

Chapter 11

LEARNING OBJECTIVES

1. Explain how and when payroll taxes are paid to the government.
2. Compute and record the employer's social security and Medicare taxes.
3. Record deposit of social security, Medicare, and employee income taxes.
4. Prepare an Employer's Quarterly Federal Tax Return, Form 941.
5. Prepare Wage and Tax Statement (Form W-2) and Annual Transmittal of Wage and Tax Statements (Form W-3).
6. Compute and record liability for federal and state unemployment taxes and record payment of the taxes.
7. Prepare an Employer's Federal Unemployment Tax Return, Form 940.
8. Compute and record workers' compensation insurance premiums.
9. Define the accounting terms new to this chapter.

NEW TERMS

Employer's Annual Federal Unemployment Tax Return, Form 940
Employer's Quarterly Federal Tax Return, Form 941
experience rating system
merit rating system
Transmittal of Wage and Tax Statements, Form W-3
unemployment insurance program
Wage and Tax Statement, Form W-2
withholding statement

 **www.newcastlehotels.com** | New Castle Hotels & Resorts is a preferred manager for Marriott, Hilton, and Starwood brand Hotels in the United States and Canada. New Castle also manages a number of independent properties like the Craftsman Inn in Syracuse, New York, and the Keltic Lodge in Ingonish Beach, Nova Scotia.

Marian Barbieri, New Castle's vice president of human resources attributes the hotel's success to employee satisfaction. "The reason we have high guest satisfaction scores is because of the great experience they have, which is tied to employee satisfaction." While national statistics for hotel employee turnover is approximately 60 percent, New Castle has been able to sustain an employee turnover rate of less than 40 percent. New Castle's executives and employees attribute their company's low numbers to the associate-centered human resources policy. One such policy is the company's "Gotcha" program (Get On The Customer Hospitality Attack), which rewards instances where an employee goes above and beyond the call of duty.

thinking critically

How does a lower staff turnover rate affect New Castle's payroll accounting department?

SECTION OBJECTIVES

>> 1. **Explain how and when payroll taxes are paid to the government.**

WHY IT'S IMPORTANT

Employers are required by law to deposit payroll taxes.

>> 2. **Compute and record the employer's social security and Medicare taxes.**

WHY IT'S IMPORTANT

Accounting records should reflect all liabilities.

>> 3. **Record deposit of social security, Medicare, and employee income taxes.**

WHY IT'S IMPORTANT

Payments decrease the payroll tax liability.

>> 4. **Prepare an Employer's Quarterly Federal Tax Return, Form 941.**

WHY IT'S IMPORTANT

Completing a federal tax return is part of the employer's legal obligation.

>> 5. **Prepare Wage and Tax Statement (Form W-2) and Annual Transmittal of Wage and Tax Statements (Form W-3).**

WHY IT'S IMPORTANT

Employers are legally required to provide end-of-year payroll information.

TERMS TO LEARN

Employer's Quarterly Federal Tax Return, Form 941

Transmittal of Wage and Tax Statements, Form W-3

Wage and Tax Statement, Form W-2

withholding statement

Social Security, Medicare, and Employee Income Tax

In Chapter 10, you learned that the law requires employers to act as collection agents for certain taxes due from employees. In this chapter, you will learn how to compute the employer's taxes, make tax payments, and file the required tax returns and reports.

>> **1. OBJECTIVE**

Explain how and when payroll taxes are paid to the government.

Payment of Payroll Taxes

The payroll register provides information about wages subject to payroll taxes. Figure 11.1 shows a portion of the payroll register for Sanchez Furniture Company for the week ending January 6.

Employers make tax deposits for federal income tax withheld from employee earnings, the employees' share of social security and Medicare taxes withheld from earnings, and the employer's share of social security and Medicare taxes. The deposits are made in a Federal Reserve Bank or other authorized financial institution. Businesses usually make payroll tax deposits at their own bank. There are two ways to deposit payroll taxes: by electronic deposit or with a tax deposit coupon.

The *Electronic Federal Tax Payment System (EFTPS)* is a system for electronically depositing employment taxes using a telephone or a computer. Any employer can use EFTPS. An employer *must* use EFTPS if the annual federal tax deposits are more than $200,000. Employers who are required to make electronic deposits and do not do so can be subject to a 10 percent penalty.

Employers who are not required to use EFTPS may deposit payroll taxes using a *Federal Tax Deposit Coupon, Form 8109.* The employer's name, tax identification number, and address are preprinted on Form 8109. The employer enters the deposit amount on the form and makes the payment with a check, money order, or cash.

FIGURE 11.1   Portion of a Payroll Register

AND ENDING	January 6, 2013						PAID	January 8, 2013				

TAXABLE WAGES			DEDUCTIONS				DISTRIBUTION			
SOCIAL SECURITY	MEDICARE	FUTA	SOCIAL SECURITY	MEDICARE	INCOME TAX	HEALTH INSURANCE	NET AMOUNT	CHECK NO.	OFFICE SALARIES	SHIPPING WAGES
400 00	400 00	400 00	24 80	5 80	19 00		350 40	1601		400 00
380 00	380 00	380 00	23 56	5 51	34 00		316 93	1602		380 00
427 50	427 50	427 50	26 51	6 20	23 00	40 00	331 79	1603		427 50
560 00	560 00	560 00	34 72	8 12	30 00	40 00	447 16	1604		560 00
480 00	480 00	480 00	29 76	6 96	49 00		394 28	1605	480 00	
2 247 50	2 247 50	2 247 50	139 35	32 59	155 00	80 00	1 840 56		480 00	1 767 50

In some cases, an employer may use Form 8109-B. *Form 8109-B* is a coupon that is *not* preprinted. Form 8109-B may be used if a new employer has been assigned an identification number but has not yet received a supply of Forms 8109, or an employer has not received a resupply of Forms 8109. Figure 11.2 shows the completed Form 8109-B for Sanchez Furniture Company.

The frequency of deposits depends on the amount of tax liability. The amount currently owed is compared to the tax liability threshold. For simplicity, this textbook uses $2,500 as the tax liability threshold.

The deposit schedules are not related to how often employees are paid. The deposit schedules are based on the amount currently owed and the amount reported in the lookback period. The *lookback period* is a four-quarter period ending on June 30 of the preceding year.

1. If the amount owed is less than $2,500, payment is due quarterly with the payroll tax return (Form 941).

   Example. An employer's tax liability is as follows:

January	$580
February	640
March	620
	$1,840

FIGURE 11.2   Federal Tax Deposit Coupon, Form 8109-B

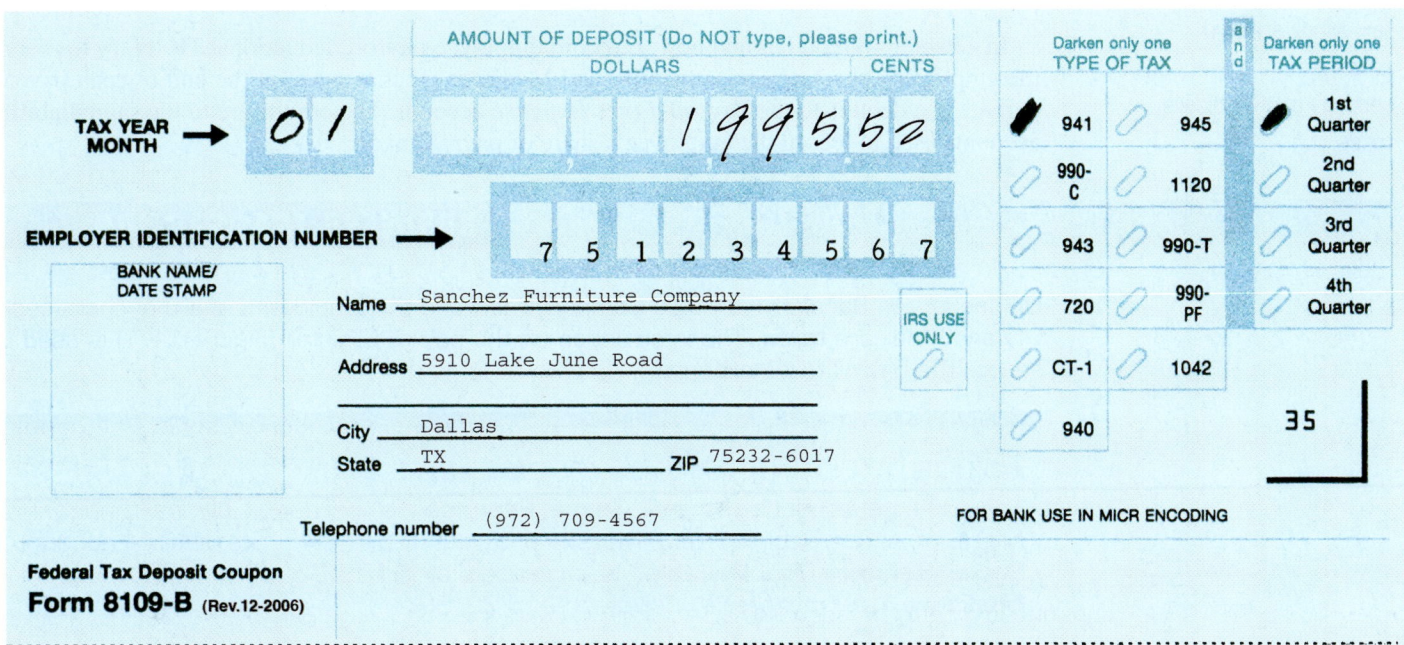

Federal Tax Deposit Coupon
Form 8109-B (Rev. 12-2006)

Since at no time during the quarter is the accumulated tax liability $2,500 or more, no deposit is required during the quarter. The employer may pay the amount with the payroll tax returns.

2. If the amount owed is $2,500 or more, the schedule is determined from the total taxes reported on Form 941 during the lookback period.

   a. If the amount reported in the lookback period was $50,000 or less, the employer is subject to the *Monthly Deposit Schedule Rule*. Monthly payments are due on the 15th day of the following month. For example, the January payment is due by February 15.

   b. If the amount reported in the lookback period was more than $50,000, the employer is subject to the *Semiweekly Deposit Schedule Rule*. "Semiweekly" refers to the fact that deposits are due on either Wednesdays or Fridays, depending on the employer's payday.

      • If payday is a Wednesday, Thursday, or Friday, the deposit is due on the following Wednesday.

      • If payday is a Saturday, Sunday, Monday, or Tuesday, the deposit is due on the following Friday.

   c. For new employers with no lookback period, if the amount owed is $2,500 or more, payments are due under the Monthly Deposit Schedule Rule.

3. If the total accumulated tax liability reaches $100,000 or more on any day, a deposit is due on the next banking day. This applies even if the employer is on a monthly or a semiweekly deposit schedule.

>>**2. OBJECTIVE**

Compute and record the employer's social security and Medicare taxes.

EMPLOYER'S SOCIAL SECURITY AND MEDICARE TAX EXPENSES

Remember that both employers and employees pay social security and Medicare taxes. Figure 11.1 shows the *employee's* share of these payroll taxes. The *employer* pays the same amount of payroll taxes. At the assumed rate of 6.2 percent for social security and 1.45 percent for Medicare tax, the employer's tax liability is $343.88.

important!

Tax Liability

The employer's tax liability is the amount owed for:

• employee withholdings (income tax, social security tax, Medicare tax);

• employer's share of social security and Medicare taxes.

	Employee (Withheld)	Employer (Matched)
Social security	$139.35	$139.35
Medicare	32.59	32.59
	$171.94	$171.94
Total	$343.88	

In Chapter 10, you learned how to record employee payroll deductions. The entry to record the employer's share of social security and Medicare taxes is made at the end of each payroll period. The debit is to the *Payroll Taxes Expense* account. The credits are to the same liability accounts used to record the employee's share of payroll taxes.

BUSINESS TRANSACTION

On January 8, Sanchez Furniture Company recorded the employer's share of social security and Medicare taxes. The information on the payroll register (Figure 11.1) is used to record the payroll taxes expense.

ANALYSIS

The expense account, **Payroll Taxes Expense**, is increased by the employer's share of social security and Medicare taxes, $171.94. The liability account, **Social Security Tax Payable**, is increased by $139.35. The liability account, **Medicare Tax Payable**, is increased by $32.59.

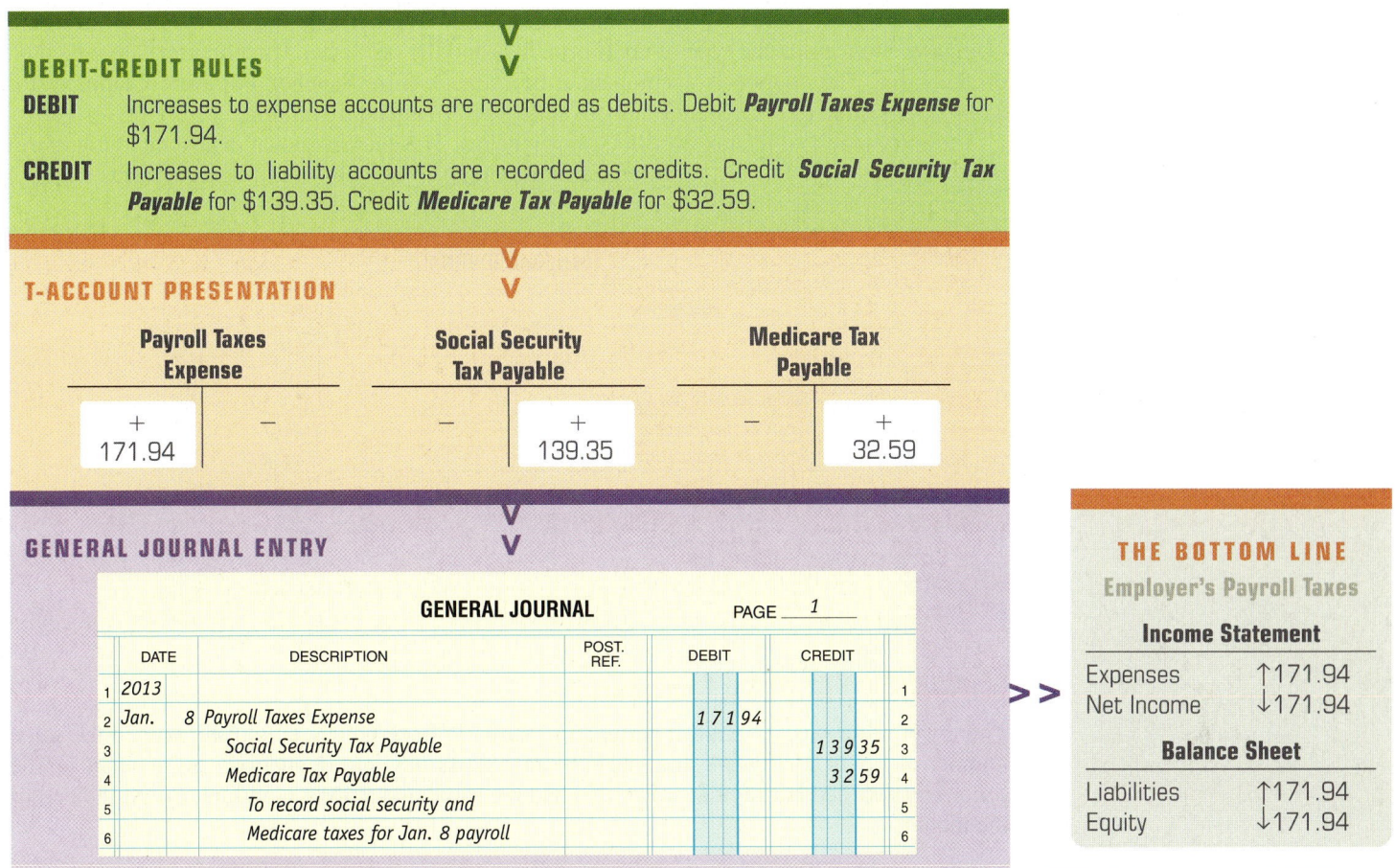

DEBIT-CREDIT RULES

DEBIT   Increases to expense accounts are recorded as debits. Debit *Payroll Taxes Expense* for $171.94.

CREDIT   Increases to liability accounts are recorded as credits. Credit *Social Security Tax Payable* for $139.35. Credit *Medicare Tax Payable* for $32.59.

T-ACCOUNT PRESENTATION

Payroll Taxes Expense		Social Security Tax Payable		Medicare Tax Payable	
+	−	−	+	−	+
171.94			139.35		32.59

GENERAL JOURNAL ENTRY

GENERAL JOURNAL   PAGE ___1___

	DATE	DESCRIPTION	POST. REF.	DEBIT	CREDIT	
1	2013					1
2	Jan. 8	Payroll Taxes Expense		171 94		2
3		Social Security Tax Payable			139 35	3
4		Medicare Tax Payable			32 59	4
5		To record social security and				5
6		Medicare taxes for Jan. 8 payroll				6

>>

THE BOTTOM LINE

Employer's Payroll Taxes

Income Statement

Expenses	↑171.94
Net Income	↓171.94

Balance Sheet

Liabilities	↑171.94
Equity	↓171.94

According to the American Payroll Association, the Social Security Administration provides benefits to approximately 44 million men, women, and children. It is essential that earnings are correctly reported so that future benefits can be calculated accurately.

RECORDING THE PAYMENT OF TAXES WITHHELD

>>**3. OBJECTIVE**

Record deposit of social security, Medicare, and employee income taxes.

At the end of January, the accounting records for Sanchez Furniture Company contained the following information:

	Employee (Withheld)	Employer (Matched)	Total
Social security	$ 557.40	$557.40	$1,114.80
Medicare	130.36	130.36	260.72
Federal income tax	620.00	—	620.00
Total	$1,307.76	$687.76	$1,995.52

Sanchez Furniture Company is on a monthly payment schedule. The amount reported in the lookback period is less than $50,000. The payroll tax liability for the quarter ending March 31, 2013, is more than $2,500. (Recall that this textbook uses $2,500 as the tax liability threshold.) A tax payment is due on the 15th day of the following month, February 15.

Figure 11.2 on page 337 shows the Federal Tax Deposit Coupon for Sanchez Furniture Company. Notice that the type of tax (Form 941) and the tax period (first quarter) are indicated on the form. The coupon is accompanied by a check from Sanchez Furniture Company for $1,995.52 written to First State Bank, an authorized financial institution.

The entry to record the tax deposit is shown below. The entry is shown in general journal form for illustration purposes only. (Sanchez Furniture Company actually uses a cash payments journal.)

	DATE		DESCRIPTION	POST. REF.	DEBIT	CREDIT	
1	2013						1
21							21
22	Feb.	15	Social Security Tax Payable		1 1 1 4 80		22
23			Medicare Tax Payable		2 6 0 72		23
24			Employee Income Tax Payable		6 2 0 00		24
25			Cash			1 9 9 5 52	25
26			Deposit of payroll taxes withholding				26
27			at First State Bank				27
28							28

GENERAL JOURNAL   PAGE **2**

FEBRUARY PAYROLL RECORDS

There were four weekly payroll periods in February. Each hourly employee worked the same number of hours each week and had the same gross pay and deductions as in January. The office clerk earned her regular salary and had the same deductions as in January. At the end of the month:

- the individual earnings records were updated;
- Form 8109, Federal Tax Deposit Coupon, was prepared, and the taxes were deposited before March 15;
- the tax deposit was recorded in the cash payments journal.

MARCH PAYROLL RECORDS

There were five weekly payroll periods in March. Assume that the payroll period ended on March 31, and the payday was on March 31. Also assume that the earnings and deductions of the employees were the same for each week as in January and February. At the end of the month, the individual earnings records were updated, the taxes were deposited, and the tax deposit was recorded in the cash payments journal.

QUARTERLY SUMMARY OF EARNINGS RECORDS

At the end of each quarter, the individual earnings records are totaled. This involves adding the columns in the Earnings, Deductions, and Net Pay sections. Figure 11.3 shows the earnings record, posted and summarized, for Alicia Martinez for the first quarter.

Table 11.1 shows the quarterly totals for each employee of Sanchez Furniture Company. This information is taken from the individual earnings records. Through the end of the first quarter, no employee has exceeded the social security earnings limit ($106,800) and the FUTA/SUTA limit ($7,000) has only been exceeded by Cecilia Wu.

>>**4. OBJECTIVE**

Prepare an Employer's Quarterly Federal Tax Return, Form 941.

EMPLOYER'S QUARTERLY FEDERAL TAX RETURN

Each quarter an employer files an **Employer's Quarterly Federal Tax Return, Form 941** with the Internal Revenue Service. Form 941 must be filed by all employers subject to federal income tax withholding, social security tax, or Medicare tax, with certain exceptions as specified in *Publication 15, Circular E*. This tax return provides information about employee earnings, the tax liability for each month in the quarter, and the deposits made.

FIGURE 11.3   Individual Earnings Record

EARNINGS RECORD FOR _2013_

NAME _Alicia Martinez_   **RATE** _$10 per hour_   **SOCIAL SECURITY NO.** _123-45-6789_

ADDRESS _1712 Windmill Hill Lane, Dallas TX 75232-6002_   **DATE OF BIRTH** _October 31, 1979_

WITHHOLDING ALLOWANCES _1_   **MARITAL STATUS** _M_

PAYROLL NO.	DATE WK. END.	DATE PAID	RG	OT	REGULAR	OVERTIME	TOTAL	CUMULATIVE	SOCIAL SECURITY	MEDICARE	INCOME TAX	OTHER	NET PAY
1	1/06	1/08	40		400 00		400 00	400 00	24 80	5 80	19 00		350 40
2	1/13	1/15	40		400 00		400 00	400 00	24 80	5 80	19 00		350 40
3	1/20	1/22	40		400 00		400 00	400 00	24 80	5 80	19 00		350 40
4	1/27	1/29	40		400 00		400 00	400 00	24 80	5 80	19 00		350 40
	January				1600 00		1600 00	1600 00	99 20	23 20	76 00		1401 60
1	2/03	2/05	40		400 00		400 00	400 00	24 80	5 80	19 00		350 40
2	2/10	2/12	40		400 00		400 00	400 00	24 80	5 80	19 00		350 40
3	2/17	2/19	40		400 00		400 00	400 00	24 80	5 80	19 00		350 40
4	2/24	2/25	40		400 00		400 00	400 00	24 80	5 80	19 00		350 40
	February				1600 00		1600 00	1600 00	99 20	23 20	76 00		1401 60
1	3/03	3/05	40		400 00		400 00	400 00	24 80	5 80	19 00		350 40
2	3/10	3/12	40		400 00		400 00	400 00	24 80	5 80	19 00		350 40
3	3/17	3/19	40		400 00		400 00	400 00	24 80	5 80	19 00		350 40
4	3/24	3/26	40		400 00		400 00	400 00	24 80	5 80	19 00		350 40
5	3/31	3/31	40		400 00		400 00	400 00	24 80	5 80	19 00		350 40
	March				2000 00		2000 00	2000 00	124 00	29 00	95 00		1752 00
					5200 00		5200 00	5200 00	322 40	75 40	247 00		4555 20
	First Quarter												

The Social Security Administration administers the Old Age and Survivors, Disability Insurance, and Supplemental Security Income Programs. These programs are funded by the social security taxes collected from employees and matched by employers. The system currently takes in more in revenue from the 12.4 percent payroll taxes than it pays out in benefits. The trust fund is expected to begin paying out more in benefits than it collects in 2016.

TABLE 11.1

Summary of Earnings, Quarter Ended March 31, 2013

| | Taxable Earnings | | | | Deductions | | |
Employee	Total Earnings	Social Security	Medicare	SUTA & FUTA	Social Security	Medicare Tax	Income Tax
Alicia Martinez	5,200.00	5,200.00	5,200.00	5,200.00	322.40	75.40	247.00
Jorge Rodriguez	4,940.00	4,940.00	4,940.00	4,940.00	306.28	71.63	442.00
George Dunlap	5,557.50	5,557.50	5,557.50	5,557.50	344.57	80.58	299.00
Cecilia Wu	7,280.00	7,280.00	7,280.00	7,000.00	451.36	105.56	390.00
Cynthia Booker	6,240.00	6,240.00	6,240.00	6,240.00	386.88	90.48	637.00
Totals	29,217.50	29,217.50	29,217.50	28,937.50	1,811.49	423.65	2,015.00

When to File Form 941   The due date for Form 941 is the last day of the month following the end of each calendar quarter. If the taxes for the quarter were deposited when due, the due date is extended by 10 days.

Completing Form 941   Figure 11.4 on pages 343 and 344 shows Form 941 for Sanchez Furniture Company. Form 941 is prepared using the data on the quarterly summary of earnings records, Table 11.1 on page 341. Let's examine Form 941.

- Use the preprinted form if it is available. Otherwise, enter the employer's name, address, and identification number at the top of Form 941. Check the applicable quarter.
- *Line 1* is completed for each quarter. Enter the number of employees for the pay periods indicated.
- *Line 2* shows total wages and tips subject to withholding. For Sanchez Furniture Company the total subject to withholdings is $29,217.50.
- *Line 3* shows the total employee income tax withheld during the quarter, $2,015.00.
- *Line 4* is checked if no wages or tips are subject to social security or Medicare tax.
- *Line 5a* shows the total amount of wages that are subject to social security taxes, $29,217.50. The amount is multiplied by the combined social security rate, 12.4 percent.

Social Security Tax:	
Employee's share	6.2%
Employer's share	6.2
Total	12.4%

The amount of taxes is $3,622.97 ($29,217.50 × 12.4%).

- *Line 5b* is left blank since no employees at Sanchez Furniture Company had taxable social security tips.
- *Line 5c* shows the total amount of wages that are subject to Medicare taxes, $29,217.50. The amount is multiplied by the combined Medicare tax rate, 2.9 percent.

Medicare Tax:	
Employee's share	1.45%
Employer's share	1.45
Total	2.90%

The amount of taxes is $847.31 ($29,217.50 × 2.90%).

- *Line 5d* shows the total social security and Medicare taxes, $4,470.28.
- *Line 6* shows the total tax liability for withheld income taxes, social security, and Medicare Taxes, $6,485.28.
- *Lines 7a* through *7h* are for adjustments. Sanchez Furniture Company had no adjustments this quarter. If there is a difference due to rounding that difference can be adjusted on line 7a.
- *Line 8* shows total taxes after adjustments, $6,485.28.
- *Line 9* is for deducting the amount of any advance earned income credit payments to employees. Sanchez Furniture Company had no advance payments for earned income credit payments to employees.
- *Line 10* shows total taxes after adjustments, $6,485.28.
- *Line 11* shows total deposits made during the quarter including overpayments applied from a prior quarter, $6,485.28.
- Any balance due is entered on *Line 12* or overpayment is entered on *Line 13*.
- The state where deposits were made is entered on *Line 14*.
- *Line 15* shows the monthly deposits made by Sanchez Furniture Company.

FIGURE 11.4   Employer's Quarterly Federal Tax Return, Form 941

Form **941 for 2013:** Employer's Quarterly Federal Tax Return   9901

(Rev. January 2007)   Department of the Treasury — Internal Revenue Service

OMB No. 1545-0029

Employer identification number   7 5 — 1 2 3 4 5 6 7

Name (not your trade name)   Sarah Sanchez

Trade name (if any)   Sanchez Furniture Company

Address   5910 Lake June Road

Number   Street   Suite or room number

Dallas   TX   75232-6017

City   State   ZIP code

Report for this Quarter ...
(Check one.)

☑ **1:** January, February, March

☐ **2:** April, May, June

☐ **3:** July, August, September

☐ **4:** October, November, December

Read the separate instructions before you fill out this form. Please type or print within the boxes.

Part 1: Answer these questions for this quarter.

1 Number of employees who received wages, tips, or other compensation for the pay period
   including: *Mar. 12* (Quarter 1), *June 12* (Quarter 2), *Sept. 12* (Quarter 3), *Dec. 12* (Quarter 4)   **1**   5

2 Wages, tips, and other compensation . . . .   **2**   29,217 . 50

3 Total income tax withheld from wages, tips, and other compensation . . . .   **3**   2,015 . 00

4 If no wages, tips, and other compensation are subject to social security or Medicare tax .   . ☐ Check and go to line 6.

5 Taxable social security and Medicare wages and tips:

	Column 1		Column 2	
5a Taxable social security wages	29,217 . 50	× .124 =	3,622 . 97	
5b Taxable social security tips	.	× .124 =	.	
5c Taxable Medicare wages & tips	29,217 . 50	× .029 =	847 . 31	

5d Total social security and Medicare taxes (*Column 2,* lines 5a + 5b + 5c = line 5d) . .   **5d**   4,470 . 28

6 Total taxes before adjustments (lines 3 + 5d = line 6) . . . .   **6**   6,485 . 28

7 Tax adjustments (If your answer is a negative number, write it in brackets.):

7a Current quarter's fractions of cents . . . .

7b Current quarter's sick pay . . . .

7c Current quarter's adjustments for tips and group-term life insurance   .

7d Current year's income tax withholding (Attach Form 941c) . . .   .

7e Prior quarters' social security and Medicare taxes (Attach Form 941c)   .

7f Special additions to federal income tax (reserved use) . . . . .   .

7g Special additions to social security and Medicare (reserved use)   .

7h Total adjustments (Combine all amounts: lines 7a through 7g.) . . . .   **7h**   .

8 Total taxes after adjustments (Combine lines 6 and 7h.) . . . .   **8**   6,485 . 28

9 Advance earned income credit (EIC) payments made to employees . . . .   **9**   .

10 Total taxes after adjustment for advance EIC (lines 8 – 9 = line 10) . . . .   **10**   6,485 . 28

11 Total deposits for this quarter, including overpayment applied from a prior quarter . . . .   **11**   6,485 . 28

12 Balance due (lines 10 – 11 = line 12) Make checks payable to the *United States Treasury* . .   **12**   0 .

13 Overpayment (If line 11 is more than line 10, write the difference here.)   .   Check one ☐ Apply to next return.
    ☐ Send a refund.

Next ➡

For Privacy Act and Paperwork Reduction Act Notice, see the back of the Payment Voucher.   Cat. No. 17001Z   Form **941**

FIGURE 11.4 (concluded)

9902

Name (not your trade name)	Employer identification number
Sarah Sanchez	**75-1234567**

Part 2: Tell us about your deposit schedule for this quarter.

If you are unsure about whether you are a monthly schedule depositor or a semiweekly schedule depositor, see *Pub. 15 (Circular E)*, section 11.

14 **T** **X** Write the state abbreviation for the state where you made your deposits OR write "MU" if you made your deposits in *multiple* states.

15 Check one: ☐ Line 10 is less than $2,500. Go to Part 3.

☑ You were a monthly schedule depositor for the entire quarter. Fill out your tax liability for each month. Then go to Part 3.

Tax liability:	Month 1	1,995 . 52
	Month 2	1,995 . 52
	Month 3	2,494 . 24
	Total	6,485 . 28	Total must equal line 10.

☐ You were a semiweekly schedule depositor for any part of this quarter. Fill out *Schedule B (Form 941): Report of Tax Liability for Semiweekly Schedule Depositors*, and attach it to this form.

Part 3: Tell us about your business. If a question does NOT apply to your business, leave it blank.

16 If your business has closed and you do not have to file returns in the future . . . . ☐ Check here, and

enter the final date you paid wages [/ /] .

17 If you are a seasonal employer and you do not have to file a return for every quarter of the year . . ☐ Check here.

Part 4: May we contact your third-party designee?

Do you want to allow an employee, a paid tax preparer, or another person to discuss this return with the IRS? See the instructions for details.

☐ Yes. Designee's name [   ]

Phone ( ) – Personal Identification Number (PIN) [ ][ ][ ][ ][ ]

☑ No.

Part 5: Sign here

Under penalties of perjury, I declare that I have examined this return, including accompanying schedules and statements, and to the best of my knowledge and belief, it is true, correct, and complete.

X Sign your name here *Sarah Sanchez*

Print name and title **Sarah Sanchez, Owner**

Date 04 / 30 / 13 Phone (972) 709 – 4567

Part 6: For paid preparers only (optional)

Preparer's signature	
Firm's name	
Address		EIN	
		ZIP code	
Date / / Phone ( ) –	SSN/PTIN	

☐ Check if you are self-employed.

Notice that on Line 15 if the amount of taxes is less than $2,500, the amount may be paid with the return or with a financial depositor. There is no need to complete the record of monthly deposits. Since the amount of taxes due for Sanchez Furniture Company is greater than $2,500, and Sanchez is a monthly depositor, the record of monthly tax deposits must be completed on Line 15. The total deposits shown on Line 15 must equal the taxes shown on Line 10.

If the employer did not make sufficient deposits, a check for the balance due is mailed to the Internal Revenue Service with Form 941. An employer may instead make a deposit at an authorized financial institution.

If the employer did not deduct enough taxes from an employee's earnings, the business pays the difference. The deficiency is debited to *Payroll Taxes Expense.*

Wage and Tax Statement, Form W-2

Employers provide a **Wage and Tax Statement, Form W-2,** to each employee by January 31 of the following year. Form W-2 is sometimes called a **withholding statement.** Form W-2 contains information about the employee's earnings and tax withholdings for the year. The information for Form W-2 comes from the employee's earnings record.

Employees who stop working for the business during the year may ask that a Form W-2 be issued early. The Form W-2 must be issued within 30 days after the request or after the final wage payment, whichever is later.

Figure 11.5 on page 346 shows Form W-2 for Alicia Martinez. This is the standard form provided by the Internal Revenue Service (IRS). Some employers use a "substitute" Form W-2 that is approved by the IRS. The substitute form permits the employer to list total deductions and to reconcile the gross earnings, the deductions, and the net pay. If the firm issues 250 or more Forms W-2, the returns must be filed electronically.

At least four copies of each of Form W-2 are prepared:

1. One copy for the employer to send to the Social Security Administration, which shares the information with the IRS.

2. One copy for the employee to attach to the federal income tax return.

3. One copy for the employee's records.

4. One copy for the employer's records.

If there is a state income tax, two more copies of Form W-2 are prepared:

5. One copy for the employer to send to the state tax department.

6. One copy for the employee to attach to the state income tax return.

Additional copies are prepared if there is a city or county income tax.

Annual Transmittal of Wage and Tax Statements, Form W-3

The **Transmittal of Wage and Tax Statements, Form W-3,** is submitted with Forms W-2 to the Social Security Administration. Form W-3 reports the total social security wages; total Medicare wages; total social security tax withheld; total Medicare tax withheld; total wages, tips, and other compensation; total federal income tax withheld; and other information.

A copy of Form W-2 for each employee is attached to Form W-3. Form W-3 is due by the last day of February following the end of the calendar year. The Social Security Administration shares the tax information on Forms W-2 with the Internal Revenue Service. Figure 11.6 on page 347 shows the completed Form W-3 for Sanchez Furniture Company.

>>**5. OBJECTIVE**

Prepare Wage and Tax Statement (Form W-2) and Annual Transmittal of Wage and Tax Statements (Form W-3).

important!

Form W-2

The employer must provide each employee with a Wage and Tax Statement, Form W-2, by January 31 of the following year.

ABOUT
ACCOUNTING

IRS Electronic Filing
More than 19 million taxpayers have filed their tax returns electronically. Returns that are filed electronically are more accurate than paper returns. Electronic filing means refunds in half the time, especially if the taxpayer chooses direct deposit of the refund.

FIGURE 11.5   Wage and Tax Statement, Form W-2

The amounts on Form W-3 must equal the sums of the amounts on the attached Forms W-2. For example, the amount entered in Box 1 of Form W-3 must equal the sum of the amounts entered in Box 1 of all the Forms W-2.

The amounts on Form W-3 also must equal the sums of the amounts reported on the Forms 941 during the year. For example, the social security wages reported on the Form W-3 must equal the sum of the social security wages reported on the four Forms 941.

The filing of Form W-3 marks the end of the routine procedures needed to account for payrolls and for payroll tax withholdings.

FIGURE 11.6

Transmittal of Wage and Tax Statements, Form W-3

a Control number 33333	For Official Use Only ▶ OMB No. 1545-0008		
b Kind of Payer ▶ 941 [X] Military ☐ 943 ☐ CT-1 ☐ Hshld. emp. ☐ Medicare govt. emp. ☐ Third-party sick pay ☐	1 Wages, tips, other compensation 116,870.00	2 Federal income tax withheld 8,060.00	
	3 Social security wages 116,870.00	4 Social security tax withheld 7,245.96	
c Total number of Forms W-2 5	d Establishment number	5 Medicare wages and tips 116,870.00	6 Medicare tax withheld 1,694.60
e Employer identification number 75-1234567		7 Social security tips	8 Allocated tips
f Employer's name Sanchez Furniture Co.		9 Advance EIC payments	10 Dependent care benefits
		11 Nonqualified plans	12 Deferred compensation
5910 Lake June Road Dallas, TX 75232-6017		13 For third-party sick pay use only	
		14 Income tax withheld by third-party sick pay	
g Employer's address and ZIP code			
h Other EIN used this year			
15 State TX	Employer's state I.D. no. 12-9876500	16 State wages, tips, etc.	17 State income tax
		18 Local wages, tips, etc.	19 Local income tax
Contact person Sarah Sanchez		Telephone number (972) 709-4567	For Official Use Only
E-mail address Sanchez@aol.net		Fax number ( )	

Under penalties of perjury, I declare that I have examined this return and accompanying documents, and, to the best of my knowledge and belief, they are true, correct, and complete.

Signature ▶ *Sarah Sanchez*   Title ▶ *Owner*   Date ▶ *February 10, 2014*

Form **W-3** Transmittal of Wage and Tax Statements   **2013**   Department of the Treasury Internal Revenue Service

---

Section 1   Self Review

QUESTIONS

1. What is the purpose of Form W-2?
2. Where does a business deposit federal payroll taxes?
3. What is the purpose of Form 941?

EXERCISES

4. Which tax is shared equally by the employee and employer?
   a. Federal income tax
   b. State income tax
   c. Social security tax
   d. Federal unemployment tax

5. Employers usually record social security taxes in the accounting records at the end of:
   a. each payroll period.
   b. each month.
   c. each quarter.
   d. the year.

ANALYSIS

6. Your business currently owes $2,910 in payroll taxes. During the lookback period, your business paid $10,000 in payroll taxes. How often does your business need to make payroll tax deposits?

(Answers to Section 1 Self Review are on page 370.)

SECTION OBJECTIVES

>> 6. Compute and record liability for federal and state unemployment taxes and record payment of the taxes.

WHY IT'S IMPORTANT

Businesses need to record all payroll tax liabilities.

>> 7. Prepare an Employer's Federal Unemployment Tax Return, Form 940.

WHY IT'S IMPORTANT

The unemployment insurance programs provide support to individuals during temporary periods of unemployment.

>> 8. Compute and record workers' compensation insurance premiums.

WHY IT'S IMPORTANT

Businesses need insurance to cover workplace injury claims.

TERMS TO LEARN

Employer's Annual Federal Unemployment Tax Return, Form 940

experience rating system

merit rating system

unemployment insurance program

Unemployment Tax and Workers' Compensation

In Section 1, we discussed taxes that are withheld from employees' earnings and, in some cases, matched by the employer. In this section, we will discuss payroll related expenses that are paid solely by the employer.

Unemployment Compensation Insurance Taxes

The unemployment compensation tax program, often called the **unemployment insurance program,** provides unemployment compensation through a tax levied on employers.

COORDINATION OF FEDERAL AND STATE UNEMPLOYMENT RATES

The unemployment insurance program is a federal program that encourages states to provide unemployment insurance for employees working in the state. The federal government allows a credit—or reduction—in the federal unemployment tax for amounts charged by the state for unemployment taxes.

This text assumes that the federal unemployment tax rate is 6.2 percent less a state unemployment tax credit of 5.4 percent; thus, the federal tax rate is reduced to 0.8 percent (6.2% − 5.4%). The earnings limits for the federal and the state unemployment tax are usually the same, $7,000.

A few states levy an unemployment tax on the employee. The tax is withheld from employee pay and remitted by the employer to the state.

For businesses that provide steady employment, the state unemployment tax rate may be lowered based on an **experience rating system,** or a **merit rating system.** Under the experience rating system, the state tax rate may be reduced to less than 1 percent for businesses that provide steady employment. In contrast, some states levy penalty rates as high as 10 percent for employers with poor records of providing steady employment.

The reduction of state unemployment taxes because of favorable experience ratings does not affect the credit allowable against the federal tax. An employer may take a credit against the federal unemployment tax as though it were paid at the normal state rate even though the employer actually pays the state a lower rate.

Because of its experience rating, Sanchez Furniture Company pays state unemployment tax of 4.0 percent, which is less than the standard rate of 5.4 percent. Note that the business may take the credit for the full amount of the state rate (5.4%) against the federal rate, even though the business actually pays a state rate of 4.0%.

COMPUTING AND RECORDING UNEMPLOYMENT TAXES

Sanchez Furniture Company records its state and federal unemployment tax expense at the end of each payroll period. The unemployment taxes for the payroll period ending January 6 are as follows:

Federal unemployment tax	($2,247.50 × 0.008)	=	$ 17.98
State unemployment tax	($2,247.50 × 0.040)	=	89.90
Total unemployment taxes		=	$107.88

>>**6. OBJECTIVE**
Compute and record liability for federal and state unemployment taxes and record payment of the taxes.

The entry to record the employer's unemployment payroll taxes follows.

	DATE		DESCRIPTION	POST. REF.	DEBIT	CREDIT	
GENERAL JOURNAL					PAGE 1		
1	2013						1
8	Jan.	8	Payroll Taxes Expense		107 88		8
9			Federal Unemployment Tax Payable			17 98	9
10			State Unemployment Tax Payable			89 90	10
11			Unemployment taxes on				11
12			weekly payroll				12

REPORTING AND PAYING STATE UNEMPLOYMENT TAXES

In most states, the due date for the unemployment tax return is the last day of the month following the end of the quarter. Generally, the tax is paid with the return.

Employer's Quarterly Report Figure 11.7 on the next page shows the Employer's Quarterly Report for the State of Texas filed by Sanchez Furniture Company in April for the first quarter. The report for Texas is similar to the tax forms of other states. The top of the form contains information about the company.

■ *Block 4* at the top of the form shows the tax rate assigned by the state based on the experience rating. The tax rate for Sanchez Furniture Company is 4.0 percent.

■ *Block 10* (3 boxes) shows the number of employees in the state on the 12th day of each month of the quarter.

■ *Line 13* shows the total wages paid during the quarter to employees in the state, $29,217.50.

■ *Line 14* shows the total *taxable* wages paid during the quarter, $28,937.50. Note that the limit on taxable wages is $7,000. Table 11.1 on page 341 shows that at the end of the first quarter, one employee, Cecilia Wu, earned more than $7,000. All other wages and salaries are taxable for state unemployment. Actually, the base in Texas is $9,000. We use a base of $7,000 for the sake of simplicity.

■ *Line 15* shows the total tax for the quarter. Taxable wages are multiplied by the tax rate ($28,937.50 × 0.04 = $1,157.50).

■ *Lines 16a* and *b* are a breakdown of the amount on Line 15. In Texas, part of the 4 percent tax is set aside for job training and other incentive programs. Box 4a contains the tax rate for the unemployment tax (3.9%). Box 4b contains the tax rate for training incentives or *Smart Jobs Assessment* (0.1%).

■ *Lines 17* and *18* are blank. There are no penalties or interest because no taxes or reports are past due.

■ *Line 19* is blank. There is no balance due from prior periods.

■ *Line 20* shows the tax due.

FIGURE 11.7   Employer's Quarterly Report Form for State Unemployment Taxes

TEXAS WORKFORCE COMMISSION AUSTIN, TEXAS 78714-9037 (512)-463-2222	**EMPLOYER'S QUARTERLY REPORT**				**11111**

1. ACCOUNT NUMBER	2. COUNTY CODE	3. TAX AREA	4. TAX RATE	5. SIC CODE	6. FEDERAL I.D. NUMBER	7. QTR. YR.
12-9876500	121	2	4.0 %	59	75-1234567	1st/2013

8. EMPLOYER NAME AND ADDRESS (SEE ITEM 25 FOR CHANGES TO NAME, ADDRESS, ETC.)

9. TELEPHONE NUMBER

(972) 709-4567

Sarah Sanchez

Sanchez Furniture Company

5910 Lake June Road

Dallas, TX 75232-6017

4a. UI TAX RATE	4b. SMART JOBS ASSESSMENT
3.9 %	.1 %

ALIGNMENT   9A. QUARTER ENDING

1st Month	2nd Month	3rd Month
5	5	5

9B. PENALTIES WILL BE ASSESSED IF REPORT IS NOT POSTMARKED BY

10. Enter in the boxes above the number of employees both full-time and part-time, in pay periods that include 12th day of the calendar month. (ENTER NUMERALS ONLY)

11. SHOW THE COUNTY CODE (see list on the back of this form) in which you had the greatest number of employees. **121**

12. IF you have employees in more than one county in TEXAS, how many are outside the county shown in Item 11?

	DOLLARS	CENTS
13. Total (Gross) Wages Paid During this Quarter to Texas Employees	29,217	50
14. Taxable Wages paid this quarter to each employee up to $7000, the annual maximum amount. **(If none, enter "0")**	28,937	50
15. Tax Due (Multiply Taxable Wages By Tax Rate, Item 4 Above)	1,157	50
16a. UI TAX 1128 56 b. Smart Jobs Assessment 28 94		
17. Interest, If Tax is Past Due		
18. Penalty, If Report Is Past Due		
19. Balance Due From Prior Periods (Subtract Credit Or Add Debit)		
20. Total Due - Make Remittance Payable To TEXAS WORKFORCE COMMISSION	1,157	50

You must FILE this return even though you had no payroll this quarter. If you had no payroll show '0' in item 13 and sign the declaration (Item 26) on this form.

14a. Mark box with an 'X' if reporting wages to another state during the year for employees listed in Item 22.

FOR TWC USE ONLY

	MONTH	DAY	YEAR
POSTMARK DATE C3			
POSTMARK DATE S			
EX DATE C3			
EX DATE S			

Est

DOLLARS	CENTS	INITIALS

AMOUNT RECEIVED

	21. SOCIAL SECURITY NUMBER	1ST INIT	2ND INIT	22. EMPLOYEE NAME LAST NAME	23. TOTAL WAGES PAID THIS QUARTER
1	587-XX-XXXX			C. Booker	6,240 00
2	427-XX-XXXX			G. Dunlap	5,557 50
3	687-XX-XXXX			A. Martinez	5,200 00
4	123-XX-XXXX			J. Rodriguez	4,940 00
5	587-XX-XXXX			C. Wu	7,280 00
6					
7					
8					
9					
10					

26. I DECLARE that the information herein is true and correct to the best of my knowledge and belief.

SIGNATURE   *Sarah Sanchez*

TITLE   Owner   DATE   4/29/2013

PREPARERS NAME   Sarah Sanchez

PREPARERS PHONE NUMBER   (972) 709-4567

For assistance in completing form call,

24. PAGE TOTAL	29,217 50

MAIL REPORT AND REMITTANCE TO:
CASHIER
TEXAS WORKFORCE COMMISSION
P.O. BOX 149037
AUSTIN, TEXAS 78714-9037
DO NOT STAPLE REPORT
(Write Account No. On Check)

FORM C - 3 (6/99)
SCANC3

25. MAKE CHANGES TO EMPLOYER INFORMATION USING C-3 **INSTRUCTION SHEET.** CHANGES NOTED ON THIS FORM MAY NOT BE CAPTURED DURING PROCESSING.

Sanchez Furniture Company submits the report and issues a check payable to the state tax authority for the amount shown on Line 20. The entry is recorded in the cash payments journal. The transaction is shown here in general journal form for purposes of illustration:

GENERAL JOURNAL   PAGE _____

	DATE	DESCRIPTION	POST. REF.	DEBIT	CREDIT	
1	2013					1
2	Apr. 29	State Unemployment Tax Payable		1 1 5 7 50		2
3		Cash			1 1 5 7 50	3
4		Paid SUTA taxes for quarter				4
5		ending March 31				5
6						6

Earnings in Excess of Base Amount State unemployment tax is paid on the first $7,000 of annual earnings for each employee. Earnings over $7,000 are not subject to state unemployment tax.

For example, Cecilia Wu earns $560 every week of the year. Table 11.1 on page 341 shows that she earned $7,280 at the end of the first quarter. In the four weeks of January, February, and March, she earned $2,240 ($560 × 4).

	Earnings	Cumulative Earnings
January	$2,240	$2,240
February	2,240	4,480
March	2,240	6,720
March, week 5	560	7,280

In the fifth week of March, Wu earned $560, but only $280 of it is subject to state unemployment tax ($7,000 earnings limit − $6,720 cumulative earnings = $280). For the rest of the calendar year, Wu's earnings are not subject to state unemployment tax.

REPORTING AND PAYING FEDERAL UNEMPLOYMENT TAXES

The rules for reporting and depositing federal unemployment taxes differ from those used for social security and Medicare taxes.

Depositing Federal Unemployment Taxes There are two ways to make federal unemployment tax deposits: with electronic deposits using EFTPS or with a Federal Tax Deposit Coupon, Form 8109, at an authorized financial institution. Deposits are made quarterly and are due on the last day of the month following the end of the quarter.

The federal unemployment tax is calculated at the end of each quarter. It is computed by multiplying the first $7,000 of each employee's wages by 0.008. A deposit is required when more than $500 of federal unemployment tax is owed. If $500 or less is owed, no deposit is due.

For example, suppose that a business calculates its federal unemployment tax to be $325 at the end of the first quarter. Since it is not more than $500, no deposit is due. At the end of the second quarter, it calculates its federal unemployment taxes on second quarter wages to be $200. The total undeposited unemployment tax now is more than $500, so a deposit is required.

First quarter undeposited tax	$325
Second quarter undeposited tax	200
Total deposit due	$525

In the case of Sanchez Furniture Company, the company owed $231.50 in federal unemployment tax at the end of March. Since this is less than $500, no deposit is due.

Month	Taxable Earnings Paid	Rate	Tax Due	Deposit Due Date
January	$ 8,990.00	0.008	$ 71.92	April 30
February	8,990.00	0.008	71.92	April 30
March	10,957.50	0.008	87.66	April 30
Total	$28,937.50		$231.50	

The payment of federal unemployment tax is recorded by debiting the Federal Unemployment Tax Payable account and crediting the Cash account.

>>7. OBJECTIVE

Prepare an Employer's Federal Unemployment Tax Return, Form 940.

Reporting Federal Unemployment Tax, Form 940 Tax returns are not due quarterly for the federal unemployment tax. The employer submits an annual return. The **Employer's Annual Federal Unemployment Tax Return, Form 940,** is a preprinted government form used to report unemployment taxes for the calendar year. It is due by January 31 of the following year. The due date is extended to February 10 if all tax deposits were made on time.

The information needed to complete Form 940 comes from the annual summary of individual earnings records and from the state unemployment tax returns filed during the year.

Figure 11.8 shows Form 940 prepared for Sanchez Furniture Company. Refer to it as you learn how to complete Form 940.

PART 1: Asks the filer if he or she was required to pay SUTA tax in more than one state.

PART 2: Determine your FUTA tax before adjustments

- *Line 3* shows the total compensation paid to employees, $116,870.00.
- *Line 4* is blank because there were no exempt payments for Sanchez Furniture Company.
- *Line 5* shows the compensation that exceeds the $7,000 earnings limit, $81,870 ($116,870 − $35,000).
- *Line 6* shows the wages not subject to federal unemployment tax, $81,870.
- *Line 7* shows the taxable wages for the year, $35,000. This amount must agree with the total taxable FUTA wages shown on the individual employee earnings records for the year.
- *Line 8* shows the FUTA tax, $280 ($35,000 × 0.008).

PART 3: Determine your adjustments.

- *Lines 9, 10, and 11* are blank because Sanchez Furniture Company had no adjustments.

PART 4: Determine your FUTA tax and balance due or over payment.

- *Line 12* shows the total FUTA tax, after adjustments, $280.
- *Line 13* shows the FUTA tax deposited during the year, $0.
- *Line 14* shows the balance due.
- *Line 15* is blank because there is no overpayment.

PART 5: Report your FUTA tax liability by quarter. This section is not applicable to Sanchez Furniture Company, because its total FUTA liability is less than $500.

>>8. OBJECTIVE

Compute and record workers' compensation insurance premiums.

WORKERS' COMPENSATION INSURANCE

Workers' compensation provides benefits for employees who are injured on the job. The insurance premium, which is paid by the employer, depends on the risk involved with the work performed. It is important to classify earnings according to the type of work the employees perform and to summarize labor costs according to the insurance premium classifications.

FIGURE 11.8   Employer's Annual Federal Unemployment Tax Return, Form 940

Form **940 for 2013:** **Employer's Annual Federal Unemployment (FUTA) Tax Return**   850109

Department of the Treasury — Internal Revenue Service

OMB No. 1545-0028

(EIN)
Employer identification number   7 5 – 1 2 3 4 5 6 7

Name *(not your trade name)*   **Sarah Sanchez**

Trade name *(if any)*   **Sanchez Furniture Company**

Address   **5910 June Lake Road**
Number   Street   Suite or room number
Dallas   **TX**   **75322-6017**
City   State   ZIP code

Type of Return
(Check all that apply.)

- [ ] **a.** Amended
- [ ] **b.** Successor employer
- [ ] **c.** No payments to employees in 2009
- [ ] **d.** Final: Business closed or stopped paying wages

Read the separate instructions before you fill out this form. Please type or print within the boxes.

Part 1: Tell us about your return. If any line does NOT apply, leave it blank.

1 If you were required to pay your state unemployment tax in ...

1a **One state only,** write the state abbreviation . . . . **1a** | T | X |
  - OR -
1b **More than one state** (You are a multi-state employer) . . . . **1b** [ ] Check here. Fill out Schedule A.

2 If you paid wages in a state that is subject to **CREDIT REDUCTION** . . . . . **2** [ ] Check here. Fill out Schedule A (Form 940), Part 2.

Part 2: Determine your FUTA tax before adjustments for 2013. If any line does NOT apply, leave it blank.

3 Total payments to all employees . . . . **3**   116870 . 00

4 Payments exempt from FUTA tax . . . . **4**   .

Check all that apply: **4a** [ ] Fringe benefits **4c** [ ] Retirement/Pension **4e** [ ] Other
  4b [ ] Group-term life insurance **4d** [ ] Dependent care

5 Total of payments made to each employee in excess of $7,000 . . . . **5**   81870 . 00

6 Subtotal (line 4 + line 5 = line 6) . . . . **6**   81870 . 00

7 Total taxable FUTA wages (line 3 – line 6 = line 7) . . . . **7**   35000 . 00

8 FUTA tax before adjustments (line 7 × .008 = line 8) . . . . **8**   280 . 00

Part 3: Determine your adjustments. If any line does NOT apply, leave it blank.

9 If ALL of the taxable FUTA wages you paid were excluded from state unemployment tax, multiply line 7 by .054 (line 7 × .054 = line 9). Then go to line 12 . . . . **9**   .

10 If SOME of the taxable FUTA wages you paid were excluded from state unemployment tax, **OR** you paid ANY state unemployment tax late (after the due date for filing Form 940), fill out the worksheet in the instructions. Enter the amount from line 7 of the worksheet . . . . . . **10**   .

11 If credit reduction applies, enter the amount from line 3 of Schedule A (Form 940) . . . . . **11**   .

Part 4: Determine your FUTA tax and balance due or overpayment for 2009. If any line does NOT apply, leave it blank.

12 Total FUTA tax after adjustments (lines 8 + 9 + 10 + 11 = line 12) . . . . **12**   280 . 00

13 FUTA tax deposited for the year, including any overpayment applied from a prior year . . **13**   0 . 00

14 Balance due (If line 12 is more than line 13, enter the difference on line 14.)
  ● If line 14 is more than $500, you must deposit your tax.
  ● If line 14 is $500 or less, you may pay with this return. For more information on how to pay, see the separate instructions . . . . **14**   280 . 00

15 Overpayment (If line 13 is more than line 12, enter the difference on line 15 and check a box below.) . . . . **15**   .

Check one: [ ] Apply to next return.
  [ ] Send a refund.

▶ You **MUST** fill out both pages of this form and **SIGN** it.

Next ➡

For Privacy Act and Paperwork Reduction Act Notice, see the back of Form 940-V, Payment Voucher.   Cat. No. 11234O   Form **940** (2009)

FIGURE 11.8 (concluded)

850209

Name *(not your trade name)*	Employer identification number (EIN)
Sarah Sanchez	75-123456

Part 5: Report your FUTA tax liability by quarter only if line 12 is more than $500. If not, go to Part 6.

16 Report the amount of your FUTA tax liability for each quarter; do NOT enter the amount you deposited. If you had no liability for a quarter, leave the line blank.

    16a **1st quarter** (January 1 – March 31) . . . . 16a [.   ]

    16b **2nd quarter** (April 1 – June 30) . . . . 16b [.   ]

    16c **3rd quarter** (July 1 – September 30) . . . . 16c [.   ]

    16d **4th quarter** (October 1 – December 31) . . . . . . 16d [.   ]

17 Total tax liability for the year (lines 16a + 16b + 16c + 16d = line 17) 17 [.   ] Total must equal line 12.

Part 6: May we speak with your third-party designee?

Do you want to allow an employee, a paid tax preparer, or another person to discuss this return with the IRS? See the instructions for details.

☐ **Yes.** Designee's name and phone number [   ] (   )   –

    Select a 5-digit Personal Identification Number (PIN) to use when talking to IRS [ ][ ][ ][ ][ ]

☑ **No.**

Part 7: Sign here. You MUST fill out both pages of this form and SIGN it.

Under penalties of perjury, I declare that I have examined this return, including accompanying schedules and statements, and to the best of my knowledge and belief, it is true, correct, and complete, and that no part of any payment made to a state unemployment fund claimed as a credit was, or is to be, deducted from the payments made to employees. Declaration of preparer (other than taxpayer) is based on all information of which preparer has any knowledge.

X Sign your name here *Sarah Sanchez*

Print your name here	Sarah Sanchez
Print your title here	Owner

Date 01 / 31 / 2014

Best daytime phone (972) 123 – 8766

Paid preparer's use only   Check if you are self-employed . . . ☐

Preparer's name		Preparer's SSN/PTIN	
Preparer's signature		Date	/ /
Firm's name (or yours if self-employed)		EIN	
Address		Phone	( ) –
City		State		ZIP code	

Form **940** (2009)

There are two ways to handle workers' compensation insurance. The method a business uses depends on the number of its employees.

Estimated Annual Premium in Advance. Employers who have few employees pay an estimated premium in advance. At the end of the year, the employer calculates the actual premium. If the actual premium is more than the estimated premium paid, the employer pays the balance due. If the actual premium is less than the estimated premium paid, the employer receives a refund.

Sanchez Furniture Company has two work classifications: office work and shipping work. The workers' compensation premium rates are:

| Office workers | $0.45 per $100 of labor costs |
| Shipping workers | 1.25 per $100 of labor costs |

The insurance premium rates recognize that injuries are more likely to occur to shipping workers than to office workers. Based on employee earnings for the previous year, Sanchez Furniture Company paid an estimated premium of $1,000 for the new year. The payment was made on January 15.

GENERAL JOURNAL   PAGE _____

	DATE		DESCRIPTION	POST. REF.	DEBIT	CREDIT	
1	2013						1
14	Jan.	15	Prepaid Workers' Compensation Insurance Expense		1 0 0 0 00		14
15			Cash			1 0 0 0 00	15
16			Estimated workers' compensation				16
17			insurance for 2013				17
18							18

At the end of the year, the actual premium was computed, $1,261.20. The actual premium was computed by applying the proper rates to the payroll data for the year:

- The office wages were $24,960.

  ($24,960 ÷ $100) × $0.45 =

  249.60 × $0.45 = $ 112.32

- The shipping wages were $91,910.

  ($91,910 ÷ $100) × $1.25 =

  919.1 × $1.25 = $1,148.88

- Total premium for year = $1,261.20

Classification	Payroll	Rate	Premium
Office work	$24,960	$0.45 per $100	$ 112.32
Shipping work	91,910	1.25 per $100	1,148.88
Total premium for year			$1,261.20
Less estimated premium paid			1,000.00
Balance of premium due			$ 261.20

PAYROLL TAXES

- Management must ensure that payroll taxes are computed properly and paid on time.
- In order to avoid penalties, it is essential that a business prepares its payroll tax returns accurately and files the returns and required forms promptly.
- The payroll system should ensure that payroll reports are prepared in an efficient manner.
- Managers need to be familiar with all payroll taxes and how they impact operating expenses.

- Managers must be knowledgeable about unemployment tax regulations in their state because favorable experience ratings can reduce unemployment tax expense.
- Management is responsible for developing effective internal control procedures over payroll operations and ensuring that they are followed.

THINKING CRITICALLY

What accounting records are used to prepare Form 941?

On December 31, the balance due to the insurance company is recorded as a liability by an adjusting entry. Sanchez Furniture Company owes $261.20 ($1,261.20 − $1,000.00) for the workers' compensation insurance.

	DATE		DESCRIPTION	POST. REF.	DEBIT	CREDIT	
1	2013						1
2	Dec.	31	Workers' Compensation Insurance Expense		2 6 1 20		2
3			Workers' Compensation Insurance Payable			2 6 1 20	3
4							4

GENERAL JOURNAL   PAGE _____

Additionally, an adjusting journal would be recorded on December 31, 2013, for prepaid workers' compensation insurance expired.

Suppose that on January 15, Sanchez Furniture Company had paid an estimated premium of $1,400 instead of $1,000. The actual premium at the end of the year was $1,261.20. Sanchez Furniture Company would be due a refund from the insurance company for the amount overpaid, $138.80 ($1,400.00 − $1,261.20).

Deposit and Monthly Premium Payments Employers with many employees use a different method to handle workers' compensation insurance. At the beginning of the year, they make large deposits, often 25 percent of the estimated annual premium. From January through November, they pay the actual premium due based on an audit of the month's wages. The premium for the last month is deducted from the deposit. Any balance is refunded or applied toward the following year's deposit.

Internal Control over Payroll Operations

Now that we have examined the basic accounting procedures used for payrolls and payroll taxes, let's look at some internal control procedures that are recommended to protect payroll operations.

1. Assign only highly responsible, well-trained employees to work in payroll operations.
2. Keep payroll records in locked files. Train payroll employees to maintain confidentiality about pay rates and other information in the payroll records.
3. Add new employees to the payroll system and make all changes in employee pay rates only with proper written authorization from management.
4. Make changes to an employee's withholding allowances based only on a Form W-4 properly completed and signed by the employee.

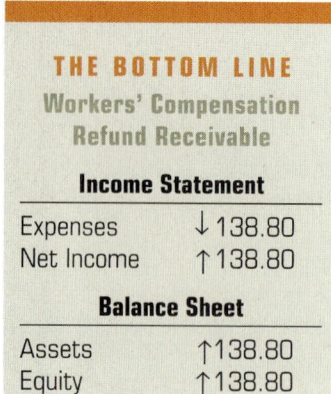

THE BOTTOM LINE

Workers' Compensation Refund Receivable

Income Statement

Expenses	↓ 138.80
Net Income	↑ 138.80

Balance Sheet

Assets	↑138.80
Equity	↑138.80

5. Make voluntary deductions from employee earnings based only on a signed authorization from the employee.

6. Have the payroll checks examined by someone other than the person who prepares them. Compare each check to the entry for the employee in the payroll register.

7. Have payroll checks distributed to the employees by someone other than the person who prepares them.

8. Have the monthly payroll bank account statement received and reconciled by someone other than the person who prepares the payroll checks.

9. Use prenumbered forms for the payroll checks. Periodically the numbers of the checks issued and the numbers of the unused checks should be verified to make sure that all checks can be accounted for.

10. Maintain files of all authorization forms for adding new employees, changing pay rates, and making voluntary deductions. Also retain all Forms W-4.

Section 2 Self Review

QUESTIONS

1. Why is it important for workers' compensation wages to be classified according to the type of work performed?

2. Who pays the federal unemployment tax? The state unemployment tax?

3. How does a favorable experience rating affect the state unemployment tax rate?

EXERCISES

4. The federal unemployment taxes are reported on:
   a. Form 941.
   b. Form 8109.
   c. Form W-3.
   d. Form 940.

5. State unemployment taxes are filed:
   a. monthly.
   b. quarterly.
   c. yearly.
   d. at the end of each pay period.

ANALYSIS

6. At the end of the year, the business has a balance due for workers' compensation insurance. If no adjusting entry is made, will the amount of net income reported be correct? If not, how will it be wrong?

(Answers to Section 2 Self Review are on page 370.)

11 Chapter REVIEW Chapter Summary

Employers must pay social security, SUTA, FUTA, and Medicare taxes. They must also collect federal and state taxes from their employees and then remit those taxes to the appropriate taxing authorities. In this chapter, you have learned how to compute the employer's taxes and how to file the required tax returns and reports.

Learning Objectives

1 Explain how and when payroll taxes are paid to the government.

Employers act as collection agents for social security, Medicare, and federal income taxes withheld from employee earnings. Employers must remit these sums, with their own share of social security and Medicare taxes, to the government. The taxes must be deposited in an authorized depository, usually a commercial bank. The methods and schedules for deposits vary according to the sums involved.

2 Compute and record the employer's social security and Medicare taxes.

Employers should multiply the social security and Medicare tax rates by taxable wages to compute the employer's portion of taxes due.

3 Record deposit of social security, Medicare, and employee income taxes.

As taxes are paid to the government, the accounting records should be updated to reflect the payment, thereby reducing tax liability accounts.

4 Prepare an Employer's Quarterly Federal Tax Return, Form 941.

The Form 941 reports wages paid, federal employee income tax withheld, and applicable social security and Medicare taxes.

5 Prepare Wage and Tax Statement (Form W-2) and Annual Transmittal of Wage and Tax Statements (Form W-3).

By the end of January, each employee must be given a Wage and Tax Statement, Form W-2, showing the previous year's earnings and withholdings for social security, Medicare, and employee income tax. The employer files a Transmittal of Wage and Tax Statements, Form W-3, with copies of employees' Forms W-2. Form W-3 is due by the last day of February following the end of the calendar year.

6 Compute and record liability for federal and state unemployment taxes and record payment of the taxes.

Unemployment insurance taxes are paid by the employer to both state and federal governments. State unemployment tax returns differ from state to state but usually require a list of employees, their social security numbers, and taxable wages paid. The rate of state unemployment tax depends on the employer's experience rating. The net federal unemployment tax rate can be as low as 0.8 percent.

7 Prepare an Employer's Federal Unemployment Tax Return, Form 940.

An Employer's Annual Federal Unemployment Tax Return, Form 940, must be filed in January for the preceding calendar year. The form shows the total wages paid, the amount of wages subject to unemployment tax, and the federal unemployment tax owed for the year. A credit is allowed against gross federal tax for unemployment tax charged under state plans, up to 5.4 percent of wages subject to the federal tax.

8 Compute and record workers' compensation insurance premiums.

By state law, employers might be required to carry workers' compensation insurance. For companies with a few employees, an estimated premium is paid at the start of the year. A final settlement is made with the insurance company on the basis of an audit of the payroll after the end of the year. Premiums vary according to the type of work performed by each employee. Other premium payment plans can be used for larger employers.

9 Define the accounting terms new to this chapter.

Glossary

Employer's Annual Federal Unemployment Tax Return, Form 940 (p. 352) Preprinted government form used by the employer to report unemployment taxes for the calendar year

Employer's Quarterly Federal Tax Return, Form 941 (p. 340) Preprinted government form used by the employer to report payroll tax information relating to social security, Medicare, and employee income tax withholding to the Internal Revenue Service

Experience rating system (p. 348) A system that rewards an employer for maintaining steady employment conditions by reducing the firm's state unemployment tax rate

Merit rating system (p. 348) See Experience rating system

Transmittal of Wage and Tax Statements, Form W-3 (p. 345) Preprinted government form submitted with Forms W-2 to the Social Security Administration

Unemployment insurance program (p. 348) A program that provides unemployment compensation through a tax levied on employers

Wage and Tax Statement, Form W-2 (p. 345) Preprinted government form that contains information about an employee's earnings and tax withholdings for the year

Withholding statement (p. 345) See Wage and Tax Statement, Form W-2

Comprehensive **Self Review**

1. What is Form W-3?

2. Is the ceiling on earnings subject to unemployment taxes larger than or smaller than the ceiling on earnings subject to the social security tax?

3. How do the FUTA and SUTA taxes relate to each other?

4. Under the monthly deposit schedule rule, when must deposits for employee income tax and other withheld taxes be made?

5. Which of the following factors determine the frequency of deposits of social security, Medicare, and income tax withholdings?

   a. Experience rating.

   b. Amount of taxes reported in the lookback period.

   c. Company's net income.

   d. Amount of taxes currently owed.

   e. How often employees are paid.

(Answers to Comprehensive Self Review are on page 370.)

Discussion Questions

1. Which of the following are withheld from employees' earnings?

   a. FUTA

   b. income tax

   c. Medicare

   d. social security

   e. SUTA

   f. workers' compensation

2. What does "monthly" refer to in the Monthly Deposit Schedule Rule?

3. What does "semiweekly" refer to in the Semiweekly Deposit Schedule Rule?

4. What is EFTPS? When is EFTPS required?

5. When is the use of Form 8109-B permitted?

6. What is a business tax identification number?

7. What are the four taxes levied on employers?

Review and Applications

8. What is the lookback period?

9. What is the purpose of Form W-3? When must it be issued? To whom is it sent?

10. When must Form W-2 be issued? To whom is it sent?

11. What happens if the employer fails to deduct enough employee income tax or FICA tax from employee earnings?

12. What government form is prepared to accompany deposits of federal taxes?

13. How can an employer keep informed about changes in the rates and bases for the social security, Medicare, and FUTA taxes?

14. When is the premium for workers' compensation insurance usually paid?

15. Who pays for workers' compensation insurance?

16. What is Form 941? How often is the form filed?

17. Is the employer required to deposit the federal unemployment tax during the year? Explain.

18. A state charges a basic SUTA tax rate of 5.4 percent. Because of an excellent experience rating, an employer in the state has to pay only 1.0 percent of the taxable payroll as state tax. What is the percentage to be used in computing the credit against the federal unemployment tax?

19. What is the purpose of Form 940? How often is it filed?

20. What is the purpose of allowing a credit against the FUTA for state unemployment taxes?

21. Why was the unemployment insurance system established?

APPLICATIONS

Exercises

Exercise 11.1

Objective 1

▶ **Depositing payroll taxes.**

The amounts of employee income tax withheld and social security and Medicare taxes (both employee and employer shares) shown below were owed by different businesses on the specified dates. In each case, decide whether the firm is required to deposit the sum in an authorized financial institution. If a deposit is necessary, give the date by which it should be made. The employers are monthly depositors.

1. Total taxes of $550 owed on July 31, 2013.

2. Total taxes of $1,650 owed on April 30, 2013.

3. Total taxes of $1,200 owed on March 31, 2013.

4. Total taxes of $8,750 owed on February 28, 2013.

Exercise 11.2

Objective 3

▶ **Recording deposit of social security, Medicare, and income taxes.**

After Beam Corporation paid its employees on July 15, 2013, and recorded the corporation's share of payroll taxes for the payroll paid that date, the firm's general ledger showed a balance of $19,700 in the *Social Security Tax Payable* account, a balance of $4,196 in the *Medicare Tax Payable* account, and a balance of $18,260 in the *Employee Income Tax Payable* account. On July 16, the business issued a check to deposit the taxes owed in the First Texas Bank. Record this transaction in general journal form. Use 24 as the page number for the general journal.

Exercise 11.3

Objectives 2, 6

▶ **Computing employer's payroll taxes.**

At the end of the weekly payroll period on June 30, 2013, the payroll register of Cordts Consultants showed employee earnings of $70,900. Determine the firm's payroll taxes for the period. Use a social security rate of 6.2 percent, Medicare rate of 1.45 percent, FUTA rate of 0.8 percent, and SUTA rate of 5.4 percent. Consider all earnings subject to social security tax and Medicare tax and $40,850 subject to FUTA and SUTA taxes.

Depositing federal unemployment tax.

On March 31, 2013, the *Federal Unemployment Tax Payable* account in the general ledger of The Argosy Company showed a balance of $1,497. This represents the FUTA tax owed for the first quarter of the year. On April 30, 2013, the firm issued a check to deposit the amount owed in the First Security National Bank. Record this transaction in general journal form. Use 14 as the page number for the general journal.

◀ **Exercise 11.4**
Objective 6

Computing SUTA tax.

On April 30, 2013, Chung Furniture Company prepared its state unemployment tax return for the first quarter of the year. The firm had taxable wages of $100,550. Because of a favorable experience rating, Chung pays SUTA tax at a rate of 1.4 percent. How much SUTA tax did the firm owe for the quarter?

◀ **Exercise 11.5**
Objective 6

Paying SUTA tax.

On June 30, 2013, the *State Unemployment Tax Payable* account in the general ledger of Alan Office Supplies showed a balance of $2,098. This represents the SUTA tax owed for the second quarter of the year. On July 31, 2013, the business issued a check to the state unemployment insurance fund for the amount due. Record this payment in general journal form. Use 30 as the page number for the general journal.

◀ **Exercise 11.6**
Objective 6

Computing FUTA tax.

On January 31, Giovanni Accountancy Corp. prepared its Employer's Annual Federal Unemployment Tax Return, Form 940. During the previous year, the business paid total wages of $396,500 to its nineteen employees. Of this amount, $128,692 was subject to FUTA tax. Using a rate of 0.8 percent, determine the FUTA tax owed and the balance due on January 31, 2013, when Form 940 was filed. A deposit of $750 was made during the year.

◀ **Exercise 11.7**
Objective 6

Computing workers' compensation insurance premiums.

Canzano Medical Supplies estimates that its office employees will earn $205,000 next year and its factory employees will earn $960,000. The firm pays the following rates for workers' compensation insurance: $0.57 per $100 of wages for the office employees and $8.31 per $100 of wages for the factory employees. Determine the estimated premium for each group of employees and the total estimated premium for next year.

◀ **Exercise 11.8**
Objective 8

PROBLEMS

Problem Set A

Computing and recording employer's payroll tax expense.

The payroll register of Total Garden Care showed total employee earnings of $3,500 for the payroll period ended July 14, 2013.

◀ **Problem 11.1A**
Objectives 2, 6
eXcel

INSTRUCTIONS

1. Compute the employer's payroll taxes for the period. Use rates of 6.2 percent for the employer's share of the social security tax, 1.45 percent for Medicare tax, 0.8 percent for FUTA tax, and 5.4 percent for SUTA tax. All earnings are taxable.

2. Prepare a general journal entry to record the employer's payroll taxes for the period. Use journal page 30.

Analyze: Which of the above taxes are paid by the employee and matched by the employer?

Computing employer's social security tax, Medicare tax, and unemployment taxes.

A payroll summary for Fronke Consulting Company, owned by Mark Fronke, for the quarter ending June 30, 2013, appears on page 362. The firm prepared the required tax deposit forms and issued checks as follows:

a. Federal Tax Deposit Coupon, Form 8109, check for April taxes, paid on May 15.

b. Federal Tax Deposit Coupon, Form 8109, check for May taxes, paid on June 17.

◀ **Problem 11.2A**
Objectives 2, 3
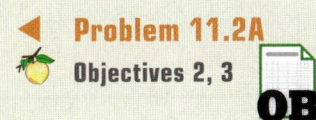

Date Wages Paid	Total Earnings	Social Security Tax Deducted	Medicare Tax Deducted	Income Tax Withheld
April 8	$ 2,332.00	$ 144.58	$ 33.81	$ 231.00
15	2,420.00	150.04	35.09	238.00
22	2,332.00	144.58	33.81	231.00
29	2,376.00	147.31	34.45	235.00
	$ 9,460.00	$ 586.51	$137.16	$ 935.00
May 5	$ 2,288.00	$ 141.86	$ 33.18	227.00
12	2,332.00	144.58	33.81	231.00
19	2,332.00	144.58	33.81	231.00
26	2,376.00	147.31	34.45	235.00
	$ 9,328.00	$ 578.33	$135.25	$ 924.00
June 2	$ 2,420.00	$ 150.04	$ 35.09	$ 238.00
9	2,332.00	144.58	33.81	231.00
16	2,376.00	147.31	34.45	235.00
23	2,332.00	144.58	33.81	231.00
30	2,288.00	141.86	33.18	227.00
	$11,748.00	$ 728.37	$170.34	$1,162.00
Total	$30,536.00	$1,893.21	$442.75	$3,021.00

INSTRUCTIONS

1. Using the tax rates given below, and assuming that all earnings are taxable, make the general journal entry on April 8, 2013, to record the employer's payroll tax expense on the payroll ending that date. Use journal page 12.

Social security	6.2 percent
Medicare	1.45
FUTA	0.8
SUTA	5.4

2. Prepare the entries in general journal form to record deposit of the employee income tax withheld and the social security and Medicare taxes (employee and employer shares) on May 15 for April taxes and on June 17 for May taxes.

Analyze: How were the amounts for *Income Tax Withheld* determined?

CONTINUING >>>
Problem

Problem 11.3A ▶

Objectives 4, 6

This is a continuation of Problem 11.2A for Fronke Consulting Company; recording payment of taxes and preparing employer's quarterly federal tax return.

1. On July 15, the firm issued a check to deposit the federal income tax withheld and the FICA tax (both employee and employer shares for the third month [June]). Based on your computations in Problem 11.2A, record the issuance of the check in general journal form. Use journal page 24.

2. Complete Form 941 in accordance with the discussions in this chapter. Use a 12.4 percent social security rate and a 2.9 percent Medicare rate in computations. Use the following address for the company: 2300 East Ocean Blvd., Long Beach, CA 90802. Use 75-4444444 as the employer identification number. Date the return July 31, 2013. Mr. Fronke's phone number is 562-709-3654.

Analyze: Based on the entries that you have recorded, what is the balance of the *Employee Income Tax Payable* account at July 15?

Computing and recording unemployment taxes; completing Form 940.

◄ **Problem 11.4A**
Objectives 6, 7

Certain transactions and procedures relating to federal and state unemployment taxes follow for Fashion Sense, a retail store owned by Nancy Roberts. The firm's address is 2007 Trendsetter Lane, Dallas, TX 75268-0967. The firm's phone number is 972-456-1200.The employer's federal and state identification numbers are 75-9462315 and 37-9462315, respectively. Carry out the procedures as instructed in each of the following steps.

INSTRUCTIONS

1. Compute the state unemployment insurance tax owed on the employees' wages for the quarter ended March 31, 2013. This information will be shown on the employer's quarterly report to the state agency that collects SUTA tax. The employer has recorded the tax on each payroll date. Although the state charges a 5.4 percent unemployment tax rate, Fashion Sense's rate is only 1.7 percent because of its experience rating. The employee earnings for the first quarter are shown below. All earnings are subject to SUTA tax.

Name of Employee	Total Earnings
Terri Chu	$ 5,810
Jeri Guyton	3,775
Gloria Bermudez	4,098
Stacee Scott	5,270
Anita Thomas	4,000
Terri Wong	2,910
Total	$25,863

2. On April 30, 2013, the firm issued a check to the state employment commission for the amount computed above. In general journal form, record the issuance of the check. Use journal page 82.

Analyze: Why is the business experience rating important with regard to the state unemployment tax rate?

This is a continuation of Problem 11.4A for Fashion Sense; computing and recording unemployment taxes; completing Form 940.

◄ **Problem 11.5A**
Objectives 6, 7

Problem

1. Complete Form 940, the Employer's Annual Federal Unemployment Tax Return. Assume that all wages have been paid and that all quarterly payments have been submitted to the state as required. The payroll information for 2013 appears below. The required federal tax deposit forms and checks were submitted as follows: a deposit of $206.90 on April 21, a deposit of $198.72 on July 22, and a deposit of $240 on October 21. Date the unemployment tax return January 28, 2014. A check for the balance due as per line 14, Part 4, will be sent with Form 940.

Quarter Ended	Total Wages Paid	Wages Paid in Excess of $7,000	State Unemployment Tax Paid
Mar. 31	$ 25,863.00	–0–	$ 439.67
June 30	58,915.00	$ 4,075.00	932.28
Sept. 30	29,880.00	20,550.00	158.61
Dec. 31	31,350.00	28,910.00	41.48
Totals	$146,008.00	$53,535.00	$1,572.04

2. In general journal form, record issuance of a check on January 28, 2014, for the balance of FUTA tax due for 2013. Use journal page 15.

Analyze: What total debits were made to liability accounts for entries you recorded in Problem 11.4A and Problem 11.5A?

Problem 11.6A ▶
Objective 8

Computing and recording workers' compensation insurance premiums.

The following information relates to Ponte Manufacturing Company's workers' compensation insurance premiums for 2013. On January 15, 2013, the company estimated its premium for workers' compensation insurance for the year on the basis of that data.

Work Classification	Amount of Estimated Wages	Insurance Rates
Office work	$ 54,000	$0.40/$100
Shop work	298,000	$5.00/$100

INSTRUCTIONS

1. Compute the estimated premiums.

2. Record in general journal form payment of the estimated premium on January 15, 2013. Use 8 as the page number.

3. On January 4, 2014, an audit of the firm's payroll records showed that it had actually paid wages of $59,960 to its office employees and wages of $305,320 to its shop employees. Compute the actual premium for the year and the balance due the insurance company or the credit due the firm.

4. Prepare the general journal entry on December 31, 2013, to adjust the **Workers' Compensation Insurance Expense** account. Use 98 as the page number.

Analyze: If all wages were attributable to shop employees, what premium estimate would have been calculated and recorded on January 15, 2013?

Problem Set B

Problem 11.1B ▶
Objectives 2, 6

Computing and recording employer's payroll tax expense.

The payroll register of Cliff's Auto Detailers showed total employee earnings of $4,000 for the week ended April 8, 2013.

INSTRUCTIONS

1. Compute the employer's payroll taxes for the period. The tax rates are as follows:

Social security	6.2 percent
Medicare	1.45
FUTA	0.8
SUTA	2.2

2. Prepare a general journal entry to record the employer's payroll taxes for the period. Use journal page 28.

Analyze: If the FUTA tax rate had been 1.2 percent, what total employer payroll taxes would have been recorded?

Problem 11.2B ▶
Objectives 2, 3

Computing employer's social security tax, Medicare tax, and unemployment taxes.

A payroll summary for Styles for Less, owned by Nikki Parikh, for the quarter ending September 30, 2013, appears below. The business prepared the tax deposit forms and issued checks as follows during the quarter:

a. Federal Tax Deposit Coupon, Form 8109, check for July taxes, paid on August 15.

b. Federal Tax Deposit Coupon, Form 8109, check for August taxes, paid on September 15.

Date Wages Paid	Total Earnings	Social Security Tax Withheld	Medicare Tax Withheld	Income Tax Withheld
July 7	$ 1,980.00	$ 122.76	$ 28.71	$ 192.50
14	1,980.00	122.76	28.71	192.50
21	2,310.00	143.22	33.50	225.50
28	1,980.00	122.76	28.71	192.50
	$ 8,250.00	$ 511.50	$119.63	$ 803.00
Aug. 4	$ 2,310.00	$ 143.22	$ 33.50	225.50
11	2,970.00	184.14	43.07	291.50
18	2,970.00	184.14	43.07	291.50
25	2,640.00	163.68	38.28	258.50
	$10,890.00	$ 675.18	$157.92	$1,067.00
Sept. 2	$ 1,980.00	$ 122.76	$ 28.71	$ 192.50
9	2,310.00	143.22	33.50	225.50
16	2,310.00	143.22	33.50	225.50
23	2,310.00	143.22	33.50	225.50
30	1,980.00	122.76	28.71	192.50
	$10,890.00	$ 675.18	$157.92	$1,061.50
Total	$30,030.00	$1,861.86	$435.47	$2,931.50

INSTRUCTIONS

1. Prepare the general journal entry on July 7, 2013, to record the employer's payroll tax expense on the payroll ending that date. Use journal page 31. All earnings are subject to the following taxes:

Social security	6.2	percent
Medicare	1.45	
FUTA	0.8	
SUTA	2.2	

2. Make the entries in general journal form to record deposit of the employee income tax withheld and the social security and Medicare taxes (both employees' withholding and employer's matching portion) on August 15 for July taxes and on September 15 for the August taxes.

Analyze: How much would a SUTA rate of 1.5 percent reduce the tax for the payroll of July 7?

This is a continuation of Problem 11.2B for Styles for Less; recording payment of taxes and preparing employer's quarterly federal tax return.

◀ **Problem 11.3B**
Objectives 4, 6
CONTINUING >>>
Problem

1. On October 15, the firm issued a check to deposit the federal income tax withheld and the FICA tax (both employees' withholding and employer's matching portion). Based on your computations in Problem 11.2B, record the issuance of the check in general journal form. Use journal page 31.

2. Complete Form 941 in accordance with the discussions in this chapter and the instructions on the form. Use a 12.4 percent social security rate and a 2.9 percent Medicare rate in computations. Use the following address for the company: 12001 Pioneer Blvd., Artesia, CA 90650. The firm's phone number is 562-860-5451. Use 75-5555555 as the employer identification number. Date the return October 31, 2013. (Hint: Enter $0.07 on line 7a.)

Analyze: What total taxes were deposited with the IRS for the quarter ended September 30, 2013?

Problem 11.4B

Objectives 6, 7

▶ **Computing and recording unemployment taxes; completing Form 940.**

Certain transactions and procedures relating to federal and state unemployment taxes are given below for The Game Wizard, a retail store owned by Helen Kim. The firm's address is 4560 LBJ Freeway, Dallas, TX 75232-6002. The firm's phone number is 972-456-1201. The employer's federal and state identification numbers are 75-9999999 and 37-6789015, respectively. Carry out the procedures as instructed in each step.

INSTRUCTIONS

1. Compute the state unemployment insurance tax owed for the quarter ended March 31, 2013. This information will be shown on the employer's quarterly report to the state agency that collects SUTA tax. The employer has recorded the tax expense and liability on each payroll date. Although the state charges a 5.4 percent unemployment tax rate, The Game Wizard has received a favorable experience rating and therefore pays only a 2.3 percent state tax rate. The employee earnings for the first quarter are given below. All earnings are subject to SUTA tax.

Name of Employee	Total Earnings
Brian Morris	$ 3,880
Stan Cantu	3,650
Alicia Chiu	3,225
Yvonne Martinez	3,780
Patricia Jones	2,890
John Phan	2,910
Total	$20,335

2. On April 30, 2013, the firm issued a check for the amount computed above. Record the transaction in general journal form. Use journal page 21.

Analyze: If Brian Morris made the same amount for the quarter ended June 30, 2013, how much of his earnings would be subject to the federal unemployment tax?

Problem 11.5B

Objectives 6, 7

CONTINUING ▶▶▶
Problem

▶ **This is a continuation of Problem 11.4B for The Game Wizard; computing and recording unemployment taxes; completing Form 940.**

1. Complete Form 940, the Employer's Annual Federal Unemployment Tax Return. Assume that all wages have been paid and that all quarterly payments have been submitted to the state as required. The payroll information for 2013 appears below. The firm's FUTA tax liability by quarter follows. 1st quarter, $162.68; 2nd quarter, $170.00; third quarter, $102.00; and fourth quarter, $116.40. The firm made no FUTA deposits in 2013. Date the unemployment tax return January 27, 2014. A check for the balance due will be sent with Form 940.

Quarter Ended	Total Wages Paid	Wages Paid in Excess of $7,000	State Unemployment Tax Paid
Mar. 31	$20,335.00	–0–	$ 467.71
June 30	21,250.00	–0–	488.75
Sept. 30	22,050.00	$ 9,300.00	293.25
Dec. 31	34,800.00	20,250.00	334.65
Totals	$98,435.00	$29,550.00	$1,584.36

2. On January 27, 2014, the firm issued a check for the amount shown on line 14, Part 4 of form 940. In general journal form, record issuance of a check. Use journal page 48.

Analyze: What is the balance of the *Federal Unemployment Tax Payable* account on January 27, 2014?

Computing and recording premiums on workers' compensation insurance.

◀ **Problem 11.6B**
Objectives 8

The following information is for Union Express Delivery Service workers' compensation insurance premiums. On January 15, 2013, the company estimated its premium for workers' compensation insurance for the year on the basis of the following data:

Work Classification	Amount of Estimated Wages	Insurance Rates
Office work	$ 50,000	$0.50/$100
Delivery work	308,000	$6.00/$100

INSTRUCTIONS

1. Use the information to compute the estimated premium for the year.

2. A check was issued to pay the estimated premium on January 17, 2013. Record the transaction in general journal form. Use 7 as the page number.

3. On January 19, 2014, an audit of the firm's payroll records showed that it had actually paid wages of $52,970 to its office employees and wages of $316,240 to its delivery employees. Compute the actual premium for the year and the balance due the insurance company or the credit due the firm.

4. Give the general journal entry to adjust the *Workers' Compensation Insurance Expense* account. Date the entry December 31, 2013. Use 88 as the page number.

Analyze: What is the balance of the *Workers' Compensation Insurance Expense* account at December 31, 2013, after all journal entries have been posted?

Critical Thinking Problem 11.1

Determining Employee Status

In each of the following independent situations, decide whether the business organization should treat the person being paid as an employee and should withhold social security, Medicare, and employee income taxes from the payment made.

1. Tony Jacobs owns and operates a crafts shop, as a sole proprietor. Jacobs withdraws $2,000 a week from the crafts shop.

2. Guy Gagliardi is a court reporter. He has an office at the Metroplex Court Reporting Center but pays no rent. The manager of the center receives requests from attorneys for court reporters to take depositions at legal hearings. The manager then chooses a court reporter who best meets the needs of the client and contacts the court reporter chosen. The court reporter has the right to refuse to take on the job, and the court reporter controls his or her working hours and days. Clients make payments to the center, which deducts a 30 percent fee for providing facilities and rendering services to support the court reporter. The balance is paid to the court reporter. During the current month, the center collected fees of $30,000 for Guy, deducted $7,500 for the center's fee, and remitted the remainder to Guy.

3. Ken, a registered nurse, has retired from full-time work. However, because of his experience and special skills, on each Monday, Wednesday, and Thursday afternoon he assists Dr. Grace Liu, a dermatologist. Ken is paid an hourly fee by Dr. Liu. During the current week, his hourly fees totaled $800.

4. After working several years as an editor for a magazine publisher, Lisa quit her job to stay at home with her two small children. Later, the publisher asked her to work in her home performing editorial work as needed. Lisa is paid an hourly fee for the work she performs. In

some cases, she goes to the publishing company's offices to pick up or return a manuscript. In other cases the firm sends a manuscript to her, or she returns one by mail. During the current month, Lisa's hourly earnings totaled $2,500.

5. Investor Corporation carries on very little business activity. It merely holds land and certain assets. The board of directors has concluded that they need no employees. They have decided instead to pay Ron Christie, one of the shareholders, a consulting fee of $20,000 per year to serve as president, secretary, and treasurer and to manage all the affairs of the company. Christie spends an average of one hour per week on the corporation's business affairs. However, his fee is fixed regardless of how few or how many hours he works.

Analyze: What characteristics do the persons you identified as "employees" have in common?

Critical Thinking Problem 11.2

Comparing Employees and Independent Contractors

The *Town Record Chronicle* is a local newspaper that is published Monday through Friday. It sells 90,000 copies daily. The paper is currently in a profit squeeze, and the publisher, Brenda Davis, is looking for ways to reduce expenses.

A review of current distribution procedures reveals that the *Town Record Chronicle* employs 110 truck drivers to drop off bundles of newspapers to 1,300 teenagers who deliver papers to individual homes. The drivers are paid an hourly wage while the teenagers receive 4 cents for each paper they deliver.

Davis is considering an alternative method of distributing the papers, which she says has worked in other cities the size of Flower Mound (where the *Town Record Chronicle* is published). Under the new system, the newspaper would retain 30 truck drivers to transport papers to five distribution centers around the city. The distribution centers are operated by independent contractors who would be responsible for making their own arrangements to deliver papers to subscribers' homes. The 30 drivers retained by the *Town Record Chronicle* would receive the same hourly rate as they currently earn, and the independent contractors would receive 20 cents for each paper delivered.

1. What payroll information does Davis need in order to make a decision about adopting the alternative distribution method?

2. Assume the following information:

    a. The average driver earns $48,000 per year.

    b. Average employee income tax withholding is 18 percent.

    c. The social security tax is 6.2 percent of the first $106,800 of earnings.

    d. The Medicare tax is 1.45 percent of all earnings.

    e. The state unemployment tax is 5 percent, and the federal unemployment tax is 0.8 percent of the first $7,000 of earnings.

    f. Workers' compensation insurance is 70 cents per $100 of wages.

    g. The paper pays $310 per month for health insurance for each driver and contributes $250 per month to each driver's pension plan.

    h. The paper has liability insurance coverage for all teenage carriers that costs $110,000 per year.

    Prepare a schedule showing the costs of distributing the newspapers under the current system and the proposed new system. Based on your analysis, which system would you recommend to Davis?

3. What other factors, monetary and nonmonetary, might influence your decision?

BUSINESS CONNECTIONS

Payroll

1. Davis Company recently discovered that a payroll clerk had issued checks to nonexistent employees for several years and cashed the checks himself. The firm does not have any internal control procedures for its payroll operations. What specific controls might have led to the discovery of this fraud more quickly or discouraged the payroll clerk from even attempting the fraud?

2. Johnson Company has 20 employees. Some employees work in the office, others in the warehouse, and still others in the retail store. In the company's records, all employees are simply referred to as "general employees." Explain to management why this is not an acceptable practice.

3. Why should management be concerned about the accuracy and promptness of payroll tax deposits and payroll tax returns?

4. What is the significance to management of the experience rating system used to determine the employer's tax under the state unemployment insurance laws?

Ghost Employee

Johan Jones owns a dress shop that has been very successful. He employs 3 sales associates who get paid $10 per hour for a 40-hour week. He decides to open up another dress shop on the other side of town. He hires three more sales associates with the same pay arrangements. After three months, Johan notices he is not making the same profit he did. His sales have doubled and his expenses are the same proportion except for wages. He knows that each sales associate should receive $1,720 each month yet his total wages expense for the month is $12,040. He worries that he is not paying close enough attention to the old store. What is his problem? Should he discuss this problem with all the sales associates?

Employee Data

The Home Depot, Inc. reported the following data in its *2009 Annual Report (for the fiscal year ended January 31, 2010)*:

Number of employees at January 31, 2010	317,000
Percentage of employees employed full-time	61%
Contributions to employees' retirement plans during the year ended January 31, 2010	$161 million

Analyze:

1. Based on the data above, how many employees were employed full-time at January 31, 2010?
2. Assume only full-time employees receive contributions to their retirement plan. What was the average retirement plan contribution made by The Home Depot for full-time employees?

Determining Information

Wages and payroll tax expense are the largest cost that a company incurs. At times, a company has a problem paying wages and cash deposits for payroll taxes. Your company has a cash flow problem. In a group of 4 employees, brainstorm ways to cut the costs of wages and payroll taxes.

Internal Revenue Service

Go to the Internal Revenue Web site at www.irs.gov. Does the Web site contain the necessary federal forms? Can you use these forms to submit your report? What reports must be obtained from the IRS in an original, not downloaded, form?

Answers to **Self Reviews**

Answers to Section 1 Self Review

1. Form W-2 provides information to enable the employees to complete their federal income tax return. Copies are given to the employee and to the federal government (and to other governmental units that levy an income tax).

2. Federal Reserve Bank or a commercial bank that is designated as a federal depository.

3. Form 941 shows income taxes withheld, social security and Medicare taxes due for the quarter, and tax deposits. The form is due on the last day of the month following the end of the quarter.

4. **c.** Social security tax

5. **a.** each payroll period

6. Monthly

Answers to Section 2 Self Review

1. The amount of the premium depends on the type of work the employee performs.

2. The employer pays FUTA. Usually the employer pays SUTA, although a few states also levy SUTA on employees.

3. It reduces the rate of SUTA tax that must actually be paid.

4. **d.** Form 940

5. **b.** quarterly

6. Expenses will be understated. Net income will be overstated.

Answers to Comprehensive Self Review

1. Form W-3 is sent to the Social Security Administration. It reports the total social security wages; total Medicare wages; total social security and Medicare taxes withheld; total wages, tips, and other compensation; total employee income tax withheld; and other information.

2. Smaller

3. A credit, with limits, is allowed against the federal tax for unemployment tax charged by the state.

4. By the 15th day of the following month.

5. **b.** Amount of taxes reported in the lookback period

   d. Amount of taxes currently owed

Accruals, Deferrals, and the Worksheet

LEARNING OBJECTIVES

1. Determine the adjustment for merchandise inventory, and enter the adjustment on the worksheet.
2. Compute adjustments for accrued and prepaid expense items, and enter the adjustments on the worksheet.
3. Compute adjustments for accrued and deferred income items, and enter the adjustments on the worksheet.
4. Complete a 10-column worksheet.
5. Define the accounting terms new to this chapter.

NEW TERMS

accrual basis
accrued expenses
accrued income
deferred expenses
deferred income
inventory sheet

net income line
prepaid expenses
property, plant, and equipment
unearned income
updated account balances

Urban Outfitters, Inc.
www.urbanoutfittersinc.com

Urban Outfitters, Inc., is an innovative specialty retail company that targets highly defined customer niches. The brands—Urban Outfitters, Anthropologie, Free People, Leifsdottir, and Terrain—are all distinct. The company designs innovative stores that resonate with the target audience. Stores offer an eclectic mix of merchandise and unique product displays that incorporate found objects into creative selling vignettes.

The strategy is working. While many retailers struggled through tough economic times in the past five years, net sales at Anthropologie, Free People, and Urban Outfitters have shown respectable increases. Glen T. Senk, chief executive officer explains, "Given the context of an uncertain economic environment, the company continues to focus on superior creative execution combined with disciplined inventory and expense management."

thinking critically
What types of adjustments do you think Urban Outfitters might have made when consumer spending declined in the past decade?

SECTION OBJECTIVES

>> 1. **Determine the adjustment for merchandise inventory, and enter the adjustment on the worksheet.**

   WHY IT'S IMPORTANT
   The change in merchandise inventory affects the financial statements.

>> 2. **Compute adjustments for accrued and prepaid expense items, and enter the adjustments on the worksheet.**

   WHY IT'S IMPORTANT
   Each expense item needs to be assigned to the accounting period in which it helped to earn revenue.

>> 3. **Compute adjustments for accrued and deferred income items, and enter the adjustments on the worksheet.**

   WHY IT'S IMPORTANT
   The accrual basis of accounting states that income is recognized in the period it is earned.

TERMS TO LEARN

accrual basis
accrued expenses
accrued income
deferred expenses
deferred income
inventory sheet
prepaid expenses
property, plant, and equipment
unearned income

Calculating and Recording Adjustments

In Chapter 5, you learned how to make adjustments so that all revenue and expenses that apply to a fiscal period appear on the income statement for that period. In this chapter, you will learn more about adjustments and how they affect Whiteside Antiques, a retail merchandising business owned by Bill Whiteside.

The Accrual Basis of Accounting

Financial statements usually are prepared using the **accrual basis** of accounting because it most nearly attains the goal of matching expenses and revenue in an accounting period.

- *Revenue is recognized when earned, not necessarily when the cash is received.* Revenue is recognized when the sale is complete. A sale is complete when title to the goods passes to the customer or when the service is provided. For sales on account, revenue is recognized when the sale occurs even though the cash is not collected immediately.

- *Expenses are recognized when incurred or used, not necessarily when cash is paid.* Each expense is assigned to the accounting period in which it helped to earn revenue for the business, even if cash is not paid at that time. This is often referred to as *matching revenues and expenses.*

Sometimes cash changes hands before the revenue or expense is recognized. For example, insurance premiums are normally paid in advance, and the coverage extends over several accounting periods. In other cases, cash changes hands after the revenue or expense has been recognized. For example, employees might work during December but be paid in January of the following year. Because of these timing differences, adjustments are made to ensure that revenue and expenses are recognized in the appropriate period.

Using the Worksheet to Record Adjustments

The worksheet is used to assemble data about adjustments and to organize the information for the financial statements. Figure 12.1 on pages 374–375 shows the first two sections of the worksheet for Whiteside Antiques. Let's review how to prepare the worksheet:

- Enter the trial balance in the Trial Balance section. Total the columns. Be sure that total debits equal total credits.

- Enter the adjustments in the Adjustments section. Use the same letter to identify the debit part and the credit part of each adjustment. Total the columns. Be sure that total debits equal total credits.

- For each account, combine the amounts in the Trial Balance section and the Adjustments section. Enter the results in the Adjusted Trial Balance section, total the columns, and make sure that total debits equal total credits.

- Extend account balances to the Income Statement and Balance Sheet sections and complete the worksheet.

ADJUSTMENT FOR MERCHANDISE INVENTORY

Merchandise inventory consists of the goods that a business has on hand for sale to customers. An asset account for merchandise inventory is maintained in the general ledger. During the accounting period, all purchases of merchandise are debited to the **Purchases** account. All sales of merchandise are credited to the revenue account **Sales.**

Notice that no entries are made directly to the **Merchandise Inventory** account during the accounting period. Consequently, when the trial balance is prepared at the end of the period, the **Merchandise Inventory** account still shows the *beginning* inventory for the period. At the end of each period, a business determines the *ending* balance of the **Merchandise Inventory** account. The first step in determining the ending inventory is to count the number of units of each type of item on hand. As the merchandise is counted, the quantity on hand is entered on an inventory sheet. The <mark>inventory sheet</mark> lists the quantity of each type of goods a firm has in stock. This process is called a physical inventory. For each item, the quantity is multiplied by the unit cost to find the totals per item. The totals for all items are added to compute the total cost of merchandise inventory.

The trial balance for Whiteside Antiques shows **Merchandise Inventory** of $52,000. Based on a count taken on December 31, merchandise inventory at the end of the year actually totaled $47,000. Whiteside Antiques needs to adjust the **Merchandise Inventory** account to reflect the balance at the end of the year.

The adjustment is made in two steps, using the accounts **Merchandise Inventory** and **Income Summary.**

1. The beginning inventory ($52,000) is taken off the books by transferring the account balance to the **Income Summary** account. This entry is labeled **(a)** on the worksheet in Figure 12.1 and is illustrated in T-account form below.

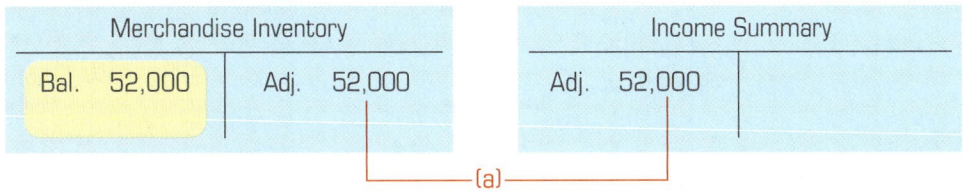

2. The ending inventory ($47,000) is placed on the books by debiting **Merchandise Inventory** and crediting **Income Summary.** This entry is labeled **(b)** on the worksheet in Figure 12.1.

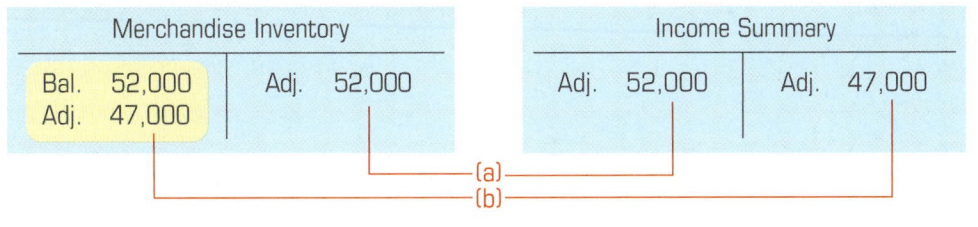

>>1. OBJECTIVE
Determine the adjustment for merchandise inventory, and enter the adjustment on the worksheet.

FIGURE 12.1   10-Column Worksheet—Partial

Whiteside Antiques

Worksheet

Year Ended December 31, 2013

	ACCOUNT NAME	TRIAL BALANCE DEBIT	TRIAL BALANCE CREDIT	ADJUSTMENTS DEBIT	ADJUSTMENTS CREDIT
1	Cash	13 136 00			
2	Petty Cash Fund	100 00			
3	Notes Receivable	1 200 00			
4	Accounts Receivable	32 000 00			
5	Allowance for Doubtful Accounts		250 00		(c) 800 00
6	Interest Receivable			(m) 30 00	
7	Merchandise Inventory	52 000 00		(b) 47 000 00	(a) 52 000 00
8	Prepaid Insurance	7 350 00			(k) 2 450 00
9	Prepaid Interest	225 00			(l) 150 00
10	Supplies	6 300 00			(j) 4 975 00
11	Store Equipment	30 000 00			
12	Accumulated Depreciation—Store Equipment				(d) 2 400 00
13	Office Equipment	5 000 00			
14	Accumulated Depreciation—Office Equipment				(e) 700 00
15	Notes Payable—Trade		2 000 00		
16	Notes Payable—Bank		9 000 00		
17	Accounts Payable		24 129 00		
18	Interest Payable				(i) 20 00
19	Social Security Tax Payable		1 084 00		(g) 74 40
20	Medicare Tax Payable		250 00		(g) 17 40
21	Employee Income Taxes Payable		990 00		
22	Federal Unemployment Tax Payable				(h) 9 60
23	State Unemployment Tax Payable				(h) 64 80
24	Salaries Payable				(f) 1 200 00
25	Sales Tax Payable		7 200 00		
26	Bill Whiteside, Capital		61 221 00		
27	Bill Whiteside, Drawing	27 600 00			
28	Income Summary			(a) 52 000 00	(b) 47 000 00
29	Sales		561 650 00		
30	Sales Returns and Allowances	12 500 00			
31	Interest Income		136 00		(m) 30 00
32	Miscellaneous Income		366 00		
33	Purchases	321 500 00			
34	Freight In	9 800 00			
35	Purchases Returns and Allowances		3 050 00		
36	Purchases Discounts		3 130 00		
37	Salaries Expense—Sales	78 490 00		(f) 1 200 00	
38	Advertising Expense	7 425 00			
39	Cash Short or Over	125 00			
40	Supplies Expense			(j) 4 975 00	

FIGURE 12.1   10-Column Worksheet—Partial (concluded)

| | TRIAL BALANCE | | ADJUSTMENTS | |
ACCOUNT NAME	DEBIT	CREDIT	DEBIT	CREDIT
41 Depreciation Expense—Store Equipment			(d) 2 400 00	
42 Rent Expense	27 600 00			
43 Salaries Expense—Office	26 500 00			
44 Insurance Expense			(k) 2 450 00	
45 Payroll Taxes Expense	7 205 00		(g) 91 80	
46			(h) 74 40	
47 Telephone Expense	1 875 00			
48 Uncollectible Accounts Expense			(c) 800 00	
49 Utilities Expense	5 925 00			
50 Depreciation Expense—Office Equipment			(e) 700 00	
51 Interest Expense	600 00		(i) 20 00	
52			(l) 150 00	
53 Totals	674 456 00	674 456 00	111 891 20	111 891 20

The effect of this adjustment is to remove the beginning merchandise inventory balance and replace it with the ending merchandise inventory balance. Merchandise inventory is adjusted in two steps on the worksheet because both the beginning and the ending inventory figures appear on the income statement, which is prepared directly from the worksheet.

ADJUSTMENT FOR LOSS FROM UNCOLLECTIBLE ACCOUNTS

Credit sales are made with the expectation that the customers will pay the amount due later. Sometimes the account receivable is never collected. Losses from uncollectible accounts are classified as operating expenses.

Under accrual accounting, the expense for uncollectible accounts is recorded in the same period as the related sale. The expense is estimated because the actual amount of uncollectible accounts is not known until later periods. To match the expense for uncollectible accounts with the sales revenue for the same period, the estimated expense is debited to an account named *Uncollectible Accounts Expense.*

Several methods exist for estimating the expense for uncollectible accounts. Whiteside Antiques uses the *percentage of net credit sales* method. The rate used is based on the company's past experience with uncollectible accounts and management's assessment of current business conditions. Whiteside Antiques estimates that four-fifths of 1 percent (0.80 percent) of net credit sales will be uncollectible. Net credit sales for the year were $100,000. The estimated expense for uncollectible accounts is $800 ($100,000 × 0.0080).

The entry to record the expense for uncollectible accounts includes a credit to a contra asset account, *Allowance for Doubtful Accounts.* This account appears on the balance sheet as follows.

Accounts Receivable	$32,000
Allowance for Doubtful Accounts ($800 + $250)	1,050
Net Accounts Receivable	$30,950

Adjustment **(c)** appears on the worksheet in Figure 12.1 for the expense for uncollectible accounts.

>>**2. OBJECTIVE**

Compute adjustments for accrued and prepaid expense items, and enter the adjustments on the worksheet.

THE BOTTOM LINE

Uncollectible Accounts Expense

Income Statement

Expenses	↑ 800
Net income	↓ 800

Balance Sheet

Assets	↓ 800
Equity	↓ 800

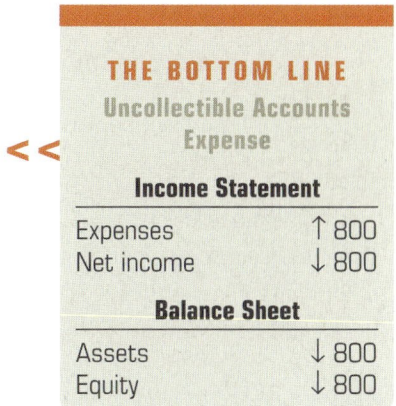

When a specific account becomes uncollectible, it is written off:

■ The entry is a debit to *Allowance for Doubtful Accounts* and a credit to *Accounts Receivable.*

■ The customer's account in the accounts receivable subsidiary ledger is also reduced.

Uncollectible Accounts Expense is not affected by the write-off of individual accounts identified as uncollectible. It is used only when the end-of-period adjustment is recorded.

Notice that net income is decreased at the end of the period when the adjustment for *estimated* expense for uncollectible accounts is made. When a specific customer account is written off, net income is *not* affected. The write-off of a specific account affects only the balance sheet accounts *Accounts Receivable* (asset) and *Allowance for Doubtful Accounts* (contra asset).

The balance of *Allowance for Doubtful Accounts* is reduced throughout the year as customer accounts are written off. Notice that *Allowance for Doubtful Accounts* already has a credit balance of $250 in the Trial Balance section of the worksheet. When the estimate of uncollectible accounts expense is based on sales, any remaining balance from previous periods is not considered when recording the adjustment.

ADJUSTMENTS FOR DEPRECIATION

Most businesses have long-term assets that are used in the operation of the business. These are often referred to as **property, plant, and equipment.** Property, plant, and equipment includes buildings, trucks, automobiles, machinery, furniture, fixtures, office equipment, and land.

Property, plant, and equipment costs are not charged to expense accounts when purchased. Instead, the cost of a long-term asset is allocated over the asset's expected useful life by depreciation. This process involves the gradual transfer of acquisition cost to expense. There is one exception. Land is not depreciated.

There are many ways to calculate depreciation. Whiteside Antiques uses the straight-line method, so an equal amount of depreciation is taken in each year of the asset's useful life. The formula for straight-line depreciation is:

$$\frac{\text{Cost} - \text{Salvage value}}{\text{Estimated useful life}} = \text{Depreciation}$$

Salvage value is an estimate of the amount that could be obtained from the sale or disposition of an asset at the end of its useful life. Cost minus salvage value is called the *depreciable base.*

Depreciation of Store Equipment   The trial balance shows that Whiteside Antiques has $30,000 of store equipment. Estimated salvage value is $6,000. What is the amount of annual depreciation expense using the straight-line method?

Cost of store equipment	$30,000
Salvage value	(6,000)
Depreciable base	$24,000
Expected useful life	10 years

$$\frac{\$30,000 - \$6,000}{10 \text{ years}} = \$2,400 \text{ per year}$$

The annual depreciation expense is $2,400. Adjustment **(d)** appears on the worksheet in Figure 12.1 for the depreciation expense for store equipment.

important!

Depreciation
To calculate monthly straight-line depreciation, divide the depreciable base by the number of months in the useful life.

Depr. Expense—Store Equipment		Accum. Depr.—Store Equipment	
Adj. 2,400			Adj. 2,400

(d)

Depreciation of Office Equipment
Whiteside Antiques reports $5,000 of office equipment on the trial balance. What is the amount of annual depreciation expense using the straight-line method if estimated salvage value is $800 and estimated life is 6 years?

Cost of office equipment	$5,000
Salvage value	(800)
Depreciable base	$4,200
Expected useful life	6 years

$$\frac{\$5,000 - \$800}{6 \text{ Years}} = \$700 \text{ per year}$$

Annual depreciation expense is $700. Adjustment **(e)** appears on the worksheet in Figure 12.1 for depreciation expense for office equipment.

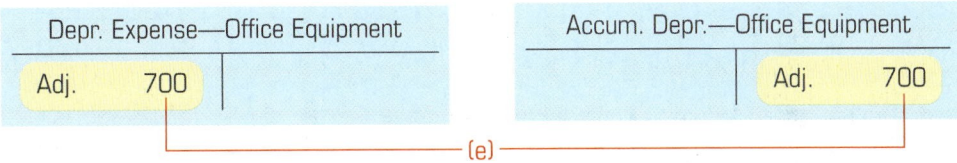

ADJUSTMENTS FOR ACCRUED EXPENSES

Many expense items are paid for, recorded, and used in the same accounting period. However, some expense items are paid for and recorded in one period but used in a later period. Other expense items are used in one period and paid for in a later period. In these situations, adjustments are made so that the financial statements show all expenses in the appropriate period.

Accrued expenses are expenses that relate to (are used in) the current period but have not yet been paid and do not yet appear in the accounting records. Whiteside Antiques makes adjustments for three types of accrued expenses:

- accrued salaries
- accrued payroll taxes
- accrued interest on notes payable

Because accrued expenses involve amounts that must be paid in the future, the adjustment for each item is a debit to an expense account and a credit to a liability account.

Accrued Salaries
At Whiteside Antiques, all full-time sales and office employees are paid semimonthly—on the 15th and the last day of the month. The trial balance in Figure 12.1 shows the correct salaries expense for the full-time employees for the year. From December 28 to January 3, the firm hired several part-time sales clerks for the year-end sale. Through December 31, 2013, these employees earned $1,200. The part-time salaries expense has not yet been recorded because the employees will not be paid until January 3, 2014. An adjustment is made to record the amount owed, but not yet paid, as of the end of December.

Adjustment **(f)** appears on the worksheet in Figure 12.1 for accrued salaries.

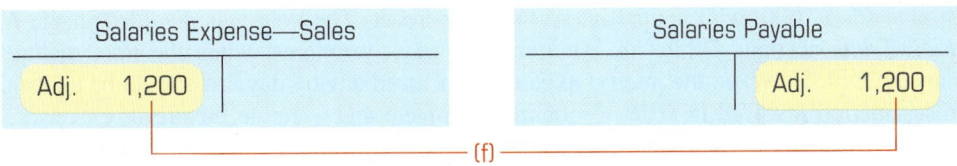

Accrued Payroll Taxes
Payroll taxes are not legally owed until the salaries are paid. Businesses that want to match revenue and expenses in the appropriate period make adjustments to accrue the

employer's payroll taxes even though the taxes are technically not yet due. Whiteside Antiques makes adjustments for accrued employer's payroll taxes.

The payroll taxes related to the full-time employees of Whiteside Antiques have been recorded and appear on the trial balance. However, the payroll taxes for the part-time sales clerks have not been recorded. None of the part-time clerks have reached the social security wage base limit. The entire $1,200 of accrued salaries is subject to the employer's share of social security and Medicare taxes. The accrued employer's payroll taxes are:

Social security tax	$1,200	×	0.0620	=	$74.40
Medicare tax	$1,200	×	0.0145	=	17.40
Total accrued payroll taxes					$91.80

Adjustment **(g)** appears on the worksheet in Figure 12.1 for accrued payroll taxes.

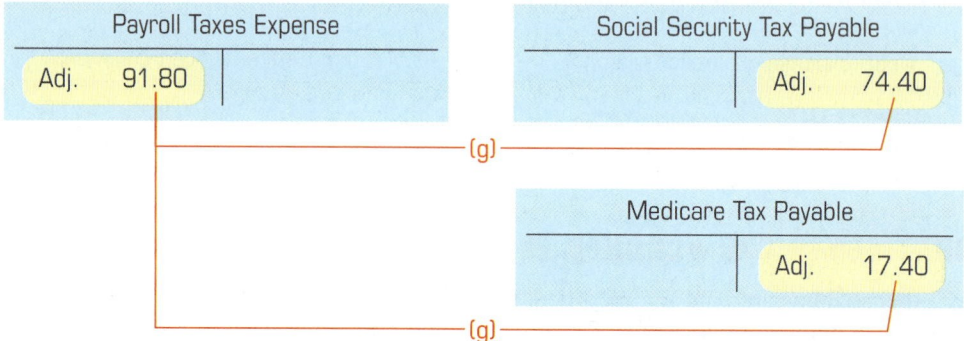

The entire $1,200 of accrued salaries is also subject to unemployment taxes. The unemployment tax rates for Whiteside Antiques are 0.8 percent for federal and 5.4 percent for state.

Federal unemployment tax	$1,200	×	0.008	=	$ 9.60
State unemployment tax	$1,200	×	0.054	=	64.80
Total accrued taxes					$74.40

Adjustment **(h)** appears on the worksheet in Figure 12.1 for accrued unemployment taxes.

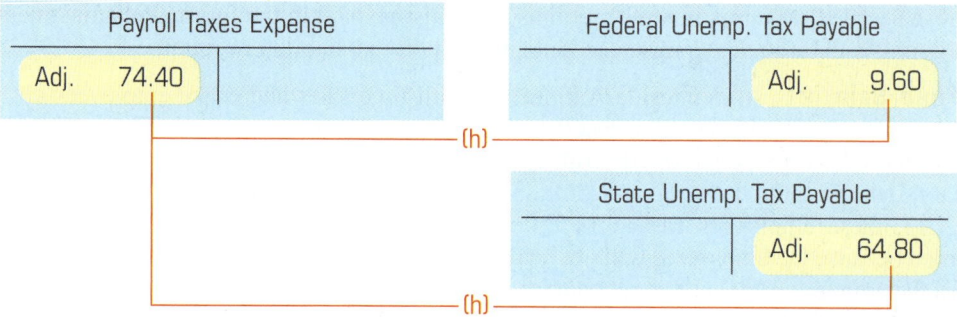

Accrued Interest on Notes Payable   On December 1, 2013, Whiteside Antiques issued a two-month note for $2,000, with annual interest of 12 percent. The note was recorded in the *Notes Payable—Trade* account. Whiteside Antiques will pay the interest when the note matures on February 1, 2014. However, the interest expense is incurred day by day and should be allocated to each fiscal period involved in order to obtain a complete and accurate picture of expenses. The accrued interest amount is determined by using the interest formula Principal × Rate × Time.

Principal	×	**Rate**	×	**Time**		
$2,000	×	0.12	×	1/12	=	$20

The fraction $\frac{1}{12}$ represents one month, which is 1/12 of a year.

Adjustment (i) appears on the worksheet in Figure 12.1 for the accrued interest expense.

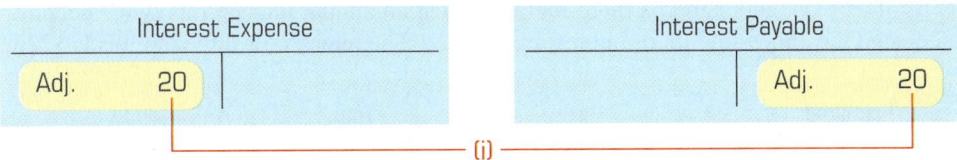

Other Accrued Expenses

Most businesses pay property taxes to state and local governments. They accrue these taxes at the end of the accounting period. Adjustments might also be necessary for commissions, professional services, and many other accrued expenses.

ADJUSTMENTS FOR PREPAID EXPENSES

Prepaid expenses, or **deferred expenses,** are expenses that are paid for and recorded before they are used. Often a portion of a prepaid item remains unused at the end of the period; it is applicable to future periods. When paid for, these items are recorded as assets. At the end of the period, an adjustment is made to recognize as an expense the portion used during the period. Whiteside Antiques makes adjustments for three types of prepaid expenses:

- prepaid supplies
- prepaid insurance
- prepaid interest on notes payable

> In its balance sheet for January 30, 2010, American Eagle Outfitters reported total current liabilities of $409 million. Included in that total were these items (all expressed in millions of dollars): Accounts Payable, $158.5; Current Portion of Deferred Lease Credits, $17.4; Accrued Compensation and Payroll Taxes, $55.1; Accrued Rent, $68.9; Accrued Income and Other Taxes, $20.6; Unredeemed Gift Cards and Gift Certificates, $39.4; Other Liabilities and Accrued Expenses, $19.1; and Note Payable, $30.

Supplies Used

When supplies are purchased, they are debited to the asset account *Supplies.* On the trial balance in Figure 12.1, *Supplies* has a balance of $6,300. A physical count on December 31 showed $1,325 of supplies on hand. This means that $4,975 ($6,300 − $1,325) of supplies were used during the year. An adjustment is made to charge the cost of supplies used to the current year's operations and to reflect the value of the supplies on hand.

Adjustment (j) appears on the worksheet in Figure 12.1 for supplies expense.

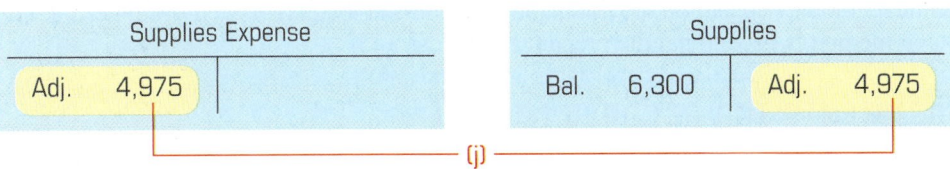

Expired Insurance

On January 2, 2013, Whiteside Antiques wrote a check for $7,350 for a three-year insurance policy. The asset account *Prepaid Insurance* was debited for $7,350. On December 31, 2013, one year of insurance had expired. An adjustment for $2,450 ($7,350 × 1/3) was made to charge the cost of the expired insurance to operations and to decrease *Prepaid Insurance* to reflect the prepaid insurance premium that remains.

Adjustment (k) appears on the worksheet in Figure 12.1 for the insurance.

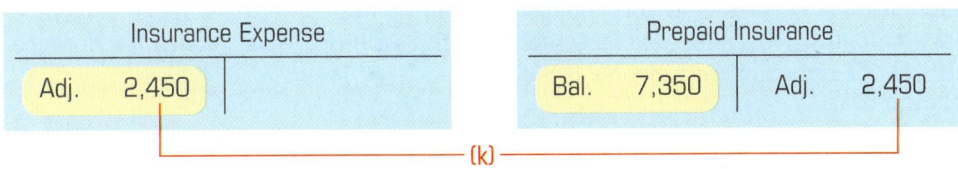

Prepaid Interest on Notes Payable On November 1, 2013, Whiteside Antiques borrowed $9,000 from its bank and signed a three-month note at an annual interest rate of 10 percent. The bank deducted the entire amount of interest in advance. The interest for three months is $225.

Principal	×	Rate	×	Time		
$9,000	×	0.10	×	3/12	=	$225

Whiteside Antiques received $8,775 ($9,000 − $225). The transaction was recorded as a debit to **Cash** for $8,775, a debit to **Prepaid Interest** for $225, and a credit to **Notes Payable—Bank** for $9,000.

On December 31, two months of prepaid interest ($225 × 2/3 = $150) had been incurred and needed to be recorded as an expense. The adjustment consists of a debit to **Interest Expense** and a credit to **Prepaid Interest.**

Adjustment (**l**) appears on the worksheet in Figure 12.1 for the interest expense.

Interest Expense		Prepaid Interest	
Adj. 150		Bal. 225	Adj. 150

(l)

important!

Some assets and liabilities always require adjustments
Although prepaid expenses are usually charged to an asset account when they are paid, some businesses charge most prepayments to expense. In either case, at the time financial statements are prepared the accounts must be adjusted to show the correct expense and prepayment.

>>3. OBJECTIVE

Compute adjustments for accrued and deferred income items, and enter the adjustments on the worksheet.

Other Prepaid Expenses Other common prepaid expenses are prepaid rent, prepaid advertising, and prepaid taxes. When paid, the amounts are debited to the asset accounts **Prepaid Rent, Prepaid Advertising,** and **Prepaid Taxes.** At the end of each period, an adjustment is made to transfer the portion used from the asset account to an expense account. For example, the adjustment for expired rent would be a debit to **Rent Expense** and a credit to **Prepaid Rent.**

Alternative Method Some businesses use a different method for prepaid expenses. At the time cash is paid, they debit an expense account (not an asset account). At the end of each period, they make an adjustment to transfer the portion that is not used from the expense account to an asset account.

Suppose that Whiteside used this alternative method when purchasing the two-year insurance policy. On January 1, 2013, the transaction would have been recorded as a debit to **Insurance Expense** for $7,350 and a credit to **Cash** for $7,350. On December 31, 2013, after the insurance coverage for one year had expired, coverage for two years remained. The adjustment would be recorded as a debit to **Prepaid Insurance** for $4,900 ($7,350 × 2/3) and a credit to **Insurance Expense** for $4,900.

Identical amounts appear on the financial statements at the end of each fiscal period, no matter which method is used to handle prepaid expenses.

ADJUSTMENTS FOR ACCRUED INCOME

Accrued income is income that has been earned but not yet received and recorded. On December 31, 2013, Whiteside Antiques had accrued interest on notes receivable.

Accrued Interest on Notes Receivable Interest-bearing notes receivable are recorded at face value and are carried in the accounting records at this value until they are collected. The interest income is recorded when it is received, which is normally when the note matures. However, interest income is earned day by day. At the end of the period, an adjustment is made to recognize interest income earned but not yet received or recorded.

On November 1, 2013, Whiteside Antiques accepted from a customer a four-month, 15 percent note for $1,200. The note and interest are due on March 1, 2014. As of December 31, 2013, two months (November and December) of interest income was earned but not received. The amount of earned interest income is $30.

Principal	$\times$	Rate	$\times$	Time		
$1,200	$\times$	0.15	$\times$	2/12	=	$30

Adjustment (**m**) appears on the worksheet in Figure 12.1 for the interest income. To record the interest income of $30 earned, but not yet received, an adjustment debiting the asset account *Interest Receivable* and crediting a revenue account called *Interest Income* is made.

Interest Receivable		Interest Income	
Adj. 30		Bal. 136	
		Adj. 30	

————————————————(m)————————————————

ADJUSTMENTS FOR UNEARNED INCOME

Unearned income, or **deferred income,** exists when cash is received before income is earned. Under the accrual basis of accounting, only income that has been earned appears on the income statement. Whiteside Antiques has no unearned income. The following is an example of unearned income for another business.

Unearned Subscription Income for a Publisher   Magazine publishers receive cash in advance for subscriptions. When the publisher receives the cash, it is unearned income and is a liability. It is a liability because the publisher has an obligation to provide magazines during the subscription period. As the magazines are sent to the subscribers, income is earned and the liability decreases.

Tech Publishing Corporation publishes *Consumer Technology Today.* When subscriptions are received, *Cash* is debited and *Unearned Subscription Income,* a liability account, is credited. At the end of the year, *Unearned Subscription Income* had a balance of $450,000. During the year, $184,000 of magazines were delivered; income was earned in the amount of $184,000. The adjustment to recognize income is a debit to *Unearned Subscription Income* for $184,000 and a credit to *Subscription Income* for $184,000.

After the adjustment, the *Unearned Subscription Income* account has a balance of $266,000, which represents subscriptions for future periods.

Unearned Subscription Income		
12/31 Adj. 184,000	12/31 Bal. 450,000	
	12/31 Bal. 266,000	

Other Unearned Income Items   Other types of unearned income include management fees, rental income, legal fees, architectural fees, construction fees, and advertising income. The cash received in advance is recorded as unearned income. As the income is earned, the amount is transferred from the liability account to a revenue account.

Alternative Method   Some businesses use a different method to handle unearned income. At the time the cash is received, a credit is made to a revenue account (not a liability account). At the end of each period, the adjustment transfers the portion that is not earned to a liability account. For example, suppose Tech Publishing Corporation uses this method. When cash for subscriptions is received, it is credited to *Subscription Income.* At the end of the period, an adjustment is made to transfer the unearned income to a liability account. The entry is a debit to *Subscription Income* and a credit to *Unearned Subscription Income.*

Identical amounts appear on the financial statements at the end of each fiscal period no matter which method is used to handle unearned income.

recall

Two Ways to Record Transactions

Earlier in this chapter you learned that prepaid expenses are usually charged to an asset account when paid, but may be charged to an expense account at that time. Likewise, unearned income is usually credited to a liability account when received, but may be credited to an income account. Be sure to understand how the transaction was originally entered before you begin making the adjusting entry.

Section 1 Self Review

QUESTIONS

1. Why is a 10-column worksheet used as part of the procedures for adjusting and closing accounts and preparing financial statements?

2. Why are there two amounts (a debit and a credit) in the adjustments column on the line for Merchandise Inventory in the 10-column worksheet?

3. Why are adjusting entries necessary?

EXERCISES

4. Samek Company adjusts and closes its accounts and prepares financial statements each month. In the December 31 Trial Balance column for debit balances, a balance of $6,000 is found in the Prepaid Rent account. A payment of $12,000 for prepayment of six months' rent was made on September 1.

   a. What is the amount of the adjusting entry for this item?

   b. What account would be debited and what account would be credited in the December 31 adjustments?

5. In Samek's December 31 trial balance, a credit balance of $14,000 appears in Unearned Fee Income. This amount represents a part of $21,000 received from a customer on November 1 covering work to be performed by Samek in November through January. What account will be debited and what account will be credited in the adjusting entry on December 31? What is the amount of the adjustment?

ANALYSIS

6. Your company prepares financial statements each month, using a 10-column worksheet to assemble data. What is the primary difference between the adjustments made on a monthly basis and those made on an annual basis?

(Answers to Section 1 Self Review are on pages 408–409.)

SECTION OBJECTIVES

TERMS TO LEARN

net income line
updated account balances

>> 4. **Complete a 10-column worksheet.**

WHY IT'S IMPORTANT
Using the worksheet is a convenient way to gather the information
needed for the financial statements.

Completing the Worksheet

After all adjustments have been entered on the worksheet, total the Adjustments Debit and Credit columns and verify that debits and credits are equal. The next step in the process is to prepare the Adjusted Trial Balance section.

Preparing the Adjusted Trial Balance Section

Figure 12.2 on pages 384–386 shows the completed worksheet for Whiteside Antiques. The Adjusted Trial Balance section of the worksheet is completed as follows:

>>**4. OBJECTIVE**
Complete a 10-column worksheet.

1. Combine the amount in the Trial Balance section and the Adjustments section for each account.

2. Enter the results in the Adjusted Trial Balance section. The accounts that do not have adjustments are simply extended from the Trial Balance section to the Adjusted Trial Balance section. For example, the balance of the *Cash* account is recorded in the Debit column of the Adjusted Trial Balance section without change.

3. The accounts that are affected by adjustments are recomputed. Follow these rules to combine amounts on the worksheet:

Trial Balance Section	Adjustments Section	Action
Debit	Debit	Add
Debit	Credit	Subtract
Credit	Credit	Add
Credit	Debit	Subtract

■ If the account has a debit balance in the Trial Balance section and a debit entry in the Adjustments section, add the two amounts. Look at the *Salaries Expense—Sales* account. It has a $78,490 debit balance in the Trial Balance section and a $1,200 debit entry in the Adjustments section. The new balance is $79,690 ($78,490 + $1,200). It is entered in the Debit column of the Adjusted Trial Balance section.

■ If the account has a debit balance in the Trial Balance section and a credit entry in the Adjustments section, subtract the credit amount. Look at the *Supplies* account. It has a $6,300 debit balance in the Trial Balance section and a $4,975 credit entry in the Adjustments section. The new balance is $1,325 ($6,300 − $4,975). It is entered in the Debit column of the Adjusted Trial Balance section.

FIGURE 12.2 Ten-Column Worksheet—Complete

Whiteside Antiques

Worksheet

Year Ended December 31, 2013

	ACCOUNT NAME	TRIAL BALANCE DEBIT	TRIAL BALANCE CREDIT	ADJUSTMENTS DEBIT	ADJUSTMENTS CREDIT
1	Cash	13 1 3 6 00			
2	Petty Cash Fund	1 0 0 00			
3	Notes Receivable	1 2 0 0 00			
4	Accounts Receivable	32 0 0 0 00			
5	Allowance for Doubtful Accounts		2 5 0 00		(c) 8 0 0 00
6	Interest Receivable			(m) 3 0 00	
7	Merchandise Inventory	52 0 0 0 00		(b) 47 0 0 0 00	(a) 52 0 0 0 00
8	Prepaid Insurance	7 3 5 0 00			(k) 2 4 5 0 00
9	Prepaid Interest	2 2 5 00			(l) 1 5 0 00
10	Supplies	6 3 0 0 00			(j) 4 9 7 5 00
11	Store Equipment	30 0 0 0 00			
12	Accumulated Depreciation—Store Equipment				(d) 2 4 0 0 00
13	Office Equipment	5 0 0 0 00			
14	Accumulated Depreciation—Office Equipment				(e) 7 0 0 00
15	Notes Payable—Trade		2 0 0 0 00		
16	Notes Payable—Bank		9 0 0 0 00		
17	Accounts Payable		24 1 2 9 00		
18	Interest Payable				(i) 2 0 00
19	Social Security Tax Payable		1 0 8 4 00		(g) 7 4 40
20	Medicare Tax Payable		2 5 0 00		(g) 1 7 40
21	Employee Income Taxes Payable		9 9 0 00		
22	Federal Unemployment Tax Payable				(h) 9 60
23	State Unemployment Tax Payable				(h) 6 4 80
24	Salaries Payable				(f) 1 2 0 0 00
25	Sales Tax Payable		7 2 0 0 00		
26	Bill Whiteside, Capital		61 2 2 1 00		
27	Bill Whiteside, Drawing	27 6 0 0 00			
28	Income Summary			(a) 52 0 0 0 00	(b) 47 0 0 0 00
29	Sales		561 6 5 0 00		
30	Sales Returns and Allowances	12 5 0 0 00			
31	Interest Income		1 3 6 00		(m) 3 0 00
32	Miscellaneous Income		3 6 6 00		
33	Purchases	321 5 0 0 00			
34	Freight In	9 8 0 0 00			
35	Purchases Returns and Allowances		3 0 5 0 00		
36	Purchases Discounts		3 1 3 0 00		
37	Salaries Expense—Sales	78 4 9 0 00		(f) 1 2 0 0 00	
38	Advertising Expense	7 4 2 5 00			
39	Cash Short or Over	1 2 5 00			
40	Supplies Expense			(j) 4 9 7 5 00	

	ADJUSTED TRIAL BALANCE		INCOME STATEMENT		BALANCE SHEET		
	DEBIT	CREDIT	DEBIT	CREDIT	DEBIT	CREDIT	
	13 1 3 6 00				13 1 3 6 00		1
	1 0 0 00				1 0 0 00		2
	1 2 0 0 00				1 2 0 0 00		3
	32 0 0 0 00				32 0 0 0 00		4
		1 0 5 0 00				1 0 5 0 00	5
		3 0 00				3 0 00	6
	47 0 0 0 00				47 0 0 0 00		7
	4 9 0 0 00				4 9 0 0 00		8
		7 5 00				7 5 00	9
	1 3 2 5 00				1 3 2 5 00		10
	30 0 0 0 00				30 0 0 0 00		11
		2 4 0 0 00				2 4 0 0 00	12
	5 0 0 0 00				5 0 0 0 00		13
		7 0 0 00				7 0 0 00	14
		2 0 0 0 00				2 0 0 0 00	15
		9 0 0 0 00				9 0 0 0 00	16
		24 1 2 9 00				24 1 2 9 00	17
		2 00				2 00	18
		1 1 5 8 40				1 1 5 8 40	19
		2 6 7 40				2 6 7 40	20
		9 9 0 00				9 9 0 00	21
		9 60				9 60	22
		6 4 80				6 4 80	23
		1 2 0 0 00				1 2 0 0 00	24
		7 2 0 0 00				7 2 0 0 00	25
		61 2 2 1 00				61 2 2 1 00	26
	27 6 0 0 00				27 6 0 0 00		27
	52 0 0 0 00	47 0 0 0 00	52 0 0 0 00	47 0 0 0 00			28
		561 6 5 0 00		561 6 5 0 00			29
	12 5 0 0 00		12 5 0 0 00				30
		1 6 6 00		1 6 6 00			31
		3 6 6 00		3 6 6 00			32
	321 5 0 0 00		321 5 0 0 00				33
	9 8 0 0 00		9 8 0 0 00				34
		3 0 5 0 00		3 0 5 0 00			35
		3 1 3 0 00		3 1 3 0 00			36
	79 6 9 0 00		79 6 9 0 00				37
	7 4 2 5 00		7 4 2 5 00				38
	1 2 5 00		1 2 5 00				39
	4 9 7 5 00		4 9 7 5 00				40

(continued)

FIGURE 12.2   Ten-Column Worksheet—Complete (concluded)

	ACCOUNT NAME	TRIAL BALANCE DEBIT	TRIAL BALANCE CREDIT	ADJUSTMENTS DEBIT	ADJUSTMENTS CREDIT
41	Depreciation Expense—Store Equipment			(d) 2 4 0 0 00	
42	Rent Expense	27 6 0 0 00			
43	Salaries Expense—Office	26 5 0 0 00			
44	Insurance Expense			(k) 2 4 5 0 00	
45	Payroll Taxes Expense	7 2 0 5 00		(g) 9 1 80	
46				(h) 7 4 40	
47	Telephone Expense	1 8 7 5 00			
48	Uncollectible Accounts Expense			(c) 8 0 0 00	
49	Utilities Expense	5 9 2 5 00			
50	Depreciation Expense—Office Equipment			(e) 7 0 0 00	
51	Interest Expense	6 0 0 00		(i) 2 0 00	
52				(l) 1 5 0 00	
53	Totals	674 4 5 6 00	674 4 5 6 00	111 8 9 1 20	111 8 9 1 20
54	Net Income				

- ■ If the account has a credit balance in the Trial Balance section and a credit entry in the Adjustments section, add the two amounts. Look at ***Allowance for Doubtful Accounts.*** It has a $250 credit balance in the Trial Balance section and an $800 credit entry in the Adjustments section. The new balance is $1,050 ($250 + $800). It is entered in the Credit column of the Adjusted Trial Balance section.

- ■ If the account has a credit balance in the Trial Balance section and a debit entry in the Adjustments section, subtract the debit amount. Whiteside Antiques had no such adjustments.

The Adjusted Trial Balance section now contains the **updated account balances** that will be used in preparing the financial statements.

Look at the ***Income Summary*** account. Recall that the debit entry in this account removed the *beginning* balance from ***Merchandise Inventory*** and the credit entry added the *ending* balance to ***Merchandise Inventory.*** Notice that the debit and credit amounts in ***Income Summary*** are not combined in the Adjusted Trial Balance section.

Once all the updated account balances have been entered in the Adjusted Trial Balance section, total and rule the columns. Confirm that total debits equal total credits.

Preparing the Balance Sheet and Income Statement Sections

To complete the Income Statement and Balance Sheet sections of the worksheet, identify the accounts that appear on the balance sheet. On Figure 12.2, the accounts from ***Cash*** through ***Bill Whiteside, Drawing*** appear on the balance sheet. For each account enter the amount in the appropriate Debit or Credit column of the Balance Sheet section of the worksheet.

For accounts that appear on the income statement, ***Sales*** through ***Interest Expense,*** enter the amounts in the appropriate Debit or Credit column of the Income Statement section. The ***Income Summary*** debit and credit amounts are also entered in the Income Statement section of the worksheet. Notice that the debit and credit amounts in ***Income Summary*** are not combined in the Income Statement section.

Calculating Net Income or Net Loss

Once all account balances have been entered in the financial statement sections of the worksheet, the net income or net loss for the period is determined.

	ADJUSTED TRIAL BALANCE		INCOME STATEMENT		BALANCE SHEET		
	DEBIT	CREDIT	DEBIT	CREDIT	DEBIT	CREDIT	
	2 400 00		2 400 00				41
	27 600 00		27 600 00				42
	26 500 00		26 500 00				43
	2 450 00		2 450 00				44
	7 371 20		7 371 20				45
							46
	1 875 00		1 875 00				47
	800 00		800 00				48
	5 925 00		5 925 00				49
	700 00		700 00				50
	770 00		770 00				51
							52
	726 772 20	726 772 20	564 406 20	615 362 00	162 366 00	111 410 20	53
			50 955 80			50 955 80	54
			615 362 00	615 362 00	162 366 00	162 366 00	55
							56

1. Total the Debit and Credit columns in the Income Statement section. For Whiteside Antiques, the debits total $564,406.20 and the credits total $615,362.00. Since the credits exceed the debits, the difference represents net income of $50,955.80.

2. To balance the Debit and the Credit columns in the Income Statement section, enter $50,955.80 in the Debit column of the Income Statement section. Total each column again and record the final total of each column ($615,362.00) on the worksheet.

3. Total the columns in the Balance Sheet section. Total debits are $162,366.00 and total credits are $111,410.20. The difference must equal the net income for the year, $50,955.80.

MANAGERIAL IMPLICATIONS <<

EFFECT OF ADJUSTMENTS ON FINANCIAL STATEMENTS

- If managers are to know the true revenue, expenses, and net income or net loss for a period, the matching process is necessary.

- If accounts are not adjusted, the financial statements will be incomplete, misleading, and of little help in evaluating operations.

- Managers need to be familiar with the procedures and underlying assumptions used by the accountant to make adjustments because adjustments increase or decrease net income.

- Managers need information about uncollectible accounts expense in order to review the firm's credit policy. If losses are too high, management might tighten the requirements for obtaining credit. If losses are very low, management might investigate whether easing credit requirements would increase net income.

- The worksheet is a useful device for gathering data about adjustments and for preparing the financial statements.

- Managers are keenly interested in receiving timely financial statements, especially the income statement, which shows the results of operations.

- Managers are also interested in the prompt preparation of the balance sheet because it shows the financial position of the business at the end of the period.

THINKING CRITICALLY

What are some possible consequences of not making adjusting entries?

4. Enter $50,955.80 in the Credit column of the Balance Sheet section. Total each column again and record the final total in each column ($162,366.00).

5. Rule the Debit and Credit columns in all sections to show that the worksheet is complete.

Notice that the net income is recorded in two places on the **net income line** of the worksheet. It is recorded in the Credit column of the Balance Sheet section because net income *increases* owner's equity. It is recorded in the Debit column of the Income Statement section to balance the two columns in that section.

Section 2 Self Review

QUESTIONS

1. In the adjusting entry for depreciation, is the **Depreciation Expense** account increased or decreased? Is the book value of the asset being depreciated increased or is it decreased?

2. In its December 31, 2013, financial reports, St. Claire Company's accountant made two errors: (1) failed to record interest of $300 accrued on a note payable; and (2) failed to record interest of $800 accrued on a note receivable. What is the net effect of these two errors on assets, on liabilities, on expenses, on income, and on owner's equity?

3. The trial balance in the first two columns of the worksheet balances and the adjustments in the next two columns balance. However, the adjusted trial balance does not balance. What is the likely source of the trouble?

EXERCISES

4. The amount of net income appears on the worksheet in the:

   a. Credit column of the balance sheet section.

   b. Debit column of the balance sheet section.

   c. Credit column of the income statement section.

   d. Debit column of the income statement section.

5. What account is debited and what account is credited to accrue interest on notes payable?

ANALYZE

6. Explain why an error in the amount of an adjusting entry usually affects at least two accounting periods.

(Answers to Section 2 Self Review are on page 409.)

REVIEW   Chapter Summary

Accrual basis accounting requires that all revenue and expenses for a fiscal period be matched and reported on the income statement to determine net income or net loss for the period. In this chapter, you have learned the techniques used to adjust accounts so that they accurately reflect the operations of the period.

Learning Objectives

1 Determine the adjustment for merchandise inventory, and enter the adjustment on the worksheet.

Merchandise inventory consists of goods that a business has on hand for sale to customers. When the trial balance is prepared at the end of the period, the *Merchandise Inventory* account still reflects the beginning inventory. Before the financial statements can be prepared, *Merchandise Inventory* must be updated to reflect the ending inventory for the period. The actual quantity of the goods on hand at the end of the period must be counted. Then the adjustment is completed in two steps:

1. Remove the beginning inventory balance from the *Merchandise Inventory* account. Debit *Income Summary;* credit *Merchandise Inventory.*

2. Add the ending inventory to the *Merchandise Inventory* account. Debit *Merchandise Inventory;* credit *Income Summary.*

2 Compute adjustments for accrued and prepaid expense items, and enter the adjustments on the worksheet.

Expense accounts are adjusted at the end of the period so that they correctly reflect the current period. Examples of adjustments include provision for uncollectible accounts and depreciation. Other typical adjustments of expense accounts involve accrued expenses and prepaid expenses.

- Accrued expenses are expense items that have been incurred or used but not yet paid or recorded. They include salaries, payroll taxes, interest on notes payable, and property taxes.

- Prepaid expenses are expense items that a business pays for and records before it actually uses the items. Rent, insurance, and advertising paid in advance are examples.

3 Compute adjustments for accrued and deferred income items, and enter the adjustments on the worksheet.

Revenue accounts are adjusted at the end of the period so that they correctly reflect the current period.

- Adjustments can affect either accrued income or deferred income.

- Accrued income is income that has been earned but not yet received and recorded.

- Deferred, or unearned, income is income that has not yet been earned but has been received.

4 Complete a 10-column worksheet.

When all adjustments have been entered on the worksheet, the worksheet is completed so that the financial statements can be prepared easily.

1. Figures in the Trial Balance section are combined with the adjustments to obtain an adjusted trial balance.

2. Each item in the Adjusted Trial Balance section is extended to the Income Statement and Balance Sheet sections of the worksheet.

3. The Income Statement columns are totaled and the net income or net loss is determined and entered in the net income line.

4. The amount of net income or net loss is entered in the net income line in the Balance Sheet section. After net income or net loss is added, the total debits must equal the total credits in the Balance Sheet section columns.

5 Define the accounting terms new to this chapter.

Glossary

Accrual basis (p. 372) A system of accounting by which all revenues and expenses are matched and reported on financial statements for the applicable period, regardless of when the cash related to the transaction is received or paid

Accrued expenses (p. 377) Expense items that relate to the current period but have not yet been paid and do not yet appear in the accounting records

Accrued income (p. 380) Income that has been earned but not yet received and recorded

Deferred expenses (p. 379) See Prepaid expenses

Deferred income (p. 381) See Unearned income

Inventory sheet (p. 373) A form used to list the volume and type of goods a firm has in stock

Net income line (p. 388) The worksheet line immediately following the column totals on which net income (or net loss) is recorded in two places: the Income Statement section and the Balance Sheet section

Prepaid expenses (p. 379) Expenses that are paid for and recorded before they are used, such as rent or insurance

Property, plant, and equipment (p. 376) Long-term assets that are used in the operation of a business and that are subject to depreciation (except for land, which is not depreciated)

Unearned income (p. 381) Income received before it is earned

Updated account balances (p. 386) The amounts entered in the Adjusted Trial Balance section of the worksheet

Comprehensive **Self Review**

1. Why is the accrual basis of accounting favored?

2. What is meant by the term "accrued income"?

3. How, if at all, does "accrued income" differ from "unearned income"?

4. On July 1, 2013, a landlord received $24,000 cash from a tenant, covering rent from that date through June 30, 2014. The payment was credited to *Rent Income.* Assuming no entry has been made in the income account since receipt of the payment, what would be the adjusting entry on December 31, 2013?

5. A completed worksheet for Holiday Company on December 31, 2013, showed a total of $930,000 in the debit column of the Income Statement section and a total credit of $905,000 in the credit column. Does this represent a profit or a loss for the year? How much?

(Answers to Comprehensive Self Review are on page 409.)

Discussion Questions

1. When a specific account receivable is deemed uncollectible it is written off by debiting _____ and crediting _____.

2. Income Summary amounts are extended to which statement columns on the worksheet?

3. What adjustment is made to record the estimated expense for uncollectible accounts?

4. Why is depreciation recorded?

5. What types of assets are subject to depreciation? Give three examples of such assets.

6. Explain the meaning of the following terms that relate to depreciation:
   a. Salvage value
   b. Depreciable base
   c. Useful life
   d. Straight-line method

7. What adjustment is made for depreciation on office equipment?

8. What is an accrued expense? Give three examples of items that often become accrued expenses.

9. What adjustment is made to record accrued salaries?

10. What is a prepaid expense? Give three examples of prepaid expense items.

11. How is the cost of an insurance policy recorded when the policy is purchased?

12. What adjustment is made to record expired insurance?

13. What is the alternative method of handling prepaid expenses?

14. What is accrued income? Give an example of an item that might produce accrued income.

15. What adjustment is made for accrued interest on a note receivable?

16. What is unearned income? Give two examples of items that would be classified as unearned income.

17. How is unearned income recorded when it is received?

18. What adjustment is made to record income earned during a period?

19. What is the alternative method of handling unearned income?

20. How does the worksheet help the accountant to prepare financial statements more efficiently?

21. *Unearned Fees Income* is classified as which type of account?

APPLICATIONS

Exercises

Determining the adjustments for inventory.   ◀ **Exercise 12.1**

The beginning inventory of a merchandising business was $121,000, and the ending inventory is $102,519. What entries are needed at the end of the fiscal period to adjust *Merchandise Inventory?*

Objective 1

Determining the adjustments for inventory.   ◀ **Exercise 12.2**

The Income Statement section of the worksheet of Smith Company for the year ended December 31, has $179,000 recorded in the Debit column and $203,344 in the Credit column on the line for the *Income Summary* account. What were the beginning and ending balances for *Merchandise Inventory?*

Objective 1

Computing adjustments for accrued and prepaid expense items.   ◀ **Exercise 12.3**

For each of the following independent situations, indicate the adjusting entry that must be made on the December 31, 2013, worksheet. Omit descriptions.

Objective 2

a. During the year 2013, Sam & Sons Company had net credit sales of $941,000. Past experience shows that 0.6 percent of the firm's net credit sales result in uncollectible accounts.

b. Equipment purchased by One Stop Shops for $29,355 on January 2, 2013, has an estimated useful life of nine years and an estimated salvage value of $1,743. What adjustment for depreciation should be recorded on the firm's worksheet for the year ended December 31, 2013?

c. On December 31, 2013, Parrish Plumbing Supply owed wages of $6,546 to its factory employees, who are paid weekly.

d. On December 31, 2013, Parrish Plumbing Supply owed the employer's social security (6.2%) and Medicare (1.45%) taxes on the entire $6,546 of accrued wages for its factory employees.

e. On December 31, 2013, Parrish Plumbing Supply owed federal (0.8%) and state (5.4%) unemployment taxes on the entire $6,546 of accrued wages for its factory employees.

Computing adjustments for accrued and prepaid expense items.   ◀ **Exercise 12.4**

For each of the following independent situations, indicate the adjusting entry that must be made on the December 31, 2013, worksheet. Omit descriptions.

Objective 2

a. On December 31, 2013, the *Notes Payable* account at King Manufacturing Company had a balance of $14,000. This balance represented a three-month, 9 percent note issued on November 1.

b. On January 2, 2013, Wayland's Word Processing Service purchased flash drives, paper, and other supplies for $5,950 in cash. On December 31, 2013, an inventory of supplies showed that items costing $1,517 were on hand. The **Supplies** account has a balance of $5,950.

c. On August 1, 2013, North Texas Manufacturing paid a premium of $12,324 in cash for a one-year insurance policy. On December 31, 2013, an examination of the insurance records showed that coverage for a period of five months had expired.

d. On April 1, 2013, Connie Crafts signed a one-year advertising contract with a local radio station and issued a check for $12,960 to pay the total amount owed. On December 31, 2013, the **Prepaid Advertising** account has a balance of $12,960.

Exercise 12.5
Objective 2

▶ **Recording adjustments for accrued and prepaid expense items.**

On December 1, 2013, Joe's Java Joint borrowed $31,000 from its bank in order to expand its operations. The firm issued a four-month, 11 percent note for $31,000 to the bank and received $29,864 in cash because the bank deducted the interest for the entire period in advance. In general journal form, show the entry that would be made to record this transaction and the adjustment for prepaid interest that should be recorded on the firm's worksheet for the year ended December 31, 2013. Omit descriptions. Round your answers to the nearest dollar.

Exercise 12.6
Objective 2

▶ **Recording adjustments for accrued and prepaid expense items.**

On December 31, 2013, the **Notes Payable** account at Beth's Boutique Shop had a balance of $52,000. This amount represented funds borrowed on a six-month, 9 percent note from the firm's bank on December 1. Record the journal entry for interest expense on this note that should be recorded on the firm's worksheet for the year ended December 31, 2013. Omit descriptions.

Exercise 12.7
Objective 3

▶ **Recording adjustments for accrued and deferred income items.**

For each of the following independent situations, indicate the adjusting entry that must be made on the December 31, 2013, worksheet. Omit descriptions.

a. On December 31, 2013, the **Notes Receivable** account at Monroe Materials had a balance of $16,000, which represented a six-month, 12 percent note received from a customer on September 1.

b. During the week ended June 7, 2013, Taylor Magazine Publishing received $40,000 from customers for subscriptions to its magazine *Modern Business.* On December 31, 2013, an analysis of the **Unearned Subscription Revenue** account showed that half of the subscriptions were earned in 2013.

c. On November 1, 2013, Peacock Realty Company rented a commercial building to a new tenant and received $48,000 in advance to cover the rent for six months. Upon receipt, the $48,000 was recorded in the Unearned Rent account.

d. On November 1, 2013, the Mighty Bucks Hockey Club sold season tickets for 40 home games, receiving $4,800,000. Upon receipt, the $4,800,000 was recorded in the Unearned Season Tickets Income account. At December 31, 2013, the mighty Bucks Hockey Club had played 5 home games.

PROBLEMS

Problem Set A

Problem 12.1A
Objectives 2, 3

▶ **Recording adjustments for accrued and prepaid items and unearned income.**

Based on the information below, record the adjusting journal entries that must be made for John Gavone Consulting on June 30, 2013. The company has a June 30 fiscal year-end. Use 18 as the page number for the general journal.

a.–b. Merchandise Inventory, before adjustment, has a balance of $7,500. The newly counted inventory balance is $8,000.

c. Unearned Seminar Fees has a balance of $6,000, representing prepayment by customers for five seminars to be conducted in June, July, and August 2013. Two seminars had been conducted by June 30, 2013.

d. Prepaid Insurance has a balance of $12,000 for six months insurance paid in advance on May 1, 2013.

e. Store Equipment costing $5,000 was purchased on March 31, 2013. It has a salvage value of $500, and a useful life of five years.

f. Employees have earned $250 that has not been paid at June 30, 2013.

g. The employer owes the following taxes on wages not paid at June 30, 2013: SUTA, $7.50; FUTA, $2,00; Medicare, $3.63; and Social Security, $15.50.

h. Management estimates uncollectible accounts expense at 1% of sales. This year's sales were $2,000,000.

i. Prepaid Rent has a balance of $6,600 for six months rent paid in advance on March 1, 2013.

j. The supplies account in the general ledger has a balance of $400. A count of supplies on hand at June 30, 2013 indicated $150 of supplies remain.

k. The company borrowed $6,000 from First Bank on June 1, 2013 and issued a four-month note. The note bears interest at 7%.

Analyze: After all adjusting entries have been journalized and posted, what is the balance of the **Prepaid Rent** account?

Recording adjustments for accrued and prepaid expense items and unearned income.

 **Problem 12.2A**

Objectives 2, 3

On July 1, 2013, Shawn Smith established his own accounting practice. Selected transactions for the first few days of July follow.

INSTRUCTIONS

1. Record the transactions on page 1 of the general journal. Omit descriptions. Assume that the firm initially records prepaid expenses as assets and unearned income as a liability.

2. Record the adjusting journal entries that must be made on July 31, 2013, on page 2 of the general journal. Omit descriptions.

DATE		TRANSACTIONS
July	1	Signed a lease for an office and issued Check 101 for $13,200 to pay the rent in advance for six months.
	1	Borrowed money from First National Bank by issuing a four-month, 12 percent note for $24,000; received $23,040 because the bank deducted the interest in advance.
	1	Signed an agreement with Young Corp. to provide accounting and tax services for one year at $6,000 per month; received the entire fee of $72,000 in advance.
	1	Purchased office equipment for $17,000 from Office Outfitters; issued a two-month, 12 percent note in payment. The equipment is estimated to have a useful life of six years and a $1,160 salvage value. The equipment will be depreciated using the straight-line method.
	1	Purchased a one-year insurance policy and issued Check 102 for $1,620 to pay the entire premium.
	3	Purchased office furniture for $16,600 from Office Warehouse; issued Check 103 for $8,400 and agreed to pay the balance in 60 days. The equipment has an estimated useful life of five years and a $1,000 salvage value. The office furniture will be depreciated using the straight-line method.
	5	Purchased office supplies for $1,810 with Check 104. Assume $800 of supplies are on hand July 31, 2013.

Analyze: What balance should be reflected in **Unearned Accounting Fees** at July 31, 2013?

Problem 12.3A ▶

Objectives 2, 3

Recording adjustments for accrued and prepaid expense items and earned income.

On July 31, 2013, after one month of operation, the general ledger of Michael Brady, Consultant, contained the accounts and balances given below.

INSTRUCTIONS

1. Prepare a partial worksheet with the following sections: Trial Balance, Adjustments, and Adjusted Trial Balance. Use the data about the firm's accounts and balances to complete the Trial Balance section.

2. Enter the adjustments described below in the Adjustments section. Identify each adjustment with the appropriate letter.

3. Complete the Adjusted Trial Balance section.

ACCOUNTS AND BALANCES

Cash	$25,010	Dr.
Accounts Receivable	1,340	Dr.
Supplies	860	Dr.
Prepaid Rent	9,000	Dr.
Prepaid Insurance	1,620	Dr.
Prepaid Interest	360	Dr.
Furniture	12,050	Dr.
Accumulated Depreciation—Furniture		
Equipment	6,400	Dr.
Accumulated Depreciation—Equipment		
Notes Payable	16,700	Cr.
Accounts Payable	4,500	Cr.
Interest Payable		
Unearned Consulting Fees	4,800	Cr.
Michael Brady, Capital	28,220	Cr.
Michael Brady, Drawing	2,000	Dr.
Consulting Fees	8,000	Cr.
Salaries Expense	3,200	Dr.
Utilities Expense	220	Dr.
Telephone Expense	160	Dr.
Supplies Expense		
Rent Expense		
Insurance Expense		
Depreciation Expense—Furniture		
Depreciation Expense—Equipment		
Interest Expense		

ADJUSTMENTS

a. On July 31, an inventory of the supplies showed that items costing $580 were on hand.

b. On July 1, the firm paid $9,000 in advance for six months of rent.

c. On July 1, the firm purchased a one-year insurance policy for $1,620.

d. On July 1, the firm paid $360 interest in advance on a four-month note that it issued to the bank.

e. On July 1, the firm purchased office furniture for $12,050. The furniture is expected to have a useful life of seven years and a salvage value of $1,550.

f. On July 1, the firm purchased office equipment for $6,400. The equipment is expected to have a useful life of five years and a salvage value of $1,600.

g. On July 1, the firm issued a three-month, 8 percent note for $7,800.

h. On July 1, the firm received a consulting fee of $4,800 in advance for a one-year period.

Analyze: By what total amount were the expense accounts of the business adjusted?

Recording adjustments and completing the worksheet.

◀ **Problem 12.4A**

Objectives 1, 2, 3, 4

e**X**cel

The Green Thumb Gallery is a retail store that sells plants, soil, and decorative pots. On December 31, 2013, the firm's general ledger contained the accounts and balances that appear below.

INSTRUCTIONS

1. Prepare the Trial Balance section of a 10-column worksheet. The worksheet covers the year ended December 31, 2013.

2. Enter the adjustments below in the Adjustments section of the worksheet. Identify each adjustment with the appropriate letter.

3. Complete the worksheet.

ACCOUNTS AND BALANCES

Cash	$ 5,700	Dr.
Accounts Receivable	2,600	Dr.
Allowance for Doubtful Accounts	52	Cr.
Merchandise Inventory	11,300	Dr.
Supplies	1,200	Dr.
Prepaid Advertising	960	Dr.
Store Equipment	8,100	Dr.
Accumulated Depreciation—Store Equipment	1,500	Cr.
Office Equipment	1,600	Dr.
Accumulated Depreciation—Office Equipment	280	Cr.
Accounts Payable	2,625	Cr.
Social Security Tax Payable	430	Cr.
Medicare Tax Payable	98	Cr.
Federal Unemployment Tax Payable		
State Unemployment Tax Payable		
Salaries Payable		
Beth Argo, Capital	25,457	Cr.
Beth Argo, Drawing	20,000	Dr.
Sales	90,048	Cr.
Sales Returns and Allowances	1,100	Dr.
Purchases	46,400	Dr.
Purchases Returns and Allowances	430	Cr.
Rent Expense	6,000	Dr.
Telephone Expense	590	Dr.
Salaries Expense	14,100	Dr.
Payroll Taxes Expense	1,270	Dr.
Income Summary		
Supplies Expense		
Advertising Expense		
Depreciation Expense—Store Equipment		
Depreciation Expense—Office Equipment		
Uncollectible Accounts Expense		

ADJUSTMENTS

a.–b. Merchandise inventory on December 31, 2013, is $12,321.

c. During 2013, the firm had net credit sales of $35,000; the firm estimates that 0.6 percent of these sales will result in uncollectible accounts.

d. On December 31, 2013, an inventory of the supplies showed that items costing $275 were on hand.

e. On October 1, 2013, the firm signed a six-month advertising contract for $960 with a local newspaper and paid the full amount in advance.

f. On January 2, 2012, the firm purchased store equipment for $8,100. At that time, the equipment was estimated to have a useful life of five years and a salvage value of $600.

g. On January 2, 2012, the firm purchased office equipment for $1,600. At that time, the equipment was estimated to have a useful life of five years and a salvage value of $200.

h. On December 31, 2013, the firm owed salaries of $1,830 that will not be paid until 2014.

i. On December 31, 2013, the firm owed the employer's social security tax (assume 6.2 percent) and Medicare tax (assume 1.45 percent) on the entire $1,830 of accrued wages.

j. On December 31, 2013, the firm owed federal unemployment tax (assume 0.8 percent) and state unemployment tax (assume 5.4 percent) on the entire $1,830 of accrued wages.

Analyze: By what total amount were the net assets of the business affected by adjustments?

Problem 12.5A ▶ **Recording adjustments and completing the worksheet.**

Objectives 1, 2, 3, 4

CONTINUING >>> Problem

Healthy Habits Foods Company is a distributor of nutritious snack foods such as granola bars. On December 31, 2013, the firm's general ledger contained the accounts and balances that follow.

INSTRUCTIONS

1. Prepare the Trial Balance section of a 10-column worksheet. The worksheet covers the year ended December 31, 2013.

2. Enter the adjustments in the Adjustments section of the worksheet. Identify each adjustment with the appropriate letter.

3. Complete the worksheet.

Note: This problem will be required to complete Problem 13.4A in Chapter 13.

ACCOUNTS AND BALANCES

Cash	$ 30,100	Dr.
Accounts Receivable	35,200	Dr.
Allowance for Doubtful Accounts	420	Cr.
Merchandise Inventory	86,000	Dr.
Supplies	10,400	Dr.
Prepaid Insurance	5,400	Dr.
Office Equipment	8,300	Dr.
Accum. Depreciation—Office Equipment	2,650	Cr.
Warehouse Equipment	28,000	Dr.
Accum. Depreciation—Warehouse Equipment	9,600	Cr.
Notes Payable—Bank	32,000	Cr.
Accounts Payable	12,200	Cr.
Interest Payable		
Social Security Tax Payable	1,680	Cr.
Medicare Tax Payable	388	Cr.
Federal Unemployment Tax Payable		
State Unemployment Tax Payable		
Salaries Payable		
Phillip Tucker, Capital	108,684	Cr.

ACCOUNTS AND BALANCES (CONT.)

Phillip Tucker, Drawing	56,000	Dr.
Sales	653,778	Cr.
Sales Returns and Allowances	10,000	Dr.
Purchases	350,000	Dr.
Purchases Returns and Allowances	9,200	Cr.
Income Summary		
Rent Expense	36,000	Dr.
Telephone Expense	2,200	Dr.
Salaries Expense	160,000	Dr.
Payroll Taxes Expense	13,000	Dr.
Supplies Expense		
Insurance Expense		
Depreciation Expense—Office Equip.		
Depreciation Expense—Warehouse Equip.		
Uncollectible Accounts Expense		
Interest Expense		

ADJUSTMENTS

a.–b. Merchandise inventory on December 31, 2013, is $78,000.

c. During 2013, the firm had net credit sales of $560,000; past experience indicates that 0.5 percent of these sales should result in uncollectible accounts.

d. On December 31, 2013, an inventory of supplies showed that items costing $1,180 were on hand.

e. On May 1, 2013, the firm purchased a one-year insurance policy for $5,400.

f. On January 2, 2011, the firm purchased office equipment for $8,300. At that time, the equipment was estimated to have a useful life of six years and a salvage value of $350.

g. On January 2, 2011, the firm purchased warehouse equipment for $28,000. At that time, the equipment was estimated to have a useful life of five years and a salvage value of $4,000.

h. On November 1, 2013, the firm issued a four-month, 12 percent note for $32,000.

i. On December 31, 2013, the firm owed salaries of $5,000 that will not be paid until 2014.

j. On December 31, 2013, the firm owed the employer's social security tax (assume 6.2 percent) and Medicare tax (assume 1.45 percent) on the entire $5,000 of accrued wages.

k. On December 31, 2013, the firm owed the federal unemployment tax (assume 0.8 percent) and the state unemployment tax (assume 5.4 percent) on the entire $5,000 of accrued wages.

Analyze: When the financial statements for Healthy Habits Foods Company are prepared, what net income will be reported for the period ended December 31, 2013?

Recording adjustments and completing the worksheet.

◀ **Problem 12.6A**
Objectives 1, 2, 3, 4

The Wine Shop is a retail store selling vintage wines. On December 31, 2013, the firm's general ledger contained the accounts and balances below. All account balances are normal.

Cash	28,386
Accounts Receivable	500
Prepaid Advertising	480
Supplies	300
Merchandise Inventory	15,000
Store Equipment	25,000
Accumulated Depreciation—Store Equipment	3,000
Office Equipment	5,000

Accumulated Depreciation—Office Equipment	1,500
Notes Payable, due 2014	20,000
Accounts Payable	2,705
Wages Payable	
Social Security Tax Payable	
Medicare Tax Payable	
Unearned Seminar Fees	6,000
Interest Payable	
Vincent Arroyo, Capital	32,700
Vincent Arroyo, Drawing	14,110
Income Summary	
Sales	153,970
Sales Discounts	200
Seminar Fee Income	
Purchases	91,000
Purchases Returns and Allowances	1,000
Freight In	225
Rent Expense	13,200
Wages Expense	24,000
Payroll Taxes Expense	3,324
Depreciation Expense—Store Equipment	
Depreciation Expense—Office Equipment	
Advertising Expense	
Supplies Expense	
Interest Expense	150

INSTRUCTIONS

1. Prepare the Trial Balance section of a 10-column worksheet. The worksheet covers the year ended December 31, 2013.

2. Enter the adjustments below in the Adjustments section of the worksheet. Identify each adjustment with the appropriate letter.

3. Complete the worksheet.

ADJUSTMENTS

a.–b. Merchandise inventory at December 31, 2013, was counted, and determined to be $12,000.

c. The amount recorded as prepaid advertising represents $480 paid on September 1, 2013, for 12 months of advertising.

d. The amount of supplies on hand at December 31 was $100.

e. Depreciation on store equipment was $3,125 for 2013.

f. Depreciation on office equipment was $1,000 for 2013.

g. Unearned Seminar Fees represents $6,000 received on November 1, 2013, for six seminars. At December 31, two of these seminars had been conducted.

h. Wages owed but not paid at December 31 were $500.

i. On December 31, 2013, the firm owed the employer's social security tax ($31.25) and Medicare tax ($7.25).

j. The note payable bears interest at 6% per annum. One month interest is owed at December 31, 2013.

Analyze: What was the amount of revenue earned by conducting seminars during the year ended December 31, 2013?

Problem Set B

Recording adjustments for accrued and prepaid items and unearned income.

◀ **Problem 12.1B**
Objectives 2, 3

Based on the information below, record the adjusting journal entries that must be made for June Kang Consulting Services on December 31, 2013. The company has a December 31 fiscal year-end. Use 18 as the page number for the general journal.

a.–b. Merchandise Inventory, before adjustment, has a balance of $9,000. The newly counted inventory balance is $10,500.

c. Unearned Seminar Fees has a balance of $10,000, representing prepayment by customers for four seminars to be conducted in December 2013 and January 2014. Three seminars had been conducted by December 31, 2013.

d. Prepaid Insurance has a balance of $12,000 for six months insurance paid in advance on October 1, 2013.

e. Store Equipment costing $5,000 was purchased on September 1, 2013. It has a salvage value of $500, and a useful life of five years.

f. Employees have earned $500 of wages not paid at December 31, 2013.

g. The employer owes the following taxes on wages not paid at December 31, 2013: SUTA, $15.00; FUTA, $4.00; Medicare, $7.25; and Social Security, $31.00.

h. Management estimates uncollectible accounts expense at 1.5% (0.015) of sales. This year's sales were $3,000,000.

i. Prepaid Rent has a balance of $13,200 for six months rent paid in advance on October 1, 2013.

j. The Supplies account in the general ledger has a balance of $500. A count of supplies on hand at December 31, 2013, indicated $225 of supplies remain.

k. The company borrowed $8,000 on a two-month note payable dated December 1, 2013. The note bears interest at 6%

Analyze: After all adjusting entries have been journalized and posted, what is the balance of the *Unearned Seminar Fees* account?

Recording adjustments for accrued and prepaid expense items and unearned income.

◀ **Problem 12.2B**
Objectives 2, 3

On June 1, 2013, Penelope Bermudez established her own advertising firm. Selected transactions for the first few days of June follow.

1. Record the transactions on page 1 of the general journal. Omit descriptions. Assume that the firm initially records prepaid expenses as assets and unearned income as a liability.

2. Record the adjusting journal entries that must be made on June 30, 2013, on page 2 of the general journal. Omit descriptions.

DATE	TRANSACTIONS
2013	
June 1	Signed a lease for an office and issued Check 101 for $18,000 to pay the rent in advance for six months.
1	Borrowed money from National Trust Bank by issuing a three-month, 10 percent note for $18,000; received $17,550 because the bank deducted interest in advance.
1	Signed an agreement with Glass Decorations, Inc. to provide advertising consulting for one year at $4,550 per month; received the entire fee of $54,600 in advance.
1	Purchased office equipment for $15,400 from The Equipment Depot; issued a three-month, 12 percent note in payment. The equipment is estimated to have a useful life of five years and a $1,000 salvage value and will be depreciated using the straight-line method.
1	Purchased a one-year insurance policy and issued Check 102 for $1,944 to pay the entire premium.
3	Purchased office furniture for $17,400 from Office Gallery; issued Check 103 for $8,400 and agreed to pay the balance in 60 days. The equipment is estimated to have a useful life of five years and a $1,200 salvage value and will be depreciated using the straight-line method.
5	Purchased office supplies for $2,810 with Check 104; assume $1,150 of supplies are on hand June 30, 2013.

Analyze: At the end of the year, 2013, how much of the rent paid on June 1 will have been charged to expense?

Problem 12.3B
Objectives 2, 3

▶ **Recording adjustments for accrued and prepaid expense items and unearned income.**

On September 30, 2013, after one month of operation, the general ledger of Cross Timbers Company contained the accounts and balances shown below.

INSTRUCTIONS

1. Prepare a partial worksheet with the following sections: Trial Balance, Adjustments, and Adjusted Trial Balance. Use the data about the firm's accounts and balances to complete the Trial Balance section.

2. Enter the adjustments described below in the Adjustments section. Identify each adjustment with the appropriate letter. (Some items may not require adjustments.)

3. Complete the Adjusted Trial Balance section.

ACCOUNTS AND BALANCES

Cash	$26,460	Dr.
Supplies	740	Dr.
Prepaid Rent	4,200	Dr.
Prepaid Advertising	3,750	Dr.
Prepaid Interest	450	Dr.
Furniture	4,840	Dr.
Accumulated Depreciation—Furniture		
Equipment	9,000	Dr.
Accumulated Depreciation—Equipment		
Notes Payable	20,250	Cr.
Accounts Payable	4,400	Cr.

ACCOUNTS AND BALANCES (CONT.)

Interest Payable		
Unearned Course Fees	22,000	Cr.
Scott Nelson, Capital	6,730	Cr.
Scott Nelson, Drawing	2,000	Dr.
Course Fees		
Salaries Expense	1,600	Dr.
Telephone Expense	120	Dr.
Entertainment Expense	220	Dr.
Supplies Expense		
Rent Expense		
Advertising Expense		
Depreciation Expense—Furniture		
Depreciation Expense—Equipment		
Interest Expense		

ADJUSTMENTS

a. On September 30, an inventory of the supplies showed that items costing $705 were on hand.

b. On September 1, the firm paid $4,200 in advance for six months of rent.

c. On September 1, the firm signed a six-month advertising contract for $3,750 and paid the full amount in advance.

d. On September 1, the firm paid $450 interest in advance on a three-month note that it issued to the bank.

e. On September 1, the firm purchased office furniture for $4,840. The furniture is expected to have a useful life of five years and a salvage value of $340.

f. On September 3, the firm purchased equipment for $9,000. The equipment is expected to have a useful life of five years and a salvage value of $1,200.

g. On September 1, the firm issued a two-month, 8 percent note for $5,250.

h. During September, the firm received $22,000 fees in advance. An analysis of the firm's records shows that $7,000 applies to services provided in September and the rest pertains to future months.

Analyze: What was the net dollar effect on income of the adjustments to the accounting records of the business?

Recording adjustments and completing the worksheet.

◄ **Problem 12.4B**
Objectives 1, 2, 3, 4

Fun Depot is a retail store that sells toys, games, and bicycles. On December 31, 2013, the firm's general ledger contained the following accounts and balances.

INSTRUCTIONS

1. Prepare the Trial Balance section of a 10-column worksheet. The worksheet covers the year ended December 31, 2013.

2. Enter the adjustments below in the Adjustments section of the worksheet. Identify each adjustment with the appropriate letter.

3. Complete the worksheet.

ACCOUNTS AND BALANCES

Cash	$ 26,400	Dr.
Accounts Receivable	22,700	Dr.
Allowance for Doubtful Accounts	320	Cr.
Merchandise Inventory	138,000	Dr.
Supplies	11,600	Dr.

ACCOUNTS AND BALANCES (CONT.)

Prepaid Advertising	5,280	Dr.
Store Equipment	32,500	Dr.
Accumulated Depreciation—Store Equipment	5,760	Cr.
Office Equipment	8,400	Dr.
Accumulated Depreciation—Office Equipment	1,440	Cr.
Accounts Payable	8,600	Cr.
Social Security Tax Payable	5,920	Cr.
Medicare Tax Payable	1,368	Cr.
Federal Unemployment Tax Payable		
State Unemployment Tax Payable		
Salaries Payable		
Janie Fielder, Capital	112,250	Cr.
Janie Fielder, Drawing	100,000	Dr.
Sales	1,043,662	Cr.
Sales Returns and Allowances	17,200	Dr.
Purchases	507,600	Dr.
Purchases Returns and Allowances	5,040	Cr.
Rent Expense	125,000	Dr.
Telephone Expense	4,280	Dr.
Salaries Expense	164,200	Dr.
Payroll Taxes Expense	15,200	Dr.
Income Summary		
Supplies Expense		
Advertising Expense	6,000	Dr.
Depreciation Expense—Store Equipment		
Depreciation Expense—Office Equipment		
Uncollectible Accounts Expense		

ADJUSTMENTS

a.–b. Merchandise inventory on December 31, 2013, is $148,000.

c. During 2013, the firm had net credit sales of $440,000. The firm estimates that 0.7 percent of these sales will result in uncollectible accounts.

d. On December 31, 2013, an inventory of the supplies showed that items costing $2,960 were on hand.

e. On September 1, 2013, the firm signed a six-month advertising contract for $5,280 with a local newspaper and paid the full amount in advance.

f. On January 2, 2012, the firm purchased store equipment for $32,500. At that time, the equipment was estimated to have a useful life of five years and a salvage value of $3,700.

g. On January 2, 2012, the firm purchased office equipment for $8,400. At that time, the equipment was estimated to have a useful life of five years and a salvage value of $1,200.

h. On December 31, 2013, the firm owed salaries of $8,000 that will not be paid until 2014.

i. On December 31, 2013, the firm owed the employer's social security tax (assume 6.2 percent) and Medicare tax (assume 1.45 percent) on the entire $8,000 of accrued wages.

j. On December 31, 2013, the firm owed federal unemployment tax (assume 0.8 percent) and state unemployment tax (assume 5.4 percent) on the entire $8,000 of accrued wages.

Analyze: If the adjustment for advertising had not been recorded, what would the reported net income have been?

Recording adjustments and completing the worksheet.

Whatnots is a retail seller of cards, novelty items, and business products. On December 31, 2013, the firm's general ledger contained the following accounts and balances.

◄ **Problem 12.5B**
Objectives 1, 2, 3, 4

Problem

INSTRUCTIONS

1. Prepare the Trial Balance section of a 10-column worksheet. The worksheet covers the year ended December 31, 2013.

2. Enter the adjustments in the Adjustments section of the worksheet. Identify each adjustment with the appropriate letter.

3. Complete the worksheet.

Note: This problem will be required to complete Problem 13.4B in Chapter 13.

ACCOUNTS AND BALANCES

Cash	$ 3,235	Dr.
Accounts Receivable	6,910	Dr.
Allowance for Doubtful Accounts	600	Cr.
Merchandise Inventory	16,985	Dr.
Supplies	750	Dr.
Prepaid Insurance	2,400	Dr.
Store Equipment	6,000	Dr.
Accumulated Depreciation—Store Equip.	2,000	Cr.
Store Fixtures	15,760	Dr.
Accumulated Depreciation—Store Fixtures	4,100	Cr.
Notes Payable	4,000	Cr.
Accounts Payable	600	Cr.
Interest Payable		
Social Security Tax Payable		
Medicare Tax Payable		
Federal Unemployment Tax Payable		
State Unemployment Tax Payable		
Salaries Payable		
Preston Allen, Capital	39,780	Cr.
Preston Allen, Drawing	8,000	Dr.
Sales	236,560	Cr.
Sales Returns and Allowances	6,000	Dr.
Purchases	160,000	Dr.
Purchases Returns and Allowances	2,000	Cr.
Income Summary		
Rent Expense	18,000	Dr.
Telephone Expense	2,400	Dr.
Salaries Expense	40,000	Dr.
Payroll Tax Expense	3,200	Dr.
Supplies Expense		
Insurance Expense		
Depreciation Expense—Store Equipment		
Depreciation Expense—Store Fixtures		
Uncollectible Accounts Expense		
Interest Expense		

ADJUSTMENTS

a.–b. Merchandise inventory on hand on December 31, 2013, is $15,840.

c. During 2013, the firm had net credit sales of $160,000. Past experience indicates that 0.8 percent of these sales should result in uncollectible accounts.

d. On December 31, 2013, an inventory of supplies showed that items costing $245 were on hand.

e. On July 1, 2013, the firm purchased a one-year insurance policy for $2,400.

f. On January 2, 2011, the firm purchased store equipment for $6,000. The equipment was estimated to have a five-year useful life and a salvage value of $1,000.

g. On January 4, 2011, the firm purchased store fixtures for $15,760. At the time of the purchase, the fixtures were assumed to have a useful life of seven years and a salvage value of $1,410.

h. On October 1, 2013, the firm issued a six-month, $4,000 note payable at 9 percent interest with a local bank.

i. At year-end (December 31, 2013), the firm owed salaries of $1,450 that will not be paid until January 2014.

j. On December 31, 2013, the firm owed the employer's social security tax (assume 6.2 percent) and Medicare tax (assume 1.45 percent) on the entire $1,450 of accrued wages.

k. On December 31, 2013, the firm owed federal unemployment tax (assume 1.0 percent) and state unemployment tax (assume 5.0 percent) on the entire $1,450 of accrued wages.

Analyze: After all adjustments have been recorded, what is the net book value of the company's assets?

Problem 12.6B ▶
Objectives 1, 2, 3, 4

Recording adjustments and completing the worksheet.

The Game Place is a retail store that sells computer games, owned by Matt Huffman. On December 31, 2013, the firm's general ledger contained the accounts and balances below. All account balances are normal.

ACCOUNTS AND BALANCES

Cash	32,465
Accounts Receivable	669
Prepaid Advertising	480
Supplies	425
Merchandise Inventory	18,500
Store Equipment	30,000
Accumulated Depreciation—Store Equipment	3,000
Office Equipment	4,800
Accumulated Depreciation—Office Equipment	1,500
Notes Payable, due 2014	22,500
Accounts Payable	3,725
Wages Payable	
Social Security Tax Payable	
Medicare Tax Payable	
Unearned Seminar Fees	7,500
Interest Payable	
Matt Huffman, Capital	43,000
Matt Huffman, Drawing	18,000
Income Summary	
Sales	162,660
Sales Discounts	180
Seminar Fee Income	
Purchases	92,500
Purchases Returns and Allowances	770
Freight In	275
Rent Expense	26,400
Wages Expense	18,000

ACCOUNTS AND BALANCES (CONT.)

Payroll Taxes Expense	1,811
Depreciation Expense—Store Equipment	
Depreciation Expense—Office Equipment	
Advertising Expense	
Supplies Expense	
Interest Expense	150

INSTRUCTIONS

1. Prepare the Trial Balance section of a 10-column worksheet. The worksheet covers the year ended December 31, 2013.
2. Enter the adjustments below in the Adjustments section of the worksheet. Identify each adjustment with the appropriate letter.
3. Complete the worksheet.

ADJUSTMENTS

a.–b. Merchandise inventory at December 31, 2013, was counted, and determined to be $20,000.

c. The amount recorded as prepaid advertising represents $480 paid on September 1, 2013, for six months of advertising.

d. The amount of supplies on hand at December 31 was $150.

e. Depreciation on store equipment was $4,500 for 2013.

f. Depreciation on office equipment was $1,500 for 2013.

g. Unearned Seminar Fees represents $7,500 received on November 1, 2013, for five seminars. At December 31, four of these seminars had been conducted.

h. Wages owed but not paid at December 31 were $800.

i. On December 31, 2013, the firm owed the employer's social securtity tax ($49.60) and Medicare tax ($11.60).

j. The note payable bears interest at 8% per annum. One month interest is owed at December 31, 2013.

Analyze: How did the balance of merchandise inventory change during the year ended December 31, 2013?

Critical Thinking Problem 12.1

Completing the Worksheet

The unadjusted trial balance of Ben's Jewelers on December 31, 2013, the end of its fiscal year, appears on page 406.

INSTRUCTIONS

1. Copy the unadjusted trial balance onto a worksheet and complete the worksheet using the following information:

   a.–b. Ending merchandise inventory, $98,700.

   c. Uncollectible accounts expense, $1,000.

   d. Store supplies on hand December 31, 2013, $625.

   e. Office supplies on hand December 31, 2013, $305.

   f. Depreciation on store equipment, $11,360.

   g. Depreciation on office equipment, $3,300.

   h. Accrued sales salaries, $4,000, and accrued office salaries, $1,000.

   i. Social security tax on accrued salaries, $310; Medicare tax on accrued salaries, $73. (Assumes that tax rates have increased.)

   j. Federal unemployment tax on accrued salaries, $40; state unemployment tax on accrued salaries, $270.

2. Journalize the adjusting entries on page 30 of the general journal. Omit descriptions.

3. Journalize the closing entries on page 32 of the general journal. Omit descriptions.

4. Compute the following:

    a. net sales

    b. net delivered cost of purchases

    c. cost of goods sold

    d. net income or net loss

    e. balance of *Ben Waites, Capital* on December 31, 2013.

Analyze: What change(s) to *Ben Waites, Capital* will be reported on the statement of owner's equity?

BEN'S JEWELERS		
Trial Balance		
December 31, 2013		
Cash	$ 13,050	Dr.
Accounts Receivable	49,900	Dr.
Allowance for Doubtful Accounts	2,000	Cr.
Merchandise Inventory	105,900	Dr.
Store Supplies	4,230	Dr.
Office Supplies	2,950	Dr.
Store Equipment	113,590	Dr.
Accumulated Depreciation—Store Equipment	13,010	Cr.
Office Equipment	27,640	Dr.
Accumulated Depreciation—Office Equipment	4,930	Cr.
Accounts Payable	4,390	Cr.
Salaries Payable		
Social Security Tax Payable		
Medicare Tax Payable		
Federal Unemployment Tax Payable		
State Unemployment Tax Payable		
Ben Waites, Capital	166,310	Cr.
Ben Waites, Drawing	30,000	Dr.
Income Summary		
Sales	862,230	Cr.
Sales Returns and Allowances	7,580	Dr.
Purchases	504,810	Dr.
Purchases Returns and Allowances	4,240	Cr.
Purchases Discounts	10,770	Cr.
Freight In	7,000	Dr.
Salaries Expense—Sales	75,950	Dr.
Rent Expense	35,500	Dr.
Advertising Expense	12,300	Dr.
Store Supplies Expense		
Depreciation Expense—Store Equipment		
Salaries Expense—Office	77,480	Dr.
Payroll Taxes Expense		
Uncollectible Accounts Expense		
Office Supplies Expense		
Depreciation Expense—Office Equipment		

Critical Thinking Problem 12.2

Net Profit

When Sandra Costello's father died suddenly, Sandra had just completed the semester in college, so she stepped in to run the family business, Costello's Delivery Service, until it could be sold. Under her father's direction, the company was a successful operation and provided ample money to meet the family's needs.

Sandra was majoring in biology in college and knew little about business or accounting, but she was eager to do a good job of running the business so it would command a good selling price. Since all of the services performed were paid in cash, Sandra figured that she would do all right as long as the *Cash* account increased. Thus, she was delighted to watch the cash balance increase from $25,000 at the beginning of the first month to $73,028 at the end of the second month—an increase of $48,028 during the two months she had been in charge. When she was presented an income statement for the two months by the company's bookkeeper, she could not understand why it did not show that amount as income but instead reported only $19,100 as net income.

Knowing that you are taking an accounting class, Sandra brings the income statement, shown below, to you and asks if you can help her understand the difference.

COSTELLO'S DELIVERY SERVICE Income Statement Months of June and July, 2013		
Operating Revenues		
Delivery Fees		$205,018
Operating Expenses		
Salaries and Related Taxes	$128,224	
Gasoline and Oil	32,000	
Repairs Expense	6,570	
Supplies Expense	2,268	
Insurance Expense	2,856	
Depreciation Expense	14,000	
Total Operating Expense		185,918
Net Income		$ 19,100

In addition, Sandra permits you to examine the accounting records, which show that the balance of *Salaries Payable* was $12,680 at the beginning of the first month but had increased to $25,040 at the end of the second month. Most of the balance in the *Insurance Expense* account reflects monthly insurance payments covering only one month each. However, the *Prepaid Insurance* account had decreased $300 during the two months, and all supplies had been purchased before Sandra took over. The balances of the company's other asset and liability accounts showed no changes.

1. Explain the cause of the difference between the increase in the *Cash* account balance and the net income for the two months.
2. Prepare a schedule that accounts for this difference.

BUSINESS CONNECTIONS

Out of Balance

Ethical DILEMMA

The president of Murray Stainless Steel Corporation has told you to go out to the factory and count merchandise inventory. He said the stockholders were coming for a meeting and he wanted to put on a good show. He asked you to make the inventory a bit heavy by counting one row twice. The higher ending inventory will show a higher net income. What should you do?

Financial Statement ANALYSIS

Balance Sheet

McCormick and Company, Incorporated reported the following in its *2009 Annual Report:*

Consolidated Balance Sheet		
at November 30 (millions)	*2009*	*2008*
Assets		
Cash and cash equivalents	*$ 39.5*	*$ 38.9*
Trade accounts receivable, net	*365.3*	*380.7*
Inventories	*445.9*	*439.0*
Prepaid expenses and other current assets	*119.8*	*109.7*
Total current assets	*970.5*	*968.3*
Property, plant, and equipment, net	*489.8*	*461.1*

Analyze:

1. Based on the information presented above, which categories might require adjusting entries at the end of an operating period?

2. List the potential adjusting entries. Disregard dollar amounts.

3. By what percentage did McCormick's inventories increase from 2008 to 2009?

TEAMWORK

Both Sellers and Servers Adjust

Accruals and deferrals can vary for each company. The adjusting entries for a service company will differ from those of a merchandising company. Brainstorm the adjusting entries similarities and differences for a service company and a merchandising company.

Internet CONNECTION

There Is Help for Preparing a Trial Balance

The trial balance worksheet is an organizational tool to view the accruals and deferrals on one piece of paper. Use your search engine to search for *Trial Balance Worksheet Templates.* Download several different forms of worksheets and notice the number of helpful excel templates available to download.

Answers to Self Reviews

Answers to Section 1 Self Review

1. The worksheet facilitates the end-of-period activities by assembling in one document all data needed. The worksheet provides a place for the trial balance, for entering the necessary adjusting entries, an adjusted trial balance to greatly reduce the chance for mathematical errors, and all the information necessary for closing entries and preparing the income statement and balance sheet.

2. Both the beginning and ending inventory are presented in the income statement, so both should ultimately appear in the Income Statement columns. In the adjusting entries, in effect the beginning balance is closed and transferred to the Income Summary. The ending inventory is entered in the Inventory account by a debit in the Adjustments column and a credit to Income Summary because it reduces the cost of goods sold.

3. Adjusting entries are necessary because the amounts shown for many accounts in the trial balance reflect old data that ignore the fact that assets shown have been partially consumed, that expenses and incomes have not been entered in the accounts even though they have been incurred or earned, and that some liabilities and assets are not reflected in the accounts.

4. **a.** The amount of adjustments is $2,000 ($12,000 ÷ 6).

    b. *Rent Expense* will be debited and *Prepaid Rent* will be credited.

5. *Unearned Fee Income* will be debited for $7,000 and *Fee Income* will be credited for that amount.

6. There is no difference except that the amounts will be different because in one case they reflect only one month's activities and in the other case they reflect 12 months' activities.

Answers to Section 2 Self Review

1. The *Depreciation Expense* account is increased. The book value of the asset is decreased.

2. The net effects are:

    a. Assets are understated by $800.

    b. Liabilities are understated by $300.

    c. Expenses are understated by $300.

    d. Income is understated by $800.

    e. Owner's equity is understated by $500.

3. It appears that there is an error in adding the adjustment amount, or subtracting that amount from, some trial balance amount(s).

4. **a.** "credit" balance sheet column

    d. "debit" income statement column

5. *Interest Expense* is debited and *Interest Payable* is credited.

6. Adjusting entries almost invariably involve the assignment of revenues or expenses to a specific accounting period. If the revenue or expense is not assigned to the correct period, it is assigned to an incorrect period. Thus, both periods are incorrectly stated.

Answers to Comprehensive Self Review

1. The accrual method properly matches expenses with revenues in each accounting period so that statement users can rely on the financial statements prepared for each period.

2. Accrued income is income that has been earned but which has not yet been received in cash or other assets.

3. Accrued income is income earned but not yet received. Unearned income is the reverse of accrued income: It is an amount that has been received, but which has not yet been earned.

4. *Rent Income* will be debited for $12,000 and *Unearned Rent Income* will be credited for that amount.

5. This represents a loss because expenses are greater than income. The loss is $25,000.

Financial Statements and Closing Procedures

Chapter 13

LEARNING OBJECTIVES

1. Prepare a classified income statement from the worksheet.
2. Prepare a statement of owner's equity from the worksheet.
3. Prepare a classified balance sheet from the worksheet.
4. Journalize and post the adjusting entries.
5. Journalize and post the closing entries.
6. Prepare a postclosing trial balance.
7. Journalize and post reversing entries.
8. Define the accounting terms new to this chapter.

NEW TERMS

classified financial statement
current assets
current liabilities
current ratio
gross profit
gross profit percentage
inventory turnover
liquidity
long-term liabilities
multiple-step income statement
plant and equipment
reversing entries
single-step income statement
working capital

Whole Foods www.wholefoodsmarket.com

Founded in 1980 in Austin, Texas, Whole Foods Market® is the world's leading retailer of natural and organic foods. In 2009, the company reported sales of $8 billion. The company operates approximately 284 stores in the United States, Canada, and the United Kingdom.

The volatile U.S. economy has impacted many businesses, including Whole Foods. For the first time in 30 years, Whole Foods experienced a decline in its comparable store sales. Due to the execution of a conservative growth and business strategy implemented in 2008, the company was able to adjust operationally to lower sales volumes and eventually delivered a 16 percent increase in adjusted EBITDA* on a 1 percent increase in sales.

---

*Earnings before income taxes, depreciation, and amortization

thinking critically

If you owned stock in Whole Foods Market, what types of financial information would be most important to you?

SECTION OBJECTIVES

>> 1. **Prepare a classified income statement from the worksheet.**

>> **WHY IT'S IMPORTANT**
To help decision makers, financial information needs to be presented in a meaningful and easy-to-use way.

>> 2. **Prepare a statement of owner's equity from the worksheet.**

>> **WHY IT'S IMPORTANT**
The statement of owner's equity reports changes to and balances in the owner's equity account.

>> 3. **Prepare a classified balance sheet from the worksheet.**

>> **WHY IT'S IMPORTANT**
Grouping accounts helps financial statement users to identify total assets, equity, and financial obligations of the business.

TERMS TO LEARN

classified financial statement
current assets
current liabilities
gross profit
liquidity
long-term liabilities
multiple-step income statement
plant and equipment
single-step income statement

Preparing the Financial Statements

The information needed to prepare the financial statements is on the worksheet in the Income Statement and Balance Sheet sections. At the end of the period, Whiteside Antiques prepares three financial statements: income statement, statement of owner's equity, and balance sheet, based on the worksheet you studied in Chapter 12. The income statement and the balance sheet are arranged in a classified format. On **classified financial statements,** revenues, expenses, assets, and liabilities are divided into groups of similar accounts and a subtotal is given for each group. This makes the financial statements more useful to the readers.

> The annual report of the Coca-Cola Company includes Consolidated Balance Sheets, Consolidated Statements of Income, and Consolidated Statements of Share-Owners' Equity. The annual report also contains a table of Selected Financial Data that reports five consecutive years of summarized financial information.

The Classified Income Statement

A classified income statement is sometimes called a **multiple-step income statement** because several subtotals are computed before net income is calculated. The simpler income statement you learned about in previous chapters is called a **single-step income statement.** It lists all revenues in one section and all expenses in another section. Only one computation is necessary to determine the net income (Total Revenue − Total Expenses = Net Income).

Figure 13.1 shows the classified income statement for Whiteside Antiques. Refer to it as you learn how to prepare a multiple-step income statement.

>>1. OBJECTIVE

Prepare a classified income statement from the worksheet.

OPERATING REVENUE

The first section of the classified income statement contains the revenue from operations. This is the revenue earned from normal business activities. Other income is presented separately near the bottom of the statement. For Whiteside Antiques, all operating revenue comes from sales of merchandise.

FIGURE 13.1   Classified Income Statement

Whiteside Antiques
Income Statement
Year Ended December 31, 2013

Operating Revenue						
Sales						561 650 00
Less Sales Returns and Allowances						12 500 00
Net Sales						549 150 00
Cost of Goods Sold						
Merchandise Inventory, Jan. 1, 2013				52 000 00		
Purchases			321 500 00			
Freight In			9 800 00			
Delivered Cost of Purchases			331 300 00			
Less Purchases Returns and Allowances	3 050 00					
Purchases Discounts	3 130 00		6 180 00			
Net Delivered Cost of Purchases				325 120 00		
Total Merchandise Available for Sale				377 120 00		
Less Merchandise Inventory, Dec. 31, 2013				47 000 00		
Cost of Goods Sold						330 120 00
Gross Profit on Sales						219 030 00
Operating Expenses						
Selling Expenses						
Salaries Expense—Sales			79 690 00			
Advertising Expense			7 425 00			
Cash Short or Over			125 00			
Supplies Expense			4 975 00			
Depreciation Expense—Store Equipment			2 400 00			
Total Selling Expenses				94 615 00		
General and Administrative Expenses						
Rent Expense			27 600 00			
Salaries Expense—Office			26 500 00			
Insurance Expense			2 450 00			
Payroll Taxes Expense			7 371 20			
Telephone Expense			1 875 00			
Uncollectible Accounts Expense			800 00			
Utilities Expense			5 925 00			
Depreciation Expense—Office Equipment			700 00			
Total General and Administrative Expenses				73 221 20		
Total Operating Expenses						167 836 20
Net Income from Operations						51 193 80
Other Income						
Interest Income			166 00			
Miscellaneous Income			366 00			
Total Other Income				532 00		
Other Expenses						
Interest Expense			770 00			
Net Nonoperating Expense						238 00
Net Income for Year						50 955 80

Because Whiteside Antiques is a retail firm, it does not offer sales discounts to its customers. If it did, the sales discounts would be deducted from total sales in order to compute net sales. The net sales amount is computed as follows:

```
Sales
(Sales Returns and Allowances)
(Sales Discounts)
―――――――――――――――――
Net Sales
```

The parentheses indicate that the amount is subtracted. Net sales for Whiteside Antiques are $549,150 for 2013.

COST OF GOODS SOLD

The Cost of Goods Sold section contains information about the cost of the merchandise that was sold during the period. Three elements are needed to compute the cost of goods sold: beginning inventory, net delivered cost of purchases, and ending inventory. The format is:

```
    Purchases
+   Freight In
    (Purchases Returns and Allowances)
    (Purchases Discounts)
    ―――――――――――――――――――――――
    Net Delivered Cost of Purchases

    Beginning Merchandise Inventory
+   Net Delivered Cost of Purchases
    ―――――――――――――――――――――――
    Total Merchandise Available for Sale
    (Ending Merchandise Inventory)
    ―――――――――――――――――――――――
    Cost of Goods Sold
```

For Whiteside Antiques, the net delivered cost of purchases is $325,120 and the cost of goods sold is $330,120. **Merchandise Inventory** is the one account that appears on both the income statement and the balance sheet. Beginning and ending merchandise inventory balances appear on the income statement. Ending merchandise inventory also appears on the balance sheet in the Assets section.

GROSS PROFIT ON SALES

The **gross profit** on sales is the difference between the net sales and the cost of goods sold. For Whiteside, net sales is the revenue earned from selling antique items. Cost of goods sold is what Whiteside paid for the antiques that were sold during the fiscal period. Gross profit is what is left to cover operating expenses and provide a profit. The format is:

```
Net Sales
(Cost of Goods Sold)
―――――――――――――――――
Gross Profit on Sales
```

The gross profit on sales is $219,030.

OPERATING EXPENSES

Operating expenses are expenses that arise from normal business activities. Whiteside Antiques separates operating expenses into two categories: *Selling Expenses* and *General and Administrative Expenses.* The selling expenses relate directly to the sale and delivery of goods. The general and administrative expenses are necessary for business operations but are not directly connected with the sales function. Rent, utilities, and salaries for office employees are examples of general and administrative expenses.

FIGURE 13.2

Statement of Owner's Equity

Whiteside Antiques									
Statement of Owner's Equity									
Year Ended December 31, 2013									
Bill Whiteside, Capital, January 1, 2013						61	2 2 1	00	
Net Income for Year	50	9 5 5	80						
Less Withdrawals for the Year	27	6 0 0	00						
Increase in Capital						23	3 5 5	80	
Bill Whiteside, Capital, December 31, 2013						84	5 7 6	80	

NET INCOME OR NET LOSS FROM OPERATIONS

Keeping operating and nonoperating income separate helps financial statement users learn about the operating efficiency of the firm. The format for determining net income (or net loss) from operations is:

Gross Profit on Sales
(Total Operating Expenses)
_____
Net Income (or Net Loss) from Operations

For Whiteside Antiques, net income from operations is $51,193.80.

OTHER INCOME AND OTHER EXPENSES

Income that is earned from sources other than normal business activities appears in the Other Income section. For Whiteside Antiques, other income includes interest on notes receivable and one miscellaneous income item.

Expenses that are not directly connected with business operations appear in the Other Expenses section. The only other expense for Whiteside Antiques is interest expense.

NET INCOME OR NET LOSS

Net income is all the revenue minus all the expenses. For Whiteside Antiques, net income is $50,955.80. If there is a net loss, it appears in parentheses. Net income or net loss is used to prepare the statement of owner's equity.

The Statement of Owner's Equity

>>2. OBJECTIVE
Prepare a statement of owner's equity from the worksheet.

The statement of owner's equity reports the changes that occurred in the owner's financial interest during the period. Figure 13.2 shows the statement of owner's equity for Whiteside Antiques. The ending capital balance for Bill Whiteside, $84,576.80, is used to prepare the balance sheet.

The Classified Balance Sheet

>>3. OBJECTIVE
Prepare a classified balance sheet from the worksheet.

The classified balance sheet divides the various assets and liabilities into groups. Figure 13.3 on the next page shows the balance sheet for Whiteside Antiques. Refer to it as you learn how to prepare a classified balance sheet.

CURRENT ASSETS

Current assets consist of cash, items that will normally be converted into cash within one year, and items that will be used up within one year. Current assets are usually listed in order of liquidity. Liquidity is the ease with which an item can be converted into cash. Current assets

FIGURE 13.3

Classified Balance Sheet

Whiteside Antiques
Balance Sheet
December 31, 2013

Assets				
Current Assets				
Cash				13 1 3 6 00
Petty Cash Fund				1 0 0 00
Notes Receivable				1 2 0 0 00
Accounts Receivable		32 0 0 0 00		
Less Allowance for Doubtful Accounts		1 0 5 0 00	30 9 5 0 00	
Interest Receivable				3 0 00
Merchandise Inventory				47 0 0 0 00
Prepaid Expenses				
Supplies		1 3 2 5 00		
Prepaid Insurance		4 9 0 0 00		
Prepaid Interest		7 5 00	6 3 0 0 00	
Total Current Assets				98 7 1 6 00
Plant and Equipment				
Store Equipment	30 0 0 0 00			
Less Accumulated Depreciation	2 4 0 0 00	27 6 0 0 00		
Office Equipment	5 0 0 0 00			
Less Accumulated Depreciation	7 0 0 00	4 3 0 0 00		
Total Plant and Equipment				31 9 0 0 00
Total Assets				130 6 1 6 00
Liabilities and Owner's Equity				
Current Liabilities				
Notes Payable—Trade		2 0 0 0 00		
Notes Payable—Bank		9 0 0 0 00		
Accounts Payable		24 1 2 9 00		
Interest Payable		2 0 00		
Social Security Tax Payable		1 1 5 8 40		
Medicare Tax Payable		2 6 7 40		
Employee Income Tax Payable		9 9 0 00		
Federal Unemployment Tax Payable		9 60		
State Unemployment Tax Payable		6 4 80		
Salaries Payable		1 2 0 0 00		
Sales Tax Payable		7 2 0 0 00		
Total Current Liabilities				46 0 3 9 20
Owner's Equity				
Bill Whiteside, Capital				84 5 7 6 80
Total Liabilities and Owner's Equity				130 6 1 6 00

recall

Book Value

Book value is the portion of the original cost that has not been depreciated. Usually, book value bears no relation to the market value of the asset.

are vital to the survival of a business because they provide the funds needed to pay bills and meet expenses. The current assets for Whiteside Antiques total $98,716.

PLANT AND EQUIPMENT

Noncurrent assets are called *long-term assets*. An important category of long-term assets is plant and equipment. **Plant and equipment** consists of property that will be used in the business for longer than one year. For many businesses, plant and equipment represents a sizable investment. The balance sheet shows three amounts for each category of plant and equipment:

Asset
(Accumulated depreciation)

Book value

For Whiteside Antiques, total plant and equipment is $31,900.

CURRENT LIABILITIES

Current liabilities are the debts that must be paid within one year. They are usually listed in order of priority of payment. Management must ensure that funds are available to pay current liabilities when they become due in order to maintain the firm's good credit reputation. For Whiteside Antiques, total current liabilities are $46,039.20.

LONG-TERM LIABILITIES

Long-term liabilities are debts of the business that are due more than one year in the future. Although repayment of long-term liabilities might not be due for several years, management must make sure that periodic interest is paid promptly. Long-term liabilities include mortgages, notes payable, and loans payable. Whiteside Antiques had no long-term liabilities on December 31, 2013.

OWNER'S EQUITY

Whiteside Antiques prepares a separate statement of owner's equity that reports all information about changes that occurred in Bill Whiteside's financial interest during the period. The ending balance from that statement is transferred to the Owner's Equity section of the balance sheet.

Section 1 Self Review

QUESTIONS

1. Why are financial statements prepared in classified form?

2. What is the distinction between current liabilities and long-term liabilities?

3. What is gross profit on sales?

EXERCISES

4. Which of the following is not a current asset?

   a. Merchandise inventory

   b. A note receivable due in 13 months

   c. Prepaid insurance covering the next eight months

   d. A note receivable due in eight months

5. How should purchases returns and allowances be shown on the income statement?

   a. As Other Income

   b. As a deduction from the delivered cost of purchases

   c. As an addition to Sales

   d. As Other Expenses

ANALYSIS

6. Assume that a business listed the *Freight In* account in the Operating Expense section of the income statement. What is the effect on net purchases? On total operating expenses? On net income from operations?

(Answers to Section 1 Self Review are on page 451.)

TERMS TO LEARN

current ratio
gross profit percentage
inventory turnover
reversing entries
working capital

Completing the Accounting Cycle

The complete accounting cycle was presented in Chapter 6 (pages 168–169). In this section, we will complete the accounting cycle for Whiteside Antiques.

>>**4. OBJECTIVE**

Journalize and post the adjusting entries.

Journalizing and Posting the Adjusting Entries

All adjustments are shown on the worksheet. After the financial statements have been prepared, the adjustments are made a permanent part of the accounting records. They are recorded in the general journal as adjusting journal entries and are posted to the general ledger.

JOURNALIZING THE ADJUSTING ENTRIES

Figure 13.4 shows the adjusting journal entries for Whiteside Antiques. Each adjusting entry shows how the adjustment was calculated. Supervisors and auditors need to understand, without additional explanation, why the adjustment was made.

Let's review the types of adjusting entries made by Whiteside Antiques:

Type of Adjustment	Worksheet Reference	Purpose
Inventory	(a–b)	Removes beginning inventory and adds ending inventory to the accounting records.
Expense	(c–e)	Matches expense to revenue for the period; the credit is to a contra asset account.
Accrued Expense	(f–i)	Matches expense to revenue for the period; the credit is to a liability account.
Prepaid Expense	(j–l)	Matches expense to revenue for the period; the credit is to an asset account.
Accrued Income	(m)	Recognizes income earned in the period. The debit is to an asset account *(Interest Receivable).*

FIGURE 13.4

Adjusting Entries in the General Journal

GENERAL JOURNAL   PAGE ___25___

	DATE		DESCRIPTION	POST. REF.	DEBIT	CREDIT	
1			*Adjusting Entries*				1
2	2013		*(Adjustment a)*				2
3	Dec.	31	Income Summary	399	52 000 00		3
4			Merchandise Inventory	121		52 000 00	4
5			To transfer beginning inventory				5
6			to Income Summary				6
7							7
8			*(Adjustment b)*				8
9		31	Merchandise Inventory	121	47 000 00		9
10			Income Summary	399		47 000 00	10
11			To record ending inventory				11
12							12
13			*(Adjustment c)*				13
14		31	Uncollectible Accounts Expense	685	800 00		14
15			Allowance For Doubtful Accounts	112		800 00	15
16			To record estimated loss				16
17			from uncollectible accounts				17
18			based on 0.80% of net				18
19			credit sales of $100,000				19
20							20
21			*(Adjustment d)*				21
22		31	Depreciation Expense—Store Equip.	620	2 400 00		22
23			Accum. Depreciation—Store Equip.	132		2 400 00	23
24			To record depreciation				24
25			for 2013 as shown by				25
26			schedule on file				26
27							27
28			*(Adjustment e)*				28
29		31	Depreciation Expense—Office Equip.	689	700 00		29
30			Accum. Depreciation—Office Equip.	142		700 00	30
31			To record depreciation				31
32			for 2013 as shown by				32
33			schedule on file				33
34							34
35			*(Adjustment f)*				35
36		31	Salaries Expense—Sales	602	1 200 00		36
37			Salaries Payable	229		1 200 00	37
38			To record accrued salaries				38
39			of part-time sales clerks				39
40			for Dec. 28–31				40

(continued)

FIGURE 13.4

Adjusting Entries in the General
Journal (continued)

GENERAL JOURNAL   PAGE ___26___

	DATE		DESCRIPTION	POST. REF.	DEBIT	CREDIT	
1			*Adjusting Entries*				1
2	*2013*		*(Adjustment g)*				2
3	*Dec.*	*31*	*Payroll Taxes Expense*	*665*	*9 1 80*		3
4			*Social Security Tax Payable*	*221*		*7 4 40*	4
5			*Medicare Tax Payable*	*223*		*1 7 40*	5
6			*To record accrued payroll*				6
7			*taxes on accrued salaries*				7
8			*for Dec. 28–31*				8
9							9
10			*(Adjustment h)*				10
11		*31*	*Payroll Taxes Expense*	*665*	*7 4 40*		11
12			*Fed. Unemployment Tax Payable*	*225*		*9 60*	12
13			*State Unemployment Tax Payable*	*227*		*6 4 80*	13
14			*To record accrued payroll*				14
15			*taxes on accrued salaries*				15
16			*for Dec. 28–31*				16
17							17
18			*(Adjustment i)*				18
19		*31*	*Interest Expense*	*695*	*2 0 00*		19
20			*Interest Payable*	*216*		*2 0 00*	20
21			*To record interest on a*				21
22			*2-month, $2,000, 12%*				22
23			*note payable dated*				23
24			*Dec. 1, 2013*				24
25							25
26			*(Adjustment j)*				26
27		*31*	*Supplies Expense*	*615*	*4 9 7 5 00*		27
28			*Supplies*	*129*		*4 9 7 5 00*	28
29			*To record supplies used*				29
30							30
31			*(Adjustment k)*				31
32		*31*	*Insurance Expense*	*660*	*2 4 5 0 00*		32
33			*Prepaid Insurance*	*126*		*2 4 5 0 00*	33
34			*To record expired*				34
35			*insurance on 3-year*				35
36			*policy purchased for*				36
37			*$7,350 on Jan. 2, 2013*				37
38							38
39							39
40							40

FIGURE 13.4

Adjusting Entries in the General
Journal (concluded)

	DATE		DESCRIPTION	POST. REF.	DEBIT	CREDIT	
1	2013		(Adjustment l)				1
2	Dec.	31	Interest Expense	695	1 5 0 00		2
3			Prepaid Interest	127		1 5 0 00	3
4			To record transfer of 2/3				4
5			of prepaid interest of				5
6			$225 for a 3-month,				6
7			10% note payable issued				7
8			to bank on Nov. 1, 2013				8
9							9
10			(Adjustment m)				10
11		31	Interest Receivable	116	3 0 00		11
12			Interest Income	491		3 0 00	12
13			To record accrued interest				13
14			earned on a 4-month,				14
15			15% note receivable				15
16			dated Nov. 1, 2013				16
17			($1,200 x 0.15 x 2/12)				17
18							18

GENERAL JOURNAL   PAGE __27__

POSTING THE ADJUSTING ENTRIES

After the adjustments have been recorded in the general journal, they are promptly posted to the general ledger. The word *Adjusting* is entered in the Description column of the general ledger account. This distinguishes it from entries for transactions that occurred during that period. After the adjusting entries have been posted, the general ledger account balances match the amounts shown in the Adjusted Trial Balance section of the worksheet in Figure 12.2.

Journalizing and Posting the Closing Entries

At the end of the period, the temporary accounts are closed. The temporary accounts are the revenue, cost of goods sold, expense, and drawing accounts.

JOURNALIZING THE CLOSING ENTRIES

The Income Statement section of the worksheet in Figure 12.2 on pages 384–386 provides the data needed to prepare closing entries. There are four steps in the closing process:

1. Close revenue accounts and cost of goods sold accounts with credit balances to *Income Summary.*
2. Close expense accounts and cost of goods sold accounts with debit balances to *Income Summary.*
3. Close *Income Summary,* which now reflects the net income or loss for the period, to owner's capital.
4. Close the drawing account to owner's capital.

Step 1: **Closing the Revenue Accounts and the Cost of Goods Sold Accounts with Credit Balances.** The first entry closes the revenue accounts and other temporary income statement accounts with credit balances. Look at the Income Statement

>>5. OBJECTIVE

Journalize and post the
closing entries.

section of the worksheet in Figure 12.2. There are five items listed in the Credit column, not including *Income Summary.* Debit each account, except *Income Summary,* for its balance. Credit *Income Summary* for the total, $568,362.

GENERAL JOURNAL PAGE __28__

	DATE		DESCRIPTION	POST. REF.	DEBIT	CREDIT	
1	2013		Closing Entries				1
2	Dec.	31	Sales	401	561 650 00		2
3			Interest Income	491	1 66 00		3
4			Miscellaneous Income	493	3 66 00		4
5			Purchases Returns and Allowances	503	3 050 00		5
6			Purchases Discounts	504	3 130 00		6
7			Income Summary			568 362 00	7

Step 2: **Closing the Expense Accounts and the Cost of Goods Sold Accounts with Debit Balances.** The Debit column of the Income Statement section of the worksheet in Figure 12.2 shows the expense accounts and the cost of goods sold accounts with debit balances. Credit each account, *except Income Summary,* for its balance. Debit *Income Summary* for the total, $512,406.20.

GENERAL JOURNAL PAGE __28__

	DATE		DESCRIPTION	POST. REF.	DEBIT	CREDIT	
1	2013						1
9	Dec.	31	Income Summary	399	512 406 20		9
10			Sales Returns and Allowances	451		12 500 00	10
11			Purchases	501		321 500 00	11
12			Freight In	502		9 800 00	12
13			Salaries Expense—Sales	602		79 690 00	13
14			Advertising Expense	605		7 425 00	14
15			Cash Short or Over	610		1 25 00	15
16			Supplies Expense	615		4 975 00	16
17			Depreciation Expense—Store Equip.	620		2 400 00	17
18			Rent Expense	640		27 600 00	18
19			Salaries Expense—Office	645		26 500 00	19
20			Insurance Expense	660		2 450 00	20
21			Payroll Taxes Expense	665		7 371 20	21
22			Telephone Expense	680		1 875 00	22
23			Uncollectible Accounts Expense	685		8 00 00	23
24			Utilities Expense	687		5 925 00	24
25			Depreciation Expense—Office Equip.	689		7 00 00	25
26			Interest Expense	695		7 70 00	26

Step 3: **Closing the Income Summary Account.** After the first two closing entries have been posted, the balance of the *Income Summary* account is equal to the net income or net loss for the period. The third closing entry transfers the *Income Summary* balance to the owner's capital account. *Income Summary* after the second closing entry has a balance of $50,955.80.

		Income Summary			
Adjusting Entries (a–b)	12/31	52,000.00	12/31	47,000.00	
Closing Entries	12/31	512,406.20	12/31	568,362.00	
		564,406.20		615,362.00	
			Bal.	50,955.80	

For Whiteside Antiques, the third closing entry is as follows. This closes the *Income Summary* account, which remains closed until it is used in the end-of-period process for the next year.

		GENERAL JOURNAL	PAGE	28	
	DATE	DESCRIPTION	POST. REF.	DEBIT	CREDIT
28	Dec. 31	Income Summary	399	50 955 80	
29		Bill Whiteside, Capital	301		50 955 80

Step 4: Closing the Drawing Account. This entry closes the drawing account and updates the capital account so that its balance agrees with the ending capital reported on the statement of owner's equity and on the balance sheet.

		GENERAL JOURNAL	PAGE	28	
	DATE	DESCRIPTION	POST. REF.	DEBIT	CREDIT
31	Dec. 31	Bill Whiteside, Capital	301	27 600 00	
32		Bill Whiteside, Drawing	302		27 600 00

POSTING THE CLOSING ENTRIES

The closing entries are posted from the general journal to the general ledger. The word *Closing* is entered in the Description column of each account that is closed. After the closing entry is posted, each temporary account balance is zero.

Preparing a Postclosing Trial Balance

After the closing entries have been posted, prepare a postclosing trial balance to confirm that the general ledger is in balance. Only the accounts that have balances—the asset, liability and owner's capital accounts—appear on the postclosing trial balance. The postclosing trial balance matches the amounts reported on the balance sheet. To verify this, compare the postclosing trial balance, Figure 13.5 on the next page, with the balance sheet, Figure 13.3 on page 416.

If the postclosing trial balance shows that the general ledger is out of balance, find and correct the error or errors immediately. Any necessary correcting entries must be journalized and posted so that the general ledger is in balance before any transactions can be recorded for the new period.

>>6. OBJECTIVE

Prepare a postclosing trial balance.

FIGURE 13.5

Postclosing Trial Balance

ACCOUNT NAME	DEBIT	CREDIT
Cash	13 136 00	
Petty Cash Fund	100 00	
Notes Receivable	1 200 00	
Accounts Receivable	32 000 00	
Allowance for Doubtful Accounts		1 050 00
Interest Receivable	30 00	
Merchandise Inventory	47 000 00	
Supplies	1 325 00	
Prepaid Insurance	4 900 00	
Prepaid Interest	75 00	
Store Equipment	30 000 00	
Accumulated Depreciation—Store Equipment		2 400 00
Office Equipment	5 000 00	
Accumulated Depreciation—Office Equipment		700 00
Notes Payable—Trade		2 000 00
Notes Payable—Bank		9 000 00
Accounts Payable		24 129 00
Interest Payable		20 00
Social Security Tax Payable		1 158 40
Medicare Tax Payable		267 40
Employee Income Taxes Payable		990 00
Federal Unemployment Tax Payable		9 60
State Unemployment Tax Payable		64 80
Salaries Payable		1 200 00
Sales Tax Payable		7 200 00
Bill Whiteside, Capital		84 576 80
Totals	134 766 00	134 766 00

Whiteside Antiques
Postclosing Trial Balance
December 31, 2013

Interpreting the Financial Statements

Interested parties analyze the financial statements to evaluate the results of operations and to make decisions. Interpreting financial statements requires an understanding of the business and the environment in which it operates as well as the nature and limitations of accounting information. Ratios and other measurements are used to analyze and interpret financial statements. Four such measurements are used by Whiteside Antiques.

The **gross profit percentage** reveals the amount of gross profit from each sales dollar. The gross profit percentage is calculated by dividing gross profit by net sales. For Whiteside, for every dollar of net sales, gross profit was almost 40 cents.

$$\frac{\text{Gross profit}}{\text{Net sales}} = \frac{\$219,030}{\$549,150} = 0.3988 = 39.9\%$$

Working capital is the difference between total current assets and total current liabilities. It is a measure of the firm's ability to pay its current obligations. Whiteside Antiques' working capital is $52,676.80, calculated as follows:

Current assets − Current liabilities = $98,716.00 − 46,039.20 = $52,676.80

The **current ratio** is a relationship between current assets and current liabilities that provides a measure of a firm's ability to pay its current debts. Whiteside has $2.14 in current assets for every dollar of current liabilities. The current ratio may also be compared to other firms in the same business. The current ratio is calculated in the following manner:

$$\frac{\text{Current assets}}{\text{Current liabilities}} = \frac{\$98,716.00}{\$46,039.20} = 2.14 \text{ to } 1$$

important!

Current Ratio

Banks and other lenders look closely at the current ratio of each loan applicant.

Caterpillar Inc. reported current assets of $26.8 billion and current liabilities of $19.3 billion on December 31, 2009. The current ratio shows that the business has $1.39 of current assets for each dollar of current liabilities.

Inventory turnover shows the number of times inventory is replaced during the accounting period. Inventory turnover is calculated in the following manner:

$$\text{Inventory turnover} = \frac{\text{Cost of goods sold}}{\text{Average inventory}}$$

$$\text{Average inventory} = \frac{\text{Beginning inventory} + \text{Ending inventory}}{2}$$

$$\text{Average inventory} = \frac{\$52{,}000 + \$47{,}000}{2} = \$49{,}500$$

$$\text{Inventory turnover} = \frac{\$330{,}120}{\$49{,}500} = 6.67 \text{ times}$$

For Whiteside Antiques, the average inventory for the year was $49,500. The inventory turnover was 6.67; that is, inventory was replaced about seven times during the year.

Journalizing and Posting Reversing Entries

Some adjustments made at the end of one period can cause problems in the next period. **Reversing entries** are made to reverse the effect of certain adjustments. This helps prevent errors in recording payments or cash receipts in the new accounting period.

Let's use adjustment **(f)** as an illustration of how reversing entries are helpful. On December 31, Whiteside Antiques owed $1,200 of salaries to its part-time sales clerks. The salaries will be paid in January. To recognize the salaries expense in December, adjustment **(f)** was made to debit *Salaries Expense—Sales* for $1,200 and credit *Salaries Payable* for $1,200. The adjustment was recorded and posted in the accounting records.

By payday on January 3, the part-time sales clerks have earned $1,700:

$1,200   earned in December
$ 500   earned in January

The entry to record the January 3 payment of the salaries is a debit to *Salaries Expense—Sales* for $500, a debit to *Salaries Payable* for $1,200, and a credit to *Cash* for $1,700. This entry recognizes the salary expense for January and reduces the *Salaries Payable* account to zero.

Salaries Expense—Sales		
1/3	500	

Cash			
12/31	13,136	1/3	1,700
Bal.	11,436		

Salaries Payable			
1/3	1,200	12/31	1,200
		Bal.	0

>>**7. OBJECTIVE**
Journalize and post reversing entries.

recall

Accrual Basis
Revenues are recognized when earned, and expenses are recognized when incurred or used, regardless of when cash is received or paid.

To record this transaction, the accountant had to review the adjustment in the end-of-period records and divide the amount paid between the expense and liability accounts. This review is time consuming, can cause errors, and is sometimes forgotten.

Reversing entries provide a way to guard against oversights, eliminate the review of accounting records, and simplify the entry made in the new period. As an example of a reversing entry, we will analyze the same transaction (January 3 payroll of $1,700) if reversing entries are made.

First, record the adjustment on December 31. Then record the reversing entry on January 1. Note that the reversing entry is the exact opposite (the reverse) of the adjustment. After the reversing entry is posted, the **Salaries Payable** account shows a zero balance and the **Salaries Expense—Sales** account has a credit balance. This is unusual because the normal balance of an expense account is a debit.

GENERAL JOURNAL   PAGE ___25___

	DATE	DESCRIPTION	POST. REF.	DEBIT	CREDIT	
1	2013	*Adjusting Entries*				1
35		*(Adjustment f)*				35
36	Dec. 31	Salaries Expense—Sales	602	1 2 0 0 00		36
37		Salaries Payable	229		1 2 0 0 00	37

GENERAL JOURNAL   PAGE ___29___

	DATE	DESCRIPTION	POST. REF.	DEBIT	CREDIT	
1	2014	*Reversing Entries*				1
2	Jan. 1	Salaries Payable	229	1 2 0 0 00		2
3		Salaries Expense—Sales	602		1 2 0 0 00	3

ACCOUNT _Salaries Payable_   ACCOUNT NO. _229_

DATE	DESCRIPTION	POST. REF.	DEBIT	CREDIT	BALANCE DEBIT	BALANCE CREDIT
2013						
Dec. 31	Adjusting	J25		1 2 0 0 00		1 2 0 0 00
2014						
Jan. 1	Reversing	J29	1 2 0 0 00			–0–

ACCOUNT _Salaries Expense—Sales_   ACCOUNT NO. _602_

DATE	DESCRIPTION	POST. REF.	DEBIT	CREDIT	BALANCE DEBIT	BALANCE CREDIT
2013						
Dec. 31	Balance				78 4 9 0 00	
31	Adjusting	J25	1 2 0 0 00		79 6 9 0 00	
31	Closing	J28		79 6 9 0 00	–0–	
2014						
Jan. 1	Reversing	J29		1 2 0 0 00		1 2 0 0 00

On January 3, the payment of $1,700 of salaries is recorded in the normal manner. Notice that this entry reduces cash and increases the expense account for the entire $1,700. It does not allocate the $1,700 between the expense and liability accounts.

GENERAL JOURNAL   PAGE ___30___

	DATE	DESCRIPTION	POST. REF.	DEBIT	CREDIT	
1	2014					1
2	Jan. 3	Salaries Expense—Sales	602	1 7 0 0 00		2
3		Cash	101		1 7 0 0 00	3

After this entry is posted, the expenses are properly divided between the two periods: $1,200 in December and $500 in January. The **Salaries Payable** account has a zero balance. The accountant did not have to review the previous records or allocate the payment between two accounts when the salaries were paid.

ACCOUNT _Salaries Expense—Sales_   ACCOUNT NO. _602_

DATE		DESCRIPTION	POST. REF.	DEBIT	CREDIT	BALANCE DEBIT	BALANCE CREDIT
2013							
Dec.	31	Balance				78 4 9 0 00	
	31	Adjusting	J25	1 2 0 0 00		79 6 9 0 00	
	31	Closing	J28		79 6 9 0 00	—0—	
2014							
Jan.	1	Reversing	J29		1 2 0 0 00		1 2 0 0 00
	3		J30	1 7 0 0 00		5 0 0 00	

IDENTIFYING ITEMS FOR REVERSAL

Not all adjustments need to be reversed. Normally, reversing entries are made for accrued items that involve future payments or receipts of cash. Reversing entries are not made for uncollectible accounts, depreciation, and prepaid expenses—if they are initially recorded as assets. However, when prepaid expenses are initially recorded as expenses (the alternative method), the end-of-period adjustment needs to be reversed.

Whiteside Antiques makes reversing entries for:

- accrued salaries—adjustment **(f),**
- accrued payroll taxes—adjustments **(g)** and **(h),**
- interest payable—adjustment **(i),**
- interest receivable—adjustment **(m).**

JOURNALIZING REVERSING ENTRIES

We just analyzed the reversing entry for accrued salaries, adjustment **(f).** The next two reversing entries are for accrued payroll taxes. Making these reversing entries means that the accountant does not have to review the year-end adjustments before recording the payment of payroll taxes in the next year.

GENERAL JOURNAL   PAGE _29_

	DATE		DESCRIPTION	POST. REF.	DEBIT	CREDIT	
1	2014						1
6	Jan.	1	Social Security Tax Payable	221	7 4 40		6
7			Medicare Tax Payable	223	1 7 40		7
8			Payroll Taxes Expense	665		9 1 80	8
9			To reverse adjusting entry				9
10			(g) made Dec. 31, 2013				10
11							11
12		1	Federal Unemployment Tax Payable	225	9 60		12
13			State Unemployment Tax Payable	227	6 4 80		13
14			Payroll Taxes Expense	665		7 4 40	14
15			To reverse adjusting entry				15
16			(h) made Dec. 31, 2013				16

The next reversing entry is for accrued interest expense. The reversing entry that follows prevents recording difficulties when the note is paid on February 1.

GENERAL JOURNAL   PAGE ___29___

	DATE		DESCRIPTION	POST. REF.	DEBIT	CREDIT	
18	Jan.	1	Interest Payable	216	2 0 00		18
19			Interest Expense	695		2 0 00	19
20			To reverse adjusting entry				20
21			(i) made Dec. 31, 2013				21

In addition to adjustments for accrued expenses, Whiteside Antiques made two adjustments for accrued income items. The next reversing entry is for accrued interest income on the note receivable. Whiteside will receive cash for the note and the interest on March 1. The reversing entry eliminates any difficulties in recording the interest income when the note is paid on March 1.

GENERAL JOURNAL   PAGE ___29___

	DATE		DESCRIPTION	POST. REF.	DEBIT	CREDIT	
23	Jan.	1	Interest Income	491	3 0 00		23
24			Interest Receivable	116		3 0 00	24
25			To reverse adjusting entry				25
26			(m) made Dec. 31, 2013				26

After the reversing entry has been posted, the **Interest Receivable** account has a zero balance and the **Interest Income** account has a debit balance of $30. This is unusual because the normal balance of **Interest Income** is a credit.

On March 1, Whiteside Antiques received a check for $1,260 in payment of the note ($1,200) and the interest ($60). The transaction is recorded in the normal manner as a debit to **Cash** for $1,260, a credit to **Notes Receivable** for $1,200, and a credit to **Interest Income** for $60.

Refer to the **Interest Income** general ledger account below. After this entry has been posted, interest income is properly divided between the two periods, $30 in the previous year and $30 in the current year. The balance of **Interest Receivable** is zero. The accountant does not have to review the year-end adjustments before recording the receipt of the principal and interest relating to the note receivable on March 1.

ACCOUNT __Interest Receivable__   ACCOUNT NO. __116__

DATE		DESCRIPTION	POST. REF.	DEBIT	CREDIT	BALANCE DEBIT	BALANCE CREDIT
2013							
Dec.	31	Adjusting	J27	3 0 00		3 0 00	
2014							
Jan.	1	Reversing	J29		3 0 00	—0—	

ACCOUNT __Interest Income__   ACCOUNT NO. __491__

DATE		DESCRIPTION	POST. REF.	DEBIT	CREDIT	BALANCE DEBIT	BALANCE CREDIT
2013							
Dec.	31	Balance					1 3 6 00
	31	Adjusting	J27		3 0 00		1 6 6 00
	31	Closing	J28	1 6 6 00			—0—
2014							
Jan.	1	Reversing	J29	3 0 00		3 0 00	
Mar.	1		CR3		6 0 00		3 0 00

Review of the Accounting Cycle

In Chapters 7, 8, and 9, Maxx-Out Sporting Goods was used to introduce accounting procedures, records, and statements for merchandising businesses. In Chapters 12 and 13, Whiteside Antiques was used to illustrate the end-of-period activities for merchandising businesses. Underlying the various procedures described were the steps in the accounting cycle. Let's review the accounting cycle.

1. ***Analyze transactions.*** Transaction data comes into an accounting system from a variety of source documents—sales slips, purchase invoices, credit memorandums, check stubs, and so on. Each document is analyzed to determine the accounts and amounts affected.

2. ***Journalize the data about transactions.*** Each transaction is recorded in either a special journal or the general journal.

3. ***Post the data about transactions.*** Each transaction is transferred from the journal to the ledger accounts. Merchandising businesses typically maintain several subsidiary ledgers in addition to the general ledger.

4. ***Prepare a worksheet.*** At the end of each period, a worksheet is prepared. The Trial Balance section of the worksheet is used to prove the equality of the debits and credits in the general ledger. Adjustments are entered in the Adjustments section so that the financial statements will be prepared using the accrual basis of accounting. The Adjusted Trial Balance section is used to prove the equality of the debit and credits of the updated account balances. The Income Statement and Balance Sheet sections are used to arrange data in an orderly manner.

5. ***Prepare financial statements.*** A formal set of financial statements is prepared to report information to interested parties.

6. ***Journalize and post adjusting entries.*** Adjusting entries are journalized and posted in the accounting records. This creates a permanent record of the changes shown on the worksheet.

7. ***Journalize and post closing entries.*** Closing entries are journalized and posted in order to transfer the results of operations to owner's equity and to prepare the temporary accounts for the next period. The closing entries reduce the temporary account balances to zero.

8. ***Prepare a postclosing trial balance.*** The postclosing trial balance confirms that the general ledger is still in balance and that the temporary accounts have zero balances.

9. ***Interpret the financial information.*** The accountant, owners, managers, and other interested parties interpret the information shown in the financial statements and other less formal financial reports that might be prepared. This information is used to evaluate the results of operations and the financial position of the business and to make decisions.

In addition to the nine steps listed here, some firms record reversing entries. Reversing entries simplify the recording of cash payments for accrued expenses and cash receipts for accrued income.

Figure 13.6 on the next page shows the flow of data through an accounting system that uses special journals and subsidiary ledgers. The system is composed of subsystems that perform specialized functions.

The accounts receivable area records transactions involving sales and cash receipts and maintains the individual accounts for credit customers. This area also handles billing for credit customers.

The accounts payable area records transactions involving purchases and cash payments and maintains the individual accounts for creditors.

The general ledger and financial reporting area records transactions in the general journal, maintains the general ledger accounts, performs the end-of-period procedures, and prepares financial statements. This area is the focal point for the accounting system because all transactions eventually flow into the general ledger. In turn, the general ledger provides the data that appear in the financial statements.

ABOUT
ACCOUNTING

Professional Conduct
In September 1998, the Securities and Exchange (SEC) defined improper professional conduct by accountants. The new rule allowed the SEC to censure, suspend, or bar accountants who violate it. The American Institute of Certified Public Accountants (AICPA) supported the rule. The rule led to the dissolution of one of the nation's "big five" accounting firms (Arthur Andersen) in 2003 following the imposition of severe sanctions of the firm in the "Enron Affair," in which Arthur Andersen was the auditor for Enron. The Sarbanes-Oxley Act has further strengthened the SEC's power over professional conduct by accountants.

MANAGERIAL IMPLICATIONS <<

FINANCIAL STATEMENTS

- Managers carefully study the financial statements to evaluate the operating efficiency and financial strength of the business.

- A common analysis technique is to compare the data on current statements with the data from previous statements. This can reveal developing trends.

- In large businesses, financial statements are compared with the published financial reports of other companies in the same industry.

- In order to evaluate information on classified financial statements, managers need to understand the nature and significance of the groupings.

- Management ensures that closing entries are promptly made so that transactions for the new period can be recorded. Any significant delay means that valuable information, such as the firm's cash position, will not be available or up to date.

- The efficiency and effectiveness of the adjusting and closing procedures can have a positive effect on the annual independent audit. For example, detailed descriptions in the general journal make it easy for the auditor to understand the adjusting entries.

THINKING CRITICALLY

How can managers use the financial statements to learn about a company's operating efficiency?

FIGURE 13.6 Flow of Financial Data through an Accounting System

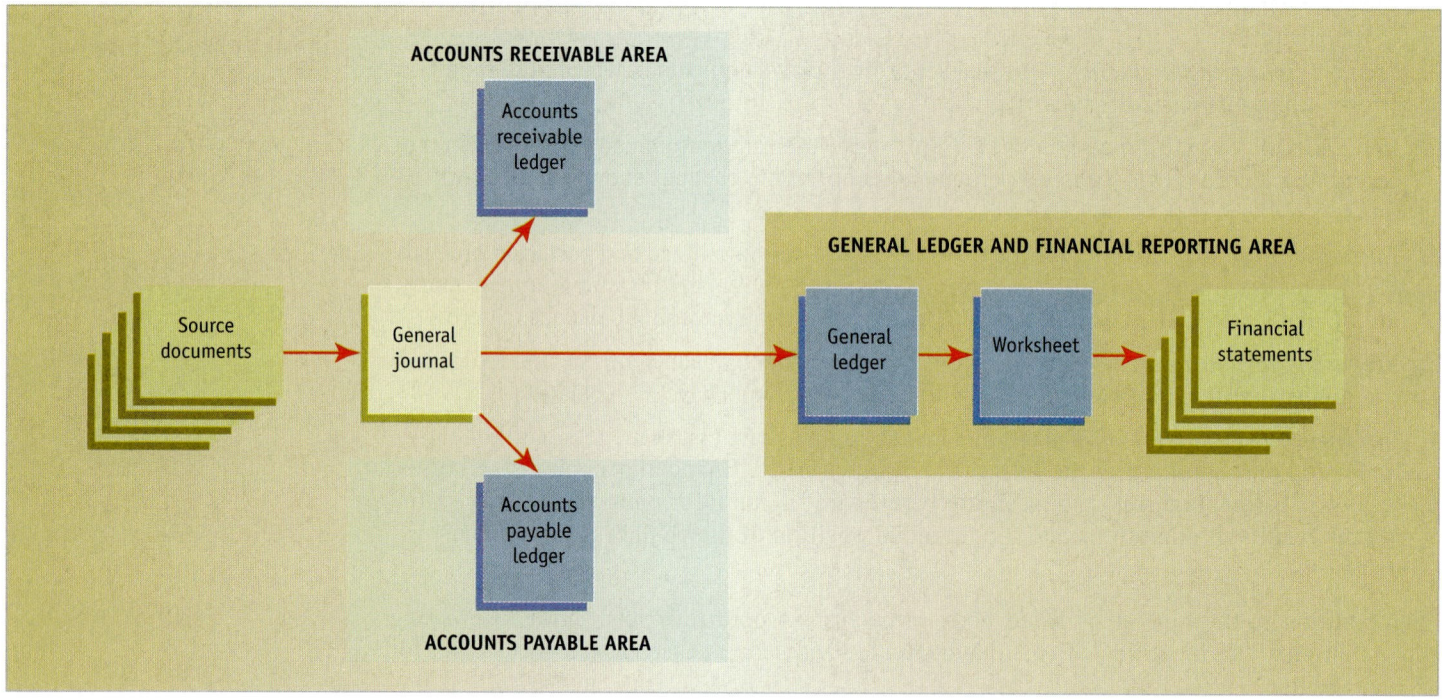

Section 2 Self Review

QUESTIONS

1. Which adjusting entries should be reversed?

2. Why do adjusting entries need detailed explanations in the general journal?

3. What do the four steps in the closing process accomplish?

EXERCISES

4. A reversing entry is made for an end-of-period adjustment that recorded:

   a. estimated bad debts for the period.

   b. an accrued expense that involves future cash payments.

   c. a transfer of an amount from a prepaid expense account to an expense account.

   d. the change in merchandise inventory.

5. The current ratio is:

   a. current liabilities divided by current assets,

   b. the sum of Cash, Accounts Receivable and Notes Receivable, divided by Current Liabilities.

   c. current assets divided by total liabilities.

   d. current assets divided by current liabilities.

ANALYSIS

6. At the end of the previous accounting period, an adjusting entry to record accrued employer's payroll taxes was made. Reversing entries were not made for the current accounting period. What effect will this have on the current period's financial statements?

(Answers to Section 2 Self Review are on page 451.)

13 Chapter REVIEW Chapter Summary

In this chapter, you have learned how to prepare classified financial statements from the worksheet and how to close the accounting records for the period.

Learning Objectives

1 Prepare a classified income statement from the worksheet.

- A classified income statement for a merchandising business usually includes these sections: Operating Revenue, Cost of Goods Sold, Gross Profit on Sales, Operating Expenses, and Net Income.

- To make the income statement even more useful, operating expenses may be broken down into categories, such as selling expenses and general and administrative expenses.

2 Prepare a statement of owner's equity from the worksheet.

A statement of owner's equity is prepared to provide detailed information about the changes in the owner's financial interest during the period. The ending owner's capital balance is used to prepare the balance sheet.

3 Prepare a classified balance sheet from the worksheet.

- Assets are usually presented in two groups—current assets, and plant and equipment. Current assets consist of cash, items to be converted into cash within one year, and items to be used up within one year. Plant and equipment consists of property that will be used for a long time in the operations of the business.

- Liabilities are also divided into two groups—current liabilities and long-term liabilities. Current liabilities will normally be paid within one year. Long-term liabilities are due in more than one year.

4 Journalize and post the adjusting entries.

When the year-end worksheet and financial statements have been completed, adjusting entries are recorded in the general journal and posted to the general ledger. The data comes from the worksheet Adjustments section.

5 Journalize and post the closing entries.

After the adjusting entries have been journalized and posted, the closing entries should be recorded in the records of the business. The data in the Income Statement section of the worksheet can be used to journalize the closing entries.

6 Prepare a postclosing trial balance.

To confirm that the general ledger is still in balance after the adjusting and closing entries have been posted, a postclosing trial balance is prepared.

7 Journalize and post reversing entries.

At the start of each new period, most firms follow the practice of reversing certain adjustments that were made in the previous period.

- This is done to avoid recording problems with transactions that will occur in the new period.

- Usually, only adjusting entries for accrued expenses and accrued income need be considered for reversing. Of these, usually only accrued expense and income items involving future payments and receipts of cash can cause difficulties later and should therefore be reversed.

- The use of reversing entries is optional. Reversing entries save time, promote efficiency, and help to achieve a proper matching of revenue and expenses in each period.

- With reversing entries, there is no need to examine each transaction to see whether a portion applies to the past period and then divide the amount of the transaction between the two periods.

8 Define the accounting terms new to this chapter.

Glossary

Classified financial statement (p. 412) A format by which revenues and expenses on the income statement, and assets and liabilities on the balance sheet, are divided into groups of similar accounts and a subtotal is given for each group

Current assets (p. 415) Assets consisting of cash, items that normally will be converted into cash within one year, or items that will be used up within one year

Current liabilities (p. 417) Debts that must be paid within one year

Current ratio (p. 424) A relationship between current assets and current liabilities that provides a measure of a firm's ability to pay its current debts (current ratio = current assets ÷ current liabilities)

Gross profit (p. 414) The difference between net sales and the cost of goods sold (gross profit = net sales − cost of goods sold)

Gross profit percentage (p. 424) The amount of gross profit from each dollar of sales (gross profit percentage = gross profit ÷ net sales)

Inventory turnover (p. 425) The number of times inventory is purchased and sold during the accounting period (inventory turnover = cost of goods sold ÷ average inventory)

Liquidity (p. 415) The ease with which an item can be converted into cash

Long-term liabilities (p. 417) Debts of a business that are due more than one year in the future

Multiple-step income statement (p. 412) A type of income statement on which several subtotals are computed before the net income is calculated

Plant and equipment (p. 416) Property that will be used in the business for longer than one year

Reversing entries (p. 425) Journal entries made to reverse the effect of certain adjusting entries involving accrued income or accrued expenses to avoid problems in recording future payments or receipts of cash in a new accounting period

Single-step income statement (p. 412) A type of income statement where only one computation is needed to determine the net income (total revenue − total expenses = net income)

Working capital (p. 424) The difference between current assets and current liabilities. It is a measure of the firm's ability to pay current obligations.

Comprehensive **Self Review**

1. Explain the difference between a single-step income statement and a multiple-step income statement. Which is normally favored?

2. What journal entry(ies) is (are) made in the adjustment column for beginning and ending inventories?

3. Why would a fax machine used in the office not be considered a current asset?

4. Immediately after closing entries are posted, which of the following types of accounts will have zero balances?

    a. asset accounts

    b. expense accounts

    c. liability accounts

    d. owner's drawing account

    e. *Income Summary* account

    f. owner's capital account

    g. revenue accounts

5. Give the sequence in which the following journal entries are posted to the accounts.

    a. adjusting entries

    b. entries to close expense accounts

    c. entries to close revenue accounts

    d. reversing entries

6. Describe the entry that would be made to close the *Income Summary* account in each of the following cases. The owner of the firm is Dorothy Hitt.

    a. There is net income of $38,000.

    b. There is a net loss of $18,000.

7. Which of the following accounts should have debit balances in the adjusted trial balance?

    a. *Sales Returns and Allowances*

    b. *Purchases Discounts*

    c. *Salaries Payable*

    d. *Unearned Rental Income*

(Answers to Comprehensive Self Review are on pages 451–452.)

Discussion Questions

1. What is the difference, if any, between the classification Other Revenue and Expense and the classification Extraordinary Gains and Losses?

2. What are operating expenses?

3. Which section of the income statement contains information about the purchases made during the period and the beginning and ending inventories?

4. What is the purpose of the balance sheet?

5. What are current assets that usually are classified as Current Assets on the balance sheet?

6. How do current liabilities and long-term liabilities differ?

7. What information is provided by the statement of owner's equity?

8. What account balances or other amount are included on two different financial statements for the period? Which statements are involved?

9. What is the purpose of the postclosing trial balance?

10. What accounts appear on the postclosing trial balance?

11. If the totals of the adjusted trial balance Debit and Credit columns are equal, but the postclosing trial balance does not balance, what is the likely cause of the problem?

12. What types of adjustments are reversed?

13. On December 31, Klien Company made an adjusting entry debiting *Interest Receivable* and crediting *Interest Income* for $300 of accrued interest. What reversing entry, if any, should be recorded for this item on January 1?

14. Various adjustments made at Acres Company are listed below. Which of the adjustments would normally be reversed?
    a. Adjustment for accrued payroll taxes expense
    b. Adjustment for supplies used
    c. Adjustment for depreciation on the building
    d. Adjustment for estimated uncollectible accounts
    e. Adjustment for accrued interest income
    f. Adjustment for beginning inventory
    g. Adjustment for ending inventory
    h. Adjustment to record portion of insurance premiums that have expired

15. What are the steps in the accounting cycle?

16. If the owner invests additional capital in the business during the month, how would that new investment be shown in the financial statements?

APPLICATIONS

Exercises

Exercise 13.1

Objective 1

▶ ### Classifying income statement items.

The accounts listed on the next page appear on the worksheet of Giddy's Craft Store. Indicate the section of the classified income statement in which each account will be reported.

SECTIONS OF CLASSIFIED INCOME STATEMENT

a. Operating Revenue

b. Cost of Goods Sold

c. Operating Expenses

d. Other Income

e. Other Expenses

ACCOUNTS

1. Purchases Returns and Allowances
2. Telephone Expense
3. Sales Returns and Allowances
4. Purchases
5. Interest Income
6. Merchandise Inventory
7. Interest Expense
8. Sales
9. Depreciation Expense—Store Equipment
10. Rent Expense

Classifying balance sheet items.

◄ **Exercise 13.2**
Objective 3

The following accounts appear on the worksheet of Giddy's Craft Store at December 31, 2013. Indicate the section of the classified balance sheet in which each account will be reported.

SECTIONS OF CLASSIFIED BALANCE SHEET

a. Current Assets
b. Plant and Equipment
c. Current Liabilities
d. Long-Term Liabilities
e. Owner's Equity

ACCOUNTS

1. Accounts Receivable
2. Delivery Van
3. Prepaid Insurance
4. Notes Payable, due 2014
5. Store Supplies
6. Accounts Payable
7. Merchandise Inventory
8. Ray Lynch, Capital
9. Cash
10. Unearned Subscriptions Income

Preparing a classified income statement.

◄ **Exercise 13.3**
Objective 1

The worksheet of Alec's Office Supplies contains the following revenue, cost, and expense accounts. Prepare a classified income statement for this firm for the year ended December 31, 2013. The merchandise inventory amounted to $58,775 on January 1, 2013, and $51,725 on December 31, 2013. The expense accounts numbered 611 through 617 represent selling expenses, and those numbered 631 through 646 represent general and administrative expenses.

ACCOUNTS

401	Sales	$245,600	Cr.
451	Sales Returns and Allowances	4,250	Dr.
491	Miscellaneous Income	300	Cr.
501	Purchases	102,600	Dr.

ACCOUNTS (CONT.)

502	Freight In	1,875	Dr.
503	Purchases Returns and Allowances	3,500	Cr.
504	Purchases Discounts	1,700	Cr.
611	Salaries Expense—Sales	44,300	Dr.
614	Store Supplies Expense	2,210	Dr.
617	Depreciation Expense—Store Equipment	1,410	Dr.
631	Rent Expense	12,500	Dr.
634	Utilities Expense	2,900	Dr.
637	Salaries Expense—Office	20,100	Dr.
640	Payroll Taxes Expense	5,000	Dr.
643	Depreciation Expense—Office Equipment	470	Dr.
646	Uncollectible Accounts Expense	620	Dr.
691	Interest Expense	540	Dr.

Exercise 13.4
Objective 2

▶ **Preparing a statement of owner's equity.**

The worksheet of Alec's Office Supplies contains the following owner's equity accounts. Use this data and the net income determined in Exercise 13.3 to prepare a statement of owner's equity for the year ended December 31, 2013. No additional investments were made during the period.

ACCOUNTS

301	Alec Patel, Capital	$62,760	Cr.
302	Alec Patel, Drawing	40,200	Dr.

Exercise 13.5
Objective 3

▶ **Preparing a classified balance sheet.**

The worksheet of Alec's Office Supplies contains the following asset and liability accounts. The balance of the **Notes Payable** account consists of notes that are due within a year. Prepare a balance sheet dated December 31, 2013. Obtain the ending capital for the period from the statement of owner's equity completed in Exercise 13.4.

ACCOUNTS

101	Cash	$9,780	Dr.
107	Change Fund	400	Dr.
111	Accounts Receivable	5,040	Dr.
112	Allowance for Doubtful Accounts	760	Cr.
121	Merchandise Inventory	51,250	Dr.
131	Store Supplies	1,000	Dr.
133	Prepaid Interest	80	Dr.
141	Store Equipment	10,200	Dr.
142	Accum. Depreciation—Store Equipment	1,080	Cr.
151	Office Equipment	3,200	Dr.
152	Accum. Depreciation—Office Equipment	400	Cr.
201	Notes Payable	5,400	Cr.
203	Accounts Payable	3,625	Cr.
216	Interest Payable	60	Cr.
231	Sales Tax Payable	1,790	Cr.

Exercise 13.6
Objective 5

▶ **Recording closing entries.**

On December 31, 2013, the Income Statement section of the worksheet for Thomason Company contained the following information. Give the entries that should be made in the general journal to close the revenue, cost of goods sold, expense, and other temporary accounts. Use journal page 16.

INCOME STATEMENT SECTION

	Debit	Credit
Income Summary	$ 38,600	$ 41,900
Sales		254,500
Sales Returns and Allowances	3,900	
Sales Discounts	2,900	
Interest Income		170
Purchases	134,400	
Freight In	2,200	
Purchases Returns and Allowances		2,000
Purchases Discounts		1,530
Rent Expense	8,500	
Utilities Expense	2,930	
Telephone Expense	1,540	
Salaries Expense	66,100	
Payroll Taxes Expense	5,270	
Supplies Expense	1,700	
Depreciation Expense	2,500	
Interest Expense	340	
Totals	$270,880	$300,100

Assume further that the owner of the firm is Bobby Thomason and that the **Bobby Thomason, Drawing** account had a balance of $26,200 on December 31, 2013.

Journalizing reversing entries.

◀ **Exercise 13.7**
Objective 7

Examine the following adjusting entries and determine which ones should be reversed. Show the reversing entries that should be recorded in the general journal as of January 1, 2014. Include appropriate descriptions.

2013	(Adjustment a)		
Dec. 31	Uncollectible Accounts Expense	3,625.00	
	Allowance for Doubtful Accounts		3,625.00
	To record estimated loss from uncollectible accounts based on 0.5% of net credit sales, $725,000		
	(Adjustment b)		
Dec. 31	Supplies Expense	4,700.00	
	Supplies		4,700.00
	To record supplies used during the year		
	(Adjustment c)		
31	Insurance Expense	1,350.00	
	Prepaid Insurance		1,350.00
	To record expired insurance on 1-year $5,400 policy purchased on Oct. 1		
	(Adjustment d)		
31	Depreciation. Exp.—Store Equipment	14,300.00	
	Accum. Depreciation—Store Equip.		14,300.00
	To record depreciation		
	(Adjustment e)		
31	Salaries Expense—Office	2,800.00	
	Salaries Payable		2,800.00
	To record accrued salaries for Dec. 29–31		

	(Adjustment f)		
31	Payroll Tax Expense	214.20	
	Social Security Tax Payable		173.60
	Medicare Tax Payable		40.60
	To record accrued payroll taxes on accrued salaries: social security, 6.2% × 2,800 = $173.60; Medicare, 1.45% × 2,800 = $40.60		
	(Adjustment g)		
31	Interest Expense	200.00	
	Interest Payable		200.00
	To record accrued interest on a 4-month, 6% trade note payable dated Nov. 1: $20,000 × 0.06 × 2/12 = $200		
	(Adjustment h)		
31	Interest Receivable	215.00	
	Interest Income		215.00
	To record interest earned on 6-month, 10% note receivable dated Oct. 1: $8,600 × 0.10 × 3/12 = $215		

Exercise 13.8
Objective 6

▶ **Preparing a postclosing trial balance.**

The Adjusted Trial Balance section of the worksheet for Harmon Farm Supply follows. The owner made no additional investments during the year. Prepare a postclosing trial balance for the firm on December 31, 2013.

ACCOUNTS

	Debit	Credit
Cash	$ 18,600	
Accounts Receivable	59,800	
Allowance for Doubtful Accounts		$ 120
Merchandise Inventory	186,200	
Supplies	7,140	
Prepaid Insurance	3,060	
Equipment	51,000	
Accumulated Depreciation—Equipment		17,800
Notes Payable		9,500
Accounts Payable		8,700
Social Security Tax Payable		1,392
Medicare Tax Payable		324
Ken Harmon, Capital		267,964
Ken Harmon, Drawing	74,000	
Income Summary	180,000	186,200
Sales		773,000
Sales Returns and Allowances	14,400	
Purchases	486,900	
Freight In	5,400	
Purchases Returns and Allowances		8,500
Purchases Discounts		5,300
Rent Expense	33,800	
Telephone Expense	6,246	

ACCOUNTS (CONT.)

	Debit	Credit
Salaries Expense	123,140	
Payroll Taxes Expense	11,734	
Supplies Expense	6,600	
Insurance Expense	1,560	
Depreciation Expense—Equipment	8,100	
Uncollectible Accounts Expense	1,120	
Totals	$1,278,800	$1,278,800

Calculating ratios.

◀ **Exercise 13.9**
Objective 6

The following selected accounts were taken from the financial records of Santa Barbara Distributors at December 31, 2013. All accounts have normal balances.

Cash	$ 22,500
Accounts receivable	46,700
Note receivable, due 2014	8,500
Merchandise inventory	34,700
Prepaid insurance	2,250
Supplies	1,310
Equipment	42,500
Accumulated depreciation, equipment	22,500
Note payable to bank, due 2014	25,000
Accounts payable	21,134
Interest payable	250
Sales	525,000
Sales discounts	2,200
Cost of goods sold	392,100

Merchandise inventory at December 31, 2012 was $57,558. Based on the account balances above, calculate the following:

a. The gross profit percentage

b. Working capital

c. The current ratio

d. The inventory turnover

PROBLEMS

Problem Set A

Preparing classified financial statements.

◀ **Problem 13.1A**
Objectives 1, 2, 3

Wood Design Company distributes hardwood products to small furniture manufacturers. The adjusted trial balance data given below is from the firm's worksheet for the year ended December 31, 2013.

INSTRUCTIONS

1. Prepare a classified income statement for the year ended December 31, 2013. The expense accounts represent warehouse expenses, selling expenses, and general and administrative expenses.

2. Prepare a statement of owner's equity for the year ended December 31, 2013. No additional investments were made during the period.

3. Prepare a classified balance sheet as of December 31, 2013. The mortgage and the loans extend for more than a year.

ACCOUNTS

	Debit	Credit
Cash	$ 23,100	
Petty Cash Fund	400	
Notes Receivable	10,800	
Accounts Receivable	86,164	
Allowance for Doubtful Accounts		$ 5,000
Merchandise Inventory	224,000	
Warehouse Supplies	2,760	
Office Supplies	1,320	
Prepaid Insurance	7,200	
Land	36,000	
Building	168,000	
Accumulated Depreciation—Building		48,000
Warehouse Equipment	32,000	
Accumulated Depreciation—Warehouse Equipment		14,400
Delivery Equipment	46,000	
Accumulated Depreciation—Delivery Equipment		17,600
Office Equipment	20,000	
Accumulated Depreciation—Office Equipment		9,000
Notes Payable		19,200
Accounts Payable		38,000
Interest Payable		480
Mortgage Payable		56,000
Loans Payable, Long-term		12,000
Chuck Kirby, Capital (Jan. 1)		397,640
Chuck Kirby, Drawing	126,000	
Income Summary	234,000	224,000
Sales		1,665,884
Sales Returns and Allowances	17,200	
Interest Income		1,480
Purchases	757,000	
Freight In	12,800	
Purchases Returns and Allowances		7,440
Purchases Discounts		10,160
Warehouse Wages Expense	189,600	
Warehouse Supplies Expense	6,100	
Depreciation Expense—Warehouse Equipment	4,800	
Salaries Expense—Sales	259,200	
Travel and Entertainment Expense	20,500	
Delivery Wages Expense	59,330	
Depreciation Expense—Delivery Equipment	8,800	
Salaries Expense—Office	69,600	
Office Supplies Expense	3,000	
Insurance Expense	5,200	
Utilities Expense	8,290	

ACCOUNTS (CONT.)

	Debit	Credit
Telephone Expense	5,520	
Payroll Taxes Expense	54,000	
Property Taxes Expense	4,600	
Uncollectible Accounts Expense	4,800	
Depreciation Expense—Building	8,000	
Depreciation Expense—Office Equipment	3,000	
Interest Expense	7,200	
Totals	$2,526,284	$2,526,284

Analyze: What is the current ratio for this business?

Preparing classified financial statements.

Good to Go Auto Products distributes automobile parts to service stations and repair shops. The adjusted trial balance data that follows is from the firm's worksheet for the year ended December 31, 2013.

◄ **Problem 13.2A**
Objectives 1, 2, 3
eXcel

INSTRUCTIONS

1. Prepare a classified income statement for the year ended December 31, 2013. The expense accounts represent warehouse expenses, selling expenses, and general and administrative expenses.

2. Prepare a statement of owner's equity for the year ended December 31, 2013. No additional investments were made during the period.

3. Prepare a classified balance sheet as of December 31, 2013. The mortgage and the long-term notes extend for more than one year.

ACCOUNTS

	Debit	Credit
Cash	$ 98,000	
Petty Cash Fund	500	
Notes Receivable	10,000	
Accounts Receivable	139,200	
Allowance for Doubtful Accounts		$ 2,800
Interest Receivable	100	
Merchandise Inventory	127,500	
Warehouse Supplies	2,300	
Office Supplies	600	
Prepaid Insurance	3,640	
Land	15,000	
Building	102,000	
Accumulated Depreciation—Building		16,200
Warehouse Equipment	18,800	
Accumulated Depreciation—Warehouse Equipment		9,000
Office Equipment	8,400	
Accumulated Depreciation—Office Equipment		3,400
Notes Payable—Short-Term		14,000
Accounts Payable		55,900
Interest Payable		300
Notes Payable—Long-Term		12,000
Mortgage Payable		15,000
Colin O'Brien, Capital (Jan. 1)		317,020
Colin O'Brien, Drawing	69,650	

ACCOUNTS (CONT.)

	Debit	Credit
Income Summary	130,400	127,500
Sales		1,090,300
Sales Returns and Allowances	7,400	
Interest Income		480
Purchases	453,000	
Freight In	8,800	
Purchases Returns and Allowances		12,650
Purchases Discounts		8,240
Warehouse Wages Expense	107,600	
Warehouse Supplies Expense	4,800	
Depreciation Expense—Warehouse Equipment	2,400	
Salaries Expense—Sales	150,700	
Travel Expense	23,000	
Delivery Expense	36,425	
Salaries Expense—Office	84,000	
Office Supplies Expense	1,120	
Insurance Expense	8,875	
Utilities Expense	7,000	
Telephone Expense	3,180	
Payroll Taxes Expense	30,600	
Building Repairs Expense	2,700	
Property Taxes Expense	15,400	
Uncollectible Accounts Expense	2,580	
Depreciation Expense—Building	4,600	
Depreciation Expense—Office Equipment	1,520	
Interest Expense	3,000	
Totals	$1,684,790	$1,684,790

Analyze: What percentage of total operating expenses is attributable to warehouse expenses?

Problem 13.3A ▶ **Preparing classified financial statements.**

Objectives 1, 2, 3

Obtain all data necessary from the worksheet prepared for The Wine Shop in Problem 12.6A at the end of Chapter 12. Then follow the instructions to complete this problem.

INSTRUCTIONS

1. Prepare a classified income statement for the year ended December 31, 2013. The company does not classify its operating expenses as selling expenses and general and administrative expenses.

2. Prepare a statement of owner's equity for the year ended December 31, 2013. No additional investments were made during the year.

3. Prepare a classified balance sheet as of December 31, 2013.

Analyze: What is the inventory turnover for The Wine Shop?

Problem 13.4A ▶ **Journalizing adjusting, closing, and reversing entries.**

Objectives 4, 5, 7

Obtain all data that is necessary from the worksheet prepared for Healthy Habits Foods Company in Problem 12.5A at the end of Chapter 12. Then follow the instructions to complete this problem.

INSTRUCTIONS

1. Record adjusting entries in the general journal as of December 31, 2013. Use 25 as the first journal page number. Include descriptions for the entries.

2. Record closing entries in the general journal as of December 31, 2013. Include descriptions.

3. Record reversing entries in the general journal as of January 1, 2014. Include descriptions.

Analyze: Assuming that the firm did not record a reversing entry for salaries payable, what entry is required when salaries of $5,000 are paid on January 3?

Journalizing adjusting and reversing entries.

◄ **Problem 13.5A**

Objectives 4, 7

The data below concerns adjustments to be made at Vaughn Company.

INSTRUCTIONS

1. Record the adjusting entries in the general journal as of December 31, 2013. Use 25 as the first journal page number. Include descriptions.

2. Record reversing entries in the general journal as of January 1, 2014. Include descriptions.

ADJUSTMENTS

a. On October 1, 2013, the firm signed a lease for a warehouse and paid rent of $17,700 in advance for a six-month period.

b. On December 31, 2013, an inventory of supplies showed that items costing $1,840 were on hand. The balance of the **Supplies** account was $11,120.

c. A depreciation schedule for the firm's equipment shows that a total of $8,200 should be charged off as depreciation for 2013.

d. On December 31, 2013, the firm owed salaries of $4,400 that will not be paid until January 2014.

e. On December 31, 2013, the firm owed the employer's social security (6.2 percent) and Medicare (1.45 percent) taxes on all accrued salaries.

f. On September 1, 2013, the firm received a five-month, 8 percent note for $4,500 from a customer with an overdue balance.

Analyze: After the adjusting entries have been posted, what is the balance of the **Prepaid Rent** account on January 1, 2014?

Problem Set B

Preparing classified financial statements.

◄ **Problem 13.1B**

Objectives 1, 2, 3

Lite Speed Electronics is a retail store that sells computers and computer supplies. The adjusted trial balance data given below is from the firm's worksheet for the year ended December 31, 2013.

INSTRUCTIONS

1. Prepare a classified income statement for the year ended December 31, 2013. The expense accounts represent warehouse expenses, selling expenses, and general and administrative expenses.

2. Prepare a statement of owner's equity for the year ended December 31, 2013. No additional investments were made during the period.

3. Prepare a classified balance sheet as of December 31, 2013. The mortgage and the loans extend for more than one year.

ACCOUNTS

	Debit	Credit
Cash	$ 10,200	
Petty Cash Fund	100	
Notes Receivable	3,200	

ACCOUNTS (CONT.)

	Debit	Credit
Accounts Receivable	21,250	
Allowance for Doubtful Accounts		$ 2,250
Merchandise Inventory	35,400	
Warehouse Supplies	775	
Office Supplies	780	
Prepaid Insurance	2,200	
Land	7,642	
Building	48,500	
Accum. Depr.—Building		13,000
Warehouse Equipment	8,000	
Accumulated Depreciation—Warehouse Equipment		2,300
Delivery Equipment	16,400	
Accumulated Depreciation—Delivery Equipment		3,600
Office Equipment	6,000	
Accumulated Depreciation—Office Equipment		2,500
Notes Payable		5,000
Accounts Payable		13,140
Interest Payable		240
Mortgage Payable		15,950
Loans Payable		4,000
Toshi Takahashi, Capital (Jan. 1)		60,940
Toshi Takahashi, Drawing	24,000	
Income Summary	33,125	35,400
Sales		429,800
Sales Returns and Allowances	3,150	
Interest Income		462
Purchases	179,600	
Freight In	2,200	
Purchases Returns and Allowances		2,520
Purchases Discounts		2,350
Warehouse Wages Expense	38,900	
Warehouse Supplies Expense	1,790	
Depreciation Expense—Warehouse Equipment	1,400	
Salaries Expense—Sales	67,200	
Travel and Entertainment Expense	6,300	
Delivery Wages Expense	26,900	
Depreciation Expense—Delivery Equipment	2,440	
Salaries Expense—Office	15,900	
Office Supplies Expense	1,150	
Insurance Expense	1,500	
Utilities Expense	2,400	
Telephone Expense	1,380	
Payroll Taxes Expense	15,250	
Property Taxes Expense	1,750	
Uncollectible Accounts Expense	1,050	
Depreciation Expense—Building	3,000	

ACCOUNTS [CONT.]

	Debit	Credit
Depreciation Expense—Office Equipment	1,020	
Interest Expense	1,600	
Totals	$593,452	$593,452

Analyze: What is the gross profit percentage for the period ended December 31, 2013?

Preparing classified financial statements.

◀ **Problem 13.2B**
Objectives 1, 2, 3

Hog Wild is a retail firm that sells motorcycles, parts, and accessories. The adjusted trial balance data given below is from the firm's worksheet for the year ended December 31, 2013.

INSTRUCTIONS

1. Prepare a classified income statement for the year ended December 31, 2013. The expense accounts represent warehouse expenses, selling expenses, and general and administrative expenses.

2. Prepare a statement of owner's equity for the year ended December 31, 2013. No additional investments were made during the period.

3. Prepare a classified balance sheet as of December 31, 2013. The mortgage and the long-term notes extend for more than one year.

ACCOUNTS

	Debit	Credit
Cash	$ 14,350	
Petty Cash Fund	200	
Notes Receivable	6,000	
Accounts Receivable	54,600	
Allowance for Doubtful Accounts		$ 5,000
Interest Receivable	200	
Merchandise Inventory	87,915	
Warehouse Supplies	3,700	
Office Supplies	1,800	
Prepaid Insurance	6,900	
Land	20,400	
Building	53,100	
Accumulated Depreciation—Building		8,400
Warehouse Equipment	24,000	
Accumulated Depreciation—Warehouse Equipment		4,000
Office Equipment	12,800	
Accumulated Depreciation—Office Equipment		1,800
Notes Payable—Short-Term		8,000
Accounts Payable		32,500
Interest Payable		1,800
Notes Payable—Long-Term		6,000
Mortgage Payable		35,875
Nick Henry, Capital (Jan. 1)		198,710
Nick Henry, Drawing	56,000	
Income Summary	88,980	87,915
Sales		608,417

ACCOUNTS (CONT.)

	Debit	Credit
Sales Returns and Allowances	9,400	
Interest Income		720
Purchases	230,050	
Freight In	9,600	
Purchases Returns and Allowances		6,420
Purchases Discounts		5,760
Warehouse Wages Expense	64,300	
Warehouse Supplies Expense	4,300	
Depreciation Expense—Warehouse Equipment	2,400	
Salaries Expense—Sales	78,900	
Travel Expense—Sales	21,000	
Delivery Expense	35,400	
Salaries Expense—Office	57,500	
Office Supplies Expense	1,360	
Insurance Expense	9,500	
Utilities Expense	6,912	
Telephone Expense	4,370	
Payroll Taxes Expense	19,200	
Building Repairs Expense	3,100	
Property Taxes Expense	11,700	
Uncollectible Accounts Expense	2,900	
Depreciation Expense—Building	3,200	
Depreciation Expense—Office Equipment	1,680	
Interest Expense	3,600	
Totals	$1,011,317	$1,011,317

Analyze: What is the inventory turnover for Hog Wild?

Problem 13.3B ▶
Objectives 1, 2, 3

Preparing classified financial statements.

Obtain all data necessary from the worksheet prepared for The Game Place in Problem 12.6B at the end of Chapter 12. Then follow the instructions to complete this problem.

INSTRUCTIONS

1. Prepare a classified income statement for the year ended December 31, 2013. The company does not classify its operating expenses as selling expenses and general and administrative expenses.

2. Prepare a statement of owner's equity for the year ended December 31, 2013. No additional investments were made during the year.

3. Prepare a classified balance sheet as of December 31, 2013.

Analyze: What is the amount of working capital for The Game Place?

Problem 13.4B ▶
Objectives 4, 5, 7

CONTINUING >>>
Problem

Journalizing adjusting, closing, and reversing entries.

Obtain all data that is necessary from the worksheet prepared for Whatnots in Problem 12.5B at the end of Chapter 12. Then follow the instructions to complete this problem.

INSTRUCTIONS

1. Record adjusting entries in the general journal as of December 31, 2013. Use 29 as the first journal page number. Include descriptions for the entries.

2. Record closing entries in the general journal as of December 31, 2013. Include descriptions.

3. Record reversing entries in the general journal as of January 1, 2014. Include descriptions.

Analyze: Assuming that the company did not record a reversing entry for salaries payable, what entry is required when salaries of $2,600 are paid on January 4? (Ignore payroll taxes withheld.)

Journalizing adjusting and reversing entries.

◄ **Problem 13.5B**
Objectives 4, 7

The data below concerns adjustments to be made at Ramos Company.

INSTRUCTIONS

1. Record the adjusting entries in the general journal as of December 31, 2013. Use 25 as the first journal page number. Include descriptions.

2. Record reversing entries in the general journal as of January 1, 2014. Include descriptions.

ADJUSTMENTS

a. On August 1, 2013, the firm signed a one-year advertising contract with a trade magazine and paid the entire amount, $17,700, in advance. *Prepaid Advertising* had a balance of $17,700 on December 31, 2013.

b. On December 31, 2013, an inventory of supplies showed that items costing $2,840 were on hand. The balance of the *Supplies* account was $11,120.

c. A depreciation schedule for the firm's store equipment shows that a total of $9,200 should be charged off as depreciation for 2013.

d. On December 31, 2013, the firm owed salaries of $4,400 that will not be paid until January 2014.

e. On December 31, 2013, the firm owed the employer's social security (6.2 percent) and Medicare (1.45 percent) taxes on all accrued salaries.

f. On December 1, 2013, the firm received a five-month, 8 percent note for $4,500 from a customer with an overdue balance.

Analyze: After the adjusting entries have been posted, what is the balance of the Prepaid Advertising account on December 31?

Critical Thinking Problem 13.1

Year-End Processing

Programs Plus is a retail firm that sells computer programs for home and business use. On December 31, 2013, its general ledger contained the accounts and balances shown below:

ACCOUNTS	BALANCES	
Cash	$ 15,280	Dr.
Accounts Receivable	26,600	Dr.
Allowance for Doubtful Accounts	95	Cr.
Merchandise Inventory	62,375	Dr.
Supplies	6,740	Dr.
Prepaid Insurance	2,380	Dr.
Equipment	34,000	Dr.
Accumulated Depreciation—Equipment	10,100	Cr.
Notes Payable	7,264	Cr.
Accounts Payable	6,500	Cr.
Social Security Tax Payable	560	Cr.
Medicare Tax Payable	130	Cr.
Yasser Tousson, Capital	93,620	Cr.
Yasser Tousson, Drawing	50,000	Dr.
Sales	514,980	Cr.

Sales Returns and Allowances	9,600	Dr.
Purchases	319,430	Dr.
Freight In	3,600	Dr.
Purchases Returns and Allowances	7,145	Cr.
Purchases Discounts	5,760	Cr.
Rent Expense	14,500	Dr.
Telephone Expense	2,164	Dr.
Salaries Expense	92,000	Dr.
Payroll Taxes Expense	7,300	Dr.
Interest Expense	185	Dr.

The following accounts had zero balances:

Interest Payable
Salaries Payable
Income Summary
Supplies Expense
Insurance Expense
Depreciation Expense—Equipment
Uncollectible Accounts Expense

The data needed for the adjustments on December 31 are as follows:

a.–b. Ending merchandise inventory, $67,850.

c. Uncollectible accounts, 0.5 percent of net credit sales of $245,000.

d. Supplies on hand December 31, $1,020.

e. Expired insurance, $1,190.

f. *Depreciation Expense—Equipment,* $5,600.

g. Accrued interest expense on notes payable, $325.

h. Accrued salaries, $2,100.

i. *Social Security Tax Payable* (6.2 percent) and *Medicare Tax Payable* (1.45 percent) of accrued salaries.

INSTRUCTIONS

1. Prepare a worksheet for the year ended December 31, 2013.
2. Prepare a classified income statement. The firm does not divide its operating expenses into selling and administrative expenses.
3. Prepare a statement of owner's equity. No additional investments were made during the period.
4. Prepare a classified balance sheet. All notes payable are due within one year.
5. Journalize the adjusting entries. Use 25 as the first journal page number.
6. Journalize the closing entries.
7. Journalize the reversing entries.

Analyze: By what percentage did the owner's capital account change in the period from January 1, 2013, to December 31, 2013?

Critical Thinking Problem 13.2

Classified Balance Sheet

Kim-Yi Wei is the owner of Kim-Yi Jewelry, a store specializing in gold, platinum, and special stones. During the past year, in response to increased demand, Kim-Yi doubled her selling space by expanding into the vacant building space next door to her store. This expansion has been expensive because of the need to increase inventory and to purchase new store fixtures and equipment, including carpeting and state-of-the-art built-in fixtures. Kim-Yi notes that the company's cash position has gone down and she is worried about future demands on cash to finance the growth.

Kim-Yi presents you with a statement showing the assets, liabilities, and her equity for year-end 2012 and 2013, and asks your opinion on the company's ability to pay for the recent expansion. She did not have income and expense data available at the time. She commented that she had not made any new investment in the business in the past two years and was not financially able to do so presently. The information presented is shown below:

	December 31, 2012	December 31, 2013
Assets		
Cash	$150,000	$ 35,000
Accounts Receivable	45,000	96,000
Inventory	105,000	236,000
Prepaid Expenses	6,000	9,000
Store Fixtures and Equipment	180,000	390,000
Total Assets	$486,000	$766,000
Liabilities and Owner's Equity		
Liabilities		
Notes Payable (due in 4 years)	$ 90,000	$246,500
Accounts Payable	132,000	176,000
Salaries Payable	18,000	19,500
Total Liabilities	$240,000	$442,000
Owner's Equity		
Kim-Yi Wei, Capital	246,000	324,000
Total Liabilities and Owner's Equity	$486,000	$766,000

INSTRUCTIONS

1. Prepare classified balance sheets for Kim-Yi Jewelry for December 31, 2012, and December 31, 2013. (Ignore depreciation.)

2. Based on the information presented in the classified balance sheets, what is your opinion of Kim-Yi Jewelry's ability to pay its current bills in a timely manner?

3. What is the advantage of a classified balance sheet over a balance sheet that is not classified?

BUSINESS CONNECTIONS

Understanding Financial Statements

Managerial | FOCUS

1. Why should management be concerned about the efficiency of the end-of-period procedures?

2. Spector Company had an increase in sales and net income during its last fiscal year, but cash decreased and the firm was having difficulty paying its bills by the end of the year. What factors might cause a shortage of cash even though a firm is profitable?

3. For the last three years, the balance sheet of Desai Hardware Center, a large retail store, has shown a substantial increase in merchandise inventory. Why might management be concerned about this development?

4. Why is it important to compare the financial statements of the current year with those of prior years?

5. Should a manager be concerned if the balance sheet shows a large increase in current liabilities and a large decrease in current assets? Explain your answer.

6. The latest income statement prepared at Wilkes Company shows that net sales increased by 10 percent over the previous year and selling expenses increased by 25 percent. Do you think that management should investigate the reasons for the increase in selling expenses? Why or why not?

7. Why is it useful for management to compare a firm's financial statements with financial information from other companies in the same industry?

Helping Your Boss May Be Wrong

Ethical DILEMMA

It is standard accounting procedures, or GAAP, to make an adjusting entry to remove the current year's principle from the long-term liabilities. This entry reduces the long-term liabilities and increases the current liabilities. You are the bookkeeper for Biker's Business. Biker's Business has a bank loan that requires a current ratio of 1.5 times. The owner has asked that you do not make the adjusting entry to take the current portion from the long-term liabilities. You know if you make the adjusting entry Biker's Business' loan will need to be repaid immediately (or the loan called). What should you do?

Balance Sheet

Financial Statement ANALYSIS

McCormick and Company, Incorporated reported the following in its *2009 Annual Report:*

Consolidated Balance Sheet		
	November 30	
(in millions)	*2009*	*2008*
Total Current Assets	$ 970.5	$ 968.3
Total Assets	$3,387.9	$3,220.3
Total Current Liabilities	$ 818.2	$ 1,034.1
Total Liabilities	$2,053.2	$2,165.0

Analyze:

1. What is the current ratio for both 2009 and 2008?

2. Did the current ratio improve from 2008 to 2009?

3. The company reported net sales of $3,192 million and gross profit of $1,327 million for its fiscal year ended November 30, 2009. What is the gross profit percentage for this period?

Analyzing The Home Depot

TEAMWORK

Ratios are an important part of financial analysis. Divide into groups of two or three. Each person should choose one year from The Home Depot *2009 Annual Report (for the fiscal year ended January 31, 2010)* in Appendix A. Calculate the current ratio, gross profit percentage, and inventory turnover. Is The Home Depot doing better or worse than the previous year? What account is causing this change?

Using Financial Statements from the Internet

Choose the Web site of a corporation. You can find most corporate Web sites by typing the corporation's name after www., then .com. Find the 10K or annual report. Locate the Income Statement, Balance Sheet, and Cash Flow statements for the corporation. Notice the current assets and current liabilities. Calculate the current ratio, gross profit percentage, and inventory turnover.

Internet CONNECTION

Answers to **Self Reviews**

Answers to Section 1 Self Review

1. Classified statements permit users to better interpret the statements and analyze operations and financial conditions.
2. Current liabilities are those that fall due within one year. Long-term liabilities are those that will be due in more than one year.
3. Gross profit is the difference between net sales and the cost of goods sold.
4. **b.** A note receivable due in 13 months
5. **b.** As a deduction from the delivered cost of purchases
6. Net delivered cost of purchases is understated. Operating expenses are overstated. The net income from operations is unchanged.

Answers to Section 2 Self Review

1. Adjustments that include entries in asset and liability accounts that have not been used during the period.
2. So that anyone who needs to examine the entries at a later date will understand how and why the adjustments were made.
3. They provide a systematic and uniform method for closing all accounts that affect profit or loss for the period and transferring that profit or loss, adjusted for owner's withdrawals, to the owner's capital account.
4. **b.** an accrued expense that involves future cash payments.
5. **d.** current assets divided by current liabilities.
6. If the accountant correctly allocates the entire future payment to the payroll taxes expense account and the accrued liability account, there will be no effects on the proper allocation of expense between periods. If the accountant debits the payment in the subsequent month to the payroll taxes expense account, payroll tax expense will be correctly stated in the earlier period and overstated in the current period. *Payroll Taxes Payable* will be overstated during the later period.

Answers to Comprehensive Self Review

1. Single-step: all revenues listed in one section and all related costs and expenses in another section. Multiple-step: various sections in which subtotals and totals are computed in arriving at net income. Multi-step statements are generally preferred.
2. An entry in the debit column on the *Income Summary* line and a credit to *Merchandise Inventory* for the amount of beginning inventory closes the beginning inventory. A debit on the *Merchandise Inventory* line and a credit to *Income Summary* for the amount of ending inventory sets up the ending inventory.

3. It generally has a life of more than one year and is used in carrying on the business.

4. **b.** expense accounts   **e.** *Income Summary* account

   d. owner's drawing account   **g.** revenue accounts

5. **a.** adjusting entries; **c.** entries to close revenue accounts; **b.** entries to close expense accounts; **d.** reversing entries

6. **a.** Debit *Income Summary* and credit *Dorothy Hitt, Capital* for $38,000.

   b. Debit **Dorothy Hitt, Capital** for $18,000 and credit **Income Summary** for $18,000.

7. **a.** *Sales Returns and Allowances*

Mini-Practice Set 2

Merchandising Business Accounting Cycle

The Fashion Rack

The Fashion Rack is a retail merchandising business that sells brand-name clothing at discount prices. The firm is owned and managed by Teresa Lojay, who started the business on April 1, 2013. This project will give you an opportunity to put your knowledge of accounting into practice as you handle the accounting work of The Fashion Rack during the month of October 2013.

The Fashion Rack has a monthly accounting period. The firm's chart of accounts is shown below and on the next page. The journals used to record transactions are the sales journal, purchases journal, cash receipts journal, cash payments journal, and general journal. Postings are made from the journals to the accounts receivable ledger, accounts payable ledger, and general ledger. The employees are paid at the end of the month. A computerized payroll service prepares all payroll records and checks.

INTRODUCTION

INSTRUCTIONS

1. Open the general ledger accounts and enter the balances for October 1, 2013. Obtain the necessary figures from the postclosing trial balance prepared on September 30, 2013, which is shown on page 456. (If you are using the *Study Guide & Working Papers,* you will find that the general ledger accounts are already open.)

2. Open the subsidiary ledger accounts and enter the balances for October 1, 2013. Obtain the necessary figures from the schedule of accounts payable and schedule of accounts receivable prepared on September 30, 2013, which appear on page 457. (If you are using the *Study Guide & Working Papers,* you will find that the subsidiary ledger accounts are already open.)

3. Analyze the transactions for October and record each transaction in the general journal. (Use 16 as the number for the first page of the general journal.)

4. Post the individual entries from the general journal to the general ledger and the subsidiary ledgers.

5. Check the accuracy of the subsidiary ledgers by preparing a schedule of accounts receivable and a schedule of accounts payable as of October 31, 2013. Compare the totals with the balances of the *Accounts Receivable* account and the *Accounts Payable* account in the general ledger.

The Fashion Rack Chart of Accounts	
Assets	**Liabilities**
101 Cash	203 Accounts Payable
111 Accounts Receivable	221 Social Security Tax Payable
112 Allowance for Doubtful Accounts	222 Medicare Tax Payable
121 Merchandise Inventory	223 Employee Income Tax Payable
131 Supplies	225 Federal Unemployment Tax Payable
133 Prepaid Insurance	227 State Unemployment Tax Payable
135 Prepaid Advertising	229 Salaries Payable
141 Equipment	231 Sales Tax Payable
142 Accumulated Depreciation—Equipment	

The Fashion Rack Chart of Accounts (continued)	
Owner's Equity	**Expenses**
301 Teresa Lojay, Capital	611 Advertising Expense
302 Teresa Lojay, Drawing	614 Depreciation Expense—Equipment
399 Income Summary	617 Insurance Expense
Revenues	620 Uncollectible Accounts Expense
401 Sales	623 Janitorial Services Expense
402 Sales Returns and Allowances	626 Payroll Taxes Expense
Cost of Goods Sold	629 Rent Expense
501 Purchases	632 Salaries Expense
502 Freight In	635 Supplies Expense
503 Purchases Returns and Allowances	638 Telephone Expense
504 Purchases Discounts	644 Utilities Expense

6. Check the accuracy of the general ledger by preparing a trial balance in the first two columns of a 10-column worksheet. Make sure that the total debits and the total credits are equal.

7. Complete the Adjustments section of the worksheet. Use the following data. Identify each adjustment with the appropriate letter:

   a. During October, the firm had net credit sales of $9,610. From experience with similar businesses, the previous accountant had estimated that 1.0 percent of the firm's net credit sales would result in uncollectible accounts. Record an adjustment for the expected loss from uncollectible accounts for the month of October.

   b. On October 31, an inventory of the supplies showed that items costing $2,840 were on hand. Record an adjustment for the supplies used in October.

   c. On September 30, 2013, the firm purchased a one-year insurance policy for $8,400. Record an adjustment for the expired insurance for October.

   d. On October 1, the firm signed a four-month advertising contract for $3,600 with a local cable television station and paid the full amount in advance. Record an adjustment for the expired advertising for October.

   e. On April 1, 2013, the firm purchased equipment for $83,000. The equipment was estimated to have a useful life of five years and a salvage value of $12,500. Record an adjustment for depreciation on the equipment for October.

   f.–g. Based on a physical count, ending merchandise inventory was determined to be $80,400.

8. Complete the Adjusted Trial Balance section of the worksheet.

9. Determine the net income or net loss for October and complete the worksheet.

10. Prepare a classified income statement for the month ended October 31, 2013. (The firm does not divide its operating expenses into selling and administrative expenses.)

11. Prepare a statement of owner's equity for the month ended October 31, 2013.

12. Prepare a classified balance sheet as of October 31, 2013.

13. Journalize and post the adjusting entries using general journal page 17.

14. Prepare and post the closing entries using general journal page 18.

15. Prepare a postclosing trial balance.

DATE	TRANSACTIONS
Oct. 1	Issued Check 601 for $4,200 to pay City Properties the monthly rent.
1	Signed a four-month radio advertising contract with Cable Station KOTU for $3,600; issued Check 602 to pay the full amount in advance.
2	Received $520 from Megan Greening, a credit customer, in payment of her account.
2	Issued Check 603 for $17,820 to remit the sales tax owed for July through September to the State Tax Commission.
2	Issued Check 604 for $7,673.40 to A Fashion Statement, a creditor, in payment of Invoice 9387 ($7,830), less a cash discount ($156.60).
3	Sold merchandise on credit for $2,480 plus sales tax of $124 to Dimitri Sayegh, Sales Slip 241.
4	Issued Check 605 for $1,050 to BMX Supply Co. for supplies.
4	Issued Check 606 for $8,594.60 to Today's Woman, a creditor, in payment of Invoice 5671 ($8,770), less a cash discount ($175.40).
5	Collected $1,700.00 on account from Emily Tran, a credit customer.
5	Accepted a return of merchandise from Dimitri Sayegh. The merchandise was originally sold on Sales Slip 241, dated October 3; issued Credit Memorandum 18 for $630, which includes sales tax of $30.
5	Issued Check 607 for $1,666 to Classy Threads, a creditor, in payment of Invoice 3292 ($1,700), less a cash discount ($34).
6	Had cash sales of $18,100 plus sales tax of $905 during October 1–6.
8	Received a check from James Helmer, a credit customer, for $832 to pay the balance he owes.
8	Issued Check 608 for $1,884 to deposit social security tax ($702), Medicare tax ($162), and federal income tax withholding ($1,020) from the September payroll.
9	Sold merchandise on credit for $2,050 plus sales tax of $102.50 to Emma Maldonado, Sales Slip 242.
10	Issued Check 609 for $2,225 to pay *The City Daily* for a newspaper advertisement that appeared in October.
11	Purchased merchandise for $4,820 from A Fashion Statement, Invoice 9422, dated October 8; the terms are 2/10, n/30.
12	Issued Check 610 for $300 to pay freight charges to Ace Freight Company, the trucking company that delivered merchandise from A Fashion Statement on September 27 and October 11.
13	Had cash sales of $12,300 plus sales tax of $615 during October 8–13.
15	Sold merchandise on credit for $1,940 plus sales tax of $97 to James Helmer, Sales Slip 243.
16	Purchased discontinued merchandise from Acme Jobbers; paid for it immediately with Check 611 for $5,250.
16	Received $510 on account from Dimitri Sayegh, a credit customer.
16	Issued Check 612 for $4,723.60 to A Fashion Statement, a creditor, in payment of Invoice 9422 ($4,820.00), less cash discount ($96.40).
18	Issued Check 613 for $6,500 to Teresa Lojay as a withdrawal for personal use.
20	Had cash sales of $12,800 plus sales tax of $640 during October 15–20.
22	Issued Check 614 to City Utilities for $881 to pay the monthly electric bill.
24	Sold merchandise on credit for $820 plus sales tax of $41 to Megan Greening, Sales Slip 244.

(continued)

DATE	TRANSACTIONS (CONT.)
Oct. 25	Purchased merchandise for $3,380 from Classy Threads, Invoice 3418, dated October 23; the terms are 2/10, n/30.
26	Issued Check 615 to Regional Telephone for $520 to pay the monthly telephone bill.
27	Had cash sales of $13,240 plus sales tax of $662 during October 22–27.
29	Received Credit Memorandum 175 for $430 from Classy Threads Inc. for defective goods that were returned. The original purchase was made on Invoice 3418, dated October 25.
29	Sold merchandise on credit for $2,920 plus sales tax of $146 to Emily Tran, Sales Slip 245.
29	Recorded the October payroll. The records prepared by the payroll service show the following totals: earnings, $10,800; social security, $702.00; Medicare, $162.00; income tax, $1,020; and net pay, $8,916. The excess withholdings corrected an error made in withholdings in September.
29	Recorded the employer's payroll taxes, which were calculated by the payroll service: social security, $702; Medicare, $162; federal unemployment tax, $118; and state unemployment tax, $584. This, too, reflects an understatement of taxes recorded in September and corrected in this month.
30	Purchased merchandise for $2,920 from Today's Woman, Invoice 5821, dated October 26; the terms are 1/10, n/30.
31	Issued Checks 616 through 619, totaling $8,916.00, to employees to pay October payroll. For the sake of simplicity, enter the total of the checks on a single line.
31	Issued Check 620 for $275 to Handy Janitors for October janitorial services.
31	Had cash sales of $1,700 plus sales tax of $85 for October 29–31.

The Fashion Rack
Postclosing Trial Balance
September 30, 2013

ACCOUNT NAME	DEBIT	CREDIT
Cash	59 8 0 0 00	
Accounts Receivable	6 2 1 0 00	
Allowance for Doubtful Accounts		4 2 0 00
Merchandise Inventory	88 9 9 6 00	
Supplies	4 1 0 0 00	
Prepaid Insurance	8 4 0 0 00	
Equipment	83 0 0 0 00	
Accumulated Depreciation—Equipment		7 0 5 0 00
Accounts Payable		18 3 0 0 00
Social Security Tax Payable		7 0 2 00
Medicare Tax Payable		1 6 2 00
Employee Income Tax Payable		1 0 2 0 00
Federal Unemployment Tax Payable		5 1 2 00
State Unemployment Tax Payable		1 2 6 8 00
Sales Tax Payable		17 8 2 0 00
Teresa Lojay, Capital		203 2 5 2 00
Totals	250 5 0 6 00	250 5 0 6 00

The Fashion Rack
Schedule of Accounts Payable
September 30, 2013

A Fashion Statement	7	8	3	0	00
Classy Threads	1	7	0	0	00
Today's Woman	8	7	7	0	00
Total	18	3	0	0	00

The Fashion Rack
Schedule of Accounts Receivable
September 30, 2013

Jennifer Brown		7	9	5	00
Megan Greening		5	2	0	00
James Helmer		8	3	2	00
Emma Maldonado		2	3	2	00
Jim Price	1	6	2	1	00
Dimitri Sayegh		5	1	0	00
Emily Tran	1	7	0	0	00
Total	6	2	1	0	00

APPENDIX

APPENDIX A

The Home Depot 2009 Financial Statements (for the fiscal year ended January 31, 2010)

Appendix A

The Home Depot 2009 Financial Statements (for the fiscal year ended January 31, 2010)

Item 8.   Financial Statements and Supplementary Data.

Management's Responsibility for Financial Statements

The financial statements presented in this Annual Report have been prepared with integrity and objectivity and are the responsibility of the management of The Home Depot, Inc. These financial statements have been prepared in conformity with U.S. generally accepted accounting principles and properly reflect certain estimates and judgments based upon the best available information.

The financial statements of the Company have been audited by KPMG LLP, an independent registered public accounting firm. Their accompanying report is based upon an audit conducted in accordance with the standards of the Public Company Accounting Oversight Board (United States).

The Audit Committee of the Board of Directors, consisting solely of independent directors, meets five times a year with the independent registered public accounting firm, the internal auditors and representatives of management to discuss auditing and financial reporting matters. In addition, a telephonic meeting is held prior to each quarterly earnings release. The Audit Committee retains the independent registered public accounting firm and regularly reviews the internal accounting controls, the activities of the independent registered public accounting firm and internal auditors and the financial condition of the Company. Both the Company's independent registered public accounting firm and the internal auditors have free access to the Audit Committee.

Management's Report on Internal Control over Financial Reporting

Our management is responsible for establishing and maintaining adequate internal control over financial reporting, as such term is defined in Rule 13a-15(f) promulgated under the Securities Exchange Act of 1934, as amended (the "Exchange Act"). Under the supervision and with the participation of our management, including our Chief Executive Officer and Chief Financial Officer, we conducted an evaluation of the effectiveness of our internal control over financial reporting as of January 31, 2010 based on the framework in *Internal Control – Integrated Framework* issued by the Committee of Sponsoring Organizations of the Treadway Commission (COSO). Based on our evaluation, our management concluded that our internal control over financial reporting was effective as of January 31, 2010 in providing reasonable assurance regarding the reliability of financial reporting and the preparation of financial statements for external purposes in accordance with U.S. generally accepted accounting principles. The effectiveness of our internal control over financial reporting as of January 31, 2010 has been audited by KPMG LLP, an independent registered public accounting firm, as stated in their report which is included on page 30 in this Form 10-K.

/s/   FRANCIS S. BLAKE
                      /s/   CAROL B. TOMÉ
Francis S. Blake   **Carol B. Tomé**
Chairman &   **Chief Financial Officer &**
Chief Executive Officer   **Executive Vice President – Corporate Services**

Report of Independent Registered Public Accounting Firm

The Board of Directors and Stockholders
The Home Depot, Inc.:

We have audited the accompanying Consolidated Balance Sheets of The Home Depot, Inc. and subsidiaries as of January 31, 2010 and February 1, 2009, and the related Consolidated Statements of Earnings, Stockholders' Equity and Comprehensive Income, and Cash Flows for each of the fiscal years in the three-year period ended January 31, 2010. These Consolidated Financial Statements are the responsibility of the Company's management. Our responsibility is to express an opinion on these Consolidated Financial Statements based on our audits.

We conducted our audits in accordance with the standards of the Public Company Accounting Oversight Board (United States). Those standards require that we plan and perform the audit to obtain reasonable assurance about whether the financial statements are free of material misstatement. An audit includes examining, on a test basis, evidence supporting the amounts and disclosures in the financial statements. An audit also includes assessing the accounting principles used and significant estimates made by management, as well as evaluating the overall financial statement presentation. We believe that our audits provide a reasonable basis for our opinion.

In our opinion, the Consolidated Financial Statements referred to above present fairly, in all material respects, the financial position of The Home Depot, Inc. and subsidiaries as of January 31, 2010 and February 1, 2009, and the results of their operations and their cash flows for each of the fiscal years in the three-year period ended January 31, 2010, in conformity with U.S. generally accepted accounting principles.

We also have audited, in accordance with the standards of the Public Company Accounting Oversight Board (United States), The Home Depot, Inc.'s internal control over financial reporting as of January 31, 2010, based on criteria established in *Internal Control – Integrated Framework* issued by the Committee of Sponsoring Organizations of the Treadway Commission (COSO), and our report dated March 25, 2010 expressed an unqualified opinion on the effectiveness of the Company's internal control over financial reporting.

/s/ KPMG LLP

Atlanta, Georgia
March 25, 2010

THE HOME DEPOT, INC. AND SUBSIDIARIES
CONSOLIDATED STATEMENTS OF EARNINGS

amounts in millions, except per share data	Fiscal Year Ended[1]		
	January 31, 2010	February 1, 2009	February 3, 2008
NET SALES	$ 66,176	$ 71,288	$ 77,349
Cost of Sales	43,764	47,298	51,352
GROSS PROFIT	22,412	23,990	25,997
Operating Expenses:			
Selling, General and Administrative	15,902	17,846	17,053
Depreciation and Amortization	1,707	1,785	1,702
Total Operating Expenses	17,609	19,631	18,755
OPERATING INCOME	4,803	4,359	7,242
Interest and Other (Income) Expense:			
Interest and Investment Income	(18)	(18)	(74)
Interest Expense	676	624	696
Other	163	163	—
Interest and Other, net	821	769	622
EARNINGS FROM CONTINUING OPERATIONS BEFORE PROVISION FOR INCOME TAXES	3,982	3,590	6,620
Provision for Income Taxes	1,362	1,278	2,410
EARNINGS FROM CONTINUING OPERATIONS	2,620	2,312	4,210
EARNINGS (LOSS) FROM DISCONTINUED OPERATIONS, NET OF TAX	41	(52)	185
NET EARNINGS	$ 2,661	$ 2,260	$ 4,395
Weighted Average Common Shares	1,683	1,682	1,849
BASIC EARNINGS PER SHARE FROM CONTINUING OPERATIONS	$ 1.56	$ 1.37	$ 2.28
BASIC EARNINGS (LOSS) PER SHARE FROM DISCONTINUED OPERATIONS	$ 0.02	$ (0.03)	$ 0.10
BASIC EARNINGS PER SHARE	$ 1.58	$ 1.34	$ 2.38
Diluted Weighted Average Common Shares	1,692	1,686	1,856
DILUTED EARNINGS PER SHARE FROM CONTINUING OPERATIONS	$ 1.55	$ 1.37	$ 2.27
DILUTED EARNINGS (LOSS) PER SHARE FROM DISCONTINUED OPERATIONS	$ 0.02	$ (0.03)	$ 0.10
DILUTED EARNINGS PER SHARE	$ 1.57	$ 1.34	$ 2.37

(1)Fiscal years ended January 31, 2010 and February 1, 2009 include 52 weeks. Fiscal year ended February 3, 2008 includes 53 weeks.

See accompanying Notes to Consolidated Financial Statements.

THE HOME DEPOT, INC. AND SUBSIDIARIES
CONSOLIDATED BALANCE SHEETS

amounts in millions, except share and per share data	January 31, 2010	February 1, 2009
ASSETS		
Current Assets:		
Cash and Cash Equivalents	$ 1,421	$ 519
Short-Term Investments	6	6
Receivables, net	964	972
Merchandise Inventories	10,188	10,673
Other Current Assets	1,321	1,192
Total Current Assets	13,900	13,362
Property and Equipment, at cost:		
Land	8,451	8,301
Buildings	17,391	16,961
Furniture, Fixtures and Equipment	9,091	8,741
Leasehold Improvements	1,383	1,359
Construction in Progress	525	625
Capital Leases	504	490
	37,345	36,477
Less Accumulated Depreciation and Amortization	11,795	10,243
Net Property and Equipment	25,550	26,234
Notes Receivable	33	36
Goodwill	1,171	1,134
Other Assets	223	398
Total Assets	$ 40,877	$ 41,164
LIABILITIES AND STOCKHOLDERS' EQUITY		
Current Liabilities:		
Accounts Payable	$ 4,863	$ 4,822
Accrued Salaries and Related Expenses	1,263	1,129
Sales Taxes Payable	362	337
Deferred Revenue	1,158	1,165
Income Taxes Payable	108	289
Current Installments of Long-Term Debt	1,020	1,767
Other Accrued Expenses	1,589	1,644
Total Current Liabilities	10,363	11,153
Long-Term Debt, excluding current installments	8,662	9,667
Other Long-Term Liabilities	2,140	2,198
Deferred Income Taxes	319	369
Total Liabilities	21,484	23,387
STOCKHOLDERS' EQUITY		
Common Stock, par value $0.05; authorized: 10 billion shares; issued: 1.716 billion shares at January 31, 2010 and 1.707 billion shares at February 1, 2009; outstanding: 1.698 billion shares at January 31, 2010 and 1.696 billion shares at February 1, 2009	86	85
Paid-In Capital	6,304	6,048
Retained Earnings	13,226	12,093
Accumulated Other Comprehensive Income (Loss)	362	(77)
Treasury Stock, at cost, 18 million shares at January 31, 2010 and 11 million shares at February 1, 2009	(585)	(372)
Total Stockholders' Equity	19,393	17,777
Total Liabilities and Stockholders' Equity	$40,877	$ 41,164

See accompanying Notes to Consolidated Financial Statements.

THE HOME DEPOT, INC. AND SUBSIDIARIES

CONSOLIDATED STATEMENTS OF STOCKHOLDERS' EQUITY AND COMPREHENSIVE INCOME

amounts in millions, except per share data	Common Stock Shares	Common Stock Amount	Paid-In Capital	Retained Earnings	Accumulated Other Comprehensive Income (Loss)	Treasury Stock Shares	Treasury Stock Amount	Stockholders' Equity	Total Comprehensive Income
BALANCE, JANUARY 28, 2007	2,421	$ 121	$ 7,930	$33,052	$310	(451)	$(16,383)	$ 25,030	
Cumulative Effect of the Adoption of FIN 48	—	—	—	(111)	—	—	—	(111)	
Net Earnings	—	—	—	4,395	—	—	—	4,395	$4,395
Shares Issued Under Employee Stock Plans	12	1	239	—	—	—	—	240	
Tax Effect of Sale of Option Shares by Employees	—	—	4	—	—	—	—	4	
Translation Adjustments	—	—	—	—	455	—	—	455	455
Cash Flow Hedges, net of tax	—	—	—	—	(10)	—	—	(10)	(10)
Stock Options, Awards and Amortization of Restricted Stock	—	—	206	—	—	—	—	206	
Repurchase of Common Stock	—	—	—	—	—	(292)	(10,815)	(10,815)	
Retirement of Treasury Stock	(735)	(37)	(2,608)	(24,239)	—	735	26,884	—	
Cash Dividends ($0.90 per share)	—	—	—	(1,709)	—	—	—	(1,709)	
Other	—	—	29	—	—	—	—	29	
Comprehensive Income									$4,840
BALANCE, FEBRUARY 3, 2008	1,698	$ 85	$ 5,800	$11,388	$755	(8)	$ (314)	$ 17,714	
Net Earnings	—	—	—	2,260	—	—	—	2,260	$2,260
Shares Issued Under Employee Stock Plans	9	—	68	—	—	—	—	68	
Tax Effect of Sale of Option Shares by Employees	—	—	7	—	—	—	—	7	
Translation Adjustments	—	—	—	—	(831)	—	—	(831)	(831)
Cash Flow Hedges, net of tax	—	—	—	—	(1)	—	—	(1)	(1)
Stock Options, Awards and Amortization of Restricted Stock	—	—	176	—	—	—	—	176	
Repurchase of Common Stock	—	—	—	—	—	(3)	(70)	(70)	
Cash Dividends ($0.90 per share)	—	—	—	(1,521)	—	—	—	(1,521)	
Other	—	—	(3)	(34)	—	—	12	(25)	
Comprehensive Income									$1,428
BALANCE, FEBRUARY 1, 2009	1,707	$ 85	$ 6,048	$12,093	$ (77)	(11)	$ (372)	$ 17,777	
Net Earnings	—	—	—	2,661	—	—	—	2,661	$2,661
Shares Issued Under Employee Stock Plans	9	1	57	—	—	—	—	58	
Tax Effect of Sale of Option Shares by Employees	—	—	(2)	—	—	—	—	(2)	
Translation Adjustments	—	—	—	—	426	—	—	426	426
Cash Flow Hedges, net of tax	—	—	—	—	11	—	—	11	11
Stock Options, Awards and Amortization of Restricted Stock	—	—	201	—	—	—	—	201	
Repurchase of Common Stock	—	—	—	—	—	(7)	(213)	(213)	
Cash Dividends ($0.90 per share)	—	—	—	(1,525)	—	—	—	(1,525)	
Other	—	—	—	(3)	2	—	—	(1)	2
Comprehensive Income									$3,100
BALANCE, JANUARY 31, 2010	1,716	$ 86	$ 6,304	$13,226	$ 362	(18)	$ (585)	$ 19,393	

See accompanying Notes to Consolidated Financial Statements.

THE HOME DEPOT, INC. AND SUBSIDIARIES
CONSOLIDATED STATEMENTS OF CASH FLOWS

	Fiscal Year Ended[1]		
amounts in millions	January 31, 2010	February 1, 2009	February 3, 2008
CASH FLOWS FROM OPERATING ACTIVITIES:			
Net Earnings	$ 2,661	$ 2,260	$ 4,395
Reconciliation of Net Earnings to Net Cash Provided by Operating Activities:			
Depreciation and Amortization	1,806	1,902	1,906
Impairment Related to Rationalization Charges	—	580	—
Impairment of Investment	163	163	—
Stock-Based Compensation Expense	201	176	207
Changes in Assets and Liabilities, net of the effects of acquisitions and disposition:			
(Increase) Decrease in Receivables, net	(23)	121	116
Decrease (Increase) in Merchandise Inventories	625	743	(491)
Decrease (Increase) in Other Current Assets	4	(7)	109
Increase (Decrease) in Accounts Payable and Accrued Expenses	59	(646)	(465)
Decrease in Deferred Revenue	(21)	(292)	(159)
(Decrease) Increase in Income Taxes Payable	(174)	262	—
Decrease in Deferred Income Taxes	(227)	(282)	(348)
(Decrease) Increase in Other Long-Term Liabilities	(19)	306	186
Other	70	242	271
Net Cash Provided by Operating Activities	5,125	5,528	5,727
CASH FLOWS FROM INVESTING ACTIVITIES:			
Capital Expenditures, net of $10, $37 and $19 of non-cash capital expenditures in fiscal 2009, 2008 and 2007, respectively	(966)	(1,847)	(3,558)
Proceeds from Sale of Business, net	—	—	8,337
Payments for Businesses Acquired, net	—	—	(13)
Proceeds from Sales of Property and Equipment	178	147	318
Purchases of Investments	—	(168)	(11,225)
Proceeds from Sales and Maturities of Investments	33	139	10,899
Net Cash (Used in) Provided by Investing Activities	(755)	(1,729)	4,758
CASH FLOWS FROM FINANCING ACTIVITIES:			
(Repayments of) Proceeds from Short-Term Borrowings, net	—	(1,732)	1,734
Repayments of Long-Term Debt	(1,774)	(313)	(20)
Repurchases of Common Stock	(213)	(70)	(10,815)
Proceeds from Sales of Common Stock	73	84	276
Cash Dividends Paid to Stockholders	(1,525)	(1,521)	(1,709)
Other Financing Activities	(64)	(128)	(105)
Net Cash Used in Financing Activities	(3,503)	(3,680)	(10,639)
Increase (Decrease) in Cash and Cash Equivalents	867	119	(154)
Effect of Exchange Rate Changes on Cash and Cash Equivalents	35	(45)	(1)
Cash and Cash Equivalents at Beginning of Year	519	445	600
Cash and Cash Equivalents at End of Year	$ 1,421	$ 519	$ 445
SUPPLEMENTAL DISCLOSURE OF CASH PAYMENTS MADE FOR:			
Interest, net of interest capitalized	$ 664	$ 622	$ 672
Income Taxes	$ 2,082	$ 1,265	$ 2,524

(1)Fiscal years ended January 31, 2010 and February 1, 2009 include 52 weeks. Fiscal year ended February 3, 2008 includes 53 weeks.

See accompanying Notes to Consolidated Financial Statements.

NOTES TO CONSOLIDATED FINANCIAL STATEMENTS

1.   SUMMARY OF SIGNIFICANT ACCOUNTING POLICIES

Business, Consolidation and Presentation

The Home Depot, Inc. and its subsidiaries (the "Company") operate The Home Depot stores, which are full-service, warehouse-style stores averaging approximately 105,000 square feet in size. The stores stock approximately 30,000 to 40,000 different kinds of building materials, home improvement supplies and lawn and garden products that are sold to do-it-yourself customers, do-it-for-me customers and professional customers. At the end of fiscal 2009, the Company was operating 2,244 stores, which included 1,976 The Home Depot stores in the United States, including the Commonwealth of Puerto Rico and the territories of the U.S. Virgin Islands and Guam ("U.S."), 179 The Home Depot stores in Canada, 79 The Home Depot stores in Mexico and 10 The Home Depot stores in China. The Consolidated Financial Statements include the accounts of the Company and its wholly-owned subsidiaries. All significant intercompany transactions have been eliminated in consolidation.

Fiscal Year

The Company's fiscal year is a 52- or 53-week period ending on the Sunday nearest to January 31. Fiscal years ended January 31, 2010 ("fiscal 2009") and February 1, 2009 ("fiscal 2008") include 52 weeks. The fiscal year ended February 3, 2008 ("fiscal 2007") includes 53 weeks.

Use of Estimates

Management of the Company has made a number of estimates and assumptions relating to the reporting of assets and liabilities, the disclosure of contingent assets and liabilities, and reported amounts of revenues and expenses in preparing these financial statements in conformity with U.S. generally accepted accounting principles. Actual results could differ from these estimates.

Fair Value of Financial Instruments

The carrying amounts of Cash and Cash Equivalents, Receivables and Accounts Payable approximate fair value due to the short-term maturities of these financial instruments. The fair value of the Company's investments is discussed under the caption "Short-Term Investments" in this Note 1. The fair value of the Company's Long-Term Debt is discussed in Note 11.

Cash Equivalents

The Company considers all highly liquid investments purchased with original maturities of three months or less to be cash equivalents. The Company's Cash Equivalents are carried at fair market value and consist primarily of high-grade commercial paper, money market funds and U.S. government agency securities.

Short-Term Investments

Short-Term Investments are recorded at fair value based on current market rates and are classified as available-for-sale.

Accounts Receivable

The Company has an agreement with a third-party service provider who directly extends credit to customers, manages the Company's private label credit card program and owns the related receivables. We evaluated the third-party entities holding the receivables under the program and concluded that they should not be consolidated by the Company. The agreement with the third-party service provider expires in 2018, with the Company having the option, but no obligation, to purchase the receivables at the end of the agreement. The deferred interest charges incurred by the Company for its deferred financing programs offered to its customers are included in Cost of Sales. The interchange fees charged to the Company for the customers' use of the cards and the profit sharing with the third-party administrator are included in Selling, General and Administrative expenses ("SG&A"). The sum of the three is referred to by the Company as "the cost of credit" of the private label credit card program.

In addition, certain subsidiaries of the Company extend credit directly to customers in the ordinary course of business. The receivables due from customers were $38 million and $37 million as of January 31, 2010 and February 1, 2009, respectively. The Company's valuation reserve related to accounts receivable was not material to the Consolidated Financial Statements of the Company as of the end of fiscal 2009 or 2008.

Merchandise Inventories

The majority of the Company's Merchandise Inventories are stated at the lower of cost (first-in, first-out) or market, as determined by the retail inventory method. As the inventory retail value is adjusted regularly to reflect market conditions, the inventory valued using the retail method approximates the lower of cost or market. Certain subsidiaries, including retail operations in Canada, Mexico and China, and distribution centers, record Merchandise Inventories at the lower of cost or market, as determined by a cost method. These Merchandise Inventories represent approximately 18% of the total Merchandise Inventories balance. The Company evaluates the inventory valued using a cost method at the end of each quarter to ensure that it is carried at the lower of cost or market. The valuation allowance for Merchandise Inventories valued under a cost method was not material to the Consolidated Financial Statements of the Company as of the end of fiscal 2009 or 2008.

Independent physical inventory counts or cycle counts are taken on a regular basis in each store and distribution center to ensure that amounts reflected in the accompanying Consolidated Financial Statements for Merchandise Inventories are properly stated. During the period between physical inventory counts in stores, the Company accrues for estimated losses related to shrink on a store-by-store basis based on historical shrink results and current trends in the business. Shrink (or in the case of excess inventory, "swell") is the difference between the recorded amount of inventory and the physical inventory. Shrink may occur due to theft, loss, inaccurate records for the receipt of inventory or deterioration of goods, among other things.

Income Taxes

The Company provides for federal, state and foreign income taxes currently payable, as well as for those deferred due to timing differences between reporting income and expenses for financial statement purposes versus tax purposes. Deferred tax assets and liabilities are recognized for the future tax consequences attributable to temporary differences between the financial statement carrying amounts of existing assets and liabilities and their respective tax bases. Deferred tax assets and liabilities are measured using enacted income tax rates expected to apply to taxable income in the years in which those temporary differences are expected to be recovered or settled. The effect of a change in income tax rates is recognized as income or expense in the period that includes the enactment date.

The Company and its eligible subsidiaries file a consolidated U.S. federal income tax return. Non-U.S. subsidiaries and certain U.S. subsidiaries, which are consolidated for financial reporting purposes, are not eligible to be included in the Company's consolidated U.S. federal income tax return. Separate provisions for income taxes have been determined for these entities. The Company intends to reinvest substantially all of the unremitted earnings of its non-U.S. subsidiaries and postpone their remittance indefinitely. Accordingly, no provision for U.S. income taxes for these non-U.S. subsidiaries was recorded in the accompanying Consolidated Statements of Earnings.

Depreciation and Amortization

The Company's Buildings, Furniture, Fixtures and Equipment are recorded at cost and depreciated using the straight-line method over the estimated useful lives of the assets. Leasehold Improvements are amortized using the straight-line method over the original term of the lease or the useful life of the improvement, whichever is shorter. The Company's Property and Equipment is depreciated using the following estimated useful lives:

	Life
Buildings	5 – 45 years
Furniture, Fixtures and Equipment	3 – 20 years
Leasehold Improvements	5 – 45 years

Capitalized Software Costs

The Company capitalizes certain costs related to the acquisition and development of software and amortizes these costs using the straight-line method over the estimated useful life of the software, which is three to six years. These costs are included in Furniture, Fixtures and Equipment in the accompanying Consolidated Balance Sheets. Certain development costs not meeting the criteria for capitalization are expensed as incurred.

Revenues

The Company recognizes revenue, net of estimated returns and sales tax, at the time the customer takes possession of merchandise or receives services. The liability for sales returns is estimated based on historical return levels. When the Company receives payment from customers before the customer has taken possession of the merchandise or the service has been performed, the amount received is recorded as Deferred Revenue in the accompanying Consolidated Balance Sheets until the sale or service is complete. The Company also records Deferred Revenue for the sale of gift cards and recognizes this revenue upon the redemption of gift cards in Net Sales. Gift card breakage income is recognized based upon historical redemption patterns and represents the balance of gift cards for which the Company believes the likelihood of redemption by the customer is remote. During fiscal 2009, 2008 and 2007, the Company recognized $40 million, $37 million and $36 million, respectively, of gift card breakage income. This income is recorded as other income and is included in the accompanying Consolidated Statements of Earnings as a reduction in SG&A.

Services Revenue

Net Sales include services revenue generated through a variety of installation, home maintenance and professional service programs. In these programs, the customer selects and purchases material for a project and the Company provides or arranges professional installation. These programs are offered through the Company's stores. Under certain programs, when the Company provides or arranges the installation of a project and the subcontractor provides material as part of the installation, both the material and labor are included in services revenue. The Company recognizes this revenue when the service for the customer is complete.

All payments received prior to the completion of services are recorded in Deferred Revenue in the accompanying Consolidated Balance Sheets. Services revenue was $2.6 billion, $3.1 billion and $3.5 billion for fiscal 2009, 2008 and 2007, respectively.

Self-Insurance

The Company is self-insured for certain losses related to general liability, product liability, automobile, workers' compensation and medical claims. The expected ultimate cost for claims incurred as of the balance sheet date is not discounted and is recognized as a liability. The expected ultimate cost of claims is estimated based upon analysis of historical data and actuarial estimates.

Prepaid Advertising

Television and radio advertising production costs, along with media placement costs, are expensed when the advertisement first appears. Amounts included in Other Current Assets in the accompanying Consolidated Balance Sheets relating to prepayments of production costs for print and broadcast advertising as well as sponsorship promotions were not material at the end of fiscal 2009 and 2008.

Vendor Allowances

Vendor allowances primarily consist of volume rebates that are earned as a result of attaining certain purchase levels and advertising co-op allowances for the promotion of vendors' products that are typically based on guaranteed minimum amounts with additional amounts being earned for attaining certain purchase levels. These vendor allowances are accrued as earned, with those allowances received as a result of attaining certain purchase levels accrued over the incentive period based on estimates of purchases.

Volume rebates and certain advertising co-op allowances earned are initially recorded as a reduction in Merchandise Inventories and a subsequent reduction in Cost of Sales when the related product is sold. Certain advertising co-op allowances that are reimbursements of specific, incremental and identifiable costs incurred to promote vendors' products are recorded as an offset against advertising expense. In fiscal 2009, 2008 and 2007, gross advertising expense was $897 million, $1.0 billion and $1.2 billion, respectively, and is included in SG&A. Specific, incremental and identifiable advertising co-op allowances were $105 million, $107 million and $120 million for fiscal 2009, 2008 and 2007, respectively, and were recorded as an offset to advertising expense in SG&A.

Cost of Sales

Cost of Sales includes the actual cost of merchandise sold and services performed, the cost of transportation of merchandise from vendors to the Company's stores, locations or customers, the operating cost of the Company's sourcing and distribution network and the cost of deferred interest programs offered through the Company's private label credit card program.

The cost of handling and shipping merchandise from the Company's stores, locations or distribution centers to the customer is classified as SG&A. The cost of shipping and handling, including internal costs and payments to third parties, classified as SG&A was $426 million, $501 million and $571 million in fiscal 2009, 2008 and 2007, respectively.

Impairment of Long-Lived Assets

The Company evaluates its long-lived assets each quarter for indicators of potential impairment. Indicators of impairment include current period losses combined with a history of losses, management's decision to relocate or close a store or other location before the end of its previously estimated useful life, or when changes in other circumstances indicate the carrying amount of an asset may not be recoverable. The evaluation for long-lived assets is performed at the lowest level of identifiable cash flows, which is generally the individual store level.

The assets of a store with indicators of impairment are evaluated by comparing its undiscounted cash flows with its carrying value. The estimate of cash flows includes management's assumptions of cash inflows and outflows directly resulting from the use of those assets in operations, including gross margin on Net Sales, payroll and related items, occupancy costs, insurance allocations and other costs to operate a store. If the carrying value is greater than the undiscounted cash flows, an impairment loss is recognized for the difference between the carrying value and the estimated fair market value. Impairment losses are recorded as a component of SG&A in the accompanying Consolidated Statements of Earnings. When a leased location closes, the Company also recognizes in SG&A the net present value of future lease obligations less estimated sublease income.

As part of its Rationalization Charges, the Company recorded no asset impairment and $84 million of lease obligation costs in fiscal 2009 compared to $580 million of asset impairments and $252 million of lease obligation costs in fiscal 2008. See Note 2 for more details on the Rationalization Charges. The Company also recorded impairments on other closings and relocations in the ordinary course of business, which were not material to the Consolidated Financial Statements in fiscal 2009, 2008 and 2007.

Goodwill and Other Intangible Assets

Goodwill represents the excess of purchase price over the fair value of net assets acquired. The Company does not amortize goodwill, but does assess the recoverability of goodwill in the third quarter of each fiscal year, or more often if indicators warrant, by determining whether the fair value of each reporting unit supports its carrying value. The fair values of the Company's identified reporting units were estimated using the present value of expected future discounted cash flows.

The Company amortizes the cost of other intangible assets over their estimated useful lives, which range from 1 to 20 years, unless such lives are deemed indefinite. Intangible assets with indefinite lives are tested in the third quarter of each fiscal year for impairment, or more often if indicators warrant. The Company recorded no impairment charges for goodwill or other intangible assets for fiscal 2009, 2008 or 2007.

Stock-Based Compensation

The per share weighted average fair value of stock options granted during fiscal 2009, 2008 and 2007 was $6.61, $6.46 and $9.45, respectively. The fair value of these options was determined at the date of grant using the Black-Scholes option-pricing model with the following assumptions:

	Fiscal Year Ended		
	January 31, 2010	February 1, 2009	February 3, 2008
Risk-free interest rate	2.3%	2.9%	4.4%
Assumed volatility	41.5%	33.8%	25.5%
Assumed dividend yield	3.9%	3.5%	2.4%
Assumed lives of option	6 years	6 years	6 years

Derivatives

The Company uses derivative financial instruments from time to time in the management of its interest rate exposure on long-term debt and its exposure on foreign currency fluctuations. The Company accounts for its derivative financial instruments in accordance with the Financial Accounting Standards Board Accounting Standards Codification ("FASB ASC") 815-10. The fair value of the Company's derivative financial instruments is discussed in Note 5.

Comprehensive Income

Comprehensive Income includes Net Earnings adjusted for certain revenues, expenses, gains and losses that are excluded from Net Earnings under U.S. generally accepted accounting principles. Adjustments to Net Earnings and Accumulated Other Comprehensive Income consist primarily of foreign currency translation adjustments.

Foreign Currency Translation

Assets and Liabilities denominated in a foreign currency are translated into U.S. dollars at the current rate of exchange on the last day of the reporting period. Revenues and expenses are generally translated using average exchange rates for the period and equity transactions are translated using the actual rate on the day of the transaction.

Segment Information

The Company operates within a single reportable segment primarily within North America. Net Sales for the Company outside of the U.S. were $7.0 billion for fiscal 2009 and were $7.4 billion for fiscal 2008 and 2007. Long-lived assets outside of the U.S. totaled $3.0 billion and $2.8 billion as of January 31, 2010 and February 1, 2009, respectively.

10-Year Summary of Financial and Operating Results
The Home Depot, Inc. and Subsidiaries

amounts in millions, except where noted	10-Year Compound Annual Growth Rate	2009	2008	2007[1]
STATEMENT OF EARNINGS DATA[2]				
Net sales	5.6%	$ 66,176	$ 71,288	$ 77,349
Net sales increase (decrease) (%)	—	(7.2)	(7.8)	(2.1)
Earnings before provision for income taxes	0.5	3,982	3,590	6,620
Net earnings	1.2	2,620	2,312	4,210
Net earnings increase (decrease) (%)	—	13.3	(45.1)	(20.1)
Diluted earnings per share ($)	4.5	1.55	1.37	2.27
Diluted earnings per share increase (decrease) (%)	—	13.1	(39.6)	(11.0)
Diluted weighted average number of common shares	(3.2)	1,692	1,686	1,856
Gross margin – % of sales	—	33.9	33.7	33.6
Total operating expenses – % of sales	—	26.6	27.5	24.3
Interest and other, net – % of sales	—	1.2	1.1	0.8
Earnings before provision for income taxes – % of sales	—	6.0	5.0	8.6
Net earnings – % of sales	—	4.0	3.2	5.4
BALANCE SHEET DATA AND FINANCIAL RATIOS[3]				
Total assets	9.1%	$ 40,877	$ 41,164	$ 44,324
Working capital	2.6	3,537	2,209	1,968
Merchandise inventories	6.4	10,188	10,673	11,731
Net property and equipment	9.6	25,550	26,234	27,476
Long-term debt	27.7	8,662	9,667	11,383
Stockholders' equity	4.6	19,393	17,777	17,714
Book value per share ($)	7.9	11.42	10.48	10.48
Long-term debt-to-equity (%)	—	44.7	54.4	64.3
Total debt-to-equity (%)	—	49.9	64.3	75.8
Current ratio	—	1.34:1	1.20:1	1.15:1
Inventory turnover[2]	—	4.1x	4.0x	4.2x
Return on invested capital (%)[2]	—	10.7	9.5	13.9
STATEMENT OF CASH FLOWS DATA				
Depreciation and amortization	14.6%	$ 1,806	$ 1,902	$ 1,906
Capital expenditures	(9.5)	966	1,847	3,558
Payments for businesses acquired, net	(100.0)	—	—	13
Cash dividends per share ($)	23.3	0.900	0.900	0.900
STORE DATA				
Number of stores	9.2%	2,244	2,274	2,234
Square footage at fiscal year-end	8.9	235	238	235
(Decrease) increase in square footage (%)	—	(1.3)	1.3	4.9
Average square footage per store (in thousands)	(0.3)	105	105	105
STORE SALES AND OTHER DATA				
Comparable store sales increase (decrease) (%)[4][5]	—	(6.6)	(8.7)	(6.7)
Weighted average weekly sales per operating store (in thousands)	(4.3)%	$ 563	$ 601	$ 658
Weighted average sales per square foot ($)	(4.1)	279	298	332
Number of customer transactions	4.8	1,274	1,272	1,336
Average ticket ($)	0.8	51.76	55.61	57.48
Number of associates at fiscal year-end[3]	4.6	317,000	322,000	331,000

(1)   *Fiscal years 2007 and 2001 include 53 weeks; all other fiscal years reported include 52 weeks.*

(2)   *Fiscal years 2003 through 2009 include Continuing Operations only. The discontinued operations in fiscal years prior to 2003 were not material. See Note 4 to the Consolidated Financial Statements included in Item 8, "Financial Statements and Supplementary Data."*

(3)   *Amounts for fiscal years 2009, 2008 and 2007 include Continuing Operations only. All amounts in other fiscal years reported include discontinued operations. See Note 4 to the Consolidated Financial Statements included in Item 8, "Financial Statements and Supplementary Data."*

2006	2005	2004	2003	2002	2001[1]	2000
$79,022	$ 77,019	$ 71,100	$ 63,660	$ 58,247	$ 53,553	$ 45,738
2.6	8.3	11.7	9.3	8.8	17.1	19.0
8,502	8,967	7,790	6,762	5,872	4,957	4,217
5,266	5,641	4,922	4,253	3,664	3,044	2,581
(6.6)	14.6	15.7	16.1	20.4	17.9	11.3
2.55	2.63	2.22	1.86	1.56	1.29	1.10
(3.0)	18.5	19.4	19.2	20.9	17.3	10.0
2,062	2,147	2,216	2,289	2,344	2,353	2,352
33.6	33.7	33.4	31.7	31.1	30.2	29.9
22.4	21.9	22.4	21.1	21.1	20.9	20.7
0.5	0.1	—	—	(0.1)	—	—
10.8	11.6	11.0	10.6	10.1	9.3	9.2
6.7	7.3	6.9	6.7	6.3	5.7	5.6
$52,263	$ 44,405	$ 39,020	$ 34,437	$ 30,011	$ 26,394	$ 21,385
5,069	2,563	3,818	3,774	3,882	3,860	3,392
12,822	11,401	10,076	9,076	8,338	6,725	6,556
26,605	24,901	22,726	20,063	17,168	15,375	13,068
11,643	2,672	2,148	856	1,321	1,250	1,545
25,030	26,909	24,158	22,407	19,802	18,082	15,004
12.71	12.67	11.06	9.93	8.38	7.71	6.46
46.5	9.9	8.9	3.8	6.7	6.9	10.3
46.6	15.2	8.9	6.1	6.7	6.9	10.3
1.39:1	1.20:1	1.37:1	1.40:1	1.48:1	1.59:1	1.77:1
4.5x	4.7x	4.9x	5.0x	5.3x	5.4x	5.1x
16.8	20.4	19.9	19.2	18.8	18.3	19.6
$ 1,886	$ 1,579	$ 1,319	$ 1,076	$ 903	$ 764	$ 601
3,542	3,881	3,948	3,508	2,749	3,393	3,574
4,268	2,546	727	215	235	190	26
0.675	0.400	0.325	0.26	0.21	0.17	0.16
2,147	2,042	1,890	1,707	1,532	1,333	1,134
224	215	201	183	166	146	123
4.2	7.0	9.8	10.2	14.1	18.5	22.6
105	105	106	107	108	109	108
(2.8)	3.1	5.1	3.7	(0.5)	—	4
$ 723	$ 763	$ 766	$ 763	$ 772	$ 812	$ 864
358	377	375	371	370	394	415
1,330	1,330	1,295	1,246	1,161	1,091	937
58.90	57.98	54.89	51.15	49.43	48.64	48.65
364,400	344,800	323,100	298,800	280,900	256,300	227,300

(4)   *Includes Net Sales at locations open greater than 12 months, including relocated and remodeled stores. Stores become comparable on the Monday following their 365th day of operation. Comparable store sales is intended only as supplemental information and is not a substitute for Net Sales or Net Earnings presented in accordance with generally accepted accounting principles.*

(5)   *Comparable store sales in fiscal years prior to 2002 were reported to the nearest percent.*

Glossary

Account balance The difference between the amounts recorded on the two sides of an account

Account form balance sheet A balance sheet that lists assets on the left and liabilities and owner's equity on the right (*see also* Report form balance sheet)

Accounting The process by which financial information about a business is recorded, classified, summarized, interpreted, and communicated to owners, managers, and other interested parties

Accounting cycle A series of steps performed during each accounting period to classify, record, and summarize data for a business and to produce needed financial information

Accounting system A process designed to accumulate, classify, and summarize financial data

Accounts Written records of the assets, liabilities, and owner's equity of a business

Accounts payable Amounts a business must pay in the future

Accounts payable ledger A subsidiary ledger that contains a separate account for each creditor

Accounts receivable Claims for future collection from customers

Accounts receivable ledger A subsidiary ledger that contains credit customer accounts

Accrual basis A system of accounting by which all revenues and expenses are matched and reported on financial statements for the applicable period, regardless of when the cash related to the transaction is received or paid

Accrued expenses Expense items that relate to the current period but have not yet been paid and do not yet appear in the accounting records

Accrued income Income that has been earned but not yet received and recorded

Adjusting entries Journal entries made to update accounts for items that were not recorded during the accounting period

Adjustments *See* Adjusting entries

Assets Property owned by a business

Audit trail A chain of references that makes it possible to trace information, locate errors, and prevent fraud

Auditing The review of financial statements to assess their fairness and adherence to generally accepted accounting principles

Auditor's report An independent accountant's review of a firm's financial statements

Balance ledger form A ledger account form that shows the balance of the account after each entry is posted

Balance sheet A formal report of a business's financial condition on a certain date; reports the assets, liabilities, and owner's equity of the business

Bank reconciliation statement A statement that accounts for all differences between the balance on the bank statement and the book balance of cash

Blank endorsement A signature of the payee written on the back of the check that transfers ownership of the check without specifying to whom or for what purpose

Bonding The process by which employees are investigated by an insurance company that will insure the business against losses through employee theft or mishandling of funds

Book value That portion of an asset's original cost that has not yet been depreciated

Break even A point at which revenue equals expenses

Business transaction A financial event that changes the resources of a firm

Canceled check A check paid by the bank on which it was drawn

Capital Financial investment in a business; equity

Cash In accounting, currency, coins, checks, money orders, and funds on deposit in a bank

Cash discount A discount offered by suppliers for payment received within a specified period of time

Cash Short or Over account An account used to record any discrepancies between the amount of currency and coins in the cash register and the amount shown on the audit tape

Certified public accountant (CPA) An independent accountant who provides accounting services to the public for a fee

Chart of accounts A list of the accounts used by a business to record its financial transactions

Check A written order signed by an authorized person instructing a bank to pay a specific sum of money to a designated person or business

Chronological order Organized in the order in which the events occur

Classification A means of identifying each account as an asset, liability, or owner's equity

Classified financial statement A format by which revenues and expenses on the income statement, and assets and liabilities on the balance sheet, are divided into groups of similar accounts and a subtotal is given for each group

Closing entries Journal entries that transfer the results of operations (net income or net loss) to owner's equity and reduce the revenue, expense, and drawing account balances to zero

Commission basis A method of paying employees according to a percentage of net sales

Compensation record *See* Individual earnings record

Compound entry A journal entry with more than one debit or credit

Contra account An account with a normal balance that is opposite that of a related account

Contra asset account An asset account with a credit balance, which is contrary to the normal balance of an asset account

Contra revenue account An account with a debit balance, which is contrary to the normal balance for a revenue account

Control account An account that links a subsidiary ledger and the general ledger since its balance summarizes the balances of the accounts in the subsidiary ledger

Corporation A publicly or privately owned business entity that is separate from its owners and has a legal right to own property and do business in its own name; stockholders are not responsible for the debts or taxes of the business

Correcting entry A journal entry made to correct an erroneous entry

Cost of goods sold The actual cost to the business of the merchandise sold to customers

Credit An entry on the right side of an account

Credit memorandum (banking) A form that explains any addition, other than a deposit, to a checking account

Credit terms Terms for payment on credit by buyer to seller

Creditor One to whom money is owed

Current assets Assets consisting of cash, items that normally will be converted into cash within one year, or items that will be used up within one year

Current liabilities Debts that must be paid within one year

Current ratio A relationship between current assets and current liabilities that provides a measure of a firm's ability to pay its current debts (current ratio = current assets ÷ current liabilities)

Debit An entry on the left side of an account

Debit memorandum A form that explains any deduction, other than a check, from a checking account

Deferred expenses *See* Prepaid expenses

Deferred income *See* Unearned income

Deposit in transit A deposit that is recorded in the cash receipts journal but that reaches the bank too late to be shown on the monthly bank statement

Deposit slip A form prepared to record the deposit of cash or checks to a bank account

Depreciation Allocation of the cost of a long-term asset to operations during its expected useful life

Discussion memorandum An explanation of a topic under consideration by the Financial Accounting Standards Board

Dishonored check A check returned to the depositor unpaid because of insufficient funds in the drawer's account; also called an NSF check

Double-entry system An accounting system that involves recording the effects of each transaction as debits and credits

Drawee The bank on which a check is written

Drawer The person or firm issuing a check

Drawing **account** A special type of owner's equity account set up to record the owner's withdrawal of cash from the business

Economic entity A business or organization whose major purpose is to produce a profit for its owners

Electronic funds transfer (EFT) An electronic transfer of money from one account to another

Employee A person who is hired by and works under the control and direction of the employer

Employee's Withholding Allowance Certificate, Form W-4 A form used to claim exemption (withholding) allowances

Employer's Annual Federal Unemployment Tax Return, Form 940 or 940-EZ Preprinted government form used by the employer to report unemployment taxes for the calendar year

Employer's Quarterly Federal Tax Return, Form 941 Preprinted government form used by the employer to report payroll tax information relating to social security, Medicare, and employee income tax withholding to the Internal Revenue Service

Endorsement A written authorization that transfers ownership of a check

Entity Anything having its own separate identity, such as an individual, a town, a university, or a business

Equity An owner's financial interest in a business

Exempt employees Salaried employees who hold supervisory or managerial positions who are not subject to the maximum hour and overtime pay provisions of the Wage and Hour Law

Expense An outflow of cash, use of other assets, or incurring of a liability

Experience rating system A system that rewards an employer for maintaining steady employment conditions by reducing the firm's state unemployment tax rate

Exposure draft A proposed solution to a problem being considered by the Financial Accounting Standards Board

Fair market value The current worth of an asset or the price the asset would bring if sold on the open market

Federal unemployment taxes (FUTA) Taxes levied by the federal government against employers to benefit unemployed workers

Financial statements Periodic reports of a firm's financial position or operating results

Footing A small pencil figure written at the base of an amount column showing the sum of the entries in the column

Freight In **account** An account showing transportation charges for items purchased

Full endorsement A signature transferring a check to a specific person, firm, or bank

Fundamental accounting equation The relationship between assets and liabilities plus owner's equity

General journal A financial record for entering all types of business transactions; a record of original entry

General ledger A permanent, classified record of all accounts used in a firm's operation; a record of final entry

Generally accepted accounting principles (GAAP) Accounting standards developed and applied by professional accountants

Governmental accounting Accounting work performed for a federal, state, or local governmental unit

Gross profit The difference between net sales and the cost of goods sold

Gross profit percentage The amount of gross profit from each dollar of sales (gross profit percentage = gross profit ÷ net sales)

Hourly rate basis A method of paying employees according to a stated rate per hour

Income statement A formal report of business operations covering a specific period of time; also called a profit and loss statement or a statement of income and expenses

Income Summary account A special owner's equity account that is used only in the closing process to summarize the results of operations

Independent contractor One who is paid by a company to carry out a specific task or job but is not under the direct supervision or control of the company

Individual earnings record An employee record that contains information needed to compute earnings and complete tax reports

International accounting The study of accounting principles used by different countries

Interpret To understand and explain the meaning and importance of something (such as financial statements)

Inventory sheet A form used to list the volume and type of goods a firm has in stock

Inventory turnover The number of times inventory is purchased and sold during the accounting period (inventory turnover cost of goods sold average inventory)

Journal The record of original entry

Journalizing Recording transactions in a journal

Ledger The record of final entry

Liabilities Debts or obligations of a business

Liquidity The ease with which an item can be converted into cash; the ability of a business to pay its debts when due

List price An established retail price

Long-term liabilities Debts of a business that are due more than one year in the future

Management advisory services Services designed to help clients improve their information systems or their business performance

Managerial accounting Accounting work carried on by an accountant employed by a single business in industry; the branch of accounting that provides financial information about business segments, activities, or products

Manufacturing business A business that sells goods that it has produced

Medicare tax A tax levied on employees and employers to provide medical care for the employee and the employee's spouse after each has reached age 65

Merchandise inventory The stock of goods a merchandising business keeps on hand

Merchandising business A business that sells goods purchased for resale

Merit rating system *See* Experience rating system

Multiple-step income statement A type of income statement on which several subtotals are computed before the net income is calculated

Negotiable A financial instrument whose ownership can be transferred to another person or business

Net income The result of an excess of revenue over expenses

Net income line The worksheet line immediately following the column totals on which net income (or net loss) is recorded in two places: the Income Statement section and the Balance Sheet section

Net loss The result of an excess of expenses over revenue

Net sales The difference between the balance in the Sales account and the balance in the *Sales Returns and Allowances* account

Normal balance The increase side of an account

On account An arrangement to allow payment at a later date; also called a charge account or open-account credit

Open-account credit A system that allows the sale of services or goods with the understanding that payment will be made at a later date

Outstanding checks Checks that have been recorded in the cash payments journal but have not yet been paid by the bank

Owner's equity The financial interest of the owner of a business; also called proprietorship or net worth

Partnership A business entity owned by two or more persons who carry on a business for profit and who are legally responsible for the debts and taxes of the business

Payee The person or firm to whom a check is payable

Payroll register A record of payroll information for each employee for the pay period

Permanent account An account that is kept open from one accounting period to the next

Petty cash analysis sheet A form used to record transactions involving petty cash

Petty cash voucher A form used to record the payments made from a petty cash fund

Piece-rate basis A method of paying employees according to the number of units produced

Plant and equipment Property that will be used in the business for longer than one year

Postclosing trial balance A statement that is prepared to prove the equality of total debits and credits after the closing process is completed

Postdated check A check dated some time in the future

Posting Transferring data from a journal to a ledger

Prepaid expenses Expense items acquired, recorded, and paid for in advance of their use

Promissory note A written promise to pay a specified amount of money on a specific date

Property, plant, and equipment Long-term assets that are used in the operation of a business and that are subject to depreciation (except for land, which is not depreciated)

Public accountants Members of firms that perform accounting services for other companies

Purchase allowance A price reduction from the amount originally billed

Purchase invoice A bill received for goods purchased

Purchase order An order to the supplier of goods specifying items needed, quantity, price, and credit terms

Purchase requisition A list sent to the purchasing department showing the items to be ordered

Purchase return Return of unsatisfactory goods

***Purchases* account** An account used to record cost of goods bought for resale during a period

Purchases discount A cash discount offered to customers for payment within a specified period

Receiving report A form showing quantity and condition of goods received

Report form balance sheet A balance sheet that lists the asset accounts first, followed by liabilities and owner's equity

Restrictive endorsement A signature that transfers a check to a specific party for a stated purpose

Retail business A business that sells directly to individual consumers

Revenue An inflow of money or other assets that results from the sales of goods or services or from the use of money or property; also called income

Reversing entries Journal entries made to reverse the effect of certain adjusting entries involving accrued income or accrued expenses to avoid problems in recording future payments or receipts of cash in a new accounting period

Salary basis A method of paying employees according to an agreed-upon amount for each week or month

Sales allowance A reduction in the price originally charged to customers for goods or services

Sales discount A cash discount offered by the supplier to customers for payment within a specified period

Sales invoice A supplier's billing document

Sales return A firm's acceptance of a return of goods from a customer

Sales Returns and Allowances A contra revenue account where sales returns and sales allowances are recorded; sales returns and allowances are subtracted from sales to determine net sales

Salvage value An estimate of the amount that could be received by selling or disposing of an asset at the end of its useful life

Schedule of accounts payable A list of all balances owed to creditors

Schedule of accounts receivable A listing of all balances of the accounts in the accounts receivable subsidiary ledger

Separate entity assumption The concept that a business is separate from its owners; the concept of keeping a firm's financial records separate from the owner's personal financial records

Service business A business that sells services

Service charge A fee charged by a bank to cover the costs of maintaining accounts and providing services

Single-step income statement A type of income statement where only one computation is needed to determine the net income (total revenue − total expenses = net income)

Slide An accounting error involving a misplaced decimal point

Social entity A nonprofit organization, such as a city, public school, or public hospital

Social Security Act A federal act providing certain benefits for employees and their families; officially the Federal Insurance Contributions Act

Social security tax (FICA) A tax imposed by the Federal Insurance Contributions Act and collected on employee earnings to provide retirement and disability benefits

Sole proprietorship A business entity owned by one person who is legally responsible for the debts and taxes of the business

State unemployment taxes (SUTA) Taxes levied by a state government against employers to benefit unemployed workers

Statement of account A form sent to a firm's customers showing transactions during the month and the balance owed

Statement of owner's equity A formal report of changes that occurred in the owner's financial interest during a reporting period

Statements of Financial Accounting Standards Accounting principles established by the Financial Accounting Standards Board

Stock Certificates that represent ownership of a corporation

Stockholders The owners of a corporation; also called shareholders

Straight-line depreciation Allocation of an asset's cost in equal amounts to each accounting period of the asset's useful life

Subsidiary ledger A ledger dedicated to accounts of a single type and showing details to support a general ledger account

T account A type of account, resembling a T, used to analyze the effects of a business transaction

Tax accounting A service that involves tax compliance and tax planning

Tax-exempt wages Earnings in excess of the base amount set by the Social Security Act

Temporary account An account whose balance is transferred to another account at the end of an accounting period

Time and a half Rate of pay for an employee's work in excess of 40 hours a week

Trade discount A reduction from list price

Transmittal of Wage and Tax Statements, Form W-3 Preprinted government form submitted with Forms W-2 to the Social Security Administration

***Transportation In* account** *See Freight In* account

Transposition An accounting error involving misplaced digits in a number

Trial balance A statement to test the accuracy of total debits and credits after transactions have been recorded

Unearned income Income received before it is earned

Unemployment insurance program A program that provides unemployment compensation through a tax levied on employers

Updated account balances The amounts entered in the Adjusted Trial Balance section of the worksheet

Wage and Tax Statement, Form W-2 Preprinted government form that contains information about an employee's earnings and tax withholdings for the year

Wage-bracket table method A simple method to determine the amount of federal income tax to be withheld using a table provided by the government

Wholesale business A business that manufactures or distributes goods to retail businesses or large consumers such as hotels and hospitals

Withdrawals Funds taken from the business by the owner for personal use

Withholding statement *See* Wage and Tax Statement, Form W-2

Workers' compensation insurance Insurance that protects employees against losses from job-related injuries or illnesses, or compensates their families if death occurs in the course of the employment

Working capital The measure of the ability of a company to meet its current obligations; the excess of current assets over current liabilities

Worksheet A form used to gather all data needed at the end of an accounting period to prepare financial statements

Credits

Index

Key terms and page numbers where defined in the text are in **bold**.